Ex

IN A

"Remarkable . . . *In a Different Key: The Story of Autism* tells a riveting tale about how a seemingly rare childhood disorder became a salient fixture in our cultural landscape. It features vivid portraits of people with autism and their devoted parents and recounts dramatic controversies among well-intentioned and occasionally misguided advocates and doctors who have tried to help those with the condition. These gripping personal stories give the book tremendous narrative drive."

—***Wall Street Journal***

"Fast-paced and far-reaching, this book contextualizes the arguments that autism is a horrifying epidemic with those that say it is a valuable aspect of human diversity. This is an important missing piece to the conversation about autism; no one trying to make sense of the spectrum should do so without reading this book."

—**Andrew Solomon,** author of *Far from the Tree*

"Magnificent . . . spellbinding—a fable about greed, power and betrayal told through the lens of autism . . . chock-full of suspense and hairpin turns . . . This book does what no other on autism has done: capture all the slippery, bewildering and deceptive aspects. . . . I have been the mother of an autistic son since 1988. . . . I wept and laughed and raged while reading *In a Different Key,* all the while thinking, Yes! This is my experience, including the raw and dirty parts, but also the wonder and joy."

—**Ann Bauer, *Washington Post***

"The book probes a difficult subject with intelligence and compassion. . . . The complete absence of hysteria will make it essential reading for many. . . . Its insights and quiet wisdom demand our attention, and gratitude."

—**Amy Bloom, *O, The Oprah Magazine***

"Donvan and Zucker sensitively and accurately portray the emergence of understanding of this thing we now call autism, a story that goes back hundreds of years. They make a compelling case for autistic traits—gift and disability alike—being part of the human condition. In the words of child psychiatry pioneer Leo Kanner, autism was 'always there,' even before the diagnosis was invented."

—**John Elder Robison,** author of *Look Me in the Eye* and *Switched On*

"Fascinating . . . A 560-page history of autism sounds intimidating, but fear not. [*In a Different Key*] takes an accessible approach that sheds much light on this human condition . . . through the human stories of those raising autistic children, of those trying to treat, study and research it and those who are autistic."

—*Seattle Times*

"A fascinating and comprehensive history . . . *In a Different Key* shares the often debilitating aspects of autism yet shows how those with autism can and do flourish with the right supports and environments, and how their lives, and the lives of their families, are filled with joys and triumphs and fun and irreverence, too."

—*Chicago Tribune*

"*In a Different Key* is a story about autism as it has passed through largely American institutions, shaped not only by psychiatrists and psychologists but by parents, schools, politicians, and lawyers. It shows how, in turn, the condition acquired a powerful capacity both to change those institutions and to challenge our notions of what is pathological and what is normal."

—Steven Shapin, *The New Yorker*

"A fascinating history of this confounding condition."

—*People*

"Donvan and Zucker's generous yet sharp-eyed portraits of men, women, and children—most of them unknown until now—make it stunningly clear that we all have a stake in the story of autism. We come to understand that we are all wired differently, and that how we treat those who are different than most is a telling measure of who we truly are. This is the kind of history that not only informs but enlarges the spirit."

—Susan Cain, author of *Quiet: The Power of Introverts in a World That Can't Stop Talking*

"*In a Different Key* is nothing if not judicious and fair-minded in its approach to a field harried by controversies and enmities from the very start. . . . [The book] is grounded and sensible, which in the contentious world of autism activism constitutes a kind of grace."

—Laura Miller, *Slate*

"*In a Different Key* is filled with gripping personal histories that powerfully illustrate the mistakes and malpractices in the diagnosis and treatment of autism; the courage and resilience of those who fought for better treatment and deeper understanding; and the sheer variability of people who are given the autism label and too often lumped together as 'disabled.' A fascinating and revealing read, even for those with no personal connection to the topic."

—**Stephanie Coontz,** author of *The Way We Never Were: American Families and the Nostalgia Trap*

"The authors have captured the art of storytelling and the book therefore has a broad appeal, beyond those directly involved or affected by autism. . . . Comprehensive and illuminating . . . From cover to cover this book stirs up a combination of emotions. Admiration for the parents that took a stand; incredulity at treatments and assumptions; and gratitude to scientists and activists that dedicate their expertise and devote their energy to making people with autism spectrum disorder feel part of a world that appears to fear nonconformity to what is considered normal. . . . You must read this book."

—***The Lancet***

"*In a Different Key* transports the reader back to the earlier days of autism. It is essential reading for anyone who is interested in how society treats those who are different."

—**Temple Grandin,** author of *Thinking in Pictures* and *The Autistic Brain*

"*In a Different Key* is fascinating on autism, but it also reveals a new world full of heartbreak and beauty, and a new way of looking at the world."

—**Azar Nafisi,** author of *Reading Lolita in Tehran*

"Donvan and Zucker delve deep into both the science and the politics of autism across time. They tell the story of the extreme treatments that have been tried, such as administering LSD or electric shocks in the '60s, to 'normalize' these children. They uncover the tragic 'mercy killing' of a teenager with autism by his father, and explore the MMR-vaccine-causes-autism theory, named by *Time* magazine as top of the list of 'great science frauds.' This book will make a remarkable contribution to the history of autism."

—**Simon Baron-Cohen,** director, Autism Research Centre, Cambridge University, and author of *The Essential Difference*

"A fascinating history of science, treatment, and civil rights."

—***Newsday***

"Autism is a shape changer that has continuously resisted being pinned down. This meticulously researched book leads us deeply into the history of autism and brings to life the colorful personalities and conflicting ideas that deepen the fascination of autism."

—**Uta Frith,** Emeritus Professor of Cognitive Development at University College London

"In this compelling, well-researched book, the authors weave together the heroic search by parents for treatment and services for their children with the personal stories of a fascinating cast of characters. An invaluable guide for those dealing with autism and an inspiring affirmation of every individual's contribution to 'the fabric of humanity.'"

—***Kirkus Reviews*** (starred review)

"Autism remains one of the great medical mysteries of our time and this is the first book to fully document the decades of efforts by parents, doctors and society to deal with it—so far. For, as the authors say, this is a story that is far from over. *In a Different Key* is a monumental piece of journalism that promises to be a classic, a comprehensive baseline for evidence only future research can reveal. It is written with clarity and grace, and with heart, because the authors have both lived with autism in their own families."

—**Robert Macneil,** former anchor and cofounder of *PBS NewsHour*

"Bravo to Donvan and brava to Zucker. Comically/tragically, autism's history is as emotionally dysfunctional—and as beautiful—as it gets. Finally, we all have an exhaustive reckoning."

—**Michael John Carley,** founder, GRASP, and author of *Asperger's from the Inside Out*

"This one volume captures the textured and sometimes turbulent story of autism in all of its facets: as a scholarly and scientific endeavor, as a political and legal enterprise, as a social movement. Most especially it embeds these developments within stories of people whose lives defined and shaped the course of autism. *In a Different Key* is authoritative and utterly absorbing."

—**Judith Favell,** past president, Developmental Disabilities Division, American Psychological Association

"Donvan and Zucker's tremendous study keeps autism at its center while telling an extraordinary tale of social change. . . . Viewed as a whole, the narrative ultimately reveals a transition from an emphasis on treating individual cases to a more society-wide effort for advocacy and inclusion—an effort that this book will do much to advance."

—***Publishers Weekly***

IN A DIFFERENT KEY

The Story of Autism

JOHN DONVAN

CAREN ZUCKER

B\D\W\Y
BROADWAY
NEW YORK

Published in the United States by Broadway Books, an imprint of the Crown Publishing Group, a division of Penguin Random House LLC, New York.
broadwaybooks.com

Broadway Books and its logo, B \ D \ W \ Y, are trademarks of Penguin Random House LLC.

Originally published in hardcover in slightly different form in the United States by Crown, an imprint of the Crown Publishing Group, a division of Penguin Random House LLC, New York, in 2016.

Library of Congress Cataloging-in-Publication Data
Names: Donvan, John (John Joseph) 1955– author | Zucker, Caren (Caren Brenda) 1961– author.
Title: In a different key: the story of autism / John Donvan and Caren Zucker.
Description: New York: Crown Publishers, [2016]
Identifiers: LCCN 2015024706 | ISBN 9780307985675 (hardback)
ISBN 9780307985682 (ebook)
Subjects: LCSH: Autism spectrum disorders. | Autism spectrum disorders—History. | People with disabilities. | BISAC: PSYCHOLOGY / Psychopathology / Autism Spectrum Disorders. | PSYCHOLOGY / History. | SOCIAL SCIENCE / People with Disabilities.
Classification: LCC RC553.A88 D67 2016 | DDC 616.85/882—dc23
LC record available at http://lccn.loc.gov/2015024706

ISBN 978-0-307-98570-5
Ebook ISBN 978-0-307-98568-2
International edition ISBN 978-0-8041-8938-5

Printed in the United States of America

Book design by Lauren Dong
Cover design by David Drummond
Cover photograph: Hayati Kayhan/Shutterstock

10 9 8 7 6 5 4

For Helen and Frank, for the words,
and Edna, for the spark.

—JD

For Jonah, Molly, Mickey, and John,
and Mom and Dad, for everything you taught me.

—CZ

CONTENTS

PREFACE

THE MEN WERE CRYING TOO. ALL AROUND THE THEATER. In the balcony. In the orchestra seats. On the stage, off to one side, the show's host, Jon Stewart, was seen bringing the back of his hand to his cheek, and swiping at it. Stewart was due to step back on, but for the time being, he joined with the audience, standing and clapping, and letting the moment last—this tearful, joyful ovation for the kid and the singer in the spotlight, whose duet had just topped everything.

By 2012, Night of Too Many Stars was a New York fixture, an every-eighteen-months benefit for autism, created by Robert and Michelle Smigel. They were close friends of Stewart's, but more important they were the parents of a teenager named Daniel, who had a most challenging form of autism. When Daniel was younger, and at the point where the Smigels realized they could never give him the ability to speak—or alter most of the other lasting limitations to his independence—they figured out what they *could* do. Robert, a longtime writer for and performer on *Saturday Night Live,* knew almost everybody in comedy. Michelle was a superior organizer and arm-twister.

The first time out, in 2003, by getting their friends to help them put on a show, they raised just under a million dollars for programs that would help people like Daniel get along in life. By 2012, the money was up to eight figures, and the stars invited to perform considered it an honor to be asked. They were big names—from George Clooney to Tina Fey to Tom Hanks to Chris Rock to Katy Perry.

It was Katy Perry's duet, on that night in October 2012, that brought the house to tears. The song was "Firework," one of her biggest singles ever. But it was the eleven-year-old girl who played piano and sang with her who sparked the outpouring of emotion. Jodi DiPiazza, diagnosed with autism just before turning two, had discovered music early, practiced the piano relentlessly, and idolized Katy Perry. Sitting at a massive baby grand, with Perry standing opposite, Jodi launched into the song, keeping her gaze fixed at some point in space above the keyboard. Though she never once looked up, the whole theater spotted the slight smile when, mid-song, applause broke out for the first time. When they finished the piece, Jodi leapt to her feet and threw her arms around Perry in a long, awkward hug, which everyone there recognized as the expression of a child with autism who was, in that moment, exceedingly happy. That was when everyone cried. And when Robert and Michelle, standing in the wings, knew they had just helped create a moment that would last longer than any they had created on this stage before. They were right. By 2015, more than 9 million people had watched the DiPiazza-Perry duet online.

At one time—and it was only a generation or so ago—what happened that night in the Beacon Theatre on Broadway would have been nothing short of astounding. Back then, autism was shrouded in shame, secrecy, and ignorance—certainly not a cause to which movie stars lent their names, amid lights, limousines, and paparazzi. Indeed, the diagnosis itself does not go back far, dating only to World War II. Then, once the label existed, children who were given it—and their families—were met with ignorance and bigotry. They were barred from public schools and banished to institutions, where they remained through their adult years, often until death. Their parents, and in particular their mothers, were routinely blamed for causing their autism. So little research on autism had been done that no counterargument existed. Most people did not even know of the condition, and the word "autism" prompted almost no recognition from the general public. It was a bitter irony that parents sometimes heard themselves congratulated for having such an "artistic" girl or boy.

This book tells the story of how and why cultural attitudes toward autism shifted so profoundly, from an era when autism was isolating and almost wholly misunderstood to today, when stars flock to a Broadway theater to talk about and raise millions for the cause. It is a story woven together from a range of sources—memoirs by parents and doctors, long-forgotten scientific writings and documentary films, newspaper clippings, archived documents, and interviews with more than two hundred people who have autism, have studied autism, or have raised children with the diagnosis. What emerges is an account of the heart, the sweat, the stubbornness, and the fight displayed by an always-evolving cast of players, whose commitment to changing the world, over three to four generations, turned autism from a condition that was barely recognized into the most talked-about, most controversial, diagnosis of our time.

Thousands were involved in bringing about that outcome: doctors and social workers, educators and lawyers, researchers and writers. More recently, individuals with autism have often taken a more active role, speaking for themselves. The most constant presence, however, is that of parents: mothers and fathers standing up for their children, driven sometimes by desperation, sometimes by anger, and always by love. Their two main goals—to find out why their children have autism, and to make it go away—remain unfulfilled, while recently some are challenging the worthiness of the goals themselves. Nevertheless, the paths those parents took, the hills they climbed and the valleys they entered, chart much of the landscape laid out in these pages.

The story of autism is actually many stories, set on different continents and overlapping in time, and circling back on one another, which can make the tale challenging to tell and not always easy to follow. Ideas cross-pollinate, major players make cameos in one another's stories, and entire story lines unfold at different paces thousands of miles apart. But that was just how it happened. In that way, the story of autism resembles autism itself. Both defy any sort of simple, straight-line narrative.

And yet, as much as the story zigzags or circles back, there is unmistakable forward movement. Over time, because of the efforts made by parents and activists—including the many we did not have room for in these pages—public attitudes toward people given the autism label have moved in what all would agree is the right direction. The cruelty and neglect that have marked the history of autism now seem antiquated. More and more, a new impulse has taken hold, the impulse to recognize the different among us as part of us, and to root for their full participation in the world. That project, of course, is still a work in progress. But it puts all of us in the middle of the story, right now.

PART I

AUTISM'S FIRST CHILD

1930s–1960s

1

DONALD

In 1935, five Canadian baby girls, all sisters, edged out Niagara Falls on the list of Canada's most popular tourist draws. That year, up to six thousand visitors each day took Route 11 into far northern Ontario for the sole purpose of gawking at the babies. By order of the provincial government, they had recently been removed from the care of their farmer parents, to be raised instead in a hurriedly built "hospital" situated not far from the family farmhouse. There they would have indoor plumbing, electricity, and a "scientific" upbringing overseen by a full-time doctor and two full-time nurses.

Three times a day, on cue, the girls were carried out to a grass-covered "play area" just a few yards from where a crowd waited for them. The audience was packed into a specially designed viewing arcade, tented and fitted with one-way screens so that the girls could never see who was making all the noise. Invariably, the moment they came into view, a warm sigh would float aloft, followed by coos, squeals, and scattered applause at the sight of history's first surviving identical quintuplets, who had been given only hours to live the night they were born, in May of the previous year.

Exotic by virtue of their genetic rarity, the Dionne quintuplets imprinted themselves indelibly on their generation. They were a matched set, yet unmatched in the example they set of human resilience, and the most famous children on earth. The future queen of England would visit them. Mae West, Clark Gable, and Bette Davis all made the trip north. So did Amelia Earhart, six weeks before her final flight, not to mention thousands of ordinary families on vacation.

All were transfixed, but never, apparently, troubled by the bizarreness, even cruelty, of the arrangement—the girls' separation from their parents and from other children, their confinement in a setting they were allowed to leave only three times over the course of nine years, their government's exploitation of a random biological novelty to bring tourist dollars into a depressed province. It was estimated that the public exhibition of the girls, known as Quintland, increased revenues for Ontario by $110 million over those nine years.

The family shared in some of the riches as well. By the time the girls' father sued successfully to reunite the family, well into World War II, he was driving a Cadillac. Money had also poured in from movie deals, contracts for exclusive interviews, and a series of endorsements that put the girls' faces in almost every kitchen in America—on calendars, bottles of Karo syrup, and boxes of Quaker Oats. For years to come, no seasonal ritual came or went—not Christmas Eve, not Halloween night, not Mother's Day—without glowing newspaper and magazine stories catching readers up with the Dionne quints.

It was no surprise therefore that the girls would also mean something to a little boy named Donald, who was growing up in Forest, Mississippi, a small town nearly as rural as theirs. Though only eight months older than them, Donald was already able to recite their names: Emilie, Cecile, Marie, Yvonne, and Annette.

Except that, for Donald, these were not the names of girls. They were colors inside bottles.

"Annette and Cecile make purple," he would declare as he sketched, handling his set of paint bottles. In a sense, he had it right, insofar as his "Annette" bottle contained blue paint, and "Cecile" held red. But while his color theory was sound, his reaction to the girls was peculiar. Unlike everyone else, Donald was captivated not by the girls' humanity or the astonishing fact of their survival but by the raw geometry of their sameness. They came in an identical set of five. Just like his bottles. But they were also different, like the paint inside his bottles. It seems to have been this paradox that caught and held his attention.

If it had only been a game he was playing—some deliberate silliness or make-believe—then what Donald called his paint bottles would never have mattered much to anyone but himself. Certainly it would not be a story worth telling so many decades later. But he was serious. Blue was Annette and red was Cecile, relentlessly and earnestly, whether Donald was drawing with crayons or talking about a candy cane. He was inflexible about this, and much else besides.

The word "yes," for example, always had to mean one thing and one thing only: that he wanted to be hoisted up onto his dad's shoulders. "You" was his fixed way of saying "I," and vice versa. Some words, like "chrysanthemum," "business," and "trumpet vine," he repeated endlessly, with no decipherable intention. He was once observed staring into empty space, writing letters with his fingers in the air, commenting as he went along, "Semicolon, capital, twelve, twelve, slain slain; I could put a little comma."

The way he thought about numbers was also unique. When he was seven, an examiner asked him a question from the Binet-Simon IQ test, as it was then called: "If I were to buy four cents' worth of candy and give the storekeeper ten cents, how much would I get back?" "I'll draw a hexagon," he said in reply. Internally the gears were obviously meshing, but they seemed to slip, critically, when the task was to communicate clearly with others. His was a language of hexagons and chrysanthemums, whether it made sense to others or not.

Indeed, Donald showed scant interest in the inhabitants of the outside world, and that included his parents. Of all his peculiarities, this was the most difficult for them to accept—that he never ran to his father when he came home from work, and that he almost never cried for his mother. Relatives were unable to engage him, and when Santa showed up one Christmas, in what seems to have been a calculated effort to break through to the little boy, Donald paid him no heed whatsoever.

Seemingly oblivious to the people around him, he would turn violent the instant his activities were interrupted, whether he was sketching words in the air or spinning pot lids on the floor. Over time, it became clear that he was protecting something: sameness. Pure, unadulterated routine. He could not tolerate even the slightest changes to his physical surroundings. Furniture could not be moved, walks outdoors had to retrace exactly steps already taken, and toys had to be arranged precisely as he had left them. Anything out of place would set off wild tantrums.

Of course, this meant Donald had to be able to remember the arrangements of things, and for this he relied on his astounding capacity for recall. He could watch his father put different-colored beads on a string and then reproduce the pattern without a single glance at the original. He could rebuild a tower of blocks that had been knocked over exactly as it had been, each side of each block facing in its original direction. At the age of two, having easily mastered the alphabet, he immediately learned to recite the letters in reverse. Neither was much of a challenge, since the order never changed, backward or forward.

Odder than each of these behaviors on its own was the fact that they were locked together in a distinct combination of deficits and talents. And yet this constellation of behaviors, which shaped Donald's personality so comprehensively and dramatically, had no name. For that reason, Donald's mother drew the only conclusion that made sense to her, relying on the only words she could think of. With regret and sorrow, she wrote a letter in which she confessed that her little boy was "hopelessly insane." The diagnosis of "autism" had not yet been invented.

Mary Triplett, Donald's mother, was the one who would change that. She and Donald's father intended only to get help for their son, but in doing so, they set in motion a chain of events that would culminate in the discovery of autism in Donald, and the publication of the first internationally recognized description of the condition in a medical journal.

But before any of that could happen, Donald's parents would first have to undo a mistake they had made early and regretted almost immediately. They had to get him back home.

The last time the three of them had been together as a family had been just over a year earlier. They had been driving south out of Forest, a journey of about an hour ahead of them—two at most. But Donald, not quite four years old in that late summer of 1937, could not have been expected to understand what an hour feels like, much less guess that when the ride ended, his mother and father would disappear from his life altogether.

He was a boy who dreaded riding on or in moving objects. Tricycles provoked in him a mortal terror. He fled from swings. But ensconced between his parents in the front seat of the Buick, Donald could lean against his mother if he wanted to. True, he had never really cried for her, never fixed his gaze on her and shared a moment of tenderness. Not once during this ride would he look up at her and smile, and she knew that.

That was the hardest thing for Mary—Donald's utter emotional indifference to her presence. The boy beside her did not seem to care in the slightest whether she caressed or kissed or hugged him. If she were to turn away and face the open window, lost in her own thoughts, he would never cling or whimper to win back her attention. One of the most basic pleasures a parent feels—that of being loved—seemed to elude her, even though the other young mothers in her circle took it for granted. Surely a child's love for his mother was instinctive, the conventional order of things. And if Mary knew one thing about herself, it was that she'd always been most at home within the boundaries of the conventional, and had done surpassingly well there.

That was not to say that she was average. She had been raised to get the best out of life, with the superb advantage of being born to one of Forest's leading families, with more money and education than most of those around her. Not that there was much competition. Forest called itself a city, but really it had always been a small rural town. Even after knocking on every door in the community in 1930, census takers hadn't been able to count more than 3,000 souls. True, there was a lively enough downtown—a barbershop, a beauty salon, grocery and furniture stores, several churches, a courthouse, a railroad depot, and a public high school that served white children from Forest and surrounding towns.

The dropout rate at the school, however, was always a problem, as it would remain far into the future throughout Mississippi, where poverty, illiteracy, and a shorter-than-average life expectancy were the state's enduring triple curse. Despite the presence of two strong universities in Ole Miss and archrival Mississippi State, as well as a broad talent pool of doctors, lawyers, engineers, newspapermen, and some extraordinary artists and writers, there was a cultural and political inertia—a resistance to progress, a preference for the traditional ways.

Even when the civil rights movement finally reached Mississippi in the mid-1960s, upending the status quo, the ferment came more slowly to Scott County, where Forest was located, and where African Americans generally had no opportunity to vote. As late as 1957, town elders pressed the Forest High School marching band to open a football game with "Dixie" instead of "The Star Spangled Banner," which they described as the anthem of an oppressive new order. The school administration complied.

Mary was born a McCravey, the daughter of J. R. McCravey, a founder of the Bank of Forest, which still operates today. Conservative Presbyterians, the McCraveys had little incentive to upset the social order, but her parents did have more sophisticated aspirations than raising yet another mildly educated Southern belle. They pulled Mary out of public school to send her to a private Presbyterian girls' school fifty miles away in Jackson. A few years later, still in Jackson, she enrolled in Belhaven College, a school for Christian women.

She did well at Belhaven, where she was named business manager for the yearbook, elected senior class president, and awarded a bachelor's degree in English. Graduate school was an option, but Mary chose to move directly into teaching, one of the careers most welcoming to the nation's relatively few college-educated women. She joined the English department of a public high school that prepared teenagers primarily for the farming life.

The next stage for her, it was clear, would be marriage, followed by motherhood. For the time being, she would keep working, but as with any single woman her age in Forest, her proper ambition during this phase in her life—which ideally should not run for too long—was to be courted.

She didn't have long to wait. Though not beautiful, she had an appealing confidence; her wavy bobbed hair, modest jewelry, and simple dresses signaled that she felt comfortable in her skin. And then, of course, her family owned that bank.

She had more than one suitor but settled finally for a local young man named Oliver Triplett. Known to everyone by his middle name,

Beamon, he was the former mayor's son. He was active with the Boy Scouts and regularly taught Sunday school at the Presbyterian church, where his sister was the organist. The unusual thing about Beamon was that he had left home to go north to complete his law studies at Yale, then come home again to open a one-man practice in a corner office above a storefront facing the county courthouse.

Mary and Beamon exchanged vows on June 19, 1930. She was twenty-five, and he was twenty-seven. Donald was born a little more than three years later, on September 8, 1933.

They sensed nothing amiss in the beginning, but then, they had no previous experience to go by. Physically, Donald was perfectly normal; he learned to sit up and walk according to the usual timetable, and even talked a little early. A weathered family album shows a small baby and then a toddler, who does, on occasion, look directly into the camera. In one shot, taken when he was probably not yet one, his gaze appears as intently focused forward as that of his grandfather, on whose right arm he perches. In another, in which he appears to be about two, Donald stands alone in the family garden, his body turned away from the camera, his hands occupied with some sort of toy vehicle. But his face and eyes are turned toward the camera, with a smile that seems aimed at the photographer, as though an instant earlier he had heard his name called, and was now glancing back over his shoulder to see who was there.

The album shows the moments of connection becoming less frequent as Donald gets older. He smiles less, and a discomfort creeps in—a discomfort in being held, or made to sit still, or compelled to look "natural" with the parents and aunts and grandparents who stand near him in billowing blouses, bow ties, straw hats, and suspenders. In nearly every frame, everyone grins big and focuses their attention on the camera—everyone but Donald, who peers off in random directions, his bare arms and legs limp.

Mary had to admit to herself that Donald was not "normal," whatever normal meant. Neither, any longer, was Mary's life as his mother. All her hours now belonged to Donald, even as he reached an age when children start to become more self-sufficient. Well into his third year he still could not feed himself, so she was at his side at every meal, handing him the cup, raising the spoon to his mouth, cajoling him to eat. He had no common sense about danger, yet he grew ever more competent at putting himself into dangerous situations. He could figure out the latch on a second-floor window, for example, or find his way outside and to the middle of the street, yet he was oblivious to the possibility that he might fall out the window or be mowed down by a car. He needed a guardian angel, and his mother filled the position, following him on his mysterious rounds from room to room during all his waking hours.

This required an inexhaustible supply of energy, yet somehow Mary found new ways to keep trying to reverse whatever was wrong with him. She talked to him, although it was always a one-way conversation. Yet she knew Donald must be hearing her, because he demonstrated an astounding gift for recalling what he had heard. She saw this in 1934 when, around Christmas, she started singing carols in the house. Suddenly Donald, only fifteen months old, began singing them too, word for word. Soon after, he memorized the twenty-five questions and answers of the Presbyterian catechism.

Mary also dedicated herself to learning her son's many elaborate rituals. His extreme need for sameness made him violently inflexible about a series of routines of his own invention. Many of these were verbal, such as an incantation at breakfast every morning that went like this:

"Say 'Eat it or I won't give you tomatoes, but if I don't eat it I will give you tomatoes.'" It made no obvious sense, but that wasn't important. If Mary didn't say the words, exactly as instructed, Donald would scream, every muscle visibly strained in agony. Thus, Mary became his partner in this strange performance, taking on a series of roles that kept her perpetually by his side. In a world teeming with variables, she was the one constant in his life, reliably and relentlessly there.

And so, as the three of them motored south that day on Mississippi 35, perhaps Mary let herself think that her presence next to Donald helped him relax. Perhaps, on a certain level, she was right. Inside the car, she represented the familiar. Everything outside would have hurtled at Donald in a raucous rush of unpredictability—the very thing that rattled him most. The passing sights and sounds that would go unremarked upon by most of us—the ugly belch of a tractor churning smoke in a field; a flapping mass of laundry on a clothesline; the unexpected sound of a car radio crackling from the window of an oncoming car; not to mention the rocking and rumble of the car he was in—would have unfolded in a startling, spontaneous riot, faster than Donald's mind could make sense of it. It's easy to imagine him leaning into his mother's side in the face of this onslaught, not necessarily to get her attention, but because she served as a constant in his life. She was the same as always, exactly how he needed things to be.

But Donald was leaving her, and his father too. The three of them were headed to a little town called Sanatorium, Mississippi, to a facility known as the Preventorium, established in 1930. Located on a small rise, it was a curious statement of a building, unexpectedly handsome and bold among the pines. On its driveway side, six huge white columns supported a high roof, throwing shade over the steps and veranda. Inside, the Preventorium's rooms and corridors were arranged to replicate the shape of a double crucifix.

The Preventorium housed exclusively white children between the ages of four and eleven, up to fifty at any one time, each committed to the care of the state of Mississippi to reside, parents were promised, "under constant expert medical supervision." In the most literal sense of the word, these kids were "institutionalized." Their number would soon increase by one. Since Donald was still only three, the state would be making an exception in taking him, but that had been worked out in advance.

Goodbyes at the Preventorium were managed briskly, with little time for clinging or tears. One child resident of that era, Cecile Snider, recalls that even her mother did not explain why she had been brought to this elegant dormitory that looked vaguely like a red-walled Greek temple. Cecile was six and had followed her mother trustingly between the two huge white pillars that framed the entrance. Two hours later, when her mother left without her, Cecile did not quite comprehend that she was now on her own and would not see her mother for months. One of the nurses took possession of her prized Shirley Temple doll—which she would never see again—and directed her instead to the shelves of communal toys, games, and books. Another nurse took away the clothes and shoes she had worn from home. From then on, she would dress in short white bloomers and a white sleeveless top and go barefoot, like all the children at the Preventorium. This separation would haunt her well into adulthood.

Donald, however, already appeared emotionally separated from his family and anyone else who happened to be around. He had a habit, any time he entered a new setting, of ignoring any people present and making straight for whatever inanimate objects might catch his eye: paper clips or seat cushions or an ashtray—especially anything that could be set spinning. Wholly engaged by these new objects, Donald would have missed the mood of the moment, not seen the tension in his parents' eyes as they knelt down for their final goodbye. If anything, he might have been slightly irritated by the interruption.

Mary and Beamon watched the nurse take Donald by the hand and lead him down the hall, where there was a uniform waiting for him, still crisp from the laundry. Then they turned away, passing once again through the pillars out front, and headed for the car. There could not have been much to say on the long ride home.

2

A MENACE TO SOCIETY

IT HAD NOT BEEN THEIR IDEA TO SEND HIM AWAY.

You have overstimulated him. That was a doctor's verdict on Mary's approach to childrearing, and most likely was delivered to her, word for word, in just those terms—with the clear implication that she had done something wrong. The same specialist had also advised the Tripletts that being separated from his parents was the best option for Donald—the only one, really.

There was something else that had helped convince them. In 1937, Donald stopped eating. Getting him fed had always been complicated, but then, late in his third year, Donald began refusing everything. It was this loss of appetite that finally sealed the case for sending Donald away. Mary and Beamon could tell themselves, and others, that Donald was absent from home for health reasons.

The dietary program at the Preventorium made this reassuringly plausible. Its management advertised a focus on food as its core therapeutic offering. In fact, many children were sent there specifically to eat better. Furthermore, Donald's stay at the Preventorium would not last forever. Many children returned home after three or four months. Some stayed as long as six months. Nine was not unheard of, but that was stretching it. Everyone went home, healthier than when he or she had arrived. That was all Mary and Beamon had to tell anyone who asked where Donald was.

In fact, Donald did begin to eat again at the Preventorium, if only because of its strict rule that required each child to eat everything on his plate. But his social isolation—the true reason for his placement—remained a problem, and so he stayed, past the three-month mark, then six months, nine months, and a year. At the age of four, Donald was both the youngest and the longest-term resident of the Preventorium.

Of course, the Tripletts did not have to follow the doctor's advice to send Donald away. But it would have been strange to ignore the best medical advice after they had spent so much time seeking it out.

The Tripletts had thrown everything they had at trying to find an answer for their son. They had money and, therefore, access to the best technological tools of the day: a car and a telephone. They also had the pull to get Donald seen by the best-regarded doctors. They took him to the Mayo Clinic in Minnesota, and, nearer Forest, they consulted John Bullock, the sitting vice president of the Mississippi State Pediatric Society.

In Donald's day, these doctors, upon examining him, would likely have referred to him with terms such as *defective.* And once a child had that label—whether due to Down syndrome, epilepsy, traumatic brain injury, or for reasons the doctors could not explain—parents quickly learned what they were expected to do: put their children away. Following doctors' orders, thousands did so.

To be sure, the advice to institutionalize was never meant to be cruel, any more than the word "defective" was intended to disparage. At the time, it was simply a clinical term that denoted a disparity from normal functioning, equally applicable to a defective heart valve. The same was true, initially, when the words "idiot," "imbecile," and "moron" were designated, in 1902, to describe people operating with "mental ages" of—respectively—less than three years, three to seven years, and seven to ten years.

Throughout the first half of the twentieth century, the lexicon of disability also included "cretin," "ignoramus," "simpleton," "maniac," "lunatic," "dullard," "dunce," "demented," "deranged," "schizoid," "spastic," "feebleminded," and "psychotic." Appearing in lectures and scholarly writings, these terms, when used by men of medicine, were intended only to be clinically descriptive and specific.

Inevitably, however, each of these words would be co-opted by the public and deployed out of their clinical context, used to mock, wound, and stigmatize. Such shifts in meaning forced the earliest professional organization for intellectual disability in the United States to go through five name changes in its history. Founded in 1876, the Association of Medical Officers of American Institutions for Idiotic and Feebleminded Persons became, in 1906, the American Association for the Study of the Feebleminded. In 1933, it was renamed the American Association on Mental Deficiency. In 1987, it became the American Association on Mental Retardation, and, in 2006, the American Association on Intellectual and Developmental Disabilities. "Retarded," once one of the most neutral terms in the vocabulary of disability—a high-toned way of saying "delayed"—had long since become the root word for a variety of slurs in the culture at large.

Another term in this category was "mongoloid," used to describe people born with Down syndrome. Later regarded as a double insult, because of its racial connotations, it was at one time so widely accepted that Benjamin Spock used a variant of it in the first edition of his bestselling book on parenting. The term disappeared from later editions, along with Spock's advice to parents of children with Down syndrome. His original counsel was, of course, nothing more than the conventional wisdom of the time—the advice nearly all parents were given when they were told that their child was going to grow up to be a good deal different from "normal."

For parents who planned simply to embrace the child, to make him or her part of the family, the advice from doctors was blunt.

Don't.

"You know more than you think you do," Spock told mothers in his classic book, *The Common Sense Book of Baby and Child Care,* first published in 1946. It was the most quoted line of a work that would be translated into thirty-nine languages and become one of the bestselling books in history. That reassuring sentiment, like the book itself, struck a chord with young women who felt thrown off balance by the cottage industry of "experts" giving childrearing advice that sprang up in the United States in the early 1900s. Many mothers began to fear that they were getting it all wrong—ruining their children's lives and failing at what the experts cast as a woman's most important contribution to society.

But here was Benjamin Spock—a Harvard graduate and a pediatrician—suggesting that everyone just relax. Spock scoffed at the prevailing view that babies' lives conform to strict schedules, and that too much attention and coddling was a bad thing. Spock was all for love and affection and for women trusting their own instincts.

But in his first 1946 edition, he drew the line when a "Mongolian" baby entered the picture. In a section called "Special Problems," he strongly urged that such a child be placed in an institution, and quickly. "It is usually recommended that this be done right after birth," Spock wrote. "Then the parents will not become too wrapped up in a child who will never develop very far, and they will have more attention to give to their children who need it." In a later edition, he appeared to recognize that parents might resist taking this step. "If placement in a nursing home or school is going to prove inevitable," he wrote, "it's better for the suggestion to come from the professional person rather than be left to the parents who become very guilty thinking about it."

The rush to institutionalize mentally challenged children in the early twentieth century, when so much shame was attached to a child who was not "normal," meant that very few families publicly discussed the challenges of raising these children. Memoirs of raising disabled children barely exist from this era, and the few that were published plainly show the pressure parents faced to rid their homes of children whose disabilities might burden the entire family.

Attorney John P. Frank gave a moving account of just this struggle in his 1954 book, *My Son's Story*. Frank's son Petey had been born in 1947 with a malformation in his brain that severely impaired his growth, his speech, and his intellect. The idea of sending Petey away to an institution at the age of two broke Frank's heart, but he never questioned the necessity of doing so, because it was recommended to him by every single doctor he consulted.

Frank also received heartfelt letters from not one but two justices of the Supreme Court, where he had clerked, who also urged a separation. Justice Wiley Rutledge told him of close friends who had hesitated to institutionalize a disabled girl and had come to regret it. "The parents would have been much better off throughout those long years of suffering," Rutledge told him, if they had only sent her away early. Justice Hugo Black told of a family whose decision to raise an intellectually disabled boy at home had "cast a blight over the lives of the parents and the children." Black urged his former clerk to avoid the same mistake and find a proper place for Petey. In the end, a placement was arranged, in a setting where he was looked after by nuns and where Petey's mother visited him regularly for the rest of her life. Petey died there in 2010.

Like Beamon Triplett, John Frank was a well-educated lawyer. Spock thought social class and education were important parts of the decision to institutionalize. The higher a family stood on the social ladder, the more sense it made to send a child away. In some few cases, he wrote, if the child is truly "responsive, loved and enjoyed by the family, everyone will be happier if he stays at home." But he thought that shame worked against this outcome. "Sadly enough," he wrote, the "child whose parents have had only an average amount of schooling and are living happily on a modest scale makes out better."

There were, then, squadrons of babies and toddlers, both before Spock and after, exiled from their homes, generally forever. Often families postponed the separation by a few years, because institutions tended not to take the very youngest children. It was a stage the parents passed through in isolation, confiding only to people in their inner circle. And no matter how often doctors and friends and Spock tried to talk these mothers and fathers out of feeling shame, the silence that accompanied the disappearance only reinforced that feeling. They had sent away their children in secret, and in time, the children themselves became secrets, never to be spoken of again.

THERE HAD BEEN a light in Donald's eyes before the Preventorium. Whatever his peculiarities, he had always been noisy and active, curious and creative. Yes, people seemed to baffle him, but with *things* he enjoyed a solid and satisfying relationship. He could be mesmerized by numbers and notes, or lose himself in the contemplation of lists and patterns. These objects and abstractions were his connections to the world, his points of give-and-take. Even when he was demanding and stubborn, he was an irrepressible presence. But all of that went dead at the Preventorium, and almost all at once.

A photograph of Donald exists from this period, in a small hardbound report published in 1939. It is titled *The Mississippi State Sanatorium, A Book of Information,* and on page 33, there is Donald, concrete and spiritless, posed on some steps. The photo is captioned "Preventorium Children," and in it Donald is surrounded by a dozen other kids, who are clearly reacting to something amusing. The kids are beaming, caught off guard by the joke, one girl giggling behind her fingers, the others grinning past the camera or at one another.

All but Donald. Seated in the middle, looking smaller than anyone else, he remains rigid, eyes fixed on the lens, a dead stare, lips locked in a slight frown. Donald had gone silent. The boisterous ball of fire his mother could barely contain now "faded away physically," according to a doctor who examined Donald. Though the place was a swirl of activity, the daily routine packed full with meals and lessons and playground visits and naptimes, the doctor noted that Donald "sat motionless, not paying attention to anything." Blocks, books, toy trucks, pots and pans—he stopped reaching for them. The examining doctor later concluded: "It seems that he had there his worst phase."

His parents must have been able to see how poorly Donald was doing at the Preventorium. The place allowed twice-monthly visits from families, always conducted outdoors on the grounds. One afternoon, during one of these visits, someone snapped a photo of Donald and his dad out on the great lawn together. Both are facing the photographer, Beamon crouched down so that he is glancing up at his son, his hands encircling Donald's waist. Beamon grins widely, coaxingly, straining to make the picture work. Donald wears an expression that is hard to interpret—somewhere between complaint and confusion. The boy who once smiled for the camera is no longer smiling.

Time after time, these visits would end with Donald being led back inside through the imposing white columns, and with Mary and

Beamon driving away, silencing every instinct they felt to take him back home.

In 1938, Mary and Beamon had a second child, a boy they named Oliver. He arrived in May, about nine months after they had driven with Donald to Sanatorium. It felt like they were making a new start. Over and over again, Mary had been told things like: *Move on with your life. Have more children. Devote yourself to the ones who can benefit from it.* Now she was complying with at least the second part of the prescription. And there could be no doubt that, after Donald left, and before the second baby came, the Triplett household had become more *convenient* to live in, more like the one she grew up in. One in which she and Beamon could enjoy quiet conversation over supper; where they didn't hesitate to have people over; where at last she could get a full night's sleep every night.

Once baby Oliver arrived, the three of them could go out and, to any casual passerby, look the part of a typical young American family, baby in tow, parents focused on his future. Finally, they were living the model of parenthood Mary and Beamon had imagined for themselves—the one the magazines talked about when they dispensed advice on how to survive the strains and uncertainties that could overwhelm a young mother.

For Mary, the ordinariness of those strains was a blessing. At the same time, she knew that if those casual passersby knew there was a Donald, many of them would have reassessed the "model couple" walking past with the baby in the stroller. Donald, even in exile, would be seen as a stain on the family. Reactions would range from pity to contempt, for the values of the day were unforgiving. Mary and Beamon's bloodlines, once crossed, had produced a "defective" child.

There is no way for us to know how much shame Mary and Beamon felt, but we know that during their youth, a campaign was under way, fought by intelligent, zealous, and influential Americans who believed that children like Donald were a danger to society and, worse, not fully human. This campaign had an enormous effect on how mental disability was perceived in the United States, not only when Donald was a child but for decades afterward. In a very real way, Donald, four years old and shut away, with only his parents to stand up for him, had enemies out there.

If there was a model family, it was the Kelleys of Isle of Hope, Georgia. The front-page headline in the *Savannah Press* told the story in 1924: KELLEYS WIN IN "FITTER FAMILIES" CONTEST. The medal winners were pictured as well: James Kelley, a teacher and school principal, sits unsmiling but serene, with his two well-groomed young daughters, Elizabeth and Priscilla, positioned on either side of him; his wife, also identified as a teacher but never named, stands behind them, not smiling either.

Their scores, recorded while the Kelleys were at the Georgia State Fair, had astonished the national contest organizer, a Mrs. Watts, who was struck giddy at finding such talent in a part of the South where, until then, she had not run tests. "Kansas still has the high-score family so far," she told the *Press* reporter, "but it is a question how long they can hold it. Georgia is a close second."

A matronly presence, impeccable in appearance, draped in pearls that swung to her waist, Mrs. Watts had been organizing Fitter Family Contests across the South and Midwest since 1921. Over the next several years, these contests would also take place in Texas and Louisiana, and as far north as Michigan and Massachusetts, often with a healthy dose of newspaper coverage. It was great human-interest stuff.

Mrs. Watts staged her contests at state agricultural fairs, always timed to overlap with the main event—the livestock contests. Farmers had trucked in their best-looking cattle, their most perfect pigs, to compete for blue ribbons. The judges, fellow farmers, gave prizes for breeding animals that came as close as possible to flawless examples of their species. Better-bred animals, when crossed again and again, led to unending improvement in the stock of the breed.

Mrs. Watts had the same goal for humans. "While the [cattle] judges are testing the Holsteins, Jerseys and whitefaces," Watts once said, "we are testing the Joneses, Smiths and the Johnsons." When she declared the Kelleys to be "of the highest type," she meant that they were the sort of Americans who should be encouraged—exhorted, even—to reproduce.

They had been examined by an expert team that included a dentist, a psychologist, a psychiatrist, a pathologist, a pediatrician, and a historian. They'd had their urine tested; their skulls measured; their teeth evaluated for the orderliness of their alignment and the durability of their enamel. They were asked about childhood diseases, broken bones, and bathing schedules. Mothers were required to provide a list of daily meals, which was assessed for the percentage of protein versus non-protein. And each family member was observed chewing food, with notes taken when this was performed "too slowly" or "too hastily." There was also a written IQ test—timed—that the children, as well as the adults, had to complete.

The wild card for every contestant, however, was ancestry. The Fitter Family Contests were designed to get something across to the masses: a rudimentary understanding of the way human genetics determined all that was good and evil about modern American society. A hand-painted sign hanging by the entrance to the competition booth carried an urgent warning:

> EVERY 48 SECONDS A PERSON IS BORN IN THE UNITED STATES WHO WILL NEVER GROW UP MENTALLY BEYOND THAT STAGE OF A NORMAL 8 YR. OLD BOY OR GIRL.

A second sign added perspective:

> EVERY 15 SECONDS $100 OF YOUR MONEY GOES FOR THE CARE OF PERSONS WITH BAD HEREDITY SUCH AS THE INSANE, FEEBLEMINDED, CRIMINALS AND OTHER DEFECTIVES.

And a third offered hope:

> EVERY 7½ MINUTES A HIGH-GRADE PERSON IS BORN IN THE UNITED STATES.

An electric lightbulb was affixed to each sign, flashing on at the appropriate intervals: every forty-eight seconds, every fifteen seconds, and, much too infrequently, every seven and a half minutes. Good heredity was falling behind at an alarming rate.

It had to be a rude shock for families that went into these contests concerned about the dire message of the lightbulbs, only to come out with a flunking grade. They would leave the state fairgrounds that day branded unfit for America. But this was useful knowledge, in its way, because if Mrs. Watts's hopes for these contests were to be fulfilled, a failing family would know never to procreate, for the good of society. And those from families "of good stock" would know never to let their children mate with someone from an unfortunately blighted family.

The caliber of the herd as a whole is lifted when only the best of its members are permitted to breed. Obviously, that applied to humans as well.

MARY AND BEAMON TRIPLETT came of age during the era of the Fitter Family Contests. People of lesser mental capability were portrayed as a menace to society, and extreme measures were justified to eliminate that menace. This was not merely theoretical, and not nearly as benign as the smiling Mrs. Watts made it out to be with her quaint contests. Her operation was merely the extreme retail end of a scientific, political, and philosophical movement that, in the two decades leading up to Donald's birth, had dedicated itself to the proposition that children like him didn't deserve to be born. In the movement as a whole, Mrs. Watts was a bit player, a self-appointed and enthusiastic popularizer, civic-minded and hardworking, but not a scientist, academic, or statesman.

But those levels of society were well represented in the movement as well. At Harvard and Yale, in the pages of the *New York Times* and the *Saturday Evening Post,* and in the hearing rooms of Congress, men who stood at the pinnacle of their fields and of society had embraced, in a burst of optimism, a brand-new science.

Eugenics—derived from a combination of other relatively new sciences like anthropology, zoology, genetics, and psychometrics—opened up the possibility of purging rot and impurity from the lineage of humanity. President Teddy Roosevelt himself touted a eugenics manifesto called *The Passing of the Great Race,* written by his friend, New York lawyer Madison Grant. In his book, Grant recommended a program of mass selective breeding to rid the United States of the genetic influence of "the weak, the broken, the mentally crippled," the millions of citizens he deemed "worthless" and "wretched." Roosevelt praised the book's compendium of "facts our people most need to realize." A young man wrote Grant a fan letter from Austria, announcing that his book was now his "bible." His name was Adolf Hitler.

Grant argued for the forced sterilization of people deemed not worthy of procreating. So powerful was the enthusiasm for eugenics that seventeen states legalized forced sterilization in the 1920s. These measures found support all over the political spectrum. In 1926, Margaret Sanger, the founder of Planned Parenthood and a defender of the disadvantaged, said to a Vassar College audience: "The American public is taxed, heavily taxed, to maintain an increasing race of morons, which threatens the very foundations of our civilization."

The state of Mississippi's sterilization law was written to cover hereditary "insanity, feeblemindedness, idiocy, and epilepsy." In fact, Mississippi was less aggressive in sterilizing its disabled than some other states. By 1933, the year Donald was born, twelve people had been forced to undergo the procedure, versus 1,333 in Virginia and 8,504 in California. In 1939, Mississippi's laxity seemed to bother an editorial writer for the *Delta Democrat Times* in Greenville. Envying Virginia's record, and "the money the state was set to save by practicing preventive eugenics"—which reduced the financial burden of caring for "defectives"—the writer suggested hopefully that "Mississippi might profit by Virginia's example." Donald was five years old when that editorial appeared.

Of course, Hitler, once in power, took things a great deal further. He started World War II eight months after that *Delta Democrat Times* editorial, and under his rule, following his "bible," the number of disabled Germans murdered to purify the racial stock of the Third Reich reached into the tens of thousands.

REMARKABLY, CONSIDERING that the United States was by then at war with the Nazis, a soberly worded endorsement of "mercy killing" for mentally disabled children appeared in the July 1942 issue of the *American Journal of Psychiatry,* published by the American Psychiatric Association. It was written by Robert Foster Kennedy, an Irish-born American neurologist.

"Nature's mistakes," Kennedy argued, deserved relief from the burden of a life "that at no time can produce anything good at all." He called for painless methods of killing and spelled out a careful selection process. First, the parents of such a child would need to request the death. Then, three examinations should be conducted, over time, but only after "a defective . . . has reached the age of five or more." Should it then be found "that the defective has no future nor hope of one," he wrote, "then I believe it is a merciful and kindly thing to relieve that defective—often tortured and convulsed, grotesque and absurd, useless and foolish, and entirely undesirable—of the agony of living."

Not everyone took Kennedy's side. In the very same issue of the *Journal of Psychiatry,* there appeared a six-page clarion call for the "humanization" of the mentally disabled, a recognition that each disabled person has a place in society. The author used the language of the era—*defectives, feebleminded, imbeciles*—but his compassion for the disabled and his respect for their dignity and right to exist was palpable. Indeed, he wrote, it was time that psychiatrists ceased "to treat the term mental deficiency as a swear word," and to recognize that when a society diminishes the standing of its weakest, the whole society is diminished as well. "By exonerating the feeble," he concluded, "we thus exonerate ourselves."

And so a rare gauntlet was thrown down on behalf of mentally disabled children, by a child psychiatrist from Johns Hopkins named Leo Kanner. Kanner was, at that time, less than a year away from publishing a far more important article, one that would be quoted around the world and into the next century. It began with a description of a boy who had been brought to Kanner's Baltimore office by his parents six years earlier. The boy was from Mississippi, and his name was Donald Triplett.

3

CASE 1

THE PREVENTORIUM HAD BEEN A PREMATURE SURRENDER. True, life was more serene now at the Triplett house. The new baby was so different from Donald. Oliver looked at them when he smiled, and he curved his body into their arms when they held him. Even so, either Mary or Beamon, or both of them, eventually reached the conclusion that the Preventorium was the wrong solution for Donald, and that it was far too soon to give up trying to find the right one. They had already traveled all over Mississippi, and as far north as Minnesota, in search of answers. This time, they would travel even farther, to Baltimore, to meet with a doctor by the name of Leo Kanner.

IN THE 1930S, Leo Kanner ranked as the top child psychiatrist in the United States, perhaps even the world. It had only been thirty years or so since psychiatry had discovered childhood as a subspecialty; it took the profession quite some time to cease thinking of children merely as miniature adults. Kanner's 1935 book, *Child Psychiatry,* was for many years the standard, and only, textbook on the topic. He was the first head of the department of child psychiatry at Johns Hopkins University in Baltimore, which was, in turn, the first such academic department of its kind in the United States. To American eyes, Kanner certainly looked the part. Slight and stooped, with oversized ears and a basset hound face, he spoke English in a high, reedy voice, with an accent so heavy that at times he was incomprehensible. Like Sigmund Freud, he was both Austrian and Jewish.

Kanner's move to the United States, in 1924, happened on a whim.

That was something of a pattern with him. He was once hit by a train when, on a lark, he took a stroll out onto a railroad bridge where it crossed over water. Having never learned to swim, he was lucky to be saved from drowning by a member of the train crew. He had tried, also on impulse, to join the German army as a young man to fight in World War I. Rejected due to his small stature and two missing front teeth, he headed for the recruiting office of the Austrian army, where he was accepted.

Kanner was sent to the front as a medical corpsman but, with his hands stained with the blood of men far too young to die, he quickly realized that war was not for him. He performed his hospital duties fully and well, then worked just as diligently at arranging a series of transfers for assignments farther and farther from the front. He won an honorable discharge one year into his service, granted on the premise that he would be more valuable to the Fatherland as a fully trained physician. He committed to return to Germany to start medical school.

By late 1923, Kanner, now a husband and father, had been in general practice in Berlin for three years, and his patient list was growing. It might have gone on this way had he not befriended a young American physician, Dr. Louis Holtz, who had come to Berlin to take a few medical courses. Kanner liked Holtz enormously and began bringing him home for dinners. Holtz, who had recently become a widower, took comfort in the Kanners' company and appreciated the friendship extended him in a foreign land. Over dinner, he would regale Kanner and his wife, June, with stories of the wonders of life in America. Having resolved to repay the Kanners' kindness, Holtz talked Kanner into applying for a visa to the United States—just in case he ever wanted it—and then turned up bearing a written offer of a position as a physician at the South Dakota State Hospital for the Insane, in Yankton, South Dakota. Within four weeks, Kanner had arranged for a one-year leave of absence from work and shipped the family's two featherbeds to America.

Kanner was thirty years old and fluent in seven languages when he arrived in Yankton. Unfortunately, English wasn't one of them. He worked at changing that, just as he worked hard to adopt American ways. He bought a Chevrolet, tried to take an interest in golf, and joined a weekly poker game. Soon enough, he was publishing medical articles in English. He learned to live with the fact that Americans were always either misspelling or mispronouncing his last name, which rhymed with "honor." (When they did pronounce it right, they often assumed they were talking to "Dr. Lee O'Connor.") Eventually, he became known around Yankton as "the German doctor," not a bad credential when German medicine was seen as the best in the world.

In the United States, most psychiatrists started out as garden-variety MDs who learned the specialty by going to work in mental institutions—just as Kanner was doing. The discipline of psychiatry was still young enough that doctors largely taught themselves, sorting out what worked and what didn't patient by patient, by trial and error, gradually formulating their own guiding principles for how to treat mental illness. It was at Yankton that Kanner noticed, and rejected, an institutional penchant for pigeonholing patients by syndrome. He hated this. Too much emphasis was put on figuring out what label to stick on each patient, he concluded, and not enough time was spent listening to the patients themselves. Kanner developed his own style of writing up an individual's medical history. Instead of the usual dry compendium of dates and previous illnesses, he presented his patients' histories in full sentences, with well-developed paragraphs and telling details taken from his personal observations. This would become a hallmark of his work: to appreciate the actual *stories* of his patients, and to use that understanding as the key to diagnosing and treating them.

More controversially, Kanner became increasingly impatient with medical procedures that seemed to have no rationale other than habit. One Christmas Eve, Kanner ordered that most of the restrained patients be released from their straitjackets for the evening. The floor supervisor objected strenuously and took the matter to the hospital director, but Kanner prevailed—by volunteering to spend Christmas in the ward personally. It worked out—there were no incidents—except that his wife had to spend the day without him. By the time the holiday was over, it was clear that the straitjackets were unnecessary. The patients remained unrestrained from then on.

In 1928, Kanner, ever ambitious, met and impressed Adolf Meyer, the head of psychiatry at Johns Hopkins, which led to Kanner's landing a fellowship there. Two years after arriving in Baltimore, Kanner was tasked with establishing the university's first clinical department of child psychiatry.

In short order, he became the field's most prominent figure. This was not least due to Kanner's penchant for seeking the spotlight. He wrote often for the popular press, where he positioned himself as a demystifier of the art and science of childrearing and as a defender of the weak and vulnerable—clearly relishing, and even cultivating, the recognition that came with that role. He also worked for years on an autobiography in which he related, in minute detail, his striver's story of a small-town boy who wanted to be a poet, making good instead as a man of medicine on the world stage. While he looked in vain for a publisher, the manuscript went through several rewrites. But it remained a portrait of a progressive doctor fighting with skill, wit, and humility against entrenched forces that sought to crush the human spirit.

In fact, his self-portrait was not entirely unjustified. When Jewish psychiatrists and other medical professionals were fleeing the Nazis in Germany and Austria, he personally intervened in scores of cases to ensure that the refugees were granted permission to enter the United States, and then he helped them find jobs so they could support themselves and start over again. Taking into account the families of those he aided, Kanner can be credited with saving hundreds of lives.

More publicly, Kanner blew the whistle in 1937 on a racket run out of the Baltimore Home for the Feebleminded. While working on a study of outcomes for released patients, he and a social worker named Mabel Kraus learned that ten to twenty years earlier, close to a hundred teenage girls had ended up in what he described as slavery. The scheme was engineered by a corrupt judge and a lawyer working on behalf of dozens of wealthy Baltimore families. For a fee—which the two men split—the judge authorized the release of the girls to specific families who claimed to be giving the girls homes. Instead, they put them to work as servants, scrubbing their toilets and in some cases, Kanner hinted, sexually servicing males in the family. Many of the young women ended up on the street, in prostitution. By the time

Kanner found out about this, the judge enabling this abuse had long since retired. But Kanner went public with the details anyway, in a speech to the American Psychiatric Association. After that he told the story to newspaper reporters.

The man who had released mental patients from their straitjackets also held relatively progressive views—for his day—on race. In 1938, he told a young doctor who wrote asking for "a comparison of the Negro child's mental abilities with that of the white race" that no difference existed. "The fact that a child comes into the world as a Negro does in no way serve as a barometer for his intellectual potentialities," Kanner wrote back. At the time virtually all mental hospitals were still segregated by race.

Yet for all his manifest high-mindedness, Kanner was no radical. Having worked so hard to reach the upper ranks of American society, he never took a stance that truly ruffled feathers or risked alienation from that society. Instead, he hedged. While exposing the scandal of the servant girls, for example, he rued the fact that the women were having children, who were likewise mentally disabled, and he refused to name the wrongdoers publicly. And his letter to the doctor about racial differences was private. In public, he never questioned the racial segregation that prevailed in the wards of Johns Hopkins into the 1950s. Similarly, although he spoke out against euthanasia for the disabled, and opposed the forced sterilization of those with low IQs, he described sterilization as "a desirable procedure" when parents were too intellectually impaired to care for their children safely, in which case the obligation for care would fall to society. Thus, Kanner, who clearly aspired to land on the right side of history, was still in many ways captive to the views of his day.

This then was the man Beamon and Mary turned to in 1938 to get help for their son. But before meeting the boy, the doctor who liked stories asked to know a bit more about him. So in the late summer of 1938, Beamon set out to write for America's greatest child psychiatrist the complete story of Donald.

BEAMON TRIPLETT didn't type. For that, he needed Katherine Robertson, who commanded the outer room of his one-man law practice. Hardly a word went out above Beamon's signature that did not go through Katherine. Beamon would dictate in his mild Mississippi drawl while she filled her notepad with shorthand. Then, she typed.

Kanner would later remark on the sheer amount of detail Beamon packed into the letter, which struck him, frankly, as the output of an obsessive man. Perhaps so, for Beamon did come with a few personality wrinkles of his own. There was his tendency to tune out the world when he went for walks, to the point where he couldn't remember afterward where he'd been or whom he'd seen along the way. While at Yale Law School, he had cracked under the pressure and taken to his bed with what he regarded as a nervous breakdown. A doctor he consulted diagnosed an irrational fear of teachers.

But that had been years ago. Beamon was successful now, a sharp lawyer, a man with first-rate observational skills who had every reason to want to get this letter absolutely right. And he was determined to compose a full biography of this four-year-old child trapped in the Preventorium, a place that made no sense for him. In time, Beamon's words would travel far and wide. They would be quoted in scholarly research; discussed in university classrooms; translated into multiple languages; excavated, late at night, by frantic parents scouring the Internet. But that humid day in Forest, it was just one father speaking, and it was Katherine Robertson alone who heard this story, for the first time, and got it down.

"He never seems glad," Beamon dictated, "to see father or mother. He seems almost to draw into his shell, and live within himself." In minute detail, he described Donald's eating habits, his verbal patterns, the clarity of his enunciation, the ages at which he learned to walk and count and hum and sing. And so it poured forth, what would become the seminal account of a child with autism, a term and diagnosis that did not yet exist.

The Donald that Beamon described was unreachable by any of the usual ways parents connect to their children: "He seldom comes when called but has to be picked up and carried or led wherever he ought to go." Yet, at the same time, the toddler Donald tantalized his parents with hints of a sharp intelligence. His focus on the activities that captivated him could not have been more intense. "He seems always to be thinking," Beamon observed, "thinking and thinking."

Beamon listed the things Donald had committed to memory at the age of two: the words of many songs and the melodies that went with them; the names of all of the presidents of the United States; and "most of the pictures of his ancestors and kinfolk on both sides of the house." Yet Donald could do little with these facts beyond reciting them. Conversation was impossible, Beamon said, as "he was not learning to ask questions or to answer questions."

He appeared indifferent to the company of other children, and in one episode Beamon recounted, he positively shunned them. One day, in what was meant as a pleasant surprise, a playground slide was delivered to the Triplett backyard. Donald seemed not to grasp its function, but a small crowd of neighborhood children did. As they clambered all over it, Donald held back, resisting furiously when his father picked him up and sat him at the top to show him how it worked. "When we put him up to slide down, he seemed horror-struck," he recounted.

It was different, though, when no one else was there. The next morning, he walked out, climbed the ladder, and slid down. He knew, after all, exactly how it worked. Beamon reported that Donald continued to slide on it frequently, but only when no other children were present.

Beamon also shared his own botched effort to foist a friendship upon Donald. In 1936, the year Donald turned three, he approached the Baptist Children's Home, an orphanage in Jackson, and explained to the people in charge his wish to find a companion for Donald—a boy of the same age who would be a full-time playmate. He made it clear that he did not intend to adopt the child. Nevertheless, this highly unusual arrangement was agreed to. A three-year-old named Jimmy was led outside to where the Triplett family car was waiting.

When the boy arrived at the house, Donald would not even look at him. That did not change, no matter how Mary tried to get the two of them to play together. After some weeks, the experiment was deemed a failure, and Beamon arranged for Jimmy's return to the Baptist home.

This was the essence of Donald, as Beamon described him.

Aloneness was his preferred state of being, one he protected with "a mental barrier between his inner consciousness and the outside world." Only behind that barrier, Beamon observed, in that world of his own, did his son appear content. Donald was fully capable of joy and laughter, and there were days when he seemed "constantly happy." But it was never prompted by the company of others, never by virtue of sharing a joke. It was, inevitably, only when he was "busy entertaining himself."

By the time Katherine finished typing it up, the entire thing ran to thirty-three single-spaced pages. Beamon folded it up and sent the letter off. Soon after that, a date was set: Donald would go to Baltimore to meet Dr. Leo Kanner in person the second week of October 1938.

For the last time, Mary and Beamon drove out to the Preventorium. They had resolved that, after they took Donald to Baltimore, they would not bring him back.

Donald had been there for more than a year by then. He was still the strangest boy in the building, as incomprehensible to those around him as ever. No longer the locked, motionless presence he had been at the beginning, he had developed a new habit of swinging his whole head side to side without letup. And he was once again interested in playing with objects in his unique ways, spinning and stacking and counting them. Yet he still didn't play or speak with the other children, and not because they had shut him out. In terms of connecting to others, his progress had been none to negative.

Still, when Mary and Beamon announced their intention to take Donald home for good, they were met with strenuous argument. The director admonished them to "let him alone." He was "getting along nicely" now, hardly any trouble at all anymore. Taking him home would be a terrible mistake.

This much was true: in his white bloomers and top, Donald had grown accustomed to the routines and the discipline of the place. He had adapted. But "getting along nicely" did not mean the same thing to the director as it did to Mary and Beamon. The director was telling them, in essence, that Donald was no longer disruptive to the system.

He was eating, for example, but there was nothing to be said about Donald outgrowing his aloneness.

This fruitless experiment in separation—it was enough now. Mary took Donald aside and dressed him in clothes she had brought from home. In the outer office, Beamon signed the papers and squared their account, ignoring the staff's disapproving looks. All he requested was a write-up of Donald's progress over the previous year, so that he could share it with Kanner. Not terribly motivated, apparently, the director came up with a scant half page of terse notes, in which he offered the opinion that Donald's problem was some sort of "glandular disease."

Then, having gathered up Donald's few belongings, all three Tripletts went out, for the last time, between those massive front pillars. Donald would be turning five in a few weeks, on September 8, 1938. The family would celebrate at home.

Just over a month after Donald's fifth birthday, he and his parents traveled to Baltimore by train—a journey of nearly two days, across seven states, including a stop to switch lines in Birmingham, Alabama. For Donald, the journey would have been one of those bewildering, or perhaps mesmerizing, explosions of new sensory experiences. Especially the overnight stretch of it, when from his bed, up against the high, wide windows of the Pullman, he could stare out into the night, watching the lights of the sleeping South slinging past through the blackness outside, with a rhythm that echoed the sounds of the rocking train, a gentle song of repetition that his mind would be drawn to.

For the last part of the trip, the Tripletts caught a ride outside the Lord Baltimore Hotel, which took them to the Harriet Lane Home for Invalid Children a few miles away. The Harriet Lane Home was an extension of Johns Hopkins, with staff that reported directly to Leo Kanner. Donald was to stay there for the next two weeks. He would undergo a physical exam, psychological testing, and full-time observation, which explained the little suitcase Mary brought along that morning. Yet again, Donald would be parted from his parents. But this time he would be seen by the best-known child psychiatrist in America.

When Donald Triplett and Leo Kanner were introduced, Donald, true to form, did not even acknowledge the doctor's existence. When he entered the psychiatrist's office, accompanied by his parents, he ignored the adults shaking hands and headed straight to the far wall, where Kanner kept a small collection of toys. While the grown-ups conversed, Donald stayed on the floor, counting, stacking, and lining up wooden blocks.

At a certain point, Kanner produced a pin and gave Donald a little prick with it. The boy flinched, but he seemed to make no connection between the slight sting and the man who had caused it; in other words, Donald was not frightened of the doctor because of it. Kanner was fascinated. "He was never angry at the interfering person," he wrote later. "He angrily shoved away the *hand* that was in his way or the *foot* that stepped on one of his blocks, at one time referring to the foot on the block as 'umbrella.'"

Besides relying on his own observations, Kanner would also rely a great deal on those made by the team of doctors who tracked Donald's days through the Harriet Lane Home. The place had a dormitory feel to it, with a number of other children in residence. The staff kept notes on how Donald interacted with his peers, noting especially his striking indifference to potential playmates. If one of the little girls tried to join whatever Donald was doing on his own, he invariably walked away. Occasionally, one of the boys would take a toy from his hands, which he passively allowed. Unlike when his block arrangements were disturbed, this did not seem to perturb him.

At the home, Donald's behaviors were very much as his father had described them:

> He wandered about smiling, making stereotyped movements with his fingers, crossing them about in the air. He shook his head from side to side, whispering or humming the same three-note tune. He spun with great pleasure anything he could seize upon to spin. He kept throwing things on the floor, seeming to delight in the sounds they made. He arranged beads, stick[s],

or blocks in groups of different series of colors. Whenever he finished one of these performances, he squealed and jumped up and down.

Judging by their notes, the examining team was thoroughly startled and confused by what they were seeing. On one form, in the space designated for a diagnosis, a question mark appeared, and then some guesses: "? Heller's Disease. Schizophrenia." The rest of the space was blank.

At the same time, they took favorable notice of Mary's interactions with Donald. She visited the ward daily, keeping Donald company for hours. The team was apparently impressed by her capacity for giving her taxing child nearly constant attention. It was recorded in Donald's file that "she spent all of her time developing ways of keeping him at play with her." Kanner later concluded that Mary was "the only person with whom he had any contact at all."

As the two weeks came to a close, Mary came by the home one last time to pack up the little suitcase and walk Donald out the door. The only other thing she needed before she left was Kanner's diagnosis. It was, she believed, the key that would turn the lock; the signpost that would tell them where to go next. She wanted the *name* of the thing that made Donald act the way he did.

But Kanner would disappoint her in that regard. Donald was different from any other child he had treated and unlike any description in any textbook. As a result, he had no label to give her.

After the family's return to Forest, Mary and Kanner launched a regular correspondence. Riveted by Donald's case, Kanner wanted to be kept up to date on the boy's growth and development. Mary, for her part, appreciated the psychiatrist's interest and was keen to provide him with any information that might help him solve the puzzle of her son.

For years, they communicated at least once a month. Sometimes Mary shared the strain she was feeling. It was to Kanner that Mary confessed her despair over "the fact that I have a hopelessly insane child." Kanner was quick to discourage such thinking, urging her in his next letter to "refrain from that type of gloom." That was not the only occasion when he tried to rally her spirits. Many times, he wrote to reassure her that her efforts to help Donald were "splendid and often heroic." Even his staff had been impressed by "the good sense you are using." Donald, he insisted, was fortunate in "having you for a mother." Moreover, he shared his opinion that Donald was not necessarily stuck at his present level of development—that he still had the potential to grow.

Mary brought Donald up to Baltimore for a second time in 1939, and twice more in the following years. Kanner looked forward to these visits, as Donald's case presented a real intellectual challenge. Combined with Mary's regular updates, the visits kept him on top of the development of this mystifying young boy.

Mary, however, was frustrated. In 1942, four years after the first visit to Baltimore, Mary wrote to Kanner, suggesting that he had been feeding her only "generalities" regarding Donald's condition, whereas she needed "specifics." She wondered whether his vagueness was a tactic to spare her feelings.

Once again, Kanner wrote back to reassure her. He insisted, first of all, that he was not holding anything back. But he acknowledged that on one level he had failed her and Beamon. "At no time have you or your husband been given a clear-cut and unequivocal evaluation," he wrote, "in the sense of a diagnostic term." The truth was, he confessed, that he still simply could not match Donald with any familiar or standard label, nor could he predict the boy's prospects. His behaviors comprised a mystery that Kanner had not yet been able to solve. "Nobody realizes [that] more than I do myself," Kanner confessed.

That letter, dated September 28, 1942—a carbon copy of which would sit undiscovered in the archives of Johns Hopkins for the next sixty-five years—coincided with a critical turning point in Kanner's perception of Donald's behaviors. While the portions of the letter that address Mary's frustration sound like a frank admission of diagnostic defeat, Kanner had, in fact, already begun formulating a novel type of diagnosis.

After seeing several more children with traits similar to Donald's,

Kanner told Mary that he had "come to recognize for the first time a condition which has not hitherto been described by psychiatric or any other literature." So far, he reported, he had come across "eight other cases, which are very much like Don's." He had been keeping this news to himself, he said, because he wanted to have sufficient time to observe the children and follow their development. Soon, however, he intended to go public with these findings and to give his discovery a name.

"If there is any name to be applied to this condition of Don and those other children," he told her, "I have found it best to speak of it as 'autistic disturbances of affective contact.'" This, Kanner's first recorded use of "autistic" in the context of a behavior pattern like Donald's, was followed by a brief explanation: "The main distinction lies in the inability of these children from earliest infancy to relate themselves to other people." Critically, Kanner added, this inability to relate was present in children whose overall health and "intellectual endowment" was otherwise not significantly impaired.

Thus, it was in a private letter to a mother that Kanner first announced his recognition of the condition that came to be called autism.

Donald would be his Case 1.

4

WILD CHILDREN AND HOLY FOOLS

LEO KANNER CULTIVATED PRAISE AND ATTENTION, BUT IN public he feigned indifference to the plaudits that came his way. This false modesty was on display in July 1969, long after he became famous for discovering autism, when he gave a speech to a group of parents in Washington, DC.

"I didn't go out of my way to discover this condition," he said, after being honored for doing just that. No, he protested, to praise him on those grounds was just "a bit exaggerated."

"A sample of serendipity," he called it. And then he explained how that meant being in the right place at the right time.

"I wasn't looking for anything," he insisted.

But then Kanner took the performance a little further than he usually did.

"I did not discover autism," he declared. "It was there before."

IT WAS THERE BEFORE.

In that single sentence, Kanner summed up his opinion on what remains one of the lasting questions in the field of autism: Was the collection of behaviors he described as "autistic disturbance" a phenomenon new to the mid-twentieth century, or had these behaviors always been present but simply unrecognized?

This question was unanswerable for a number of reasons. One was the fact that medical notation and archiving were rudimentary before the twentieth century. Before World War I, no database was ever compiled from systematic observation of the behavioral traits of individuals in any population of a statistically meaningful size. Indeed, until the late nineteenth century, psychiatry was barely practiced at all—to say nothing of child psychiatry—in the sense of a professional discipline embracing a scientific methodology, a shared vocabulary, and an agreed-upon body of findings rooted in research and practice. In that regard, Kanner's generation was among the pioneers. The undocumented past offered no statistical basis for asserting that autism emerged only around the time Kanner saw it in Donald.

And yet when Kanner asserted the opposite—that autism was always there—that too seemed speculative.

Kanner, however, knew that in psychiatry, the obvious often went unrecognized until someone looked at it with the right set of eyes. As he tried to explain in his speech, he had not "discovered" autism as much as found the eyes with which to see it.

KANNER'S "DISCOVERY" OF autism was not a sudden aha moment, but a slow dawning recognition, one that took nearly four years from when he first met Donald. That recognition culminated in 1943 in a groundbreaking article starring a boy he called "Donald T."

By the time Kanner published his article in April of that year, the number of cases he was tracking had increased to eleven. Eight of his subjects were boys, and three were girls. The title of the article was the same as the name he coined for the condition: "Autistic Disturbances of Affective Contact." He would soon replace this term with *infantile autism,* which merely meant, in medical terminology, that the autism was "present in earliest childhood."

He did not originate the terms *autism* or *autistic.* Rather, they were borrowed from the symptom list of a different condition altogether: schizophrenia. This would long be a source of confusion when autism was discussed, but it made sense from where Kanner sat at the time. By 1943, schizophrenia was a widely accepted label for a mental illness that included hallucinations, disordered thinking, and other breaks with reality. Swiss psychiatrist Eugen Bleuler had also documented a tendency among some schizophrenia patients—who were overwhelmingly adolescents or adults—to detach from interaction with their environment, and to engage exclusively with an interior reality.

Around 1910, Bleuler began using the term *autistic thinking* to describe this behavior. He derived it from the Greek word αυτο, which means "self." Bleuler held that a certain amount of autistic thinking happened in every person's life. It was the essence of dreaming, as well as children's pretend play. But with schizophrenia, autistic thinking could become pathological. That might mean a complete cessation of social interaction and a drastic flattening of the ill person's emotional connection to the surrounding environment and the people in it. This type of autistic thinking was rarely permanent. Like hallucinations and other symptoms of schizophrenia, episodes of Bleuler's autism came and went.

Autism, therefore, had been a part of the psychiatric vocabulary for a generation already when Kanner announced to the world that he had been seeing "a number of children whose condition differs . . . markedly and uniquely from anything reported so far." This new condition was reminiscent of the autism of schizophrenic adults, but it appeared in young children, he wrote. Moreover, it appeared to him that the condition was something that "the children have come into the world with." The condition manifested itself early in life and came with its own "fascinating peculiarities," such as flashes of a brilliance, a distinctive use of language, and a "basic desire for aloneness and sameness." Essentially, this was a description of Donald, but the article added copious supporting details from the cases of the other ten girls and boys as well.

The article also explored how psychiatry had viewed these eleven children before Kanner suggested viewing them through the lens of autism. Without that lens, it was easy to focus primarily on the differences among the eleven. Some of them could speak, for example, while others could not. Their particular skill sets were not identical to Donald's—who could sing and count and who had perfect pitch—or to one another's. These differences had produced a range of diagnoses across the group before Kanner saw them. Several were institutionalized. Two had been labeled schizophrenic. One child had been diagnosed, wrongly, as deaf. Diagnoses handed out to the others included "idiot," "imbecile," and "feebleminded." As seen in Donald's case, his evaluators at Hopkins had entertained the possibility that he had schizophrenia or Heller's syndrome, a rare neurological condition marked by a rapid degeneration of social and motor skills. In short, nearly all the children had been judged insane or intellectually impaired.

It was Kanner who identified the two defining traits common to all of them: the extreme preference for aloneness and the extreme need for sameness. It was this pairing of extremes, he decided, that formed the heart of the syndrome he was talking about, whose presence had previously been masked by the differences among the children.

It was there before.

In retrospect, it was an assertion supported even by Kanner's small sample, in the sense that all eleven of the boys and girls he wrote about, regardless of their diagnoses, had autism before he recognized it. So did dozens more children, whom Kanner would diagnose in the next few years, now that he knew what he was looking for. Beginning in the 1960s, scholars discovered a small scattering of clinical descriptions in the European medical literature, going back more than a century, of children reminiscent of Donald. Unknown, of course, was how many more children would also have been given the diagnosis if their parents had the sophistication and the financial means to seek consultations with the top child psychiatrist in the United States.

Even more unknowable was the number of people born decades and centuries earlier, whose traits, in retrospect, fit Kanner's diagnosis.

But perhaps not entirely unknowable. In the decades after Kanner "found" autism, a small group of scholars investigated whether autism had a "pre-history." While acknowledging the speculative nature of retrospective diagnosis, the researchers turned to legends and ledger books to find compelling accounts of long-gone individuals whose odd behaviors earned them, during their lifetimes, the status of outsiders, sometimes for the better, but often for the worse. Once labeled fools, idiots, or madmen, they were reevaluated through the lens of Kanner's description of autism. Viewed this way, their stories lent intriguing support to Kanner's assertion that autism, as one permutation of being human, was nothing new.

Half a millennium ago, a Russian shoemaker named Basil, born around 1469, was spotted walking about naked in winter, spouting incomprehensible utterances, while remaining inattentive to his own needs, even for food. The populace did not see this as madness. They thought, rather, that they were witnessing extreme holiness. The Russians called this "foolishness for Christ" and regarded Basil's self-abnegation as a courageous, difficult, and pious path, which Basil took in order to allow Christ to speak through him. Even the tsar—Ivan the Terrible—who was known to have waiters executed for serving the wrong drink at dinner, let Basil criticize him in public. He believed Basil could read his thoughts, and he took it to heart when the wandering shoemaker scolded him for letting his mind wander in church. It was said that Basil was the only man Ivan truly feared.

In 1974, a pair of Russian-speaking scholars at the University of Michigan suggested that something other than pure foolishness or holiness might have been at work in Basil, and in a few others with similar stories. Natalia Challis and Horace Dewey dove deeply into the available accounts of Basil's life and some thirty-five other "Holy Fools" of bygone days, all recognized as saints by the Russian Orthodox Church. Challis's and Dewey's academic specialty was Russian history and culture, not autism. But Dewey had a son, born in the 1950s, who had been diagnosed with autism, and that gave him insights into the behaviors of the ancient wanderers. He came to believe that autism, not insanity or divinity, might explain the Holy Fools' behavior.

This set of individuals, he and Challis wrote, was "unhampered by society's preconceptions" and content to live in a state of social isolation. Certain of them were wedded to rituals. They noted that Basil's tolerance of extreme cold—which let him "walk barefoot on the frozen Volga"—was reminiscent of how some people with autism appear indifferent to extremes of cold, heat, or pain. The Holy Fools were also observed to get by on limited sleep and food—again, similar to some people with autism.

While some remained mute, several were known to echo the words of others, and still others spoke in riddles. And legend has it that some blurted out whatever they were thinking into the faces of the powerful. That tendency, Challis and Dewey wrote, was a major part of what endeared the Fools to the Russian public. In a culture where few dared to question authority, their impertinence was reminiscent of the great prophets of the Old Testament.

Paradoxically, a diagnosis of autism, had it existed five hundred years ago, would have undermined the Fools' credibility as pious citizens. Awe and respect accrued to the Fools only because it was assumed that they had deliberately chosen this harsh and isolating way of life. In later centuries, some self-appointed Fools fell under suspicion of faking their piety, adopting certain behaviors only to advance their careers as beggars and con men. The resulting mistrust helped bring an end to the phenomenon of the Holy Fool. Gradually, the worship of and tolerance for such strange behaviors abated, and those who displayed such behaviors were once more neglected, if not treated with outright cruelty.

But not always.

HUGH BLAIR OF BORGUE was fussy about wigs—an accoutrement that, as a member of the landed class in 1740s Scotland, he was expected to wear whenever he ventured out in public. He did this, but not without a great deal of bother. He was always taking his wig off, plunging it into water, and trying to wash it. There it would hang, on a tree branch outside the family manse in southwest Scotland, drying in the wind while he waited. And yet, for all that, when Hugh finally did plunk the thing on his head, often as not he put it on backward, and went out in public that way. He was either unaware of the faux pas or indifferent to it.

Hugh was in his late thirties, a loner who lived with his aged mother in the stone house his grandfather had built, where his attic bedroom was cluttered with the twigs, feathers, and scraps of cloth he picked up off the ground every day. He dressed in bizarre outfits, worn and torn and mended all over with mismatched colored patches he sewed on himself. Once a piece of clothing became his favorite, he would refuse to wear anything else. Some of these were garments he came across abandoned by the road or "found" in the closets of nearby houses. Dropping in on neighbors unexpectedly, wandering through their rooms, whether they were at home or not, he tended to carry off whatever struck his fancy. He also made a habit of attending every funeral held in the community, even when he was not particularly well acquainted with the deceased.

In the small, connected world of southwest Scotland, the neighbors were aware of his odd behaviors and apparently quite understanding of them. They knew, when he came by, that it was never for a chat. People appeared to hold no interest for him, especially not in comparison with animals. With cats, for example, he was on close terms. When he sat down for supper, they draped themselves about him to share the meal, plunging paws into his spoon even as he lifted it to his mouth. Hugh didn't push them away. Instead, he pulled their paws to his lips and licked them clean.

This portrait of Hugh Blair of Borgue was pieced together in the 1990s by the two-person team of Rab Houston, a Scottish social historian, and Uta Frith, a London-based psychologist. It was Houston and Frith's contention that Hugh Blair of eighteenth-century Scotland was a clear case of what Leo Kanner learned to see only after he'd met Donald in the twentieth century. Frith put it this way: "The available evidence is rich enough and unambiguous enough to demonstrate that Hugh Blair would be given an unequivocal diagnosis of autism today."

The best evidence the eighteenth century could offer was a documented legal inquiry into Hugh's mental competence, presided over by a judge, officially transcribed, and informed by the testimony of twenty-nine witnesses, as well as that of Hugh himself. The proceedings, which lasted over several days in 1747, arose from a family dispute over inheritance. Hugh's father, a landowner, had died many years earlier, leaving a sizable estate to be divided between his two sons. Hugh's half remained under his mother's guardianship; his younger brother, John, controlled the other half. Hugh had no heirs, while John had two sons. This meant that upon Hugh's death, the entire estate would pass back to John and his progeny. John was counting on that, since he had been running up debts and had already been forced to borrow money from his mother.

Their mother, however, had gone and arranged a marriage for her odd older son. Somehow, she had persuaded a local surgeon to give his daughter's hand to a man who licked cats' paws at the dinner table. The exact inducements offered to the young woman were unknown, but likely involved a transfer of money. As for the mother's motives, she was probably worried about her son's future. Well into her sixties, she could imagine that soon Hugh might lose his primary protector in the world, the one person who had been keeping him out of trouble for his entire life. A wife could fill this role.

The wedding that took place in 1746 immediately put younger brother John's financial plans at risk. If Hugh and his new wife produced sons in wedlock, those boys would become the rightful heirs to Hugh's portion of the estate, ending any claim on it by John or John's sons. In 1747, John initiated proceedings to have the marriage annulled, on the grounds that his brother was not mentally competent enough to have entered into it in the first place.

Against this background, a hearing was called to look into Hugh's mental competence. It helped Houston and Frith in the 1990s that the court in the 1700s was gathering the same kinds of facts about Hugh that a psychologist interested in diagnosing autism would look for today. Everything contributed by the twenty-nine witnesses—clergymen, neighbors, craftsmen, laborers, and others who had contact with Hugh—pointed to his atypical behaviors.

It all fell into place: Hugh's various obsessions, his attachment to objects, his lack of connection to people, his indifference to social norms. There is striking evidence that Hugh exhibited echolalia, a frequently seen autistic trait in which a person only echoes what he has heard said by others.

Having considered the evidence, the Scottish court ruled that Hugh Blair was a "natural fool," incapable of entering into a contract, including a marriage contract. John Blair had won. The marriage was annulled. The prospect of a helpless, aging Hugh Blair, alone in the world once his mother passed on, must now have seemed a near certainty.

Yet the record shows that was not what happened. Hugh's mother must have chosen wisely, because the woman who was married to her son for a year did not leave his side once the court declared them, once again, unmarried. Hugh and his former wife remained a couple, not only living together outside the law but raising two sons as well. Hugh lived into his sixties in a family setting, where the neighbors knew who he was, and where he could collect twigs, wash out his wigs, and drop in on funerals for as long as he wished to.

Fifty-three years after a court found Hugh Blair a "natural fool," on the other side of the English Channel, a nearly naked boy walked out of the forest and immediately became the most famous child in France. The so-called Wild Boy of Aveyron, whose story was popularized in the Parisian press of 1800, became an object of fascination not just to newspaper readers but also to eminent scientists and philosophers of the day. The whole country puzzled over who he was and what state of the human condition he represented. A century and a half later, Leo Kanner's description of Donald offered new insight to historians and psychologists still pondering this question: France's Wild Boy had almost certainly been a person with autism.

He was, at best guess, a twelve-year-old, with no family, no home, no history, and no name. When he opened his mouth, all that came out was a sort of low, guttural moan or an occasional high squeal. He was small—four feet one inch tall—and bone thin. He was covered with scars, and his gait was affected by one knee that turned in hard on the other. The newspapers of the time said he had spent years in the forest, cut off from human society, naked but covered in fur, like a bear, from head to toe.

Except for the part about the fur, it was all true. He had been briefly captured by hunters around 1797 but soon escaped again. In 1800, he left the woods willingly and was taken in by a young doctor named Jean-Marc-Gaspard Itard, who gave him the name Victor. He amazed onlookers with his ability to run and climb and with his tolerance for cold and heat. Initially unwilling to wear regular clothes, he was seen rolling naked in snowdrifts. He was also known to plunge his fingers into a bed of red-hot coals to pluck out roasting potatoes, which he popped straight into his mouth before they had cooled. For a long time, this was the only food he would eat.

To the Enlightenment thinkers of the day, Victor's mysterious arrival was viewed as an opportunity to explore the operative properties of human language. There were some who anticipated that, once he was exposed to spoken French, Victor would quickly develop a full command of the language. Some hoped this could happen within months and that it would prove the key to his full blossoming as a participant in civilization—that he would stop, for example, removing his new clothes and trying to run back into nature, or stop giving in to the impulse to defecate and urinate whenever and wherever it struck him. But when early attempts at instruction proved disappointing, interest in Victor faded. A panel of experts found him to be an "idiot," not worthy of an education. He was shut away in an orphanage, where the other children bullied him.

Itard then arranged for Victor to be cared for by a couple whose own children were grown, while he himself patiently worked with him daily as his personal teacher. With Itard instructing him, Victor made measurable strides. He became toilet-trained. He learned to wash and dress himself, to sit for meals, and even to set the table for himself. Itard taught him these complex procedures by breaking them down into small steps that could be practiced one at a time, over and over again.

Teaching Victor to speak, however, was a frustrating exercise. Itard wrote of his excitement when, one day, Victor began repeating the phrase "*Mon Dieu.*" It soon became clear, however, that he was only parroting something he had heard someone else say. He did learn to manipulate a set of steel alphabet letters to spell out a few words, but his comprehension of their meaning and use was minimal. He could communicate, and often did, by pantomiming—evidence that he had something to say. These gestures always related to his immediate desires—to eat, to go outside, to play the game where he was pushed about in a wheelbarrow. But in trying to teach him to say words aloud—even just to name things—Itard got nowhere.

A key problem was Victor's unusually selective hearing. He shut out certain sounds as though he were completely deaf to them. When Itard, as an experiment, came up behind him and fired a pistol twice into the air, Victor did not even flinch. The human voice was another sound that registered with Victor only feebly. But let someone crack a nut in the next room, and his head would jerk around in that direction.

Itard, who regarded language as the essential test of Victor's intelligence, finally considered himself defeated. After five years, he stopped all teaching. "Seeing that my efforts were leading nowhere," he said, "I gave up my efforts to teach Victor to speak, and I abandoned him to a state of incurable muteness." Itard would continue to work with mentally challenged people, making contributions to the theory and methodology that became the bedrock of special education as it developed for the next 150 years.

Victor spent his last years comfortably, treated with kindness. The state paid for his upkeep under the care of the married couple, who treated him almost as a son. He died in 1828 around the age of forty, far from the wilderness, having never spoken a full sentence, and always giving the appearance, like little Donald Triplett a century later, of being happiest when left alone.

On February 26, 1848, a leather-bound report was delivered to the Massachusetts statehouse by one of the most compassionate activists the state had ever seen. Samuel Gridley Howe was the founder of the New England Asylum for the Blind, the institution that almost single-handedly changed the minds of Americans about the ability of blind people to benefit from an education. In both Europe and America, blindness was treated like deafness, lameness, epilepsy, or any apparent defect in typical organic functioning. Having a disability voided all claims to opportunity. Like those who could not hear or walk, those who could not see were written off as useless and broken. Educating them was regarded as absurd, until Howe proved otherwise.

Sometime around 1845, Howe had a new inspiration. He had learned that the French were making progress teaching people of impaired intellect, and that similar progress was being seen in Prussia.

Why shouldn't he try to educate his three new students? Even though one of the boys was mute, he was able to achieve considerable success.

When he began to speak openly of the educability of this group of people generally labeled "idiots," Howe encountered ridicule. This incensed him, as did the abuse heaped upon the mentally disabled. Writing to a powerful member of the Massachusetts legislature, Howe spoke of everyone's shared duty "to respect humanity in every form." When society failed at this, he argued, "the community . . . suffers therefore in its moral character."

The result of Howe's outrage was that leather-bound book, entitled *Report Made to the Legislature of Massachusetts upon Idiocy.* It compiled the results of an investigation he undertook in 1846 into the condition of the mentally disabled in Massachusetts. Funded by the taxpayers, Howe and two colleagues traveled on horseback to some sixty-three towns and villages across the state, examining more than five hundred people identified in each of these places as being the community's "idiots." The project took two years.

Packed with tables and data, Howe's report was astonishingly comprehensive for its time. Howe told the legislature that Massachusetts was home to approximately 1,300 men, women, and children who fit the description for mental "idiocy." This struck him as alarmingly high.

"The whole subject of idiocy is new," Howe wrote in the text accompanying his data. "Science has not yet thrown her certain light upon its remote, or even its proximate causes." He was right. Little effort had ever been made to understand the nature of intellectual disability. Society had never seen the purpose in doing so.

Howe himself was not prepared for one of the findings he made on his two-year tour: A good many of the people who had been pointed out to him as "idiots," he reported, did not seem to belong in that category. Upon close examination, he found many "who have some of the intellectual faculties well-developed, and yet are called idiots." Far from fitting the label neatly, he said, they "upset every one of these definitions."

There was the man named Billy, whom Howe listed as Case 27,

who "knows, and can sing correctly, more than two hundred tunes . . . and who will instantly detect a false note in any of them." Also notable about Billy, whose age was given as fifty-nine, was that ordinary communication appeared beyond him. "If he is told to go and milk the cows, he stands and repeats over the words, 'Billy go and milk the cows,' for hours together, or until someone tells him something else, which he will repeat over in the same way."

Billy was born about 140 years before Kanner began thinking about autism, but much of what Howe recorded—his talent for music, his apparently perfect pitch, and his seeming echolalia—would almost certainly have earned him a place on Kanner's list.

Howe's Case 360 might have made that list also: "This man has the perception of combination of numbers in an extraordinary degree of activity. Tell him your age, and ask him how many seconds it is, and he will tell you in a very few minutes. In all other respects, he is an idiot."

And Howe's Case 25: "This young man knows the name and sound of every letter, he can put the letters into words, the words into sentences, and read off a page with correctness; but he would read over that page a thousand times, without getting the slightest idea of the meaning."

Howe went on to list more examples that hint at autism, though with less detail. "What they learn, they never forget," he reported, of one particular group. Also: "There are cases, Nos. 175 and 192, idiots beyond all question, but who can count not only to 20, but to 20,000, and perform many simple arithmetical operations with a great deal more facility than ordinary persons." There is Case 277, a girl who can "learn and know letters" but can understand nothing to which they relate.

Howe's research took place during a period when the majority of "ordinary persons" in the United States were illiterate, with little experience of using the alphabet at all. Neither did most Americans have much exposure to math, beyond counting what was in front of their noses: farm animals, rows of crops, family members. Twenty was a number beyond which few had much occasion to go visiting in their imaginations. The "idiots" were, by comparison, intellectual voyagers, at least in this narrow respect.

Howe was ridiculed yet again when he presented his report to the legislature. For his idealism, he was compared to Don Quixote, tilting at windmills. He prevailed, however, where it counted—with the lawmakers, who came up with $2,500 to fund an experimental school for ten of the children in the survey, with Howe in charge. Three years later, each of the children, previously thought uneducable, had made progress. Howe was thrilled. His report had fulfilled his ambitions in his own time, even as it tucked away something more relevant to our own—his eyewitness accounts of what autism looked like, ninety years before it was "discovered" in a psychiatrist's office in Baltimore.

IF KANNER WAS RIGHT, and autism had always existed, then these stories from the past hint at some unpleasant life experiences for those who, during autism's prehistory, went through their days undiagnosed. If, in the seventeenth century, they were still burning and hanging epileptics as witches—due to their occasional fits of strange movements and sounds—that would not have boded well for a child who tonelessly parroted back whatever was said to him, or whose deep concentration on the movement of his own fingers before his eyes could not be interrupted. If mutism was confused with lunacy, then quite likely nonspeaking people with autism would have been candidates for Europe's various institutions, which included a tower in the city wall of Hamburg, where the insane were confined to a space known as the Idiot's Cage.

Samuel Gridley Howe saw a great deal of dehumanizing of the disabled on his tour of Massachusetts towns. He found parents mired in "gross ignorance" of their children's capabilities. One family kept their middle-aged son in a cage in the parents' shop. He had been there since the age of twelve. Another man, age fifty, had been chained up for twenty years.

Such outcomes were not inevitable, however. In the eighteenth century, a town of rural Scotsmen proved that through their acceptance of Hugh Blair. So, in the twentieth century, did the people of a small Mississippi town, through the way they responded to the odd child in their midst—Donald Triplett.

5

DOUBLY LOVED AND PROTECTED

IN MAY 1945, LEO KANNER TRAVELED TO MISSISSIPPI TO see, for the last time, his Case 1, who was eleven years old by this time. For a few days, Dr. Kanner would be a guest of the Triplett family.

It had been four years since Donald's last visit to Kanner's clinic in Baltimore, and seven years since his first visit. Now, sitting on the white sofas in the Triplett living room, near the baby grand piano Mary and Beamon had splurged on, the three had time to ruminate on the ups and downs of Donald's past few years, including Mary's attempts to get him to go to school.

In the late summer of 1939, when Donald was about to turn six, Mary had approached the public elementary school with the hope of enrolling him in the first-grade class starting that September. She knew what she was asking. Schools all over the country were flatly refusing children like Donald, and the law backed them up. True, there were special-education classrooms in some public school districts, whose availability varied by region, but even in these, children who did not sit quietly and follow directions readily were quickly expelled. However, in this case the school principal was a friend of Mary's. A space was found for Donald, and the first-grade teacher was made to understand that she would have to accommodate this somewhat different child.

On the first day, Donald threw tantrums. He was a little calmer the second day, and even more so in the days that followed. Given no choice but to adapt to Donald, his teacher apparently made efforts to accommodate his peculiar ways. Perhaps this meant ignoring or redirecting odd behavior rather than punishing it. Or maybe it meant finding ways to give Donald a little extra attention to help him keep up.

It seems Donald began to adapt as well. A lot of his odd behaviors, to be sure, remained, and were doubtlessly disruptive. In the first few weeks, he randomly broke out in squeals and shrieks, and when he was answering a question addressed to him directly, he sometimes jumped up and down after giving his answer, giving his head a hard shake. But at least he answered questions from time to time. By October, he could keep his place in line, answer politely when called upon in class, and follow along better with the flow of the learning day. In the evenings, he never had anything to say about what he was doing at school, but he put up no resistance to returning there in the morning. For a child with a phobia about changes to his environment, this was progress.

His use of language improved as well. While he had learned to read words aloud earlier than the other children, it appeared he had no idea of the meaning of those words. It was the same with movies. He enjoyed going to them and would recite lines of dialogue for weeks afterward, but he seemed not to understand that the characters on the screen were telling a story. After having been enrolled in school, these deficits showed signs of being corrected.

One day, during his third month in school, on a visit to the classroom, Mary was amazed to see Donald fully engaged in a reading lesson. The teacher had just written a series of sentences on the chalkboard and was explaining to the class that she would be calling on each child one at a time to step forward, find the sentence in which his or her name appeared, circle the name, and then act out the sentence. Mary saw the teacher write the sentence with her son's name: "Don may feed a fish." When it was his turn, she watched Donald stand up, accept the chalk, draw a chalk circle around "Don," and then go over to the side table where the class aquarium sat and sprinkle some fish food into the water. Donald had done it—he had made sense of both the spoken and the written word—without fuss. To Mary, his performance was so momentous that, when she got home, she immediately wrote a letter to Kanner, describing the entire scene for him.

Without a doubt, Donald still lagged behind the other first-graders, but it was obvious that he was steadily changing, growing, and discovering how to connect. Kanner had seen this happening during the family's first follow-up trip to Baltimore, in May 1939, seven months after their initial consultation and a few months before the school experiment started. Writing up his observations from that time, Kanner reported that Donald's attention and concentration were showing improvement, that he was in better contact with his environment, and that he was reacting much more appropriately to people and situations. "He showed disappointment when thwarted," Kanner observed, and "gave evidence of pleasure when praised." At the same time, there was a big part of Donald's world that remained out of reach. "He still went on writing letters with his fingers in the air," Kanner noted.

The first-grade experiment proceeded past Christmas and into winter. By spring, Donald's use of language had developed even further. At home, he began engaging in a rough approximation of conversation. Mary would ask specific questions about his day, and he would readily answer. But his responses were narrow and concrete; he never opened up about his thoughts and experiences. He did, however, insist one night on making the entire family play a game he had just learned at school. They all went along with it, following his exceedingly precise instructions. Both Mary and Beamon understood how remarkable it was that Donald was entering into a game at all. This was a first in his life—playing with other children.

Donald survived the first grade and returned to school for a second year, and then a third. In a way, the routine of the classroom may have suited his need for sameness: he went to the same building every day, at the same hour, for the same length of time. His seat was always where it was supposed to be, and a bell rang automatically, and reliably, to start and stop activities. One afternoon, when he was nine and a half, he walked into his classroom not knowing that classes had been canceled for the rest of the day. His parents were also unaware of the change. Donald spent the next few hours alone at his desk, writing in a notebook, waiting for the dismissal bell. When it rang, he packed away his things and headed home as usual. His ingrained habits had served him well.

Ultimately, however, school became more demanding, and the difference between him and the other children became more pronounced.

Around the time he turned ten, the gap between what the school expected and what Donald was capable of—both academically and socially—grew too wide.

By the spring of 1943, when his original first-grade classmates were making their way through the fourth grade, Donald was back at home, helping his mother with simple chores in return for money for the picture shows he loved. At the same time, his natural skill in arithmetic was strengthened when he made a hobby out of calculating the publication dates of *Time* magazine. By chance, he had come across a copy of *Time*'s first issue. On the cover it said "Vol. I, No. 1" and the date, "March 3, 1923." He was fascinated, and became obsessed with figuring out the exact dates on which every subsequent issue was published.

This led to an obsession with calendars. Once, when visiting his mother's friends, the Rushings, he pulled up a chair in their kitchen so that he could stand up high enough to study their big wall calendar. By the time he was done frantically rifling back and forth through its pages, it was so much the worse for wear that they took it down after he and Mary left.

Donald was stretching his mind, but the seeming impracticality of his efforts was overwhelming. What he was good at did not fit in the classroom anymore. What he was not good at—making sense of reading and history lessons—increasingly got in the way of everyone else's learning. His adjustment to life, while progressing, was not progressing quickly enough.

With Donald at home again, Mary experienced the full burden of loneliness, frustration, and exhaustion that crushed other mothers in her situation. For the second time in his life, Donald was sent away.

It was not an institution this time. And in no way was Donald abandoned. The setting, in fact, was a home—a real family home, and getting there from the Triplett residence took all of eighteen minutes by car. Located in the deep Mississippi countryside, well past the last road sign, and at the end of a network of unmarked dirt roads, it was a house on a hill where no electricity or phone lines ran. The place did not even have running water; the toilet was outdoors. But Donald's parents hoped the couple who lived there would be kind to their son, and that the outdoor setting would be good for his development.

Their names were Ernest and Josephine Lewis. They were poor farmers, without much education, but townspeople said they were decent, hardworking, and honest. Josephine was in her early forties, and Ernest was in his mid-fifties. They had no children of their own, and they lived off the land they worked themselves. The amount of money Beamon paid the couple to take in Donald was never disclosed, but their treatment of him was a matter of record, thanks to Leo Kanner.

Donald had already started living with the Lewises when Kanner came to visit the Tripletts in May 1945. He was interested in seeing how it was working out, and, of course, most curious to see how his Case 1 was doing. As it was, Donald came home to Forest many weekends and all holidays, and he was there for Kanner's visit. But at some point, they all piled into Beamon's car and hit the dusty road to visit Ernest and Josephine.

By this time, the Lewises had become almost like family to the Tripletts. Mary's father's appreciation of the couple and their way of life was apparent in a letter he sent his grandson in 1943: "Now I think Mr. & Mrs. Lewis are the very best people in the County. They are trying to train you to be a useful man. They are out for you and you must reciprocate by minding them. Bring in the stove wood for Mrs. Lewis, get the hatchet and fix the kindling wood for the kitchen fire." Granddaddy McCravey had grown up on such a farm himself before setting out at the age of twenty-two and striking it rich in finance. He respected the discipline of chores. "It is by far the best training a boy can get," he told Donald. "To live in a place like Forest is not comparable to it in any sense. You are near nature, and nature's God."

Granddaddy signed off by reminding his grandson, "I have loved lots of folks, but I love you as much as anyone I have ever known."

Leo Kanner didn't idealize country living quite as much as Granddaddy McCravey, but after getting to the farm and spending a few hours there, he formed just as high an opinion of the Lewises. Ernest and Josephine walked the psychiatrist all around the place, showed him Donald's room, and talked him through the chores Donald did regularly. As Kanner took it in, he realized that the couple had stumbled upon a kind of therapeutic solution to Donald's deficits. On the one hand, there was a rigid structure to days on the farm—the same pattern every morning, every night, every season. Donald had no choice but to abide by the schedule.

At the same time, they showed creativity and flexibility in how they accommodated his obsessions and strengths and fit them into farm life. As Kanner watched, for example, Donald ran into a cornfield, took up the reins of a heavy plow horse, and successfully put the animal through its paces—plowing one long row, then turning the horse around to begin another. As he looked on, amazed, the Lewises explained that this had all begun when Donald had started walking the cornfields, obsessively counting the rows. Then Ernest had put the reins in his hand and showed him how to control the horse and maneuver the plowshare. In this way, he was able to count the rows while working them. Kanner watched Donald pass back and forth with the horse half a dozen times and cut half a dozen field lengths in the earth; it seemed to give the boy pleasure.

Donald had also become entranced by the process of measurement and had been taking a yardstick to whatever he could find around the farm, keeping track of how long, tall, deep, or wide everything was. Again, Ernest thought about this, and when the farm needed a new well, he recruited Donald to help dig it, presenting it to him as a measuring project: How deep is the well now? How deep should it go?

Josephine and Ernest also made allowances for some of Donald's less practical preoccupations. For a time, Donald went through a phase when he was obsessed with death and brought every dead bird or bug he found back to the house. The Lewises could be tough with Donald, and they did take a switch to him when he misbehaved. But with the birds and the bugs, they understood that Donald was trying to figure out something important. Instead of punishing him for dirtying the house, they pointed to a little parcel of open ground near the house and told him he could lay all the creatures to rest there. Donald built his little graveyard enthusiastically, not only burying every deceased thing he found, but doing so with an air of formality.

When Kanner strolled into Donald's little cemetery, he saw that he had given names to all the creatures buried there, erecting small wooden markers over each grave and making them all members of the Lewis family. The one that stuck in Kanner's mind was inscribed "*John Snail Lewis. Born, date unknown.*" For the date of departure from this life, Donald listed the date on which he'd found the snail's remains.

Donald flourished under the regimen of farm life. In Kanner's estimation, living there for a period of time was one of the best things that ever happened to Donald. The farm offered an ideal balance of restrictions and freedoms. Donald became more verbal, more creative, and more accomplished at completing complex tasks. He also basked in a kind of freedom he never had in town: the freedom to explore, to go over to the next field to find birds and bugs, without giving anyone cause to worry that cars might run him down.

After a while, the Lewises began bringing him to a nearby country school every day to resume his education. It was a better fit for Donald than the school in town for one simple reason: it was a one-room schoolhouse. By its very nature, it had to tailor itself to children learning different material on different schedules. As for Donald's social peculiarities, they were accommodated without too much fuss—another benefit of being in an environment that was less caught up with appearances.

In this setting, Donald began writing letters home, using complete sentences and correct spelling—mostly—and sharing concrete details about his days with the Lewises. A few days before Mother's Day in 1944, he picked up a pencil and wrote to Mary that he had been to the town of Salem to make a purchase. "Mr. Ernest told me that I have to have a rose for Mother's Day," he wrote. "He told me that a red rose was to show that the mother was still living. A white rose is to show that the mother is dead." He also mentioned that he had been playing ball and that "the score I made was . . . 5/74." He signed it "Donald G. T. Lewis." Mary preserved this letter for the rest of her life.

Donald would always remember those years as happy ones, when he belonged to two families. It was an arrangement in which he was doubly loved and doubly protected, and was spared the awful things happening to so many other children like him—children who were stuck in large institutions, often neglected and sometimes abused, because, unlike the Tripletts, their parents lacked the resources to create something better.

Kanner was thrilled to see Donald growing and learning so much. While the boy's overall improvement could be labeled "moderate," moderate in the context of Donald's development was like a leap across an abyss. Donald was proof that at least some children could leave the most debilitating aspects of autism behind, and that it was worth trying to encourage that process.

6

SOME KIND OF GENIUS

When Donald was fourteen years old, he suddenly became very ill. He was with the Lewises when the symptoms began. It was chills at first. Then fever. Then chills again. It was so bad that the Lewises let him off from his chores and had him stay in bed. Then his joints began acting up too. It hurt to bend his arms and legs. The pain became excruciating. The Lewises, alarmed, packed Donald into their car and drove him back to his parents' house. For some days, Donald was back in his old bed, where he became extremely agitated and difficult to handle. As the family put it, he was exceedingly "nervous" again, more like his toddler self than the teenager he was. When the fevers ran still higher, he became delirious.

At the Campbell Clinic in Memphis, a doctor diagnosed Still's disease, also known as juvenile rheumatoid arthritis, an autoimmune disease. For reasons still not well understood, the body's immune system turns against itself and attacks the tissues in the joints. There are high fevers, which can be fatal. For the children who survive, there can be lasting damage to the joints, which fuse together permanently. Using a compound called gold salts and a steroid known as ACTH, doctors at the clinic pulled him back from the brink. The fevers receded, and the disease slowly loosened its grip on his joints. But it was not until the middle of 1949, a year and a half later, that Donald was up and walking again.

His recovery began in Memphis, and then, after several months, he returned home to Forest, where his convalescence continued under his parents' roof. This was a turning point for the Triplett family—the first time in years that Donald was back with them full-time. As the months passed and Donald's health returned, so did more of the personality he had been showing on the farm, before the illness. His "nervousness" faded. As it did, his improvement in language and learning resumed, and, if anything, picked up pace. With each month, he became less the boy whose extreme behaviors had overwhelmed the Triplett household in the early 1940s. Instead, he was maturing into a young man who could take his place at the table. Sixteen years old, he was home again. The Lewises would always remain close friends, but Donald would not return to the farm to live. Mary had something new in mind for Donald. That September, he would go to high school.

In the early 1950s, when Donald was a high school student, a number of local myths swirled around him. Some were more true than others, but all had something to do with numbers. The most famous was the one about the bricks.

The story goes that Donald was standing outside Forest High School one day, facing a half-circle of his classmates, who wanted him to confirm a rumor. Word was that Donald had a gift for counting things quickly, and these boys wanted him to prove it. "Okay, so how many bricks are in that wall there?" the leader challenged him, nodding toward the side of the building that housed the gymnasium, a long, high edifice of redbrick. According to legend, Donald glanced at the school and immediately announced the correct number of bricks.

Mouths fell open. *That fast?* Staggered, the boys ran off to tell everyone else what they had just seen the Triplett kid do, with their own eyes. The story spread rapidly, even as far as some of the neighboring towns. And it endured. No newcomer to town would ever hear the name Donald Triplett for the first time without also hearing that, sometime back in the early fifties, he had counted every brick on the side of the school gym in an instant.

This account was missing a vital detail or two. For one thing, no one ever seemed to remember the actual number Donald had come up with. Also, no one ever explained how the boys knew that Donald's calculation was accurate. In one version, a couple of boys ran over to the wall and spent a tedious hour or so counting the bricks one by one. In another version, one of the math-minded kids did some quick geometry. But most of the time it was simply taken for granted that Donald had it exactly right.

Whether it was true or not, the episode fit the larger story about Donald that took hold when he was in high school, and that no one who met him doubted: this Triplett boy, odd as he was, just might be some kind of genius.

The most unusual thing about Donald's experience at Forest High in the early fifties was how his fellow students, their families, and the school community treated him—this eccentric teenager who had disappeared from school for so many years.

They simply let him be.

That is saying a lot when, almost everywhere else in the United States, children as different as Donald were still banished from school and frequently deposited in institutions. It is not immediately obvious why things were different in Forest, a town with no special claim to enlightenment. When it came to race relations, Jim Crow, and civil rights, the white residents of Forest were not known to protest the status quo. None of them questioned the separate "whites only" and "colored" drinking fountains at the town courthouse. The trains Leo Kanner had ridden to Forest enforced segregated seating. Forest High itself was, by law, a "whites only" school well into the 1960s.

Given all that, it seems unlikely that Donald was permitted to enroll in high school and treated kindly by his classmates out of a commitment to inclusiveness, an idea that did not have much currency at that time. Rather, Donald's remarkably good high school experience was one of the benefits of the relative privilege he was born into.

First of all, there was the Triplett family name. In the 1950s, it carried more clout in Forest than ever. Beamon Triplett was considered the town's best lawyer and, as he moved into his fifties, was often tapped for dignitary roles such as board director of the Lions Club or chairman of the local Boy Scouts.

Mary's profile mirrored her husband's. During the 1940s, when

Donald was away, she had reengaged with her old life, returning to the rounds of luncheons and garden parties that were the backbone of conviviality among the town's female upper class, and where she was something of a queen bee. She became a member of the Fortnightly Club, a group that attracted intellectually curious women who had been discouraged from attending college. They put on plays for one another, read poetry aloud, and staged dance and piano recitals.

The Triplett home was its own social hub, and Mary often took her turn as civic hostess. In addition to women's gatherings, the Presbyterian choir sometimes came to the house to rehearse. But while most of these visitors were acquainted with the Tripletts' son Oliver, few had ever laid eyes on Donald, because he had been living on the farm all those years.

Now that Donald was home, his presence was unmissable. The Tripletts apparently refused to be shamed into hiding him—not from the choir, not from the ladies of Forest's upper crust, not from whoever might cross his path. If Donald happened to yelp from his bedroom in the middle of a poetry reading in the living room, if he gawked at a matron's bosom, if he took too much of a visitor's time talking about *Time* magazine or the calendar, then so be it—that's who he was, and guests would just have to make allowances. Implicitly, Beamon and Mary were making a clear and definitive statement: *Donald belongs. And he belongs because we say he belongs.* Done wavering, they made it clear to the community that, from now on, they expected their son to be treated as an equal.

The evidence suggests that the message was received. Forest's size was an advantage for Donald. In 1950, the population was only 2,874, so it did not take long for word to travel. It is easy to imagine parents around town advising their kids, "Don't mess with the Triplett boy. Be nice to him." Such was the social authority of the Tripletts.

But credit for Donald's happy run at high school also belongs to the teenage boys and girls who accommodated this strange kid in their midst on a day-by-day basis. It fell to them to do the simplest thing, which was to be kind to Donald, who would have been easy to tease. After all, he was two years older than everyone else in his grade and could barely hold a conversation; he could be mocked without even being aware it was happening. He walked with his arms held stiff and apart from his sides, like a big letter A. Plus, he was basically defenseless; if someone wanted to get physical with him, he was small and knew nothing about how to handle himself in a fight.

Fortunately for Donald, there were enough students at Forest High who were prepared to keep that from happening to him. The Theriot sisters in particular—Celeste, Yvonne, and Jean—kept an eye out for him. They had moved to Forest only a few years earlier, when their father was hired by the railroad to water the engines of the trains coming in and out of town. They were Cajuns from Louisiana who showed up at school speaking only French, so they were still figuring out how to blend in themselves.

It did not help that their mother, whose commitment to their education was spotty, frequently kept them home from school to assist her around the house. As a result, all three, and a brother named Paul, fell behind academically, to the point where, like Donald, they were a good year or two older than their classmates. But the girls had a streak of fierce decency, and whenever they saw Donald being teased, they put themselves in front of him, using their seniority to get the bullies to back off. In time, the lesson stuck, and picking on Donald went out of fashion. He became accepted, and more kids found it in themselves to get to know the strangest-seeming boy in the school, until he wasn't really a stranger at all. It was around this time that people stopped calling him Donald and began to call him D.G.—from Donald Gray Triplett, his full name. That was because Donald called everyone else by his or her initials.

Still, it was a challenge to be friends with Donald. He got along so well with just himself for company, and he still mostly seemed to prefer it that way. This was not so obvious when everyone was in class together and he was anchored to his desk, doing the same exercises as they were. But it was different between classes, when the hormone-hyped social swirl of Forest High was let loose. Donald moved through the hallways saying little, seemingly oblivious to the chatter, the teenage hierarchy, the cliques. None of it mattered to him.

At lunch, he ate alone, unless one of the Theriot girls plopped down beside him. When kids congregated outdoors, Donald usually wandered off toward the edge of the yard, where he stood by himself, looking upward. After a few moments, using his right index finger like a pencil, he commenced waggling it up and down and left and right, drawing figures in the air. After a while, this became such a regular sight that no one paid much attention. But kids who watched him were able to figure out what the figures were. They were numbers. Donald was doing arithmetic in the sky.

This obsession with numbers became a ticket to some extra respect from his classmates. When they saw him, usually off to one side, scribbling away in a notebook, they would peek over his shoulder and see that the book was filled with numerals, column after column, page after page. Not understanding the cipher, they leapt to the conclusion that Donald must be practicing some higher form of mathematics. More likely, he was back to making up his own peculiar number lists, which he had been doing for years. But the other kids didn't know that; to them, he was a math wizard wandering among them.

In some respects, Donald *was* a numbers whiz. He had practiced mental calculation for so long that he could instantaneously spit out an answer to any two-digit multiplication problem. Kids would approach him in the yard, clutching a slip of paper with the correct answers worked out ahead of time.

"D.G., what's eighty-four times seventeen?"

Donald would stop, close his eyes for the briefest moment, then open them again and speak.

"Uh, uh . . . One thousand four hundred and twenty-eight."

A glance down at the paper. Correct.

"What's forty-two times ninety-three?"

"Uh, uh . . . Three thousand nine hundred and six."

Right again.

Donald also had a photographic memory for numbers. He was often seen walking the square around the courthouse near his father's office, studying the license plates of the cars parked there. One time, some boys from his class bumped into him and, on a hunch, one of them asked, "So what's the number of that Plymouth?" He pointed out a car at the far end, parked at a diagonal to where they were all standing. Donald closed his eyes, took a beat, and then spit out a set of letters and numbers. The boys hustled across the square and around the back end of the Plymouth.

"Hey, D.G.," one of them called out, "you got it, D.G.!"

Before long, it was understood in Forest that Donald had a list in his head of the tag number of every car in town.

He also had a list in his head of all the people in town and *their* numbers—numbers he had personally assigned to them.

For example, Janelle Brown was a freshman when Donald, then a senior, approached her. They had not previously spoken.

"Uh, uh . . . Janelle Brown, from now on your number is one thousand four hundred and eighty-seven," he announced, then turned and walked away. The next time he saw Janelle in the hallway, Donald approached again, but this time, he greeted her not by name, but by her number. "Uh, hello, fourteen eighty-seven!" And then he wandered off.

Donald continued doing this, all over the school and always the same way. Those who were chosen were mystified, never sure how they had attracted a Donald number or what it meant. It seemed random, as did the numbers themselves. Some, like Buddy Lovett, got a three-digit number. He was 333. Others, like Janelle, got the full four digits. Various theories made the rounds. Some heard that Donald gave out numbers based on what he thought a person's chances were of getting into heaven. Others suspected the figures somehow related to the recipient's physical attractiveness.

One classmate, John Rushing, didn't think either of those explained his own number. He had his own ideas about where it came from.

John and Donald had known each other since they were little. They had grown up a few houses away from each other, and John was often invited over to play on the Tripletts' swing set. It was at John's house that Donald had made a mess of that wall calendar. Later, before Donald went to live with the Lewises, the two boys belonged to the same first-, second-, and third-grade classes at school. By the early 1950s, though, when both boys were at Forest High, John was two grades ahead of Donald and a star player on the football team, the Forest Bearcats. Compared to his schoolmates, John had turned into a giant, hard as a rock, and he was as solid morally as he was physically. Like the Theriot girls, he could not abide seeing Donald picked on, and he always intervened to stop it when it happened.

Donald may have been reciprocating when, one day, he walked up to John and announced, "John Rushing, from now on your number is one hundred ninety-three." Rushing wondered, Why 193? For days he puzzled over it. Then, one Friday night, just before a big Bearcat game, he got a look at the official program for the event. It listed the two teams' players, along with their numbers, heights, and weights. He ran his thumb down the column looking for his own name and found it; his game weight for the season was posted as 193.

Donald himself never explained what the rules were. But in his quirky way, he had invented a social interaction for himself, a transaction that took few words but was an exchange just the same. Donald's numbers were harmless, intriguing, charming, and they certainly got people's attention.

Forest was a safe place for Donald not only because he knew his way around but also because the community had been learning his ways. By the time he was fifteen or sixteen, he was often seen taking long treks down the edge of the highway leading out of town, still scribbling at the sky. People driving by would slow down, greet him, and check to see if he wanted a lift somewhere, or suggest that it might be time to head back toward town. If he said he wanted to keep walking, that was fine too. Donald had become theirs to protect, because they understood he needed it. He was a fixture and a favorite.

DONALD'S SENIOR YEAR at Forest High turned out to be his best ever. Outside of math, where he was strongest, his grades were mediocre. History and English—subjects with a human story at their hearts—were hard for him to master. Still, he was getting C's. He joined a club or two—the Future Farmers of America and the school chorus. But his crowning achievement came halfway through the second semester, when he tried out for and landed a part in the school play.

This was a landmark in his life. Among all school activities, few were more socially collaborative than a theatrical production, and suddenly Donald was fully involved. The play was called *The Monkey's Uncle*. It was a popular farce about a pretty young woman pretending to be a boy, a skunk, and some romantic mismatches. Donald played "Billy Bob Hefferfield," the thirteen-year-old son of the town busybody. Ironically, Billy Bob was also a notorious bully.

Learning lines and delivering them on cue was probably easier for Donald than for some of his fellow actors, since it played to one of his strengths: memory. And in the performance, it didn't matter that his vocal tone was a little flat and mechanical. It was a local audience, accustomed to Donald's way of talking. Townspeople knew instead to listen for the comic content of the words. No one had ever heard Donald say so much all at once as he said on that Tuesday night in 1953, when the words came from a playwright's pen. One other thing was clear by the time the curtain came down and the bows were taken: Donald did not suffer at all from stage fright. To the contrary, he seemed to like the attention.

When he graduated that June, Mary and Beamon had the entire class over to the house for a parent-sponsored "Good Luck Buffet Supper." Each of the attending graduates received a penny for good luck, and the evening gave the class of '53 one more chance to mingle. Everyone signed everyone else's yearbook. Donald did not get everyone's signature, but he managed to get to most of the young women, some of whom would be married within a year or two. Each found a different way to sound loving, almost motherly, toward their older classmate. Dorothy "Dot" Stroud took the pen and wrote, "To one of the sweetest boys I know." Margaret Smith echoed this: "To a sweet guy, remember always do as well as you have done this year." Margaret Ann Weems, who was class co-president: "Don, you have much ability and in the past year you have put it to good use . . ."

Some made a reference to the Donald they thought of as a genius. Ann Viverette: "With that brain of yours, I'm sure you will go far." And Joel Antley: "To one of my best friends, and one of the most brilliant students I've ever known."

Joel was not the only student to call Donald a best friend. Several other boys used the same words, including Gilbert Broussard, a three-letter athlete and fellow cast member. His message read, "D.G.

you are one of the best of friends, even if you did call me a thousand fools, good luck, your pal, Gilbert B." And the student body president, Tommy Huff, wrote under his own beaming face, "Don, you have been an inspiration to me these high school years. Best luck always."

Just as for everyone else in his class, change was coming for Donald now. He had been accepted at East Central Community College in Decatur, twenty-five miles from Forest. Donald would be living there, which had to be daunting. And yet there is evidence that he was looking forward to the adventure.

It exists in the form of a brief message he scribbled into that same yearbook, to the right of his own picture. It was a good photo of him. In jacket and tie, hair combed, he had his eyes trained straight at the camera, a slightly quizzical half smile on his lips. It had never been easy to know what Donald was thinking, but in this case he spelled it out for anyone who might wonder. With a fountain pen, he composed a short salutation to his own future.

D.G.
I wish myself luck.
D.G.

PART II

THE BLAME GAME

1960s–1980s

7

THE REFRIGERATOR MOTHER

THE TRUTH IS, NOT EVERY MOTHER'S BABY IS BORN BEAUTIful. Rita Tepper's mistake was admitting that to herself the week her newborn son arrived. She was twenty-four at the time, and she had expected pink and round and cuddly. Instead, her infant boy, whom she named Steven, showed up bony, unusually long, and yellow. His off-color skin was the result of jaundice, not uncommon among newborns, and generally not much to worry about. Still, he was the color of corn. His yellow hair was strange-looking too, sticking up all over in little points. No, Rita could not call Steven beautiful. If she was honest about it, the way Steven appeared right then—scrawny, yellowish, and spike-haired—made him look an awful lot like a chicken.

Two and a half years later, in 1966, Rita would be crushed by that memory, as she was made to understand the lifelong harm she had inflicted on her son by letting the thought merely enter her mind. Steven had recently been diagnosed with a condition called autism, and she was being questioned by a social worker at New York's Bellevue Hospital, who had been assigned to help her cope with the diagnosis.

Of course, Rita was the one with questions, but there wasn't much the social worker could tell her. Autism was such a rare diagnosis, and so little research had been done on it, that few medical doctors knew anything about it or had even heard of it. Dr. Taft, the psychiatrist who had examined Steven a few months earlier, when he was just past his second birthday, put it succinctly when he met with Rita and her husband, Jerry: "You have a major problem." A few minutes later, Rita heard him say that it was probably "autism." Taft talked for quite a while longer, but the words stopped making sense. Rita felt as though she were watching a soap opera, but had somehow ended up in the scene itself. When she and her husband returned home, Jerry walked into their bedroom, collapsed onto the covers, and sobbed. Rita knew immediately she would have to be the strong one, even if that meant taking all the blame.

By the time the Teppers were given the shattering news about Steven, twenty-three years—roughly a generation—had gone by since Leo Kanner had written up his account of Donald and the "novel" syndrome his behaviors suggested. By then, Donald and the other ten children Kanner wrote about were well into adulthood and scattered around the United States, and the condition we know as autism had continued to gain slow recognition as a meaningful diagnosis. Some of its criteria were still debated, and there was no consensus on the best name for it. Kanner, for example, still insisted on "infantile autism," while some paid homage to him by calling it Kanner's syndrome.

By whatever name, the concept had gained a certain clinical currency by 1966, the year of Steven's diagnosis. By that time, the medical literature contained references to hundreds more children who more or less shared the kinds of behaviors that Kanner had linked together. The vast majority lived in the United States, and the greatest concentration of cases was at Johns Hopkins in Kanner's clinic.

Still, despite the mounting numbers, almost no sustained effort was being made to scientifically explore autism's essential nature. In part, this was because scientists viewed the condition as too rare to justify much attention. The bigger factor, however, was psychiatry's blanket certainty that it already knew why some children had autism and others did not.

The verdict: autism was caused by mothers not loving their children enough.

This idea had put down roots in the late 1940s, when Rita Tepper was a child herself. It was still an article of faith in the 1960s, when she became a mother, and it was presented to her almost immediately after being informed that Steven had autism. Like all mothers of her generation trying to raise children with autism, Rita had to endure knowing that the medical profession believed her son's autism was all her fault.

SEVERAL WEEKS AFTER receiving his diagnosis of autism, Steven was enrolled in a program offered at Bellevue. But for Steven to get treatment, Rita had to agree to be treated as well. That reflected the premise of the program: the mother was part of the child's problem, and she had to be fixed too if there was to be any hope of improvement for the child. And so, while Steven was led off to a room filled with other children needing help, Rita met with a social worker. Sometimes the meetings were one-on-one. Occasionally Rita joined a small group of other women who had children in the program. On those days, they sat in a larger room, in a circle of folding chairs.

The group meetings were intense confessionals, each mother speaking in turn as the social worker offered guidance. One by one, those in the circle would comb through memories of those hazy first weeks and months in their children's young lives, trying to pinpoint when the autism started. But this was not a search for when they had first noticed signs of the condition. Rather, the women were straining to recall moments when they might have done something wrong—without even knowing it—something that had so traumatized their babies that they had withdrawn, for good, into their own version of reality. It was difficult, serious work, based on the assumption that their children had been born "normal" and then, somehow, their own mothers had inflicted a devastating psychic injury on them.

During the group sessions, ideas flowed. One mother confessed that she might have spent too much time focused on another of her children. Another acknowledged, with shame, that she might have grown overly resentful of the sleep she lost when her daughter was teething. Others racked their brains for examples of their own deficient mothering. All of them, including Rita, desperately wanted to figure out what they had done wrong. If they could just pinpoint the mistake they had made, then they could try to change their behavior and reverse the damage.

The memory of having once pictured her baby as a chicken did not come back to Rita immediately. Steven's jaundice had cleared up a few days after his birth and she had forgotten about it. Quickly, her baby had become extraordinarily beautiful in her eyes. Others saw it too. Before he could walk, when she wheeled him through their neighborhood in Rego Park, New York, passersby paid him compliments. His blue eyes were stunning, his hair golden, and his features so handsome that his face could have been used to sell baby food. But while neighbors cooed, Steven made no sound in return.

Rita began to wonder about that, especially as his first birthday came and went. Some of her friends had children his age, and those kids had started using words already. Surely Steven should be making noises, at least some effort to communicate—maybe a "mama" or "dada." But he wasn't.

He also didn't seem to understand what toys were for. His dad spent hours showing him how to stack plastic, bagel-like rings onto a set of wooden pegs, the largest ring at the bottom, smallest at the top. Steven knew how to do just one thing with those rings: bang them into the floor. It was how he played with any toy placed into his hands. Whatever it was, he only wanted to pound it. It didn't even have to be a toy. There was a set of candlesticks in the house that he liked banging more than anything else. They were made of sterling silver, and he beat them so far out of shape they could never be used again.

During visits to the pediatrician, Rita brought up the fact that Steven's development seemed off-kilter. But the doctor always told her the same thing: that she needed to let Steven grow up at his own pace. "Let him live his life!" he would say with a warm laugh meant to tell her she was worrying too much. But he was only seeing Steven for short periods, a few minutes here and there, and only in his office—not out in the world, where, in addition to banging things, Steven was now running.

It had started as soon as he learned to walk, and at that, Steven was ahead of his age group. He rolled over early, sat up early, took his first steps early, and began to run early. It was a need, it seemed, his straight-line dash. Anytime he was placed in his stroller, his only impulse was to climb out and start running—not in circles but away, in any direction, through any doorway, over or around any obstacle. When Rita took him to a fenced-in playground and set him down, he shot straight for the gate, then through it, then down the sidewalk.

This meant Rita, now pregnant with their second child, was constantly on the run too. Chasing after Steven, dragging the carriage with her, heaving herself into traffic to pull him back out of the rush of taxis and buses, she began to realize that this happened every single time they went to the playground. Meanwhile, back inside the fence, the other mothers sat, calm and chatting, almost never having to run after their kids and rescue them from traffic.

"You're not doing anything wrong," her pediatrician told her every time she asked. Again and again he encouraged her to "just relax," intending no irony.

Then one day, when paying a house call to the Teppers, the doctor suddenly changed his mind. Steven's sister, Alison, had arrived by then and was still only a few months old. The house call was a well-baby visit the pediatrician provided for all newborns in his practice. Rita had cleared some space atop a diaper table, and the pediatrician leaned over Alison, listening to her lungs and heart with his stethoscope. But his eyes kept shifting over to the corner of the room, where Steven was making a lot of noise, banging toys, and then suddenly leaping up to scale a high piece of furniture. The doctor watched all this, glancing back and forth between Steven making a ruckus and the peaceful baby girl on the table.

Rita, watching the doctor watch Steven, gave him a questioning look, to which he replied, "You know, I think we're going to send him in for a screening." It actually pleased Rita to hear this, to finally have her worries validated as more than maternal anxiety. It never would have occurred to her that whatever was wrong with Steven might be unfixable.

Weeks later, Rita sat facing the social worker at Bellevue, working through a series of questions about her earliest feelings toward Steven.

"When you first saw him," the social worker asked, "did you feel a sort of loving feeling toward him?"

"Well, the truth is . . ." Rita began. The truth, she had decided, was important. She wanted this process to work, so she decided to be completely candid. She told the chicken story.

From there, she expanded. She told the social worker that when she left the hospital after the usual five-day recuperation period prescribed for new mothers, the doctors kept Steven awhile longer, to keep an eye on the jaundice. This meant that, for several days, she had to visit the hospital to see him. It was stressful, she admitted.

Other difficulties followed after Steven came home. He immediately resisted being cuddled, pushing and straining against his mother's, or anyone's, embrace. He barely slept—never for more than an hour or so at a time. Therefore, neither did she.

There were also feeding problems. Steven was bottle-fed from the start, like most American babies of the 1960s, but he seemed unable to digest any of the formula he was given. Like clockwork, he would eat and then vomit—powerful jets of liquid that left their marks on the carpet, the furniture, and almost every piece of clothing she wore.

So, yes, he looked like a chicken at first, and, no, there were not many times when caring for him was not stressful. And yes, he had exhausted her. She was exhausted even now.

As Rita poured this all out, she could tell from the way the social worker looked at her that they must finally be getting somewhere. This recitation of all the problems between Steven and her—this was obviously what the social worker was looking for. And to Rita herself, it was now becoming clear where she had gone wrong, and where those other playground moms had gone right. As painful as it was to face up to it, she had no choice but to admit it to herself: she might not have shown Steven enough love.

The social worker let her drift toward this conclusion, then added some further perspective. She asked whether Rita had been disappointed with the appearance of her second baby, Alison. Rita had to admit that Alison had met every expectation she had for how a baby should look and act. Her little girl had been born pink and round and cuddly. When Rita hugged her, this baby melted into her arms. Rita was smart enough to see where this was leading. She had seen Alison as beautiful from the start, had hugged her warmly from the beginning, and she did not get autism.

So there it was. By picturing the infant Steven as a chicken, Rita had instilled a sense of rejection in her defenseless baby boy. Her devotion to him since then—the long nights awake, the travails over feeding him, the exhausting days chasing after him—none of it counted. He just went on being autistic, because there was something wrong with her.

Some mothers might have dismissed such an explanation out of hand. But Rita, ironically, was too well educated to be able to do that. She had graduated from Hunter College with a degree in sociology, and over the next few years, served as a caseworker in New York's Bureau of Child Welfare. She had also worked at an adult psychiatric hospital and taught fifth grade in a special-education program in the South Bronx. Along the way, she had read enough about autism to know what the experts said: where autism occurred, it was always the mother's fault.

Who thinks of her son as a chicken? she kept asking herself. She knew the answer, and sadly, she knew the outcome. She was a textbook case. She only hoped that her full admission of responsibility, and her willingness to submit to continued treatment to get at the root of her failures as a mother, would be enough, in time, to save her son.

Refrigerator mother. That was the term. And it was a slur—the first seed of which was planted in *Time* magazine's earliest-ever report on the topic of autism, which ran on April 26, 1948, under the headline "Medicine: Frosted Children." The main point of the piece was to introduce *Time*'s readers to the existence of these rare "diaper-aged schizoids," who were "happiest when left alone." But the whole thing was written with a heavy slant of blame, summed up in the magazine's rhetorical question: "Were the cold parents freezing their children" into autism? In all documented cases, according to *Time,* the mothers and fathers were of one particular type. These were parents who "hardly knew their children," who were "cold" and "undemonstrative." To put it bluntly, "there was something wrong with all of them."

An expert quoted near the end of the story offered up the image that would define most public discussion of autism for the next two decades. It was his metaphor for the fate met by these young, "pathetic patients," as *Time* called them, at the hands of their flawed, icy mothers and fathers. These children, said the expert, were "kept neatly in a refrigerator which didn't defrost."

Over time, the discussion about blame would start to look past the role of fathers and focus almost entirely on mothers. The "refrigerator" metaphor stuck to them, transforming sympathy for their difficulties into contempt. Almost the entire apparatus of American psychiatry participated in this ostracizing and debilitating portrayal of the refrigerator mother. One expert in particular, however, took the concept to such an extreme that his name became synonymous with mother blaming: Bruno Bettelheim.

8

PRISONER 15209

HE WAS CALLED *DR.* BRUNO BETTELHEIM, SOMETIMES JUST Dr. B, although he wasn't actually a doctor, not in the sense of someone who went to medical school or earned a degree in psychology. A former Austrian lumber merchant, he had earned his doctorate in art history. Still, in the 1950s and '60s, he somehow became the nation's most beloved, respected, and trusted dispenser of insight on the human psyche.

Bettelheim, by his own forlorn admission, was ugly to look at, to an extent that bothered him all his life. He acquired English late, in his thirties, when he first set foot in the United States. But he had wit, charm, intelligence, and drive, and on the strength of those qualities and a Viennese accent, he talked his way to the top of American popular culture. His books, though not easy reads, became bestsellers. He wrote cover stories for magazines, and magazines wrote cover stories about him. *Chicago Magazine*'s front-page profile called him "The Man Who Cares So Much." A BBC documentary placed him among the world's "greatest living child psychologists." He was a *Today* show guest, a "get" on late-night television, and, when Woody Allen was casting his mock documentary film *Zelig,* which came out in 1983, he contacted Bettelheim to tell him he had written in a cameo appearance for him, playing an authority on the human mind. Bettelheim took the part. After all, he had been playing it for thirty years.

PRISONER NUMBER 15209 stood before the desk of a young Gestapo captain, who gestured to the prisoner to help himself to a chair. The prisoner, who was Jewish and knew how the captain felt about people like him, declined the invitation. Despite the snub, the Gestapo officer produced a rubber stamp and, after asking a few preliminary questions, brought it down, with a proper and precise thump, onto the official document that released the prisoner from incarceration in the Buchenwald concentration camp. The stamped paper gave the freedman a limited number of days to depart Austria for the United States, with the strict condition that he never return. It was April 1939.

That was how Bettelheim told the story. As his version would have it, he was the prisoner, and the young captain was an up-and-coming Nazi named Adolf Eichmann. Such a chance encounter, between the future star of American pop psychology and the Nazi destined to hang for engineering the machinery of the Holocaust, seems almost too improbable to be believed. Perhaps it was.

As shown by Richard Pollak, his most critical biographer, Bettelheim was a prolific embellisher of the truth. Pollak's extensive research found instance after instance over several decades in which Bettelheim exaggerated or left out important facts about his work and life. For example, Pollak discovered that Bettelheim had told parts of the prisoner story on numerous occasions, but only once did he talk about facing down the engineer of the Holocaust. On all other occasions, according to Pollak, "Eichmann made no appearance." Pollak concluded that Bettelheim almost certainly never met Eichmann.

It is true that Bettelheim spent eleven months as a concentration-camp prisoner. He was picked up in a general roundup of Jews in Vienna in May 1938 and shipped off to Germany's first concentration camp, Dachau, in a cattle car. His first few months, he survived basically blind, for he was severely nearsighted, and one of the guards had smashed his thick-lensed eyeglasses.

At this stage, after Germany had annexed Austria, but before World War II began, the camps did not yet serve primarily as death factories. For Jews, the camps were a tool used to terrorize them into fleeing the Reich. Treatment was brutal, beatings were frequent and random, and prisoners died daily of disease, malnutrition, and summary executions. Buchenwald, where Bettelheim was transferred after four months, was even harsher. Yet there was, for Jews in particular, the real possibility of release in those early days, on the condition that a prisoner leave the Fatherland for good, abandoning his property to the state.

Bettelheim, upon his release, was given a week to leave the land of his birth. In May 1939, he landed in New York—traumatized, severely underweight, missing several teeth, and stripped of the better part of his life's savings. He had no job, little English, and, as far as credentials, only that doctorate in art history from the University of Vienna, which he had earned over seven years while running the family lumber business. It was not, on the face of it, the key to finding paying work in a foreign country.

He had nothing but his freedom and temporary permission to reside in the ultimate land of second chances. He made everything of the opportunity. Ten years later, he was on his way to fame, having created a new life and constructed, for public deployment, a new self. The "Dr." in front of his name was now a permanent part of his identity.

In 1950, the University of Chicago placed Bettelheim in charge of the Sonia Shankman Orthogenic School, which functioned as a working laboratory for developing new methods in the treatment of disturbed children who lived full-time within its walls.

In short order, Bettelheim was reporting extraordinary success in healing mental illness in the students under his charge. This in turn created a huge demand for his pronouncements on the best approach to raising "normal" children.

For years, in addition to writing advice articles for parenting magazines, and taking calls from reporters needing a quick quote on deadline for anything related to psychiatry or mental health, Bettelheim also held monthly sit-downs with young Chicago mothers, focused on telling them how to raise their children correctly. Forty or so women at a time would cram into a seminar room at the university in the evening, after their children were asleep, and the conversation would unfold for hours.

"He was God, we idolized him," one mother told Richard Pollak, who later interviewed as many of them as he could track down.

At least three full-length biographies of Bettelheim, ranging from hostile to sympathetic, have taken on the question of how an Austrian lumber merchant with a doctorate in art history became recognized as an eminent child psychologist and the world's leading expert on what causes autism. The answer remains elusive. Part of the explanation may be that Bettelheim actually did acquire, on his own, a meaningful knowledge of psychoanalysis, which fascinated him. He was a denizen of Jewish Vienna, where psychoanalysis was born, and where it wove itself into the fabric of intellectual discourse, affecting drama, literature, politics, and art—something Bettelheim did know a good deal about. At the University of Vienna, it appears, he took at least two psychology courses, and he read widely in the field throughout his life.

With a few clever adjustments here and there, Bettelheim nudged and stretched his life's narrative into a seductive curriculum vitae. No one, it appears, bothered to fact-check these adjustments, even as they opened doors for Bettelheim into ever-higher reaches of academia. Ultimately, Robert Hutchins, the president of the University of Chicago, would be one of his most enthusiastic patrons.

Bettelheim's ace card was his history inside the Nazi camps. On this subject, he had credentials and authenticity no American academic could match. When he wrote that Europe's Jews were partially to blame for the Holocaust—for being too unwilling to assimilate before it began, and too unwilling to put up resistance after—he felt he had the right to do so, due to the fact that he had been there and had made it out alive. American Jewish audiences who heard him say these things exploded with shock and outrage, but he never backed down.

As a survivor living in the United States, he was appalled that few Americans knew about the camps or seemed to believe the few incredible scraps of information that leaked out from time to time. He was driven to prove that what sounded unbelievable was true, and in 1942, after working on it for more than a year, he completed an essay on what he had witnessed during his imprisonment. He wrote not only about the conditions inside the barbed wire, but also about the psychology he had seen in play: why some prisoners were able to mentally withstand the nightmare, while others wilted and gave up. It was another year before he could persuade anyone to publish it.

When at last his piece, entitled "Individual and Mass Behavior in Extreme Situations," was printed in *The Journal of Abnormal and Social Psychology,* it startled readers. Soon, other, more widely read publications were reprinting large chunks of the article or reproducing it in full. Bettelheim's standing soared. For several years, it stood as the definitive account in English of the atrocities the Nazis were attempting to carry out in secret, as well as an analysis of the psyches of the prisoners. True, the author wasn't a psychiatrist; in fact, when one publisher called him that, Bettelheim wrote a short note to correct him.

By coincidence, Bettelheim's piece was published only a few months after Leo Kanner wrote for the first time about Donald and the other ten boys and girls he was seeing at Hopkins. While few Americans knew much of the camps, virtually none knew anything about autism. A decade was to pass, during which the condition remained obscure, familiar only to a small circle of psychiatrists who read Kanner and thought perhaps they were seeing cases in their own practices.

Then Bettelheim decided autism deserved his attention.

In 1955, Bettelheim applied for a grant from the Ford Foundation to bring a handful of children with autism into the Orthogenic School for a period of seven years. He proposed to track their development while figuring out the best ways to reach them, and he pointed out that the lessons learned could have wider applications. "From these children who have never made a normal emotional adjustment," he wrote, "much could be learned about both normal emotional adjustment and adjustment through mental illness." He received the funding.

TO BE SURE, Bettelheim did not intend to study the brains of these children. It was the wrong era for that sort of approach. The brain was an organ, and mainstream psychiatry put little stock in the notion of organic causes of mental misbehavior.

For Bettelheim, an autistic child, especially one who could not speak, was the perfect canvas upon which to scrawl a Freudian interpretation of behaviors. Consider, for example, his explanation of why children with autism have a hard time going to the dentist. Ask any parent of a child with severe autism: this is a classic struggle. The dentist's chair has everything wrong with it. It's unfamiliar, it's confining, it moves, it may even vibrate. Blinding lights hover. Equipment screeches and squeals. A stranger in strange clothing comes to poke strange instruments *into the child's mouth.* Sometimes there's pain.

Inspired by Freud, Bettelheim had an explanation: "From what we know of autistic children, their main anxiety is that the dentist will destroy their teeth in retaliation for their wish to bite and devour."

His theories on dentistry and autism appeared in *The Empty Fortress,* the 1967 book that catapulted him to the top of the list of autism's explainers. The book is constructed as a guided tour through a weird, wondrous corner of the "fascinating" human condition known as autism. In a detailed sketch of a handful of children under his care at the Orthogenic School, he offers their strange behaviors and obsessions as clues—clues that explain why these children might choose to run from reality.

Critics were awed by Bettelheim's devotion to helping autistic children and called the book "brilliant." *The New Republic* anointed him "a hero of our time." Eliot Fremont-Smith of the *New York Times* called *The Empty Fortress* "as much a philosophical and political book as it is a scientific one." He felt that Bettelheim, in discussing the challenge of reaching children with autism, was examining the universal challenge of communicating across barriers of all sorts. "It is inspiring," he wrote, as evidence that "the alienations in our age . . . need not be accepted as the permanent condition of man."

Bettelheim's descriptions of the children were vivid and compelling. Marcia, for example, was obsessed with the weather. "She studied it with intense fascination," Bettelheim wrote, "and for a long time it was the only thing she would talk about." People with autism can become entirely fixated by, and trapped inside, a single obsessive interest that takes over their lives. But weather had a special significance for Marcia, he explained, which could only be understood when the word itself was broken into the three smaller words it contains: "We/eat/her." Bettelheim explained that the girl's obsession with the wind, temperature, and precipitation grew out of a deep fear that her mother "intended to devour her." He reported that, after working with him, the girl "was well on her way to complete recovery" from autism.

A second, more discussed, case in *The Empty Fortress* was that of "Joey, a Mechanical Boy." Bettelheim had written previously in *Scientific American* about this same child—how, because he had been "completely ignored" by his parents when he was little, he had developed an image of himself as a piece of machinery, which in turn belonged to a larger machine, which was the world. Joey was interested primarily in mechanical things, especially fans, while avoiding contact with people.

Why fans? Because they rotate, Bettelheim theorized, and circles have a special symbolic meaning to children with autism. "I believe it to be that they circle around and around, never reaching a goal," he wrote. "The child longs for mutuality. He wants to be part of a circle consisting of him and his parents, preferably with him as the center around which their lives revolve."

Bettelheim reported that Joey broke out of "the vicious circle" on the day he spontaneously crawled under a table and imagined laying an egg that contained himself. When he symbolically pecked his way out, he was reborn and was suddenly many steps closer to a cure. "He broke through and came into this world," Bettelheim wrote. "He was no longer a mechanical contrivance but a human child." As to what was really going on, Bettelheim believed: "If the mother is the crucially dangerous person, then to be nursed by her is like being poisoned. . . . Thus a birth entailing nursing might have seemed too dangerous to Joey. But if he were born out of an egg, he could fend for himself the minute he crawled out of his shell. There would be no need to nurse from the breast."

Joey too was reported to have "recovered," returning home after nine years at the Orthogenic School, then successfully attending and completing high school.

Vicious. Dangerous. Devouring. These were some of Bettelheim's favorite expressions for conveying the causes and effects of autism. Autism, as he saw it, was a decision children made in response to the cold, nasty, threatening world in which they found themselves. Babies arrived fine and healthy, took a look around their lives, and realized they couldn't handle the ugly circumstances into which they'd been born. Before long, they "deliberately" proceeded "to turn their backs on humanity and society" in order to survive.

Bettelheim believed he had witnessed this firsthand, not in children, but in grown men, who had found themselves trapped inside one of the most vicious and devouring habitats ever constructed—the Nazi concentration camps. Symptom by symptom, Bettelheim matched the ways he saw men break down at Dachau and Buchenwald with autistic behaviors in youngsters. Children with autism often avoid eye contact? He had seen it before. "This is essentially the same phenomenon as the prisoner's averted gaze," he explained. "Both behaviors result from the conviction that it is not safe to let others see one observing." He had also seen prisoners fall into the paralysis of daydreaming. This, he knew, "was a close parallel to the self-stimulation of autistic children, as in their repetitive twiddling."

And on it went. Prisoners given to memorizing lists of names or dates to maintain their sanity were like autistic children who compulsively memorize train timetables. Inmates who clung to the hope of returning to the world that existed before their lives were destroyed evoked the autistic child's need for sameness. And so forth.

The behaviors matched up, perhaps, for readers who had no personal experience of autism and found Bettelheim's analogies intriguing. There was also the satisfaction of feeling privy to something esoteric. Above all, readers felt they had learned a brutal but necessary truth: *Mothers cause their children's autism.* This was, after all, the logical extension of his argument linking autism and the camps. If it was the Nazis who crushed the spirit of those grown men, then it was mothers who broke their children. The analogy was complete: Mothers as camp guards. Mothers as Nazis.

Bettelheim was aware of how harsh his indictment sounded. In the years to come he would take pains to point out, accurately, that he never once called mothers Nazis. That was a distortion put forward by unfriendly critics, he said, repeated by people who had never actually read his book. Moreover, he never actually used the phrase "refrigerator mother," though it was often attributed to him.

Indeed, while Bettelheim became the most eloquent proponent of the refrigerator metaphor, he was not its originator. That distinction belonged to the expert quoted in *Time* in 1948—years before Bettelheim began talking about autism—the one who described children who "never defrost." These were the words that first gave life to the canard of the mother-at-fault, and they came from a most unlikely source: Leo Kanner.

9

KANNER'S FAULT?

In 1949, Leo Kanner published his third major article on what he continued to call early infantile autism, based on his treatment of some fifty children with the condition. In it, he never mentioned Mary, or the Triplett family, by name, so she almost certainly never learned of the portrait he painted of her there. It was surprisingly unflattering.

It was not only Mary who came in for blunt treatment in the article. The other parents of the children he treated were also painted in terms that sound harsh and judgmental, certainly to modern ears. "Impossible to disregard," he wrote, were a set of features seen in "the vast majority": "coldness," "seriousness," "obsessiveness," "detachment." He went on about the "mechanical type of attention" they paid to their children and the pervasive "maternal lack of genuine warmth"—so pronounced that he could see it within seconds when new families arrived at his clinic. "As they come up the stairs," he wrote, "the child trails forlornly behind the mother, who does not even bother to look back."

At one point, his 1949 journal article turned to a scene that took place in the Triplett household in 1945. During a visit, Kanner observed the following: "Donald, the patient, sat down next to his mother on the sofa. She kept moving away from him as though she could not bear his physical proximity. When Donald moved along with her, she finally told him coldly to go and sit on a chair." Next Kanner suggested that Mary and Beamon calibrated their affection based on Donald's ability to perform. He portrayed them as pushing the young boy into pointless precocious achievements, such as memorizing lists of names.

Many of the parents shared this predilection, he wrote. "Unable to enjoy their children as they are," they focused on getting the kids to meet certain objective targets: "the attainment of goodness, obedience, quiet, good eating, earliest possible control of elimination, large vocabularies, memory feats." The frozen-out children met these performance demands, Kanner suggested, in "a plea for parental approval." And when they exploded in tantrums, this "serve[d] as an opportunity—their only opportunity—for retaliation."

In summary, he concluded that children with autism "seem to be in an act of turning away from [their home] situation to seek comfort in solitude." It was a protest against their entrapment inside the "emotional refrigerators" of their home lives.

It was confounding. If Kanner now blamed parents, that represented a significant about-face on his part. After all, one of his key insights about autism in 1943 had been that "the children's aloneness" was evident "from the very beginning of life," which is to say autism was innate and not instigated by parental behavior or other environmental factors. In his writings, Kanner contrasted autism and schizophrenia: autism was part of the child's constitution, while schizophrenia developed later in life. In the closing sentence of his landmark 1943 paper, he used the word "inborn" for emphasis: "For here we seem to have pure-culture examples of inborn autistic disturbances."

Moreover, he had previously had only the most positive things to say about Mary Triplett. He had mentioned to colleagues how capable she was as a mother. And in their own correspondence, he had repeatedly made clear that he admired her.

This much is certain: Until Kanner began using the refrigerator image in discussing autism, his discovery was largely ignored. For the first several years after his 1943 article featuring "Donald T," his description of children with inborn "infantile autism" was barely talked about in the medical literature, drawing only a handful of citations. Neither did the popular press pay any attention. Not a single newspaper or magazine article made mention of the condition Kanner described. More significantly, clinicians in other parts of the world were not confirming what he was seeing. Through 1950 or so, virtually all cases of autism were diagnosed by Leo Kanner himself.

His findings were not simply ignored; people Kanner respected told him that he hadn't, in fact, discovered anything new. Louise Despert, a New York psychiatrist whom Kanner esteemed highly, wrote him that everything in his paper about Donald read "almost word-for-word" like a case history of schizophrenia. In their lively correspondence, Kanner gamely defended his insights, but there is evidence that such critiques influenced him. Still in the early stages of formulating his thinking about the nature of autism, and never a dogmatist, Kanner nodded to his uncertainty when he revised his textbook during this period, moving infantile autism to the schizophrenia category. But even then, as if he was still having trouble making up his mind, he gave it a subhead of its own.

It is in this light that his new focus on the coldness of parents looks like a remarkable betrayal of his first intuitions, perhaps motivated by a desire to align his statements about autism more closely with mainstream psychiatric thinking. Calling autism "inborn" collided hard with psychiatry's consensus that mental illness was invariably caused by traumatic emotional experiences, in which mothers were almost always implicated. With schizophrenia, there was even a term for this: the "schizophrenogenic mother." Having moved autism into the schizophrenia column, Kanner may have felt internal pressure to retreat from his theory that autism was innate, and instead focus on family dynamics, dissecting parental behavior in the style to which his colleagues were accustomed. In short, based on what he said and wrote about parents in 1948 and 1949, there is a strong case that Kanner set aside his original convictions and became the first professional to overtly blame mothers for causing autism. This is a disappointing portrayal of Kanner that has gained and lost prominence multiple times over the years.

It has also faced vigorous opposition, particularly from people who knew and worked with Kanner, some of whom have published spirited refutations of the idea that Kanner ever believed or intended to imply that mothers cause autism. This, they say, was a misinterpretation of Kanner's words and intentions—propagated largely by an unsophisticated press, and amplified by the mother-blaming culture that already held sway. A mother-blaming Kanner, his defenders assert, simply does not conform to anything else they know about the man. They note, for example, his 1941 book, *In Defense of Mothers,* which rejected mother bashing outright and passionately.

They reject the idea that, in 1948, Kanner suddenly "switched sides"—from believing that autism was essentially genetic to thinking that autistic behaviors are the result of the parenting environment. Rather, they say, Kanner drew attention to parents' "coldness" and "obsessiveness" in order to ask how children who had been born with autism might thrive—or not—in the care of parents with social impairments of their own. Kanner's allies believe that he was pondering whether some of the parents had mild autism themselves—the assumption being that it was genetic, perhaps inherited by their children. Although Kanner did not say this explicitly at the time, which undercuts his defenders' argument, he did signal such thinking in 1954, when he wrote that he was "tempted to think of [the parents] as successfully autistic adults." Moreover, in 1956, he insisted that "innate as well as experiential factors conjoin to produce the clinical picture" of autism—the framework his supporters say he worked within all along.

By then, of course, the die was cast for mothers. Whether by design or by accident, it was Kanner's choice of words—"a refrigerator which didn't defrost"—that launched the era of the refrigerator mother. And it was the new language and approach he adopted in the late forties that finally earned his writings on autism a significant audience. As Kanner's onetime assistant Leon Eisenberg would point out decades later, "When Kanner coined the term 'refrigerator mother,' his view of autism became more fashionable." Kanner himself called 1951 the turning point for autism's stature as a concept. Some fifty-two articles and one book focused specifically on the subject between then and 1959, and autism began to be diagnosed in children overseas—first in Holland, and then elsewhere.

The problem was, most of these new writings agreed that autism was caused by mothers not loving their children.

By 1966, when every psychiatrist and social worker was telling Rita Tepper and other mothers that their children's autism was their fault, Kanner had long since stopped publishing analyses of parents. In the intervening years, he had not only come to rue the havoc those early comments unleashed; he was determined to make clear that he rejected every aspect of the refrigerator-mother theory. That determination may have been strengthened by his personal disdain for Bruno Bettelheim. No doubt it was galling that the most widely read book on autism in the 1960s had Bettelheim's name on the cover rather than his own, but it was not only that. When he looked at Bettelheim's work, he saw mostly bombast and unexamined assertions. In 1969, he openly ridiculed the book and the man before a gathering of parents in Washington, DC.

"I need not mention to you *the book,*" Kanner said, confident that his listeners, nearly all mothers and fathers of children with autism, would know that he was speaking of *The Empty Fortress.* "An empty book, I call it," he added, in case anyone missed the reference.

Kanner told the parents that he had personally combed through a forty-six-page chapter, one line at a time. "On those forty-six pages, I counted about a hundred and fifty times when the author says 'maybe,' 'perhaps,' and 'it may just be mere speculation.' One hundred fifty times! Please," he implored his audience, "beware of the sort of people who dictatorially tell you 'This is what it is because I say so.' We still have to be very cautious."

Since Kanner's audience was better informed than most, he also took a few moments to address the question of his own role in the mother-blaming fiasco. First, he denied all responsibility. "From the very first publication to the last," he insisted, "I spoke of this condition in no uncertain terms as 'innate.'" As for the refrigerator-mother myth, that was a misunderstanding. "I have been misquoted often as having said that 'it is all the parents' fault,'" he told his listeners. "I never said that." Then he delivered seven words, to electrifying effect: "Herewith I acquit you people as parents," he said.

Everyone understood what he meant. Applause ricocheted off the wall behind him and out the windows—a burst of gratitude and relief, coming first from the mothers. On their feet, clapping, some were in tears. Fathers as well. One parent would later describe the moment as "thrilling," for it was not just the sound of their shared appreciation floating up and beyond the ballroom. It was the sound of pent-up shame being released. Later, a parent newsletter referred to him as "Our beloved Dr. Kanner."

Bruno Bettelheim never renounced mother blaming. Two years after Kanner absolved parents, in the summer of 1971, Bettelheim appeared as a guest on *The Dick Cavett Show.* The refrigerator-mother theory still had standing in the psychiatric world, but there was increasing pushback. A great deal had been written by then about Bettelheim himself, who was still at the University of Chicago running the Orthogenic School and taking in children with autism. It had been reported that parents were banned from the school, and that the garden featured a sculpture of a reclining mother, which the kids were encouraged to kick as they came and went. Yet Bettelheim was still a figure of consequence, and his thoughts on autism still shaped popular thinking on the condition.

That night, hundreds of thousands were watching when Cavett asked Bettelheim to explain autism. It was, he told Cavett, "the most severe psychotic disturbance of childhood known to man." Cavett wanted to know more, so Bettelheim began to explain, gently and movingly, what autism in a child really represented: a form of despair.

"In order to survive," Bettelheim said, "you have to feel that you are terribly important to somebody."

Cavett jumped in: "That somebody cares."

Yes, that was it, Bettelheim agreed. "In the case of these extremely disturbed children, not only nobody cared, but there was a wish that it would be much better if the child wouldn't live." The next morning, across America, mothers of children with autism would be viewed differently by anyone who had watched the show the night before. Doctors, special-ed teachers, graduate students of psychology, mothers-in-law, neighbors—they had all heard it the same way. When children had autism, it was because their mothers wanted them dead.

10

BITING HER TONGUE

It was winter 1964, and they were being treated like outcasts, banished to the clump of orange plastic chairs at the far end of the hospital lobby, so close to the sliding-glass doors that whenever they shooshed open, the frozen air outside charged in to bite them. Later, a number of them would become one another's best friends and surest sources of support. That morning, though, they were still strangers to one another, exchanging only tight smiles, pleasantries, and scraps of information. They were on guard, these women—braced against the danger that the children who darted among them, making strange movements and even stranger sounds, might hurt themselves. The very thing that connected them—their children—also set them apart. Each of the children had autism.

Since the mid-1950s—the cold, dead middle of the mother-blaming era in autism—New York's Lenox Hill Hospital had been conducting research aimed at finding the causes of severe learning impairments in very young children. After a three-year pilot study, the hospital decided to extend the research indefinitely, using space on the ground floor of a nearby building as a laboratory. It was set up to resemble a nursery school, with the aim of expanding the children's capacity to learn. Only three- and four-year-olds were accepted, and families had to commit to sending them five days per week. Now a new session was starting, and a new round of children was being considered for admission.

So desperate were the parents to give their children this opportunity that some traveled an hour and a half each way every day. After all, no *real* nursery schools accepted children like theirs. This "school" within a hospital, which had few spaces available, might be their children's only chance to get inside a learning environment.

This was an interview day, when the women running the program evaluated the boys and girls applying for the next session. But it was not only the children who were being evaluated. The mothers were too.

One of them, a young woman named Audrey, had joined the other women on the chairs, holding the hand of her four-year-old daughter, Melissa. Her other arm was wrapped around Melissa's two-year-old sister, Hannah. To get there, the three of them had taken two buses and hiked four long city blocks, through slush and snow. During the walk, Melissa repeatedly kicked off her shoes and tore off her mittens. But somehow they had made it to the orange chairs. Sitting there, Audrey was still unsettled by how she had been greeted when she checked in. The receptionist, hearing the purpose of their visit, had dropped her eyes, as well as her smile, and then—Audrey was quite certain of this—looked up again with a chilly expression. Without comment, she had checked off Audrey's name on a list and then flicked her head toward the far end of the lobby, where the other mothers sat waiting. Audrey had turned away slowly, feeling defensive already.

But she had to shake it off and steel herself for the encounter ahead—her appointment with Mrs. Jaffe, the social worker. Among the mothers, Mrs. Jaffe was notorious. She was the gatekeeper, the first stop in the admissions process. Displease Mrs. Jaffe, and a child's chance of admission was ruined then and there.

The fact was that the program staff saw these children as injured, and believed that the injury had been inflicted by their mothers. The term used by the team was *psychogenic factors.* It was a way of saying that some emotional trauma had befallen these children and made them autistic. Identifying the source of the trauma and divining ways to reverse the psychic damage were among the team's chief goals. Children whose behavior was thought to have "any organic basis"—that is, a biological rather than a psychological cause—were not accepted into the program.

Women who wanted their children admitted had to submit to a battery of psychological tests. Once their children were enrolled, they had to show up weekly for mandatory "casework treatment." The staff expressed strong opinions about both the mothers and fathers:

> Among the mothers, we became aware of marked immaturity, strong hostile dependent ties to their own mothers, and depression as predominant features of their disturbed functioning. Fathers also showed markedly infantile reactions and either related on a sibling level to their children or remained withdrawn and remote from the family.

The staff found it paradoxical that, despite the many defects in their personalities, these parents were universally dedicated to finding help for their children. The mothers rarely failed to show up on their appointed day for therapy. The staff was impressed by the parents' "willingness to follow a program at a considerable sacrifice of time, energy, and money." Yet even this devotion to their children was interpreted as pathological, and "in part stimulated by guilt feelings about unconscious rejection of the child."

THE WAIT IN the orange chairs had gone on too long. Because it was so cold by the doors, Audrey pulled Melissa close, cinching her wool cap around her ears. Melissa's eyes were wide, as always. They shone like gemstones, inviting smiles even from strangers, who registered her slightly mysterious air of intelligent serenity. From a glance, they could not know what Audrey did—that this ethereal child, her firstborn, faced immense challenges.

One of those challenges had to do with being touched. When Audrey pulled Melissa toward her, Melissa went stiff and, with a powerful jerk of her body, broke out of Audrey's embrace. She could not tolerate certain kinds of contact—even, sometimes, the feeling of fabric against her skin. This turned out to be one of those times. She dashed away, stripping off her hat, coat, scarf, and gloves. In the seats nearby, a few of the other mothers faced the same struggle. Their children were tearing off their outer garments and bolting for the sliding doors, drawn to the rhythm of them and to their reflections in the glass. The cold did not matter—they did not even seem to feel it. Some of them even had their shoes off.

Once again, the sliding doors opened and two or three of the boys slipped through to the sidewalk, soaking their socks in the slush. A moment later, their mothers burst onto the sidewalk to retrieve them.

Audrey wasn't among them. Melissa, still inside, had bolted in a different direction, to the corner of the lobby that was dominated by a large potted plant. By the time Audrey spotted her, she had reached the base of the display and had one leg up on it. In that moment, the whole plant, pot and all, was starting to tip, with Melissa hanging on. Audrey sprang forward, rescuing Melissa and righting the plant. But some of the dirt spilled on the floor, and Audrey, glancing up, saw the looks on the faces of staff and passersby, who were no doubt jumping to conclusions about this "bad mother" in the hospital lobby.

"And how are we this morning?"

By the time the question was put to her by the infamous Mrs. Jaffe, Audrey was a wreck, and not just because she had very nearly missed catching Melissa when the plant keeled over. No, it was the fact that, for her, every day was like this one, and so few people seemed to understand what mothers like her—raising children like Melissa—went through.

Audrey, thirty-three, had lived with being a "refrigerator mother" a few years longer than Rita Tepper. Melissa had been born in 1959, four years before Rita's son Steven was born. The hostile attitude the two women confronted, however, was identical. The perception of mothers as the chief cause of autism was constant and unchanging, almost monolithic—the same for women who faced it in the early '50s as it was for women who faced it in the '60s.

Yet although Audrey and Rita faced the same hostility, they reacted to it very differently. Rita, who had studied psychology, was inclined to believe that she must have unintentionally done something wrong that caused her baby to retreat into his autistic world. Audrey's perspective was different. No doubt she had made mistakes, like any mother. But she knew that nothing she had done could have caused the extreme behavior Melissa had exhibited from the very first; the very idea was cruel. She sometimes felt vague twinges of guilt, of course, but virtually all mothers did. Intellectually, she was certain that those who blamed mothers relied on a distorted interpretation of psychoanalytic thought.

And yet, the near constant stress wore her down so much—to the point that she feared she was disintegrating—that she did see a psychotherapist for a time. She went on the off chance that doing so might somehow help her help Melissa, as well as her marriage, which was clearly in trouble. For more than a year, once a week, she took two buses, followed by a long walk, to get to the psychotherapist's office. He worked for an organization that offered a sliding scale and, at $1.25 a session, Audrey could just afford it. But the two of them did not click. The day she asked to borrow a dime because in her rush to get out she had forgotten her return bus fare, he insisted on analyzing why she had forgotten the fare and refused to lend her the ten cents. She walked home.

Audrey could not escape the mother-blaming message. Her husband's uncle was a Viennese-born psychiatrist in the Freudian mold, and she knew he blamed her for Melissa's behaviors. He had helped launch the Lenox Hill program, and he had been the one to tell her about it.

And so, as Audrey faced Mrs. Jaffe, who had begun asking questions, it hit her that she was in a setting where mother blaming was the starting premise. It galled her to be going through this interrogation; she wanted nothing more than to stand up and say what a sham the whole mother-blaming idea was. But she didn't. One of the other women had warned her that it was best to play along. Based on her own quick assessment of the Mrs. Jaffe situation, she knew how she had to present herself—as pliant and deferential, the kind of mother who posed no unnecessary or inconvenient questions. And so, Audrey bit her tongue. For Melissa's sake.

AUDREY WAS AN ARTIST—a painter first, and later a sculptor—whose photorealistic paintings would, a year or two later, be recognized as groundbreaking. In 1978, her painting of Anwar Sadat would be featured on the cover of *Time,* and some of her other works would be purchased for the permanent collection of the Guggenheim and other prominent art museums. But at the time she was still scraping by, largely unrecognized.

Audrey had been on fire about drawing and painting since early childhood, attending a special New York City public high school for the arts and graduating from one of the nation's leading art colleges, Cooper Union, followed by a master's program at Yale. After that, she just kept painting, though only late at night. In 1958, she married a musician, a talented cellist. But after Melissa came along, her husband was absent more than he was present, especially as Melissa's problems became more evident. To Audrey, however, Melissa's problems had always been evident, even in the first days on the maternity ward, when she had the sense that her baby's responses were off.

When the attending pediatrician stopped by, she put the question to him: "Doctor, do you think my baby can hear properly?" The doctor looked down on Melissa dozing in her bassinet, breathing easily, eyes shut. There was a pause while he bent in for what seemed to be a closer look. Then, without warning, he raised both hands, spread them wide apart, and slammed them hard into the sides of the bassinet. Melissa, startled awake, began to howl. "She can hear," he said as he left the room. Hours later, Melissa was still crying.

For the next five years, Audrey would never really rest again. The arrival of a new baby always forces parents to recalibrate their lives, but Melissa's homecoming was several orders more disruptive than that. Her first year she rarely slept, and never for more than one hour at a time. When awake, she often screamed for hours. When she babbled, she did not sound like other infants. A few words emerged when she was about a year and a half old, but those vanished, and no others followed. Audrey, meanwhile, was always with Melissa, always searching for ways to intuit her thoughts and wants, and for ways to soothe her. But Melissa flinched when Audrey held or snuggled her.

Audrey was alarmed to discover that although she was extremely sensitive to touch, Melissa seemed oblivious to pain. Once, after she had started to walk, she somehow wedged her foot under a steam radiator that Audrey knew was scalding to the touch. Melissa, however, remained still, not crying—simply staring at the invisible attractions that always seemed to captivate her. When Audrey rushed over and managed to gently release Melissa's foot, the skin was a harsh red where it had pressed against the metal. A large blister soon formed—a second-degree burn.

If left unattended in a room for more than a few minutes, Melissa invariably toppled or tore up whatever she could reach and climbed furniture to get to whatever was out of reach. Her coordination was poor as well, so even when she tried to perform small tasks, like pouring herself a glass of milk, whatever she was holding would slip from her fingers and smash on the floor. She didn't understand that food needed to be taken out of its wrappers and tried to swallow packaged food, such as cheese slices, plastic and all. When Audrey reached between Melissa's teeth to keep her from choking, Melissa bit down so hard that she drew blood. Yet Audrey knew that Melissa did not mean to hurt her.

In 1961, Hannah was born. But even with another daughter to love, Audrey felt a deep sense of loneliness. She filled the hours by pushing her two girls around the neighborhood, in and out of small shops and supermarkets—any establishment that would allow them to linger a bit. Other families in the neighborhood turned in the other direction when Melissa began making strange movements with her fingers in front of her eyes. The feeling of isolation was all-encompassing; Audrey knew no one who understood what she was going through. She didn't feel she should confide in even her closest friends in the art world, where women artists were expected to forgo motherhood if they hoped to be taken seriously. That she had a special-needs daughter would have been incomprehensible to many of her colleagues, perhaps even held against her. She had trouble making even her own extended family understand that Melissa's behavior was not something that could be fixed by a good spanking or two.

During one of many trips to the library to pore over textbooks in search of insight into Melissa, Audrey finally came across one that listed symptoms that matched those of her daughter. *Autism.* It was a relief to know there was a name for her daughter's condition. At the same time she learned that experts believed autism was more or less the mother's fault. But there was nothing in that book or any other that offered advice and support to a mother trying to raise such a child. There were days when Audrey curled up on the cold bathroom floor and wept.

She would have cracked had it not been for her painting. Somehow she found the time to keep at it, working into the early-morning hours, using the intervals when Melissa finally gave in to exhaustion and slept for an hour or two. Despite the demands on her as a mother, she made sure to maintain contact with the art world. When a gallery owner who had asked to see her work saw one of her recent paintings, he told her on the spot that he wanted it. In fact, he scheduled a gallery opening around it.

The night of the opening, Audrey was just stepping out her front door when she heard a loud crash from inside the apartment. Rushing back in past the babysitter, she threw open the door to the bathroom and found the floor a sopping mess. Melissa had both faucets running, and the toilet was somehow flushing itself over and over, overflowing the bowl. Going down on her hands and knees, Audrey yanked up her sleeve and reached into the bowl, fishing out two diapers, some wooden blocks, and a chunk of clay. She wasn't sure what had caused the crash, but Melissa seemed unhurt and so did Hannah. Audrey wiped her fingers clean, fixed her lipstick, and headed for the gallery, where for the next several hours, over wine and cheese, she accepted the compliments of a crowd of art lovers, and shook every hand offered.

Audrey must have succeeded at pretending to be the ultra-cooperative person she imagined Mrs. Jaffe required. Melissa, she was told, could start right away.

As it turned out, the best thing about the Lenox Hill program was that it introduced Audrey to some of the closest friends she would ever make: other mothers who were living with the same crushing sense of isolation. Now they became one another's allies, guardian angels, and sounding boards. Each was married, and a few were previously well connected socially—one was a published novelist, another was the wife of a prominent jazz musician. But in every case, the fathers had pulled away from the marriage. One husband was seeking a divorce while demanding custody only of the couple's non-autistic child. It depressed Audrey to see how haggard and beaten down her new friends looked. Years later, after she had lost touch with some members of the group, she would learn that three of them hadn't lived to see fifty. It saddened her to realize that her looks too reflected how she felt—stringy hair, food-stained sneakers, clothing that sagged.

But although becoming close to the other mothers would be a comfort, that day in 1964 when Audrey first brought Melissa in to start the program was perhaps the most painful moment of her life. It was a gray and rainy day. The lab school was on the ground floor of a brownstone on Seventy-Seventh Street, a few steps below street level. Audrey rang the bell, and a woman she didn't know opened the door a crack, grabbed Melissa by the wrist, pulled her inside without a word, and slammed the door shut.

There was a reason for that abruptness. The program was built around the idea of therapeutic "mothering," delivered to the child by a teacher or a social worker. Their attention and affection would be the antidote to the damaging mothering the child had received at home. The door was slammed on Audrey because no real mothers were wanted in there, contaminating the treatment.

Audrey stood in the downpour, crying, as it all hit her: Melissa was so in need of help and there was so little of it, except from people who treated Audrey as though she were poison. A passing police officer saw her and pulled over to see if she needed help. The question struck her as almost comical. She knew she needed to pull herself together.

She had become good at that, at least. She crossed Seventy-seventh Street and went into a coffee shop. She would wait there and calm down. In a few hours, Melissa would be hers again. And that night she would be back at her easel again.

In 1964, Audrey could not imagine how the medical establishment's conviction that mothers were to blame would ever change. In 1967, the most influential of all mother-blaming books, Bruno Bettelheim's *The*

Empty Fortress, would be published, leading her to feel that she must be alone in dismissing his ideas as absurd and destructive.

In fact, she was not. Even as Audrey spent her days calming Melissa and her nights making art, parents were organizing to break Bettelheim's hold on the conversation about autism. Indeed, by the time Bettelheim took his own life in March 1990, the obituaries made plain how much the tides had shifted. Though newspapers called him a "renowned figure in child psychotherapy," there was little mention of his argument that autism resulted from mothers wishing their infants dead. As the *New York Times* noted blandly, "The point of view is now regarded as outmoded."

If it was regarded as outmoded, that was due to a concerted effort, launched by parents in the 1960s, to replace mother blaming with research into the causes of autism, increased support of families, and meaningful help for their children. As the parents learned early on, the obstacles to these goals were not easily vanquished.

Then again, these parents were not easily vanquished either.

11

MOTHERS-IN-ARMS

Ruth Sullivan had no patience for sob sessions. Yet now, on this winter's evening in 1964, as she slipped out of her overcoat and began introducing herself to the thirteen other mothers in the room, she feared that was what she was in for. Like her, these other mothers had all recently been to the same psychiatrist, here in this very office building in Albany, New York, to get their "problem" child seen. Ruth's boy Joe had been to see this woman three times. Now the psychiatrist was urging the mothers to form a group, where they could get to know one another and share their feelings about the stresses at home.

Ruth, however, was not there to share her feelings with these women. She was there to recruit them. She had big plans: to get them organized, and to show what mothers like them could get done for their children. Sitting around feeling bad about how hard things were at home was not, in her mind, part of the program.

Ruth had stopped doubting herself the morning she saw Joe do a jigsaw puzzle upside down. For some time, she had been nagged by a feeling that he was not like her other children in some crucial way. Six months earlier, Joe had stopped speaking, even though, up to that point, he had seemed to be developing normally. At the same time, he was extravagantly ahead of schedule in other areas of development. He was more agile than most children his age. Only two, he was a far better runner and climber even than some older children in the neighborhood.

And then there were these puzzles. He was working on one just then, a map of the United States, whose parts were sprawled, like him, all over the kitchen floor and through the doorway into the living room. He was getting it done: New Hampshire met Maine, and New Mexico snapped in next to Arizona. But he was getting it done fast, almost *too* fast, Ruth felt, for a two-year-old. On a hunch, she knelt down to Joe's level and pulled the map apart, scattering the pieces. She also, deliberately, turned each piece upside down, so that only the gray-brown backing was showing. Then she watched what Joe did with them.

He seemed not even to notice. Pausing only for a moment, Joe peered into the pile of pieces, then reached for two of them. They were a match. He immediately snapped them together, backside-up, between his knees on the floor. It was his new starting point. From there he kept going, building, in lifeless monochrome, out of fifty pieces, a picture of nothing.

It gave Ruth a chill to see her hunch borne out so starkly.

Ruth was a faculty wife, married to a professor of English in western Louisiana. As a former army nurse with a master's in public health, she knew how to gain access to the medical system. Asking around, she learned there was a child psychiatrist practicing over the Texas border, in Beaumont, who made the two-hour drive to a clinic near her home one day a month. She got Joe in to see him in March 1963. It would be the first time she was forced to focus on the word "autism," because the doctor had no doubt about the diagnosis.

Joe was an obvious case, he told her, given his peculiar combination of skills and deficits, overlaid with the characteristic lack of interest in other people and hyper interest in objects. The fact that both Ruth and her husband were so well educated filled out the profile. Though it would later be disproved, Kanner had written about it again and again: autism appeared strongly associated with families of high-achieving, highly intelligent parents. He didn't say that to Ruth, whose only question, at that point, was what lay in store for her son. "He will always be a little odd," he added, and then began talking about perhaps putting Joe in an institution when he was older.

Five months later, when William landed a teaching post at the College of Saint Rose in Albany, the family moved to upstate New York, about 150 miles north of Manhattan. With the greater availability of child specialists there, Joe was soon seen by two more child psychiatrists and two different pediatricians, all four of whom, as it happened, had trained under Leo Kanner. All confirmed the diagnosis of autism.

Ruth was not a crier—certainly not in front of people she barely knew. The verdict frightened her, but her first instinct was to be stoic, even appreciative about having the diagnosis confirmed. Ruth was a doer by nature, a problem solver, an organizer. She was active, for example, in the League of Women Voters, a group that had worked for decades to promote civic and political engagement by women. A challenge gave her focus, and clarity gave her motivation. As a nurse, she liked to think in terms of going on the attack against illness, which required knowing what it was.

But when she asked what she was supposed to do for Joe, she found the Kanner-trained specialists frustratingly silent. At the last consultation, with the psychiatrist who urged her to attend the mothers' group, Ruth asked for recommendations for a book or two that would tell her more about autism. The woman astonished Ruth, and earned her instant dislike, by advising against doing any reading about autism on her own. She warned Ruth that this would only confuse her. Rattled, Ruth finished the appointment and headed for the exit, dragging a writhing, screaming Joe behind her. On the way, a burly psychologist belonging to the practice saw them and offered to help, hoisting Joe into his arms. For a full minute, until they reached the sidewalk, the big man was nearly overwhelmed by the little boy, but in the end, he managed to get Joe inside the car.

The unexpected kindness touched something in Ruth. For a brief second, with Joe in the backseat and the car doors locked, she let down her guard. She had started the engine, but now she leaned across to the passenger side and rolled down the window. "I hope you can help my little boy," she called out. The man she had just privately ordained a Good Samaritan turned and looked at Ruth for a long moment, in a way that made her feel studied, evaluated. "You're just an overanxious mother," he said. Ruth stepped on the gas, knowing that she was through listening to this group of experts.

Ruth went to the library at the State University of New York at Albany and read through all the books and medical journals she could find that listed "autism" in the index. At the end of it, she was no longer confused. She was furious. Were they serious, these writers? That Joe had autism because *she* was cold, rejecting, and overanxious? Where was the science, she asked herself, and where was the research on how actually to *help* her son? So many mothers before her had heard this same account of autism and been crushed by it. Even those bold enough to question it usually questioned themselves even more, because expert opinion weighed against them, and because parents of disabled children so often feel a twinge of guilt deep inside—the unbearable suspicion that their children are paying the price for something they have done.

But Ruth did not succumb to those thoughts and feelings. She knew what the theory said. But reality—the reality of her own kitchen table and the nine chairs around it—told her something much more persuasive. Ruth and her husband were full participants in the baby boom, as well as being Irish Catholics. The oldest of eight children herself, she was now the mother of seven. Seven children, all loved and mothered the same way, but only one had autism. It was an experiment with a ready-made control group. Six to one? Evidence like that was all Ruth needed. It was the shield of common sense, and common sense was how Ruth approached everything in life. Not for a moment did she entertain the thought that she had made Joe autistic—not then, or ever.

Still, she was appalled by the implications of everyone else buying into the refrigerator-mother scenario. It caused harm in so many ways. It rendered the psychiatric profession useless as a resource. It stifled any impulse to conduct research on other plausible causes of autism. It brought pain and confusion to parents, especially the mothers, who were already overwhelmed by the sheer amount of work required to raise a child with autism at home—or by the sorrow of putting that child in an institution. Above all, it wrote off the children, because the prescribed therapy, aimed at the mother, was doomed to fail from the outset.

Realizing all this awakened the doer in Ruth. It was time to lead a charge against the status quo and to do it as a mother, even if being one robbed her of credibility in the eyes of professionals. She intended to reverse that dynamic, to ensure that mothers' insights were taken seriously, and that their actual needs were addressed. She believed in the power of large numbers, the potential for a group of women to force change. She set out to put such a group together from the small universe of mothers whose children had this uncommon condition.

The problem was finding them. Autism existed almost in secret. Parents tended not to talk about it, or even to circulate much. They dropped out of activities, quit clubs, stopped going to parties, and spent less time with relatives outside their immediate families. Most mothers in this situation had no idea how many other women like them were out there, and part of their anguish sprang from the idea that they were in it on their own. Short of putting an ad in the newspaper, or stapling flyers to telephone poles, Ruth had no way to reach them.

And then, like a gift, came the invitation to join the new group being organized by the psychiatrist she disliked so much. Ruth called the woman's office and accepted. She was going back there, but for the last time.

THAT NIGHT, AS the group settled into a circle of chairs and the mothers started to talk, Ruth gave every appearance of playing along. But at a certain point she casually slipped a small piece of paper and a pen to the woman seated to her right and nodded down at it. The woman understood. She jotted down her name, address, and phone number, then passed it on. Quietly, as the paper moved around the circle, the other twelve women did the same. Ruth pocketed the paper when it came back her way. She went home that night with the seeds of a movement in her hands.

The next morning, Ruth started making calls. She saw right away that she had won this early round. Every single mother she contacted responded enthusiastically to her suggestion that they form an organization of their own. A nun of Ruth's acquaintance, on the faculty of the College of Saint Rose, found them a room in the campus library. They would meet there regularly for the next few years, not so much for emotional support but to pursue solutions to the problems they shared. They tracked down researchers working on ways to help their children communicate, strategized on changing education laws, and notified the press that they, and their children, made for a great human-interest story. Ruth turned out to be good at wooing reporters, unabashedly playing to the media's appetite for the strange and the wondrous, like stories of kids doing puzzles upside down, and for the chance to champion valiant-seeming underdogs, like parents fighting to give their children a place in the world.

For the next two decades, national media would still mention autism only rarely, but in the mid-1960s, in upstate New York, readers of several small-town newspapers became well acquainted with this mysterious condition, thanks to frequent coverage of Ruth, her group, and their children. Every now and then, the stories pushed the right button. In February 1966, a reporter named John Machacek, then with the *Albany Knickerbocker News,* wrote a piece about a boy who was "ready for school," although "school is not ready for him." Joe was the featured child. In fact, he was the only child named, as Ruth had given Machacek what he needed to make her boy's story compelling—autism's mysterious mix of skills and deficits. Machacek made Joe sound like a kid who could go far if he were only given a chance. "The six-year-old is superior to most children his age in reading, writing and other language skills," Machacek wrote, but "for autistic cases like Joseph to attend regular schools, an extra teacher or assistant would have to be in the classroom in case they became uncontrollable." Ruth had been pressing her local school district for just that remedy before the article came out. Within months of Machacek's article, she won this round also.

It was one child, one teacher, one classroom—a onetime concession, rather than a sweeping reform. But it was a valuable win for Joe, one that helped Ruth figure out where the pressure points were. And it was an early win for the model of advocacy that she was inventing as she went along. Years later, she would write up a set of guidelines for younger parents based on what she had learned during this early period. From the start, she recognized the need to get across a clear story line, so that people would "feel the heat of the autism drama." At the same time, she urged that they try to ensure that the "poignant beauty" of the kids came through as well, to make the public care.

Ruth also discovered the value of getting through to the powerful by finding shared connections to the experience of disability. She wrote about a state representative whose readiness to help stemmed from his own childhood, when he struggled because of a clubfoot. Another legislative ally's mother had been disabled by a stroke. Ruth saw him develop into "one of the most sensitive and helpful legislators in our state," while simultaneously caring for his mother. "He recognizes her," Ruth wrote, "in some of the descriptions we give him of our autistic children."

She learned to make friends with the secretaries of powerful people, who knew the best times to ask for meetings. She immersed herself in the technical details of the systems and bureaucracies that she wanted to change. "It means reading reports, budgets, studies, plans, laws, regulations, briefs, court decisions, journals, newsletters [and] going, going and going to meetings . . . seemingly unending hours on the phone, night and day . . . to persuade, dissuade, encourage, cajole," she wrote.

Ruth did not know it at first, but there were other clusters of parents in the United States fashioning their own activist responses. Jacques and Marie May, originally from France and the parents of twin boys with autism, founded a school tailored to their sons' needs on Cape Cod in 1955. Six years later, families in Suffolk County, New York, similarly started their own school, working out of the basements of their homes. They, in turn, modeled their efforts on a program next door in Nassau County, where parents restored a farmhouse and turned it into a schoolhouse. Each of these efforts was highly localized, however—not a basis for launching a national school-building movement. Most everywhere else, children with autism who were rejected by state education systems as "uneducable" remained, in a self-fulfilling way, uneducated.

It would be this way for decades to come: again and again, when something changed for the better, it was because parents had stepped up, overturning a status quo that argued against doing much to help their kids. Each generation of parents would stand on the achievements of the preceding one, but it was only this pioneering group—Ruth Sullivan and her Albany mothers, and the other organizers, scattered, isolated, and with few resources—who had to face the stubborn perception that they were part of the problem. The refrigerator-mother theory painted them as the central cause of their children's autism, thus making their voices seem not worth hearing.

Passion and organization, therefore, would not be enough. More than anything, Ruth and the others needed a counterargument to the refrigerator-mother theory, and they needed someone with unassailable credentials and credibility to stand behind it, so that the profession of psychiatry would be forced to admit the hollowness of the refrigerator-mother myth and lay it to rest.

In 1964, that person emerged. He was a onetime locksmith from San Diego who set out to learn more about autism than anyone alive, and succeeded.

12

THE AGITATOR

TO THE WORLD HE CHANGED, HE WAS BERNARD RIMLAND, PhD. To his friends, he was "Bernie." Bernie's doctorate was in the right field for someone with something to say about autism: psychology. He also had a son with autism, and, like Ruth Sullivan, his future partner-in-arms, he had a passion for organizing. Without a doubt, if the community of autism parents had been a church, they would have made Rimland their first saint.

Except that he was Jewish, so sainthood might not have sat very well on his shoulders. Then again, later in life, when he had grown a big, Santa Claus–sized beard, he was famously happy to put on the red suit at Christmastime and hand out toys at the office party, where parents were welcome to bring in their autistic kids.

Bernie's own parents were immigrants from Russia who met in Cleveland and tried to make a go of it there. Neither of them could read or write—not even in their native Russian—but his father had learned metalworking, and as World War II broke out, he moved the family to San Diego, California, where he got work in the warplane factories. Bernie, even as a young teenager, was contributing to the family finances. Starting at age fourteen, Bernie could be seen streaking by bicycle downtown into San Diego's Gaslight District every afternoon after school, where he started to work as a locksmith's assistant. Within a few years, still a teenager, he was a locksmith in his own right. He had a mind for systems and a curiosity about how their parts worked together.

He enrolled at San Diego State University, ignoring his parents' view of college as an unnecessary frill. This was where he discovered psychology, which seemed to fascinate that same part of his mind that liked taking locks apart. The internal workings of personality and the tools that had been designed to test and measure it—it was just like locks and keys, but on a higher plane. He went on to earn the school's first-ever master's degree in psychology.

Three years later, at Penn State, Rimland collected his PhD in experimental psychology; then he returned to San Diego to begin the job he would keep for the next thirty-two years. The Defense Department had just opened the Naval Personnel Research and Development Center, whose team of largely civilian social scientists was tasked with exploiting psychology to identify and address problematic military behaviors, with a heavy emphasis on psychological testing and data analysis.

Rimland was a prolific producer of data in the program, as he traveled to military bases all over the country to conduct research and published dozens of papers. It was a good period in his life, with all its parts in balance. He had married a woman, Gloria, whom he had known since they were children living in the same San Diego neighborhood. Bernie's job with the navy was secure, his income was steady, and his marriage was happy. As he turned twenty-eight, the only piece missing was fatherhood. Then, in 1956, when Gloria gave birth to their son Mark, that piece fell into place as well.

It would always strike Rimland afterward how, on the one hand, Mark was "a perfectly normal-looking infant," and on the other, how clearly he could see that there was "something dramatically wrong with him." He was walking at eight months, and speaking in full sentences at one year, very early for both of these milestones. But Mark never spoke *to* anyone, and he never said "Mommy" or "Daddy." From the start, he had cried inconsolably, been almost impossible to nurse, and went stiff against the hands of both his parents—all signs of a condition that their pediatrician, despite thirty-five years in practice, did not recognize as autism. Neither, for that matter, did Rimland, who, despite his PhD, could later say with certainty that he had never even heard the word at that point.

It was Gloria who had the first flash of insight that Mark's behaviors might have a name. While she was watching him one day, a faint memory reached her, a recollection of taking a psychology course in college, where the case of a strange child had come up—a boy who was endlessly restless, usually inconsolable, and whose language seemed disconnected from any actual intention to communicate.

When she mentioned this to Bernie, he headed straight for the garage, where they kept all their old schoolbooks. He opened a lot of boxes that day, flipping through every book with the word "psychology" on the spine, scanning for the case Gloria thought she remembered. When he finally returned to the house, he had one of the books with him, a particular page bookmarked by his thumb. "Autism," he said to Gloria. "It's called autism."

IN RIMLAND'S MIND, the diagnosis was less an answer than a question he would spend the rest of his life pursuing. Autism, this rare condition: what caused it, and—even more important to him—what would make it go away? With his two-year-old's future hanging in the balance, he headed to the library to see what more he could learn. Gloria's textbook had made it clear that the condition was extremely rare, so it was likely that its causes would be thinly researched and quite possibly unknown. To his surprise, however, the first few articles he found told him that the origin of his son Mark's autism was well established. His wife, Gloria, had caused it.

Like Ruth Sullivan, Rimland never bought it—not for a moment. He couldn't, not when he immediately saw two compelling reasons for finding the idea preposterous. One was the data—specifically, the lack of it. He was a numbers man, and he could see that no one writing about refrigerator mothers was actually offering any sort of scientific or statistical backup for it. The level of scholarship on this, he was shocked to see, was abysmal.

The other reason was Gloria herself. Bernie had seen her with Mark, how carefully she tended to him, how gently she worked with him. Besides, Mark's odd fit into the world had been obvious from birth. He had seen that too, and he had watched Gloria work to adjust to Mark's distinct ways.

So as he pondered what these books and articles on autism were saying about her, he felt himself getting angry. It wasn't just the baselessness of the refrigerator theory. It was the insult of it. These people—Bettelheim and his colleagues—were falsely accusing his own wife, this marvelous woman who had been giving up everything just to keep up with the challenge of Mark, of causing his autism. Over the next days and weeks, this ire chewed on him.

But at the same time, it awakened something in him: a resolve to clear Gloria's name, and that of all the other mothers so ridiculously and scandalously accused. In the coming years, the quiet, clean-cut, bookish man he had always been—just Bernie—would be replaced, little by little, by Rimland, the man with the big beard, the dominating presence, and the uncompromising personality: the agitator, the advocate, and the instigator.

Rimland always thought of autism itself as his primary enemy, as a foreign entity that needed to be defeated. But his war against autism necessitated a campaign against conventional thinking and those who espoused it.

In the beginning, this meant taking on the denizens of the psychiatric profession who saw mothers as the cause of autism. But in order to prove them wrong, he would need ammunition.

In 1958, Rimland set out to get his hands on every published report, every study, every case history in existence that even hinted at autism. He did this at night, on weekends, and between giving IQ tests to sailors while he was traveling. The information he needed was scattered all over the place in various books, journals, and libraries around the United States. As much as he could, he went to these places himself, relying on his handwritten notes and his own near-photographic memory, because photocopying was prohibitively expensive.

Rimland also wrote letters to investigators he could not meet in person, mailing them off to New York, London, and Amsterdam, soliciting details on their unpublished cases and seeking leads to other write-ups by other researchers that he might have overlooked. No one had done this before—pulled together all the reported cases of autism to create and analyze a profile of this little-known condition. He devoted more than two years to this search, until he was convinced there probably was not a single reported case of autism out there that he had missed. Altogether, he found somewhere in the region of 230 cases written up in some detail. Then he started reading.

Rimland's goal was to produce a document that would examine the refrigerator-mother theory as scientifically as possible. If the theory held up, he would admit it. But if, on the other hand, the evidence was weak or lacking, then he would go on the attack.

It was not even a close call. As soon as Rimland began teasing out a few basic facts about the world's known population of autistic children, the mother-blaming concept completely collapsed. This started with his discovery that nearly every mother raising a child with autism was also bringing up children who did not have the condition. It made no sense that these women, presumed to be more poisonous than wasps, would only sting once.

Rimland also noted the complete failure of psychotherapy to make autism disappear. Presumably, an illness that was psychogenic in origin would yield to such treatment. The attempt had been made several times, Rimland found, and always with dismal results. In one group of 42 children, the 29 who underwent a supposedly high-quality cycle of psychotherapy showed no progress at all. They "went nowhere," according to the study Rimland read. The remaining 13 children had received either inadequate therapy or none at all. Ironically, only some children in this second group made enough progress to start school.

The refrigerator-mother theory presumed that some sort of trauma had occurred early in the life of the child. This might include the birth of a sibling, a stay in the hospital, or the absence of a parent. But there was no pattern of such inciting events in the lives of the 230 children he had read about. On the flip side, neither could Rimland find evidence of children who had acquired autism as a result of such events occurring early in their lives. He also found that the much-reported observation that parents of autistic children were cold, distant, and self-absorbed personalities did not apply to at least twenty-three of the families in his database, who were described as noticeably warm, vivid personalities.

As for the mothers observed handling their child with uncertainty in a doctor's office or answering a clinician's questions in a voice that sounded flat and spiritless, Rimland reasoned that these behaviors, taken as evidence of "coldness," could just as plausibly have been the result of exhaustion and confusion, a result of the child's seeming indifference to his mother's loving words and touches.

Yet another possibility that occurred to Rimland was that the behaviors observed in parents might be clues to a genetic component to autism. Perhaps both parent and child were manifesting variations of the same underlying predisposition, inborn in both, passed down from parent to child as a matter of inheritance. Or perhaps, if not strictly genetic, it could be the result of something in the environment acting upon both parent and child with differing severity.

At bottom, Rimland's database was throwing off all sorts of clues that autism might be rooted in the human organism itself, and none to suggest that bad mothering had anything to do with it. He was sure that the psyche was beside the point, and that autism was biology.

Knowing he was getting out of his depth, the experimental psychologist went back to reading, and began to teach himself genetics, biochemistry, neurophysiology, nutrition, and child psychology, which he had specifically avoided in graduate school, because he never saw it coming in handy for the career he had planned. To reassure himself, perhaps, that he was not wandering too far off course himself, he decided to start running his ideas by a noted expert in the field: Leo Kanner.

Rimland started writing to Kanner at least as early as 1960, with a deference befitting the situation. Rimland was a young, unknown experimenter with a lot of questions he wanted to ask. Kanner was the world's leading child psychiatrist, Berlin-trained, with four decades in practice and a condition named after him in the textbooks. Indeed, in his earliest letters, Rimland was downright fawning. "Only Churchill comes to mind when I think of writers," he wrote of Kanner's scholarly prose, "whose . . . rhetoric demonstrate[s] similar mastery."

The flattery worked. Kanner clearly read Rimland's letters closely, as well as at least one "brief paper presenting my findings in very rough form." He encouraged Rimland to keep going.

Over time, as their relationship developed, their correspondence took on a more relaxed tone, like that between mentor and protégé.

Kanner must have known that Rimland's investigations were moving the younger man in a direction that would correct the sullied record on mothers and autism—much of which had been Kanner's doing in the first place. Kanner had not yet found the opportunity to recant. But he was making amends another way: by taking Rimland seriously, nudging him along in his efforts, encouraging him to continue developing the theory that autism was organic in nature. It was an extraordinary act of mentorship toward a man he had never met and whose work risked discrediting his own to some extent.

Rimland hit a wall, however, when he approached Bruno Bettelheim. Rimland's first letter to Bettelheim was a request for names of families he could contact in the Chicago area, where Rimland had found a lab that could run blood tests for some chromosome studies he was trying to organize. By this time, 1965 to 1966, Bettelheim had read some of Rimland's writing and knew he was being directly challenged on his own psychogenic theory of autism.

"I . . . shall give you no help," Bettelheim wrote in response to Rimland's request. He told Rimland he could never cooperate with someone capable of such "ill-conceived . . . erroneous and biased judgments."

Rimland wrote a second time, asking Bettelheim for copies of "any reprints, reports or references" related to his cases—a routine professional courtesy. This time, Rimland hit a much deeper nerve, possibly on purpose. Rimland knew that while Bettelheim wrote often for the popular press about autism, he never exposed his work at the Orthogenic School to peer review. Even the progress reports Bettelheim was supposed to provide annually to his main funder, the Ford Foundation, had shrunk in size over the years to just two or three pages.

Bettelheim's response was scathing. He informed Rimland that the progress he was making with the children in his care required no written proof: what he saw with his own eyes was evidence enough. Then he threw in a dash of analysis of Rimland himself: "You see, feelings are unimportant to you, and to me they are the most important thing in dealing with human beings."

Bettelheim was likely rattled because, in 1964, Rimland had pulled all of his research together and turned it into the book that would become the definitive takedown of the mother-blaming theory of autism.

Putting his findings between hard covers had been Gloria's idea. She had watched Bernie's "paper" grow, over four years, into a treatise hundreds of pages long. Sometime during 1962, she mentioned that he should start thinking of it as a book. Rimland took her point and began pulling it all into shape, with chapters and a title—*Kanner's Syndrome of Apparent Autism*. Only one copy existed at that point, and it was all in Rimland's own handwriting—he didn't even know how to type.

He approached his secretary at the navy lab, asking if she would be willing to take on the job for some extra cash. She agreed, and over the course of several nights and some weekends, she typed her boss's words onto a "ditto master," which Rimland then ran through a ditto machine—cranking out duplicates one page at a time. Once the "books" had been stapled and the envelopes stuffed and stamped, Rimland headed to the post office with dozens of thick envelopes addressed to researchers and psychiatrists around the country, specifically ones he hoped would take the time to read his work, including Bettelheim and Kanner.

He also sent a copy to a small scientific publishing house, Appleton-Century-Crofts. The timing was a fluke; the firm's publishers had recently come up with the idea of giving out an award that year, honoring the best new "distinguished manuscript in psychology" that it could find. They wanted to make the award an annual prize, no doubt to bring some honor and prestige to the firm itself, so they hoped to find a truly dazzling and deserving manuscript to start with.

Rimland's manuscript must have struck whoever read it as just the thing they were looking for, because soon enough, Rimland received a letter informing him that he had won the Century Psychology Series Award of 1962. There was no check in the envelope—it wasn't that kind of prize—but the letter promised something of far greater value to Rimland than any amount of cash: publication.

Two years later, in 1964, after a good deal more editing, revising, and narrowing down, Rimland's book finally made its public appearance with a new title. It was called *Infantile Autism: The Syndrome and Its Implications for a Neural Theory of Behavior.* Kanner's name wasn't in the title any longer, but he gave Rimland an immeasurable boost by agreeing to write a foreword to the book. There could be no better endorsement than one from the man already known as the "father of autism."

In his foreword, Kanner shared that he and Rimland had been in touch for four years already, and that Kanner himself believed the book's contents deserved a fair hearing. His tone made it obvious to readers that, on top of professional respect, Kanner also *liked* Rimland. The "father of autism" was anointing Rimland a member of the family.

WHEN AN OBSCURE specialist house prints a small run of a technical book with a subtitle offering a "Neural Theory of Behavior," it can't be considered a publishing event. At the time Rimland's work appeared, in 1964, there was no splash made—no talk-show bookings, no newspaper reviews. There were some brief notices in an academic journal or two, which came across as cordial and mildly interested, but those took months to reach print.

Despite the lack of fanfare, it was clear that there was an audience out there who knew about Rimland's book. It was parents who were snapping it up—mothers like Audrey Flack who saw, in Rimland's book, the possibility of deliverance from the story of the ice-cold mother, which had caused them so much guilt and invited so much disapproval from outsiders. Flack and others read Rimland and could see at least the beginning of the end of that damaging stereotype.

Rimland later heard that parents were actually stealing his book off the shelves of libraries, and not just to read it. They were ripping out the final pages and mailing them to Rimland. Years before the concept became popular, he had accidentally made his book interactive.

He had included a seventeen-page questionnaire, bound between his last full chapter and the start of the bibliography. It comprised seventy-six questions, a "diagnostic checklist": "Is the child destructive?" "Will the child readily accept new sweaters, pajamas, etc.?" "Does he consistently use the word 'you' when he should say 'I'?"

He called it Form E-1—the "E" standing for "experimental." This was, of course, his area of true expertise—test design and experimental psychology. It was intended as a draft, to show his fellow psychologists a prototype version of the kind of survey he believed could pinpoint autism in children and distinguish it from, say, schizophrenia. Naturally, he wrote, such investigators would recognize that "the form is designed for completion by the children's parents." Parents read that as an instruction that they were to fill out the form, and they took Rimland's closing line—"correspondence with the author is invited"—to mean he personally wanted to see the results.

It was only a week after the book was published that the first letters started arriving. Not everybody out there was pulling the library trick. Those who happened to learn of the book's existence early had ordered it outright from Appleton-Century-Crofts, but they too were scissoring out the questionnaire and sending it, completed, to San Diego. Some chose to type out the whole questionnaire instead; others sent carbon copies around to other families they happened to know with a child like theirs. Sometimes Rimland opened an envelope to find a single sheet, with a name, an address, and the answers to his seventy-six questions.

Autism had no central gathering place, and the book had only word of mouth to drive its marketing, so it was hit or miss as to whom Rimland heard from. In upstate New York, for example, Ruth Sullivan, as active as she was, would hear nothing of the book for quite some time.

Along with each letter Rimland received came a story. Mothers and fathers unburdened themselves to him, the only person they'd ever known carrying the title "Dr." who also knew which questions really applied to their kids' unusual natures. Not all of them realized they were writing to a fellow parent, because Rimland never mentioned the autism in his own family in his book. He'd done that so as not to undermine his credibility among scientific and professional readers.

The parents only knew that they'd found a sympathetic expert, who then turned out to be one of them. Rimland, for his part, treated each one of these letters as the beginning of a relationship; there was not a single family who did not receive a long letter in Rimland's handwriting in response, and most ended up getting a phone call as well, long distance from San Diego. Some would come to know Rimland as a dear friend.

Right from the start, Rimland recognized what these parents represented—the beginning of a movement. In the same way that Ruth Sullivan, in the smaller orbit of Albany, New York, began emerging as a force by organizing mothers, Rimland now had a connection to all these families, whose numbers climbed into the several hundreds as the months passed and their letters continued to arrive in his mailbox. Soon Rimland began organizing his navy travel schedule, which took him to bases all around the United States, to squeeze in visits to the homes of these parents. Sometimes he would pull together several families at once, giving them the comfort of knowing they were far less alone with autism than they had thought.

These families were giving Rimland something else vital as well: data. As their answers to his Form E-1 continued piling up on his desk at home, Rimland found himself, unexpectedly, the holder of more raw information on more cases of autism in children than anyone anywhere—far more even than Kanner, who was in the habit of calling his Baltimore clinic autism's "clearinghouse."

This allowed Rimland to start working on studies of his own, particularly in the area of possible treatments. In 1965, he completed a special one-year program at Stanford University's Center for Advanced Behavioral Research. Largely on the strength of his book and the publisher's prize, he'd been awarded a one-year fellowship there, which came with no obligations other than to think and write on whatever interested him—with free secretarial support as part of the package. Naturally, he upped his reading and writing on autism.

His stature in the field of autism was growing exponentially, to the point where, in a few years, the *Salt Lake City Tribune* would refer to him as "one of the nation's leading authorities on autism," and the *Oxnard Press Courier* would call him "a recognized authority on communication and behavioral disorders."

More important, his argument about the nature of autism as the result of something organic was making headway. When *Washington Post* writer Ellen Hoffman put together a short piece about autism in July 1969, she wrote about the conflict of views between the "two major schools of thought on the causes and treatment of autism"—essentially Rimland versus Bettelheim. Hoffman didn't take sides. For the first time, the two men—one a parent, the other a blamer of parents—were being presented as public equals.

Bernard Rimland had the standing and credibility, and Ruth Sullivan had the drive and skills to organize. But in 1964, he was in San Diego, she was in Albany, and neither knew the other existed. It took a TV show, and an autism dad neither of them knew personally, to help them find each other.

Robert Crean was a playwright and a television scriptwriter during the last years of TV's first Golden Age, when networks staged live, intelligent, challenging dramas that tended to set the bar high for everything else—for science-fiction shows like *The Twilight Zone* and courtroom dramas like *The Defenders,* each of which Crean wrote several scripts for.

Shortly after one p.m. on Sunday, February 7, 1965, a show called *Directions 65* aired on ABC. The episode was called "Conall," and it was about an eight-year-old boy of that name who, according to the television listing, was "severely retarded." Actually, Conall had autism, and he was not an actor. Robert Crean, who had written the script, was his father.

The program aired, telling the story, through still photographs and tape-recorded interviews with Conall's many brothers and sisters, of how the entire family was affected by their younger sibling's autism. Little noticed at the time was how truly groundbreaking the program was: this was the first instance of network television broadcasting an extended profile of a person with autism. Once again, it was a parent who was behind the precedent-setting effort, motivated, one of his sons would say later, by the passion to have his family's situation understood, both the good and the bad of it.

There was no television in the Sullivan house. Ruth had banned it, having decided TV was bad for the kids. But that afternoon, an excited relative called to let her know that she had just seen a show about autism, and that the boy in it had reminded her a great deal of Ruth's son Joe. Disappointed that she had missed something so monumental, Ruth decided to track down Crean himself. When she finally got him on the phone, it was a long, spirited conversation—the kind autism parents had on those rare instances when they first found one another. Crean kept referring to the "Rimland book," which he had just finished reading. When Sullivan confessed to having never heard of it, Crean explained to her that this book was very important, that it was the first thing he'd ever read on autism that wasn't the same old nonsense about mothers being to blame.

Ruth wrote down the name. Bernard Rimland. San Diego. A long-distance call would cost too much. But when she and Crean hung up, she sat down and wrote Rimland a long letter.

Ruth and Rimland would click instantly. Right away, the two saw each other as natural allies. Sullivan knew how to work legislators and the media; Rimland was masterful at digesting research and could talk to doctors and scientists in their own language. Both wanted to force major change in how their children were perceived, treated, and educated. And both had been piecing together a network of parents as best they could.

In late summer of 1965, after much correspondence back and forth between them, it occurred to Sullivan, the natural organizer, that it was past time to rally these many isolated families into a single nationwide society of some sort. She pushed these ideas around on paper for a while, and then shaped them into another letter for Rimland. But it crossed in the mail with a letter from him to her, in which he informed her that he had decided, on his own, to launch a national organization, and that he would like her help.

THE NATIONAL SOCIETY for Autistic Children was born on the evening of November 14, 1965, in a private home in Teaneck, New Jersey, just over the George Washington Bridge from Manhattan. Over the previous weeks, calls had been made and letters sent to parents in several states, giving the time and date, and the address of a couple named Herbert and Roslyn Kahn. The Kahns' five-year-old son, Jerry, had been diagnosed with autism by Leo Kanner himself. Ever since, the couple, who had two daughters as well, had not done much entertaining, so they were a little out of practice at hosting more than a few visitors at a time. On the other hand, given that this evening event fell on a Tuesday, not during school vacation, it was probably optimistic to expect many parents to turn up in Teaneck at all.

But a little after seven p.m., the first cars—some bearing license plates from as far away as Maryland and Massachusetts—began turning onto Essex Road, heading for the white-brick house standing next to where the woods stopped, across from the church, and down the street from the public school. Coincidentally, that school signified something important the Kahns had in common with all the parents arriving that night from all over. Even in Teaneck, which that year became the first school system in the United States to desegregate its all-white schools voluntarily, children with autism had no legal right to go to public school.

As eight o'clock approached, somewhere between thirty and sixty people—accounts vary—had already assembled in the Kahns' family room. If standing up all night was going to be an inconvenience, nobody cared. Instead, in the moment when the guests finally laid eyes on one another and grasped that they had actually filled an entire house with people who knew what autism was, and what it was like to be raising a child who had the condition, the feeling in the room changed to something electric. After all those years of loneliness and blame, the parents leaned on one another, letting go in a way they never could, or ever had, even among their extended families or closest friends.

It would be this way ever after whenever and wherever autism parents got together: insiders sharing stories, swapping advice, and taking pleasure in actually getting to laugh, for a change, about autism—about those few but real moments when they find the stuff their kids do more uproariously funny than sad. On that Tuesday night in 1965, that's what they were, for the first time—a whole house full of insiders.

At the center of the energy was the pair who had pulled the group together: Bernie Rimland, who had flown in from California, and Ruth Sullivan, who had driven down from Albany. The agenda for the evening included a talk by Mary Goodwin, a pediatrician who had been experimenting with a communication device called the "talking typewriter," and a presentation by Rimland on new advances in behavioral work being done with kids with autism. But the main event was the decision, by acclamation, to create the nationwide organization Rimland and Sullivan had in mind: the National Society for Autistic Children—or NSAC—which was almost immediately referred to as "n-sack" for colloquial purposes. Their logo would be a puzzle piece, as from a jigsaw puzzle.

A few initial bylaws were discussed and officers were appointed. A mother of autistic twin girls from the Washington, DC, area, Mooza Grant, was named NSAC's first president. Everyone there resolved to establish local chapters back home, looping in local parents and reaching out to already established groups, such as Ruth's in Albany, encouraging them to join.

Finally, there was a discussion of launching an NSAC newsletter. Other than paying dues of two dollars a year and carrying an official NSAC membership card, that mailer would be the parents' principal means of keeping in touch on a nationwide scale. That was key to the whole enterprise—to create a sense that, from now on, they had one another, and that they were all part of something bigger.

It was after midnight when the women finally turned to emptying the ashtrays and busing drinking glasses back into the kitchen while their husbands hunted down hats and overcoats. Then they dispersed, stepping outside the Kahn home, and crossing the darkness to their cars.

Looking back at that night, Ruth Sullivan would always say the parents felt that something had changed as they drove away from Essex Road. Now they had one another, and now their kids' future suddenly looked different.

"For the first time," she would say later, "we had hope."

13

HOME ON A MONDAY AFTERNOON

SHE ONLY KNEW HE WAS BLIND. THAT'S WHAT THE AD IN the back of the newspaper had said. "Blind Child Slow Learner." The word "autism" wasn't mentioned. Not that it would have meant anything to Alice Barton, who also had no notion at all of adopting a child when she'd picked up the paper that morning to peruse over coffee. But the boy's photo on the back page caught her eye.

"Blind Child Slow Learner." On Alice, the headline worked like an incantation. Partly, it was the fluky fact that Alice knew Braille. In the late 1960s, for no reason other than the challenge of it, she'd set out to become a fluent reader of Braille. She took classes, acquired a Braille-imprinting machine, and joined a group of volunteers who translated whole chapters of schoolbooks into pages readable by fingertip.

Though her skills were only rudimentary, she could suddenly see herself teaching this young boy to read, opening his life to books and much more. But of course, when she phoned the number in the paper, she had some questions.

"So just how slow is this little boy?"

There was a pause. "Actually," the agency woman finally puffed out, "he's kind of retarded."

Actually, it was more complicated than that, but the woman likely didn't know that herself. Frankie was six years old already, with dark features that hinted at a Mexican heritage. He was, according to anyone who laid eyes on him, a gorgeous little boy. The orphanage he lived in was located in Santa Maria, California, some sixty miles away from the Bartons' home in Santa Barbara. He was in school there, placed in a class with other "slow learners," and given the label "TMR." It stood for "trainable mentally retarded."

Alice listened to all of this, uncertain what she was feeling. The social-services woman took that as a cue to push. "Just come up and meet him," she urged, "and then we can talk about it."

"I don't think I can tackle a retarded child," her husband, George, said when Alice had hung up.

"Well, we made the appointment," she replied.

She and George drove up California 101 to Santa Maria on a June morning in 1970. While Alice went inside to meet Frankie's caseworker, George, not wanting to encourage this process at all, remained outside, killing time by wandering around on the porch, then down the side of the building to the fenced-in play area out back. There, rocking on a swing, sat Frankie, all alone.

Inside, Alice was getting the full picture of Frankie's situation. He was not blind, it turned out, but he had serious vision problems, though not so serious that he'd ever have to turn to reading with his fingertips. Then the caseworker began discussing the mental difficulties he faced, using over and over this unfamiliar term—*autism.* Alice, as she'd say later, "didn't have the foggiest" when it came to understanding what the word meant. So the caseworker put it in terms of how much Frankie was unable to do: *he doesn't talk, he doesn't learn, he's violent at times.* What's more—*it may never get better.*

Alice was shaken. This didn't sound like mental retardation as she understood it. It just sounded strange and a little scary. She was invited outside and around the back to see for herself what autism looked like, and then it hit her fully. *George was right.* They couldn't tackle this. A graceful escape—that's all she wanted now, to get George and get back to Santa Barbara as quickly as possible.

But George didn't want to escape. To this day he can't really explain it, but sitting out there that afternoon with Frankie, just the two of them—one a former marine, strong and able; the other a boy with autism, fragile and vulnerable—George just fell for the kid. And when Alice pulled her husband aside, the voice of pragmatism trying to talk her husband back to reality and back to their car parked out front, she could see it in his eyes, in how he kept looking back at the boy on the swing. They were about to become a family of three. "Let's do it," he said.

They took Frankie home on July 3, 1970, a date that, along with his birthday, they would celebrate with a cake and candles every year after that. But the first few months were an ordeal. "An endurance contest" was George's judgment on it, as they learned for themselves what severe autism looks like up close.

Alice had the days alone with Frankie, so George wasn't there the first time he put his head through the wall. When he came home and saw the damaged wall, and Alice told him how it got there, all he could say was: "You're kidding!" But the implications were beginning to dawn on him. A six-year-old boy had mustered enough raw strength—along with a startling indifference to pain—to break an eight-inch opening in a plaster wall, using only his skull.

At the same time, Frankie had started wandering the house at night, scared to be left alone in his bedroom. But because he spoke not a word, there was no way they knew to reassure him with words. George announced that a line had to be drawn, otherwise the household would be at the mercy of an unspeaking child who, a few years on, could actually hurt them, even if only by accident. Starting that night, the ex-marine posted himself outside Frankie's bedroom, seated on the carpet, to play sentry to a six-year-old.

"No, Frank, you can't get up," he'd repeat each time Frankie arose, gently leading him back to bed, settling him again under the blankets. Inevitably, as George turned his back to leave, Frankie would already be on his tail. "No, Frank, not during the night," he'd whisper, "back you go." This went on for weeks, exhausting all three of them, but in the end, Frankie finally learned to stay in bed.

George also won the battle of the nail clippers. The first time George brought them out, Frankie spiraled into a tantrum of pure fear. But George held that Frankie both had to be and could be taught to tolerate having his fingernails clipped. Little by little, George trained Frankie out of this particular phobia. At first, he'd just show Frankie the clippers, then put them away. After a while, he started using them only on himself. Next, he made brief passes at the little boy's fingernails, making only the most minuscule clips. Finally, Frankie relaxed enough to have his nails clipped whenever necessary and without resistance. The process took eight months.

George, of course, had no idea that he was accomplishing the impossible. The overwhelming professional opinion of the time defined Frankie as a lost cause, not worth trying to educate. But unaware that he wasn't supposed to try, he and Alice continued to operate on the principle that "kids will get away with whatever they want to get away with as long as you let them."

George was improvising, more than anything else, falling back on the instincts that all parents in his situation had to work with. But he was trusting those instincts, and Alice could see that Frankie was making progress—painstakingly, but also unmistakably. Now it was both of them in love with Frankie—a kid who still never had spoken, nor ever would speak, a recognizable word. That was one of the hardest parts—the silence in between all the otherwise incomprehensible sounds that came out of Frankie's mouth. Figuring out Frankie's wants, his fears, his moods—it was like trying to read messages in a passing cloud. They could find it frustrating, exhausting, and all-consuming, feelings that would have been all too recognizable to Mary Triplett, Rita Tepper, or Audrey Flack.

Of course, as they were foster parents and he was a foster child, they had an escape available—an open path back to their old lives. *They could send him back.* "It's not working out," they could say. Or, "He needs more than we can give him." That option dangled in the air they breathed every day. Yet they chose not to use it and did the opposite instead. They filed to adopt Frankie, and he became their son for good, loved and legal, and with a new last name—Barton.

In all of this, crucially, George and Alice were *not* alone—not in the all-encompassing way the preceding generation of parents had been. To be sure, in 1970, parents like them were still standing in a cold rain when it came to society understanding their children and what they needed. But in Santa Barbara, the Bartons knew they had company in the small circle of other parents living nearby who were also dealing with autism in their families.

These families had found one another and, by banding together and offering support, gave one another reasons to believe that something could change for their kids—and that maybe they could make the change happen. There were not many of them in the circle, a couple dozen parents at most. But for George and Alice, and many of the others, knowing they were part of a community gave them the energy to hang on and to fight. And that, in the story of autism, was something new.

In the middle of a California morning in 1971, the idle lawn sprinklers out front of the Santa Barbara County Education Building suddenly spit and gurgled and spun into action. Within seconds, they had soaked a couple of people who, up until that moment, had posted themselves near the front entrance, waving hand-drawn signs and grousing about school policy. When the water hit them, they scooped up their leaflets and wet cardboard and retreated down toward the street, beyond the spray's reach, pausing there to pull themselves together.

Inside, the superintendent of schools, watching from his office window, turned back to his desk, satisfied. He had ordered the sprinklers switched on, just as a prank, of course. The two parents down there would never know that getting sprayed was no accident. Then too, perhaps this annoyingly relentless pair, George and Alice Barton, would finally get the message: *Back off and stop wasting the school system's time.* Wouldn't that be a relief?

It almost never occurs to people raising kids of "normal" health and abilities to ask where all the *other* children are. Unseen, they are not likely to be missed. It was true when George and Alice Barton were attending elementary school themselves in the 1930s: kids at their desks had no reason to wonder about the absence of children who were too far off the mark to be there—like the boy they would adopt decades later. It therefore came as a shock in the early 1970s when, as parents, they went to enroll Frankie in the Santa Barbara schools, only to learn that by law and long-standing practice, the schools could and would bar him. That realization instantly turned them into activists.

That, and a night listening to Bernard Rimland talk. These were the years when Rimland was going from town to town, spreading the gospel of autism parent power. By 1970, when he scheduled a meeting to talk with parents in Ventura, about thirty-five miles from Santa Barbara, the autism advocacy movement was on solid footing. But before that, for a time, he'd had to work at keeping the movement from foundering off course and possibly collapsing. During NSAC's first year of existence, tensions had developed within the leadership over style as much as substance. Some of the founding members had come to see NSAC's president, Mooza Grant, as overly bossy, disorganized, and of questionable accountability in her handling of the organization's money.

Grant had grievances of her own, born of the belief that she alone was shouldering most of the day-to-day workload of the movement, without sufficient support from other parents. Plus, it was her husband, Leslie, who was doing the lion's share of the fund-raising, which took him away from home more than she liked. She was, after all, also raising twin girls with autism, one of whom was severely self-injurious—a chronic head banger, constantly at risk of cracking open her own skull. After two years, with Grant's term expiring, an election was held to replace her. The National Society for Autistic Children began 1968 with a new president—Ruth Sullivan.

But the schism was lasting. Even before the election, Mooza Grant had secretly been laying the groundwork to launch a competing organization, a rival for NSAC even in the name she chose for it—the American Foundation for Autistic Children, which she incorporated in Maryland. When NSAC learned of this, it threatened legal action to prevent Grant from taking the group's mailing list with her. It was an early harbinger of the tragic tendency of autism advocacy groups, or the individuals in them, all supposedly dedicated to the same cause, to turn against one another. It had been there at the beginning, and it would flare up, again and again, to the detriment of the greater cause, in every decade to follow.

Rimland himself would also be drawn into this unfortunate sport as years passed, but on that night in Ventura, with the Bartons and a handful of other area families gathered to hear him speak, Rimland was still living up to his saintly reputation, a defender of mothers and the lead architect of a better future for their kids. He urged parents there to organize, to agitate, to learn how to make demands. He talked them through the steps of organizing their own chapter of NSAC and urged them not to take no for an answer. When they started to deal with the important issues—getting their children both treated and educated, which NSAC argued were usually one and the same thing—they needed to push back against the authorities. He encouraged them to bring pressure to bear on the schools and on state legislatures, not to mention on public opinion.

These were not born revolutionaries Rimland was addressing. They were middle-class Californians in their thirties or forties—people who had grown up trusting authority and its representatives—presidents, priests, school superintendents, bankers, doctors, and policemen—and decent, ordinary people usually did not put themselves in the position of challenging that authority.

Rimland had been the same way until he lost his trust in psychiatry. Coincidentally, around this time, psychiatry had also been losing trust in itself. One reason Rimland received such a warm embrace at Stanford during his fellowship there was the fact that his book had dealt psychiatry—and its cousin, psychology—a satisfying punch in the nose. While the Freudians still ruled in the plush settings of private practice, a younger generation of psychiatrists and psychologists, at Stanford and elsewhere, were pushing back against the authoritarian certainty of their elders. Psychology departments had caught the rebellious spirit of the day and were impatient to have their work actually benefit society, broadly and urgently. In this pursuit, experimentation boomed, and the walls began crumbling that had kept apart fields like neurology and computer science, biochemistry and genetics. The time was ripe for iconoclasts.

And here was Rimland persuasively daring families to challenge authority alongside him. Shortly after his speech, some of those families established the Santa Barbara Society for Autistic Children, a chapter of NSAC. The women took the lead, with mothers elected to the posts of president, vice president, and so on. At first, they embarked onto more familiar ground, holding yard sales to raise funds for the group. But soon they moved on to demanding meetings with school officials and making the rounds of pediatricians' offices in town, seeking support and understanding, and leaving behind leaflets to explain autism to other parents.

Among the dads, George became perhaps the most active, launching a letter-writing campaign he wouldn't give up for years. He wrote the board of education, the newspaper, even the governor, Ronald Reagan. And he went along with Alice when she came up with the idea of picketing the school superintendent's office. The superintendent had, after all, received them in his office, more than once, and heard them out as they presented their pleas for some kind of educational support for Frankie. But nothing had changed for Frankie. He was still stuck at home. And so Alice had decided it was time to experiment with some political theater.

Maybe, to passersby, they looked comical out there, with their mini-protest in the sunshine—especially when the sprinkler came on and sent them hightailing it for dry ground. But to Alice and George, and the other parents who were also getting nowhere with the schools, there wasn't much about the fight for their kids that they found humorous. Unfortunately, before their desperate pleas on behalf of their children's need for education received a fair hearing, tragedy would ensue.

Alice Barton remembers precisely the moment she heard that Alec Gibson, her friend Velna's husband, had snapped. Alice was up on a stepladder in the living room, one ear on the television as she set about taking down the Christmas tree. It was the first week of January 1971, and Frankie had been with Alice and George for six months. Then the news came—an urgent story about a man named Gibson and a shooting in the neighborhood. She turned to look and then began shrieking. "Oh my God, George! Look at this! It's Alec Gibson!" As they stared, overcome, at the TV, Alice still perched on the ladder, George could only breathe out the obvious: "My God, what's he done?"

Perhaps only Velna Gibson, secretary of the Santa Barbara chapter of NSAC, had been aware of the darkness that had been gathering inside her husband. Alec Gibson had once been a content man, confident in his ability to provide for his family, competent in his career as a machinist in the aerospace industry. In 1958, Alec and Velna had relocated from Cape Canaveral to Lompoc, California, along with their girls, Junie and Sandy—who were thirteen and eleven—and the baby, Dougie, who'd been born the previous November. There was a job connected to the nearby Vandenberg Air Force Base, and a new home, where Alec himself, who was good at these things, set to work putting in a new yard.

It was his first heart attack—the first of several—that seemed to change Alec Gibson forever. It was a severe episode, and it meant abandoning not just the yard project but also his job at the plant. Gibson, practically overnight, went from feeling robust and confident to seeing himself, in his mid-fifties, as a near invalid. Then Dougie was diagnosed with autism.

By the age of three, their son was displaying classic symptoms. Before that, Velna had thought that Dougie, if anything, was ahead of most other children his age. He climbed out of his playpen at six months. At twenty months, he had toilet-trained himself. At twenty-four months, he knew how to work the dials on the washing machine.

His way with toys, however, was strange from the start. He'd have them spread out on the floor, and then, methodically, he would pick each one up in turn, play with it awhile, and then move on to the next toy in line. Eventually, he abandoned conventional toys altogether and started spinning things—pot lids and so forth. This became his new, all-consuming pastime—that, and banging his head against the wall.

Language never came. He had a phrase—*coolacoolacoola*—that he recited singsong to himself on and off—and a single word he reserved to address the rest of the world: "muh." It was his answer to any question or statement from his mother and father. "Are you cold?" "Muh." "We're putting on your socks now." "Muh." "Come over here, Dougie." "Muh."

That sharp intelligence Velna thought she saw early on was still there. It showed in his beautiful eyes, which were alert and inquisitive. Still a toddler, he developed a taste for recorded music, and he figured out the complicated stereo system his father had built from parts out in the garage. When the overture from *The Sound of Music* could be heard through the kitchen window, Velna knew where Dougie had disappeared to. He also managed to overcome the sliding bolt system Alec had installed high up on his daughter Junie's bedroom door, supposedly out of Dougie's reach, to keep him away from her record collection.

Another specific like: Coke and French fries. A specific dislike: the sight of airplanes, which set off tantrums. This mysterious blend of strong likes and stronger dislikes instilled in his mother the belief that there was a "normal" Dougie trapped somewhere beyond the strange behaviors, operating inside his body but just out of her reach. To Velna, Dougie became a boy waiting to be rescued, or perhaps healed by God. She had, shortly after his diagnosis, converted to Christian Science, and spent a good deal of time in prayer for her son.

But Velna wasn't just waiting for a miracle. She threw herself into getting whatever professional help she could find in and around Lompoc. There were some promising leads in the beginning. Now and then, in one special-ed program or another, a space would become available, and she would pack Dougie into the car for the obligatory trial day in the classroom. But it never worked out. Some places rejected Dougie outright as beyond help. Others agreed to give him a chance, but it wouldn't be long before Velna, arriving for pickup in the afternoon, would be pulled aside, and gently but firmly informed that a mistake had been made and that Dougie should not come back.

His sister Junie moved out in 1964, marrying young and not at all selectively, to escape the sorrow at home. Dougie had moved past his toddler years, showing almost no improvement, while the search for help and the cost of programs ate through the family savings. Alec sold the Pepsi stock he'd held for years to guarantee his retirement. Then he sold his beloved homemade stereo system. Then, one at a time, the family parted with their better pieces of furniture.

Ultimately, when Velna finally found a program that would take Dougie, the household itself had to be broken up. The Kennedy Institute, three hours away in Los Angeles, specialized in educating the mentally retarded. Again, it was an imperfect fit for a boy with autism, but the institute had committed to taking Dougie when no other place would. The Gibsons had to sell the house to pay for it. It was a day program, and Dougie would need someplace to spend nights. So Velna and Dougie moved to Los Angeles, where she found part-time work in day care, while Alec and his younger daughter, Sandy, stayed behind in Lompoc in a rented apartment. The goal was to give Dougie language, but two years later, he still only said "Muh." Alec was discouraged. "This isn't working," he said to Velna during one of their few weekend visits together. "We have to try something else."

Velna wasn't ready to give up, but when Alec suffered another heart attack, she and Dougie came home. Not long after that, with little to hold them in Lompoc, they all moved north to Santa Barbara, where they had relatives. The city's then progressive reputation also gave them hope that Dougie might have a shot in the public school system. Instead, they found themselves beating the same path George and Alice had traveled with Frankie. Meetings with the Santa Barbara schools were followed by vague promises, then rejections from one classroom after another.

Finally, they took the step they'd been trying to avoid all along and placed their now eleven-year-old son in the one institution they knew would never turn him down—the state mental hospital in Camarillo. There would be no bills to pay, at least. It was the only place they could afford.

It was Alec who cut this experiment short. Since driving Dougie to Camarillo for his initial commitment there, he and Velna had been making two round-trips there each week, taking Dougie home on Fridays, and then back to the institution on Sunday afternoons. The pickups went fine. Dougie always rushed into their arms to give them hugs, evidence all by itself that he was making the type of connection to them that autism was supposed to hinder. Velna took it as a sign that Camarillo was doing him some good.

But then came Sunday, and the return trip, which was torture for everyone involved. Without fail, the moment the institution walls came into view, Dougie would explode. Screaming and flailing, he had to be dragged into the building by white-jacketed attendants. It ripped into Alec's already weak heart to see this, week after week, and after nearly three months of it, he called a halt. One Friday, he and Velna picked Dougie up from Camarillo and never brought him back.

Their home life settled down into an immutable pattern. Dougie needed twenty-four-hour supervision, and since only Velna could work, Alec looked after him during the days. The two of them apparently grew quite close in this period, as they would have to, given that playdates with other children were not an option, and that Alec, now nearly penniless, had also turned rather reclusive. When he and Dougie weren't alone together for hours in the upstairs apartment of the two-family home they rented on East Figueroa Street, they were out on walks together, just the two of them. Neighbors noticed them but didn't interact much with the lonely-looking pair—the unusually good-looking boy, somewhat tall for his age, who made strange sounds as he passed by; and the lean, gray-haired man who was always by his side, saying little.

It was sometime during this period that Alec got hold of a Beretta .45. Exactly when and how has never been clear. Alec took his last walk with Dougie on January 4, 1971. They went to McDonald's, Dougie's favorite place, for his favorite meal, which, at age thirteen, was still French fries and Coke. It was around one thirty p.m. when they returned home. The street outside was quiet, as the neighborhood children had just gone back to school after Christmas break. Dougie lay down for a nap on a small cot in the dayroom, and Alec went into the kitchen and wrote a note:

> *I have done a terrible thing. I know that I cannot be forgiven.*
> *Don't want to see you or anyone.*

He left the note standing up against the telephone on the kitchen counter and went in to look at his sleeping son. It is not known how long he stood there, but at some point, Alec lifted the Beretta and shot Dougie in the head.

Dougie did not die right away. That would happen later, in the ambulance. When the ambulance team first saw him, they reported that he was still gurgling for breath on the daybed.

Alec likely didn't see any of that. Immediately after firing, he'd returned to the kitchen, placed the gun in its original box next to the note, and then called the police. Then he stepped outside and sat down on the front steps, waiting for the first sound of sirens to carry in on the afternoon breeze.

"Retarded Son Is Dead," the *Santa Barbara Press* reported the next morning on an inside page. The day after that, school officials gave interviews attempting to correct the record, but they also got it wrong. "Douglas was not mentally retarded," one of them informed the paper; he "had been diagnosed as emotionally disturbed." A source at the Camarillo State Hospital, where he'd spent three months, came up with yet a third variant: "schizophrenic reaction, childhood type," someone told the reporter who called.

Finally, a letter to the editor appeared in the *Press* that clarified the nature of Dougie's condition. The woman who wrote it, Mary Ellen Nava, identified herself "as the parent of an autistic child like Dougie." Actually, she and Alice Barton had worked on the letter together, but only Mary Ellen's name appeared in print. She opened her letter by posing a question about the father who had shot his son: "What went through the mind of this man?"

It was the obvious thing to ask. Nava was president of the Santa Barbara Society for Autistic Children and one of the mothers who had attended that Ventura meeting with Bernard Rimland. Her son Eddie, three years younger than Velna's Dougie, was almost as disabled as Dougie. He didn't speak and had a tendency to attack his own skin with his fingernails, scratching himself raw till bleeding, which often led to infections. He had been luckier, though, in finding placement in a special-education class where his behaviors were just barely tolerated. Dougie's, on the other hand, were always just too extreme, and Mary Ellen could see what Velna, now a good friend, had to go through each time another school expelled him.

What went through the mind of this man?

Mary Ellen phrased her response carefully. Velna had told her that Alec had convinced himself that killing Dougie was the only way to spare him. One of the police officers who made the arrest had quickly formed the same impression. After sizing up the situation at the house and taking Alec's statement, he told a reporter that the suspect had intended a "mercy killing."

At the trial, a sympathetic psychiatrist corroborated this account of the defendant's thought process, noting that it fed darkly on the strangling depression that had seized on Alec as his own health problems worsened. Alec had become certain his heart would soon fail for good, and he had become obsessed with thoughts of the cruelty the world would visit upon his son when he was no longer there to protect him, as well as with the burden that would shift fully onto Velna. The harsh indifference of the schools toward Dougie already served to confirm these fears, but it was an incident some weeks before the shooting that may have triggered Alec's final lunge toward despair.

It was the day Dougie, who had just turned thirteen, had suddenly dropped his pants and begun playing with his genitals, out in the open, in front of a group of children in their own backyard. It caused a momentary uproar among the kids, who reported it immediately to their mother, a friend of the Gibsons named Aggie. If anyone in the Gibsons' world was capable of avoiding an all-out panic over this turn of events, it was Aggie. She was one of the few mothers around who was not put off by seeing Dougie walk up her front path with his parents. When the Gibsons came over, her kids always included Dougie in their games, because Aggie encouraged it. Perhaps she didn't know much about autism, but she knew enough never to hold Alec or Velna at fault when Dougie did something that crossed the boundaries of what was considered socially acceptable.

When he started masturbating in the sunlight that day, Alec was on Dougie in an instant, jerking his pants back up to his waist, embarrassed for him, scolding him, while making apologies to Aggie, who in fact didn't require any. She understood: Dougie, just entering puberty, was only doing what came naturally. *Coolacoolacoola.* That was all this tall, handsome young man had to say for himself, then and always. It was hard to imagine his indiscretion was a deliberate attempt to create a scandal by the sandbox—not when these physical feelings were so new to him, and "the rules" about them so far past his comprehension.

Someone like Aggie could forgive and forget the awkward episode. But Alec couldn't let it go. It began to haunt him—the realization that sex represented a thousand new ways Dougie could find himself dangerously out of sync with the world. More of this kind of thing, and his boy could easily be branded something he wasn't: a deviant, a threat. People like that get arrested or beaten to death. *And he was only thirteen.* Adolescence still stretched in front of Dougie, followed by manhood. The social complexities he would need to negotiate seemed overwhelming. Alec could not conceive of Dougie ever being able to learn to observe the boundaries set by concepts like privacy or modesty. Instead, he foresaw the thicket of autism, sex, and etiquette as a wilderness that would swallow his son whole. It would only get worse, he had to assume, as Dougie got older, bolder, and stronger. The world was cruel. He was convinced of that.

Alec killed Dougie to put him out of a misery he believed to be inevitable, following a distorted logic he developed while profoundly depressed. That, at least, was his legal defense. Charged with murder in the first degree, he entered a plea of not guilty, and his lawyer argued temporary insanity. The district attorney never bought the story, and neither, in the end, did the jury. The DA's competing story—that Alec Gibson was a father who killed his mentally disabled son because he was tired of the sacrifices required and just wanted his freedom back—appealed more to a common sense that knew nothing of raising a child with severe autism. No members of the jury had such experience. Alec was found guilty and given a life sentence.

Mary Ellen Nava, on the other hand, understood what Alec had been up against and why he had snapped. That's how she saw it: her friend's husband had, indeed, done a terrible thing, something that could never be justified. But she doubted he did it out of selfishness. Other autism parents, when they heard about the murder, reacted the same way. They were horrified by it, but at the same time, they recognized something familiar in the despair Alec surrendered to. At times, they too had felt chipped down almost to nothing by their inability to find a safe place for their kids—whether in a school now, or out in the world after they were gone. Nava was speaking for many of them when she tried to explain this world without options to readers of the *Santa Barbara Press.*

"This . . . boy was home on a Monday afternoon," she wrote, "because the doors of public education were closed to him. Why?

"Probably," she wrote, Alec looked at his son, "his own flesh and blood," and asked, "what future does my boy have?" Then, to a world who still had little notion of autism, she appealed for understanding—not just of Alec, but of all of them: "Won't you PLEASE help before our small group of children gets smaller? Ask—WHY?—WHO?—WHAT?—of your Special Education Department, your Mental Health Center, your doctor, wherever your voice will be heard. The next autistic baby could be yours."

THOUGH FORGOTTEN OVER time, Dougie's death did shake something loose in the edifice of official indifference that the Santa Barbara families had been facing. Mary Ellen Nava may have been the first to get the phone call, because she had written that letter to the editor, but soon, it was all the parents in her group. Within days of Alec's trial starting, people in the state capital, officials from the California Department of Education, were asking to meet with them, the sooner the better, to discuss urgently the needs of Santa Barbara families dealing with autism. Soon a delegation from Sacramento had arrived in the city, shuttling from family to family in a small somber convoy of black cars, sitting down in living rooms and at kitchen tables, pulling out notepads to write down the answers to the questions they had brought. They had a lot of questions: about autism, about what these kids could learn, about what had already been tried, about what the parents would want to see if the school system committed to coming up with something better.

The sudden spotlight on their struggles was startling for Mary Ellen and the others. They had no doubt that it was because of what had happened to their friends, the Gibsons. At the trial, Alec's lawyer had laid out the long, dreary story of Dougie's rejection by one school after another. It must have tweaked somebody's conscience up in Sacramento, or embarrassed somebody in charge, because all of a sudden, instead of turning sprinklers on the parents, these state people were sipping coffee with them, leafing through their photo albums, and smiling appreciatively when it was pointed out how glowingly beautiful the kids had been as babies. The officials left vowing that something would be done in response to the absence of support that had driven Alec Gibson over the edge.

It was not an empty promise. A year later, the *Los Angeles Times* could report: "Partly because of what happened," the University of

California at Santa Barbara and the County of Santa Barbara school system "are cooperating on a model program for autistic children financed by a $200,000 federal grant." Overseen by a young UCLA-trained psychologist named Robert Koegel, who showed up with a willingness to experiment, it was a model that persisted, evolved, and expanded. Today the UCSB Koegel Autism Center dominates the West Coast of the United States in autism treatment, assessment, and research, and sees children by the thousands, from all around the world.

In that first year, it took in twenty children, mostly Santa Barbara kids, Mary Ellen's Eddie among them. The year after that, a Los Angeles TV station reported in a documentary that more than half of those children (not including Eddie) had progressed to where they were able to attend regular public school classes. "But for the tragic circumstances," explained the documentary's narrator—autism parent and Hollywood actor Lloyd Nolan—the program "probably would not have been."

It was the last time the Dougie story would be broached in public, and then the world moved on. But the wheels had been set in motion; the battle for education reform had begun.

PART III

THE END OF INSTITUTIONS

1970s–1990s

14

"BEHIND THE WALLS OF THE WORLD'S INDIFFERENCE"

In 1919, when five-year-old Archie Casto's parents moved him into an institution in West Virginia, the number of words in his vocabulary matched his age. Fifty years later, as the 1970s were just starting to unfold, he was still inside institutional walls, living at Spencer State Hospital in Roane County, West Virginia. Change was overtaking the United States, upending traditional thinking about identity and power in so many areas of American life: race, religion, gender—and disability, where the ideas behind the practice of institutionalization were starting to be questioned.

But this wave of change had not reached Spencer State yet, or Archie. He was middle-aged by then, and his parents were long gone. As no one had ever tried to teach Archie anything, or even talked to him much, language had abandoned him. His five words had dwindled to zero. He had never grown much past the height of a typical third-grader. Chronologically an adult, he had a small head, small hands and feet, and not a single tooth in his mouth. It was a known response by some state institutions to yank out the teeth of children who could not help biting—either other people or themselves. Archie might have gotten himself into that kind of trouble; compulsive self-biting sometimes goes together with severe autism.

But in 1919, when Archie was first institutionalized, that diagnosis did not exist. By the time the label was invented midcentury, Archie was still locked away, in the prime of his life, and no one thought to reassess him to see if autism explained his behaviors. As far as the bureaucracy that controlled his life was concerned, he already had a label adequate for its purposes. He was a clinical "idiot"—although, by the 1970s, a more enlightened culture had switched to the shorthand "MR," for "mentally retarded." As far as the existing staff at Spencer knew, many of whom were not even born when he first entered the system, Archie had just always been there, one of the fixtures of the place—one among hundreds of residents who were there for life, many destined to be buried in the hospital's own hillside cemetery.

Through the first two-thirds of the twentieth century, the impulse to institutionalize dominated the response to real or apparent impairment of the faculties of intelligence. A broad range of conditions were represented by the people who were "put away" as children during these years. Epilepsy, cerebral palsy, and intellectual disability were among these. Autism too—once the diagnosis was coined—became grounds for commitment. This impulse arose from shame, and from the perception that such children were burdens that no decent hardworking family should be expected to shoulder at home. States stepped in with a taxpayer-funded solution: massive fenced-in compounds that herded huge numbers of such people together, out where they could not gum up the works of normal daily existence for everyone else.

The states referred to these places as schools and hospitals, but in effect they became human warehouses. These institutions packed in hundreds of thousands of people across the country. The residents without an actual treatable mental illness became more or less lifetime detainees, because they never showed improvement and tended only to get worse. Nearly every state ran such institutions, and many had more than one.

Without question, the institutions swept up many of the people who today would be diagnosed with autism, at least up into the 1970s. This happened to most of the first eleven children Kanner wrote about in 1943. When he tracked down ten of them nearly three decades later, he discovered that five had passed their entire lives up until then at state mental hospitals, and most of the others—excluding Donald Triplett and a boy named Henry, who lived on a farm—had also spent years in institutions, sometimes several different ones, before other arrangements were finally found.

Bernard Rimland, meanwhile, wrote that those who were not at home were passing their years "in empty hopelessness" inside institutions. A 1967 British study put a number on the hopelessness, reporting that three-fourths of the several dozen individuals with autism it tracked from adolescence into adulthood ended up that way. As late as 1982, another British study of a single "mental handicap hospital" found that 9 percent of the permanent residents under age thirty-five had classic autism, while many others showed autistic traits.

This offers part of the answer to the oft-asked question: Where were all the people with autism before? For a good part of the twentieth century, they were institutionalized—if not kept hidden at home. Some were swept up into "training schools" for the mentally retarded on the assumption that they were feebleminded. Others went to a separate class of institution, the residential mental hospital, to be grouped with those said to be insane. At one time, many of these nineteenth-century institutions legitimately claimed for themselves the aspirational name of "asylum"—a place of refuge and protection. But that founding generosity of spirit withered over many decades under the pressures of overcrowding, limited budgets, and a growing despair that anything much could be done to treat, cure, or educate the clientele. Instead, institutions shifted to a custodial function, merely keeping watch over their charges, keeping them fed, but not necessarily occupied, and not always even clothed.

The year after World War I ended, an institution became five-year-old Archie Casto's whole world.

Archibald Casto was born in Huntington, West Virginia, on February 17, 1913. He was Herman and Clara Louise Casto's fourth child, and also, they could tell immediately, their healthiest, most robust baby. He was also particularly beautiful. A mischief-maker as soon as he could walk, he was in motion all the time, poking into everything, wandering off the moment no grown-up was watching him. As a toddler, he started putting himself into dangerous situations, running toward fires, into the path of trotting horses, out into thunderstorms. His mother's voice had no effect—he'd neither slow down nor come back when she called out to him.

By the age of three, when he still wasn't speaking, it began to seem plausible that Archie might be deaf—a devastating thought to his parents, as it meant a childhood of special schools and limited horizons later on, in terms of the jobs he could get and the families whose daughters would agree to let him court them. It was not a diagnosis Clara wanted to hear, but she was exhausted from trying to keep up with Archie and needed guidance on what to do. Clara set an appointment with the family doctor sometime after Archie's fifth birthday.

When they returned from the appointment a few hours later, school was out, and their daughter Harriet was home. Harriet, who was thirteen years old, had never seen a look on anyone's face like the one on her mother's that afternoon. And she had never heard her mother cry so uncontrollably. Clara was shaking with grief, sobbing. Then Harriet learned why. The doctor had just pronounced Archie insane.

The next few days were difficult in the Casto home. Harriet, not fully understanding what was happening, became frightened when her distraught mother confided in her that "some things are worse than death, and this is one of them." Her parents made a somber, silent trip to the courthouse, and upon their return, Clara told Harriet that Archie would be leaving the family to go live in another part of town. Harriet had seen the place, which had opened some years earlier on the eastern edge of town. Originally known as the Home for Incurables, it was now the Huntington State Hospital. Surrounded by a high wire fence, with iron gates and a guardhouse controlling access, it resembled a prison, but it was officially designated an insane asylum by the state legislature. Commitment to the place required a judge's approval, which explained the trip to the courthouse. The doctor had urged the Castos not to delay. The state agreed to commit Archie, a move that, in some of its practical implications, was like an adoption in reverse. Archie was broken off from the family, taken off his parents' hands, and legally joined to the state. The Castos would follow the doctor's advice—they would move on with their lives without a five-year-old insane boy in the family. The papers were signed, a bag was packed, and then Archie was gone, never to return again to a household that now had to figure out how to forget him.

Harriet was given the new rules of the Casto household where they concerned Archie. She was never to mention him again to anyone beyond the family; she was to act as if she had no brother. Harriet was obedient. She learned to keep the secret.

Once Archie stepped through the hospital gates, he ceased to have a history. There would be no letters home, and he would make no friends to tell stories about his childhood later. No one would ever take his picture. The local school district never even opened a file in his name.

The thin evidence of his continuing presence under the institution's roof appeared only once every ten years, when a federal census taker appeared at the hospital gate, and Archie's name and age were recorded by law. The 1920 census tables listed seven-year-old Archie as the youngest resident in a sex-segregated ward where nearly all the others were men in middle or old age. Now and then, at intervals spaced years apart, the local courts checked in on him, requiring that he be brought in for a personal appearance before a judge. These several minutes per decade were the only time an outside authority checked in on his well-being. One year, he was brought in wearing a woman's coat, as if that were the easiest thing to grab for whoever escorted him that day.

At Huntington, each resident's universe amounted mostly to the same two or three ward rooms: an area for sleeping, another for eating, another perhaps for pacing from corner to corner, behind windows screened with wire mesh. Archie shared these spaces, at all times, with dozens of other people. The doors, of course, were always latched—from the outside. These three rooms would be their universe, forever.

Parents who sent their children to institutions, who were usually following doctors' orders, could only pray that the place chosen was not one of the "snake pits." With sickening regularity, stories of the extreme neglect and outright abuse at many of these institutions broke out into daylight. Yet the outrage and indignation these stories stirred up almost always, with the same regularity, faded away fast, with little or nothing done to improve conditions. It was a scandal when the *New York Times* reported that attendants at the Western

Pennsylvania Hospital for the Insane were "kicking and beating patients until they were unconscious," denying them food, and controlling them by squeezing wet towels around their necks, "pulling at it until the breath is choked out of the victim and he sinks to the floor." The dateline on this particular story was March 30, 1890. It was a scandal again, thirteen years later, when the papers in Los Angeles gave coverage to nurses blowing the whistle on abusive practices at the Patton Institution, a mental hospital where women patients were allegedly disciplined for transgressions as minor as making faces or talking back to the staff by being tied under a heavy canvas sheet for up to three weeks at a time. Some, it was also alleged, were given injections of a compound that induced severe cramps and vomiting.

Another four decades after that, the nation was shocked anew when conscientious objectors, who had been forced to work in mental hospitals in lieu of fighting in World War II, came forward with photographic evidence of the wide range of atrocities they had witnessed inside the institutions. They saw men chained to beds, residents sitting naked in rows in their own excrement, and the use of beatings to keep order or simply to let off steam. They also reported that the wet-towel chokehold was still in use, half a century later. Some of the pictures became the subject of a 1946 photo essay in *LIFE* magazine, with accompanying text by Albert Maisel. Titled "Bedlam," Maisel's essay raged against these "relics of the dark ages . . . concentration camps that masquerade as hospitals." He lifted direct quotes from the conscientious objectors' eyewitness reports that painted scene after horrifying scene. This one took place in New York State:

> These four attendants slapped patients in the face as hard as they could, pummeled them in their ribs with fists, some being knocked to the floor and kicked. One 230-pound bully had the habit of bumping patients on the back of the head with the heel of his hand—and on one occasion had the patient put his hands on a chair, then [struck] his fingers with a heavy passkey.

Maisel took care to point out that not every asylum in America deserved his "concentration camp" label, though he insisted that most were implicated. He also thought that the true bullies on staff were probably few in number, but that cruelty was inherent in the conditions that both residents and staff had to share together. "We jam-pack men, women and sometimes even children into hundred-year-old firetraps in wards so crowded that the floors cannot be seen between the rickety cots, while thousands more sleep on ticks, on blankets or on the bare floors." Maisel reported that the decision to tie up patients or put them in solitary confinement was unwisely left up to badly trained and completely outnumbered staff members, who used last-resort methods too early and too often.

Each time stories like this emerged, it was as if the people on the outside were hearing it for the first time. After the 1946 *LIFE* report, the needle twitched slightly on the meter of public outrage. Congress called hearings, and Maisel testified. Hollywood made a movie called *The Snake Pit,* which was nominated for nine Oscars, about a woman confined to a state mental hospital and the indignities she suffers there. In 1948, *Time* put *The Snake Pit* on its cover. "The large, hidden population of the mentally ill lives amid squalor, dirt and creeping fear," *Time* roared, "behind the walls of the world's indifference."

As always, little changed in the aftermath. The institutions remained, and Archie Casto remained in an institution. It can never be known what sorts of abuse he personally endured, beyond what they did to his teeth. As it happened, however, a portrait of the very place he lived was put together by a newspaper reporter named Charles Armentrout, who wrote for the *Charleston Gazette.* Armentrout snuck into the Huntington State Hospital in 1949, to report on what he saw there simply by walking its "wood-rotting room[s]" and "dimly lighted hallway[s]."

He was shocked by what he experienced. It is very likely that he saw Archie, who, at thirty-six, was by then one of the "lifers." But it was the plight of the children that most disturbed Armentrout—children with nothing to do all day, with no toys, and with little or no clothing, covered in their own filth. Their lack of toilet training appalled Armentrout, and the resulting odor of the place—what he called the "odor of the mentally ill"—seemed to overpower him.

To Armentrout's eyes, the wards looked like a sure firetrap. "Locked up like common criminals," he reported, "the girl[s] mentally deficient, like the boys, must find their play on the wooden, fire-hazardous corridor floor." Elsewhere, he again referred to the "quarters of the youngsters" as "fire-trap structures."

He was prescient. One cold November night, three years after his exposé, Armentrout stood on the grass of the hospital grounds looking up at the flames chewing through the female-only building, regretting, as he listened to the screams, that his story's early warning had changed nothing. In fact, when his 1949 story appeared, six state legislators had banded together vowing to "provide needed relief." But the effort led nowhere, and a spending bill to fireproof the hospital, finally approved in 1952, was dropped just before the fire broke out.

It started just before seven o'clock on the night before Thanksgiving eve, in the basement of a three-story building housing some 275 female patients—four times the population the architects had planned for. The mattresses were an easy feast for the flames. An eighty-nine-year-old woman was swallowed by fire, still tangled in her bedsheets, unable to rise. Those who were up and able to walk, however, could not reach the rickety spiral staircase on the back of the building, the only remaining escape route, because the doors of the ward were locked.

Their faces could be seen pressed against the wire mesh over the top-floor windows. Ladders were quickly raised and reached the windows easily, but then firefighters had to climb back down to get blowtorches to cut through the mesh. Once inside the building, firefighters ran from ward to ward, unlocking the doors, giving nearly three hundred patients a chance to run for it. Not all made it. In addition to Ada Carver, the old woman in the bed, another thirteen lost their lives that night. Five girls, all under the age of sixteen, were suffocated by smoke. One—Lena Wentz—was only eleven.

Yet even this tragic fire did not bring about a reversal in the pattern of short memories and indecent neglect. In 1967, a new generation was stunned by a photo-essay published in *Look* magazine exposing the appalling treatment of children and adults locked away in several institutions for the mentally disabled. Authored by Burton Blatt, an educator; Charles Mangel, a journalist; and Fred Kaplan, a photographer, it was based on a book Blatt and Kaplan had published a year earlier with the unforgettable title *Christmas in Purgatory.*

Over the holidays in 1965, Kaplan had clipped a hidden camera on his belt, and he and Blatt had entered five different institutions. The photos, along with Blatt's accompanying text, reported the same story that "Bedlam" had, twenty years earlier. It was the same "dirt and filth, odors, naked patients groveling in their own feces, children in locked cells, horribly crowded dormitories, and understaffed and wrongly-staffed facilities." Blatt and Kaplan's account provided still more evidence of the nation's unthinking abandonment of the disabled, creating, Blatt wrote, "a hell on earth . . . a special inferno . . . the land of the living dead."

"We now have a deep sorrow, one that will not abate," Blatt wrote, "until the American people are aware of—and do something about—the treatment of the severely mentally retarded in our state institutions." In accordance with the times, Blatt and Kaplan's vocabulary relied much on the word "retarded," but in all other ways they were pleading for a real break with the past. Before long, Blatt would conclude that the only answer was to close down the institutions altogether.

Still, the institutions remained, so that in 1972 they were discovered yet again by a young lawyer-turned-journalist named Geraldo Rivera, who reported his first big story by sneaking onto the grounds of a New York City institution called Willowbrook. Rivera became an overnight star partly for the way he communicated what television never captures. "I can show you what it looked like and what it sounded like," he told his viewers, "but I can never show you how it smelled. It smelled of filth. It smelled of disease. And it smelled of death."

ABUSE, NEGLECT, INDIFFERENCE, DEPRIVATION—these were never consciously designed into institutional life, but they ultimately defined it. During his long life behind the walls, Archie Casto lost the little bit of language he once possessed. He failed to grow and pulled deeper inside himself. His ability to smile began to flicker out, and one day simply disappeared. Now, his sister Harriet noticed, his face fell permanently into what she would think of as his "stony look," an expression of pure hopelessness.

Harriet knew this because she had continued making discreet visits to the institution, encouraged to and sometimes accompanied by their mother. Clara Casto might have believed her son's insanity to be "worse than death"—requiring lifelong secrecy—but she still wanted to maintain contact with him.

Harriet never did see the back wards at Huntington. For visits, patients were always made to look presentable, then brought down to the front reception area—a clean, orderly space where Harriet could sit face-to-face with her brother. Archie was fully mute now, and his stony look didn't offer much encouragement. But she made it a point to speak on the assumption that he understood what she was saying.

When she ran out of things to say, whether news from home or comments on the weather, she would chat instead with some of the attendants nearby, who sometimes had bits of information to share on her little brother's life upstairs. That's how she learned that Archie had picked up several institutional survival tricks, like rolling up his clothes at night to make a pillow out of them, so they would not be stolen, and always eating with one arm shielding his plate of food, for the same reason. These stories, while far from uplifting, at least showed a boy capable of learning and surviving.

The attendants she spoke with remarked that it was rare to see family members dropping by as often as Harriet did. They told her that most relatives simply "dumped" their loved ones in the institution and never came back. Archie's family, they said, was "unusual" that way. It was unclear whether Harriet was being complimented or gently chided. Either way, her presence in the visiting room told the staff something unusual about Archie himself: though institutionalized, he still had family who cared about him.

The perception that nobody cared was the ever-present danger in the lives of all institutionalized patients like Archie. Never was there a constituency so denied the chance to be heard—or even seen—than the occupants of these massive warehouses for people. Geographically, they were out of earshot. Physically or developmentally, many were unable to speak. Politically, they had no chance to vote. In short, those on the inside needed someone on the outside to battle for them, and such outsiders hardly existed. For all her commitment to visiting Archie, it never occurred to Harriet, in the 1930s and 1940s, when she herself was a professional woman working in university administration, to challenge the decision-making authorities. That's not what decent people did, not in that era.

At least Archie had those visits from his sister. And then, suddenly, they stopped. One day, when Harriet dropped by the hospital, she was informed that the state had transferred her brother to Spencer State Hospital, more than 100 miles away. The family had not been informed, probably because it no longer had any say over Archie's fate. He belonged to the state. Conditions at Archie's new home, Spencer State, were described by a therapist who began working there in 1964 as "the worst I've seen anywhere that I have ever worked."

This, then, was where Archie Casto was to vanish, yet one more time—not just from the outside world, but this time, from his sister Harriet's life as well. Though in her forties, Harriet had never learned to drive and had no way to get there. For all intents and purposes, Archie was now lost for good, lost in a system that would never be kind to him, never help him grow, learn in school, or explore—and never understand that he had autism.

15

THE RIGHT TO EDUCATION

TOM GILHOOL WAS NEVER, STRICTLY SPEAKING, AN AUTISM guy. He never did much reading on it, never had relatives who dealt with it. Before he became involved, he probably would not have been able to say with certainty what autism looked like.

Not that it mattered in the long run, because Tom Gilhool was an underdog guy, a champion for the disadvantaged. He was also a smart lawyer. It was this combination that thrust him, in the early 1970s, into a decisive legal battle on the side of an organization known as PARC. It stood for the Pennsylvania Association for Retarded Children. It was these parents' children Gilhool would fight for. The state had failed to provide them with an education, leaving the children whose families could not afford private school to languish at home all day, or to waste their days confined inside the massive state-run institution known as Pennhurst.

This was at a time before the word "retarded" had fully acquired its toxic connotations. This was also at a time when the parents of children with intellectual disabilities—as opposed to parents from the autism community—were the more experienced, battle-scarred trailblazers in the fight to reform how society responded to developmental disability. Their activism had begun decades earlier, with the founding of the National Association for Retarded Children in 1950, of which PARC was a state chapter.

In those years, the parents of children labeled "MR," for mentally retarded, and the parents of children with the lesser-known condition called autism represented two separate camps, and were also to some degree rivals. They both wanted to be first in line for the attention of politicians, and they both wanted to be first in line for donor dollars. The divide between them gave rise to multiple ironies, as the two sets of kids actually showed a large overlap. In the late 1960s, for example, epidemiologists showed that roughly three-quarters of children diagnosed with autism were also intellectually impaired.

Yet certain autism activists, Bernie Rimland among them, seemed to prefer to keep a distance between autism and the question of intellectual disability. Like Leo Kanner in the beginning, Rimland believed that autism always came with relatively normal intellectual functioning. When making this case, Rimland betrayed some biases of his own, contrasting the "dull, vacuous expression" of the truly "feeble-minded" with the "beautiful and well-formed" child with autism, whose facial expressions he described as "strikingly intelligent."

Another irony lay in the fact that the two sets of parents faced nearly identical obstacles. Institutionalization, as the default solution, had failed all of their children. So had the school systems. But in 1969, the parents from the MR side of the divide—the group in Pennsylvania—set out to force change by taking the Commonwealth to court, citing a dereliction of duty to educate *all* children. They did so without the involvement of autism parents, who were still only beginning to organize. But autism parents everywhere would soon owe a great debt to the group from Pennsylvania—and the lawyer they turned to.

TOM GILHOOL WAS not familiar with PARC when, in the winter of 1969, two parents representing the organization dropped by his office to discuss the prospects of bringing a lawsuit against the state of Pennsylvania, which owned and operated the Pennhurst State School. When Gilhool confessed to not even knowing what the letters of PARC stood for, one of his visitors, Dennis Haggerty, said, "Tom, I guess now I'm going to have to teach you about mental retardation."

That's where he was wrong. "Dennis," Gilhool said back to Haggerty, "you don't need to explain it, because my brother is retarded."

It went further than that, actually. Gilhool had been out to Pennhurst many times during his youth. His mother had committed his brother Bobby there in 1953, the year Tom turned fifteen. Bobby was nine then. On visits to his brother, Gilhool had not seen a "snake pit" institution—not quite. He found the staff he encountered generally pleasant, and there were some attendants Bobby was particularly fond of. But it was clear someone was beating Bobby up from time to time. He would show up for visits with swollen ears, like boxers have. Tom was against keeping Bob in an institution at all, but after his father died, his mother, who belonged to a different generation, insisted it was best for him and for the family.

As he explained this to the two men from PARC, Gilhool could see past them, through the single long window of his narrow, corridor-shaped office, down to the neighborhoods of South Philadelphia. The streets of South Philly were where he had spent many years building his activist skills. A Lehigh and Yale man in bow tie and sideburns, he was part of that generation of young people who felt summoned to put some skin in the game by President John F. Kennedy's challenge to "ask what you can do for your country."

Gilhool, when he finished law school in 1963, was already planning to work on behalf of the disadvantaged, because of his brother Bobby. The great cause of the day was civil rights, so Gilhool dove into campaigns like the Philadelphia Tutorial Project, which brought tutors out of Philadelphia's elite universities into poor neighborhoods; worked with Community Legal Services, a provider of legal expertise to the poor; advised a successful Welfare Rights Organization campaign to convince Pennsylvania's governor to increase state assistance to needy families; and helped in the establishment of a network of "self-help centers" that negotiated a truce among Philadelphia's street gangs, ending the most deadly streak of intergang killings in the nation at that time. In the changing role of lawyer as agent of social change, Tom Gilhool, at a young age, could boast plenty of battle scars.

The parents from PARC had sought him out for this very reason. They wanted a "rights" lawyer, and they wanted a "rights" argument. Constitution-based arguments were defeating policies like racial segregation in the schools and ensuring minorities the right to vote. In court, as opposed to legislatures and governors' offices, it seemed that the weak stood a fighting chance.

PARC's parents, for some time, had been demanding reforms at the

Pennhurst School. Recently, the mother of a boy named John Stark Williams had only been informed of his death upon her arrival to visit him, although he had died nearly a year earlier. PARC investigated the school's claim that he had slipped in the shower and discovered that he had actually died of burns. When confronted by a PARC representative, a school administrator responded, "Well, these things happen. We've got twenty-eight hundred people here."

When that story was told at PARC's annual convention in Pittsburgh that year, and slides from the autopsy were shown, the outraged group immediately moved to initiate proceedings against the state of Pennsylvania. Its goal was to force the state to shut Pennhurst down, or to require the state to demonstrate just cause for its continuance as a state facility.

The meeting in Gilhool's office lasted two hours. A few days later, Haggerty picked Gilhool up in his car and drove him out to the state capital, Harrisburg, to meet PARC's full board. "I can do this," Gilhool told them.

GILHOOL WAS AN intellectual tortoise. He spent most of the rest of that year reading widely, talking with experts and activists in the field of intellectual disability, and thinking through the kinds of constitutional arguments that would move him, if he were a judge.

Nine months later, he thought he had it. He presented his clients with a nine-page battle plan whose key words were "the right to education." Gilhool wanted to build an argument around the fact that children kept locked up in the so-called state schools were not really at school at all. He believed this would resonate in court because education was a topic on which federal judges had been well briefed in a long series of cases stemming from the civil rights movement. The denial of full educational services at Pennhurst, and in school districts across the state, Gilhool wanted to argue, amounted to a violation of the Fourteenth Amendment's guarantee of equal protection under the law.

Such an argument would challenge all kinds of conventional wisdom. It would assert, first of all, that people inside institutions had full rights to begin with, and that segregation behind their walls amounted to a denial of those rights. He would also need to challenge assumptions that it was a waste of effort to educate people labeled "ineducable." These seemed enormous barriers to get across. But PARC wanted to try, and so did Gilhool.

The surprise came in just how quickly the barriers fell. The trial commenced on August 12, 1971, eight months after Gilhool first filed with the court. A three-judge panel had set aside two days for argument. A large team of lawyers, representing the state, sat together at a table to the judges' right. Gilhool, in bow tie as always, sat alone at the table opposite. He had seven witnesses to present—all experts on special education and human development. They had all prepared fastidiously, but in the end, some of them did not even get the chance to testify.

Early on the afternoon of the trial's first day, after Gilhool's first four witnesses had testified, an attorney for the state, the assistant attorney general of Pennsylvania, interrupted the proceedings and asked to address the court. "Your Honors, we surrender," the opposing counsel told the judges. Gilhool was stunned. That was it. The trial was over.

The sudden surrender was prompted by a morning of compelling testimony from a variety of educators with impeccable credentials. These educators had worked with retarded children, been in classrooms with them, carried out research on their development, created innovative teaching programs—and they testified that they had always seen the kids learn, grow, and become happier. Each witness portrayed the noneducation of the kids as an unjustifiable and scandalous waste of their potential, and affirmed, from the front lines, that all so-called retarded children were capable of learning. What's more, they came with empirical evidence so persuasive that, in the view of the judges, the state's surrender was "an intelligent response to overwhelming evidence against their position."

GILHOOL HAD WON, on behalf of the parents of PARC. Now he was handed a rare opportunity to sketch in the details of a better future for the mentally disabled of the state of Pennsylvania. He was delegated to write the first draft of a so-called consent decree—the document that, when an agreement is reached between two contesting parties, spells out what that settlement specifies. For two months, he labored over the terms, crafting a set of undertakings by the state and its thirteen school districts that would make a clean break with the past and a swift transition to the future.

Gilhool demanded, first, that every child in Pennsylvania who could qualify for the label "mentally retarded" be searched for and found—whether at home, at Pennhurst, at some other institution, or at school. The deadline for this was set for June of the following year, and part of its purpose was to let parents know their child was now entitled to a free public education. After that, school systems would be required to put together a plan specifying how they would begin offering each of them education and training, "appropriate to his learning capacities." He made clear what this was supposed to mean: programs were tailored to the individual child, and the programs themselves were to be held in settings as "normal" as possible. Specifically, "placement in a regular public school class is preferable to placement in a special public school class, and placement in a special public school class is preferable to placement in any other type of program of education and training."

The terms of the decree, which the state began putting into effect in 1973, were immediately recognized as a landmark advance for disability rights and education. The ripple effects were felt almost immediately as lawyers representing parents rushed to bring like-minded lawsuits across the nation. Most of them borrowed some of their intellectual framework—and, in some cases, exact language—from Gilhool's Pennsylvania suit. By the end of 1973, some thirty federal court decisions had affirmed the principles established in Gilhool's case. Meanwhile, legislatures in statehouses across the nation were starting to update laws to guarantee education for the mentally disabled through the public school system. State officials were making public pronouncements to show they recognized that the right to education was real, and that adjustments to the way things had been done for decades were required.

There was just one catch, in all this, for autism families: everything good that was happening all of a sudden, and in so many places, was driven by a sense of outrage on behalf of one distinct group of kids—those with so-called mental retardation. To be sure, it had been these children's parents who pushed the legal action, and it had been these children's plight, and potential, that had received unflaggingly sympathetic media coverage.

But unheard in the outcry was any mention of the terms *autism* or *autistic.* These terms were as unfamiliar to the larger public as kids with the condition were invisible. Overlooked in the outrage, they were also missing from the agenda of motivated legislatures.

It was clear what autism parents needed to do, to become part of this moment, and this important conversation. They had to change the subject, maybe a little, maybe a lot, to make their kids a part of it.

16

GETTING ON THE BUS

FOR EXACTLY SEVEN DAYS IN 1974, THE MOST VISIBLE PERson with autism in the world was a handsome, brown-haired boy named Shawn Lapin. Beginning on April 8, every newsstand in America carried the issue of *Newsweek* whose cover story, "The Troubled Child," sounded the alarm about a major outbreak of "emotional disorders" in American children. The article profiled a small number of children struggling with various kinds of mental health challenges—from schizophrenia to depression to various "neurotic symptoms." But the one the editors chose to focus on, with four photos and a sidebar, was the six-year-old with autism, Shawn Lapin. That had a lot to do with who his parents were.

Connie and Harvey Lapin had made it their mission to push for maximum attention for their son, and for access to the top people anywhere in a position to help him. Movers and shakers—they all heard from the Lapins, sooner or later—whether these were lawyers like Tom Gilhool, who had just won the PARC case; leading researchers like Ivar Lovaas, who was then experimenting with a promising therapy at UCLA; officeholders like Gov. Ronald Reagan, who had something to say about how government funds were spent; or even just other influential parents like Bernard Rimland and Ruth Sullivan. The Lapins worked at making direct connections to all of them. Connie and Harvey embodied the new paradigm for the autism parent—out to create an opening in the world for their own kid, which they took to mean changing the world itself.

Harvey and Connie Lapin were incessant doers—one of the many ways in which they were a matched set. Both were fit and good-looking: Connie, light, spry, and brunette—model-like; Harvey, tall and broad, a big smiler with a big 1970s handlebar mustache, a bear-hug-type guy rather than a handshaker, and a ceaseless narrator of whatever was on his mind. Holding a conversation with Harvey was like a riding a Ping-Pong ball through a championship match. The thoughts came fast and urgently, and never in one direction for very long. Connie, however, had a gift for translating Harvey's word stream, or reining it in. In their early thirties, they were passionate about each other, entertaining storytellers, and superb at making friends.

In the mid-1960s, Harvey had a thriving dental practice in the San Fernando Valley, on the north side of Los Angeles. Famous Hollywood types were coming in to get their teeth seen. Dr. Lapin was good, and a total charmer, much as their life in the Valley seemed charmed.

Their first son, Brad, was born in 1964. Shawn was born in 1968. In 1970, he was diagnosed with autism.

Connie and Harvey were among those autism parents who experienced the heart-piercing sense of having seen their child regress. That is, Shawn had appeared to both his parents to be developing as he was supposed to, and then, suddenly, his behavior began to change.

With Shawn, it seemed to happen in the space of a day or so, when he was around thirteen months old. He had walked early and learned to use three or four words. He did have trouble holding things before that—a bottle put in his hands would hit the floor within seconds—but other than that, he had every competency an early toddler was expected to possess.

Then, before Connie's eyes, he suddenly tuned out. The words vanished, he pushed her away when she or anyone else reached for him, and he started crying, practically full-time. The sleeping problems started then too. The four hours a night he'd sleep were interspersed with constant crying. Whenever dawn came, more often than not, he would still be at it.

His parents rushed him from doctor to doctor, who ran through the usual list of possible explanations—ear troubles, childhood psychosis, brain damage, countless others. Tests were done; theories proved false;

new ones conceived; more tests done. Throughout, Shawn kept crying through the night. He was a screamer and a runner, almost impossible to control. Every small task in his day was a pitched battle. Dressing him—because he hated to be touched. Giving him lunch—because he would fly into a rage if the items on his plate were touching. He destroyed the furniture. And escaped through the windows. And defecated on the kitchen floor. Months went by, then more than a year. And then, finally, Connie and Harvey heard the word "autism."

It was just by chance that, half an hour from their own front door, a group of young psychologists, all working at the University of California at Los Angeles, had sometime earlier become fascinated with children who had autism. Based at UCLA's Neuropsychiatric Institute, they were among the first anywhere to persist in actual research on methods for treating autism, without reference to any notion that bad mothering was involved. Getting Shawn in for a consult took some doing, but once he was seen, the diagnosis took no time at all. Shawn's autistic symptoms came straight out of Leo Kanner's original write-up on his first eleven cases. The term *classic autism* described cases like him.

The UCLA people had read Rimland, they knew the kids, and they had long ago dismissed the refrigerator-mother idea, so Connie never had to endure any mother blaming. The battle she faced would be on a different front, and it would define a new era for autism advocacy.

She wanted Shawn to go to school.

But no school wanted him, or any child with autism.

As in nearly every other state at the time, the law in California granted public school authorities the unchallenged power to refuse education to children they deemed "ineducable." Even in special-education classes—which often lumped together, in one classroom, the intellectually disabled with the epileptic, the speech-impaired, and so on—there was a cutoff for kids who seemed too disabled, physically or mentally. Schools didn't like doing it, but it was the reality: they could and did say, "Go away."

The Lapins collided with this reality only after they started Shawn, then three years old, in a Los Angeles district public school early intervention special-education class. After three days, when Connie arrived to take Shawn home, she was informed that his teachers had consulted with their superiors, and that "it was decided" that he should not return the next day, or ever. He had been running around disruptively, biting other children, and refusing to do anything he was asked.

Connie started talking fast, begging the school head to give Shawn another chance. She was refused on the spot. A boy with autism, she was told, who was so wildly out of control, could not be let loose among so many vulnerable children. It was dangerous and not conducive to learning.

Chastened, hurt, Connie took Shawn home, and began making calls, careful not to mention the word "autism" as she scrounged for alternatives. She found another public school, farther away, with a program similar to the first. Not that she believed there was much actual education happening at either place. *Conducive to learning.* That was a bit of a joke, she thought. From what she'd seen of the first classroom, it resembled group babysitting more than schooling. Still, something was better than nothing. At this second school, however, Shawn was asked to leave after only one day.

At a third school, the same thing happened. After that, word was out about Shawn in the public school system, and about his mother. Connie was asked, and not very politely, to stop wasting everyone's time.

This was a low point for Connie. She had dodged and weaved, begged and bent the truth, but she had failed to find a publicly funded preschool program willing to take her son. After that, she and Harvey began a search for alternatives, stumbling upon a small private nursery-school program for children labeled "mentally retarded," and a research program seeking children with autism to experiment with the use of behavior-modification techniques using rewards and punishments.

For a time, they had Shawn enrolled in both programs, but neither did him any good. The nursery program was expensive, and in no way addressed his autism. As for the experimental program, Connie was horrified by the punishments the researchers used to change behavior.

Shawn was slapped and had diluted mustard squirted into his face. Connie felt he was coming home every day traumatized rather than educated.

By this point, Connie and Harvey felt close to collapse. Essentially, they had a four-year-old boy with nowhere to go, and a home life fully controlled by a condition that could not be controlled itself.

AND SO, IN 1972, she and Harvey took the first steps toward placing Shawn in an institution. They had two reasons for doing so. The first was their feeling that Shawn's behaviors added up to an emergency beyond their expertise as parents. They admitted to themselves that if his problems had been purely medical—if he had been unable to breathe, or to stop bleeding, or to stop vomiting—they would not have hesitated to place him in professional hands.

The other reason was the need for some rescue from the strain, which was nonstop. Shawn was a struggle through every night, into every morning, and then all over again. This was taxing the whole family, which by now included another baby boy. Both Harvey and Connie feared what would happen when they reached their respective breaking points, when the sleep deprivation, confusion, and psychic pain of not knowing how to help their struggling middle child finally drained off their last reserves of optimism and energy.

Connie and Harvey were also, in some way, grieving over the upending of their own lives, which had changed so dramatically and unexpectedly. Being a parent is hard enough when a child does not have a serious disability. But when he does, and it is so acute that grandparents or babysitters cannot step in to provide respite, the unrelenting pressure cannot help but take its toll. Indeed, there had been some truth all along in the argument doctors made to parents through the decades when they prescribed institutionalization. It was no solution for the child, but it did address, in one stroke, a large part of the parents' problem, which was real and acute. For some families, twenty-four hours a day of handling severe autism, unrelieved, is a challenge beyond what love alone can handle.

Early one morning, the entire Lapin family drove out of the Valley, one hour west out to the Camarillo State Hospital, to inquire about a space for Shawn in the children's ward. Connie felt numb as they turned their car onto the grounds, following the same driveway that Alec Gibson had taken with his son Dougie a few years earlier. She had never seen herself as a mother who would have her son committed. Harvey, she knew, felt the same way. Shawn, in the backseat, didn't understand where they were, but eight-year-old Brad, sitting beside him, was scared. He had figured out that in some way, this trip was about his little brother leaving home.

But Harvey and Connie were pleasantly surprised when they stepped out of their car. They had not been prepared for how beautiful Camarillo's campus was, or for the warmth of the greeting extended them by Norbert Rieger, chief of the children's psychiatric section. Rieger personally showed them around, with a tour and talk that lasted the entire morning. He showed them cheerily decorated classrooms and residential cottages that looked clean and orderly. For Harvey, it was both reassuring and disorienting at the same time, not to see the "snake pit" asylum he had imagined. Making his way down the intersecting corridors, climbing the connecting stairwells, Harvey felt not so much regret or sorrow as just plain confusion—as if he were walking through a maze. Had the place been horrible, it would have simplified things: he would have walked away.

Rieger showed them the cottage Shawn would live in. It was reserved for children with autism. Researchers from nearby UCLA and elsewhere were drawn to Camarillo because of its population of children who could be used as study subjects. As a result, Camarillo had picked up a reputation for running the best autism program of any state hospital in the nation, and a good part of the academic literature published on autism in the late 1960s and early 1970s mentioned Camarillo as a primary research site. The Lapins understood that was not necessarily saying much, as there was not much competition in this area. Still, Rieger was perhaps the most empathetic authority figure the two of them had yet encountered, and he was showing them genuine concern and respect. Maybe this *was* the right place for Shawn.

Shawn acted up throughout the visit. He screamed, tried to run away, and grabbed at whatever fell within his field of vision. Connie, for once, didn't feel pressured to make him behave. Part of the purpose of this visit was to let Rieger take his measure of Shawn's disability.

Harvey and Connie didn't realize it at the time, but Rieger had come to the conclusion that institutionalization set children up for failure. "All the children who come to us at a state hospital have one thing in common—the difficulty in relating with other people," he told a reporter in 1971. "They do not learn to do this in state hospitals." Instead, many children would enter Camarillo and never go home again. Once the patients "aged out" of the children's program, like the one he ran, they often simply transferred to the adult wards, where stories of abuse and neglect continued to surface. Rieger saw very little rationale for placing a boy like Shawn at an institution like Camarillo.

At the end of the Lapins' tour, back in Rieger's office, he took the lead in the conversation.

"You've looked around," he said. "You've seen the whole setup."

They nodded and waited. Rieger took another moment, looking from one parent to the other.

"Harvey, Connie," he finally said quietly, "go home and figure it out. This is the *last* place you want your son," he said. "Take him home."

The two parents looked at each other, shocked and confused. Rieger had just spent half a day observing Shawn. He had to have seen how severe his symptoms were.

In fact, Rieger had been paying attention, and not just to Shawn. He had also watched Connie and Harvey and how they handled him. He had listened to Connie's war stories about her dealings with the school district and taken measure of Harvey's unusually winning personality. Maybe because of some gut instinct, and based on what he had just seen and heard, he repeated the phrase that still puzzled the two of them.

"You'll figure it out," he said.

DRIVING AWAY FROM Camarillo, Harvey felt an overwhelming sense of relief. The option neither of them truly wanted to see through—sending Shawn away—had just been taken off the table. At the same time, Harvey felt Rieger had handed him a mission: to find a better solution for Shawn, or to create one if none could be found. Connie had heard it the same way.

That day changed both parents' perspective permanently. From then on, they refused to feel helpless in the face of Shawn's autism. Instead, they would emerge, within two or three years, as two of the most adamant and persistent autism parent activists of their generation. They worked, first, for the good of Shawn, but always with the additional purpose of improving the odds for all people with autism. It sounds like altruism, but there was a clear, pragmatic logic to their approach: whatever project or program they launched or contributed to—if they made it last for everybody, that meant it would last for Shawn.

Harvey soon approached the Los Angeles chapter of the National Society for Autistic Children (NSAC), told them he was interested in volunteering, and within a year, he was the LA chapter president. Two years later, he became the chief of publicity for the national organization. Three years after that, he was elected national president—the position once held by Ruth Sullivan.

Harvey would be instrumental in moving the organization's national office from Albany, New York, to Washington, DC, with office space rented on Massachusetts Avenue a short cab ride from the halls of Congress. Harvey believed it critical to have access to power, and the right address for that was one close to where political power actually lived. He was also a believer in star power, and as he lacked inhibition about asking for favors, he pressed even his dental patients who might know somebody to help him get in touch with Hollywood's big names. Once introduced to the famous, he wouldn't let go until he'd wrangled a commitment to help the cause.

During his time as publicity chairman for NSAC, he managed to put together the first autism walks and telethons in the mid-1970s, with participation from film stars like Paul Newman and Joanne Woodward, singers like Johnny Cash and Frankie Avalon, and television actors like Joe Campanella. One day in 1973, Harvey showed up at a Northridge, California, post office with eight hundred large envelopes addressed to TV and radio stations and newspapers across the United Sates. Each contained a press release about autism and an upcoming national conference, a recorded announcement by legendary character actor Lloyd Nolan, and a poster featuring a photograph of that year's honorary national NSAC chairperson, Jean Peters—the actress and former wife of billionaire Howard Hughes. Peters was shown sitting with a child on her lap—a young boy in sneakers and a turtleneck sweater. The boy was Shawn Lapin.

Once again, Shawn's visibility was calculated. For so long, the reality of autism had been kept out of sight by parents' shame, with institutionalization as the response of choice. Now leading activists were seeing how counterproductive that reflex was. In 1972, NSAC's president at the time, Clarence Griffith, implored parents, "Let your child be photographed." Activist Clara Park, who wrote about her daughter in *The Siege,* made a similar appeal in a letter to parents. "The public can't care about our children unless they know they're there," she wrote. "Hiding their faces is not the way to help." During the photo shoot with Jean Peters, Shawn urinated while sitting on her lap. The Lapins, while embarrassed, were also amused, as well as impressed with how unfazed and forgiving the actress was. There was no evidence of the mishap in the final photo. Shawn, sitting on the lap of a smiling Peters, looked handsome and appealing. And that was the point.

For Harvey and Connie, committing to work for Shawn's future helped to peel away the layers of sorrow they had felt on his behalf, letting them appreciate more of the odd and unexpected moments that come with parenthood in an autism family. They could laugh more easily, roll their eyes at Shawn's foibles, and sometimes actually enjoy them. Harvey began building up a repertoire of "unbelievable true tales" of adventures with Shawn, which he could launch into at a moment's notice.

"Now, this is a good one," he'd say, and a grin would dance into his eyes. "Twice," he would announce, holding up two fingers, "two years running," the IRS had audited his tax returns. Both times the agency had come to him with challenges about the amounts of medical deductions he was claiming, which must have looked excessive. "Sure, I take lots for medical," he would protest. *"I have a kid with autism."* Both years, after sitting down with an auditor sent from the local IRS office, and painstakingly presenting him with all the supporting paperwork—which took hours—Harvey passed his audits and was granted the deductions.

Then he got another audit notice: *"Third year in a row!"* His eyebrows would lift with disbelief, then the grin would resurface.

On the day of the audit, Harvey "happened" to bring Shawn along with him to the meeting. "I hope you don't mind," he said to the IRS agent, who was already opening his briefcase on the table, pulling out forms and documents from the hefty stack of papers inside it.

"He'll just sit over on the side here and be quiet, won't you, Shawn?" At that moment, Shawn was, in fact, quiet, as Harvey led him to a seat at the far end of the table, where, remarkably, he cooperated and sat down. The IRS man nodded, smiled, and turned back to his briefcase.

Harvey made to pull out a chair for himself so they could get started, but just as he was lowering himself into the seat, he stopped, stood upright again, and slapped himself on the forehead.

"Oh, man," he said, "I forgot some papers we're gonna need downstairs in the car. Would you mind keeping an eye on Shawn for a minute?"

"Sure," the IRS man replied, with a quick glance down the table at Shawn, who was still sitting quietly, looking lost in his thoughts. "No problem. Happy to do it."

"Great, appreciate it," Harvey said. "I'll be right back." With that, Harvey stepped out, closed the door gently behind him and leaned against the wall. He tilted one ear toward the room he had just left, lit up a cigarette, and listened.

For the first few seconds, he heard only the sounds of the street traffic outside and the shuffling of papers from the other side of the door.

Then, a voice.

"Now, just what are you doing there?" The tone was friendly, but a little forced, and mildly disapproving.

"No, little boy, those are mine. . . ."

Harvey, in the hallway, blew out a plume of smoke, watching it fold and float in front of his eyes.

"I think I just said those are mine. . . ."

By Harvey's estimate, less than a minute had gone by.

"Young man, didn't you hear me?"

Harvey was enjoying this smoke. He wasn't going to rush it.

"Stop it! Where's your father?! Stop!"

The next sounds were, clearly, that of paper being thrown around and furniture hitting the floor.

"Give me that! Give me that!"

All right, enough, Harvey decided, and put out his cigarette.

"Oh my goodness! What's *happened* in here?" Harvey had flung open the door to the office to discover the IRS man holding Shawn by the wrist, trying to loosen his grip on a clutch of government forms. Papers were scattered across the table and on the floor, and two chairs were knocked over on their backs. And then there was a new sound: Shawn had started screeching.

"Suffice it to say," Harvey would always wrap up, "the guy was suddenly in a huge hurry to get the hell out of there." The point had been made. Harvey did indeed have a son whose condition justified all those medical bills. This third audit took less than an hour. It was also the final audit Harvey would face over Shawn's medical bills.

Harvey's stories, thoroughly amusing to Harvey himself, were also something he used to entertain, charm, and lure support to their cause. The IRS tale was a perfect vehicle for explaining the depth of Shawn's disability and the challenges his family faced because of it, but in a way that invited the listener to laugh, like an insider, or an ally. And finding and nurturing allies was a key part of the strategy. He and Connie were always working on the next connection to be made, the next string to pull, keeping an eye out for anyone who could make a difference for Shawn—and, by extension, every kid with autism.

A good many of the people who were making a mark on autism activism and understanding in the 1970s—Bernie Rimland, UCLA psychiatrist Edward Ritvo, Anne Donnellan of the University of Wisconsin, documentary filmmaker Mike Gavin, disability rights activist Dr. Bill Bronsten, and many others—could attest to long, wine-filled evenings over good food and spirited storytelling at the Lapins' dining room table in Northridge, because they had become friends. And outside of that intimate circle, it was still true that anyone else who "mattered," whether in science, education, law, and disability activism in general, could also count on hearing from Connie and Harvey eventually. They got to know everyone, and everyone got to know them.

Naturally, therefore, they soon established a relationship with Tom Gilhool, who became such a good friend that, once, when Gilhool landed in Los Angeles with his two children for a California vacation, only to find his hotel had botched his booking, the three of them ended up staying with the Lapins instead. Connie and Harvey, for their part, looked to their lawyer friend to counsel them through the battle they now considered unavoidable.

It was a battle they shared with other autism parents, and an unexpected result of the growing deinstitutionalization campaign. This was the dilemma they faced: while the assault on institutions was slowly forcing school districts to concede a broader obligation to educate children with disabilities, no school district regarded this obligation as encompassing every single child. Districts could, and did, continue to exclude children considered too challenging for their programs. Children with autism, in other words, though less likely to be sent to institutions, still had no right to go to school.

Shawn Lapin turned four in 1972, and though he had begun attending a pilot autism program at the county's expense, its mandate would expire in less than three years, when he would turn seven. Unless the Lapins could manage to squeeze open the door for autism in California, Shawn would be shut out of school once more.

And so, with Gilhool offering legal expertise, the Lapins sued, in parallel with autism parents elsewhere, who stood up to litigate and lobby in courtrooms and statehouses across the United States. They were all demanding the same thing: mandates for education that would explicitly spell out the word "autism." The lawsuit the Lapins filed to get their son into public school was titled, naturally, *Shawn Lapin v. State of California*.

WHILE THE LAPINS prepared their case for the courts, encouraging things were starting to happen in the chambers of another branch of government—the state legislatures. The lobbying efforts of NSAC and its local chapters around the country were starting to pay off. Around the country, lawmakers had begun to pay more attention to the autism story, and laws supporting education for kids with autism were getting passed. The NSAC June 1974 newsletter read like a celebration of parent power. Under Maryland: "The Maryland state chapters . . . were able to effect the passage and signing into law of legislation which provides for comprehensive education services." Under Oklahoma: "The Oklahoma chapter's time spent in . . . negotiation with the Tulsa Public Schools was fulfilled by establishment of the first public school class for autistic children in Oklahoma on August 27, 1973." And on it went: four new "autistic programs" in Toledo schools, seven new classes for "autistic and autistic-like" children in Northern Virginia schools, two new classes for autistic children in Lubbock, Texas, schools, and so on.

In the summer of 1974, it began to appear that California might be getting its turn next. That year, lawmakers in Sacramento encountered a campaign propelled by a group of autism mothers who were famously relentless in their efforts in pushing to get an autism education bill through both houses. Once, on the night of a crucial procedural vote, when their side looked like it might lose, they fanned out into the streets surrounding the statehouse and pulled lawmakers out of bars to get them back into the chamber before the roll was called.

Their leader was a woman named Kimberly Gund. Like the other mothers, she was a constant presence that year in lawmakers' offices but was also actively going into their constituencies, driving all over the state and giving talks at any women's club luncheon, church group, or Rotary Club meeting that would have her. She traveled with a slide projector and audio equipment, for a presentation on autism that featured her own daughter, Sherry—and a recorded narration by the stadium announcer for the San Francisco 49ers football team, who was a friend of a friend. It certainly got people's attention, as did Gund and the other mothers. By late summer of 1974, their bill had passed both houses of the California legislature.

It only needed the governor's signature. From the day it landed on his desk, a countdown started. The governor had twelve days to act—to veto the bill, or to sign it, or to do nothing, in which case it became law automatically. Several days went by and the governor had not indicated his intention. To Gund, and the whole autism community, this grew worrying. In 1974, Ronald Reagan was just completing his second and final term as governor. He had run for office determined to put the brakes on state spending, and he had made it clear that one of the sectors he suspected of budgetary extravagance was education. This did not bode well for an autism education bill that would cost the state $3,000 more *each* year for *each* child admitted to school with autism.

Gund, a Republican herself, had been selling the bill as a long-term money saver, explaining that a child who could achieve greater independence through education when young would require less state support over the course of his or her life. But she had spent so many months focused on the legislature that she had not forged any sort of relationship with the governor. And now, she had no strings left to pull. If Reagan was thinking of vetoing, the autism community needed to find a way to get him to sign instead.

Then Harvey Lapin found a string to pull.

Down in Los Angeles, the Lapins had not been nearly as involved with the education bill as Gund in Sacramento. But like her, they were fretting about the governor's intentions. Harvey, a lifelong Democrat, and no fan of Reagan's, feared the worst—a last-minute veto by an outgoing governor who was moving on to bigger things. Each day of inaction on the bill made that outcome seem more likely.

And so, Harvey called up one of his celebrity friends and asked for a favor.

Lloyd Nolan was one of the most successful character actors in Hollywood history. An Emmy winner, he was an onscreen fixture in scores of films, where he took on the role of gangster, soldier, cop, or doctor. In one ten-year period, he appeared in fifty-five movies. He was also a good friend of Reagan's, ever since they worked on films together for the War Department during World War II. Nolan, like Reagan, also leaned to the right politically. During Reagan's first run for president, Nolan made fund-raising appearances with the candidate.

Most important in this instance was that Nolan had a son, Jay, about whom he had said little to nothing publicly through most of his career. Jay had been institutionalized with a diagnosis of autism in 1956, when he was thirteen. He saw his family only occasionally for the next thirteen years, when they made visits to the privately run facility, which was located in Philadelphia. In 1969, Jay died at the age of twenty-six. He had choked while eating and could not be revived. His death was again something that Nolan did not comment upon in public at the time.

Four years later, however, in 1973, the bereaved underwent an apparent change of heart, when he told his son's story to Ursula Vils of the *Los Angeles Times*. He also testified before Congress to argue for recognizing autism as a developmental disability for the purposes of legislation. Later that year, he narrated a televised documentary on autism called *A Minority of One,* and became involved with the National Society for Autistic Children. All this happened because Harvey talked him into it. After an uncle of Connie's heard Nolan mention his son during a talk at his local school, Harvey asked the uncle to get Nolan's number. After that, the die was cast. Harvey and Connie made the movie star a good friend, and an autism activist.

In September 1974, therefore, with the education bill still unsigned, Harvey and Connie invited themselves to drop by Nolan's house, to beg him to ask his friend the governor to sign the bill into law. What happened that day became a classic in the repertoire of Harvey Lapin autism adventure stories.

After some small talk, Harvey walked Nolan over to the telephone on the bar and gestured for the famous man to pick it up. Nolan nodded. He picked up the receiver, dialed a number, and after a few moments, as Harvey and Connie looked on, asked someone on the other end to "speak to the governor, please."

"Lloyd Nolan," he said, after a moment.

A minute more passed, and then Nolan said, "Hello Ron."

Pleasantries were exchanged, then Nolan got right to it: "I know you knew that I had a son with autism, who died."

Harvey and Connie could not hear what Reagan was saying, but whatever it was, Nolan was listening for a while.

Finally, Nolan spoke again.

"I've never asked anyone for anything," he told his old friend. "But you have an education bill on your desk. Education for kids who have what my son had."

A pause.

"I would really appreciate it if you signed it."

As Harvey liked to say afterward, "And that was it. He asked. He hung up. We waited."

On September 30, 1974, the last day he could act, Reagan signed the bill into law. A photograph taken that day shows Reagan seated at his desk. Over his shoulder, beside some legislators, stands his good friend Lloyd Nolan. Bernard Rimland was there too, along with Kimberly Gund. Harvey was in his dentistry office that day, seeing patients. Connie was home, as usual, looking after their three boys.

Soon after the bill signing, the Lapins dropped their lawsuit. The new law Reagan had just signed off on, which had been pushed through by parents, meant that Shawn and other kids like him in California would finally be going to public school.

One late September afternoon in 1975, at the end of Shawn's first full day in public school under the new law, Connie strolled out to the end of the driveway to meet the school bus. But the child who clambered down the bus stairs, holding the hand of an adult aide, was a boy Connie had never seen before.

"This isn't my son," Connie said to the aide, scanning the bus windows for Shawn's face.

"Yes, this is Shawn," said the aide, smiling down at the boy, offering his hand out for Connie to take.

"No, this isn't Shawn," said Connie, looking hard at the aide.

"Yes, it is," hollered a voice from inside the bus. It was the driver. He was peering at the clipboard in his hand.

"Seriously," Connie hollered back, "I know my own child. This is *not* my son!"

"Seriously?" the aide asked.

"Yes, seriously!"

It was quickly established that at one of the preceding stops, Shawn had been handed off to some other family—who, inexplicably, had taken him in—while the boy who lived at that house had been delivered to Connie.

As the bus sped back to the earlier stop, Connie called Harvey, and told him what was going on.

"The driver kept insisting this kid off the bus was Shawn," she told Harvey on the phone, starting to laugh. "So I finally said to both of them: 'Okay, you know what? Fine. I'll take this kid—but somewhere else out there, there's a family that's in for a really bad night.'"

Harvey laughed.

"Okay," he said. "But I just need to know—this new kid—he could talk, right?"

"Yup, this one talked, and he was pretty cute too," Connie said.

"Great," Harvey said. "Let's keep *him*."

The next day, things went more smoothly. The following morning, Shawn went off to public school for the second day. The boy who got four photos in *Newsweek* would not be "sent away." Because the world had changed—to make room for him in it—just in time.

17

SEEING THE OCEAN FOR THE FIRST TIME

Archie Casto was sixty years old when Shawn Lapin started public school. At that point, Archie was still in residence at Spencer State Hospital, in Roane County, West Virginia. He would spend another fourteen years there. Then, finally, one day in 1988, he got out.

The population of America's institutions began to plunge in the 1970s, but not because older residents were getting out in large numbers. Rather, it was the relative cessation in the flow of children and younger people entering in the first place. In 1965, people under twenty-one made up 48.9 percent of the nation's institutionalized population, which was the peak for that age group. By 1977, that number had dropped to 35.8 percent, and in 1987, it was down to 12.7 percent.

In great measure, this trend resulted from the laws that gave kids somewhere else to go all day, namely school. The 1975 federal Education for All Handicapped Children Act, which was later renamed the Individuals with Disabilities Education Act (IDEA), delivered a new mandate to any public school that accepted federal funds. If they wanted to keep getting that money, they would have to provide equal access to education to any child with physical or mental disabilities. There was a list of which disabilities qualified. After 1990, autism was on it.

In 1972, Tom Gilhool had accepted a three-year position teaching law school at the University of Southern California. While there, he began work on another landmark lawsuit, *Halderman v. Pennhurst State School.* This time, he made the institution's record of abuse and neglect the core issue. The case resulted in the state of Pennsylvania agreeing in 1977 to offer services to the mentally disabled in community settings, near where they lived, rather than in some large compound out in the country. It was the beginning of the end for Pennhurst. The institution saw its population implode, as admissions of children and teenagers came to a virtual halt.

For older residents, however, including all the "lifers" like Archie Casto, deinstitutionalization would crawl forward in fits and starts, unevenly, and against some resistance, across the country. Part of the problem was the lack of better alternative arrangements for adults. "Better" was now being redefined, mostly, to mean small "group homes" inside real neighborhoods, where the residents were "clients." In these settings, ideally, they could live much more "normal" lives. Size was critical to the vision. Group homes needed to be scaled to human proportions.

Nationally, thousands upon thousands of these establishments would be needed, but few existed in the 1970s. This lack of somewhere else for their residents to go, which took roughly a quarter of a century to resolve, was a key reason that the big institutions, though mortally wounded, took so long to disappear. A good many residents died of old age waiting to leave; others only grew older, logging more years in a system whose end was now in sight.

Ruth Sullivan, who had helped start NSAC when she lived in upstate New York, had moved in 1969 to Huntington, West Virginia, where her husband had joined the faculty of Marshall University. In late 1979, she began a full-time autism information and referral service from her home, serving families around the country by phone, by mail, and now by fax machine. More and more, she was hearing from parents whose children were reaching their adult years—like her son Joe, who was in his twenties now, still living under the same roof as his mother and father. Like Ruth, the parents of these rising adults had recently been looking beyond the school issue, to the day when their children, too old for school, might be living at some different address.

Ruth decided to build a solution that would protect her own son. In her fifties, at the same time that she began pursuing a doctorate degree in psychology, speech, and special education, she set out to create the first group homes for adults with autism in the state of West Virginia. Between driving several times a week to take courses at Ohio University, she founded a new organization—the Autism Services Center—to handle the purchase of properties and offer support to adults, with herself as executive director. The organization put its first home into operation in 1979. Some years later, Joe moved into one of the ASC residences.

One day in 1988, Ruth was contacted by a local woman with an unusual request. The woman, who was in her late eighties, explained that she had recently been looking through a popular magazine and had come across an article written by Ruth, which talked about autism. She said Ruth's description of autistic traits reminded her of her brother. Though her brother had never been given an autism diagnosis, the woman had begun to think it might fit. She asked whether Ruth would be willing to meet her brother, to confirm her hunch. But Ruth would have to drive over to Roane County to pay a visit to Spencer State Hospital, where the man had been living since the early 1950s.

Harriet Casto had finally, well into middle age, reconnected with her little brother Archie—by learning to drive. She did not like being behind the wheel, but she had forced herself to get a license so that she could get to his faraway institution. It wasn't until she was in her fifties that she finally rebelled against the shame and embarrassment about Archie that she had nursed for so many years, and now regretted. She wanted to make up for those years by trying to build a new relationship with her aging brother.

Still, once she figured out the route and started visiting the state hospital regularly, it wasn't easy. Harriet found it painful at times to see him, doomed to the confines of Spencer State. And Archie, who did not speak, did not make it any easier. Harriet wanted to believe that her visits mattered to him, but at the end of each, when she bent down to hug her brother goodbye, and brought her cheek close to his, he remained frozen, that old hard look in his eyes, seemingly unmoved by his big sister's affection.

But Harriet persisted, visiting month after month, and year after year. And, ever so slowly, Archie began to pay attention when his sister was there. One day, a ward nurse told Harriet that whenever their visits ended and Harriet left the building, Archie would run to the window and watch her climb into her car, staring after it as it drove away. When Harriet heard that, she cried.

On subsequent visits, Harriet began to believe that, wordless or not, Archie had started to understand that the two of them belonged to each other. She was given permission to take him out for car rides around the nearby countryside. Later, the rides grew longer, so that she could bring him home to her house for dinner, and then back again to Spencer before lights-out. In the course of these later visits, she had already begun to question the long-standing assessment of Archie's supposed rock-bottom intelligence.

For example, whenever they set out on their road trips, he always picked out her blue car instantly from the fifty or so that might be parked in the institution's lot. Their first few times out, she had needed to walk him through the steps of putting on a seat belt, but after that, he did it automatically. One time, when the two of them arrived at her house, she asked him to help unload some tomato plants she'd picked up that day, and to leave them in the garage while she stepped into the main house to take care of something else. When it suddenly occurred to her that he probably had no idea what the word "garage" meant, she rushed outside. But she saw that he had carried all the plants in from the car and lined them up in even rows on the cement floor. On yet another occasion, she saw Archie, unprompted, wander into her front yard, pick up some odd pieces of litter that had strayed across it, and carry them out to the trash. Obviously, there was more of a mind behind Archie's stolid silence than he had ever been given credit for.

He continued, when she went to hug him, to freeze. He still didn't like to be touched. And yet, as brother and sister, they were concocting their own unique version of friendship. For a flickering instant, when he spotted her at the start of each of their visits, Harriet could see the dead look on his face lift away—replaced, momentarily, by the briefest smile. Gone again in a blink, it was never much, but for Harriet it was enough.

The day she and Ruth Sullivan drove out together to Spencer State, it took almost no time for Ruth to see that Harriet was right. Archie's autism was indisputable. Ruth was sure of it, and her opinion mattered. Her stature now, since she had completed her PhD and become *Dr.* Sullivan, was such that her verdict on Archie's diagnosis faced no challenge from the authorities at Spencer State.

But it was a different reaction when she and Harriet set about trying to get Archie transferred out of Spencer and into one of the group homes Ruth's organization was just then getting ready to open. Spencer's superintendent put up a fight, insisting that, precisely because Archie had spent his entire life within the bosom of the state hospital system, he would be lost anywhere else. It would be overwhelming for Archie, the superintendent argued. It would kill him.

As it turned out, it didn't. At the age of seventy-four, thanks to the persistence of his sister and the reputation of Ruth Sullivan, Archie was granted leave to move to a house in Huntington, West Virginia, where, instead of sharing an address with three thousand people, he would be living with five. For the first time since 1919, he had a room to himself. Rather than die as predicted, it was as though he embarked on the childhood he had missed at the century's start. A teddy bear became his first toy in seventy years. He clung to it constantly. He learned to ride a tricycle. He jumped up and down on his bed with such a passion that the staff immediately set to work to discourage it, because they were afraid he would hit his head on the ceiling and get hurt. He was in his seventies, after all. Their success at this was limited.

For the next several years, Archie continued to grow within the community the Autism Services Center had provided. He learned, as an old man, to dress himself, to bathe himself, and to keep his room in order—all skills he was missing when he left Spencer State. He began to paint and to color. Once, a kind handyman taught him how to hammer nails into boards, and this became one of his favorite activities. In 1995, he was taken, with everyone else in the house, to the Outer Banks of North Carolina. He was eighty-one, seeing the ocean for the first time.

And he finally learned to accept his sister's touch. A frequent visitor to his new home, Harriet had watched the hard-faced Archie turn into a man who smiled all the time. She saw too how he sometimes pulled himself up close to the staff members' faces, fascinated by their teeth, which of course he lacked. He would tap on their incisors with his fingers, then brush his palms over their cheeks. One day, as Harriet leaned over him to say goodbye, he did the same thing to her. He brought his hand up and touched her cheek. Then she touched his. After that, this became the way they always said goodbye to each other.

Harriet died a few weeks after turning ninety. That was in 1993. By chance, that was the year the institution that had held her brother for half his life, Spencer State Hospital, saw its last patients leave. After that, an auction was held, in which everything inside the place was put up for sale and carried off, including furniture, kitchen utensils, trees from the lawns, and patient X-rays. The buildings, used for a time by a rubber company, went under the wrecking ball some years later. Since 2000, the site has been home to a Walmart superstore.

Archie lived in the group home until his death at age eighty-three, in 1997. At the time, someone referred to him as being the oldest-known person with autism. More than one hundred people attended his funeral, and the house he lived in was named for him posthumously: Casto House.

Rescued near the end, Archie managed to get in nine years of an excellent life, and he got to leave his mark, in the house that still has his name, with cracks in the ceiling above his old bed.

PART IV

BEHAVIOR, ANALYZED

1950s–1990s

18

THE BEHAVIORIST

Before it fell from grace with the authorities—back when no one called it "acid," when possessing it was not yet a crime, and its short, mad era of being chic was still in front of it—LSD actually enjoyed a good long run of respectability.

Lysergic acid diethylamide, which was derived from a fungus, was first developed in 1938, but its mind-altering properties were unknown until 1943, when a Swiss chemist named Albert Hoffman got high on it completely by accident. Hoffman had developed the compound known as LSD-25 five years earlier as a possible respiratory stimulant for the pharmaceutical firm Sandoz. For the next few years, he kept busy with other projects, but on April 16, 1943, he synthesized it again to take another look. Suddenly, he began to feel strangely restless and dizzy. Unsettled, he went home, where he lay down on the bed and shut his eyes against the daylight, which suddenly seemed irritatingly bright. For the next two hours, he was dazzled by visions of extraordinary shapes and colors dancing before his covered eyes—a stunning imaginary show that seemed utterly real. And then it ended.

That night, thinking it over, Hoffman hypothesized that he had somehow ingested the compound he'd been working on, perhaps through the skin of his fingertips, and that this had caused the reaction. Three days later, to test this theory, he put another 250 milligrams of LSD-25 into his body—this time swallowing it. Then he went for a bike ride. The era of LSD experimentation had begun.

For the next fifteen to twenty years, it was not ordinary people testing out the drug. It was scientists. "A favorite tool of psychiatric research," *Time* magazine said of LSD in 1955. In total, some 10,000 research papers would be produced on LSD by the early 1960s, the majority of them studying its effects on human subjects—who "dropped acid" under laboratory conditions, then let their reactions be measured. Researchers were captivated by the similarity of some of LSD's effects—most obviously, hallucinations—to major symptoms of mental illness. They were excited at the possibility of using LSD to study the impact of brain chemistry on mood, cognition, and mental health in general.

It was in this spirit that, in 1959, a New York psychiatrist stirred a little LSD into the chocolate milk of an eight-year-old nonspeaking boy with autism in hopes of getting him to talk. Inspired by recent breakthroughs reported among adults, Dr. Alfred Freedman had gone to the League School in Brooklyn—a pioneer in autism education—and arranged for twelve students to take part. Five spoke mostly incomprehensibly and seven not at all.

At the time, LSD's power to crack the silence of the silent had already been well documented. There was the "catatonic woman who had been mute for some years," who, according to one write-up, began to speak again when given LSD. There was also a sixty-year-old man, identified only as Mr. G., who "responded with wild bursts of laughter, which was most unusual for him since Mr. G. never spoke." Neither of these adults had autism, but the reported vocalization effect made LSD seem worth trying on children with autism.

And so, beginning with "slender, delicate-looking" Ralph, the twelve children dropped acid, one by one, each on a different day. The LSD was administered in cups of whatever they liked best to drink. Then Freedman and two other researchers watched, waited, and wrote down what happened next.

Ralph had the classic response of someone on an LSD trip. His eyes dilated, his skin flushed, and he began acting weirdly, at least for him. He was briefly observed making eye contact with one of the adults nearby, which was unusual, but then his eyes started following something no one else in the room could see. He was hallucinating. He was definitely more perked-up than usual, even elated, until, after an hour or so, his mood turned dark, and he lost interest in everything around him, including objects placed directly in front of him. For a long time, he sat practically motionless, stroking his lips over and over, as though only just discovering them. At the four-hour mark, his alertness began to return; at five hours, he was extremely irritable until given another cup of chocolate milk. After that, "he rocked on his cot, somewhat depressed, but relaxed," while the last vestiges of his high evaporated. Observations of the remaining children showed a wide range of responses, but none of them magically began to speak.

When Dr. Freedman and his two coauthors published the findings in 1962, he sounded a defeated note. He believed the research had value as a first-time description of children with autism subjected to the LSD experience. But after filling ten pages with text, charts, and tables, he was forced to report, in the last sentence of the final paragraph: "The hoped-for change from muteness to speech did not occur." Freedman was done with LSD research, at least as the answer to autism.

Others, however, were just getting started. One leading New York psychiatrist, Dr. Lauretta Bender of Bellevue Hospital, became convinced that daily dosing with LSD was the way to go. In 1961, she chose as her subjects fourteen boys and girls, ages six to fifteen, most with symptoms that today would fit neatly into the definition of autism. The children were not volunteers; they were confined at the Creedmore State Hospital in Queens, New York, when she began injecting them with minuscule amounts of LSD—25 micrograms per week. Bender described herself and her team as "extremely cautious when first using the drug, even obtaining parents' consent."

Over the next four years, she added more children to the study and worked up to more LSD, more often—eventually reaching a whopping dose of 150 micrograms, administered orally in half doses, twice daily. Some children remained on that regimen for up to twenty-four months. This yielded for Bender years of publishing opportunities; she became the most prolific article writer among all the researchers mixing LSD with autism. By 1969, having experimented on a total of eighty-nine children, she had produced eight key articles, far more than anyone else doing experiments with kids.

Similar work was taking place at UCLA and around the country, led by both psychiatrists and psychologists, all of whom relied on captive populations of children confined to institutions. Some researchers seemed motivated more by curiosity about LSD than by an interest in autism.

The science produced from these experiments was as murky as their ethics, as most of the trials failed to meet even the basics of procedural soundness. There were almost no control groups, no objective metrics, and the researchers relied heavily on their own subjective and biased observations. In short, they wanted to see happier children, so that's what they looked for. Thus, in 1967, when Dr. Harold Abramson, an asthma doctor and leading LSD enthusiast, pulled together the results of most of the studies, he declared with confidence in *The Journal of Asthma Research* that LSD represented "new hope . . . especially to autistic and schizophrenic children."

But as the 1960s came to an end, the zeal for LSD as an autism treatment was fading. For one thing, it had become much harder to obtain. Sandoz, the Swiss manufacturer, had shut down production in 1965. And in 1968, with recreational use spreading, the US government outlawed possession of LSD except under limited circumstances. The National Institutes of Mental Health kept a supply for research purposes, but getting access to it was a laborious process.

Besides, more rigorous reviewers were looking back at studies published in the first half of the decade, and were questioning the claims that LSD had done anything good at all for children with autism.

ONE BLUNT TRUTH was cited again and again in the 1960s by researchers who resorted to outlandish measures in the effort to help kids with autism. It was the simple fact that nothing else had been found to do any good. This excuse was used to justify the LSD experiments, and it was used again by a UCLA psychologist named O. Ivar Lovaas who, in 1965, began using a battery-powered cattle prod to give electric shocks to children. The result would be as momentous as it was controversial.

Norwegian-born, Lovaas came to the United States in 1950 on a music scholarship to Iowa's Luther College, before discovering psychology, which led him into graduate studies at the University of

Washington. In the early 1960s, he had been part of a team at UCLA that had tested LSD as a treatment for autism and had been disappointed.

By that time, Lovaas had long been disillusioned with the Freudian theories he had been taught during his early days at the University of Washington. His philosophical break with those theories began when he worked for a time at Seattle's Pinel Foundation Hospital. This was a twenty-bed residence, serving primarily well-connected families, where most of the patients were diagnosed with schizophrenia and were treated with psychoanalysis. Lovaas's main role at Pinel consisted of taking the patients on walks around the grounds to calm them when they became agitated. These walks gave him an opportunity to get to know the patients, and he quickly came to the conclusion that psychoanalysis, though well-intentioned, wasn't doing them any good. One summer, two patients, on different days, committed suicide by diving headfirst from an upstairs window. As Lovaas would tell an interviewer years later, in his usual blunt way: "I knew them, and they weren't that crazy."

Lovaas was disappointed in the absence of data or testing that demonstrated the efficacy of psychoanalytic treatment, and even more so by its almost complete failure to help people with more severe forms of mental illness. He began gravitating toward a radically different approach, which led him to start in with the electricity experiments—giving shocks to disabled kids.

Lovaas's first set of what he called "punishment studies" did not employ the cattle prod. Instead, his initial experiments, which took place in 1964 at the Neuropsychiatric Institute at UCLA, involved an electrified floor. The study subjects were two boys, Mike and Marty, five-year-old twins, both of whom had autism. They did not speak or respond to speech, and 70 to 80 percent of their time awake involved behaviors that Lovaas wanted to see if he could stop: rocking, fondling themselves, or flapping their hands or arms repetitively. Lovaas also wanted to try to make them come when their names were called. He intended to produce both of these outcomes through the calculated use of pain.

To do this, he placed the boys, one at a time, in a room with two adults, who stood on opposite sides of the child. The grown-ups wore shoes, but the child was barefoot, the soles of his feet exposed to a grid of metal tapes stuck to the floor, which were hooked up to a battery. When a switch was thrown, an electric current raced through the metal tapes, dealing a shock to anyone who touched it, which Lovaas described as "definitely painful and frightening."

The experiment started with the electricity already switched on and jolting the barefoot five-year-old. Simultaneously, one of the two adults began calling out, "Come here," with arms spread. If the boy moved toward the open arms, even just by some random impulse, the electricity was immediately turned off, stopping the pain. If he did not move, after three seconds, the boy would get a little shove toward the beckoning grown-up. That too stopped the pain. Each boy went through this fifty times in the first session alone (there were three sessions over three days). The electricity went back on anytime either boy lapsed into his usual rocking or flapping. When this happened, the adults shouted a sharp "No!" at the child. The electricity, meanwhile, stayed on until the unwanted behavior ceased.

Lovaas was pleased with the results, as each boy quickly adapted his behavior to move toward the open-armed adult when invited, and each became obedient to the shouted "no." In Lovaas's view, both boys became "more alert, affectionate, and . . . surprisingly, during successful shock avoidance, they appeared happy."

But the effect was not permanent. In the absence of continual "shock-training," as Lovaas called it, both boys, within a matter of months, reverted to their previous patterns of behavior. Still, Lovaas believed he had shown that "punishment can be a very useful tool for effecting behavior change."

It was after these experiments that Lovaas procured a "Hot-Shot," which was the brand name given to a range of "electric livestock prods," manufactured in several sizes and colors by a firm located in the middle of dairy-cow country, in Savage, Minnesota. The one that Lovaas acquired was twelve inches long and delivered 1,400 volts. It had been designed for use on 2,000-pound animals. Used on humans, it caused real pain, to which he could attest because he had tried it on himself, as had a couple of his assistants. Although the pain lasted only a few seconds, they said that it was like having a tooth drilled by a dentist who had run out of Novocain.

This new round of punishment studies was carried out on three institutionalized children temporarily transferred to Lovaas's custody for research purposes—Linda and John, both age eight, and Gregg, age eleven. Lovaas described all three children as "retarded," but it is clear from his descriptions that they had severe autism, as well as other disabilities. They were entirely unable to take care of themselves and given to a variety of disturbing behaviors. John, for example, had been known to drink from the toilet and to eat his feces. Linda was functionally blind, and Gregg was unable to walk. Whenever they hit Gregg with the "Hot-Shot," they had to prop him up in a wheelchair first.

The shocks were an attempt to control the single most horrifying behavior shared by the children: physically attacking themselves. All three ferociously pummeled their own faces, especially their ears, with their fists, or slammed their heads into whatever sharp, hard edge was nearby. During one ninety-minute period, John had been observed striking himself 2,750 times. The faces and heads of all three children were a road map of scars. On the day Linda was brought in to UCLA, she had blood leaking from one ear. None of the children could talk; the violence they turned on themselves was the only message they seemed capable of sending to the outside world.

Lovaas later explained that he had intentionally chosen the most severely self-destructive children he could find. He had approached two Southern California institutions, Camarillo and Pacific State Hospital, and asked the staff to point out the children most given to harming themselves. Immediately, they singled out John, Linda, and Gregg. All three had started hurting themselves as toddlers and had since been subjected to the same last-resort method of control: physical restraints, twenty-four hours a day. Linda's wrists were kept bound to her thighs, with only a little bit of slack, to prevent her from reaching her head with her hands. She lay on her stomach, facedown in a bed all day, sunrise to sunset, awake and flopping one leg up and down. Gregg, on the other hand, was pinioned face-up, looking at the ceiling, his wrists and ankles tied to the corners of the bed. He had spent the previous two years that way. Inactivity had caused his Achilles tendon to shorten, which is why he could no longer walk.

Lovaas wanted to see whether he could stop the children's self-destructive behavior by punishing them the instant it appeared. It would be pain for the purpose of preventing pain—a paradox that, to many of Lovaas's critics, was perverse, and that he would never explain to their satisfaction.

John went first. For five minutes, he was freed of his hand and foot restraints and made to sit on the lap of an attending nurse. Lovaas sat facing them, the Hot-Shot ready. Right away, John hit himself. Lovaas reached over, touched the boy's leg with the Hot-Shot, and squeezed its trigger. The one-second-long shock surprised the eight-year-old. In instantaneous pain, John flinched and a little shudder went through his body. But this also interrupted the self-battering, at least momentarily. After a pause, John started in again, his fists flailing into his own face. Lovaas shocked his leg again. This was followed by another, longer interruption in his self-battering. The data is not entirely clear, but it seems that John and Lovaas repeated this pattern a third time, and possibly a fourth, before the five minutes were over. One result, however, was indisputable: the shock slowed the pace of John's hitting dramatically. During this one session, he went from striking himself about fifty times per minute at the beginning of the session, to almost zero strikes per minute after being shocked.

For the following two rounds, on two subsequent days, John was spared the cattle prod. Two associates of Lovaas were working with him that day, with instructions to let his behavior slide so that Lovaas could see how John responded to their leniency. Indeed, his self-injuring returned immediately and worsened from session two to session three. Interestingly, however, it was still lower overall than at the start of the experiment. During non-testing times, John was also generally less violent whenever he was in or even near the experimentation room than when he was in other parts of the institute. On the fourth day, the original discipline returned. Lovaas was back in the seat. John, placed in the nurse's lap, brought his fists up and slammed them into his own face. Lovaas shocked him, and once again, the pounding plummeted.

There were weeks of this yet to go, but one of the most dramatic revelations about John occurred not during sessions with the cattle prod. Rather, it was something that happened between sessions. On the morning of the very first day, after being shocked three or four times in a five-minute period, John was returned to his room. It was decided to leave him, for a time, without the restraints he always wore, and the door to his room was left open.

At first, John huddled, motionless, beneath the sink in a corner of the room. It was not until twenty minutes had passed that he ventured out from under the sink and walked over to a cupboard near a different corner of the room. He peeked inside briefly, then scurried back to the sink. Fifteen minutes later, he did the same thing—out and back.

At last he stood up and, with small, tentative steps, made his way to the open door and into the hallway. Following the wall, he found the room next door and entered it. A moment later, he was back in the hallway again.

Something was triggered in him at that point, because John began to run. It did not look like fear. It looked more like he was actually having fun. It was only a corridor and a couple of laboratory rooms, but it was more space than he had been able to explore at will since he had been institutionalized years earlier. As if he couldn't get enough of the feeling, he ran back and forth, over and over. From behind mirrors and through doorways, Lovaas and his team watched a little boy tasting a certain kind of childhood freedom for the first time.

Then John made a delicious discovery, which brought the frantic running to a sudden stop. He could scratch himself. Before this, his hands had always been tied behind his back. Now his hands could reach almost every inch of his body. Given the chance, he took it, and sank into the primal pleasure of it, scratching himself all over for a full hour.

A little while later, he got a bath—something that had always been impossible because of his beating arms. But in this brief hiatus from self-injury, he let Lovaas's staff plunk him into a tub of warm water. He screamed with happiness when he felt it and immediately scooted lower till he had submerged himself head to toe. Still under the water, he opened his eyes and stared with wonder at the team in white lab coats gathered around the tub, who were staring back at him in a wonder of their own.

Lovaas achieved similar mastery of the self-destructiveness of the other two children, Linda and Gregg. In their cases, however, it took only four sessions to suppress the unwanted behavior. With Linda, he added something new to the experiment: he and the other experimenters began to shout "No!" directly into her face when they were giving her a shock. Within three sessions, just the word was enough to get her to stop beating herself.

When he went back to working with John again, Lovaas expanded the experiment to see if he could crush John's self-injurious behavior not only in the lab but in a wider variety of settings. He took him to other parts of the institute, and even outside, and gave him shocks there. After that, Lovaas wrote, "John was effectively freed from self-destructive behavior outside the laboratory."

It is unknown how long the positive results lasted after the experiments ended. The children were not at UCLA for the purposes of treatment. They were laboratory specimens, chosen for research and returned at the end of the experiments to the institutions where Lovaas had found them. But he knew, and sometimes lamented, that all three resumed the self-injurious behaviors he had suppressed, and that each of them would end up once again tied down to their beds. But Lovaas was not a caregiver. His personal responsibility to the children ended when he handed them back. For him, the priority was research, which was going to mean more experiments, with more children, and perhaps, if he was smart and tenacious enough, discoveries that would lead to ways to help all of them.

Lovaas was a magnet for attention, who attracted both ardent fans and harsh critics. Over the ensuing decades, he would become—at least within the academic world—a star performer, a hot bright light, a noisy combatant, an athlete. As a professor, he knew how to play to the crowd, lacing his lectures with jokes and tales from his Norwegian childhood, like the one about how he kept his feet warm in his boots on frigid mornings in the 1940s when he had to go milk the cows. "I let the cows piss on them," he'd say.

Tan, tall, and lean, he had a whip of a body, kept in tune by constant, obsessive exercise. He was a regular at the UCLA gym in the 1960s, at a time when it was used mainly by varsity athletes. He was an ace skier, so aggressive on the slopes that, despite his advanced skills—or maybe because of them—he once broke his leg up there. Notoriously attractive to his female students, he was widely gossiped about as a professor who made full use of the opportunities presented to him. Lovaas was married twice: once early in life, when he fathered four children, and then again much later in life. In between, he had a seventeen-year run of bachelorhood that he was said to have enjoyed to the hilt. But nobody censured him for this. It was California, and it was the 1960s. The closest he came to being called out for his amorous activities was the year the students of the UCLA Psychology Department voted him winner of the "Male Chauvinist Pig Award." He regarded the designation, laughingly, as a badge of honor.

His enemies found it a challenge to ignore him or debate him. He smiled big, thought deeply, worked hard, and was entertainingly reckless in the language he used to dismiss anyone who questioned his research methods or findings. Once, at a dinner meeting, feeling challenged yet again by people he thought did not understand his work, he lifted his salad bowl for everyone to see, then announced: "There are more brains in this salad than in the people seated at this table."

At times, he was candid to a fault, as with the description he gave to an interviewer from *Psychology Today* about the kids he was working with. "They are little monsters," Lovaas said. "They have hair, a nose and a mouth—but they are not people in the psychological sense. . . . It is a test for psychology," he declared.

It was always the "test" that thrilled him, and the possibilities of what the science he practiced could produce. In his seventies, he would boast to Robert Ito of *Los Angeles Magazine:* "If I had gotten Hitler here at UCLA at the age of four or five, I could have raised him to be a nice person. A humanitarian!" Audacious, visionary, and somewhat offensive, it was classic Lovaas. Because while he was clearly joking, he also meant it. Lovaas believed deeply in the science he was practicing—a science whose claimed principles of human psychology were observable, confirmable, measurable, and reliably, relentlessly repeatable. To him, it was the antithesis of interpreting dreams or trying to divine meaning from inkblots. Lovaas's science built upon decades of work from long before his time, from labs around the world. But this science didn't discover its original working principles about the minds of people in human subjects. Instead, the major discoveries all came from experiments run on pigeons, cats, and dogs.

Not everyone liked hearing it, but what worked for animals worked for people too.

19

"SCREAMS, SLAPS, AND LOVE"

In the spring of 1965, readers of *LIFE* who picked up the May 7 issue and flipped past the cover story about actor John Wayne's rebound from lung cancer found themselves gazing at a series of disturbing photographs. The pictures showed several young boys and girls, none older than nine, undergoing what looked like an onslaught of abuse. One boy is seen in tears, his picture snapped the very instant an adult's open hand is smacking his cheek. Another girl is photographed just as a jolt of electricity is sent burning through her body. Throughout the photo spread, middle-aged men in neckties appear to be controlling this mad-seeming scenario taking place in a laboratory at UCLA. The accompanying text explains in large type what the readers are looking at: "A surprising, shocking treatment helps far-gone mental cripples."

LIFE had discovered Lovaas—and the controversy that surrounded the science he believed in.

Reinforcement and punishment. For two decades, finding the moral balance between the two would be the defining controversy of Lovaas's work with children who had autism. Often misunderstood, these terms, as used by behaviorists, were names for specific clinical and analytical tools, which had been derived from experiments on rats, mice, and pigeons.

Reinforcements worked like a reward. If they were delivered immediately following a desired behavior, they clearly encouraged the repetition of that behavior. A food pellet delivered to a pigeon stepping on a lever, for example, reinforced that behavior. It encouraged more steps on the lever by that bird in the future.

Punishment worked in nearly the opposite way. When delivered immediately following a behavior, it discouraged repetition of that behavior. Most often, punishment was "aversive," or unpleasant to experience, like a jolt of electricity. When shocked, rats tended to cease whatever behavior they had just been engaged in. If, over time, the same behavior was repeatedly followed by more shocks, they began to avoid that behavior altogether. They had "learned," through aversive experience, not to behave that way anymore. At least for a while.

Over many decades and in many labs, practitioners of this kind of psychology had painstakingly extracted the core principles of how interactions with the environment determine the behavior of virtually all organisms. Reinforcement and punishment, and other terms like *stimulus, response, shaping, operant conditioning, negative reinforcement,* and *extinction,* were the vocabulary of this science, in which study subjects learn from the environment what to do and what not to do, in order to be "rewarded" or avoid being "punished." Experimenters, meanwhile, had been perfecting their ability to control the environment of rewards and punishments in order to manipulate behavior.

This was the science of behaviorism.

Behaviorism was born, as most high-schoolers know, with an accidental observation about some dogs in Russia at the start of the twentieth century. Ivan Pavlov, a physiologist, was investigating the canine digestive system and its reflexes when he set out to measure the rate at which a dog releases saliva when food touches their tongues. He built a contraption out of a slender rubber hose, hooked up at one end to a surgically implanted tube extruding from his lab dogs' saliva glands. At the other end, a measuring beaker stood ready to collect the saliva. To get things going, Pavlov placed a fixed amount of meat powder into each animal's mouth. Saliva then flowed, giving Pavlov a readout on how much the dogs produced in a given period of time.

But a problem cropped up. After following this procedure for a few days, Pavlov noticed that the dogs were getting ahead of the experiment. They began salivating before they got a taste of the meat powder. In fact, they started drooling the instant Pavlov's assistants entered the room wearing lab coats. This was ruinous to the digestion study. It threw off all the measurements.

Then Pavlov had the flash of insight that would write him and his dogs into history. His canines, he realized, had learned from their environment. The dogs were responding not to the natural stimulus of food on the tongue but to previously neutral sights—lab assistants in white coats—they now associated with the taste of the meat powder. This would come to be called a *conditioned response.*

Pavlov devoted years to understanding this phenomenon and created other experiments to test ways the dogs' digestive responses could be manipulated by other stimuli, like the ringing of a bell. In 1904, he was awarded the Nobel Prize in Physiology or Medicine for charting the course of digestion. But in his prizewinner's lecture, Pavlov sounded more excited about his forays into the psychological realm. His discovery of some of the laws governing how the environment could be manipulated to control the behavior of dogs had, he felt, important implications for people too. Concluding his lecture, he celebrated the fact that, in his lifetime, scientists—himself included—were making new discoveries about "our psychical constitution, the mechanism of which was and is wrapped in darkness."

In the years following Pavlov's Nobel Prize, perhaps the most revolutionary of behaviorism's propositions was the idea that animal and human psychology had a great deal in common. In 1913, in a speech that came to be called "The Behaviorist Manifesto," American John Watson, destined to be hailed the "father of behaviorism," pulled no punches. "The behaviorist," he pronounced, "recognizes no dividing line between man and brute." This stand was as daring in its implications, and as insulting to notions of human uniqueness, as Darwin's theory of evolution.

But there was, in the eyes of behaviorism's critics, another, more subtle slander committed by the discipline. It projected all life experience onto a mechanistic framework, where people appeared as windup toys, all psychic gears and on-off switches, ruled by patterns of stimulus-and-response that were easily manipulated and entirely predictable. This vision seemed to rob humans of all sorts of dimensions critical to other philosophical schemes. Like free will. Or the unconscious.

Or having a soul. But those things, if they existed, could not be seen or measured. Behaviorism was only interested in what was visible and recordable. Observation and data collection were its fundamentals.

For the naysayers, perhaps the most unsettling and frustrating thing about behaviorism was that it worked. It was an astounding thing to see the great Harvard behaviorist B. F. Skinner demonstrate his ability to get a pigeon to make a 360-degree turn, using reinforcing food rewards, with only ninety seconds of conditioning. Of course, long before Skinner, conditioning was practiced by lion tamers, snake charmers, and cowboys, though they never called it that. It was also practiced by drill sergeants, school principals, and parents, who knew by instinct or experience that rewards and punishments can be extraordinarily powerful ways to shape a desired behavior in another person. To some degree, Skinner was simply dealing in common wisdom.

But led by Skinner, laboratory scientists produced thousands of studies that turned common wisdom into something quantifiable, with experiments that could be replicated. And out of these labs poured applications that put the science at the service of human need. Behavioral treatments were created for addictions and phobias. Behavioral approaches were developed for maintaining discipline in classrooms and for reinforcing learning. And behavioral methods were used by Lovaas to get children with autism to behave in ways that made them look and act less autistic.

Lovaas is sometimes mistakenly credited with having invented applied behavior analysis, or ABA, but in fact it was largely the work of a group of psychologists working at the University of Washington in the late 1950s and early 1960s. Sidney Bijou, for example, is one of the earliest researchers to test the use of ABA with children with disabilities. Bijou had worked under Skinner before becoming the director of the university's Institute of Child Development in 1948. Collaborating with Don Baer, another leader in the field—who had earned his PhD studying behavior in kittens—Bijou was a creative, hands-on researcher. Between 1957 and 1960, he was known to drive around Seattle hauling a laboratory stuffed inside a mobile home, visiting nursery schools whose kids had "volunteered" for some of his studies. His traveling lab was a fully functioning behaviorist test center, with chairs, recording gear, a one-way mirror, and a tabletop contraption of his own design with flashing blue lights and levers. The device popped out trinkets when levers were pushed in response to the lights, which he could program however he wanted. Traveling with his own lab had the advantage of creating a consistent environment for the work, even as he studied groups of kids all over the city. Eventually, he opened a nursery-school-as-laboratory on the University of Washington campus, and the mobile home was retired.

In July 1962, Bijou was contacted by Jerman Rose, the psychiatrist who ran the children's ward at the nearby Western State Hospital, a mental institution. Trained in psychoanalysis, Rose urgently sought Bijou's help with an especially troubled little boy whom no amount of psychoanalysis seemed to help. Bijou delegated the case to two University of Washington behavior analysts. One, Todd Risley, was a graduate student in the psychology department. The other, Montrose Wolf, was an assistant research professor. The boy was a three-year-old named Richard. Known to all as "Dicky," he had autism.

The "Dicky study," which appeared in the journal *Behavior Research and Therapy* in 1964, represents the first indisputably life-changing use of applied behavior analysis to instill beneficial behaviors in a child with autism while eliminating behaviors that were not only disruptive to learning but physically harmful. If it hadn't been for Wolf and his team, Dicky would have gone blind before he was five.

Dicky's severe autistic behaviors, which had become evident around nine months, made him disconnected, self-destructive, and increasingly difficult to handle. He had memorized TV commercials and could recite them verbatim for hours, but otherwise he could not use language in any normal way. He could not stand to be touched anywhere on his head. His tantrums were a few notches beyond terrifying, as he would turn on himself with such violence that, afterward, his mother said, "he was a mess, all black and blue and bleeding." In addition to all this, he had difficulty seeing. Around the same time as his autism symptoms began, cataracts began growing in both his eyes. At the age of two, he underwent a series of operations to remove them, but ultimately the doctors had been left with no choice but to take out all the tissue that serves to focus the eye naturally. Dicky would never be able to see clearly without prescription lenses.

But when he was given eyeglasses, he refused to wear them. This was especially worrisome because Dicky's ophthalmologist had warned his parents that if he went too long without corrective lenses, his retinas would lose their function permanently. Already, most of a year had passed since the operation. Nothing his parents said could get Dicky to cooperate. The typical strategies parents resort to were useless with Dicky. They could not explain the situation to him in understandable terms, nor could they bribe him or threaten punishment. All of those approaches required two-way communication and a situational understanding that Dicky didn't seem to possess.

Wolf and Risley pursued a "behavior analytical" approach. They started by observing how Dicky interacted with his mother and attendants at the state hospital. They witnessed his tantrums, which were nearly nonstop despite constant efforts by adults to calm him down. Obviously, this problem needed to be addressed before they could even start to work on the eyeglasses matter.

Inspired by two recent studies that had nothing to do with autism, they pursued a program of mild punishment and "extinction" designed to eliminate Dicky's tantrums. In the first of those studies, researchers at the University of Washington had succeeded in changing the behavior of several difficult-to-handle nursery-school children—in ways that could be enumerated and graphed—by instructing their teachers to ignore them completely whenever they displayed certain "undesirable" behaviors (which included excessive crying, isolated play, and uncontrolled self-scratching). As a result of this withdrawal of teacher attention, the undesirable behaviors quickly underwent "extinction" and were rapidly eliminated.

Conversely, when the children switched to more appropriate behaviors—cooperative play, for example—they immediately began to receive attention again from their teachers. This attention proved to be reinforcing, and these more appropriate behaviors quickly increased in frequency. "Attention" did not just mean the teachers praised the children. It was subtler than that. Moving closer to them, smiling at them, and offering to help them all counted as attention. What today is seen as conventional parenting wisdom was in fact a breakthrough discovery made at the UW labs in 1962. Previously, the powerful reinforcing effect on a child of attention from an adult had not been appreciated.

Knowing this, the team watching Dicky quickly formed the hypothesis that the attention he attracted during tantrums might be reinforcing them, even causing them to happen more often. Indeed, the hospital staff had orders to try to soothe Dicky whenever he became upset. His mother, understandably, had the same impulse. But what most people would call maternal instinct—or love—looked to the behavior analysts like the source of the problem. Dicky's mother was rewarding him for blowing up, though that was never her intention.

The other study Wolf and Risley drew upon had pigeons as its subjects, and its most interesting discovery was something of an accident. The researcher in that study did not want his pigeons pecking at the food-releasing levers in the intervals between experiments. He found that, if he shut off the lights in the space the pigeons occupied, putting them in darkness, they stopped the unwanted pecking behavior. He began using this method regularly, calling it a "time out." It was the same "time out" that was destined to become a widely adopted disciplinary tool used by parents and teachers across the United States—few of whom realized that the method had started in a behaviorist's lab, and then traveled, by word of mouth, probably by way of teachers' courses taught by psychologists with some behavioral training. In 1963, however, it was new, and only pigeon-tested. When Wolf and Risley decided to try using it as a "mild punishment" to discourage Dicky's tantrums, it was probably the first scientifically controlled use of the technique with a person.

As instructed by the behavior analysts, the hospital staff and Dicky's parents began to respond in a new way when Dicky began to act up. The adults nearby remained calm and paid him not the slightest attention, other than taking him immediately by the hand and, in a perfunctory way, leading him to a designated "time-out" room. Without fuss, without talk, without hugs, the door was closed, and Dicky was left alone in the room for a period of ten minutes.

The results were dramatic. Denied adult attention, the boy became progressively better at calming himself down during each successive time out. Over weeks, this required less and less time, and his tantrums became less and less violent. After two and a half months, Dicky was no longer scratching or slapping his face at all when he blew up. Eventually, his outbursts dwindled to so few in number that they ceased to be the defining factor in his interaction with others.

Now the two psychologists could attack the main challenge: getting eyeglasses on a three-year-old who hated anybody, or anything, touching his head. For this, Wolf and Risley turned to a classic behaviorist technique known as *shaping.* They began by getting Dicky used to the idea of simply being near eyeglasses. They placed several pairs of frames around the room, without lenses in them, and gave him a reward whenever he moved in the direction of any of them—even when the movement was clearly random. In time, this brought him closer and closer to the frames, to the point where he was reaching out and touching them. Whenever this happened, he was rewarded again—and then again when he brought them near his face. The researchers tried to keep him hungry, so that the reinforcers they were using—bits of candy and fruit at one point, breakfast in small bites at another—would motivate him. But after several days, it appeared that these reinforcers were losing their appeal. Progress slowed.

Then, late one morning, after Dicky was deliberately denied breakfast, Wolf and Risley showed up with ice cream. That changed everything. Dicky apparently loved ice cream, because soon he was letting the glasses be placed on his head and allowing them to be set more and more snugly onto the bridge of his nose, and even over and around his ears. He had a little trouble with the last part, tending to wrap them under his ears, but that was resolved over several sessions, with yet more ice cream.

Wolf and Risley had left the lenses out of the frames on purpose, concerned that it might be too intense an experience for Dicky suddenly to see things in sharp focus. But then lenses were added to the frames, and the prescription was ramped up, from weaker to stronger, all in separate sessions, and all of it shaped by spoonfuls of positive reinforcement for every right move. It took months, but in the end, before he went home, Dicky was wearing his glasses twelve hours a day. This small achievement was, in fact, a stunning outcome.

Over the next several months, Wolf and Risley continued working with Dicky, trying to teach him to talk. Working with pictures of objects, along with plenty of rewards, they gradually shaped his echolalic speech into something more obviously practical. At the beginning, his speech was no more than rote recitation—words for ice cream. But over more months and then years, with his parents joining in as teachers, Dicky's verbal skills improved to the point where he was able to ask for the things he wanted.

Having that amount of language—and being able to see—changed Dicky's life. Eventually, he was able to go to school, and then, as a young adult, to get a part-time job as a janitor and to live on his own in an apartment, with occasional supervision. The team from the University of Washington hadn't cured Dicky's autism, but they had helped him find a place in the world.

WOLF AND RISLEY got through to Dicky, in the end, with ice cream. A positive reinforcer. A reward. Actually, a frozen dessert also made a fleeting appearance in that May 1965 *LIFE* spread about Lovaas's project at UCLA. The text specified that the program relied overwhelmingly on positive reinforcers, especially food—including sherbet—and that in Lovaas's lab, the kids were shown "persistent and loving attention." A few pictures even showed kids being hugged, validating the last word in the article's title: "Screams, Slaps & Love."

But the article also revealed that the kids were kept hungry to keep them working hard for that food. And the overall impact of the pictures probably left most readers thinking that, at the heart of Lovaas's program, the children were being punished for having a condition that was described in relentlessly bleak terms.

Autism, *LIFE* explained, was a "special form of schizophrenia," which resulted in "utterly withdrawn children whose minds are sealed against all human contact and whose uncontrolled madness had turned their homes into hells." Living with autism was "a nightmare" and an "appalling gallery of madness." Certainly, it sounded worse even than the misery depicted in Lovaas's lab.

The lead-off photo shows Billy, a three-year-old who could not speak, with tears rolling down his face, as a man in a necktie, his face twisted in anger, bellows at him. The man pictured was not Lovaas but Bernard Perloff, a fellow researcher. It is Perloff's open palm that comes up against the left side of Billy's head, either grabbing it or smacking it. Either way, he appears to be furiously berating the boy. The text explained why: during a speech lesson, Billy's attention had wandered, and Perloff hit him to get him focused again. In the third picture in the sequence, the two of them are so close together, they're nearly touching noses, and Billy, though his lower lip looks like it's trembling, is looking Perloff straight in the eye.

The girl seen getting shocked with electricity is identified as Pamela, a nine-year-old. She, too, had just become distracted from the task at hand—a reading lesson with Lovaas.

By this time, Lovaas was in his second or third year of experiments using ABA with autistic children. But he was not trying to discover the nature of autism. As *LIFE* put it, "The team conducting the experiment at UCLA is not interested in causes." Instead, "by forcing a change in the child's outward behavior," according to the article, Lovaas hoped to force an inward change as well. He was trying to teach them to make eye contact, to form and use words, to read, to hug.

The work, *LIFE* made clear, was worth the time and the suffering. ABA worked. *LIFE*'s readers were told that Billy, for example, had been taught to say his own name, remarkable for a child who before had only grunted and squealed. Rewarding Billy with a steady stream of hugs and food, Lovaas had spent days teaching him to bring his lips together as if to produce the *b* sound. That achieved, the next phase was to prompt and then reward Billy for bringing his vocal cords into it—to make the silent *b* into a full-throated "Buh." If Billy's attention strayed for too long, Lovaas would slap his face. And on it went, through the rest of the sounds that made up his name until he could say "Billy" on his own—a triumph in a single word.

Over the next twenty years, Lovaas would continue to refine and experiment with his method, but a key pillar of it was on display in the *LIFE* layout: the breaking down of any task into small, teachable, learnable performances of behavior. The *LIFE* story left readers on an upbeat note, thanks to a sequence of pictures Grant took of one of the mothers who had come by the lab and was watching her son from inside a darkened room, behind a one-way mirror. On that day, her son was being taught to embrace one of the other boys, in something that at least resembled a real hug. In the dimness, she is seen biting her thumbnails as the lesson unfolds. Then the hug happens. Delighted, she throws back her head and laughs, clapping her hands at the same time. She is "overjoyed at what she sees," the caption says. In that brief instant, at least, what Lovaas was doing seemed well worth whatever tears were being shed along the way. As *LIFE* summed up the work: "Lovaas hopes he has found a way to help any child with a broken mind more quickly and simply than with methods now used."

THE MOTHER WHO laughed and clapped her hands was behind a one-way mirror, invisible to Lovaas. In fact, though, he needed parents like her. Their support for what he was doing was his best protection against the criticism that the methods he was developing were extreme, cruel, or unethical.

It could only have been heartening to Lovaas, therefore, when, within days of the *LIFE* article's appearance, parents from all over the country called and left messages via the UCLA switchboard, or sat down and wrote urgent, beseeching letters, seeking a spot in his program for their own child. Lovaas was not equipped to handle such a sudden volume of interest, and so he passed on all the letters and names to a recent acquaintance of his named Bernie Rimland. They had met several months earlier, before the *LIFE* story, in late 1964.

Rimland had yet to become a major figure in autism, since his historic book taking down the refrigerator mother had only just come out. As ever, he was continuing to track down any sort of new research that touched on autism, scarce as that was. That autumn, having heard informally about Lovaas's early punishment studies, he showed up in Lovaas's office in UCLA's Franz Hall, and introduced himself. They spent the rest of the day together, with Lovaas showing Rimland how he was teaching nonverbal children to use words. Rimland was astounded and told Lovaas as much, then he invited Lovaas to a dinner he was attending that evening.

When Rimland told Lovaas that they would be joined by a number of couples, all parents of children with autism, Lovaas immediately made his excuses. As he later confessed, he could not stand being around the parents of the kids brought to his lab. It was not that he blamed mothers for causing their autism; yes, he had at one point espoused that belief, but had long since rejected it on his own. Yet he could not help finding the parents he met to be depressingly glum, withdrawn, or vaguely hostile. As a rule, he tried to avoid them. So he declined Rimland's invitation.

Rimland, however, persisted, and turned on the charm, telling Lovaas that the parents would be dazzled by hearing what he was doing with kids like theirs. Finally, Lovaas gave in.

That night marked the turning point in Lovaas's relationship with the parents of the children he studied. The group he met, over red wine and plates of pasta, was not at all what he had expected. Away from the laboratory and their children, they impressed him as relaxed, charming, and engaging. They asked good questions. They laughed at one another's jokes. The next morning, when Lovaas returned to his lab, a new thought took shape in his mind: *These people would make excellent allies.*

That insight would prove true, again and again, in the years ahead. But in May of 1965, when the *LIFE* story appeared, it was already to Lovaas's advantage that Bernie Rimland personally was so enthusiastic about his work on ABA. Lovaas forwarded the contact information of all the parents clamoring to get into the UCLA program to Rimland, and Rimland, as he always would, reached out to every single one of them, writing long, personal, thoughtful letters.

The timing was perfect for Rimland as well; he was just then starting to recruit members for the national autism organization he was forming. In the coming months, he would be on the road often, meeting with parents in living rooms and church basements. He wanted to give them hope, so he talked often about the work in Lovaas's lab. Not every parent was convinced. Some had seen the pictures in *LIFE* and would ask, "But isn't that the place where they beat up the children?" Rimland was ready for that one. He told them that punishment was minimally used, and that positive reinforcement was the backbone of the method. He also vouched, again, for how well it worked, and he vouched for the man—the UCLA researcher—himself.

Lovaas, Rimland told all, was "one of the only professionals who really cares about these kids."

At the time, that was mostly true.

And in 1965, Lovaas was still just getting started.

20

THE AVERSION TO AVERSIVES

In 1981, Lovaas had squeezed everything he had figured out about teaching children with autism into thirty-eight short, simple chapters, put them between a set of soft covers, and published them. He had spent a decade and a half refining his method, and his book represented the culmination of that work. It was called *Teaching Developmentally Disabled Children,* but would always be better known by its quirky subtitle, *The ME Book*—a nod to the child who stood to become more fully himself, more fully "me," through correct application of the contents. It was a do-it-yourself handbook for parents who wanted to practice ABA on their own, and it was the first of its kind. In his preface, Lovaas told readers they would be practicing the very same techniques he used in his lab: breaking complex skills into small components, reinforced by frequent rewards and occasional punishments.

With *The ME Book,* Lovaas followed through on his insight that parents would make good allies by making them a vital part of their children's therapy. Doing so solved a number of problems at the same time. He had discovered, for example, that in order to make progress, children needed to be in a full-time teaching environment—as in, every waking hour. In other words, the adults in their lives needed to construct every moment so as to reinforce the lessons being taught. Lovaas had always regretted that this wasn't possible with the first groups of children he had studied in the 1960s—children like Linda, Gregg, and John, all of whom likely relapsed when they returned to the institutions where they lived. Parents, however, could reinforce lessons daily.

Additionally, Lovaas's data told him that most children needed ABA instruction on the order of twenty to sixty hours per week. Even if the state hospital had permitted him to start an ABA program on its premises, it is unlikely that the administration would have provided enough staff to work intensively with even one child for anything close to that amount of time. But a motivated mother, he reasoned, would spend all day working with her child, if that was what it took.

Lovaas had also found that location mattered. While children could master certain skills when sitting in one of his small, bare experimental rooms at UCLA, some of them proved unable to reproduce the performance in any other setting. They could point to all the chairs in the room when asked to "point at chair," as long as they were in the same lab, with the same chairs, where they had learned the lesson. But when asked to do the same in another building, with different chairs, they failed to grasp the task. In behavioral terms, they had not "generalized" the chair-recognizing skill sufficiently to use it in changed circumstances.

The ME Book program was designed to address these problems. It called for teaching the kids at home, with their mothers and fathers taking the lead, guided by the book and by a set of videotapes Lovaas had produced, which showed his students running ABA sessions. He warned parents that it was probably too much to take on the job alone, so he recommended they recruit high school and college students in order to put together a team of four to eight teachers, who would work with the child in shifts. The recommended program required twenty to sixty hours per week for two to three years early in the child's life. That, in essence, is what came to be called the "Lovaas Model" of applied behavior analysis.

THE LOVAAS MODEL faced strong headwinds when *The ME Book* arrived in 1981. The problem could be found in a single sentence on page 16: "A swat on the behind is almost always effective, if it is hard enough so that it smarts." In short, Lovaas was still advocating the use of "aversive therapy," what behaviorists also called "punishment." To be sure, *The ME Book* regarded this as a tool to be used sparingly. On an early page, a warning to readers appears inside a black box: "the authors and publishers wish to emphasize that the training programs related to aversive therapy contained herein should *not* be undertaken without professional guidance."

The book was also adamant that punishment be used in as calculated and scientific a way as possible: "You have to keep a record when you use strong discipline to make sure that the behavior you punish is decreasing. That is the only justification for using aversives." Lovaas pointed out that punishment did not necessarily have to be physical to be effective. A sharp "no" counted too.

These recommended measures seemed a good deal less harsh than the slaps across the face Lovaas had sanctioned in the 1960s—but that did not rescue his method from facing harsh criticism. As it happened, *The ME Book* arrived just as the opening salvos were being fired in the coming war over aversives. The year of its publication, 1981, was the same year that the Association for the Severely Handicapped (TASH) became the first national group to adopt an official position against the use of behavioral punishment in the education of children or adults. Other groups followed suit, in a campaign that increasingly made pain-for-progress a losing argument.

On this score, ABA had a serious image problem. It was the hangover effect of Lovaas's Hot-Shot—the cattle prod he had used on those first kids—and everything it stood for. Even Bruno Bettelheim had once attacked Lovaas by name, saying that his methods turned children into "pliable robots . . . reduced to the level of Pavlovian dogs." Throughout the 1980s, the so-called aversives issue, which centered on ABA's willingness to use punishment to change behavior, was the most controversial aspect of the practice. It nudged aside the refrigerator-mother argument—which lost steam throughout the 1970s—to become autism's next great defining conflict. In *Science,* Louisiana State University psychologist Johnny Matson would call it "perhaps the single most frequently discussed issue in the field of developmental disabilities."

The conflict began, and persisted, primarily as a battle among professionals, although parents were dragged into it too. Insults were hurled and friendships destroyed, as well-intentioned people on both sides went to war over one of the most fundamental ethical dilemmas:

When do the ends justify the means? This was reframed, in the autism argument, as an urgent and inseparable pair of questions: Was it wrong to use punishment to treat severely disabled people who are hurting themselves? Or was it wrong *not* to?

Bernie Rimland weighed in on the topic in 1988: "While the use of electric shock on an autistic person is repugnant to me also, it is not nearly so repugnant as some of the things self-injurious people do to themselves, such as causing blindness, fracturing skulls, and in one case, chewing off both thumbs." If his own son Mark had been self-injurious, he said, he would certainly have considered using aversives to stop it.

For Mooza Grant, the original president of the National Society for Autistic Children, the debate was not theoretical. She had two teenage girls with autism—the younger of whom, Linda, had mauled her own ears into permanent scar tissue by constantly slamming her head onto hard surfaces. Both parents were determined to keep their girls at home. "I couldn't envision sitting with roses growing outside my house and my child being in an institution," Mooza once said.

But Linda was violent every minute of every hour. Considering it cruel to keep her in restraints full-time or sunk inside a drug-induced fog, Mooza's husband Leslie Grant went down into the basement of their home in Chevy Chase, Maryland, and built a prototype shock-dealing device of his own design. He built a helmet with sensors inside, so that whenever Linda hit something hard with her head, the sensors would activate an electrode strapped to the girl's arm or leg, giving her a shock powered by a nine-volt battery, the intensity of which he compared to being smacked with a hard-hit tennis ball. In the 1970s, the Grants reported that their daughter, who had been hurting herself for fifteen years, stopped doing so within days of the helmet being fixed into place on her head.

Seeking to refine the device, they recruited a team at the Johns Hopkins Applied Physics Labs. Over four years, the team managed to build a more compact version with a remote-control and a counter to keep track of the number of shocks during any given time period. The resulting product, which went into small-scale commercial production at a plant in Florida, was called the SIBIS—the Self-Injurious Behavior

Inhibiting System. As of 1988, some twenty-five children were reported to have worn the SIBIS—all with positive results. Rimland told parents that self-injury was so successfully suppressed in six of these early SIBIS wearers that they no longer needed to wear the device.

But that's what made the SIBIS so dangerous, in the eyes of its opponents. It showed how seductive the employment of shock could be. Users might conclude that if *some* shock produced improved behavior, then more shock would produce additional improved behavior. Punishment could easily become a self-justifying instrument, employed indefinitely.

At the same time, the SIBIS was a superb propaganda target. A black-strapped head harness giving children shocks—it looked sinister and sounded wrong. And while there were never more than a few in use at any one time, anywhere in the country, the horror they inspired served a purpose for those who campaigned against any kind of aversive—from slaps and pinches and foul-tasting sprays aimed into people's mouths at the harsher end, to time-outs and a technique called "overcorrection." With overcorrection, a person who spilled his juice on the floor in a dining hall would be made to refill his own cup, and then to refill the cups of everyone else at the table. Even this, to critics of aversives, was inappropriate, undeserved, and an assault on dignity.

By the mid-1980s, the antiaversive backlash had been joined by disability-rights groups, parent organizations, and several prominent education specialists. This opposition would not win—not exactly—but it would greatly influence the conversation. The movement's emotional appeal was strong, and its logic was consistent with one of the more persuasive arguments then being made for shutting down large mental institutions. That argument was, simply, that the disabled have rights, just like everyone else. And that just as locking them away in big buildings merely for being different was wrong, so was forcing them into unpleasant, aversive experiences merely for being difficult to teach.

The argument caught fire among many constituencies. In 1988, the Autism Society of America adopted a position against "aversive techniques." Many parents also voiced opposition, even some who were struggling at home with children who were hurting themselves.

Unflattering comparisons were made to child abusers, Nazi doctors, and police states. "Permitting punishment is like living in Berlin," declared one activist at an open meeting of the neutral Developmental Disabilities Planning Council, "and ignoring a nuclear holocaust." Protesters threatened to picket events featuring speakers known to support aversives as a conditioning tool. The Spanish Inquisition was invoked by one influential antiaversives activist, Anne Donnellan, who coauthored an attack on Lovaas and some other behavior analysts. Their sin was to have laid out, in a paper, a set of protocols for the appropriate use of aversives. Donnellan likened this paper to a legendary treatise called the *Malleus Maleficarum,* published in Latin in 1486. The obscure reference sent all the social scientists rushing for their encyclopedias, where they learned that the *Malleus Maleficarum*—or *The Witches' Hammer*—was a witch-hunters manual, written by two German priests for the Spanish Inquisition, offering guidance on the use of torture to get their questions answered. This did not go over well with those Donnellan was criticizing.

But the mud flew in the opposite direction as well, hurled back at the antiaversive campaigners by mainstream behaviorists. Drawing comparisons with harsh but beneficial medical treatments like radical surgery or chemotherapy, this group considered it immoral not to employ pain, minimally and with strict controls, for the relief it would bring in the long run. For the most part, however, they didn't bother to disparage the morals of those who disagreed with them. Instead, they mocked their lack of scientific seriousness. Psychologist Richard Foxx would speak of the "fanaticism" of the antiaversive movement, of their reliance on ideology rather than data. He scorned their "political correctness" and their penchant for "playing fast and loose with citations."

Foxx seemed particularly peeved by Anne Donnellan. He questioned her claims to have successfully treated "severe" problem behaviors using nothing but positive reinforcements. When he got his hands on a book she coauthored—*Progress Without Punishment: Effective Approaches for Learners with Behavior Problems,* which had become something of a manifesto for the antiaversive cause—he charged that the majority of the cases she reported on there and elsewhere were actually examples of minor behavior problems: among them spitting, sticking out a tongue, hitting a teacher once or twice a week, and telling too many knock-knock jokes. Beyond that, many of Donnellan's cases were small children. Foxx implied that Donnellan may never even have laid eyes on a person with truly severe behaviors—such as a strong and difficult-to-handle adult, relentlessly battering himself, or others—people who, back in the 1970s, would likely have been in restraints and in an institution. In such settings, Foxx sniffed, anti-aversive activists "would not deign to provide treatment."

In fact, the program in *The ME Book* did rely overwhelmingly on positive reinforcement, rewarding appropriate behavior with toys, ice cream, and hugs. But behaviorism was viewed with such suspicion in some quarters that it was difficult for the Lovaas Method to gain traction. As one child psychiatrist told a curious mother, who asked his opinion of Lovaas-style operant conditioning for her son: "If you want to turn your child into a terrified trained seal, go ahead."

Cost was another obstacle to the wide adoption of the program. Keeping as many as eight college students on the payroll was an enormously expensive undertaking for the typical American family. In the 1980s, the price of a full-fledged home-based ABA program could be as much as $50,000 a year—more than half the median price of an American home in that period. The time commitment too seemed overwhelming.

And with all that, Lovaas was not promising that his method would cure autism. He discouraged "hoping and struggling for often unattainable and absolute ideal[s] of normalcy or overall excellence." Because his method would take each child only so far, Lovaas offered this piece of advice to the parents: "Often the happiest people are those that curb their ambitions a bit."

Still, in the 1980s, there were parents, mostly in the Los Angeles area, who took out a second mortgage in order to turn their homes into ABA schools, each serving one child—the parents' own. They brought in teams of college students and followed *The ME Book* religiously, consulting with staff at UCLA to make sure they were on the right track. But other than a few centers in New Jersey and Indiana,

Lovaas's work had still not traveled much beyond L.A. It did not help that there was little framework for exporting training in the proper use of his method. Aspiring therapists needed to get into the UCLA program to get exposure to it.

Neither was Lovaas well known yet outside of ABA circles. It had been twenty years since he made a splash in *LIFE* magazine, and public memory was short. The academic journals in which he published had a minute number of readers, sometimes in the low hundreds, though most were well informed. He was not a top name in autism education nationally, not even close. That position happened to belong, instead, to a psychologist and professor in North Carolina by the name of Eric Schopler, who had been researching autism almost as long as Lovaas. Already hailed as a giant in the field of autism, he would soon find himself unable to ignore Lovaas, and vice versa, as the two men launched a years-long feud—watched by everyone else in autism—over science, ideals, and which of them was right.

21

THE "ANTI-BETTELHEIM"

MANY MORNINGS, ERIC SCHOPLER STOMPED INTO HIS offices at the University of North Carolina straight from the barnyard of his farm, with the mud still on his boots. To his staff, that was part of their boss's maverick charm—that he was as unpretentious as he was smart. Schopler was a psychologist who had started working on autism at UNC in 1964, arriving there after a stint working with children in Illinois. Soon after he reached North Carolina, in his late thirties, he adopted the look that became his trademark: a lumberjack shirt and work pants, sometimes topped off with a bow tie and sports coat. And boots with mud on them. He and his second wife, Miggie—an educator—kept bees, chickens, rabbits, a horse, and a cow.

Schopler's signature contribution, among many others, was his early insistence that autism was organic and that mothers, far from being blamed, should be seen as allies in the treatment of children. Of course, Bernard Rimland had made the point first, but he was a parent. Schopler, on the other hand, was a psychologist with no conflict of interest in standing up to the teachings of Bruno Bettelheim, with whom he crossed paths more than once. "There were a good many times," one parent told author Richard Pollak, the Bettelheim critic, "when Eric Schopler was our main defense against Bettelheim."

Schopler graduated from the University of Chicago with a degree in psychology in 1949. Following a stint as a social worker for the Cook County Welfare Department in Chicago, he re-enrolled at Chicago to pursue a master's degree in social service administration, which he completed. By 1955, he was at the Emma P. Bradley hospital for troubled children, in Providence, Rhode Island, where he held the position of acting chief psychiatric social worker.

When the hospital started planning a symposium on childhood psychosis, Schopler saw the perfect opening to bring about a face-to-face meeting with Bruno Bettelheim, by nominating Bettelheim as a speaker. The hospital director rejected the idea on the grounds that Bettelheim's "offensive manner of teaching" might be bad for staff morale.

Schopler then took it upon himself to inform Bettelheim, who had probably never even heard of the Emma P. Bradley hospital, that he had been rejected by the symposium planning committee. In the letter, he even mischievously told Bettelheim that he personally regretted that the famous man's "effectiveness as a teacher was so curtailed" by his personality, because it was denying Schopler the chance to learn from him.

A few days later, Schopler received a written reply from Bettelheim inviting him to visit his Orthogenic School in Chicago for two weeks, so that he could see for himself what he "had to teach," and not "go by what other people said" about him.

This would actually be Schopler's second interaction with Bettelheim. As an undergraduate at Chicago in the late 1940s, he had attended a talk Bettelheim gave to a group of Jewish students in the university's Hillel House. Like Bettelheim himself, Schopler was a European-born Jew who had escaped the Holocaust when his family fled Germany for the United States during his early childhood. But that night, as he often did, Bettelheim chided Jews in general for not trying hard enough to submerge their Jewishness, which he blamed for anti-Semitism. In the silence that followed, according to Schopler's own account, he was the only student present who challenged Bettelheim, when he asked what difference there was, if any, between Bettelheim's views on Jews and those of any ordinary anti-Semite. Supposedly, Bettelheim became angry and sputtered, "I am only the doctor prescribing the cure!" Schopler persisted: "You mean by identifying with the disease?" Bettelheim shouted again: "Yes, by identifying with the disease!"

Apparently, Bettelheim did not make the connection when Schopler wrote him from Rhode Island, though Schopler already knew that he did not like Bettelheim when he arrived in Chicago for his two-week visit. Still, there was an allure to being offered such access to the Orthogenic School, since Bettelheim was notoriously choosy about whom he permitted past the front entrance. Parents, for example, were forever banished. Beyond that, Schopler had been forming plans to return to the University of Chicago for a PhD, and he thought there could be some advantage to knowing a recognized leader in the field, even one he did not particularly like.

Schopler found the Orthogenic School fascinating and disturbing at the same time. He took in the calculated cheeriness of the place—the gorgeous color scheme Bettelheim picked for every room, the oversized stuffed animals placed here and there, and the candy closet children could get into at almost any time. This was the physical manifestation of Bettelheim's conviction that the "psychotic" children needed to be spoiled with sweetness, as a counterbalance to the coldness of their mothers.

Schopler did not witness Bettelheim slapping children, as he was later accused of doing. But he saw him bully and badger the young women who made up his teaching staff, who struck Schopler as being in awe of the man, more acolytes than assistants. At daily staff meetings, he heard Bettelheim opine expansively on the progress of each of the forty or so children there, where he reliably spun out Freudian explanations for their autistic behaviors. Schopler found these interpretations unsatisfying; he couldn't see that anything Bettelheim was doing within the school walls was working. Sometime that second week, or after, the thought crossed his mind: *Well, shit, I can do better than that.*

Schopler began work on a doctoral degree in clinical child development in 1962, simultaneously putting in hours as a therapist at Chicago's Treatment and Research Center for Childhood Schizophrenia, which was affiliated with the Jewish Children's Bureau. At the center, Schopler saw lots of autism, because childhood schizophrenia was then a diagnostic label generally considered synonymous with autism. At the same time, after seeing Bettelheim so miss the mark with his Freudian approach, Schopler resolved to construct a study for his dissertation that would rely on empirical research, not loose theory.

Schopler had become interested in how the children at the center used their mouths and noses to examine the world—tasting dolls, smelling pencils, and so forth. He theorized that the children were taking in information using their "near" senses, which might be more meaningful for them than relying on the "distance" senses of vision and hearing. He approached Bettelheim for access to the children at the Orthogenic School in order to test his theory. Bettelheim flatly refused. "Why is it you scientists always try to prove what we knew clinically all along?" he asked Schopler.

Bettelheim probably saw that Schopler's study assumed a neurological basis to autism, which Bettelheim, with his psychoanalytic bias, considered absurd. "Of course I will not lend my children to silliness like that," he told Schopler.

Schopler did his study anyway, with a different set of boys and girls. His results clearly showed that children with autism do exhibit certain preferences for information-gathering via these "near" senses, a curious insight in its own right and one that also demonstrated a neurological idiosyncrasy at play in autism. And yet, this research, which he published as his PhD dissertation in 1964, had little to do with Schopler's later reputation as one of autism's most influential personalities. It was not in neurology that he would make his mark. It was in education, where he built the first statewide network of schools for kids with autism. In his schools, parents were always welcome.

Schopler arrived in North Carolina shortly after getting his PhD, attracted to the Southern US campus in part because his younger brother, John, was already a psychologist on the faculty there. Schopler's first position was as a consulting psychologist to a UNC experiment known as the "Psychotic Children's Group." As it turned out, taking part in this "experiment" would become one of the most bizarre experiences of his life.

Strictly speaking, it was not an autism investigation. The purpose of the experiment was to test a Freudian-inspired theory of group therapy on a set of "psychotic" three- and four-year-olds. Its designer, a psychiatrist named Rex Speers, had become intrigued by the idea that a single "group ego" could be reconstructed out of the kids' "damaged" and fragmented egos, by having them interact several hours a week in a 14-by-20-foot laboratory space. For a child to participate, the mother had to submit to group therapy as well, "to integrate her own infantile impulses and to deal with them at a conscious level." Desperate families readily volunteered. One family drove 170 miles each way twice a week.

It did not take long for Schopler to understand exactly what he was seeing, because he had seen plenty of it already: these children had autism. He doubted that group psychotherapy for them or their mothers was going to do anybody much good.

Another young consultant, soon to become Schopler's chief collaborator, reached the same conclusion. Robert Reichler, a twenty-six-year-old graduate of the Albert Einstein College of Medicine in New York City, came to North Carolina to continue his training in psychiatry. Reichler was also sent to work with the Psychotic Child Group. On his first day, standing behind the one-way mirror that ran the length of the laboratory, he watched a scene he found reminiscent of a medieval hell. The children had been given free run of the room. They were darting, spinning, throwing things, all in a din of wordless squeals, hoots, and screams that Reichler could hear through the glass. Absolute permissiveness was part of the therapy, on the premise that it would repair the damage inflicted by lack of love. As Reichler watched, a child urinated on the floor, with no one intervening. When she also defecated on the same spot, some of the boys began handling her feces, smearing them onto their own bodies. Others were banging their heads or each other. Clothing came off as the kids pleased, with genitals displayed and mutually explored. An adult therapist was in the room with the children, observing from a raised platform. From time to time, he threw in comments over the din, along the lines of "Jimmy, I can see you're really angry with Tommy today." Given the children's obvious language deficits, Reichler could see no point in this haphazard attempt to communicate.

One four-year-old girl had a single comprehensible utterance, which she used over and over: "Goddamn. Goddamn." Throughout all this, a record player in the corner was booming out the sound of a marching band. When, as the brass blared, one boy stood naked on a table and urinated in a high arc directly at the mirror, Reichler knew he had seen enough. He decided that there was no way he would work in that room.

Schopler and Reichler got lucky. Soon after they were assigned to the Psychotic Child Group, funding for the program expired and was not renewed. But parents kept calling UNC. One of these calls, which came in the second half of 1965, was passed through to Schopler. Like Reichler, he was looking for something to do, and so, a few days later, the two of them met a mother named Mardy, who had a three-year-old who had been diagnosed with autism.

Mardy's son, David, was on a drug called Stelazine, which had been prescribed by the last psychiatrist they had consulted. Reichler felt like he was meeting a zombie. But without the Stelazine, Mardy explained, David was uncontrollable. He was a screamer and a runner and a head banger. He could say only one thing—*ka-ga-ka*—which he repeated ceaselessly. Mardy confided her belief that Stelazine was the only thing keeping her son out of an institution. But she also hated seeing what the drug turned her son into—he was constantly in a trance, lifeless and lost. She wanted him off of it.

Reichler, as the MD, stopped the Stelazine immediately, and he and Schopler set a date to begin working with the boy in the space abandoned by the discontinued study. Off the drug, David quickly returned to his wild self. On the first day, he filled the room with the strange, blunt sound of his sobbing, and kept breaking for the corridor. Reichler, not knowing what else to do, scooped him up, caging him loosely with his arms, and dropped to a seated position on the floor. He was improvising, trying to keep David in one place long enough to get and hold his attention, while he danced anything within reach in front of the boy's eyes—a toy car, blocks, his own eyeglasses. He was also watching closely. When he saw David's glance lock even briefly onto whatever he was holding, Reichler gave out a cheer and a hug, then tried to get David to do it again.

Schopler stood behind the one-way mirror, noting everything that was happening. The next several sessions were much like the first: Reichler fumbled for a connection, and David, fleetingly, showed that he might be making one. At night, the two men sat up for hours, discussing how to enhance this intensive one-on-one interaction. Eventually, they discovered that David had a sweet tooth, and they began using this to reinforce any sort of imitative behavior he demonstrated. Every time he stacked two blocks into a tower, Reichler placed a piece of candy on his tongue. When Reichler started asking him to name things—and make sounds other than his *ka-ga-ka* sound—they rewarded him again. David began to grasp this and soon was also naming objects appearing in pictures: dog, boy, tree, house. Unaware of it, Reichler, by instinct, was practicing a sort of behavior analysis.

Six months into it, they began to record the sessions on videotape. From then on, when the camera was on, Reichler had to work at keeping David within the frame. By this point, David appeared to like playing the games this grown-up doctor kept coming up with. In one videotaped session, Reichler, puffing on a thin cigar, crawled around on the floor pushing a toy car, making a low *vrooooom* sound. It was yet another small breakthrough when David did the same thing.

On another day, when David pointed directly at Reichler's cigar, Reichler treated the gesture like a question. "Yes," he said quickly, "that's my cigar," and took it out of his mouth to let David take a closer look. David, pointing again, echoed Reichler's last spoken syllable, posing it like a question: *"Gaaarr?"* This was new: David was inquiring. Reichler jumped on the moment. He took a hard drag on the cigar, and as they sat there cross-legged on the floor, face-to-face, he started letting out small puffs into the air between them.

David was entranced, watching the smoke curl in front of his eyes. When the wisps had melted away to nothing, a smile began to play on his face. Then, ever so quietly, he giggled.

"Give me your hands," Reichler commanded. Now this boy, who had rarely heeded the human voice, stuck his arms out. Reichler used his own big hands to guide David's fingers into the shape of a bowl. Bending over, he put his face down into the bowl and filled it with another, puffier cloud of smoke. David, surprised, snapped upright, snatched his hands back, and then broke out laughing. It had happened. For those few minutes in that small room, the boy with autism was locked onto his grown-up playmate, enjoying being engaged with a person.

Schopler and Reichler saw that David responded best when some sort of structure was imposed on the sessions, when it was clear that activities were for set amounts of time and in a set order. They also saw how useful it was to pay close attention to what interested David himself, as Reichler had done during the smoke game. It was obvious that David worked better with visual stimuli, as opposed to information communicated verbally. They began using picture cards increasingly as a language-building tool. Within six months, David went from having zero words to having a vocabulary of about 1,000 words.

One morning, when Mardy dropped David off for another session and asked Schopler if she could join him behind the one-way mirror, he saw no reason to refuse. That decision would be momentous.

Mardy, another mother drained by the strain of raising a child with autism, nevertheless began staying for every session. She took careful note of what Reichler was doing with David in the lab and began repeating it with him at home. More than that, she began to innovate, trying a new game, adding new pictures and words, or creating some sort of puzzle. Schopler encouraged this heartily. Without question, her direct involvement, and her constant reinforcement of the lab work, was magnifying its beneficial effects on David.

Those effects were profound. After two and a half years, David had become a five-year-old boy who could talk, relate to people, and take care of himself at an age-appropriate level. Most remarkably, he soon started attending a regular kindergarten. As far as Mardy was concerned, the two men at UNC had given her son a chance at a life that would have been impossible had he stayed on Stelazine or been put away in an institution.

David gave something to Schopler and Reichler too. In 1967, they turned the videotapes of his sessions into a twenty-four-minute-long film and applied for a grant from the National Institute of Mental Health (NIMH) to continue finding ways to help children with autism learn. Covering twenty months in David's life, the film concluded dramatically with David leading a group of kids at his regular kindergarten through a game of Simon Says. The grant came through, and the NIMH agreed to fund a five-year pilot study, based at UNC and overseen by Schopler.

The money gave Schopler the chance to hire a tiny staff and set up shop in a construction trailer—number 18—parked outside UNC's medical school, whose interior was cut up into cramped offices and compressed lab spaces. It was far from well appointed, but it did, at least, have electricity and a telephone.

The modest scale of the program's resources was counterbalanced by a decision Schopler made early and stuck to faithfully ever after: to recognize parents as a critical part of the therapeutic team. In some ways, it foreshadowed Ivar Lovaas's recognition that teaching parents to perform ABA multiplied that therapy's benefits, while helping to contain its dollar cost. But Schopler's commitment to parents ran deeper than seeing them as inexpensive and trainable adjuncts. Schopler called parents *co*-therapists, and he argued that professionals had as much to learn from them as the other way around. At autism conferences, he was the one professional known to be the most approachable, the one who, at the end of a long day of presentations and testimonials, would stay up late to talk with the mothers and fathers.

His commitment to involving parents would remain a mainstay of his work. In a 1971 article he published in the *Journal of Contemporary Psychotherapy,* called "Parents of Psychotic Children as Scapegoats," he publicly informed his colleagues that, in his program, parents "have been effectively engaged as co-therapists in the successful socialization of their child." The same year, in the first-ever issue of the *Journal of Autism and Childhood Schizophrenia,* he and Reichler wrote, "It is time to recognize the autistic child's parent as the integral agent to the solution of his child's problems rather than as having caused them."

This early and public stance on the side of parents, by a professional who was not an autism parent himself, established Schopler almost as the "anti-Bettelheim." In return, Schopler enjoyed a degree of trust and affection from the parents that became ballast for his reputation in the field. Parents would do anything to support Schopler in his work, which became especially important when his program, at one point, faced extinction. Two mothers in particular proved to be highly motivated and effective frontrunners in the efforts to save his program: Betty Camp and Mary Lou "Bobo" Warren. Betty was a special-education teacher married to a college dean. At a time when African American children were only rarely given an autism diagnosis—they were often labeled mentally retarded instead—their son, Norman V. Camp IV, or "Normie," was an exception. Like Connie Lapin out west, Betty had expended a great of deal of effort cajoling schools to take Normie, only to be told, after he had been enrolled a short while, that he was not welcome back. Normie, who had been unable to talk since the age of two and had a great deal of trouble staying focused on a task or sitting still at a desk, was not a true troublemaker. Though tall for his age, he was gentle, and usually calm and compliant. Betty was certain that he was capable of learning, so she pressed hard to get him into Schopler's program at UNC, where he was accepted in 1968.

Mary Lou Warren's son George, likewise, had no language. But unlike Normie, George was always getting into trouble, because he was a runner and a climber. Mary Lou, known to all by her childhood nickname "Bobo," was one of those mothers who lived in a state of constant sleep deprivation, and who had been treated badly in her experiences with the psychiatric profession. One of her most vivid memories of George's early years took place on Easter Sunday, 1965, when she and her invited guests—her husband's parents and other family—retired after dessert to the garden to watch her two other children, Duncan and MacCrae, hunt for eggs. It was a rare moment of family relaxation, of feeling "normal." Suddenly, her mother-in-law screamed and pointed up at the second story of the house. George, then three, was teetering high above the ground atop the narrow railing that enclosed an upstairs porch. With everyone watching in terror from below, he blithely jumped back onto the porch, just as his father arrived, breathless from running upstairs to rescue him.

Her other most vivid memory concerned the doctor at a major North Carolina teaching hospital who, on March 24, 1967—a date she could never forget—told her that George had "a very severe, atypical emotional disorder." He tersely explained that whatever the boy had, it was untreatable. Then he excused himself to go keep another appointment. On his way out, he told Bobo that she should send George away and "try to forget about him."

Bobo got George an appointment in Schopler's Trailer 18 in 1968, around the same time that Betty Camp took Normie there. George had recently begun hurting himself, and Bobo had no idea how to stop it. But the local paper had just run a story about autism, and she saw that the symptoms closely matched George's. The same article mentioned Schopler and his program at UNC, so she had called immediately. She was not sure what to make of Schopler when she met him and noted the caked-on mud on his boots. *Seriously? This guy is a psychologist?*

Still learning and improvising themselves, Schopler and Reichler gave Betty and Bobo detailed instructions on how to work on their own with their boys. Her first week, for example, Betty went home with half a page of typewritten instructions for repeating some of the sorting and shape-discrimination activities she had seen at Trailer 18. The instructions also called for her to design her own activities based on what she thought would work best for her son. The guidelines here were deliberately vague. "Aim for enjoyment for yourself as well as his," they said, "and keep it simple, structured and consistent once you get something that seems to be working."

Normie and George did not have the same results as David, Mardy's son who starred in Schopler and Reichler's movie. Though both remained at UNC for several years, they did not learn to speak or become functionally independent as adults. But both mothers considered the boys' time at UNC to have been the turning point in their children's lives, the place where both boys learned how to connect to others, a skill they might never have learned otherwise. Never much fixated on "curing" autism, Schopler believed that such hard-earned achievements were, in and of themselves, reason to celebrate.

Betty and Bobo certainly thought so. Ever grateful to Schopler and Reichler, they were quick to return the favor when the UNC program needed to be rescued too.

The NIMH had agreed in 1966 to fund the Child Research Project for only five years, on the principle that if the work proved itself worthy, some other funder would surface. In early 1970, at their regular monthly meeting with all the parents, Schopler and Reichler mentioned in passing that no other funder had yet been found, which put the program less than a year away from vanishing.

Normally, these meetings were about the therapy, what was working for different kids and what was not. But that night, Bobo Warren stood up and took the meeting in a different direction. The group, she insisted, had to figure out a way to keep the program going and growing. Heads nodded. Someone made a comment that they should launch a campaign to get the state of North Carolina to pay, which brought about a boisterous round of applause. The goal was set.

Over the next several months, in Trailer 18, the psychologist and the psychiatrist worked at drafting a law—a task for which neither Schopler nor Reichler had any prior experience. A friend of Bobo Warren's journalist husband, Frank, Senator Charles Larkins, had agreed to sponsor a bill on the parents' behalf, but only if Schopler and Reichler wrote most of it.

Knowing nothing about how politics worked, the two men, in their naïveté, wrote a bill that asked for everything they could possibly think of. They conceived of a broad, school-based, statewide program that would extend the services available in Trailer 18 to children and their families all across North Carolina. It would be run out of three large regional centers, which would be located in regular public schools. It would deliver a curriculum of structured activities in structured spaces but with a student-teacher ratio of nearly one-to-one. And it would allow for tailoring of the program to the strengths of each child—who would, henceforth, be considered a student, not a patient. Parents and home instruction would of course remain vital to the program. They even came up with a catchy acronym: TEACCH. It would stand for "Treatment and Education of Autistic and Related Communication Handicapped Children."

Larkins, after reading the nonlawyers' draft, was still in. The bill's language was burnished to make it more legislatively appropriate, and the parents started to organize a lobbying campaign. Bobo Warren raised funds, while Betty Camp and David's mother, Mardy, rallied fellow parents to unleash a flood of mail on the state legislature. They came up with talking points, which they circulated via a newsletter conceived by Bobo and put together by her husband, Frank, a newspaper reporter. Parents were urged to ask all their friends, and their friends' friends, to contact their representatives.

Schopler and Reichler, meanwhile, learned that North Carolina's commissioner of mental health was furious that two upstarts from UNC were writing legislation and encroaching on his territory. They were summoned to a meeting with him, where he warned them to back off. Rattled, the pair headed over to see Larkins, who immediately placed a call to the commissioner to talk him out of trying to sabotage the bill.

Passage of the bill was far from certain. Then Betty Camp and some other mothers came up with the idea of cooking breakfast for the entire membership of the legislature—bacon, ham, eggs, grits, coffee, and juice—in order to lure as many lawmakers as possible to a talk by Schopler and Reichler. They secured a church basement near the statehouse. The politicians were told that a lot of reporters would be present; the reporters were told that a lot of lawmakers would be present.

On the morning of the breakfast, the basement was filled with parents, their kids, lawmakers, and press. As each elected official entered the basement, he or she was guided to one of the seats next to one or another of the kids. A half dozen tables filled up with legislators, parents, and a bunch of boys and girls with autism.

Reichler led off the presentation, pointing out that the TEACCH idea was viewed favorably by the biggest name in autism—Dr. Leo Kanner of Johns Hopkins. He spoke a little about the condition, and about education. Mostly, he laid out an economic argument, pointing out that helping kids become more independent now could make them less dependent on the state later in life.

Suddenly, in mid-sentence, Reichler stopped speaking and stared, mouth agape, at the table where Bobo Warren's son George was sitting. At that very moment, George had just attempted to feed grits to the second-highest-ranking elected official in the state. Lt. Gov. Hoyt Taylor Jr. had arrived a little late to the breakfast and slipped quietly into the empty seat next to George. While his attention was focused up front, George had hit him just below the chin with a spoonful of grits. Bobo rushed to pull George back and started apologizing. Taylor smiled, insisting he was fine. He motioned for Reichler to carry on. When Reichler resumed, Taylor smoothly, unobtrusively, unknotted his tie and slipped it into his pocket.

It turned out to be a good omen. When Mary Lou bumped into her friend Senator Larkins the next day, he excitedly told her that the lieutenant governor had received the message: these kids and their families needed help. Taylor had promised Larkins "not to rest until something was done."

THE BILL AUTHORIZING and funding the program known as TEACCH was passed by the North Carolina state legislature on Wednesday, January 13, 1971. Signed into law by the governor, the act immediately turned North Carolina into an oasis of compassion, offering generous support services for families dealing with autism, in stark contrast to the rest of the United States. Over the next several years, the program expanded steadily. The number of classrooms would rise from ten at the start to approximately three hundred. UNC began offering TEACCH-centered internships and postdoctoral programs, and the program hosted visitors from all over the United States and around the world. As changes in legislation increasingly began to require US school districts to offer programs appropriate for children with autism, the TEACCH curriculum was among the most often adopted. TEACCH-based programs also became prominent in the UK, Israel, Singapore, and elsewhere around the world.

Schopler's eminence in the field increased to the point where he took over as editor of the *Journal of Autism and Childhood Schizophrenia* in 1974, the year Leo Kanner stepped down. He held that post for the next twenty-four years. At UNC, among the parents, he continued to be loved, held up as the model of what an autism professional should be. Among his colleagues, his opinion carried enormous weight. His conviction that the children were educable, and that parents were part of that process, became conventional wisdom, across the field. Thus, it was hardly surprising when, in Los Angeles, Lovaas also started using parents as therapists.

The two men did not, as it turned out, ever agree on much else. Schopler in the mid-1980s, was known and liked everywhere. Lovaas, however, had a talent for making enemies, and was not so well-known. But that changed dramatically for Lovaas in 1987, when he published an article updating the autism world on what he had been up to.

The results were stunning, and they made him famous. They also made him a new, and lifelong, enemy: Eric Schopler.

22

47 PERCENT

On March 10, 1987, Ivar Lovaas made national news for the first time since his appearance in *LIFE* more than two decades earlier. That morning, the front page of the *New York Times* science section ran a piece entitled "Researcher Reports Progress Against Autism." The headline was small, but the news was huge.

Lovaas, according to the *Times,* had figured out a way "to transform a large proportion of autistic children into apparently normal children"—with a success rate of 47 percent. Lovaas described what the kids were like after he worked with them to *Times* reporter Daniel Goleman: "If you met them now that they are teenagers, you would never know there was anything wrong with them."

The 1987 study stands as a landmark. It covered work that began at UCLA in 1970, when Lovaas had launched what he called the "Young Autism Project." It was a program delivering Lovaas-style ABA to children at radically young ages, in extremely high doses. Lovaas had taken nineteen children between two and three years old and exposed them to at least forty hours per week of the kind of chair-bound, knee-to-knee-with-an-adult therapy that was one of the hallmarks of his approach. The kids were put through hundreds of different exercises tens of thousands of times. Rewards, a cookie or a cracker, came when they performed as commanded: *Raise arms! Touch cup! Give doll! Take book!*

Unwanted behavior, when it didn't yield to the persuasion of one of those rewards, brought punishment. Hitting oneself, for example, or letting one's gaze lock onto the spinning fan in the corner of the room, could provoke a loud, sharp *No!* Other times, Lovaas told the *Times* genially, "We give the kids an occasional smack on the butt if they get too far out of hand."

Lovaas was winding down his use of punishment in these years—there were no electric shocks, no slaps in the face. Still, it was a relentless regimen, during which, according to Lovaas's own report on the research, the process persisted through "almost all the subjects' waking hours, 365 days a year." Two full years of each child's life were devoted to this; some went even longer.

For nine of them—47 percent of the group of nineteen—it was well worth it, according to Lovaas. All nine achieved "normal functioning," by a variety of measures, including a battery of tests of their social skills and intellectual levels. Indeed, their IQs spiked upward, by as much as 25 to 30 points in some cases. All had been accepted at and survived regular first-grade classes, rather than special-education classes.

Lovaas reported that one of the children had achieved a new IQ of 130 and now, as a teenager, aspired to a career in meteorology. This young man, and the other kids who succeeded, did so by learning how to learn, according to Lovaas. ABA had forced them to pay attention, to imitate, to engage.

Lovaas avoided the term "cured," which would have implied he had repaired whatever might be autism's underlying organic cause. Instead, he said that the kids were "recovered," meaning that their autistic behaviors had been eliminated. For all practical purposes, it sounded like nearly the same thing as a cure, which was the very outcome he had warned parents not even to hope for six years earlier when he came out with *The ME Book*.

The key, Lovaas hypothesized, had been the intensity of the treatment in the Young Autism Project—its long duration and the high number of hours of therapy per week. To be sure, the ten children who did not achieve "normal functioning" had been exposed to the same intensity, but without "recovery." Yet they had made progress nevertheless, certainly more than a control group of children who had been given only ten hours per week of ABA.

The bottom line did not need much spelling out: ABA worked, the more of it the better, and a whole lot of it held out a nearly 50/50 possibility of achieving the previously impossible.

BERNARD RIMLAND COULD barely get off the phone the day the *Times* story broke. Parents were calling from all over the country. A second wave hit when CBS News reported the findings. Everyone was asking him the same two questions: "Is it true?" and "Should we get our child to UCLA?"

Rimland was just then launching a quarterly newsletter, *The Autism Research Review International* (ARRI), to track relevant research from around the world. Rimland reported the 47 percent breakthrough on page 2 without commentary. On page 3, however, he published an editorial that offered his own verdict. "The Lovaas study," he declared, "is credible."

But as Rimland knew, Lovaas and his claim were already under attack. Skeptics were speaking up all over the autism world, and the criticism was aggressive. "One prominent professional," Rimland reported, "went so far as to call Lovaas another Bruno Bettelheim." This, of course, was the ultimate slur, "implying that what Lovaas had done is destructive to autistic children and their families."

Rimland did not identify the expert in question, but it was not hard to guess. Eric Schopler had never much liked Ivar Lovaas. Now it was war.

SCHOPLER AND LOVAAS had first bumped into each other years earlier, at a small autism symposium held at the University of Indiana. That year, 1968, autism was still a research backwater. The twenty-six people in attendance, including three from Britain, comprised almost everybody working in the field. The TEACCH program did not yet exist, and Lovaas was still using electric shock therapy.

Schopler gave a presentation that harkened back to his dissertation work on sensory patterns. Lovaas updated the group on what he was doing with applied behavior analysis. After Lovaas concluded his points, he said something that Schopler took as a swipe at his presentation. "Why do we have to talk about these children as having neurological problems?" he recalled Lovaas as saying. Lovaas then argued that any normal child locked up in a bare room, with no one to talk to, would soon be exhibiting self-stimulating behaviors—just like any child with autism. "Even my own son," Lovaas supposedly went on to say. "So let's not talk about autistics, but just about autistic behavior."

To Schopler, this was preposterous, to posit no meaningful difference between a normal boy deprived of his toys for a while and children like those he was now treating in North Carolina, who were disabled for life. His opinion of Lovaas plummeted.

Over the years, at other conferences, Schopler hardened his disapproving view of Lovaas's character, watching him give talks and then skip out when other people got their time onstage. He often observed that Lovaas showed up "with a different woman at each conference" and spent no time with the parents. "He would just stay for his presentation and leave."

In the second issue of his ARRI newsletter, Rimland published a letter in which Schopler expressed that he was "dismayed to read [Rimland's] uncritical reporting" of the new Lovaas claim. He charged Rimland with repeating the same mistake the news media were making with their "exaggerated and misleading . . . coverage" of Lovaas's assertion of "recovery."

In the letter, Schopler claimed that Lovaas's study should not be trusted and laid out a catalog of problems with it. The measurements Lovaas used to gauge the children's progress were invalid. His control groups were not soundly constructed. Most critically, the group that included all those supposedly "recovered" kids was packed with "high-functioning" children to start with.

In no other arena did the phrase "high-functioning" constitute fighting words. But every autism expert knew what Schopler was implying: that Lovaas had stacked the deck to produce the results he wanted. First, such kids were already closer to "normal" to begin with. Second, it was accepted that high-functioning kids with autism, especially kids with language, nearly always made better net progress than those who were lower functioning and unspeaking. According to

Schopler, Lovaas's kids were anything but a random sample, representative of the full range of autism.

Rimland gave Lovaas space to respond. "We believe that Dr. Schopler is mistaken in his analysis of the study," Lovaas wrote. Then he refuted everything Schopler had said was wrong with his paper, point by point. He dwelled especially on the suggestion that he had cherry-picked high-functioning kids to tilt the outcome. Rather, he said, children were chosen for his study depending on whether he had therapists free to work with them at the point where they entered his program.

The battle between the two men, instead of dying down, would only ramp up from here. Over the next seven to eight years, their feud went through round after round of attack and counterattack, with personal smears, threats of lawsuits, and attempts to build alliances with other researchers against one another. Just as remarkable was both men's preferred setting for their sniping: the pages of various academic journals. These publications had lead times of several months, which was one reason the battle dragged on for so long. It could take half a year to take a punch, and then just as long to jab back again.

Lovaas's side was sometimes represented by people who appeared to be proxies, handling the attack on Schopler on his behalf. Schopler, for his part, made a concerted but unsuccessful effort to forge a coalition of well-known autism figures who would condemn Lovaas openly. Lovaas, on his side, dug deep into Schopler's early writing, looking for dirt. He unearthed an early Schopler paper reporting his one-on-one work with a five-year-old girl, lifting quotes from it in a way that unfairly hinted at an improper sexual relationship. Schopler was happy to frequently remind people that Lovaas had used a cattle prod on five-year-olds.

None of this was doing much to serve science. Unquestionably, Schopler was the main instigator, keeping the feud alive when Lovaas seemed willing to let it die. His personal disapproval of Lovaas and their professional competition for both the affection of the parents and the scientific limelight drove a good deal of the feud. But associates of Schopler's also thought his fundamental grievance was a sincere belief that Lovaas had played fast and loose with the scientific truth and that people would get hurt as a result.

A book chapter in which Schopler and his deputy, Gary Mesibov, chastised researchers who "foster unrealistic expectations and promises for improvement," was so clearly aimed at Lovaas that, once again, Lovaas threatened a libel suit. Lovaas also tried to turn the "unrealistic expectation" argument back on Schopler, bemoaning "the consensus of researchers that little can be done to help autistic children."

In fact, however, it was not just Schopler who questioned Lovaas's results. UCLA psychiatrist Edward Ritvo, another respected authority on autism, was heard complaining that a "lot of that stuff comes out under the label of UCLA is unfortunately disseminated widely and untrue." Michael Rutter, the UK's first professor of child psychiatry, as unimpeachable a voice as there was in autism, also expressed doubts about "claims of a cure [that] run counter to both clinical experience and what might be expected on a basis from prevailing theories." For Lovaas, too, a main problem was that no one else, anywhere, was going to be able to replicate his results quickly—if at all.

Lovaas's love of the limelight was catching up to him. He had never used the word "cure," nor would he; that term had no relevance in the ABA universe. But the media kept the talk of "cure" alive, their preferred translation for "recovered"—a word that Lovaas did use. As critics piled on, Lovaas stopped using even that term, substituting a more precise but less dramatic formulation: the kids had achieved "normal levels of intellectual and educational functioning."

To an ordinary person, that represented a big difference. The word "recovery" painted an image of previously silent and isolated kids becoming ordinary, trading baseball cards, and horsing around on the playground. "Normal levels" instead only suggested kids getting better at doing math and standing in line to pick up their own lunch. In truth, such achievements would be life-changing for any child previously incapable of them, but they were not the same thing as not having autism anymore.

When Lovaas published a follow-up study on the same group of kids in 1993 with colleagues John McEachin and Tristram Smith, he was a great deal more cautious in the tone he took. This time, there was no boasting to the *New York Times.* Yet his results were as impressive as the first time around—better, even. All but one of the children he had called "normal" in 1987 had held on to their gains in intellectual and educational functioning, and they continued to do better intellectually and socially than the nineteen kids in his original control group. Even Eric Schopler's trusted deputy Gary Mesibov tipped his hat upon hearing the update, conceding that Lovaas had confirmed "that behavioral interventions are effective in the long run."

But Mesibov also raised the perennial question: *Compared to what?* Lovaas's inability to answer that question mattered. ABA already faced serious obstacles to its acceptance. Its use of punishment remained controversial, as did the money it cost and the time it demanded. The reality was that Lovaas's method was still purely experimental. In terms of clinical trials, the intense effort represented by the Young Autism Project was something one scientist had tried one time in one lab. That was not good enough for science, which always demands that experimental results be replicable. Some other researcher—at best several of them at several sites—had to run the Lovaas experiment all over again to see if they came up with similar results.

Even one of Lovaas's most ardent supporters, fellow behaviorist Richard Foxx, chided Lovaas about this, writing that unless he successfully replicated his findings, Lovaas would be denied the full-throated standing ovation that was quite possibly his due. Foxx urged Lovaas and his partners to do everything possible to facilitate an independent research group to run his experiment again. Absent such replication, Foxx predicted, Lovaas's work would remain stuck in "a kind of scientific limbo."

Without question, Schopler's attack on the Lovaas ABA "story" succeeded for a time in raising doubts, lowering the excitement that Lovaas had aroused, and drawing parents' attention away from what he dismissed as another "mindless fad." To be sure, Lovaas still had disciples, parents and graduate students, mostly concentrated around Los Angeles, but acceptance of the Lovaas Model did not suddenly take off after his landmark study of 1987.

TEACCH, on the other hand, did. Even a close Lovaas collaborator acknowledged this. In a review of what methodologies were in use in the autism universe in the 1990s, Tristram Smith wrote that Schopler's program, "implemented throughout the United States and Europe, has been the most influential special education program for children with autism."

Richard Foxx was right. As the 1990s began, Lovaas's answer to autism, his version of ABA, was in limbo. Then a mother named Catherine Maurice wrote a book called *Let Me Hear Your Voice.*

23

LOOK AT ME

ON A MIDWINTER AFTERNOON IN 1988, WHILE TAKING THE elevator down to the first floor in Whittier Hall at Columbia University, a master's degree candidate named Bridget Taylor overheard two other students mentioning a name she recognized. "It's hanging in the job placement office," one of them was saying. "They're looking for somebody Lovaas-trained." When the elevator doors opened, Taylor took the turn toward Room 120, where Columbia's Teachers College posted employment opportunities for current students. She found the notice quickly, tacked up on a bulletin board: "Seeking a practitioner of Lovaas-based intervention." She kept reading. The work would be with a child in Manhattan, and the family was ready to pay $60 per hour. That was *six* times what she had been getting working with kids with autism the past few years. Taylor ripped the notice off the board, pocketed it, and went looking for a phone booth.

BRIDGET TAYLOR GREW up with disability in her own family. Her brother John, younger by two years, was born in 1966 and diagnosed with Down syndrome. When his parents brought him home—resisting the pressure to have him institutionalized—he was the fourth child in the household. He and Bridget, now the second youngest, shared a bedroom and quickly became inseparable.

Only two when John joined the family, Taylor did not see her baby brother as different. In a fundamental way, that never really changed, even as they grew older together. She adapted readily to the duty that falls to every older sibling to "show the ropes" to a younger kid—the essentials like how to climb a tree, or keep out of sight in hide-and-seek. It became second nature for Bridget to slow down when John had trouble following, or to figure out some other way to spell things out for him. In this manner, unimpressed with her brother's diagnosis of Down syndrome, she actually taught him to read when he was five and she was seven.

That is not to say they never had their battles. John, as he grew older, became obsessive about certain things, like music. He would lie on the floor beside the radio, listening for hours. He also had a habit, once Taylor moved into a bedroom of her own, of standing outside her door and echoing one word over and over again relentlessly. She couldn't stand this, but screaming at him—her first response—only seemed to encourage the behavior. One day, though, in a stroke of early behaviorist instinct—or just sisterly pique—she pulled the knob off the radio he loved listening to. She refused to put it back until the echoing stopped. She had figured it out: rather than reward him with her attention, she would keep quiet and use an aversive experience to shut him up. Gradually, John seemed to forget about how much he had once enjoyed repeating himself, and the behavior stopped for good.

In the fourth grade, she already knew that she wanted to be "a psychologist that helps families," as she wrote in a school essay, though she wasn't entirely sure what psychology entailed beyond that. As a teenager, when her friends were taking summer jobs in restaurants and clothing stores, she always looked for opportunities to work with kids, especially those with challenges like learning problems. Her high school offered her the chance to take advanced placement courses in psychology, and she paid for college by working two related jobs—at a preschool for mentally challenged children and as a substitute support aide taking shifts in group homes.

In 1983, as a nineteen-year-old psychology major, she was recruited for a new program starting up in Ridgewood, New Jersey, a short ride over the George Washington Bridge from Manhattan. It was an autism program—Appropriate Living for the Autistic—that was designed to give parents an occasional two- or three-hour "respite" from their kids, while the children were placed with a trustworthy person capable of handling them. This would mark the first time Bridget would encounter the condition.

Before starting, she and a group of other young hires were given a day of training, led by a young PhD candidate at Rutgers University named Carolyn Bruey—later the author of several books on autism—who showed up for the session with *The ME Book* under her arm. Over the next several hours, Bruey walked the group through the concepts of shaping, reinforcement, prompting, and extinction, giving examples of how to break complex skills into small component parts. They were taught that rewards for correct performance had to be delivered within a split second to have any impact. They also practiced honing the language they would use during sessions with the kids, to an unnatural-sounding bare minimum. "Please hand me that ball," for example, would be pared back to "Give ball."

It was a lot to take in for one day, but to Taylor, it was energizing. She had not realized there was such a specific and well-researched set of tools to use with children with autism, whom she had heard were extremely difficult to reach. She got her own copy of *The ME Book* and wore out its pages learning its contents.

The first child she encountered in the program was a three-year-old named Jeffrey, who was unspeaking, uncooperative, and easily upset. He hated the feeling of clothing on his skin and would strip himself bare whenever given the chance, no matter where he was, regardless of the weather.

Jeffrey had been attending the Douglass Developmental Disabilities Center at Rutgers for some time. But now, after school, Taylor extended his day with outings to the park, where, with no one looking over her shoulder, she began trying out some of what she had learned from Bruey and *The ME Book.* That first day, she broke up a cookie into small pieces and, using the techniques she had just learned, taught Jeffrey to sit when asked. Taylor knew this was something he had never done before, so she was both astonished and delighted to discover that he liked cookies and was, apparently, willing to sit when told in order to get a piece of one.

From there, she got Jeffrey to sit on a swing—also something brand-new—and then to use his legs to get himself moving, and, finally, to experience the full first-time pleasure of riding up to the sky all by himself. Soon she had him working puzzles and playing simple games. When she led him home after every session out together, she would throw him onto his bed over and over, which he loved. All this, they accomplished without the use of any punishment whatsoever.

Jeffrey's mother's reaction was similar to Taylor's, with gratitude layered on top of delight and astonishment. It was the first time she could recall seeing a "professional"—someone from outside the family—pay real attention to her son. Soon other parents in the program were booking Taylor for private sessions with their children outside of the established program hours.

Then she was fired.

It seems her popularity had led to some organizational strife, beginning when the agency was besieged by parents demanding that "this Bridget girl" be reassigned to their child. Taylor was called in and ordered to drop the private work, or else. She refused. And then she was out. In her view, she quit.

For the next few years, while working toward her master's in education at Columbia University, Taylor continued working with families on a private basis. She had become a complete convert to applied behavior analysis, though she still found that few people she knew had even heard of ABA. Fewer still were familiar with anyone named Lovaas.

THE JOB NOTICE had been posted at Columbia and a few other locations by a New York mother who lived in one of Manhattan's poshest neighborhoods. Affluent and well educated—with a PhD in French literature and literary criticism—Catherine Maurice (a pseudonym) would later describe herself as feeling lost and frightened that early winter of 1988. Weeks earlier, just before Christmas, she had given birth to a boy, Michel. That made three children at home now, all under the age of four years old. But it was not the burden of managing all three at once that weighed on her. A child specialist had recently informed her and her husband, Marc, that their middle child, their only girl, Anne-Marie, had autism.

Maurice had already sensed something was not right with Anne-Marie. Not quite two years old, the girl had given her parents the impression of slipping away with each month that followed her first birthday. At one point, she had built up to a vocabulary of about ten words, including "Hi, Daddy," but then she stopped using all of them. She was ignoring the sound of her mother's voice and not even looking up when her name was called. She did not play with toys in any normal way. Given a Big Bird doll, she used its beak to touch points on the wall. Most recently, she had begun banging her head on the floor during long stretches when she did nothing but cry inconsolably.

When Anne-Marie was diagnosed with autism, Maurice was terrified for her.

Everything she read told her that autism was a lifelong condition and that there was no such thing as recovery. She was offered play therapy for Anne-Marie, which was much in vogue at the time, though it had little track record as being successful for autism. She also tried something called "holding therapy," which involved the two of them keeping a close embrace for long periods of time.

Then, one morning, her sister called from Chicago, where a day earlier, her husband happened to glance at a slightly dated copy of *Psychology Today* in the waiting room of his dentist's office. Flipping through it, he had come across an article called "Saving Grace," which told the story of an astounding breakthrough in autism treatment documented at UCLA, where children were actually recovering from autism. *Recovered*—that's how the magazine put it. It was the very thing Maurice had read was impossible. But her sister was telling her that the impossible was being done by someone named Ivar Lovaas.

Maurice immediately called Lovaas's clinic in California for an appointment. An empathetic staffer named Joanne broke it to Maurice gently that, at the present time, the clinic had no open slots. Ever since the *Psychology Today* story, they had been overwhelmed with inquiries and were fully booked for months to come. But Joanne mentioned that Maurice could order *The ME Book,* and that the accompanying videotapes would guide her in setting up a home-based ABA program, while using clinic staff as long-distance consultants.

When the package arrived, Maurice and her husband sat down

together to watch the tapes. They both found them disturbing, with their scenes of kids forced into repetitions of meaningless-seeming actions, like raising their arms over their heads. The book unsettled Maurice too. It referred to using spanking and sharp reprimands to keep the kids focused. Never, she thought to herself, would she subject Anne-Marie to a regimen of such punishment. Still, she and Marc talked it over, and they decided to run an ABA program out of their apartment.

Then Bridget Taylor walked into their lives. She phoned the very day she found the job listing. When she arrived for the interview, she struck Maurice as perhaps too young to know much about teaching a child with autism. Taylor sold herself, however, the moment Maurice mentioned the name Lovaas and produced her brand-new copy of *The ME Book.* Taylor broke in to explain that she knew all about the UCLA work and told Maurice that she had been using the methods Lovaas developed for several years already, though with some modifications. She did not, for example, use aversives. Maurice hired Taylor on the spot.

Look at me. Those were the words Bridget Taylor used to kick off the first of hundreds of hours of discrete trial sessions for Anne-Marie. In *The ME Book,* "look at me" is lesson one, based on the premise that eye contact with the teacher assured attention, and that attention was a prerequisite to learning. That first day, Taylor sat with a weeping, struggling Anne-Marie, who appeared deeply unhappy about this stranger making her sit back down whenever she tried to stand up to leave. Taylor sat in front of her repeating the same phrase—"Look at me"—over and over again. If Anne-Marie looked at her, she got a Goldfish cracker and a smile from Taylor, who called out delightedly, "Good looking, Anne-Marie!"

Maurice, watching, was torn. Her motherly instinct was to intervene, to rescue Anne-Marie from a situation that was obviously making her miserable, day after day. In the first few weeks of it, she seriously considered pulling the plug and telling Taylor not to come back.

But week by week, slowly at first, Maurice could see that Anne-

Marie was beginning to connect in new ways to the world around her. First, Anne-Marie began looking at Taylor. Then, she was looking at her mother. She was learning to point, and to hug, and to use words again. A turning point was reached when Anne-Marie's steady advances started to accelerate. More words came, more eye contact, and then, one day, when her mother was in the kitchen fixing a bottle for her baby brother, Anne-Marie wandered in, calling out "Mommy, Mommy"—truly seeking out her mother.

A short time after that, once the ABA had been proceeding for several months, her parents took Anne-Marie to one of the specialists who had confirmed her autism diagnosis at the start of this journey. The doctor was astonished at the progress the little girl had made and offered his opinion that in all the basic measurable skill levels—"in communication, in social behavior, in motor skills, in daily living skills"—Anne-Marie "has moved into the clearly normal range."

In essence, after approximately half a year of intensive ABA, plus other therapies including speech and occupational therapy, Anne-Marie's autistic behaviors were in retreat. Evaluations conducted roughly another six months later confirmed this, while allowing for the persistence of a few quite minor trace elements of autistic personality, referred to as "residua"—essentially, leftovers. But in the important ways—in her connection to people, and her ability to reason, to learn, and to grow independently—Anne-Marie was one of the "recovered." Thanks to Bridget Taylor and the team of therapists she led—and the methods in *The ME Book*—Anne-Marie had joined Lovaas's 47 percent.

And then, amazingly, Taylor and the team did it a second time—a second child, and a second recovery, in the same family. Just as Anne-Marie was shedding her autism diagnosis, her baby brother, Michel, was given one. Like his sister before him, Michel had first acquired words as a toddler and then quickly lost them while appearing to detach from the people around him. After a series of evaluations, doctors told Maurice it was definite: Michel's behaviors added up to autism.

While devastated by this, Maurice was anything but defeated. Taylor started all over again. More therapists were brought in and trained to perform ABA with Michel. As before, Maurice also employed a speech therapist. Michel proved, in some ways, more difficult than his sister, as he was given to sudden and intense tantrums. Yet, once again, the program produced spectacular results. Michel, evaluated again after more than a year of treatment, joined his sister in the ranks of the "recovered."

In 1991, Catherine Maurice began writing an account of what her family had gone through, and what ABA had achieved for her children. To be sure, other individual writers before her had managed to reshape the narrative of autism completely, for better or for worse. Bruno Bettelheim had told the bestselling story of mother blaming. Bernard Rimland's book took down Bettelheim and his theories. Clara Park's 1966 *The Siege,* the first mother's memoir, had inspired many young people, including Bridget Taylor, to enter the field, and also helped build a parent community. *The ME Book,* of course, launched many a would-be ABA therapist onto the scene.

But the book Maurice produced, in terms of its impact on the autism world, was in a class by itself. Maurice, it turned out, was a superbly good writer, and more important, she knew how to inspire hope. Published in 1993, it was called *Let Me Hear Your Voice.* Its influence would be felt in homes, in schools, in research laboratories, and ultimately, in courtrooms across the country.

Its subtitle captured the reason why: "A Family's Triumph over Autism." Triumph equals recovery—this was a recovery story. To be sure, Maurice took pains to put her family's experience with ABA in a realistic perspective. She was careful to make clear that ABA was no cure and that recovery was not guaranteed. She portrayed ABA as costly, lengthy, exhausting, and, most important, unpredictable in its effects on any particular child. She was firm on that point: ABA was a gamble in terms of its outcome.

But to the readers of the book, Bridget Taylor and ABA couldn't be a mere fluke—their techniques had resulted in two recoveries in one family. When *Let Me Hear Your Voice* hit the market, it was all autism families could talk about. Immediately, Maurice's book jumped to the top of the list of books that autism parents had to read. It became the book pediatricians recommended to parents on the day their child was diagnosed. It was a bestseller at autism conferences everywhere, making its author the great explainer of Lovaas ABA to the autism "masses."

Lovaas himself even provided the book its afterword. Wrapped as it was inside a genuine love story, Maurice's ABA memoir endowed Lovaas's method with the extra layers of respectability it had always been lacking. Bernard Rimland, meanwhile, wrote the book's foreword, where he praised the power and honesty of Maurice's writing and made a prediction.

"*Let Me Hear Your Voice,*" he pronounced, "will send a powerful and long overdue message to parents and professionals alike."

It was a prophecy fulfilled both immediately and enduringly, but at the cost of much strife and anguish.

24

FROM COURTROOM TO CLASSROOM

On June 19, 1996, Lilli Mayerson arrived at a branch office of the Westchester County Department of Health. The division for children with special needs was located on Bradhurst Avenue in the town of Hawthorne, New York. Gary, Lilli's husband, was tied up in business meetings in Denver, but no one had wanted to risk postponing the appointment. Time suddenly mattered too much.

A few weeks earlier, Lilli's son had been evaluated, at county expense, by a developmental psychologist who had recommended "immediate and intense intervention" for autism. Hearing this, Lilli and Gary saw only one option. Every passing day cost their son his future. He needed ABA right away.

The county had assigned the Mayersons a case coordinator named SueAnn Galante, who would lead the session that day. The county, as mandated by law, would present a treatment plan for the year ahead, which required the parents' signature. After pleasantries were exchanged and introductions made with other staffers consulted in her son's case, they handed Lilli the paper on which Galante had sketched out what the county had come up with.

What she read stunned her.

She and Gary had been expecting, based on their own research into ABA, that the county would be offering upward of twenty-five, thirty, possibly forty hours of that therapy for their boy.

The numbers on the sheet didn't even come close.

One and a half hours of speech therapy per month. Two hours

monthly of something called family therapy. Forty-five minutes of occupational therapy per week. And eight hours of ABA a week.

Lilli Mayerson refused to sign.

A few days later, Galante took a phone call from a livid Gary Mayerson. He called the department's offer "despicable" and told Galante that he was a lawyer, one who knew that parents all over the country were suing for ABA funding and winning. Mayerson's message was clear: unless his son was offered at least twenty hours of ABA per week, the county would have a fight on its hands, with a motivated father who knew his way around a courtroom.

The era of ABA litigation had begun.

THE FEW YEARS that followed Catherine Maurice's book saw a profound shift in how parents approached the "experts" in their lives. Previously, most parents had shown deference to doctors, school principals, psychiatrists, and other professionals, not wanting to risk alienating these power-wielders whose support they needed to help their kids. It was one thing to be persistent and assertive, but being pushy and aggressive could backfire.

That changed in the 1990s, when autism parents acquired a new weapon: the law. The passage of the Individuals with Disabilities Education Act in 1990 had updated the fifteen-year-old Education for All Handicapped Children Act, which had mandated that public schools deliver an appropriate education for all children with disabilities who wanted it. The 1990 version, for the first time, named *autism* as a specific category of disability. This was pivotal. From then on, schools were required to offer programs specifically tailored to the needs of kids with autism. If parents did not agree with the offering, the law gave them the right to sue.

There had always been education-based lawsuits. Parents had sued the schools to change how their kids were disciplined or to start a girls' basketball squad. Only rarely had autism education been at issue up until now. But in the 1990s, schools were hit with a wave of "Lovaas cases," as legal scholars tagged them. ABA funding had become "a legally hot topic" and "a high stakes issue for both parents and schools," in the words of legal and medical writers. One analysis showed the proportion of all special-education litigation centering on autism was now ten times the actual proportion of special-ed students with autism. In other words, autism parents had begun disproportionately seeking legal recourse to get more ABA for their kids.

No one relished these battles. They were corrosive to the school-parent relationship, and there was something demoralizing about the prospect of seeing a school system's budget drained to pay legal fees, with both sides putting so much effort into defeating the other. One family employed an expert witness for their lawsuit who ended up billing taxpayers $135,832.67 for his expertise. On the other side, a mother and father in Oswego County, New York, showed up for a hearing to get ABA funding, only to find that the school district had lined up seventeen witnesses to testify against spending the money. That schools would go to such extraordinary lengths to fight against parents—parents of children with disabilities, at that—showed them in a most unflattering light. Parents who bought in early to Lovaas's ABA—who went online and read the stories of a 47 percent "recovery" rate—could conceive of no legitimate reason for schools not to fund it. When their requests for the therapy met official resistance—as they almost always did—it was a short leap from stunned disbelief to the suspicion that something rotten was happening inside the system. Gary Mayerson actually used an even more extreme word later when he talked about "the banality of evil" he saw himself fighting when he took on Westchester County.

Plenty of parents felt the same way. A parental movement as much as a therapy, ABA now had its own mantra, which showed up in online forums, in speeches at ABA conferences, and in brochures: "ABA is the only scientifically-based, medically-backed treatment that is proven effective." To frantic parents, for whom time was critical, the truth of the statement was self-evident: their children needed lots of ABA immediately. Parents could see no valid argument to the contrary.

But quite a few counterarguments existed, left over from both the antiaversive debate and the doubts about Lovaas's methodology that had been raised by a wide array of his colleagues over the years. In professional circles, as of the early 1990s, what Lovaas had been doing in his UCLA lab for the previous three decades still appeared, to many, to be extreme, unproven, and slightly fanatical. This alone gave school districts reason to question it.

There were other arguments as well. American education relies on professional credentialing—degrees in social work, teaching licenses, and so forth—but Lovaas's program called for the therapy to be carried out by teams of high school and college students who would work in an autistic child's home. This raised the major issue of quality control. To many in the special-education bureaucracy, it seemed irresponsible, possibly even dangerous, to fund thinly supervised, unprofessional first-time therapists working offsite with vulnerable children.

Indeed, in the first few years after Maurice's book appeared, more experienced ABA practitioners had become concerned about the sudden flood of novice, lightly trained therapists entering the field. Slowly they started to establish stricter standards and certifications, but by the time the Mayersons asked for ABA, these were in place in only a handful of states. New York was not one of them.

School administrators also knew what ABA would cost: up to $50,000 per child, to fund a team of teachers devoted just to that one child. That could only come at the cost of cutting back somewhere else in their budget, probably in some program—art, music, physical education—that served the entire student body. On top of misgivings about Lovaas's approach in the first place, this seemed a high price to pay for what might be just another fad treatment. Besides, many districts across the country were already running autism programs that came with certified personnel who worked inside school walls and did not threaten to bust the education budget. Some of these were based on North Carolina's TEACCH program or other variations that the schools knew and, more important, trusted.

AND SO, ACROSS the country, the battle increased in fury. At first, it seemed certain that the parents were the disadvantaged side. As litigants, they were taking on an opponent—school districts—that came with attorneys already on their payrolls and contingency funds to cover legal costs. Under the terms of a 1986 amendment to the IDEA law, parents, on the other hand, could only expect state reimbursement if they won their cases. If they lost, they would have to live with those legal bills forever.

Parents faced another built-in disadvantage. Courts had a tendency, in education litigation, to defer to professional educators. When the issue was the actual content of the curriculum, judges, as a rule, did not want to be in the position of telling schools what or how to teach children. Given all this, when the "Lovaas cases" started to hit the system, the die seemed cast for the schools to win and for the parents to lose.

But something surprising began to happen starting around 1994. The schools started losing. Parents did not *always* win, and even if they did, they did not get everything they wanted. But it was a clear trend: families were starting to win. Before 1996, they were winning more than half the cases brought to court. By 1996, it was 75 percent. Each win emboldened more parents to take the risk, especially as they saw the result. More kids like theirs were getting ABA services funded as schools complied with judges' orders. In Monroe County, New York, for example, one parents group, which in 1996 had reported only four families' kids getting ABA, was able to boast that more than thirty families were getting it just a year later. Indeed, due to the same group's pressure, every single school district in the 1,300 square miles surrounding Rochester, New York, was funding ABA for at least one child in 1997.

Suddenly, schools and county health departments were in a defensive crouch, sometimes spending more to fight parents than if they had just funded an ABA program in the first place. It was a bad position to be in. And it ensured that when Gary Mayerson made that phone call to his son's caseworker, SueAnn Galante, in June of 1996, there was some muscle behind his threat. He was a lawyer, and he was not bluffing.

Mayerson's call that morning had created quite a stir. Galante, who was furiously taking notes while Mayerson yelled in her ear, had hung up and immediately hurried down the hall to the office of her boss, Susanne Kaplan, who held the post of Director of Services for Children with Disabilities. Kaplan was not especially familiar with the Mayerson case, as she generally left individual program details to her caseworkers, trusting their expertise to create appropriate plans for the children under their purview.

But after hearing what Mayerson had said to Galante, Kaplan decided to contact her department's attorney to ask how she and her staff should talk to the Mayersons from now on. They were still responsible for getting services for this child, but if this furious father was serious about suing, then anything her staff said could become ammunition to be used against them.

Kaplan, Galante, and two other staffers worked together on a memo to the county attorney, laying out their concerns. Galante would later describe it as "a law alert." They outlined the program the Mayersons' boy had been offered versus what the parents wanted for him. They made sure to mention that Mayerson himself was "savvy legally" and repeated his remark about parents successfully suing school districts all over the United States to get ABA.

Having to worry about lawyers and lawsuits was not what any of these women had in mind when they went into special ed. Certainly not Susanne Kaplan, who had been in the field longer than any of them—and who had no clue, the moment she put her name on that memo, that she was stepping into a storm.

DESPITE HOW SHE would soon be depicted, Susanne Kaplan was not known to be an enemy to parents, or in any way derelict in her duty to deliver services to children with disabilities. Her attainment of a middle-management position in Westchester, overseeing early intervention program delivery, was more a testament to her long tenure in the field than to any sort of politicking personality. Kaplan was, if anything, a mild-mannered, taciturn person, who had entered the disabilities field twenty-seven years earlier as a kindergarten teacher. She later earned a master's degree in special ed and moved over into administration, the previous ten years of which she'd spent with Westchester

County. She was studious in affect, nonconfrontational in manner, and utterly lacking, by her own admission, a thick skin.

Neither was Kaplan an enemy of applied behavior analysis. In 1994, she had started talking to Professor Janet Twyman, director of the Fred S. Keller School in Yonkers, New York, where the special-ed curriculum was designed around behavior analysis. At a time when other administrators around the country were mounting legal defenses against parent pressure for ABA, Kaplan was reaching out to Twyman as a potential partner for providing additional ABA services to families in Westchester.

Unfortunately, the Keller School lacked a deep enough bench of trained therapists to be able to deliver these additional services to the county with adequate monitoring and without compromising quality. Indeed, the "quality" question loomed large in Kaplan's conversations with Twyman, who tried to impress upon her that an inflexible forty hours per week was too arbitrary a standard for framing an ABA program, and that the quality of therapists was a more meaningful benchmark than the quantity of the therapy.

Kaplan did eventually make the explicit request that Lovaas-style ABA be added to the official menu of services the state would pay for as of March 1994. Her main reason for doing so was that parents were already spending their own money to start programs, and she wanted to help.

Sure enough, the Mayersons, in July 1996, started their own ABA program. In the few weeks since Gary Mayerson's furious phone call to county headquarters, there had been no resolution over the question of hours. The county had revised the Mayersons' son's proposed plan twice—first, increasing the ABA offer from eight to ten hours weekly, and later, adding ten hours weekly of "family training," which involved a therapist instructing the parents on interacting with their son within an ABA framework. At one point, Gary Mayerson countered with an offer to pay almost half the cost of his son's ABA if the department would go higher than thirty hours, but to no avail. The haggling dragged on, but the Mayersons felt they had no more time to waste. Their son needed therapy immediately.

In remarkably short order, Lilli Mayerson managed to pull an ABA team together—all women with solid experience, with bachelor's and master's degrees. The first session began at their home in Mamaroneck on a Wednesday morning. Intensive meant intensive; by autumn, her son was getting twenty-five to thirty hours per week of ABA. And Gary was writing a lot of checks, averaging about $3,400 a month.

The work was exhausting for everyone, but it was exhilarating at the same time. Almost from the first day, the boy began to respond. Within two weeks, he started making and holding eye contact, while some of his classically autistic behaviors—such as flapping his hands—began to subside. Words began to have meaning for him, and he started to follow simple commands. After a few months, little by little, he began to mouth some words himself. It was painstaking, and primitive as communication goes, but each and every time it happened, it was a triumph. For this child, and for the argument in favor of ABA.

But during the hours when the child was not getting therapy—and was not the focus of some adult's intense interaction—the flapping would return. Left to his own devices, he would pull back into his own world again. He would, to some degree, "regress," in ABA terms. Not all the way to where he had started from, but still, it was a backslide.

The calculus seemed clear to the Mayersons: the more ABA their son got, the faster he would connect, and the less time he would have to lose ground. So Gary Mayerson asked for a due process hearing, which would get the argument in front of a judge. He also decided that he would act as his son's lawyer and handle the case himself. He wanted to be the one who showed the program for what he thought it was—inadequate, unresponsive, unfair. All he needed was some ammunition.

WHEN SUSANNE KAPLAN wrote that "law alert" memo to the county attorney, she had specifically raised the concern that Mayerson would attempt to use her or her staff's words against them. Her worry would prove to be justified when Gary Mayerson ended up making the memo itself the primary exhibit in his case against the county.

When she composed the alert, Kaplan had added a sentence for the edification of the county attorney. "Currently," she had written, "we are following a policy that limits [early intervention] ABA therapy to ten hours a week."

There was a problem with her use of the words "policy" and "limits." Everyone knew what the law required, especially after several court rulings on IDEA cases in the 1980s. Schools had to offer each child with a disability an individualized program, tailored to his or her specific needs. The court required that the program be reasonably calculated to deliver a "meaningful educational benefit." That did not mean that it had to be the best program imaginable. Indeed, in creating what was known as the "Cadillac-Chevrolet" standard, the courts had told schools that a "Cadillac" program was unnecessary. Giving a kid a "Chevrolet" program was adequate, as long as the vehicle provided was decked out meaningfully and adequately for each different child. The customization aspect was critical. Judges did not look fondly upon school systems falling back on one-size-fits-all offerings.

But Kaplan, in a confidential memo, had used language that could easily be read that way. *A policy that limits.* These words, in their most straightforward interpretation, suggested that in the early intervention program she ran for Westchester County, any child seeking ABA would be handed the same predetermined package of hours, one that came with a set ceiling. This, to Gary Mayerson, did not sound individualized at all.

BY A TOTAL FLUKE, the law-alert memo fell into Mayerson's hands in the late summer of 1996. The hearing on his son's ABA was set for October, and Mayerson, a trial lawyer, had been preparing. He read more deeply on IDEA, studied similar cases fought by parents in New York State, and met personally with Ivar Lovaas to deepen his understanding of the method. He had found an expert witness he liked, Dr. Ira Cohen, a psychologist who appeared in Catherine Maurice's *Let Me Hear Your Voice.* Dr. Cohen was ready to testify that the Mayersons' son needed forty hours of ABA per week.

One weekend afternoon, Mayerson broke open a box of documents he had requested from the county. It contained a copy of his son's file, which, under New York State's Freedom of Information law, he was entitled to see. Most of it was familiar to him already, but when he picked up two documents that were stuck together, he found himself reading something he had never seen before: Susanne Kaplan's memo—the law alert. Or, as Mayerson always liked to call it afterward, the "smoking gun."

Mayerson quickly understood that someone in Kaplan's office had made a big mistake; this was not a document he was ever meant to see. It was most likely protected by client-attorney privilege and should not have been included in the papers sent to his house. But now it was too late; they had handed it to him, so the privilege was moot.

On the second page, Mayerson found the words that he would build his case around: "Currently we have a policy that limits . . ."

He could not quite believe that Susanne Kaplan had actually put that in writing. It made him both furiously indignant and fiercely exultant at the prospects of using it to prove what he believed: that the County of Westchester was screwing every child with autism out of what they all desperately needed: as many hours of ABA as possible.

He could hardly wait to get Susanne Kaplan in a witness chair, get her under oath, and confront her.

ALL MORNING LONG, Mayerson had made his disdain for the soft-spoken woman in the witness chair so obvious that even the judge thought it was too much. It was clear that even the lawyer's looks and shrugs were rattling her.

"I am *trying* to answer," Kaplan protested, "to the best of my ability."

"Your body language is editorializing," Judge Gerald Liepshutz scolded Mayerson. "I would ask you not to do that."

It was, without doubt, the most acrimonious bout of questioning ever seen at 136 Prospect Avenue, in Mamaroneck, New York, which was not a courthouse but a public library whose conference room happened to be available for the day.

Kaplan was stunned. She had testified at due-process hearings before, but nothing remotely like this had ever happened. Her testimony had been going on for over an hour. "I am here to facilitate," she had said early in the questioning. She had arrived hoping to be helpful, but suddenly, she was being pilloried in front of people she didn't know, by a parent, a lawyer, who was casting doubt on both her character and her ethics.

When Mayerson had started raising his voice at Kaplan again, Judge Liepshutz, reading the situation, counseled Mayerson to be careful.

"You are playing two roles, and I know it is hard to separate them," Liepshutz broke in. "But that doesn't change the fact," Leipshutz continued, "that you are going to have to separate the parent's role from the lawyer role."

Mayerson apologized and resumed his line of questioning.

"Explain this one," Mayerson demanded, holding up a copy of the "law alert" memo as he read aloud the sentence Kaplan had written about the county limiting ABA to ten hours a week.

The answer Kaplan gave would never satisfy Mayerson, but she would maintain, from that moment and ever afterward, that it was the truth. The ten hours, she said, were not an upper limit on ABA. They were just a starting point, a baseline. "We look at it as a way of beginning," she said. This was the number they started out with for very young children, to see whether they could handle the intensity of the therapy before considering an increase in hours.

As a guideline, it sounded reasonable. But Mayerson quickly reminded Kaplan of her memo's telltale sentence—*we have been following a policy that limits.* That said nothing about starting low and going higher.

"It doesn't say that here on the memo," Mayerson pressed. "You are telling me it means something different than what it says on the paper, right?"

What mattered wasn't the memo language, Kaplan tried to explain, but that her staff was trying to balance concerns about overstressing the twelve- and eighteen-month-old children who might get ABA.

"This is our way of beginning," she repeated.

And yet again, and for the last time, Mayerson said what was obvious—not just to him, but now also to the judge, to the county attorney, and to Kaplan herself.

"It doesn't say that on the memo, does it?" he asked.

"No," Kaplan finally responded, realizing that continuing to argue the point was futile. "It does not."

Mayerson spent the rest of that morning painting Kaplan as one of the bad guys, in every way he could—by asking her directly, again and again, if she was trying to mislead everyone, and by rattling her with questions she had already answered at least once already. Weary, wounded, and flustered, Kaplan, in the middle of an exchange concerning what factors went into the design of Mayerson's son's program, finally blurted out, "I don't know what you're searching for."

Mayerson took the moment for what it was—the perfect setup for the perfect courtroom line.

"I am searching for the truth," he intoned. "That's all I am searching for."

The Mayersons' due-process hearing took up nine full days of testimony, spread over two months. In April 1997, Judge Liepshutz found that the county's program for the Mayersons' son had been inadequate, and that the family was owed $20,287.50 for the ABA they had already paid for themselves. He then ordered the county to continue funding their home program through August of 1997 for "32 to 40 hours per week." As for ABA, he concluded that "ABA therapy is appropriate for autistic children and is extremely effective with these children." It was everything Gary Mayerson had set out to get for his son.

Gary Mayerson had seen the lack of adequate funding for ABA as an emergency requiring urgent attention. He knew that to get anywhere, he would need to create an emergency for the county, which he did, by pummeling a midlevel executive who only had the best intentions. The feeling among Susanne Kaplan's colleagues was that she was a good woman who had not deserved to be demonized. Her professional record supported that. But it was highly likely that if Gary Mayerson had not played so rough, he would not have made much headway in getting the ABA money. Even absent the conspiracy he seemed to think was in place, plain bureaucratic inertia and the shortage of qualified ABA therapists would likely have kept his son from getting more hours than the county was prepared to give.

His performance may have seemed harsh to those in the school district, but to the autism community, Mayerson's win in Westchester made him a hero. Autism parents all over the United States wanted Mayerson to be their lawyer too. Not long after, he resigned from his big New York firm to become a specialist attorney, representing families in special-education battles. Nearly two decades later, his son, who once could not speak, vindicated his father's fight by starting college.

MUCH AS CATHERINE MAURICE had almost single-handedly made Ivar Lovaas's name famous among autism parents, these "Lovaas cases," brought to court by parents, pushed ABA into the consciousness of the government entities that ran education and health policy. Although they were resistant at first, the policymakers ultimately did a turnabout on the therapy.

In 1999, the New York Department of Health published its first-ever set of "Clinical Practice Guidelines" for early intervention, in which it endorsed ABA as "an important element in any intervention program for young children with autism." A few months later, the first-ever US Surgeon General's Report on Mental Health, a mammoth review of the mental health landscape, declared that "thirty years of research demonstrated the efficacy of applied behavioral methods." It even called Lovaas's 1987 study a "well-designed" piece of research. As the new millennium began, more schools than ever were agreeing to offer ABA.

But not all schools had waved the white flag. After losing so often in the mid-1990s, education authorities had wised up about how to start winning again. Paradoxically, saying yes to ABA became part of a strategy counseled by legal consultants such as Melinda Baird. Formerly an in-house attorney for Tennessee's Office of Special Education Programs, Baird went out on her own in 1996, on the gamble that a business existed around advising individual school districts and representing them in hearings. By 2001, she had handled cases all over Tennessee, Alabama, and Florida, and run hundreds of workshops for school personnel on how to avoid litigation. In 2000, she composed a paper called "Building a Blueprint for an Appropriate and Defensible Autism Program." Among measures for avoiding seeing autism parents in litigation, she encouraged schools to strive to use an "eclectic approach," using a variety of methods, including ABA, based on the needs of the individual child.

This so-called eclectic approach was adopted in many parts of the United States, resulting in individualized programs in which ABA is offered in small doses—only one or two hours a week in some places—but in concert with other services, such as speech or occupational therapy, sensory integration, playtime, music therapy, or time in a TEACCH classroom. The argument used here was that a combination of therapies was better than just one—a claim that remained debatable. However, the eclectic approach did clearly benefit school administrators, because it offered a shield against the charge that they were denying children some vital therapy.

Some communities, however, made a greater commitment to ABA. Indiana, New Jersey, New York, Massachusetts, and to some degree California became known as places where the programs were relatively generous with the hours the schools would fund. These local differences were in part due to aggressive parent activism—the Gary Mayerson effect—and in part due to sympathetic local judiciaries that backed the parents in litigation. Some families relocated to these states for that reason alone, just as earlier autism parents once moved to North Carolina to get access to TEACCH.

At the same time, the term *ABA* began to have different meanings in different places. Even as the "Lovaas cases" opened the schoolhouse door, competing versions of applied behavior analysis slipped through it and gained a foothold. They had acronyms of their own—PRT and SCERTS and DRI and RDI and VBA and PBS and ESDM—yet all legitimately claimed to be based on applied behavior analysis. Many tried to be more "naturalistic" than the Lovaas approach, less rigid and more open to taking cues from the students. Today, even the Lovaas Institute—which owns rights to the original method—strives to make its exercises more child-centered and more fun.

In the end, ABA, once regarded as a fringe, faddish, overhyped approach to autism, had become mainstream. It was taken as a given—backed up by numerous studies—that some ABA was far better than none, and that some children made enormous progress because of it. Their IQ scores went up and their language skills improved. As for the controversial finding that had set off the huge demand for ABA in the first place—the 47 percent recovery rate Lovaas claimed in 1987—nearly two decades would pass before it was credibly replicated. In 2005, Glen Sallows and Tamlynn Graupner, founders of the Wisconsin Early Autism Project, published the results of a four-year controlled study of the efficacy of a treatment that was a close variant of Lovaas's ABA. They reported that 48 percent of the children achieved higher IQs and fluent speech, and were, by the age of seven, performing well and making friends in regular classrooms. The treatment was not a letter-perfect reproduction of Lovaas's techniques. For example, Sallows and Graupner used no aversives, and other therapies were added to the mix. Nevertheless, the study received high marks for its methodology, even from skeptics, and it was seen as bolstering Lovaas's original claim.

In a practical sense, however, the new proof was superfluous. ABA had already won the war for acceptance. And few doubted that Lovaas had discovered something important while at UCLA. That said, his work did not shed much light on what autism was at its core—a question that Lovaas did not even try to tackle, and that behavior analysts considered largely irrelevant to the effectiveness of their treatment.

But they were not the only scientists to focus their energies on children with autism. Another group of investigators, on the other side of the Atlantic, took the study of autism in a new direction. To them, understanding the essential nature of autism was not beside the point. It *was* the point.

PART V

THE QUESTIONS ASKED IN LONDON

1960s–1990s

25

THE QUESTIONS ASKED

FOR YEARS, ONLY POLICEMEN EVER SLEPT INSIDE THE BRICK house that sat halfway down Florence Road, a short street of mostly single-family homes located in the London neighborhood of Ealing. Crammed full of beds, it served as a dormitory for employees of Britain's National Railway—specifically, for its uniformed police force. That ended, however, in 1965, when the train cops moved out, and children with autism moved in.

After that, the place was used to make autism history.

IN THE 1960S AND 1970S, Britain was as short on autism researchers as the United States. The few who did study the topic were concentrated around London, and most knew one another well. They were also in fruitful contact with their colleagues in the States. Indeed, after World War II, British and American scientists had come to dominate the investigation of the human mind, unseating their German-speaking colleagues as the leading influences in the field.

Not surprisingly, the scant literature on autism that existed focused almost exclusively on American or British children. Mention of other nationalities in the autism literature was so rare for so long that the mere fact of speaking English could almost have been mistaken for a risk factor for autism.

Yet despite their common language, American and British researchers had noticeably different priorities. Americans sought to treat—and even cure—autism. Among researchers in the United States, there was a sense of emergency, a drive to find solutions as soon as possible. In

Britain, the approach was calmer, aimed more at finding an explanation for autism. Driven more by curiosity, British researchers sought to map the contours of autism and understand the autistic mind.

The British approach—which they stuck with for the next five decades—produced a distinctive set of outcomes. A small group of British-trained experimental psychologists and research psychiatrists came up with insights that permanently altered how autism was perceived and understood around the world.

The British, too, always kept one eye on a larger question: What does autism reveal about the workings of the human mind in general? That is not to suggest that these scientists were not motivated by the wish to bring relief to the children and their families. But at the same time, the children were considered rare and fascinating subjects, fortuitously available in one place—that house on Florence Road.

Indeed, hardly an autism study took place in Britain in the 1960s that did not take the researcher to that address. First, though, the parents had to get the place up and running.

It does not do justice to the early organizing efforts of British autism parents to say they merely paralleled those of American parents. That is because, in many important respects, the British parents were the actual innovators. They did it first, and then the American parents consciously followed their lead. The British were the first, for example, to organize a national society in 1962. They were the first to use the newspapers to get their story told. They were the first to pick a puzzle piece for their logo—which would be copied again and again by autism groups around the world.

They did not, however, build the first autism school. A few had already been established in and around New York City around 1960. But the school they did build was the first to develop a global reputation, drawing visitors from around the world. Originally called the Society School for Autistic Children, it became renowned for proving that such children *could* be educated. For that, much of the credit must go to the matronly woman who lived on the top floor—a naturally gifted teacher named Sybil Elgar.

For Elgar, working with children with autism was a second chance in life. She had trained as a mortician just after World War II, but only ever worked as a government clerk, and then as a school secretary. In middle age, she was obliged to leave the paid workforce entirely to care full-time for her sick mother. In these narrowing circumstances, well into her forties, Elgar signed up for a Montessori correspondence course on how to be a teacher.

It was a slow and tedious way to enter a new profession, since her contact with professors took place entirely through the mail. It did require, however, that she get some periods of exposure to actual children in a classroom. In 1958, she fulfilled part of that requirement by spending a day at the Marlborough Day Hospital in London's St. John's Wood neighborhood, on the ward designated for children labeled "severely emotionally disturbed." She did not then realize it, but many of the children she saw that day would have qualified for diagnoses of autism.

Her day at Marlborough sickened Elgar emotionally. It was a classic scene of institutional life: the children were bereft of attention or meaningful stimulation, and they certainly were not learning anything useful. Elgar confided in friends that the place was "soul-destroying." Haunted by the memory, she made a return visit in 1960, hoping to see improvement. When she saw none, she resolved to start a school of her own for exactly these sorts of children, ones who had no champion. She was forty-six years old.

Two years later, Elgar began working with six boys in the basement of her North London home, all six of whom had been labeled "severely emotionally disturbed." The diagnosis of autism, which would have fit at least some of them, was still not familiar to most clinicians. Elgar had never heard of it. By 1963, however, she was recognizing the relevance of the concept to her work. She approached three London-based child psychiatrists to offer spaces in her school to any of their patients with the condition. Unimpressed by her credentials, not to mention her working-class accent, none of them took her seriously.

The mother of a boy with autism did, however. Helen Green Allison was an American in London whose son Joe, born in 1957, was diagnosed with autism by the age of four. Allison worked for US military intelligence in several postings abroad during World War II, before she arrived to study at Oxford in 1950, where she met her husband, a fellow student. In 1961, she went on the BBC *Women's Hour* radio program to talk about her son.

After that appearance, she was contacted by families from all over Britain with similar stories. Meanwhile, Michael Baron, father of an autistic boy, caught a British television program featuring four or five children whose behaviors seemed reminiscent of his son's. Baron reached out to Mencap, the UK's long-established and highly regarded support organization for people with learning disabilities. Through Mencap, Baron was introduced to the families of the children he had seen on TV, as well as Allison. This was the genesis of the tiny group which, in 1962, met in a private home in the London borough of Finchley and founded the world's first autism advocacy group. Initially they called themselves the Society for Psychotic Children, and operated as an affiliate of Mencap. In less than a year, however, they became a standalone organization, and came up with a more apt name: the Society for Autistic Children. Baron was its first chairman.

By this time, Allison had Joe in Sybil Elgar's little school. On his first day there, he smashed every lightbulb in the basement schoolroom. Elgar was unperturbed. She replaced the bulbs, then set out to connect with this wildly behaving boy. Watching, and improvising, she soon saw that Joe learned better when he was shown how to do something—even simple-seeming tasks like sitting down in a chair—rather than having it explained to him with words. By instinct, Elgar had stumbled onto an important insight: visual processing tends to trump auditory processing in some children with autism. In itself, this was evidence of a neurological basis to the condition, but in 1963, it was a possibility that university researchers were barely beginning to consider. Elgar also experimented with imposing structure on the children's activities. She set strict schedules and established boundaries around work and play areas. By doing so, the self-taught teacher was overruling the professional psychoanalysts, who were still recommending environments of unlimited freedom to unshackle egos boxed in by unloving mothers. When that failed to work, as it invariably did, their next suggestion was usually an institution.

But Elgar's method got results. Joe settled down and even began using words for the first time. When Helen Allison shared this with other parents, Elgar found her teaching in much higher demand. The Society decided to fund a bigger school, because Elgar's basement had run out of space. Elgar's husband, Jack, a former railway clerk, happened to hear about a policemen's dormitory coming up for sale in 1964. The society put in a timely bid, and the Elgars ended up living on the top floor of the house at 10 Florence Road.

The Society School for Autistic Children soon expanded into the two houses on either side of number 10. Money came from government and from private donors, including celebrities, among which were three of the Beatles, who spent hours playing with the kids. Eric Schopler crossed the Atlantic for a look inside, taking home new ideas that he blended into his own program in North Carolina. This master teacher, Sybil Elgar, would eventually be honored by the queen. The parents honored her as well, when they renamed her school "The Sybil Elgar School" in gratitude for what she was doing there every single day: proving that children with autism could be taught.

Over the next decades, hundreds of children were educated there. Meanwhile, many of them made cameo appearances in some of the most forward-thinking research ever undertaken in the quest to understand what autism really is.

ONE DAY IN 1967, a woman and a man, both of them scientists, showed up at Florence Road hauling along a heavy wooden box, roughly the size of a window air conditioner. A hole cut in one side was just large enough for a child's head to poke through. For the next several hours, a long line of boys and girls with autism sat down in a chair in front of the box and did just that—they stuck their heads inside, as the pair watched and took notes.

Data was everything to the two scientists who, in the compact universe of London experimental psychologists, were already research legends. The Australian-born Neil O'Connor and the German-born Beate Hermelin were seen as superb designers of brilliant experiments that shed light on how the minds of children with autism worked—and how they worked differently from everyone else's. Before O'Connor and Hermelin, almost no one had bothered to ask these questions.

The pair worked out of Maudsley Hospital, a psychiatric facility in South London. Redbrick and baronial, "the Maudsley," as it was always called, was paired operationally with Bethlem Royal Hospital, the direct descendant of the notorious thirteenth-century insane asylum known as "Bedlam." In the twentieth century, the Maudsley's wards were used for teaching by the Institute of Psychiatry, the country's top postgraduate training program. Most of Britain's leading psychiatrists passed through on the way to becoming fully certified.

O'Connor and Hermelin, who were psychologists, both spent time at the Maudsley. But starting around 1963, their desks were shifted to a set of wobbly wooden huts that stood in the big building's shadow. Thrown up after the war, those rough structures became home to a research group known as the Social Psychiatry Unit. An undertaking of Britain's Medical Research Council—the equivalent of the National Institutes of Health in the United States—the SPU brought together a disparate collection of laboratory psychiatrists, social scientists, statisticians, and graduate students. They all wanted to make a mark.

The unit became an intellectual hothouse. It was London, after all, and it was the 1960s. Iconoclasm ruled. Everything "establishment"—art, music, fashion, humor—was being frisked, mocked, shaken up, and made to account for itself. Something parallel was happening in the social sciences in Britain, especially at the Maudsley. The researchers in the huts—colleagues, friends, and competitors all—egged one another on in pursuit of the same shared objective: to challenge every known tenet of psychiatric and psychological dogma by putting it to the test of experimentation. That was the ethos and the essence of experimental psychology, which was the specialty of Hermelin and O'Connor: Test everything. Demand data.

In 1963, the pair turned their attention to autism. They wanted to give the kids tests—actual small tasks—so that they could measure performance. At the time, this was generally considered a futile proposition, since so many of the kids did not communicate in a recognizable way or were otherwise uncooperative. Hermelin and O'Connor, however, believed that there were still ways to elicit observable physical and mental responses that could be measured and quantified, ones that did not require much cooperation or conversational communication. They built that odd wooden box with these goals in mind.

THE INSIDE OF the box was painted completely black. Besides the large hole on one side for the children to put their heads through, there was a tiny peephole-sized one on the opposite side that let the researchers watch the children's faces while they were in there. That day, more than two dozen kids were brought into a small room set aside for the researchers. Some stuck their heads into the box because they were curious, others because they wanted the candy that was being used as a bribe.

For the first few seconds, the kids saw only total blackness. Then suddenly, a spotlight flashed on, revealing a human face floating in the far dark corner—actually a live person around back, pressed up against a third opening. For ten seconds, the person's eyes closed; then they opened again. After thirty seconds, the light was cut, and the box went black again.

O'Connor and Hermelin were interested in the kids' eye movements. They wanted to see where the children looked when the light came on and for how long, then contrast this with what happened when the same children were run through the experiment several more times, albeit with a key difference. In these trials, instead of a real live person's face, the light revealed pairs of upright white cards displaying various images, abstract geometric shapes, plus one that showed a photograph of a face.

It took a few hours to run the paces with all twenty-eight children who cooperated that day. Then, on a second day, Hermelin and O'Connor took the box to another school to run the tests on a roughly equivalent number of younger children who were matched with the first group in so-called mental age. The children in this second, control, group did not have autism.

When the experiment was over, O'Connor and Hermelin analyzed the data and found that the children with autism, as a group, differed significantly from the control group in the attention they gave to the dark and empty areas of the box. The control group paid almost no attention to the darkness, but the children with autism, judging by where their eyes went, were quite curious about the shapeless voids and shadows.

It was a paper-thin distinction, but it was real. And it was typical of the line of inquiry Hermelin and O'Connor pursued. Over a five-year period, through similarly exacting experiments, the pair continued to discover narrow yet quantifiable ways in which children with autism processed the world differently from other children. They discovered, for example, that many children with autism relied on their sense of touch more than they did hearing or seeing. In all, their experiments produced an array of data making clear that autism had a neurological basis. Here at last was proof that autism had to do with the brain, not with a mother's love.

Hermelin and O'Connor exerted a profound influence on their colleagues in the huts outside of Maudsley—both by the kinds of questions they asked and the discipline they brought to seeking answers. It was an ethic of inquiry that would persist as the researchers grew in numbers and took on still more novel questions. These included what seemed one of the most elementary of all: How common was autism?

It was not, and would never be, an easy question to answer. But London was the first place anyone would even try.

26

WHO COUNTS?

VICTOR LOTTER LEFT SOUTH AFRICA FOR LONDON IN 1963 to find out how much autism there might be in the world. He was late getting into psychology because he was late to enter the University of Cape Town—that lateness a result of a case of ankylosing spondylitis that hit him when he was fourteen. A severely painful autoimmune assault on the bones, it knocked him out of school for years and left him with lifelong chronic pain. By the time he applied to the university, he was in his late twenties and mostly self-educated. He graduated with a bachelor's degree, his school's top prize for anthropology, and a job offer from Neil O'Connor, to work in the huts outside the Maudsley in London.

Lotter arrived, clean-cut and buttoned up in a jacket and tie, eager to take on something challenging and worthwhile for his PhD thesis. O'Connor was happy to oblige, giving him the gargantuan task of attempting to determine the prevalence of autism in Middlesex County. British health authorities were beginning to come under parental pressure to deliver support services to children with autism, so they had approached the team at the Social Psychiatry Unit to help them figure out how big the need was. Supervised by O'Connor and John Wing, director of the Social Psychiatry Unit, Lotter was assigned to count the number of children with autism in a densely inhabited swath of England that skirted the former County of London.

Remarkably, no one, not even a veteran researcher like Neil O'Connor, had any idea how much autism existed—not in Middlesex County or anywhere else in the world. No one had ever attacked the question in any systematic way. It would have to be an epidemiological study, working with a sample population small enough to permit an actual count of everyone in it, yet big enough to have statistical significance. For that purpose, Victor Lotter decided to include only children born in the years 1953, 1954, and 1955, which gave him a set of 78,000 children, who at that point were between eight and ten years old.

Lotter would have to slog his way door to door, record office to record office, child to child, in person in order to uncover a good deal of the data he would need. That, in itself, was not a small task. But he faced another challenge of an entirely different kind.

Lotter was supposed to count kids with autism, but the question of whom to count—the matter of deciding whether a given individual had autism—was a mess of diagnostic confusion. When he turned to the medical literature to put together a simple list of defining symptoms for his survey, he discovered a tangle of competing syndromes, each with its own name, laying claim to the same traits Leo Kanner had described years earlier as being autism. In addition to Kanner's "infantile autism," there was also Loretta Bender's "childhood schizophrenia," Beata Rank's "atypical child," Margaret Mahler's "symbiotic psychosis," and a long list of other contenders, including "schizophrenic psychosis of childhood," "dementia praecocissima," "dementia infantilis," "prepubertal schizophrenia," "pseudo-psychopathic schizophrenia," "infantile psychosis," and "latent schizophrenia." These terms were all being used interchangeably to describe children showing the same sorts of behaviors. As the British child psychiatrist Michael Rutter wrote in this period, "It is by no means clear that all these authors are talking about the same condition."

It had been twenty years since Leo Kanner laid down his first description of the condition of autism using Donald Triplett and the other ten children as a model. But during the intervening two decades, the outlines of the condition, the definition of what autism looked like, had blurred and wavered continuously as other expert voices chimed in. As early as 1955, Kanner himself was grousing about the fact that there were too many inaccurate, sloppy autism diagnoses being handed out based on little more than "one or another isolated symptom." He fretted that his whole concept was being watered down by inconsistent standards. As he wrote later of that time, "Almost overnight the country seemed to be populated by a multitude of autistic children."

Such a state of affairs could only be mystifying to people outside of psychiatry. Any lay observer might think that autism was autism—simply, objectively and always.

But that was not the case, and never would be.

There was no biological marker for autism (then or now): it could not be determined by a blood test or confirmed by a cheek swab. It could only be diagnosed through the observation and interpretation of a person's behaviors, which meant it was next to impossible to avoid subjectivity in judgment. This was especially true when some of the key indicators Kanner listed were as vague as "an intelligent and pensive" expression and an "affectionate relation to objects." Doctors interpreting behaviors by those measures were bound to disagree on whether to use the label of autism.

Autism was, and would long remain, a diagnosis in the eye of the beholder.

In the end, then, since no authority clearly spelled out for him what autism looked like, it came down to Victor Lotter to define that for himself. The burden was historic. A young psychologist-in-training with only a bachelor's degree, Lotter, with guidance from his advisors, became the final arbiter of who counted and who did not in history's first-ever prevalence study of autism.

Lotter designed a questionnaire—a basic tool of epidemiology—that he mailed out to every age-appropriate school in Middlesex County and every mental hospital, along with a letter to the staff in those places requesting that they use his checklist of behaviors and report back to him the names of any children who might be showing autistic traits. This would give him his first big pass at the population of 78,000 and help him narrow down his study population. His checklist included twenty-two items, such as

Spends most of the time on his/her own
Carries or collects curious objects such as stones or tins
Often uses a 'special' or peculiar voice
Very clumsy or awkward in bodily movements
Tries to examine things in odd ways . . . by sniffing or biting them

Lotter constructed this list by improvising. First, he relied on the two criteria Leo Kanner claimed were the essence of autism: extreme self-isolation and obsessive insistence on the preservation of sameness. But he went beyond Kanner and borrowed a second diagnostic framework that went by the oddly delightful name "Creak's Nine Points." Published in the *British Medical Journal* in May 1961, these nine criteria purported to define something called "schizophrenic syndrome in childhood," which was another of those terms being used interchangeably for children with autistic behaviors.

A renowned London psychiatrist named Mildred Creak had chaired a panel of thirteen British experts, who spent nine months arguing over and negotiating a symptom list that added traits like "acute, excessive and seemingly illogical anxiety," odd movements and postures, and "apparent unawareness of [one's] own personal identity" to the overall picture. But the Nine Points, despite their creators' best efforts, also proved vague and confusing in practice. "Apparent unawareness," for example, was not a behavior that lent itself to precise and objective assessment. The list's inherent blurriness was emphasized by the critic who disparaged them as "an artificially contrived cluster of symptoms." Even Creak conceded that "subjective judgment" in their application "obviously led to divergences in interpretation."

Nevertheless, using these nine points, along with his own interpretation of Leo Kanner's thinking, Lotter cobbled together his own definition of what autism looks like, so that he could go out and count it.

THE RETURN RATE on Lotter's questionnaire was superb. By the time he finished opening up all the envelopes, 97 percent of the entire population of eight- to ten-year-olds in Middlesex County was accounted for. In this first pass, teachers flagged some 666 children as hitting at least some of the marks on his twenty-two-item autism checklist. Relying on his advisors' expertise and a closer review of each return, Lotter winnowed this group down to 88 children suspected of having autism, at least as he was defining it.

Next, he headed out to see each of these 88 children himself. He added to his list another 47 whose names he found by scouring the records at fourteen government medical centers for children who were not at school, most likely because of disability, for a total of 135 children. In the autumn of 1963, Lotter and his wife, Ann, who was also a psychologist and acting as his research assistant, launched the study. Together they went to public schools, mental hospitals, and the so-called training schools where some of these children had been placed. They observed each child, ran intelligence and language tests, and talked to the staff, who presumably knew the children as well as anyone. This process took months, but by the spring of 1964, it allowed the Lotters to eliminate more than half of the 135 children as candidates for the diagnosis of autism.

Next came the most emotionally trying part of the investigation as the Lotters began visiting the homes of the sixty-one children still remaining. The purpose of the home visits was to collect detailed medical and behavioral histories from the parents. Some of the children still lived at home, but in other cases, the child was absent, residing in an institution somewhere. In both situations, the Lotters could see the strain the families lived under and could feel their despair. Indeed, by virtue of this long journey and their tour of institutions and these households, the Lotters were collectively experiencing a larger dose of the reality of autism in the lives of families than anyone ever had before. Victor Lotter could not have called himself an autism expert when he started his project, but these months of study certainly made him one.

All sixty-one children still left on his list showed some autistic traits, but Lotter now had to make a judgment call of his own: which children's traits added up to autism, for the purposes of his count?

His solution was yet one more improvisation—a kind of decree on his part. He simply split the children into two groups. He organized their sixty-one names into a list that had the children with the highest levels of impairment at the top and those least impaired at the bottom. Then, under the thirty-fifth name, he drew a line. The children above the line, he would count as having autism; the children below the line, he would exclude. The full rationale of this selection was not clear even to Lotter himself. His top thirty-five, he wrote, were merely those "it was thought should be included." But he was bluntly honest about the subjective nature of the choice he made. "The point where a line is drawn," he wrote, was merely "arbitrary."

Thirty-five kids out of 78,000. Or 4.5 in 10,000. It was autism's first so-called prevalence rate. In subsequent years, its importance would grow—not just as a matter of historical interest but as the baseline against which all subsequent measurements of autism prevalence would be compared. Regardless of when or where later prevalence rates were published, they would invariably be cited in contrast to Lotter's rate, often as if it were a solid, objective, and universal truth.

Lotter never saw it that way. He made it clear in his 1966 paper summarizing his survey that with only a few minor alterations in the assumptions he made along the way—a few different choices about where to draw the line around symptoms and their varying intensity—his 4.5 statistic could have come out significantly higher or lower.

If anything, Lotter's intelligent and honest account of his epidemiological adventure exposed the quandary that would present itself whenever an attempt was made to measure the "rate of autism," at that time and in the future. Blurred definitions led to unanswerable questions about whether different studies at different times were even talking about the same people. The inconsistency in deciding what autism looks like would persistently undermine certainty about who should be counted. Lotter made this point bluntly when summing up everything he had learned in his journey among the autism families of Middlesex County: " 'True' prevalence may not be a useful concept," he wrote in 1966, "in the case of a syndrome . . . so poorly defined."

That lesson, learned first in London, was a lesson that would repeat itself countless times over the next fifty years.

27

WORDS UNSTRUNG

SCIENTIFIC RESEARCH IS A MENTOR-DRIVEN FIELD. EVERY established researcher can list the teachers upon whose shoulders he or she stands. Some can even remember the first meeting, that pivotal moment of connection where the fateful bond was formed.

For a young German woman named Uta Aurnhammer, that moment came at the Maudsley in 1964. A year earlier, Aurnhammer had received a diploma in psychology from Saarland University in Germany, though she had no real intention of making a career in the social sciences. That changed when she reached London. Initially, she came over only for a little English-language study, but the energy of 1960s London appealed to her, and she began looking for a way to stay longer. Tipped off about a slot in a work-study program in research psychology, she applied, but with little expectation of being accepted. To her great good fortune, not only was she chosen, but the position turned out to be in the Institute of Psychiatry, which meant she would be working at the Maudsley.

Aurnhammer found the place to be an intellectual banquet. Its spirit of iconoclasm suited her perfectly, as did the view shared by everyone at the institute that they were engaged in work that mattered, that they were probing previously uncrossed frontiers. Aurnhammer loved being taken along for the ride, and when she wasn't doing coursework or staying up late with a dictionary plowing through the especially arcane English of psychology research reports, she could be found in the Maudsley's canteen, kicking around ideas with fellow grad students and faculty. She even met her future husband, British-born psychologist Chris Frith, during her first few months at the Maudsley. As he spoke no German, their friendship became a full-time immersion in English, to her benefit. A year after their first meeting, she became Uta Frith.

It was her participation in a "journal club" that led Frith to find her mentors. Weekly, she and a group of other young psychology apprentices got together and reported on particularly interesting research papers they had each picked off an assigned list. The week Frith's turn came around, she arrived excited to discuss a paper she had chosen at random, one that had been published the year before. It covered some experiments into the perceptual differences of children labeled "psychotic"—the term that eventually would be replaced by "autistic."

Frith had been around a few such "psychotic" children at the Maudsley, and she had personally observed what the paper was talking about. Often the kids would look straight through the person sitting right in front of them—or they seemed to be deaf to someone slamming a book onto a desktop just behind them. They never turned around or even flinched, yet their hearing was perfectly intact. This selective imperviousness to interruption was one of those associated traits of autism—like the indifference some kids showed to extreme hot or cold—that disturbed parents but tantalized inquisitive psychologists.

On the ward, Frith had heard some psychiatrists attributing these behaviors to a malfunctioning parental relationship. She found this explanation unconvincing but knew of no data supporting alternative theories. In the paper Frith chose to discuss, though, the authors had constructed an experiment that identified cognitive patterns unique to children with autism, in relation to how they registered the shape, size, brightness, and orientation of line drawing. To be sure, it was a narrow, almost esoteric, discovery. But it was solid, experiment-based, and indisputably indicative of a neurological component to autism.

Frith brought the paper to her journal club not knowing that its authors worked out of the same Maudsley campus where she was doing her clinical training. As soon as she realized this, she had someone point them out to her—O'Connor and Hermelin. One day at lunch, Frith approached them in the hospital canteen. Speaking German gave Frith a quick "in" with Hermelin and made it easy for her to have a fluent, deep conversation about experimental psychology. The two professors were immediately impressed by Frith's boldness and curiosity as she framed some penetrating questions about their study. By the end of that meeting, Frith had found her mentors. Soon afterward, Hermelin and O'Connor invited her to pursue a PhD in experimental psychology under their guidance.

That was how, in 1966, Frith came to make her own journey out to the school on Florence Road, to carry out an experiment whose results would rank among the most intriguing and influential of its era.

The night before, Frith had stayed up late readying her materials, preparing a large set of hand-drawn cards. Though the experiment had been designed primarily by her new thesis advisors, Frith was to take the lead on its execution. It was set up like a memory game. Frith would read through a list of eight words. After each list, she would ask the children to repeat the words they had heard in the same order she had used.

But there was a twist. In some lists, the words were presented in a wholly random order. For example: "day she farm when cat fall back rake." But in some lists, the words actually made a little bit of sense as parts of sentences, such as: "ride home by car write to us now." As always, there was to be a control group—children without autism matched for "mental age." Each child in each group would go through eight lists in eight "trials."

The results were unambiguous. With the random word lists, the kids with autism were on par with the other kids at repeating back most of the eight words, and were actually better at retaining the last few words from each list in their memories.

With the non-random lists, however, the kids without autism had a tremendous advantage. They were obviously recognizing those partial sentences inside the word strings, then using that recognition as an aid to remember all the words in those lists.

But for the kids in the autism group, it was as if "write to us now" was just as random as "cat fall back rake." Failing to spot the organizing presence of language, their brains got no memory help from words that actually did make sense together. They just didn't hear it.

But then Frith pulled out the cards she had worked on the night before. These contained pictures—little line drawings of ordinary objects like a house, a duck, a pair of scissors, or an umbrella. She placed these cards face-up in sets of four in front of a child in a certain order. She paused, scrambled the cards, and then asked each child to restore them to their original order.

This time too there were clues built in to assist memory. Certain cards fit together in the logical sequence of an unfolding process. For example, when Frith laid down a picture of a burning candle, next to it she placed a picture of a similar candle nearly melted down to a stub. Or, next to a drawing of an egg in an eggcup, she placed a drawing of a similar egg in a similar cup, only the egg was cracked open and half-eaten.

In this purely visual memory test, the kids without autism again did well when such visual clues to meaning were provided. But so did the kids with autism. Indeed, their scores were virtually identical to those of the control group.

This intriguing experimental outcome became a classic of the autism world and pointed to a powerful hypothesis: that while children with autism may miss some of the intricacies of language and the meaning contained therein, they were strikingly capable of deriving meaning from information provided through nonlinguistic means. Moreover, these results suggested again that autistic children were better attuned to visual rather than auditory learning. These insights were repeatedly confirmed by other experiments and integral to ways in which teaching methods were shaped in the years to come.

Generously, when O'Connor and Hermelin published this research, they named Frith as a collaborator in a front-page footnote: "This work was carried out by Uta Frith in collaboration with the authors." Such a prominent acknowledgment of a graduate student was not common in that era; perhaps this spoke to her mentors' conviction that Frith, their protégée, was going to go far in her field.

They were right about that. Uta Frith would go on to become one of the biggest names in the field of autism research. In addition to composing her own probing questions about the nature of the condition and designing experiments to answer them, she became the field's leading "explainer" of autism to the general public. She hosted numerous television programs and was quoted often in the press. Her book, *Autism, Explaining the Enigma,* was the first one by a hands-on researcher to explain the condition as a matter of scientific interest to a general audience. In its pages, Frith wrote about the experiments performed on Florence Road with the same sense of wonder that had first attracted her and her mentors to autism, the same wonder she then passed down to some of her own brilliant students. She described, in plain English, the nuances of their experiments and framed their findings in a way that suggested that the study of the "autistic" brain was actually the study of all brains. The book would be translated into ten languages and go through several reprints.

Popular curiosity about autism was starting to catch on. The questions asked in London, which picked up pace in the 1970s, were stoking the fire at just the right time. The researchers weren't finding all the answers; instead, the questions kept leading to more and better questions.

28

THE GREAT TWIN CHASE

In the early 1970s, a general practitioner named M. P. Carter, who lived and worked mostly in the east of England, passed away. Later, when his wife went through the doctor's personal effects, she found in his desk a list of names of twins with autism. Carter had been putting this list together since 1967, when he placed notices in several medical journals, asking "any doctor knowing of such a twin pair [to] please contact" him. Carter was active in Britain's National Society for Autistic Children as its East Anglia organizer, and had been in touch with Bernard Rimland in the United States. The two men had been discussing some sort of joint study on autistic twins, but Carter had died before getting around to it.

Carter's wife, recognizing that the short list of names was probably important, sought to get it into the hands of someone who could make use of it. That was how the names came to be given to a London professor of psychiatry named Michael Rutter.

Rutter, then in his early forties, was already the superstar of British child psychiatry and the first person in Britain named to a professorship in that discipline. Destined to be knighted by the queen later in his career, Rutter was recognized for his exacting intellect and for the rare and blunt clarity of his academic writing. Autism was but one of his interests, in which, as a thinker and researcher, he played a leading role throughout five decades, beginning in the 1960s.

In 1973, when Rutter first saw Carter's list of twins, he saw the possibilities in it immediately. Other researchers had written about twins and autism, but only minimally, with only a few cases mentioned here or there and always with sparse data. But with a sufficient number of cases, Rutter thought he might be able to answer two intriguing questions at the same time: How frequently was autism shared between twins? And was the rate the same for identical and fraternal twins? Numbers like that had the potential to say a great deal about the role of genetics in autism. If analysis showed that autism was shared between identical twins at a higher rate than expected, that could answer the question of whether genes helped determine who had autism and who did not.

THE QUESTION HAD been taboo for several decades, a result of the lingering scientific scandal of genetic arguments used by the Nazis to justify the murder of people with mental disabilities. For many years after World War II, seeking a link between a person's DNA signature and signs of mental illness or intellectual disability was not an endeavor that appealed to many researchers. Particularly in American psychiatry, nothing was more politically incorrect than the suggestion that there was any genetic dimension to the mind's functioning. Feeding the taboo was the presence in America of many European-born psychiatrists who had escaped the Holocaust or who had family who had died in it. On this point, passion trumped the spirit of inquiry. When Danish psychiatrist Eric Stromgren visited the United States in 1948, he found it depressing that even "the possibility of genetic contributions" was something he was not permitted to broach with colleagues there. "Genetics had become a dirty word," he recounted.

Besides, the mother-blaming theory, which still dominated, obviated all need for exploring the condition's genetic or biomedical side. Taken together with the distaste for gene research, very little true scientific study of the biomedical aspect of autism was undertaken for years. But once he had the list of twins in his hands, Michael Rutter was ready to take on the taboo.

WHEN HE STARTED putting together the outlines of a study, Rutter settled on a target population: all sets of British twins—identical and fraternal—where at least one of the siblings appeared to be affected by autistic traits. That had been the organizing principle of Dr. Carter's list, whose dozen or so names gave Rutter a good starting point. Now, as Carter had once done, Rutter reached out across the medical profession to contact pediatric centers, social service agencies, and mental hospitals with the aim of tracking down any pairs of twins Carter might have missed. Rutter received remarkable cooperation—a testament to his reputation, probably. Large envelopes of documents began arriving by mail, packed with the children's full, original records.

These records all claimed autism diagnoses for at least one of the twins in each set, but Rutter wanted certainty that the diagnosis was valid. For him, that meant getting independent confirmation in each and every case. Every family on his growing list would have to be visited in person so that the children could be evaluated face-to-face. But the dozens of names on his list came from children scattered over hundreds of miles in the United Kingdom. He could not get to all these children himself; his duties at the Institute of Psychiatry demanded all of his time as it was. So he brought in an outsider.

Susan Folstein, who grew up in Missouri, was one of the five women admitted to Cornell Medical School in the class of 1970, when that was the ceiling for female enrollment. When she told a professor she hoped to become a professor herself someday, he counseled her to go "become an expert in something." By chance, this same man had studied at the Maudsley and knew Michael Rutter. He put the two of them in touch.

Thus, in the summer of 1974, Folstein found herself in the far north of England, sloshing through a soggy field toward a small encampment of mobile homes, where she spotted a mother bending down to help a naked toddler urinate in the mud. The woman's hair was waist-length and loose, the same orange-red as the child's. There was no phone service out there, or electricity or running water. Still, the woman appeared not at all surprised to have an American suddenly showing up at her trailer. Some weeks earlier, a letter had arrived, and the woman, who could not read, had walked it into town to have the doctor who looked after her kids read it to her. It was from Folstein, explaining her research interest in the woman's twin boys.

The two women took a seat inside the mobile home, surrounded by shelves of beautifully cut glass. More children joined them—lots of them. Folstein spent quite some time observing the twins, while asking their mother questions and explaining more about the purpose of the study. She also took care to inform the mother of some of what was known about autism. Over tea, the mother took all this in and then commented, "Huh! I guess there's a reason for reading, after all."

For most of 1974 and into the late spring of 1975, Folstein was on the road roughly two days out of every week, working through Rutter's list of twins, crisscrossing the United Kingdom, taking tea with every social class. Autism was in all these places. That red-maned mother belonged to a social tribe referred to, usually unkindly, as "gypsies." Folstein met other tribes, spending an afternoon in the midst of glorious gardens at the country mansion of a celebrity actress married to a famous musician, who were the parents of twins. On yet another day, she dined in the home of a retired general, grandfather to the children she'd come to see, eating bad food from silver plates. A good number of the children on the list were already institutionalized. Folstein found the grounds and the architecture of the mental hospitals picturesque but their interiors dark and dire.

In the course of these months, Folstein became the expert she aspired to be. She mastered the observation and reporting of autistic behaviors, using criteria set by Rutter. It was Rutter, though, who took command of her detailed reports to make the final determination of whether there were true autistic traits at play in these children. Working with Folstein, he eliminated cases where there might have been illness suffered, such as rubella, or physical trauma before or during birth—because those incidents could account for some of the observed behaviors. He wanted only those cases where the possibility of inheritance remained an open question, where both children were of the same sex, and where there were clear grounds for diagnosing autism in at least one of the pair.

Once Folstein's travels were complete, her long journey yielded just twenty-one sets of same-sex twins who fit the study's parameters of autism in at least one twin per set. This was not a surprisingly small number, given the relative rarity of twins in general, let alone of autism as defined by the study's rather tight criteria. In any case, it would be the numerical relationships within this group that excited the autism world when Rutter and Folstein made their findings public in July 1976, at a conference in St. Gallen, Switzerland.

With Rutter looking on from the audience, Folstein took the stage and spelled out the numbers. Twenty-one sets of twins, she reported, had made the cut. Eleven sets of identical twins and ten sets of fraternal twins, with autism in one or both children in every pair. She and Rutter were virtually certain, she told the room, that they had not missed a single pair in their sweep of Britain. That number twenty-one, she reminded everyone, covered sets of twins where at least one twin had signs of autism—a small number, yes, but one that reflected the small odds of twin births crossing paths with autism in the first place.

Then Folstein revealed the crucial finding: *all four pairings where both of the kids had autism were identical twin sets.* At the same time, among the fraternal twins, whose DNA was no more closely matched than any ordinary brother and sister, autism *never* showed up in both kids.

It was stark, even in a sample set so small, and the conclusion was crystal-clear: genetic inheritance mattered in autism. As Folstein pointed out, the known odds of two kids in one family having autism were as low as 1 in 50. But with the identical twins described in the study, the odds soared to 1 in 3. That could be no coincidence. Genetics had to be in play.

That day was a turning point in the framing of the origins of autism. Over the next twenty-five years, the genetics of the condition would become an intensively researched area of investigation. Despite early hopes that the "autism gene," or genes, would be found, no instant answers resulted. But each year, new pieces of the puzzle were consistently uncovered, coinciding with the full mapping of the human genome early in the twenty-first century. Eventually, genetic research tools were developed that were far more precise than were available to investigators when Susan Folstein took to the roads of Britain in 1974, leading to even deeper autism genome research.

The twin study was also one of the few UK-based studies of that period that did not center on the house on Florence Road, but that was only because twins with autism were few and far between. As the

1970s turned into the 1980s, researchers would continue paying visits to the children of Florence Road, as the questions they wanted to ask about autism became ever more sophisticated, and the answers ever more revealing.

This was especially true when, in the early 1980s, a young man with a briefcase stepped through the front door. He had two dolls inside the briefcase, and an idea for an experiment that would inform and intrigue anyone who had ever wondered what constituted the essence of autism.

29

FINDING THEIR MARBLES

FOR THOSE WHO EXPLORED THE INNER NATURE OF AUTISM, one of the thorniest questions was always the seemingly straightforward one of "what causes what?" It had long been obvious, for example, that the children Leo Kanner had studied all shared, at a minimum, these two traits: a difficulty processing language and a lack of social connection.

The question was: which, if either, caused the other?

Was language impairment the primary deficit, which then interfered with social development by hampering social communication? Or was the social deficit primary, which stifled language development, as so much of language learning depends on interaction with other people?

The answers that autism researchers developed to such questions gave rise over time to various working "models" for autism. These were, in the absence of empirical certainty, thoughtful guesses built out of whatever indirect and often scant data was available. Some believed that sensory challenges, for example, might be the primary driver in autism, affecting both the linguistic and social realms. But other theories abounded.

In 1984, a radically new model emerged, sparked by a conversation held in a narrow brick walk-up on Gordon Street, in London's leafy Bloomsbury neighborhood. This was where Uta Frith, who was well on her way to becoming world-renowned, had been based for some years, with a research program called the Cognitive Development Unit. She was miles from the Maudsley now, separated from it by half of London and the River Thames. Ever nostalgic, however, for the hothouse give-and-take of her own student days, Frith encouraged drop-ins by her graduate students to her Gordon Street office. There were group teas held there in the late afternoon, where discussion raged about the latest trends and controversies in cognitive psychology. Frith encouraged students to bring ideas from beyond the conventional boundaries of psychology and to keep in touch with colleagues in other disciplines. Her goal was to foster the feeling of an unstructured, nonstop seminar.

One afternoon, Frith sat sipping tea with a young man named Simon Baron-Cohen, kicking around ideas for his doctoral thesis. Baron-Cohen came to autism with the same sense of fascination as Frith had. Soon after graduating from Oxford, Baron-Cohen had worked in a school called Family Tree, which had a student body of about six small children with autism and a staff of roughly the same size. For a twenty-one-year-old who had not known autism in his own family growing up, it was an intensive first exposure to the condition. Baron-Cohen was an art teacher for art class, a pancake-maker in cooking class, and a bus driver on school outings; he spent every minute with these children, and with their autism.

The kids startled and captivated him. He found it disorienting to have one or the other of them lean in close, until their faces were only inches apart—only to realize that the child peering with fierce interest was not really seeing him at all. Not as a whole person anyway, only as sections of anatomy—or geometry. Baron-Cohen sensed that, engrossed in their own curiosity, these kids were just as oblivious to the fact that they were also being looked at by him. He was puzzled and fascinated at the same time and could not let it go. He wanted to understand how these children's minds made sense of the world.

That day when Baron-Cohen and Frith met on Gordon Street, they were joined by Alan Leslie, a psychologist from Scotland new to the CDU, whose special interest was the study of pretend play in children. They had all just read a piece in the latest issue of the academic journal *Cognition* about a concept called Theory of Mind.

The two Austrians who had written the article, Heinz Wimmer and Josef Perner, had concocted a gorgeous experiment to explore young children's ability to recognize deception. The question was how to adapt the Austrians' experiment to make potentially new discoveries about autism.

Psychologists used the term "Theory of Mind" to describe an individual's awareness that others possess independent mental states—thoughts, dreams, beliefs—distinct from the individual's own. A person lacking a Theory of Mind would go through life unable to grasp that others were experiencing their own perceptions and perspectives. This person would tend to see other people as objects without will, like leaves buffeted by the wind.

A corollary idea was that of mind reading, later renamed "mentalizing." This was the idea that, by instinct, humans are constantly making judgments based on their best estimate of what others are thinking. To mentalize well, some argued, was to survive in the evolutionary jungle. To assume that a stranger approaching at high speed swinging a club over his head was planning to kill you was probably a smart and lifesaving guess, especially if it set you running in the opposite direction.

These concepts first came to the fore in the 1970s in a scholarly article that grew out of work done at the University of Pennsylvania on communication with primates. The researchers proposed, based on experiments with a chimp named Sarah, that even animals were capable of guessing what people wanted to do next in a given situation. The paper was titled "Does the Chimpanzee Have a Theory of Mind?" Published in 1978, it became an instant classic.

The 1983 paper by the Austrians that got Baron-Cohen, Leslie, and Frith excited took the idea even further. If the Theory of Mind was operating, the authors proposed, then nothing would demonstrate this better than an experiment hinging on the human talent for deception. They reasoned that any duplicitous act, such as telling a lie, relies on having a good feel for another person's perception of reality, since lying is an attempt to manipulate that perception. The attempt to deceive shows that the deceiver is working from a Theory of Mind. To the Austrians, who were researchers in child development, the question was: how early in life does this appreciation for deception kick in?

The answer, they determined, was at around four to five years of age. However, it was not their result that intrigued the London psychologists. It was their innovative use of what was known as a false-belief test. Presented with a puppet story about kids being naughty, real children were challenged to discern when certain puppet characters had been tricked into believing something was true that was, in fact, false. The children who could recognize the deception were said to have "passed the false belief test."

As the three psychologists chatted at Alexandra House, the outlines of a PhD project for Baron-Cohen began to take shape. The experiment he hoped to design would find a way to test the ability of children with autism to recognize deception, and in that, to discover what such children experienced as Theory of Mind. The question was, what sort of experiment could be designed to work with these kids?

The answer Baron-Cohen came up with was in his briefcase when he walked through the front door of the house on Florence Road.

BARON-COHEN WAS a familiar face at the Florence Road school, as he had already been working there once a week as a teaching assistant. With his first test subject sitting next to him, he began to tell a story to the young boy, acting it out with the two dolls he held in his hands.

"This is Sally," he said, bringing the blond doll to her feet on the tabletop with his right hand. Then he stood up the dark-haired doll in his left hand. "And this is Ann."

The boy, watching, said nothing.

"Sally has a yellow box," he went on, "and Ann has a blue box." In front of each doll, he placed a two-inch-high plastic open-top box upside down.

"Sally has a little marble," Baron-Cohen announced, producing one from his pocket. "And she puts it under her yellow box."

Baron-Cohen continued acting out the story. The marble went under Sally's yellow box.

"Then, Sally decides to go outside and play."

Baron-Cohen whisked the blond doll behind his back. Now, with Sally gone, Ann came to life in Baron-Cohen's other hand and proceeded to do something naughty.

"Ann moves the marble to her own box." Baron-Cohen performed the transfer: moving the marble from Sally's yellow box to Ann's blue one.

The boy continued to watch.

The telltale moment had arrived. "Sally comes back inside." Baron-Cohen walked the doll back into the scene, positioned between the two boxes. Then he posed the critical question to the boy.

"Where will Sally look for the marble?"

He waited to see which box the boy would choose.

Beforehand, as all experimenters do, Baron-Cohen had made a prediction about this experiment's outcome. Most people, he would predict, would answer yellow. They saw Sally put the marble there, and, taking on her perspective, they would know that she would look for it there when she returned from playing.

The boy Baron-Cohen was testing saw the same thing. But Baron-Cohen predicted that he would be unable to take on Sally's perspective.

Where will Sally look for the marble?

Prompted by the question, the boy pointed to the blue box—to where he *knew* the marble actually was, not the yellow box, where Sally would mistakenly think it was still hidden. He had failed the false-belief test.

The next child Baron-Cohen tested did the same thing. And the next. Blue box, every time. Baron-Cohen was amazed at the consistency of the responses. Every kid was failing the test, and by doing so, proving his prediction right.

Then one boy actually passed the test. He pointed to Sally's yellow box. A few kids later, it happened again. Still, 85 percent of the kids, ranging in age from six to sixteen years old, came up with the wrong answer. Many of them were highly verbal, with average IQs.

Baron-Cohen then took Sally and Ann to two other London schools to run the tests again with a much younger group of kids who did not have autism. None of these control subjects was older than four. Further, one of the school's populations was made up of children with intellectual disabilities, some with IQ scores substantially lower than those of the kids in his autism group. Baron-Cohen told them the same story and asked them the same question: "Where will Sally look for the marble?"

The results were nearly the mirror image of those he got from the children with autism. The vast majority of these young children passed the test—86 percent of them, which included the children with lower IQs. Intellectual disability apparently did not interfere with the ability to assume someone else's view of the world. These children possessed, according to Baron-Cohen's hypothesis, what the autism children lacked: a working Theory of Mind.

When Baron-Cohen reported his results to Frith, she was as delighted as she was stunned. She, too, had never expected such a clear trend to emerge. Certain that Baron-Cohen had found something important, she encouraged him to gather more data.

The result was a 1985 article in *Cognition* that became one of the field's landmark papers. Baron-Cohen was the lead author, with Alan Leslie and Uta Frith taking second and third position. Nodding to the famous Theory of Mind paper about chimpanzees, they titled theirs "Does the Autistic Child Have a Theory of Mind?" In it, they made a bold statement on what they believed their data uncovered. "Our results," they wrote, "strongly support the hypothesis that autistic children as a group fail to employ a Theory of Mind."

The paper's publication had an immediate and lasting impact, not least on Baron-Cohen's standing as a researcher. At the age of twenty-five, he was suddenly launched to the front ranks of experimental psychologists. The "Sally-Ann Test" became one of those experiments taught in graduate courses.

Baron-Cohen, Leslie, and Frith had found something vital—something previously unreported and probably pivotal to the nature of autism itself. "We have demonstrated a cognitive deficit," they declared, "that is largely independent of general intellectual level and has the potential to explain both lack of pretend play and social impairment by virtue of a circumscribed cognitive failure."

THE VALIDITY OF the "Theory of Mind" theory of autism would be debated for years, as would other big ideas coming out of London. Frith, working with her students Amitta Shah and Francesca Happé, developed yet another model for autism they called "weak central coherence." Their experiments showed that individuals with autism showed superior skills at recognizing or manipulating parts of patterns and systems, but less talent for seeing how the parts worked together as a whole. In other words, they were weaker on big-picture thinking, but they could be masters of detail.

Baron-Cohen, meanwhile, also stirred new ideas into the conversation. He proposed, for example, that autism might be understood as the product of "an extreme male brain," marked by a propensity for systemized thinking, but at the price of being able to empathize well with other people. This was meant to explain the much higher ratio of men to women with autism, and why autism showed up more often in populations of engineers than in poets.

In all this, the London researchers kept spilling out data to back up their ideas, letting those ideas evolve, and expand or expire, as new data indicated. The questions asked in London continued to yield wondrous insights on how we all think, not just those of us with autism.

PART VI

REDEFINING A DIAGNOSIS

1970s–1990s

30

THE AUTISM SPECTRUM

IN THE MID-1980S, A WRITER WITH MUCH TO SAY ABOUT AUtism struck upon a word she thought perfectly captured the condition: "continuum." She felt it expressed the way that autistic traits appeared in such a wide variety of intensities and combinations, among people of such divergent intellectual and social capacities. The word "continuum," she said, described "a concept of considerable complexity, rather than simply a straight line from severe to mild."

But after she had been writing about "the autistic continuum" for a while, she decided there was an even better phrase: "the autistic spectrum." It was a decision that would radically reshape the way people interpreted and responded to autism. The repercussions would be political, social, and scientific. In short, her change of mind changed the story of autism.

The writer was Lorna Wing. A key member of the London circle of researchers, Wing was a psychiatrist with an active practice, a researcher who published groundbreaking studies, an author whose plainspoken books helped families cope with autism, and an activist on behalf of individuals with autism. During the fifty years in which she was active, from the 1960s through 2010, she outshone nearly everyone else in the field. Her unique stature among the leaders of the global conversation about autism—including the Americans—was bolstered by a key distinction between her and other researchers. Schopler and Lovaas; O'Connor and Hermelin; Rutter, Frith, and Baron-Cohen—none of them went home to autism at night.

Lorna Wing, however, did.

Wing later recalled that she had her first cold inkling that something was wrong with her six-month-old daughter Susie while the two of them were traveling on a train one day in the late 1950s, sharing a cabin with another young mother she did not know, who had brought along a baby boy about Susie's age. Typically for the era, Wing did not know a thing about autism, even though both she and her husband, John, who first met in anatomy class when they were assigned to dissect the same corpse, were already practicing psychiatrists.

Wing noticed that the boy was entranced by the sights and sounds of the journey, and that, when he spotted some sheep out the window, he pointed to them excitedly, glancing back at his mother to see her reaction. Her daughter never did this. Susie alternated between being passive and withdrawn, or extremely restless and screaming. She hardly ate. She hardly slept. And she definitely never engaged in the easygoing connection she saw this boy making with his mother. At that moment, Wing felt touched by a chill.

Just after Susie turned three, her father happened to attend a lecture by the British psychiatrist Mildred Creak, who was then involved in one of the earliest efforts to classify the collection of behaviors that added up to autism. John Wing came home with a new hunch about Susie. Shortly after that, she was diagnosed with autism.

Susie's autism was severe, and her diagnosis came at a time when severe autism led to two clear prescriptions: early institutionalization for the child and psychoanalysis for the mother.

Neither prescription interested Lorna Wing. Instead, she set out to use her training to help Susie stay out of institutional life and to assist other families in their situation. She switched her professional focus, transferring into a research setting in child psychiatry. She joined the Social Psychiatry Unit at the Maudsley, along with John, who became its director. The Wings immersed themselves in conducting studies that eventually numbered in the hundreds. One of the research projects they oversaw was Victor Lotter's landmark study that made the first attempt to measure the prevalence of autism in a population.

But science was only part of it for this autism mother. Wing also became the dominant personality in parent advocacy in Britain. She helped start Britain's National Society for Autistic Children in 1962 and was on the committee that chose Sybil Elgar to run the society's new school. She also acted as the group's science policy advisor. In this role, Wing became the go-between, connecting parents with the scientific community. She was uniquely situated for this, as the one person in London with a stake in both camps.

But that came with pitfalls too. As it was, there was an inherent challenge in being a woman trying to be taken seriously by colleagues in psychiatry, a field dominated by men. But to be the mother of a child with the very disability she was studying risked inviting skepticism of her ability to do science dispassionately.

This was not a small concern. Over in the United States, the same issue had been faced by Bernard Rimland, one of the few fathers involved in research who was then fighting the dominant mother-blaming mind-set. Rimland continued to make it a practice, when writing or speaking in a scientific setting, never to mention the existence of his son Mark. Even in his groundbreaking 1964 book, he did not specify that Mark was one of the children he described for illustrative purposes. Rimland did not want to give his critics grounds for dismissing his challenge of the status quo as the outpourings of an overwrought parent.

Wing followed this practice when, in 1970, she published *Autistic Children: A Guide for Parents and Professionals.* No expert had ever written such a book before, one that spoke directly to parents about the challenges of raising their autistic child. Previously, the question was considered moot: institutionalization negated the need for parenting advice. Further, the book that most people were still reading about autism at the time, Bruno Bettelheim's *The Empty Fortress,* hammered home the incompetence of the parents. But Wing assumed that many would at least try to keep the family together, and that mothers and fathers needed practical insights delivered in simple, straightforward language. Thus, she pointed out the importance of basic matters such as how parents should address their young children. "To begin with," she counseled, "the child's name should always be used in connection with situations which are pleasant for him."

Wing's book was received like a shaft of light in the homes of families who read it. It went through several printings and translations into other languages—some of them amateur. In Tel Aviv, for example, autism mother Edna Mishori, who cofounded Israel's first autism organization, sat up over many nights in 1971, paging through a Hebrew-English dictionary and typing up her own version of Wing's book, which she copied, stapled together, and handed out to other families in Israel.

Because of the impact *Autistic Children* had throughout the 1970s, it was true to say that, in the eyes of parents of that time, Lorna Wing had "written *the* book" on autism. And then she rewrote it.

The turning point in Wing's own thinking on autism—which led to her coining the phrase "autism spectrum"—was grounded in a set of file drawers in the basement room of an administration building inside the Maudsley Hospital complex. The drawers held a set of cards comprising a handwritten database known as the Camberwell Register. Each card carried the details of a different individual residing within the London borough of Camberwell who had required, at any time, any psychiatric service delivered by the government. All day long, a clerical staff of half a dozen women sat at desks updating this information by hand, relying on fresh field reports, so that it was always current. Reliably, whenever a child from the borough received social services for the first time anywhere in the system, a card was started for him or her right there in the basement. Wing and her husband, John, had initiated the register in the mid-1960s themselves, with the stated purpose of, first, ensuring that the government was adequately providing services to those needing them, and second, providing a database for psychiatric research.

In 1972, Wing went down to the basement with a new research project planned. She wanted to explore a particular complication frequently encountered by researchers who attempted to count the number of people in any population who had autism. It was the problem of how to account for people who were "near misses." These were individuals, often relatives of people who had been diagnosed, who also clearly showed some autistic traits, but not enough to merit a diagnosis themselves. Something about their language perhaps, or their social behavior, was resoundingly reminiscent of parts of the overall condition as it was then understood.

Or there might be individuals whose autistic traits were so mild in some areas that it was uncertain whether they completed the picture of the condition. This phenomenon was observed by Victor Lotter in the 1960s, in his count of children with autism in Middlesex, and by Susan Folstein in the 1970s, when she went looking for sets of British twins who both had autism. Folstein ended up having to exclude a number of twin sets from her final count, where one child in the pair, though obviously neurologically affected, did not meet the full set of autism criteria she was using for her study.

Wing was a mother who appreciated both the value of support services and the critical importance of having a diagnosis that justified the provision of those services. This may have been her reason for wanting to find a way to count them all: all the people who reflect any trace of autistic behavior, in any degree and in any combination. The Camberwell Register would be her launching pad.

This was far too big a project to do alone, so Wing advertised for a psychologist to work with her—someone experienced with children and in doing cognitive assessments. Judith Gould, a young psychologist then training at the Maudsley, fit the bill. Gould had been doing both of those things in an education-focused research project. After an interview with John and Lorna Wing, she was hired. On that day in 1972, the new team of Wing and Gould headed to the basement, where the records were kept.

Lifting data from the cards was not enough; Wing insisted on a stringent process of verification. She and Gould embarked on a marathon field investigation, spending nights and weekends knocking on doors in Camberwell, to see for themselves what the cards said about the individuals they described. Limiting their investigation to children who were fifteen years of age and under, they set out to see all the cases of diagnosed autism in that group. But that was just the beginning. Beyond that, they wanted to see every child who was reported as displaying any traces of developmental disability more broadly defined. That meant intellectual impairment, speech delay, or any kind of learning disability. Scattered autistic traits, such as repetitive interests, or social aloofness, also counted.

Wing and Gould conducted one-on-one interviews with more than 900 teachers of kids whose histories had been recorded on those cards in the basement. After that, they themselves spent time with more than 132 of the children and their families. Data collected by the end of any given evening would be fed back into the system the next day, then reported to the basement secretaries, who transcribed the data onto the file cards. One day, near the halfway point of the project, workmen showed up at the basement door with a desk-sized keypunch machine. Computerization had arrived at the Maudsley. It thus became the task of the clerical staff to transfer the data from those thousands of records onto punch cards. Eventually, boxes of the cards were driven to University College for processing on the mainframe there.

So labor intensive was the sheer legwork aspect of the project that it was four years before Wing and Gould were ready to start publishing. But beginning in the late 1970s, they produced a string of papers that became the foundation for Wing's own radical rethinking of the concept of autism. It was where she broke with prevailing concepts and began to change how everyone else interpreted the condition.

Wing had decided that something crucial had been missed in all the prior years of autism analysis, when the circles drawn by the condition had been too tightly inscribed. It was time to move beyond seeing autistic traits as meaningful only when they were locked together into a supposedly tight syndrome, as Kanner had done. That left out too many people who needed help, or, as she would later write, it had "the effect of excluding those who do not fit neatly into the categories." Without question, her perception was influenced by her firsthand experience of raising a child with autism, which made her ever mindful of the consequences for families of a labeling system that overlooked their need for help. By that measure, she wrote, drawing narrow definitions had "not proved helpful in prescribing types of education, behavior management, medication, or other treatment."

But just because she thought narrow definitions had failed, it did not mean Wing thought autism had no meaningful shape at all. She and Gould proposed a framework they called the "triad of impairment" to encompass the defining core of the condition. This included, first, an impairment in the usual set of social give-and-take skills. The second impairment was related to reciprocal language, including nonverbal language. The third was a failure to engage in what Wing called "social imagination," like that used in pretend play.

Key to the triad framework, however, was its flexibility and variability. Within it, Wing argued, autism's traits could appear in a huge number of combinations and infinite shades of intensity, "right up to the borderline of normality." This, she boldly asserted, was the big picture that even the great Kanner had missed. Though she first used the word "continuum" to capture this concept, including a chapter in her book called "The Continuum of Autistic Traits," by 1988 she was often using the term "spectrum" to make the same point.

By the 1990s, Wing had left "continuum" behind entirely, deciding that it was too suggestive of a sliding scale of severity. Wing wanted researchers and clinicians to break free of reliance on a simple measuring stick for autism. She hoped to encourage them to be more nimble, more discerning in how they recognized and interpreted differences that were unlikely to always appear in the same, neat, narrowly drawn boxes that diagnosticians naturally favored. As Wing would often say, repeating an adage she made her own: "Nature never draws a line without smudging it."

IF IT HAD been anyone other than Lorna Wing promoting it, the notion of an "autism spectrum" may well have remained an obscure reference in a few journal articles here and there. But Wing had both influence among her colleagues and a following among parents that no other professional could match. And she was relentless. She wanted the spectrum idea to take hold, so she did everything she could in the 1980s and 1990s to ensure that happened. She kept writing about it, and she talked it up at conferences. And when she revised her classic parent handbook, *Autistic Children,* which every autism family owned, she gave it a new name: *The Autistic Spectrum*. Among the broad community of people connected to autism, that book title, more than anything, made the term colloquial.

Wing also brought the spectrum idea with her when, in 1984, the editors of the *Diagnostic and Statistical Manual of Mental Disorders* (*DSM*)—published by the American Psychiatric Association—decided it was time to update the book. That year, because of Wing's stature in the field, she was brought in to write the first draft of the revised criteria for autism, which gave her a leading voice in the three years of debate and negotiation that followed.

When the new edition appeared in 1987, her imprint was obvious. In place of the menu of five different diagnoses the previous edition had offered to people with autistic traits—which took account of differences such as age and persistence of symptoms—this update grouped everyone together into just two categories.

One was called "autistic disorder," which applied to people whose traits were closest to what Leo Kanner would have called autism.

The other, however, was clearly spectrum-"inspired." It was a broad catchall label to serve as a diagnosis for all the "near misses"—people with impairing autistic traits that did not add up to "classic" autism. Though the label coined for it was classically clunky *DSM*-speak—"Pervasive Development Disorder Not Otherwise Specified"—PDD-NOS became an important and much-used label. One reason for this, reported anecdotally, was that pediatricians sometimes grabbed for it knowing that mothers and fathers dreaded hearing the word "autism." Parents who were wise to this practice, however, and who wanted it "given to them straight," complained that PDD should stand for "Pediatrician Didn't Decide."

But the category also caught on because it worked. As Wing had argued, not everyone who needed help fit neatly in simple boxes drawn with clean, unsmudged lines. There was a place for the diagnosis in the lives of real people, and a place for them in the diagnosis.

That was also why, once Wing pointed out the rationale for it, the concept of an autism spectrum slowly gained momentum. It captured the variability of life lived by individuals whose distinctive traits were also demonstrably and dramatically variable, yet who also shared some sort of hard-to-define touchstone of difference.

Leo Kanner, Wing thought, had spotted just a slice of the spectrum. In Wing's view, Kanner's work was historic; it brought autism to the world's attention. But she was beginning to argue that he had only found part of it, and that there was so much more to the spectrum.

It was why, at the same time she introduced the world to the concept of the autism spectrum, she also introduced another diagnostic concept that almost no one had heard of before.

It was called Asperger's syndrome.

31

THE AUSTRIAN

THEY ONLY MET ONCE, WHEN HANS ASPERGER, AN AUSTRIAN pediatrician largely unknown in the English-speaking world, was on a short visit to London. Lorna Wing had come across one of his decades-old papers and, having found it interesting, invited Asperger to drop in for a cup of tea in the canteen of the Maudsley Hospital. By Wing's later account, they communicated in English, which would have been a struggle for her elderly guest. The Austrian's manner toward her was cordial. A year or two later, in 1980, Asperger died, his name still largely unrecognized outside of Austria.

But that fact would change dramatically within a decade—and solely because of Lorna Wing. During the same years in which she was developing and promoting the concept of the autism spectrum, she also introduced the world to the work of Asperger. She was particularly intrigued by a paper he had published in German at the height of the Second World War that she felt was very relevant to the spectrum idea.

Later, Wing recognized that introducing Asperger to the world had produced a slew of consequences she never intended, which left her feeling, she said, that in lifting the lid on his legacy, she had opened a Pandora's box. But by then, she couldn't close it again.

Asperger's syndrome became famous, far better known than the man himself.

SLENDER, BESPECTACLED, and boyish-looking—even as an adult—Hans Asperger grew up on a farm outside Vienna. He was a loner in his boyhood, often taking long treks in the woods, entertaining himself by reciting long passages from poems he had memorized. As a teenager, he found some company in an outdoors and nature-oriented organization called the "Wandering Scholars." It was part of a broad youth movement called Bund Neuland, which was Roman Catholic in membership. Joining this group marked a turning point for Asperger. He later credited much of his intellectual development to its influence.

He studied medicine and became a pediatrician, working out of Vienna's University Hospital, where in 1932 he was promoted to head up a program using education as a treatment for mental and personality disorders. It was sort of a school inside a hospital. The work he did there, described in publications he produced between the years 1938 and 1944, was the basis of Lorna Wing's later interest.

Asperger's relative anonymity outside of Austria was only partly due to the fact that he wrote and published in German. The other factor was his association, by dint of his birth country, with Hitler's Third Reich. The Reich's medical science was seen as corrupted, morally and factually, by ideology. While the victorious Allies were happy to acquire Germany's rocket scientists, much of the biomedical and psychological research conducted in Germany or Austria during the Nazi era was viewed with suspicion by the rest of the world. The bad associations lingered long after the war ended.

There is no record of Asperger himself joining the Nazi Party. While he served in the German army, it was because, like many physicians, he was drafted. Having already lost a brother on the Russian front, and as a married father of five, he was not enthusiastic about having to go. His service, in any case, lasted only a matter of months. He worked in a military field hospital, in Nazi-occupied Croatia, and came home disturbed by the carnage he had seen there.

That said, the medical culture he inhabited in Vienna was permeated by Nazi ideas. Vienna was especially dangerous to children with disabilities. In 1939, the year after Austria was assimilated into the Third Reich, the state commenced a campaign of murdering disabled infants, toddlers, young children, and adolescents. Their definition of "disabled" included both mental and physical infirmities. The campaign was framed as a program of mercy killing, but it was driven by the Nazis' obsession with building a strong nation by culling its weakest citizens.

They applied an emotionless but economic and self-serving logic to this purpose. They did not insist that the presence of a disability was, by itself, the litmus test for a life-and-death decision. Rather, each disabled child's right to life was subjected to a kind of cost-benefit analysis. Medical professionals were called upon to judge which children's futures were salvageable with treatment and education, and which were not. Children found to be "educable" were those seen as having a solid chance of benefiting from remedial support. If they could become productive citizens, the state could justify an investment in them. They were channeled into special schools and given what assistance the state could afford. The "ineducable," described in Nazi literature as "worthless," were not given that chance. They were put to death.

In Vienna, this process—the judging as well as the killing—was carried out by doctors and nurses at a facility known as the Spiegelgrund, which resembled a children's hospital. Each child's murder was accomplished over the course of days and weeks, as he or she was daily dosed with the antiseizure medicine phenobarbital. It was often administered in the form of suppositories or mixed into infant formula or cocoa. Over time, the drug caused a gradual breakdown of lung function. When the end came, the cause of death was usually listed as pneumonia. The staff removed and preserved the children's brains for future research, then the families were invited to collect their children's remains.

No physician working in Vienna could avoid contact with the Nazified medical bureaucracy. Hans Asperger would have brushed up against it every day. His mentor at the University Hospital, Professor Franz Hamburger, was an enthusiastic party member. In addition, Asperger served in various advisory roles to the city, whose top administrators were loyal Hitlerites. For any Austrian with career ambitions, professional advancement required remaining in the Nazis' good graces. Getting along meant being seen as fitting in.

Each Austrian in this situation had to figure out his or her own way to navigate and survive. In the case of the pediatrician Hans Asperger, it is clear that his response was to pour most of his energy into his work with children.

On October 3, 1938—four days before Leo Kanner met Donald Triplett in Baltimore for the first time—Hans Asperger stepped before a roomful of colleagues in Vienna and began talking about a group of boys he had been studying for some time, whose personalities he described as "autistic." He used the word in a novel way, making clear that it was not meant to suggest that the boys were suffering from schizophrenia.

This was an important distinction. Until then, *autistic* had been reserved exclusively to describe one of the behaviors commonly seen in people with schizophrenia. It was a telltale social withdrawal, evidenced by a flattening of personality, a cutoff of communication, and a preference for isolation. It was a symptom of schizophrenia that appeared to come and go, in a condition that generally had its onset in young adulthood.

Just as Leo Kanner would do five years later in 1943, Asperger in 1938 consciously appropriated the word "autistic" to describe behavior that was reminiscent of schizophrenic withdrawal, but also unlike it. For one thing, it affected young children, sometimes manifesting itself as early as the age of two. The children in question did not experience hallucinations or hear voices, as was typical of schizophrenia. Further, the social deficit was more or less permanent in nature rather than fluctuating by the day.

Asperger called his boys "Autistischen Psychopathen"—autistic psychopaths. In German, the word "psychopathy" was akin to the term *personality disorder,* with none of the connotations of the deranged or criminal mind that it bore in English.

The full text of Asperger's talk was printed in a medical weekly shortly after he gave it. Six years, and most of World War II, would intervene, before he produced a second publication-worthy discourse on the boys and their behaviors. The sixty-one-page paper he published in 1944, which was actually his postgraduate thesis, told the stories of Fritz, Harro, Ernst, and Hellmuth, four Austrian boys between the ages of seven and seventeen whose behaviors captured the essence of the condition. As of 1944, Asperger had seen two hundred boys with these types of traits, but no girls.

The children Asperger described were different in important respects from Donald and the other American children Kanner had written about the year before, whose hallmark trait, in Kanner's view, was a seeming indifference to humans and a nearly full-blown disengagement from them. Most of Asperger's boys, by contrast, seemed to strive for connection with others, usually adults, but those relationships were filled with anxiety and were undermined by the boys' difficult personalities, which did not invite warmth and understanding. They failed to form friendships with other children, who teased them mercilessly. On the playground or on the way to school, Asperger reported, he had often seen such kids fighting off groups of bullies.

Sometimes the tormented children lashed back. Fritz, for example, once went after a classmate with a hammer, and several of the boys were expelled from school in the first or second year for unruly behavior. Asperger saw their alienation in their facial expressions, noting an occasional "malevolent light" in their eyes. Ernst was combative not just with other children, but also with his teachers. As for Harro, Asperger described him as an inveterate liar.

This sorry cycle of antisocial tendencies, exacerbated by other people's cruelty, grew out of specific traits Asperger ascribed to the boys. They made little eye contact, their gazes directed "into the void." Extremely literal-minded, they missed other people's nonverbal signals—the raised eyebrows, the shrugs and sighs, the half-finished sentences. They also tended to be physically clumsy, a major liability when it came to sports, thus exposing themselves to more teasing and ostracizing.

Another major difference from Kanner's cases was that most of Asperger's children were extremely verbose. But it was not simply that they were talkative; it was that they spoke more like grown-ups than like their peers, with precise grammar and large vocabularies others sometimes found strange or irritating. The boys also tended to lock on to just one or two narrow subjects that fascinated them and no one else—such as heraldry, or the layout of the railroads. They would hold forth on these topics incessantly, in a singsong, automatic way, unaware of when they were boring or exasperating others. Their very facility with words undermined their social relations.

As Asperger pointed out, their well-developed language skills were consistent with another characteristic common to all the boys: they were intellectually whole. Better than whole, in many cases. Fritz, even at the age of eight, could solve problems, analyze data, and grasp the nuances of complex systems with facility. Perhaps, Asperger posited, these intellectual gifts were not a fluke but a positive side effect of their unconventional personalities. Perhaps their ability to take a deep dive into a narrow subject went hand in hand with their ability to lock out distractions. He offered the example of a young boy obsessed with drawing geometric shapes in the sand, who went on to acquire a PhD in astronomy and to prove a mathematical error in Newton's work.

This explained why, despite their difficult experiences with people, most of the boys were more than capable of learning. Asperger cited the children he had treated who grew up to have successful careers—among them academics, musicians, and an expert on heraldry. Even though their eccentricities persisted into adulthood, he said, "they fulfill their role well, perhaps better than anyone else could."

The journal that carried Asperger's paper was dated June 3, 1944. On June 6, the Allies launched the D-Day invasion of Normandy.

Through the end of the war, and after it, Asperger's career continued to flourish. In 1944, he was named a lecturer at the University of Vienna; in 1957, a professor at the University of Innsbruck; and in 1963, the director of the children's hospital at the University of Vienna. He spent his entire career working with children, and he published more than three hundred times, often on his autistic psychopaths but also, frequently, on the subject of death. At Vienna, his classes were always a big draw for students. He continued lecturing past his official retirement, though he cut back to one lecture a week, always delivered on Wednesdays. Around 1977, he sat down for a lengthy interview with Austrian radio. In 1980, when he was seventy-four, he fell ill shortly after delivering one of his lectures. He was dead before the following Wednesday.

As established as Asperger was in his homeland, however, his name never traveled far beyond the borders of Austria and Germany during his lifetime. At the time of his death, his then thirty-six-year-old paper describing those four boys whose behaviors he saw as "autistic" had still found almost no readership in the English-speaking world. Even to those who, like Bernie Rimland, paid obsessive attention to news about autism, he was a relative nonentity. In his comprehensive 1964 book on autism, Rimland mentioned Asperger's name once, but only between parentheses. In a note that year to a genetics professor at Stanford, Rimland confessed, "I do not understand Asperger's syndrome very well."

Leo Kanner made a passing reference to Asperger in a 1971 review of someone else's autism book, but he mangled the spelling of his name. Arne Van Krevelen, an early autism researcher in the Netherlands who spoke both English and German, knew about Asperger, but cited his work only once or twice in English-language journals. Some Russian-language journal articles also mentioned Asperger here or there. In the last decades of his life, thanks at least partly to the language barrier, Asperger's relative obscurity to the rest of the world appeared destined to be permanent—a fact that apparently did not trouble him much.

Then Lorna Wing found out about him.

It was Wing's husband who first stumbled across the 1944 paper. When John, who read German, translated it for her, it dawned on Wing how closely her "triad of impairments" fit those four boys from Austria. It also struck her that several British children she was treating were a remarkably good match for Asperger's "autistic psychopaths." At the same time, she was still processing the massive amount of data she and Gould had collected from the Camberwell Register. There, too, she had found accounts of children who were quite intelligent and verbally proficient—much like Asperger's boys.

In 1981, Wing published "Asperger's Syndrome: A Clinical Account." In it she presented the Austrian's 1944 cases side by side with descriptions of children she was currently seeing, showing how the children in both groups fit the description of Asperger's "autistic psychopaths." However, she suggested a gentler-sounding nomenclature. Noting that many people associated psychopathy with sociopathic behavior, she declared that, in her paper, "the neutral term Asperger syndrome is to be preferred and will be used." With that one sentence, Wing unintentionally launched a compelling new diagnosis that would sweep the English-speaking world.

As Wing made clear many times afterward, her purpose in shining a spotlight on Asperger's paper had never been to codify his 1944 observations into a stand-alone diagnosis for the modern era. For her part, she saw "no clear boundaries separating [the syndrome Asperger identified] from other autistic disorders," and she did not foresee, or intend, that the diagnosis "Asperger syndrome"—a term she used only descriptively—would be handed out to thousands of individuals across the United States, Britain, Ireland, Australia, Canada, and many other parts of the world, or that it would be defined during the 1990s, both in practice and by the most authoritative psychiatric manuals, as distinct from the autism described by Leo Kanner.

Rather, Wing brought attention to Asperger's boys for one reason only: to bolster her idea of the spectrum. She wanted to show that the medical literature was filled with descriptions of highly verbal and intelligent individuals who, because they also manifested some autistic traits, belonged on the same spectrum with those whose language and intellects were less well developed.

In fact, as an activist determined to get services for as many people as possible, she adamantly opposed breaking up the spectrum into multiple diagnoses. "Identification of any of the eponymous behavioural syndromes," she wrote, "is not of any practical help in this process." She conceded that with some parents, and even some professionals "who often cannot believe in a diagnosis of autism" when symptoms were mild, it could be useful to employ the label Asperger's syndrome. But it would only be to "help to convince the people concerned that there is a real problem."

The real problem, Wing would always argue, should be called autism. But because she had triggered an interest in Asperger's syndrome, because she had given it its name, the world assumed she was endorsing it.

Asperger's writing helped to inspire Lorna Wing's conception of the spectrum, but ironically, it does not seem that Asperger himself agreed that it was the best way to think about autism. In fact, based on Wing's account of their meeting at the Maudsley, it seems that he resisted a key aspect of the idea. Over tea, she laid out in some detail why she was certain that both Asperger's boys in Vienna and Kanner's children in Baltimore were best understood as having the same underlying condition. For her to take this view was not at all surprising. One of the main premises of the spectrum idea was that the differences among people with autistic traits were less important than the ways in which they were like one another. Whether you were talking about those with autism whose symptoms caused severe impairment or those who seemed merely eccentric, Wing believed that there was no point in splitting them into groups based on differences in how their autism manifested itself.

Her Austrian guest argued against that way of thinking. "Asperger, despite listing numerous similarities, considered his syndrome to be different from Kanner's," Wing reported. "We cordially agreed to differ."

Asperger drew the same clear line in a March 1977 presentation to autism parents in Switzerland—emphasizing the sharp distinction between his patients and Kanner's. Reiterating points he had made in a 1968 paper, he acknowledged that there were similarities between the two sets of children, and even "complete agreement in some respects," but he insisted that Kanner's children were in a "psychotic or near psychotic state," while "the Asperger type of child is not so seriously disturbed." More than that, he emphasized, "Asperger's typical cases are very intelligent children, with extraordinary originality of thought and spontaneity of activities." To Asperger, it was clear that the two sets of children were "basically different types" and that he and Kanner were talking about two different syndromes. The word "autistic," he told his audience, can be applied to "disturbances . . . of quite different origins which can and *should be differentiated*" (our italics).

At various times, Asperger noted that typically autistic traits could appear in people of both greater and lesser mental capacity, and could be expressed in fine gradations of intensity. In contrast to Wing, he tended to brush over this observation lightly, with a single sentence or a paragraph here or there. Rather, the focus of his writing was on children with more impressive intellectual and verbal abilities. Nor did his early papers explore ways to address the challenges faced by children of lesser intellectual ability. Certainly, he never insisted on grouping them together with everyone showing autistic traits under the umbrella of "autism"—the essence of the spectrum idea.

IN THE END, Asperger's syndrome became entrenched as a diagnosis because clinicians found it useful. There are no good statistics about the number of diagnoses of Asperger's made in the 1980s, but by the 1990s the diagnosis was clearly in wide use, especially in Britain. It was also popular in Sweden, where Swedish researcher Chris Gillberg published dozens of studies of the syndrome. A number of other researchers' papers dealt drily with the question of whether Asperger's was a separate phenomenon from autism. To clinicians, the question was academic. It fit people they were seeing and, as Wing had pointed out, it was easier to deliver a diagnosis of Asperger's to parents than to tell them that their child had autism.

Notably, the diagnosis became widespread even though, as of 1991, Asperger's syndrome was not recognized in the American Psychiatric Association's *DSM*. In 1992, the World Health Organization (WHO) got out in front of the APA by including Asperger's in a massive compendium called the *International Classification of Diseases*.

With the diagnosis continuing to climb in popularity, and with the WHO having officially recognized it, the editors of the *DSM* felt pressure to follow suit. As it happened, the APA planned to publish an updated edition of the *DSM* in 1994, which made it imperative that they decide whether to include Asperger's syndrome.

But first there was an awkward question to be answered about the man the syndrome was named after.

32

THE SIGNATURE

When the question was put to Lorna Wing in 1993, in a transatlantic phone call, she was shocked by it.

Was Hans Asperger, as a young man, a Nazi?

Fred Volkmar of the Yale Child Study Center felt uncomfortable even asking the question. But he believed he should, because doubts about Asperger's character had been raised. And a decision had to be made quickly about whether to posthumously honor Asperger by naming a condition after him in the *DSM,* the "bible" of psychiatry.

For months, experts led by Volkmar had been looking at studies, running field trials, and debating with one another, in conference rooms, by phone, and by fax, whether Asperger's syndrome deserved that formal recognition. As part of the working group assigned to "pervasive developmental disorders" for the 1994 update of the *DSM,* their conclusions would be decisive.

Volkmar's Yale Child Study Center was the leader in Asperger's research in the United States. At one point, a research request for volunteers with the condition had given Yale a roster of more than eight hundred families and individuals across the country. At Yale and elsewhere, clinicians who found the concept useful and relevant had been diagnosing patients with Asperger's without waiting for the *DSM* to sanction its usage.

Yet there was still vigorous disagreement over the validity of the concept. It was unclear whether individuals with the diagnosis were truly different in presentation from those described as "high functioning autistic," an already familiar and much-used concept. Beyond that, it was evident that clinics were independently tweaking the criteria, leading to widespread inconsistency in how the Asperger's label was applied. Given this, many argued that Asperger's was not a necessary or useful addition to the diagnostic lexicon.

On the other hand, the World Health Organization had just endorsed Asperger's as a stand-alone condition. Of greater relevance, Volkmar himself was among those convinced of its validity, having seen plenty of people at the Yale Child Study Center whose symptoms appeared to justify a diagnosis of Asperger's. Volkmar, charismatic, persuasive, and thorough, would be one of the final arbiters of whether the condition would be enshrined in the *DSM.* So it mattered when, with only months left till the new manual was due, he decided to investigate the question of whether Hans Asperger had been a Nazi.

Eric Schopler, for one, was convinced of it. He was also among those who considered Asperger's ideas superfluous to the understanding of autism, not to mention sloppily conceived. His attacks on Asperger's work in the 1990s were noticeably personal, reflecting an antipathy not justified by mere professional disagreement. "The seeds for our current syndrome confusion were sown in the rich soil of his few publications," he once wrote. In Schopler's view, Asperger had never "succeeded in identifying a replicable psychiatric syndrome."

Schopler's antipathy can be understood as the bitterness of a man who, as a child, had to flee Germany with the rest of his Jewish family, and who remained suspicious of any adult—German or Austrian—whose career as a medical professional had thrived during the Nazi era. He had no more to go on than that; it was guilt by association. But this did not prevent him from launching a one-man whisper campaign to the effect that Asperger had probably been a Nazi sympathizer, if not a collaborator or actual party member. More than once, Schopler dropped such innuendoes in print, in publications he oversaw, such as the *Journal of Autism and Developmental Disorders.* There and elsewhere, he pointedly made reference to Asperger's "longstanding interest in the German Youth Movement," hinting at a connection between Asperger and the Hitler Youth. Still, perhaps because Schopler kept his allusions subtle, most people who knew of Asperger's syndrome in the 1990s were unaware of any controversy concerning Asperger's past.

Volkmar, for example, did not hear about it until late in the *DSM* review process. But it was not Schopler who brought it to his attention. During the field trials Volkmar was running in order to test the proposed criteria for Asperger's, two Yale colleagues he held in high esteem raised the subject. One, Donald Cohen, the longtime director of the Yale Child Study Center, had published widely on autism. The other was a young star in the field, a clinician and investigator named Ami Klin. As a psychology PhD candidate in London, Klin had caused a stir with a brilliantly designed study showing that autism affected children's responses to the sounds of their mothers' voices. It had been Cohen who personally recruited Klin to Yale in 1989. The two men formed a close mentor-protégé relationship based on both a fascination with autism and a powerful sense of Jewish identity. Cohen was an observant Jew and a dedicated student of the Holocaust. Klin had been born in Brazil, the son of Holocaust survivors, and had earned his undergraduate degree in history and political science at Hebrew University in Jerusalem.

The question the two men kept turning over was whether Asperger might be implicated, in any way, in the medical atrocities ascribed to the Nazis who ruled Vienna. Both knew that the medical profession had already embarrassed itself by its failure to ask this question about several doctors and researchers who had practiced under the Third Reich. Modern textbooks still carried references to diseases named for Nazi-era scientists whose ethics were repellent, if not criminal, such as neurologists whose significant discoveries were made by dissecting the brains of children and adults murdered by the Nazis. A Dr. Franz Seitelberger of Vienna had been a member of the SS, while Professor Julius Hallervorden of Berlin was known to select live patients whose brains he planned to study after their deaths by "euthanasia." Hallervorden infamously said, "If you are going to kill all these people, at least take the brains out so that the material gets some use." Yet the terms "Seitelberger disease" and "Hallervorden-Spatz disease" still appeared in academic publications.

In 1993, Asperger, dead thirteen years, never a great presence on the world stage, remained a little-known figure. Uta Frith had published a cursory review of his life and work in 1991, to accompany her translation of his big 1944 paper. In addition, a talk Asperger gave in Switzerland in 1977 had appeared in translation in the magazine of a British autism organization in 1979, but it was not widely distributed. In short, Volkmar could get little information about Asperger on his own, and had no true "Asperger expert" to turn to. It was in that context that he called Lorna Wing, the one person he knew who had met Hans Asperger, and posed the question to her: *Was Hans Asperger, as a young man, a Nazi?*

Lorna Wing gasped. "Hans Asperger, a Nazi?" He could hear her indignation. She spoke of his deep Catholic faith and lifelong devotion to young people.

"A Nazi? No," Wing said. "No, no, no! He was a very religious man."

It was a short conversation, but it settled the issue.

A few months later, the *DSM-IV* appeared. Ninety-four new mental disorders had been proposed for inclusion, but only two made it. One was Bipolar II Disorder. The other was Asperger's Disorder.

In 1993, Wing and Volkmar knew nothing, of course, of the information about Asperger that would be unearthed in the years ahead.

The first warning sign came in 1996. That year, Ami Klin, along with Volkmar and psychologist Sarah Sparrow, began putting together a book they planned to title *Asperger Syndrome.* Yet Klin still could not shake his misgivings. And, because his name would be on the cover of the book, he decided that something more than a phone call to Lorna Wing was necessary in order to establish that Asperger's hands were clean.

In late 1996, Klin began writing to archives and institutes in Germany and Austria, seeking any documentary or other information on the Austrian doctor. This yielded little. But then a professor in Cologne, Germany, referred him to Austrian historian Michael Hubenstorf, who taught at the Institute of the History of Medicine at Berlin's Free University. "We would like to be able to write that he was a benevolent doctor whose primary concern was his patient's [sic] well being," Klin wrote Hubenstorf. "But we are not sure of that."

Hubenstorf responded a few weeks later with a four-page letter and a five-page catalog of Asperger's career postings, promotions, and publications he had assembled. Klin's concerns, he wrote, were justified. While he had found no record of formal membership in the Nazi Party, Hubenstorf informed Klin that Asperger's "medical career was clearly set in a surrounding of German Nationalists and Nazis," and that he was regularly promoted within that setting. He believed the doctor might have downplayed his previous connections to known Nazis such as Professor Hamburger, his onetime mentor, whom Hubenstorf described as "the most outspoken Nazi pediatrician of them all."

"It remains unclear how much of a fellow traveler he was," Hubenstorf concluded. But his advice to Klin was to err on the side of caution. He recommended against publishing "anything before the utmost effort has been made to clear Prof. Asperger's past."

In the end, Klin chose not to take Hubenstorf's advice. Weighing everything, he recognized that no "smoking gun" had been found—no evidence that Asperger had directly participated in any Nazi medical crimes. In the meantime, Klin had received a copy of an obituary of Asperger that portrayed him as a warm, gentle doctor devoted to the care of children. Asperger's daughter, Maria Asperger Felder, also vouched for her father's reputation when Klin reached out to her. Herself a psychiatrist, she wrote that her father had been at odds with the Nazis' racial determinism, that he had been an enemy of children's suffering, and that he had never lost "his lifelong interest in and his curiosity about all living creatures."

This was the story of the benevolent doctor that Klin had hoped would turn out to be the truth. In 2000, Klin, Volkmar, and Sparrow published *Asperger Syndrome,* with a foreword by Asperger's daughter.

THE "BENEVOLENT DOCTOR" version of Asperger had strong appeal, and would inform many assessments of his work. Indeed, an overwhelmingly positive narrative of Asperger as a man of moral rectitude came into focus in the new millennium, elevating him almost to the status of hero. Increasingly, he was seen as a cautious yet brave and canny saboteur of the Nazi project to exterminate intellectually disabled children. This image of him echoed Uta Frith's assertion, in 1991, that Asperger had been an ardent defender of the "misfits" the Nazi eugenics program was designed to destroy. "Far from despising the misfits," Frith wrote in the introduction to her translation of his 1944 paper, "he devoted himself to their cause—and this at a time when allegiance to misfits was nothing less than dangerous."

The hero image was amplified by Berlin psychiatrist Brita Schirmer, who in 2002 called attention to Asperger's "humanity and his courageous commitment to the children entrusted to him in times when this was by no means obvious, or without danger."

In 2007, the Dublin-based psychologists Viktoria Lyons and Michael Fitzgerald wrote a letter to the *Journal of Autism and Developmental Disorders* that celebrated Asperger as a man who "tried to protect these children from being sent to concentration camps in World War II."

And in 2010, the British autism historian Adam Feinstein published the results of his own reporting trip to Vienna to investigate the rumors that Asperger was sympathetic to Hitler. "The very opposite is more likely to be the case," he concluded.

This view of Asperger rested on a number of compelling stories. It was said that he had twice narrowly escaped arrest by the Gestapo while working at the Vienna Hospital, and that he had risked his own safety by failing to report the names of disabled children to the authorities. An entry in his diary, written during a 1934 visit to Germany, seems to shudder at the gathering Nazi storm: "An entire nation goes in a single direction, fanatically, with constricted vision." His Catholic faith, and his membership in the Catholic youth organization known as Bund Neuland, have also been cited as evidence of his association with a progressive morality that was at odds with the Nazi agenda.

Above all, this view rested upon Asperger's clear statements, from early in the Nazi era, defending the right of mentally challenged children to society's support. During the 1938 talk in which he described his autistic cases for the first time, he declared, "Not everything that falls out of line, and thus is 'abnormal,' has to be deemed 'inferior.'" Likewise, at the conclusion of his better-known 1944 thesis, "Autistic Psychopaths," he saluted the medical profession's "duty to stand up for these children with the whole force of our personality."

Thus, the case seemed strong for Asperger as a humanitarian and liberal thinker. It was an optimistic and inspiring portrait that spoke to modern sensibilities. And it would prove to be seriously flawed.

ONE OF THE best-known laundry detergents in the world goes by the brand name Persil. Originally manufactured in Germany, Persil is the Tide of Europe. In Austria and Germany, after World War II, the word came to signify, with grim humor, the furious, sometimes ludicrous, efforts made by Germans and Austrians to clear their reputations. Prompted by the Allies' "denazification" policy, an effort to purge Nazi Party members and collaborators from positions of influence, millions scurried to track down witnesses to their innocence. Especially prized was the testimony of Jews who could vouch for some moment of kindness or decency shown as the Holocaust unfolded. Often, those seeking to clear their names portrayed themselves as having been victims also, claiming that they had been threatened with arrest by the Gestapo, or stymied in their careers for standing up to Nazi policies. Others insisted that they had gone along with the Nazis as a ruse, and that they had secretly resisted the Nazi system from within. At the end of the process, those who succeeded came away with a document called a *persilschein,* or "Persil certificate," confirming that they had been certified innocent, or "clean." Even at the time, there was much cynicism about *persilschein*.

Without doubt, there were at least some authentic secret resisters among the Austrians. But a good many of these claims were nothing more than whitewash jobs. Michael Hubenstorf's letter to Ami Klin had pointed to the possibility that Asperger's past had also been whitewashed to some degree. Indeed, a second look at the hero narrative offers reasonable grounds for skepticism. To start with, the story of Asperger's near arrest by the Gestapo had only one source, and that was Asperger himself. As far as is known, he brought it up twice in public: in a 1962 talk and during a 1974 radio appearance. To any astute Austrian familiar with the *persilschein* phenomenon, this raises the suspicion that Asperger embroidered on his experience of being politically vetted by the Nazi authorities, or perhaps even concocted the story in full. This vetting was a process most public servants had to endure under a law passed after the *Anschluss* to weed out Jews and anyone else deemed "unreliable." No doubt Asperger's being a non-party member was looked into, but in the end the Nazis cleared him.

Another flag should have been Asperger's membership in Bund Neuland, which was, by Asperger's own account, crucial to his development as a young man. While ardently pro-Catholic, this group also espoused an anti-modern, pan-Germanic nationalist philosophy, and its tensions with the Nazis stemmed primarily from the Reich's anti-Church position. Otherwise, there was a fair amount of common ground between Bund Neuland and the Nazis. For example, a 1935 issue of the *Neuland* monthly periodical highlighted the problem of "excessive Jewish influence" in the upper reaches of society, and discussed the need for "a clean separation" between the "Jews of Vienna" and the rest of the population.

Then there were Asperger's own words. His 1934 diary entry about all of Germany moving "in a single direction, fanatically" has been cited—originally by his daughter, and then by others, relying on her account—as evidence that he condemned the Nazification of Germany. Read in full, however, it seems more ambiguous, with hints of awe and admiration as well as consternation: "An entire nation goes in a single direction, fanatically, with a constricted vision, certainly, but also with enthusiasm and dedication, with tremendous discipline and control, with a terrible effectiveness. Now only soldiers—soldierly thinking—ethos—Germanic paganism . . ." Moreover, it is the sole known excerpt of Asperger's writing that suggests concern about where things might be headed as of 1934.

Four years later, on October 3, 1938, there was no ambiguity in the language he used to open a historic address he gave to an assembly of his fellow physicians. The words he used sounded startlingly pro-Nazi, and came at the beginning of the talk in which he discussed his "autistic psychopaths" for the first time. This was a full seven months after the Nazi *Anschluss,* when Austria was absorbed into the Third Reich, yet Asperger's opening lines were nothing short of a valentine to the newly Nazified Austria.

"We stand in the midst of a massive renovation of our intellectual life, which encompasses all areas of this life—not least in medicine," he began. This new thinking, he said, was "the sustaining idea of the new Reich—that the whole is greater than the parts, and that the *Volk* is more important than any single individual."

In a handful of words, this was the defining vision of German fascism, which Asperger, in the next breath, applied to his fellow doctors. This "sustaining idea," he urged, "should, where it involves the nation's most precious asset—its health—bring profound changes to our entire attitude." This applied, he said, to "the efforts being made to promote genetic health, and to prevent the passing on of diseased heredity." It was hard not to miss the clear reference to the Nazi-driven "science" of race improvement through eugenics. "We physicians must carry out the tasks that fall to us in this area with full accountability," Asperger declared.

This salute to the *Anschluss,* to the Nazis, to the suppression of individuality, and to the task of purifying the genetic lineage of the nation should by itself have dealt a fatal blow to the idea that Asperger secretly resisted the Nazi agenda. A review of other medical talks and papers printed that year in the same weekly journal where Asperger's appeared shows that the opening of his talk was far from typical. Defenders of Asperger sometimes argue that he had a hidden anti-Nazi agenda—that he sought to throw the Gestapo off his scent by paying lip service to the regime. Brita Schirmer described the preamble as a "deft chess move" on Asperger's part. His defenders usually assert, as a corollary, that the full text of Asperger's speech, together with his 1944 paper, constitute an unambiguous argument to protect and nurture *all* vulnerable children, no matter the level of their disability.

But Asperger did not, in either the talk or the paper, make that argument. Despite recognizing in passing that autistic traits can be seen in children of both stronger and weaker mental capacity, he had little to say about helping the latter. Rather, he focused on the boys who possessed what he called "social worth"—a term he did not apply to all children. The boys in the group he favored would later be known as the "Asperger's type," and decades later as "Aspies." They were those he described as being "more lightly affected," as well as not at all rare in the population. Virtually every account of Asperger has him describing his boys, with affection, as "Little Professors"—a reference to their intelligence and their sometimes pedantic style. (That turns out to be a myth; Asperger himself never actually used the term Little Professors.)

Asperger made this preference explicit in his 1938 talk, where he admitted that he "thought it more rewarding to choose two [of his] not so severe and therefore more promising cases" to present. That would always be his pattern. In 1944, when discussing his "more lightly affected" children, Asperger was effusive in celebrating how far they could go, dwelling especially on those who had the potential to reach the uppermost echelons of society. To be sure, he was convinced—and said—that autistic traits were more often a detriment than a benefit for the majority of people who had them. But he was pleased to report that, for some, autism delivered special intellectual talents, and that those so endowed could "rise to high-ranking occupations." He cited, as examples, professors and scientists and even an expert on heraldry. He also reported that some of the more able children he had treated had become assets to a country at war. During the third year of the Second World War, Asperger noted, he had received letters and reports "from many of our former children" serving on the front lines. In 1941, he wrote that these boys were "fulfill[ing] their role in the professional life, in the military, and in the party."

Thus, again, his boys had demonstrated their "social worth"—in terms that the Third Reich appreciated.

That said, Asperger's vision of special education and what it could achieve was not quite as exceptional as his supporters suggest. Contrary to popular understanding, special education had its place in Nazi

Germany. The Reich allowed that disabled children who could become productive citizens should be afforded support and education to achieve that end. Even the Hitler Youth had special units for the blind and the deaf. But the Nazis drew a line where the cost of supporting a child was expected to exceed that child's ultimate material contribution to the state. For that child the Nazis had no use; his or her life was worthless.

Asperger did not go that far in anything he published, and the Catholic faith he professed opposed sterilization and euthanasia. But he never did advocate for the children he seems to have considered less "rewarding." Indeed, he appeared to write off the possibility of improving outcomes for those whose autistic traits were accompanied by a "pronounced intellectual inferiority." Rather than lay out a path to helping them, he simply noted the "tragic" fate of such individuals, or at least a sad minority of them. "In the less favorable cases," Asperger wrote, "they roam the streets as comic originals, grotesquely unkempt, talking loudly to themselves, addressing people in the manner of the autistic." When speaking of these "less favorable cases," Asperger never celebrated their autistic differences. Rather, his tone was one of pity.

ERIC SCHOPLER NEVER made the detailed case presented here for a less heroic version of Asperger. Instead of evidence, he had instinct, which perhaps came from being a Jew who had lived part of his life in Germany.

Perhaps this instinctive suspicion also explains Leo Kanner's nearly complete silence on Asperger's work. Also a Jew—one who, as we have seen, saved Jewish lives—Kanner may have viewed Asperger as too comfortably ensconced in Nazi Vienna, and thus preferred not to recognize him. Interestingly, on the single occasion when Kanner mentioned Asperger in print, he misspelled his name

But instinct was not evidence. In short, there was still no smoking gun. And then there was.

In May 2010, a soft-spoken Austrian academic walked into Vienna's city hall and its ceremonial gathering place, the *Wappensaal,* where a symposium honoring the memory of Hans Asperger was under way. Herwig Czech was a thirty-five-year-old historian and lecturer at the University of Vienna. He had been invited to speak at the symposium by organizers from the Vienna children's hospital where Asperger had done his most important work. A number of autism's research luminaries were in attendance, and Lorna Wing herself was scheduled for an afternoon talk.

Czech's academic specialty was the role of medicine during the Third Reich. It was a hallmark of his work to unearth the discrepancies—often embarrassing—between the accounts medical professionals gave of themselves after the war and their actual conduct during it. Czech's interest in this area was perhaps connected to his dawning awareness during his boyhood that his warm and loving grandfather had been "a convinced Nazi." It was not something the old man ever talked about openly, but the knowledge lay heavily on Czech, given what he was learning at school about the darkness of those years.

Which brought Czech to city hall, some thirty years after Asperger's death. Before him, in their hands, all of the seated attendees held the day's program, its cover featuring a black-and-white photograph of a young Dr. Asperger, wearing a white lab coat and engaged in deep conversation with a young boy—presumably one of his patients. The symposium's title appeared above the photo: "On the Trail of Hans Asperger." The event had been prompted by the growing international recognition of Asperger's work. Over two days, presenters would explore the man's career and offer assessments of the latest scientific findings regarding Asperger's syndrome.

The organizers had received word beforehand that Czech had stumbled across compromising details regarding their honoree. This could not have been welcome news, but in the spirit of scientific inquiry, they encouraged him to keep digging and to report whatever he might find. But once Czech was standing in front of them, there was a slight awkwardness to the situation: among the 150 or so audience members were Asperger's daughter and some of his grandchildren. The title of Czech's talk, printed in the program brochure, was "Dr. Hans Asperger and the Nazi Child Euthanasia Program in Vienna: Possible Connections."

Awkwardness gave way to surprise, and then shock, as Czech drew a portrait of Asperger that left the hero narrative in tatters, based on a trove of original documents he had excavated. There was, for example, a 1941 letter Czech had found in the archives of the Spiegelgrund—the facility where so many children had died of "pneumonia" after being poisoned with phenobarbital. Addressed to the Spiegelgrund's administration, the letter reported on the recently conducted medical evaluation, at the University Hospital, of a little girl named Herta Schreiber. The handwriting was Asperger's. Herta was then two years old, the youngest of nine children—of whom five still lived at home—and she had been sick all spring since contracting encephalitis. Her condition did not appear to be improving, and in June her mother had brought her to be seen by Asperger at his clinic.

The letter contained an assessment of Herta's condition. It was apparent that she had suffered some sort of major insult to her brain: her mental development had halted, her behavior was disintegrating, and she was having seizures. Asperger seemed unsure of his diagnosis. He noted several possibilities: severe personality disorder, seizure disorder, idiocy. Then, in plain prose, he offered a decidedly nonmedical opinion: "When at home, this child must present an unbearable burden to the mother, who has to care for five healthy children."

Having expressed his empathy for Herta's mother, Asperger rendered his recommendation: "Permanent placement at the Spiegelgrund seems absolutely necessary." The letter was signed "Hans Asperger."

Everyone in the audience grasped the meaning of Asperger's letter. It was a death warrant. Indeed, Czech confirmed that Herta was admitted to the Spiegelgrund on July 1, 1941, and killed there on September 2, 1941, one day after her third birthday. Records state that she died of pneumonia. Notes from the hospital archives quoted her mother as agreeing, through tears, that her daughter would be better off this way, rather than living in a world where she would face constant ridicule and cruelty. It was Czech's assessment that Herta's parents supported the Nazi agenda.

The effect in the room was powerful. As they listened, members of the audience stole glances at the picture of Asperger and the boy on the cover of the program. Suddenly, the celebratory nature of their gathering seemed wildly off key, as Czech went on delivering, in a quiet, affectless voice, more disturbing news from the Nazi past.

In February 1942, he reported, Asperger was the senior pediatrician representing the city of Vienna on a commission asked to review the health status of 210 Austrian children residing in a mental hospital in lower Austria. Several months earlier, the government had begun taking steps to apply mandatory education laws even to children in these hospitals, as long as they were "educable." A panel of seven experts was charged with compiling a list of the names of those children who should, despite their mental challenges, start attending classes in either traditional academic or special-education settings. In a single day, Asperger and his colleagues went through the records of all 210 children. While 17 were found to be too young for compulsory education, and 36 too old, the panel designated 122 of them as ready for schooling.

That left 26 boys and 9 girls. Their fate, Czech reported, was known, and he believed Asperger knew it as well. A written summary detailing the commission's composition, purpose, and procedures clearly stated that those children judged to be not "educable" were to be "dispatched for Jekelius Action" as quickly as possible. When that was written, Erwin Jekelius, a former assistant to Asperger's mentor Franz Hamburger, was the fiancé of Hitler's younger sister, as well as director of the Spiegelgrund. "Jekelius Action" was a euphemism the commission's members would have understood quite well. Asperger once said he took a "great risk" by refusing to report children to the authorities. This, clearly, was not one of those times.

Czech also shared findings suggesting a greater affinity between Asperger and the Nazis than Asperger had admitted to. According to the file the Nazi Party kept on him, he was repeatedly judged to be an Austrian whom the Nazi authorities could trust, even more so as the years went by. Each time Asperger applied for a post or a promotion, he was cleared as someone who, though not a party member, abided by Nazi principles in the performance of his job. In one instance, a party official wrote that he "conforms to the principles of the policy of racial hygiene."

In the years following his talk, Czech would discover other evidence of how far Asperger went to conform. He found letters in Asperger's handwriting that used "*Heil Hitler*" as their closing salutation. This was not mandatory. He also unearthed a job application filled out in Asperger's hand in which Asperger described himself as a candidate for the Nazi Doctors Association, a group that functioned as a medical policy arm of the party and was instrumental in closing the medical practices of Jewish physicians. He also learned that Asperger had applied to be a medical consultant to the Vienna branch of the Hitler Youth, though there is no record of him having been accepted. All in all, in Czech's view, Asperger took care during the war to safeguard his career and to burnish "his Nazi credibility." Asperger, it would appear, did what was necessary.

CZECH SPOKE FOR only twenty minutes or so that day at the Vienna city hall. Then he stopped to take audience questions. In that pause, Dr. Arnold Pollak, the director of the clinic where Asperger had worked for much of his career, leapt to his feet, clearly agitated. Turning to the room, he asked that everyone present stand and observe a moment of silence in tribute to the many children whose long-forgotten murders Herwig Czech had returned to memory. The entire audience rose and joined in wordless tribute.

PART VII

DREAMS AND BOUNDARIES

1980s–1990s

33

THE DREAM OF LANGUAGE

"COMMUNICATION AT SENTENCE LEVEL." THOSE WERE THE words that leapt out at Doug Biklen when the letter from Australia arrived in 1987. By then, Biklen, based at Syracuse University, was well-known in academic and activist circles as a forward thinker on the civil rights of people with disabilities. The letter writer, an Australian lawyer named Chris Borthwick, had written him to share news of a stunning breakthrough achieved by the woman he lived with. Her name was Rosemary Crossley. Biklen had met the couple a few years earlier, when the Australian government invited him to give a series of lectures on his work in the United States. Since that time, Borthwick said in his letter, Crossley had achieved something previously considered impossible: two-way, "sentence level," English-language communication in children with autism who had never before spoken. These were children whose demeanor and verbal production—grunts, squeals, screaming, or just plain silence—suggested not only a limited capacity for language but also serious cognitive deficits.

But Crossley had tested those limits by teaching the kids to type messages on a small computerized device. Borthwick said that Crossley was eliciting sentences after as few as three sessions.

"Every single one," Borthwick emphasized. "All. The lot. One hundred percent."

Biklen was fascinated and inspired. For twenty years, since the late 1960s, he had been at the forefront of efforts to bring recognition to people with disabilities as full members of society—and to end the prejudices that saw disability as the equivalent of deficiency. As a graduate student at Syracuse University, he began joining the legendary

Burton Blatt, his mentor, in going into the back wards of New York State's large institutions to expose the appalling warehouse conditions under which intellectually disabled people were being held. In the late 1980s, he was well-established in his own right. He was on the faculty at Syracuse as the director of its Center on Human Policy, which supported research and advocacy on disability rights, and he was the author of several well-regarded books. He was also the winner of multiple rights-related awards from organizations such as the American Civil Liberties Union.

Biklen was well-known to the local public school districts around Syracuse because of his campaign, begun in the 1970s and joined by others, to open all classrooms to all children regardless of disability. Borrowing from the argument made in the landmark 1954 Supreme Court case, *Brown v. Board of Education,* which established the unconstitutionality of separate public schools for white and African American students, Biklen opposed the de facto segregation-by-disability practiced by most public schools in America—where "special education" meant usually separate classrooms and a separate curriculum. "Inclusion"—the idea that everyone should have access to the same spaces, services, and opportunities—became Biklen's watchword.

The inherent merit of his argument had been established by a number of legal victories won by Syracuse-area parents, who, with his encouragement and counsel, had successfully advocated for and even sued their schools to gain access to regular classrooms for children with disabilities. Their pressure also won for their kids a variety of supports to enhance their ability to participate academically and socially, which might include a sign language interpreter for a deaf child, or a second teacher to help a child with autism stay focused.

Not every expert agreed that inclusion was always to the individual child's benefit, and in the years to come, the efficacy of inclusion would be much debated. But Biklen was an absolutist. He argued that it was an educator's ethical responsibility to take each student's educability as a given, and he exhorted schools and teachers to approach each child with a "presumption of competence."

But a special challenge arose with bringing nonverbal children with autism into a regular classroom. Such children could only go so far, since academic progress depended so much on conversational literacy—on the vital give-and-take with teachers, and with students. Many of the kids could not demonstrate that. As Biklen recognized, it was a difference that did not seem to have a work-around.

That was why, as soon as he got the letter about "communication at sentence level," Biklen knew he had to see for himself where these words were coming from.

ROSEMARY CROSSLEY WAS a celebrity in Australia. By 1984, the story of her triumph in establishing two-way communication with a teenage girl who could not talk had been made into a movie, based on a bestselling book written by Crossley herself, with the young woman as coauthor. Annie McDonald, born in 1961, had been diagnosed with cerebral palsy and was assumed to have severe brain damage. She could not walk or feed herself. In the film, as in real life, Crossley was an assistant in the institution where Annie resided full-time in the late 1970s, when she began to suspect that the girl's intellect was, in fact, whole and vibrant. Over time, Crossley worked hard to make a connection with Annie, seeking some way to communicate using words. Ultimately, she declared that she had achieved success using a method of her own invention. She further asserted that it had vindicated her hunch that Annie was not at all mentally diminished and actually had a great deal to say. It was the cerebral palsy that kept her from speaking, by interfering with the mechanical production of speech, Crossley concluded. Then Crossley came up with a method that bypassed spoken language.

She called it "facilitated communication." It was also commonly known as FC. When Biklen flew to Australia in 1988 for a week's visit, Crossley demonstrated the method herself.

At the first session, Biklen was introduced to a twenty-four-year-old man named Louis. Louis had some speech, but it appeared to be purely echolalic, meaning that he simply repeated other people's words, without any discernible meaning. That day, Louis started out by saying, "Excuse me. Get Mommy on the bus. Excuse me," over and over, no matter what anyone else said to him. But as Biklen watched, Crossley sat down next to Louis, took hold of his right forearm, and, addressing him directly, apologized for the elementary nature of what they were about to do. Then she turned to the small electronic screen lying flat on the table in front of them and asked Louis to touch, with his finger, several small pictures displayed on the screen as a computerized voice called out the name of the object shown. With Crossley lightly supporting his arm, Louis reached out and, tentatively, hit the right target each time: *car, circle, triangle.* After a few minutes, the pictures on the screen were replaced with the words *hand, eye,* and *fish.* Crossley moved her hand up toward Louis's wrist and took hold of the top of his sleeve—again, only lightly—as she asked him to point to specific words. Again, he made all correct choices. After that, he moved on to choosing single words from full sentences and letters from a display of the full alphabet. Crossley congratulated him warmly each time he hit a mark correctly.

A half hour had already passed when Crossley produced a Canon Communicator—a small keyboard device that spooled out a thin paper tape displaying whatever was typed into it—not unlike a label maker. Crossley asked Louis to tell her his name, which he did using the keyboard. At this point, she was touching his arm only intermittently. Then she asked him if he had anything he wanted to say. His finger moved and the paper tape advanced again with each letter he pressed. It read: IM NOT RETARDED. Crossley commented, "No, I don't think you are." Louis continued pressing keys; this time the tape read: MY MOTHER THINKS IM STUPID BECAUSE I CANT USE MY VOICE PROPERLY.

Biklen was astounded. During a follow-up visit to Australia, which lasted nearly four weeks, he met with twenty-one people identified as having autism, most of whom had little to no spoken language. Via FC, he "spoke" with them. Some, new to FC, had only a limited vocabulary, producing keyboard communication that was rife with misspellings and grammatical errors. Others, who had been communicating for three or four years, seemed to have mastered the art of conversation. In each instance, a facilitator performed the role Crossley had played with Louis, offering encouragement and maintaining light physical contact with the person pressing the keys. The facilitator might support a forearm, or an elbow, or keep a hand on a shoulder. This contact was meant not to steer the letter selection, but to provide gentle resistance that slowed the process, smoothing out impulsive or involuntary movements. For example, if a person were to get locked into hitting the same key repeatedly, the facilitator would pull his hand back from the keyboard. In some cases, there was no physical contact at all, which Biklen called "independent" typing—though the facilitator always remained inches away.

Biklen found himself engaging with people who were liable to be viewed by others as profoundly uncommunicative and almost certainly intellectually disabled. But with FC, he found himself convinced that the opposite was the case. For example, he met Bette, a young woman who could not go to the toilet by herself, but was verbally sophisticated enough to ask Biklen, via keyboard, "if people like me will ever be normal . . . able to do more things that other people do." One boy explained that he had mastered reading "by being around words and by watching television." Biklen took part in facilitated conversations that wandered into jokes and wordplay and that even probed philosophical matters, such as "the social construction of reality" and the nature of disability itself. "What really does integration have to offer to some terribly retarded people?" a young woman named Polly asked him via FC. This was all the more extraordinary since many of these children and young people had been denied all education and perhaps had never even been read to. Yet they were composing full sentences, with recognizable grammar and better than passable spelling.

CROSSLEY WAS NOT the first person to claim communication with nonspeaking individuals diagnosed with autism. Various modalities had been tried in the past, with a wide range of results, some better documented than others.

The earliest-known use of attempted communication by keyboard for people with autism dated to 1964, when a pediatrician named Mary Goodwin installed a "talking typewriter" at the Bassett Medical Center in Cooperstown, New York. The device had been developed by Edison Laboratories as an experimental product for teaching beginning reading while making "learning . . . a successful, enjoyable experience for the student." Nearly as big as a refrigerator, the talking typewriter combined a keyboard with an early computer that was programmed to play a tape-recorded voice naming each letter as it was typed, while at the same time the letter was projected on the monitor. Goodwin allowed a number of children, all diagnosed with autism, to explore the keyboard, pushing keys at will.

Initially, the printouts showed only random combinations of letters. In time, however, Goodwin reported that some of the children were constructing recognizable words. For example, a boy named Robbie produced this string—downycloroxfinaltouchivoryliquidiobnkkll—which clearly yielded the words "downy," "clorox," "final," "touch," "ivory," and "liquid." It was probably no coincidence that these words, and others Robbie produced, were brand names and product descriptions he had likely seen in ads. Still, for a time, Goodwin's work caused great excitement, which died away as the verbal output of the children failed to flower beyond this typewritten version of echolalia.

Also in the 1960s, a mother named Rosalind Oppenheim published a piece in the *Saturday Evening Post* about teaching her severely impaired son to write, spell, and do arithmetic by manipulating his hand to help him grip a pencil. Though she wrote a book describing her method, it did not garner much attention or many adopters.

Ivar Lovaas, of course, had used ABA to instill speech skills in previously nonspeaking children. With some children—more often those who had higher intelligence to begin with—recognizable fluency was achieved. With children of lesser intelligence, more modest gains were made: small working vocabularies, which let children ask for what they wanted verbally. This was not an insignificant achievement, and helped lessen much of the daily frustration that came with not being able to communicate one's most basic wants and needs. A boy named Reeve, for example, after hours upon hours of ABA-based teaching, learned to form simple sentences that started with "I want . . ." and to answer the question "What are you doing?" with specific and correct answers, such as "I am drawing." Unquestionably, this marked a major leap forward in his ability to interact with the world. But it did not, as the researchers had hoped, lay the groundwork for the boy's own brain to take over the language acquisition process. Reeve never learned a new word simply by hearing it, and he never made any spontaneous attempts to practice his skills. He did not become a person able to pour out his inner thoughts.

In the 1980s, a different and wholly nonverbal approach produced authentic communication on par with Reeve's. Two Delaware educators, speech pathologist Lori Frost and behavior analyst Andrew Bondy, created small picture symbols depicting objects or actions, each the approximate size of a credit card. These constituted the system's vocabulary. A child trained in its use, who wanted, say, a cup of juice, would pick up the picture displaying juice and hand it to the person of whom the request was being made. The physical act of touching and delivering the picture bypassed the need for speech and overcame the weakness some children displayed in pointing with their fingers. Simple and effective, the Picture Exchange Communication System (PECS) acquired many users. (Many years later, a comparable visual approach was adapted to create stunningly sophisticated applications for the iPad and other touchscreen computers. Like PECS, these applications enabled communication without speech, and without the necessity of mastering complex English grammar.)

But by the late 1980s, some twenty-five years' worth of experiments in communication with nonverbal people with autism had not yet yielded anything approximating the rich, complex experience of fully realized language.

Then FC came along.

DOUG BIKLEN CAME back from Australia convinced. In August 1990, in the *Harvard Educational Review,* he published an account of what he had seen Rosemary Crossley do. He acknowledged being skeptical at first, noting that FC yielded uneven results, where children produced language with some facilitators but not others. He noted, too, that some children appeared not always to be looking at the keyboard as they typed. This raised the possibility that the facilitators were steering the letter selection. "Perhaps it is such behaviors," Biklen wrote, "that cause some people to worry that facilitated communication is no more real than a Ouija board."

But Biklen, in the end, bought in. Conceding that he was not sure why FC worked, he asserted that he had seen "enough to justify the continuing assumption of its validity." Indeed, he wrote, facilitated communication had "forced" him "to redefine autism." It was an audacious statement, as he had never been, strictly speaking, an authority on autism. But his enthusiasm was contagious, as teachers and speech language therapists in the Syracuse schools began to use facilitated communication, consulting with Biklen in after-hours meetings. As word of this spread, the excitement was echoed in news coverage, where FC was almost invariably described as a miracle. The *New York Times* published a wrenching feature article in 1991 titled "The Words They Can't Say," describing the heartbreaking messages kids were typing. "Tell my mother that I'm sorry that I could never learn how to talk," read one. "I'll die if I don't get a friend," read another. In 1992, *Prime Time Live*'s Diane Sawyer personally spent a week in Syracuse with Biklen and some of his students. The resulting story won an Emmy Award.

Meanwhile, hundreds of aspiring facilitators signed up for training in the method through a program Biklen established at Syracuse University. In less than a year, eight hundred people had completed the course. Soon workshops were being offered at Temple University, the University of Maine, and the University of Buffalo. FC experience became a selling point for new hires in special-ed departments. One New York State school district placed an ad for a speech therapist in the local newspaper and specified "Knowledge of augmentative and facilitated communication desired."

Those learning the method felt like they were an integral part of a revolution in special education. Certainly, that was what a teacher in Maine believed when she started using FC in late 1992, never expecting the words she coaxed out of a young girl to bring catastrophe along with them.

34

THE CHILD WITHIN

AFTERWARD, JANYCE BOYNTON BLAMED HERSELF MOST OF all.

For the words that came out.

For what that family went through.

For believing.

In 1992, Boynton had eight years of experience as a special-needs teacher and, more recently, as a speech clinician. The job never paid much, but she had not gone into teaching for the money. For her, helping severely disabled children improve their odds of finding a place in the world was reward enough. Boynton, who worked for the Ellsworth public schools in Maine's Hancock County, was routinely given the "difficult" cases, like sixteen-year-old Betsy Wheaton. Boynton first started looking into FC to find some way to communicate with Betsy, who had autism.

One of her colleagues, a teacher's aide who had taken a workshop in FC, had recommended it. She sat down with Betsy and, using a photocopy of a keyboard laminated in plastic, showed Boynton how the method worked. Almost immediately, Betsy's finger was touching letters in coherent patterns, giving coherent answers to simple "yes/no" questions. Briefly, Boynton doubted. It was far more likely that it was the aide holding her hand—not Betsy—who was coming up with these answers. But then, after watching some more and seeing how convinced the aide was, she reconsidered.

If this were real, it would be so wonderful for Betsy. She was a restless girl and occasionally aggressive, but Boynton had always had a gut feeling that this combative behavior came from a frustration at her inability to communicate. Sometimes she would catch Betsy staring at her with an intensity that suggested she had something she wanted to say. Now, when she sat down and took Betsy's hand lightly to try FC for the first time, she felt it: this was real. Their two hands might have been moving as a paired set, but Boynton's was only along for the ride, merely providing support.

Words didn't come right away. At first, most of what she and Betsy produced together were strings of apparently random letters. But after a few weeks, single words began to emerge, appropriate to the context, as when Boynton would ask her a series of "fill in the blank"–type questions. One of the first times this happened, it was the word "t-o-u-r-i-s-t-s," when someone had asked Betsy, "Who climbs mountains?" Another time, asked to build a sentence around the verb "fell," from a card pulled out of a deck of vocabulary words, her finger typed out, "t-h-e-s-o-n-o-f-a-b-i-t-c-h." Then she pointed to the card—*fell*—and then her finger returned to the keyboard, typing letters that completed a sentence: "o-n-t-h-e-g-r-o-u-n-d." Boynton was amazed, delighted to discover a sense of humor in her young student. Even if the whole process was plodding and lacking in fluency, Boynton took these productions as proof that hidden behind Betsy's silence was a functioning intellect. And that was thrilling.

The child within. It had always been the most tantalizing conception of autism, this idea of the "real" son or daughter hidden behind the mask of autism. Although Leo Kanner never used the phrase, he helped inspire it by drawing attention to the looks on the faces of the eleven children he first treated. Kanner wrote of "the impression of serious-mindedness," "an expression of beatitude," and the "good cognitive potentialities" with which "all [were] unquestionably endowed." As he wondered about the "placid smile" he saw play across the lips of the children when they were most content, which was when they were left in their inner worlds, it was as if he were wondering who these children really were—or would be—if they were no longer constrained or confined by their autism.

The power of this idea was reflected in how often it entered the dreams of autism parents—literally. *"Last night, I dreamed my son could speak."* Such statements would appear, with slightly different wording, again and again in memoirs, in online forums, and in conversations with mothers and fathers who teetered between hope and anguish. The possibility of "liberating" their child lifted them up with hope. The impossibility of it left them feeling crushed with guilt, convinced that they must not be trying hard enough to break through. It was as though autism was a locked room and they were constantly in search of the key.

The fierce desire to locate "the child within" was in many ways unique to families dealing with autism. In families dealing with other developmental conditions, such as Down syndrome, love translated into embracing a child as he or she was, and providing as many opportunities as possible without hoping for a radical transformation. The parents of children with autism loved their children no less, but many of them felt a strong impulse to rescue them, and sought out breakthrough treatments to help them do so.

This was especially true of the parents of newly diagnosed children, who were likely to be under five years old. After all, the one point on which nearly all experts agreed was the need to start early intensive therapy before the age of five. New autism parents did not even want to be near older parents who might advise them not to raise their hopes too high. Neither did they appreciate the cautions voiced by scientists, who were apt to suggest that the fad treatment of the moment lacked empirical support. The newcomers shut out these warnings. When there was no time to waste, when there was a child to save, surely it made more sense to try something instead of nothing—as long as the idea seemed reasonable and no one was likely to get hurt. Thus, in every decade after the 1960s, parents tried all manner of alternative therapies, which came and went, causing excitement and then, usually, disappointment.

In South Africa, they gave their children enemas with diluted bleach as a way to rid the body of evil spirits; elsewhere, the same method was used to kill "bacteria" caused by autism. Parents signed up for "holding therapy," promoted by a New York psychiatrist named Martha Welch and endorsed by a Nobel Prize–winning zoologist.

It involved mothers hugging their children as tightly as possible while shouting at them until the children calmed down, which was seen as the beginning of healing. In France, parents tried "packing therapy," in which the child is wrapped tightly in wet, refrigerated sheets, like a cocoon, with only his or her head sticking out.

Other approaches involved megavitamin regimens, special diets, and exposure to dolphins and horses. All of these came with a plausible theory, and always with reports from parents who, at least for their own kids, had seen some good come from the method. The news most often spread by word of mouth, but sometimes a new therapy surfaced through massive news media coverage.

That was the case in 1993, when Victoria Beck, a New Hampshire mother, took her three-year-old son five hundred miles to a research hospital in Maryland looking for treatment that might relieve his constant and severe gastrointestinal pain. As part of a diagnostic test, Parker, who had autism, received a pig hormone called secretin. Within days, his digestion, speech, and sociability had drastically improved. Beck began telling her son's story to the media, after which a massive demand for secretin developed. In some places, the price shot up as high as $8,000 for four doses, for a drug that costs less than $180 to produce. Clinical trials would never demonstrate any benefit comparable to the progress made by Parker.

As with secretin, virtually all of these therapies failed to pass scientifically controlled tests of their validity, and most parents who tried them were disappointed. Wiser after such experiences, many of those parents concluded that their time and energy would be better spent not chasing the latest miracle cure.

But not everybody reached that conclusion. Many of the alternative approaches considered discredited stayed alive indefinitely, out of the media limelight, practiced by parents who made only the modest claim that they saw improvement in their own kids. But no one could ever refute with certainty the possibility that, perhaps for some extremely small number of people, something real and therapeutic did take place at one time, or at least appeared to. Neither can anyone accuse the parents still engaged with such practices of not trying hard enough to find the key to unlocking the child within.

As she continued working with Betsy, Janyce Boynton, reading some of the literature published by the FC movement, was learning that successful communication depended on much more than mere mechanical technique. It required an almost spiritual commitment as well, as FC theory held that effective facilitation rested on a deep level of trust between the person typing and his or her facilitator. It further required the facilitator's absolute faith in the process and in the reality of the facilitated individual's intellectual capacity. This meant that, at all times, Boynton was to address Betsy as she would any person who could fully understand every word spoken to her. This could be wearying, as Boynton had to do all the talking, but she found the effort and the hours profoundly rewarding. She also took deep satisfaction from Betsy's growing trust in her—as evidenced by the increasing quality of the language Betsy was producing. Boynton reciprocated that trust with loyalty. Betsy became her main priority. As the girl's crucial link to the world, Boynton would stand by her and stand up for her, no matter what.

And then, mysteriously, Betsy started hitting Boynton. It began during the first week of January 1993, at around the same time that Boynton had made arrangements to take a course in FC given at the University of Maine to improve her skills. Over the course of several sessions, Betsy showed signs of agitation, scratching Boynton and slapping her hand away. Boynton persisted, knowing that the FC literature warned facilitators to expect periods when frustration and anger might surface. One day, however, Betsy smacked Boynton in the face so hard that it took Boynton several moments to regain her composure. In that moment, the thought that crossed her mind was that Betsy was trying to tell her something—something for which she had not yet found words. Then she had an intuition. The blow, she thought, must be a sign of trouble at home.

Among Boynton's colleagues in special education, it was a given that, when a disabled child began acting out, the behavior could be the result of abuse, and that it was a teacher's duty to be alert to that possibility. Also at that time there was something of a nationwide panic over accusations of widespread sexual abuse in child day-care centers around the country, with several teachers convicted and sentenced to lengthy prison terms. These cases, nearly all of which were ultimately debunked, nevertheless made educators extremely vigilant about the possibility of abuse.

Then, to Boynton's horror, the words spelled out by Betsy's pointing finger turned decidedly dark and lurid. It started with curse words and a few relatively benign complaints about her father. Then, a few sessions later, in blunt and harsh language, explicit references to Betsy's father emerged—references to his touching her genitals and breasts.

Sickened, and frightened for Betsy, Boynton took her own handwritten transcripts of the FC sessions to the head of the high school's special-education department, who in turn delivered them to the head of guidance. Two days later, Boynton, Betsy, a police officer, and a worker from the state Department of Human Services (DHS) sat clustered behind the closed door of a small room used for speech therapy, where the DHS investigator wanted to conduct an interview with Betsy. Boynton was nervous, unsure whether outsiders would understand her role as Betsy's facilitator, or recognize that the typed messages were really the words of a capable, intelligent, but upset sixteen-year-old.

Boynton was relieved when the DHS investigator began the interview by addressing Betsy directly. She looked at her and said, simply, "Hi."

At this, Betsy's hand, supported by Boynton's, moved to the keyboard and typed out two letters. *HI.*

The investigator smiled, and Boynton relaxed.

But as Boynton facilitated the next part of the exchange, a new feeling took hold of those in the room. It was horror. As Betsy's finger pounded at one key after another, Boynton transcribed a shockingly explicit description: *HE FUCKS ME AND AND HHE FUCKS ME AND HE MAKES ME HOLD HIS PENISSS.*

"Who touched you?" the DHS woman asked aloud. "Where did they touch you?"

MY FATHER.

"When?" Betsy was asked.

AFTER SCHOOL.

"Where?"

IN MY HOUSE.

More questions elicited even more disturbing details.

SOMETHING GOES OFF

"What something goes off?"

HIS FUCK

"What does that look like?"

IT LOOKS LIKE

S F A A SLIMY AND.

. . . DDAA WHITE

I'M A FRAID I AM AFRAID RAID

"What are you afraid of?"

MY FATHER AND MY MOTH . . .

"Are you afraid of Jamie?"

YES

Repeatedly, Jamie, her brother, was described as abusing Betsy, as well as being abused himself by his mother and father.

"Where is Jamie?"

HE IS FUCKED AND HE GAF FF A FF

"Who fucks your brother?"

MY FATHER AND THE BITCH

With breaks, the interview went on for four hours, with increasingly graphic details. At one point, Betsy was shown anatomically correct drawings of the male and female bodies, side by side, and asked to indicate where her father's "thing" was. She appeared to miss this question, pointing to the pubic area on the drawing of the woman. Asked a second time, a little later, Betsy pointed to the man's penis and then typed *PENIS.*

Betsy was not permitted to go home to her parents that night. Within hours, a judge had issued an emergency order transferring her and her brother into the state's care. Arrangements were made to place each into foster care—but separately, because fourteen-year-old Jamie was considered not only a victim but a suspect. The police thought he had been "brainwashed" by his parents into being a sex abuser. A willing family was quickly found for Jamie, but the DHS had difficulty placing a girl as disabled as Betsy. This was resolved when a friend of Boynton's brother agreed to shelter her on a temporary basis.

Betsy's parents were distraught. Her father, Jim, an assistant to a ferryboat captain, and her mother, Suzette, who worked at a local market cleaning fish, had not only lost both their children. They now faced the real possibility of being prosecuted for the rape of their children. In their fear and confusion, they knew only one thing with certainty—the allegations were pure fabrications. So confident were they that this obvious fact would be established quickly that they waived their right to an attorney and agreed to cooperate fully.

But that put them in the terrible position of having to call their own daughter a liar. Because, like Boynton—and the school authorities and the police—Jim and Suzette believed in FC. They had found it exhilarating, over these past several months, to learn for the first time what their silent girl was thinking. Like many parents whose children were now "speaking" through FC, they had been unsuccessful as facilitators themselves. For some reason, the words did not come when they themselves held Betsy's hand. So they were grateful that Boynton had established the trust to make the method work. The pain of hearing these terrible falsehoods was all the worse because of their certainty that they came from Betsy herself.

Then a skeptic stepped into the investigation. Phil Worden was a local attorney appointed to serve as temporary legal guardian for the two children. Worden was a father himself, with two boys only slightly younger than Betsy's brother, Jamie. Worden did not come at this assignment with an adversarial mind-set. Determined to understand the real threat to Betsy, he sat down and talked with all the adults in the case, including Betsy's parents. They struck him as forthright, and it impressed him that they were as anxious as anyone for the investigation to move forward. Boynton also impressed him as honest and passionate about her duty to do what was best for Betsy. He could tell that she was terribly upset about seeing the Wheaton family split apart. Unlike Boynton and Betsy's parents, however, he was not sure that he trusted FC.

From the first time he saw Boynton and Betsy together, he spotted things in their interaction that everyone else seemed determined to overlook. The three of them met with the DHS caseworker and a detective from the state police in the same small room in the high school. The meeting had been called so that he could hear the story from Betsy herself. With Boynton supporting her hand and index finger, Betsy's fingertip tapped out *HI PHIL* on the laminated image of a keyboard. Worden was taken aback. In that moment, it seemed so obvious to him that Boynton was directing the typing, and just as obvious that every other adult in the room thought otherwise. It felt surreal, as if by not drawing attention to the fiction in front of him, he was participating in it. Nevertheless, he kept his doubts to himself and proceeded to ask Betsy some questions.

The way she reacted made him even more of a doubter. Throughout the session, Betsy was agitated, flinging herself around so vigorously that she was not even looking at the keyboard, even in the moments when, her hand in Boynton's, her index finger continued to press on keys, spelling out words. Suddenly, she punched Boynton so hard in the face that her glasses went flying. Boynton chided her: "Betsy, it hurts me when you hit me. I want to talk with you but I cannot do so if you hit me." To Worden, none of this looked like anything he would call communication with words. He was not sure he had seen Betsy press even a single letter on the keyboard on her own.

The caseworker must have picked up on Worden's doubt, because she invited him to join her on the side of the table where Boynton was transcribing, character by character, the letters Betsy's finger touched. Gazing at the sheet of paper, Worden was amazed to read a coherent message, supposedly composed by Betsy just then, lobbing more accusations at her father. It said that she was afraid of her father, that he "fucked" her, and that she needed protection. Worden felt compelled to ask how the girl could possibly have delivered so much information when she was not even looking at the keyboard. The answer was not persuasive. Betsy, Boynton said, had memorized the layout, so she did not have to look anymore.

After this meeting, Worden could not shake the feeling that the true victims in Betsy's case might be her parents. He set out to give himself an expedited education on the literature on FC. He turned to Betsy's other teachers, who provided him with several laudatory articles about FC, one of which was written by Doug Biklen. On his own, though, Worden came across an unfavorable reference to FC in Bernie Rimland's quarterly autism newsletter. Soon he was on the phone with Rimland himself, who let loose a tirade against both FC and Doug Biklen, charging that the method was misleading and destructive. Filling Worden in on FC's origins and the problems with it, Rimland revealed that the Wheatons were not the first family to find themselves facing charges of sexual abuse of their own child—with the accusations communicated via facilitated messages.

Indeed, as Worden learned, the false sexual-abuse scenario had played out again and again in the three years since FC had been in use. It was an echo, in a way, of the day-care sexual-abuse hysteria, which was still at a high pitch in several parts of the country. Rimland cited several cases where fathers, teachers, and even social workers had been falsely accused via FC. Innocent fathers had been jailed while their alleged crimes were investigated, Rimland told him, because police were persuaded that facilitated communication was real. What Worden needed to do, Rimland advised, was to arrange for a rigorous test to determine whether the words attributed to Betsy came from her or from Boynton.

This made sense to Worden, and he thought it would also make sense to Boynton. Their conversations until then had been respectful, professional, and frank, and now they continued in this manner. Worden pointed out that it would serve everyone involved if the authorship of Betsy's words could be definitively confirmed. Boynton saw his point. Also, she had no doubt that a reliable test would prove that the words were Betsy's. Nevertheless, she hesitated, because she knew that in the broad FC community to which she belonged, testing FC's validity was frowned upon. It was almost seen as an act of betrayal, because to ask whether the communication was real was to violate the "presumption of competence" principle. Every facilitator was expected to feel not only an emotional but a philosophical commitment to that principle. At the training session at the University of Maine that Boynton had recently attended, the "don't test" imperative had been voiced again and again. Trainers even made the argument that no valid test could exist for FC, because the process of testing would itself undermine the bonds of trust that made FC work. It was a profoundly unscientific position, but to true believers in FC, it was dogma.

THREE WEEKS LATER, the Wheatons were still a broken family. Neither Jim nor Suzette Wheaton had been arrested, largely because Worden insisted that no steps be taken against them until Betsy's ability to communicate via FC had been validated. In the meantime, he had contacted a Harvard speech pathologist named Howard Shane, whose program at Harvard specialized in developing hardware and software to enable communication by people whose ability to manufacture speech was dysfunctional—due to brain damage, perhaps, or a degenerative disease such as multiple sclerosis. It was technology like this that allowed British physicist Stephen Hawking to communicate. In Hawking's case, his eyeglasses contained electronics that responded to movements of his cheek, which then produced verbal output by a computer. Shane had no complaint with presuming competence. But he believed in technology, not FC.

Shane had already been an expert witness at several trials where FC had been used to provide testimony accusing parents or others of sexual abuse. Shane was always there as a defense witness, and he always succeeded in discrediting the method. From the stand, he would explain in detail why the claims made for FC flew in the face of everything known about autism, which FC had not "redefined," despite Biklen's claims. Further, he argued that the sophisticated poetry and prose reported to be the work of young children strained credulity—as did the fact that so often the kids' fingers were pressing the keys while looking anywhere but at the keyboard.

But Shane's most significant contribution in such trials was his construction of vivid, simple experiments that could be carried out in front of a judge and jury to help them understand, in minutes, if they could trust FC when considering whether to sentence someone to prison. When Phil Worden called him, Shane outlined a testing procedure in which he would simultaneously display pictures to both Betsy and Boynton. They would sit side by side, to enable facilitation, but a divider would prevent each from viewing the picture shown to the other. Then Shane would ask Betsy to name the thing in the picture. The catch was that, sometimes, Betsy and Boynton would be shown the identical picture, sometimes two different ones. If FC was real, it should not matter what Boynton saw, as she was merely the facilitator. If FC was real, the messages should name only the items in the pictures shown to Betsy, every time.

Worden had to work at breaking down Boynton's resistance to having FC—and, effectively, Boynton herself—put on trial in this way. He appealed to her rational side, and to her sense of decency, arguing that, considering what was at stake for the family, eliminating the questions about FC was the humane thing to do. Boynton took this all in, and, after a good deal of soul-searching, she agreed with Worden that, in this situation, the method needed to be vindicated. At some level, she too wanted to know for certain whether she or Betsy was the author of these awful allegations. She gave her consent, and a date was set for Howard Shane to fly up from Boston to put FC on trial.

By now, it had been more than a month since Betsy's first alarming accusations. When Boynton arrived at the school for the test, she found an anonymous note on her desk, which read: "That student is lucky to have you in her life." In that moment, Boynton was not so sure. As she entered the room designated for the test—the same room where she and Betsy had often worked together—she saw the teenager already seated, holding a stuffed animal, and she once again felt a deep connection and love for this girl.

Shane smiled at Boynton and told her not to be nervous. Then he took out the pictures. One by one, he showed one set to Betsy and another to Boynton. In the first round, he showed each of them a picture of a key. Asked by Shane to identify the thing in the picture, Betsy, with Boynton touching her arm, typed *KEY.*

Next Betsy was shown a cup. But this time, with Boynton still helping, she typed *HAT.* After that, she was shown a picture of a dog but typed *SNEAKERS.* And when shown a boat, she typed *SANDWICH.* Each of these answers was wrong, but not arbitrary. Each wrong answer corresponded precisely to the images *Boynton* was seeing on her side of the divide. It went on like this for a while, with a wrong answer produced every single time Boynton saw a picture different from what Betsy saw. And every time, that wrong answer matched the picture in front of Boynton.

The testing continued for three hours, with breaks. Shane had Boynton leave the room, for example, while he blew up a balloon, released it, and let it buzz around everyone's heads. Then Boynton was brought back in and Betsy was asked what Shane had just shown her. *BANANA,* she typed.

The result was unequivocal. There was no real verbal communication from Betsy that day. And the implication was damning: there never had been any communication.

Boynton left without being told the outcome. It was only several hours later, when she reached her apartment and checked her answering machine, that she heard the message telling her the results. She curled up into a ball and sobbed.

Several months later, PBS broadcast a documentary called *Prisoners of Silence,* in which actors reenacted, nearly verbatim, the experiment carried out between Shane, Betsy, and Boynton. There had been some negative coverage of the case before, but the broadcast marked a turning point, after which FC's fall from grace was nearly instantaneous, not just in Maine but nationwide. Viewers who saw Shane's simple, intuitive experiment with their own eyes felt they had just witnessed the debunking of a complete sham. As media coverage turned universally hostile toward FC, skeptical school districts across the nation dropped it as quickly as they had embraced it three years earlier. Enrollment in FC training courses plummeted, and students with autism who had been sitting through advanced classes in math and physics—because their "facilitated" selves performed so well there—were pulled back into their former special-education classes, where their ability to use words was assumed to be nonexistent. They once again became children for whom the presumption of competence was likely to be denied the benefit of the doubt.

Douglas Biklen was pilloried by the press and in academia. His early claim that FC forced the "redefinition" of autism had never sat well with those who had spent years closely studying the condition.

Now that FC had been revealed as bogus in such a public fashion, they thought it was unforgivable that Biklen would not admit that he had been wrong about the method.

But Biklen did not believe he had been wrong. In 1994, as a series of studies debunking FC appeared in peer-reviewed journals, Biklen began attacking the methods of the debunkers, reiterating the distinction he said existed between well-executed and poorly executed FC. He also strove to set the record straight about what, exactly, he was claiming for FC. "I'm not walking around saying everybody's smart, or that everybody who uses FC is brilliant," he told the Associated Press. "What I am saying is that we need to realize that not being able to speak is not the same as having nothing to say."

Fortunately for Biklen, Syracuse University stood behind him, despite the widespread disparagement the school faced for having established a Facilitated Communication Institute for him to run. In 2006, the institute was still there, and Biklen was promoted to the post of dean of the School of Education. In 2007, his work on FC was cited as a point of pride for the university by its chancellor, Nancy Cantor, who noted blandly that "the controversy about facilitated communication in the research literature in psychology and education never seems to tire." It was also true that the institute—renamed the Institute on Communication and Inclusion in 2010—remained a beacon for outside funding for the university, drawing significant contributions, estimated to be in the millions, from private foundations whose faith in FC, like Biklen's, never wavered.

In 2014, Biklen retired.

Remarkably, Janyce Boynton did not stop her use of FC immediately after the failed picture test. Embarrassed and shaken by the stunning failure of a method she believed in so deeply, Boynton at first had hopes of proving that it had been Shane's test, not FC, that was at fault. For several weeks, she continued to hold FC sessions with Betsy, during which still more allegations of sexual abuse poured out. When Boynton duly reported these, Betsy's parents requested her removal as their daughter's teacher.

And then, after briefly wondering whether she was losing her mind, Boynton began to read more deeply about FC. Racked with guilt over the harm that had come to the Wheatons, she discovered how easily facilitators could steer word production without even realizing they were doing so. It sounded impossible, but experiments showed it happening again and again. Reading these papers, Boynton realized something about herself: that all along, she had desperately wished for the words to be Betsy's because she so wanted her to have a voice. The rest of it—the ugly fantasies about Betsy's home life—remained opaque to her.

Close to the end of the 1993 school year, Boynton informed her superiors of her change of heart about FC and urged the school district to suspend all use of FC in its curriculum. In a statement, the district announced it was doing just that.

The PBS documentary debunking FC aired in October 1993. Boynton had declined to be interviewed for it, and the program did not use her name when it re-created the picture test. Soon, however, she felt a backlash against her personally. A commentator in the local newspaper demanded that she be publicly named and ousted from the school system. At the same time, Boynton learned that the larger FC community wanted nothing to do with her. She heard herself being described in FC circles as a "bad facilitator," with the implication that she had brought enormous damage to the movement by her ineptitude. Somehow, in the standoff over FC, Boynton had been cast as the villain of the piece by both sides.

In 1994, Janyce Boynton was filmed apologizing to Betsy's parents in person for a television story looking back at the case. Following the debacle, it was the one and only time they met, but in that one meeting, the Wheatons were gracious and forgiving. Some years later, the family took another brutal hit, when Betsy's younger brother, Jamie, committed suicide. He was in his early twenties, and he killed his nineteen-year-old wife on the same day. His mother, Suzette, later said that Jamie was never the same after the trauma of the temporary family breakup in 1993.

Janyce Boynton worked in the Ellsworth schools for six more years, then moved to a new town, where she began making and selling arts and crafts.

In January 2012, Boynton was tracked down by a reporter from ABC News. She was seeking Boynton's comment on a story airing that night on the *20/20* magazine show. Boynton was stunned when she was told the reason why: the catastrophe had repeated itself—yet again.

That night, Boynton watched as *20/20* told the story of a family named Wendrow, who lived in West Bloomfield, Michigan, and who, almost fifteen years after her own disastrous experience with FC, had pressed their local school district into funding a facilitator for their fourteen-year-old daughter, Aislinn, who had autism and could not speak. Despite the broad scientific consensus that the technique had been discredited, FC had quietly retained a small following among families who, like Doug Biklen at Syracuse University—where FC continued to be taught—maintained that the blanket condemnation was too broad and overlooked instances where the method really worked. Practicing at the margins of respectable therapies, facilitators and the families, not surprisingly, formed a self-reinforcing subculture of support for the practice. Julian and Tal Wendrow, Aislinn's parents, joined this subculture in 2005, after putting their hope in a wide variety of other therapies—from ABA to PECS to supplements to music therapy to craniosacral massage—none of which did much to alleviate Aislinn's difficulties.

When they tried FC, and the words began to come, the Wendrows celebrated. In part, it was because they saw how quickly the rest of the world changed its attitude toward their daughter, once people believed that she could use words and was intellectually intact. They also loved chatting with her and seeing her doing so well in school.

But then, just as in Maine, the facilitated child began to allege sexual abuse by her father. The police and prosecutors bought into the validity of the communication and threw Julian Wendrow behind bars for nearly three months, including, bizarrely, seventy-four days in solitary confinement.

Then, as *20/20* reported, Howard Shane, now nearly twenty years older, showed up in Michigan and demonstrated that the communication was an illusion, inadvertently conjured by the facilitator. By the time of the broadcast, Julian Wendrow had been set free, and the family was reunited. The Wendrows were now suing the law enforcement authorities, which is what had prompted the *20/20* coverage.

Boynton had not talked about FC in public for nearly two decades. But when the ABC reporter asked for comment, she wanted to answer. She was sad, she said, that it had happened again. She explained that it was easy for facilitators and families to delude themselves, and to forget to suspend disbelief about a patently improbable process, because they so badly wanted it to be real. She told the ABC reporter that she had tried to be optimistic, after her own role in the earlier catastrophe, that at least that episode would serve as a lesson to others to be skeptical about FC, and to stay away from it. That night, however, after watching the *20/20* story in full, Boynton's heart sank at seeing yet another family learn about the dangers of FC the hard way.

Having broken her silence already, Boynton decided that she wanted to say more. Later in 2012, she published an article in an academic journal devoted to clinical and educational solutions for communication impairments. Her article was entitled "Facilitated Communication—What Harm It Can Do: Confessions of a Former Facilitator." It was a broadside against what she called "the myth of FC." She publicly regretted her own gullibility, and appealed for hard-nosed realism in situations where the dream of reaching the child within can blind all reason.

That hope, though, can persist even in those who have been hurt by nurturing it. Even in Julian Wendrow. After his daughter accused him of sexual abuse, and after he nearly ended up in jail for years because of it, he was forced to abandon his faith in FC. But he confessed that he did so only with great reluctance, and that the price he paid was worth the joy he experienced for as long as he believed that FC was real, and that his daughter was really talking to him.

Because he saw how people treated her differently when they still thought the words were hers.

And because he had so loved hearing everything she had to say.

The dream was that powerful.

35

AN ELUSIVE DEFINITION

"IT FORCED ME TO REDEFINE AUTISM." WHEN DOUGLAS Biklen spoke these words, in 1990, about facilitated communication, he did not realize how insolent it sounded to the psychiatrists and psychologists who had labored in the field for decades. With nothing more than a degree in special education, Biklen was challenging "the received knowledge coming from almost fifty years of energetic and sustained research into the condition of autism." To the established experts, it was appalling that Biklen, whom Eric Schopler called an "ideologue," would dare claim the right to *redefine* autism.

And yet that was exactly what the experts had been doing since the time of Leo Kanner—debating one another and jockeying to advance their own definitions and redefinitions of autism: its shape, its scope, its causes. This continuing push and pull happened mostly out of sight of the lay public, which assumed that when people with PhDs and MDs used the word "autism," they all meant the same thing. But that was never true, because the definition of autism has always been malleable—determined by consensus, or by whoever among the jockeying experts was most persuasive at any given moment. All the big ideas about autism over the years—from mother blaming to concepts with more solid science behind them, like mindblindness, weak central coherence, and the unifying spectrum—were still only hypotheses. Yet most were treated, at the height of their popularity, as objective fact. At least until the next big idea came along.

Given the elasticity of the definition, it has been easy for competing interests to cast autism as what they want it to be, which has at times led to enormous strife. Over the decades, autism has been seen as a behavioral, or a medical, or a psychogenic challenge. It has been blamed on mothers and it has been blamed on vaccines. It has been answered with "substitute mothering," megavitamins, facilitated communication, slaps in the face, hugging therapy, and, in some African countries, with exorcism. At this writing, autism is viewed as occurring on a spectrum, a concept that has the virtue of promoting inclusiveness but has also caused acrimony between those who see autism as a tragedy and those who claim it as a gift and an identity.

For years, many of the most respected figures in the autism community have complained about the lack of a single, incontrovertible definition of autism. In 1968, for example, Michael Rutter lamented the "hopelessly confused state of affairs . . . more confusing than it need be." A full ten years later, in 1978, Eric Schopler warned that scientists were critically misunderstanding one another's work "because criteria for diagnosis are different." One more decade after that, in 1988, Fred Volkmar and Donald Cohen wrote in frustration about the "long and controversial history of the concepts surrounding autism." And in 1998, Volkmar and Ami Klin complained about "the confusion and the plethora of diagnostic concepts" surrounding autism, and, by then, Asperger's syndrome as well.

One of the autism community's favorite adages has long been "If you've met one person with autism, you've met *one* person with autism," which captures the essence of the problem even as it affirms the complex variability of autistic traits. It is this enormous variability of autistic traits that makes defining autism so challenging. That was what hampered Victor Lotter's effort to count people with autism in the early 1960s, when he had to draw a line to define autism that even he considered arbitrary, or at least subjective, given that it was based on only his own observations. Nevertheless, the subjective judgments of Lotter and other researchers had real consequences, especially in the field of epidemiology. Valid comparisons among populations in different eras and places are impossible when definitions are highly inconsistent. Lotter thought the lesson worth sharing in 1966, when he cautioned that the true prevalence of autism would remain impossible to determine until everyone agreed on what it was they were trying to count.

Debates about who counted as autistic were not only academic; they had a profound effect on the lives of individuals. After all, a person must be diagnosed with autism before he or she can gain access to support services.

Repeatedly, one researcher or another would design a set of criteria intended to bring an end to the chaos—proposing a definition or working model meant to stand as the last word on the matter of what is meant by *autism*. The effort put into this was enormous. The goal, however, remained elusive.

Mildred Creak had tried to bring order to chaos in 1961, when she published her Nine Points. These were quickly found wanting by the clinical world, which tore them to shreds. She likened the experience to feeling as if she were "throwing them to the wolves."

Michael Rutter also tried to make sense of the mess in 1972, when he successfully campaigned to retire the diagnosis of "childhood schizophrenia," which had long competed with the diagnosis of autism in children. It was "high time," Rutter argued, for that troublesome concept to be "politely and respectfully, but firmly, put into its proper place in the section on 'the history of psychiatry.'" Still unsatisfied, he produced a new framework for autism, which became known as the "Rutter criteria," in the early 1970s. Based on Rutter's and other researchers' epidemiological and clinical studies, the criteria specified that autism manifested itself in three domains, in varying degree—through language impairment; social impairment; and restrictive, repetitive patterns of behavior. An inspiration for Lorna Wing and Judith Gould's later "triad of impairments," the Rutter criteria gained a following, and for several years thereafter they were often cited by researchers as the standard they relied on. Some of this acceptance was due, no doubt, to Rutter's standing as one of academic psychiatry's most lucid thinkers and writers. He was adept at defining the parameters of a topic, and he had a clear, unpretentious style that made his conclusions that much more forceful. "The question was not how to differentiate autism from normality. The hospital porter could do that without skilled assistance," he once wrote, on the challenge of clarifying what autism looked like in children seen at the Maudsley.

By 1977, however, the National Society for Autistic Children was promoting its own definition, which added a fourth domain: sensory processing. Developed by UCLA researchers Edward Ritvo and B. J. Freeman, this definition made "abnormal responses to sensations" also central to the experience of having autism.

And then there was the American Psychiatric Association's *DSM,* which constituted its own saga.

IN 1993, WHEN Fred Volkmar and his colleagues were trying to get Asperger's syndrome into the *DSM,* the book had already been in print for more than forty years, with revised editions published whenever psychiatry changed its mind, which was surprisingly often.

After 1980, for example, the *DSM* was overhauled at least once a decade, with whole diagnoses heavily revised or dropped altogether, and new diagnoses added. Most famously, after much pressure from the gay community and its allies, and despite the vociferous objections of a contingent of mostly older psychiatrists, the *DSM* retired the diagnosis of homosexuality as a mental illness in 1972. Though this and other amendments were billed as the positive consequences of better research and understanding, they revealed the extent to which psychiatric diagnosis is influenced not only by scientific data but by cultural, political, and other factors.

Autism was not included in the *DSM* until 1980, in the edition known as *DSM-III,* which appeared nearly forty years after Leo Kanner published his first paper on the condition. It proved to be a protean definition—altered significantly in 1987, and again in 1994. Although it was changed only slightly in 2000, it underwent a dramatic rewrite, accompanied by much angst, in 2013. Throughout this process, the length of the definition waxed and waned. The number of words in its symptom checklist, originally about seventy, jumped to more than six hundred in one edition, shrank to three hundred in the next, and then expanded again, to almost nine hundred words, two editions later. The name kept changing too—from *Infantile Autism* to *Autistic Disorder* to *Autism Spectrum Disorder.* Most critically, the symptom checklist the *DSM* writers developed to identify those with autism kept being revised. In one edition, a patient had to match a minimum of 8 out of 16 criteria to receive the diagnosis. In another, he or she had to match at least 6 out of 12. In the second case, according to Volkmar and Brian Reichow at Yale, there were more than two thousand different symptom combinations that could produce an autism diagnosis. The addition of Asperger's disorder as a separate diagnosis in 1994 further complicated the diagnostic picture.

Very often, the *DSM*'s zigzags on autism have reflected the almost philosophical divide between two camps of experts: the "lumpers" and the "splitters." This tension was on display when Lorna Wing and Hans Asperger disagreed as to whether his cases and Leo Kanner's were more alike than different, or the other way around. Asperger, it will be remembered, believed that he saw two distinctly different syndromes in his cases and Kanner's cases. His insistence on splitting his and Kanner's children into separate groups, according to key differences, made him a classic splitter. Wing, on the other hand, always spoke like a true lumper, arguing that virtually everyone with some trace or combination of autistic behaviors belonged to the same group, since the core mechanisms of autistic behavior operated in all of them in the same way, albeit to varying degrees. This thinking is what led to her construction of the highly influential "spectrum" model of autism. Today this quintessentially lumper idea is widely accepted, to the point where even popular culture appears to embrace it as unassailable truth.

But if history is a guide, that could change. As with any previous understanding of autism, the spectrum construct is not without drawbacks, and a swing back to the splitters is quite possible if, for example, further scientific inquiry determines that clusters of autistic behaviors that *look* similar in fact arise from divergent causes—environmental, genetic, or other. The study of cancer offers an analogy. For years "cancer" survived as an umbrella term for all cancers, until the field of oncology learned that different cancers are in fact radically different, each with its own signature and its own distinct biological process—and was thus forced down the path of the splitters. Autism too might turn out to be a plural entity. Researchers might discover that there are in fact *autisms,* each with its own genetic "fingerprint," each significantly unrelated to the others. If that were to happen, the idea of a broad spectrum, which smudges those differences, would have less explanatory power, and might lose some of its currency in the conversation about autism.

Such lines of inquiry, however, would require a commitment to research into the biomedical aspects of autism rather than a focus on psychiatric or behavioral interventions. Yet at the beginning of the 1990s, there was virtually no biological research into autism, and the few scientists studying it had little financial support. That is, until four parents, living on opposite coasts of the United States, decided to do something about it.

36

MEETING OF THE MINDS

THE TWO HUSBANDS WERE ARGUING BEFORE THE APPETIZers arrived. By the meal's end, it appeared the merger idea was in trouble. For reasons of philosophy and personality, it was beginning to look obvious that two of the most ambitious parent organizations ever to join the autism cause would not, after all, be getting married.

It was disappointing, perhaps, because both couples and both organizations were after exactly the same goal: to inspire the biomedical research community to take autism seriously. Because as of their sitdown in late 1995, at a restaurant near Princeton University, that was definitely not happening.

Not biology-based researchers anyway. Not the geneticists, the allergists, the endocrinologists, or the gastroenterologists. For researchers in these and other biomedical fields, autism was a non-topic, a dead-end children's condition best left to the psychologists, psychiatrists, and pediatricians.

By remarkable coincidence, these two sets of parents, on opposite coasts of the United States, had both recently set out to alter this reality with a level of ambition and energy that would, together, galvanize a movement. Unaware the other existed, both couples had had the same idea for changing the world, at almost exactly the same time.

One couple lived in Hillsborough, New Jersey, but used a mailbox in nearby Princeton for their group's address. Husband and wife were both Ivy Leaguers, and they liked the implied association with Princeton University. The other couple, who had flown in from Los Angeles for this lunch, both made their living in the movie industry. A mutual acquaintance had encouraged the four of them to get together at this table to discuss joining forces. On the face of it, this meeting of the minds made perfect sense.

After all, they had so much in common.

KAREN LONDON, A corporate lawyer, had stopped practicing law when her son, Zach, was diagnosed with autism in 1987. Her husband, Eric, a research psychiatrist, had continued his work, which focused on Alzheimer's disease and geriatric psychiatry, although now, of course, he read anything new hitting the medical literature that shed light on his son's condition. Colleagues like his friend and fellow psychiatrist Arvan Mirrow also kept an eye out for relevant research and brought it to Eric's attention now and then.

In November 1993, Mirrow showed up at the doorstep of the Londons' New Jersey home hauling three thick binders in his arms. He had just returned from the annual meeting of the Society for Neuroscience, held that year in Washington, DC. The binders contained the full set of short, descriptive "abstracts" for every piece of new research that had been presented and discussed at the conference. In total, there were some eleven thousand abstracts, all connected to brain research, which was becoming a hotter topic all the time. Mirrow had grabbed the binders thinking Eric and Karen might want to scan the abstracts for any new brain studies that focused on autism.

For the next few hours, the three of them flipped through the pages, running a finger down the index at the back end of each binder, searching for the word "autism." As hits were made, one of them kept a running tally.

The result struck the Londons as pathetic. Eleven hits, out of eleven thousand papers. What was worse: not one of these papers was about autism. The word came up only in passing, in phrases like *in contrast with autism* or *unlike autism*. Karen and Eric found it difficult to fathom that the world's leading brain scientists had just assembled, and autism had not come up.

Once, back in 1974, a concerted effort had been made to investigate how autism influenced and was influenced by the organ systems of the body, the brain included. In June of that year, a group of parents attending the annual meeting of the National Society for Autistic Children in Washington had brought along their children for the express purpose of extracting the maximum amount of data about their brains and bodies that the five-day time span would allow.

It went a little like a fire drill. As the regular parent meeting proceeded inside the hotel ballroom, a van pulled up to the lobby every forty-five minutes to transport another group of four children and their parents to a nearby clinic. Once there, each child was rushed through a battery of body measurements, blood draws, urine collection, and some quick psychological testing, while the parents filled out questionnaires on behaviors and family history. Then everybody cleared out again in time to make room for the next van load. In this way, biomedical data was gathered on a total of seventy-eight children with autism—more than had ever been collected in a single research project.

While the book of papers based on this data, published in 1976, produced no breakthroughs, it yielded some intriguing findings. The biologically based observations included an increased presence of antibodies to the herpes simplex virus, higher zinc levels, and a higher-than-expected degree of intestinal irritation—among many others. Any of these was a potential lead for further research.

But the leads were never followed, except, perhaps, by one of the parents who organized the effort, Bernie Rimland. This was not because the work was disparaged. It was because, in 1976, with the exception of Rimland and very few others, the scientific community was almost entirely uninterested in the biology of autism.

That had not changed much by the time Eric and Karen London met a scientist named Margaret Bauman for dinner in the fall of 1993. Bauman, a pediatric neurologist with Massachusetts General Hospital, was one of the very few scientists from that period interested in studying the physical brains of children with autism. She had access to a small but precious store of brain tissue, a gift to science from some bereaved but generous parents of children with autism who had died young. For a while, Bauman had been able to carry out a small number of studies detailing what appeared as distinct anatomical anomalies in their brains. But she confessed to the Londons that funding for her research was not easy to come by, as few foundations saw cause for understanding autism at that level. Right then, with no new money lined up, the brains were sitting in a laboratory freezer, unused.

The Londons shook their heads at this. Bauman confided that she had held this conversation before, and that lots of parents were as bothered by it as she was. She also mentioned that she would be speaking to some of them the next night, when she was the scheduled keynote speaker at the annual conference of the New Jersey Center for Outreach and Services for the Autism Community, which was already under way.

In fact, the Londons had been attending the conference in shifts, so that one of them could always be home looking after Zach. It was Eric who was there the next day when Bauman delivered her talk. Afterward she started taking questions.

"Why can't we get funding to do autism research?" one parent stood and asked.

Bauman paused and started to scan the audience.

"Is Dr. London here?" she asked.

Surprised, Eric slowly raised his hand—or, really, just his finger.

"Oh, well, good," Bauman said, "because *he's* starting an organization!"

A few minutes later, when Bauman's talk ended, Eric found himself surrounded by parents. Some were thanking him already. Others asked how they could help.

London excused himself, found a pay phone, and called home to tell Karen that, as of now, the two of them had just become activists for autism research.

Jon Shestack always had a photo of his son Dov, in his wallet, keeping it in reserve for situations in which a little emotional punch was called for, when he wasn't getting his way. In a room full of legislators who needed some persuading to vote for more funding for autism research, for example, he would pull out the picture and hold it high, as if to say, *Here's one of the kids I'm asking you to help. There are half a million like him.*

Shestack was a movie producer. One of his biggest credits would be a thriller about a fictional hijacking of *Air Force One,* the president's plane. His wife, Portia Iversen, was a television producer, and also a writer, an art director, and a set decorator, who had already won an Emmy. They met in the mid-1980s and were married in 1992. Their son Dov, born later that year, was diagnosed with autism in 1994. On that day, the developmental psychologist who delivered the diagnosis gave them what he said was his best advice: "Hold on to each other and cry, then get on with your lives." It was as bizarre as it was shocking. The traditional institutions had all been shutting down during the preceding decade. They could not believe that a professional was recommending a throwback solution like sending their two-year-old boy away, then trying to forget he ever existed. Dov, the doctor warned, would destroy their lives if they did not put him away fast.

They never even considered it. They did not know much about autism yet, but they knew that surely, by that point, scientists must understand more about it—and what to do about it—than this ill-informed pediatrician. Shestack and Iversen, well educated, solvent, and confident of their professional skills at "producing" their way out of difficult situations, resolved together to find that science and those scientists. Together, they would all bring Dov back from autism.

That was how they conceived of autism—as the invader they felt had snatched their son. Not even two yet, Dov had dark half circles under his eyes from lack of sleep. He was unable to digest food, and the diarrhea that had begun at birth had never subsided. He did not make eye contact. He stared at shadows on the floor or rays of light shining though the kitchen blinds. He spoke no words.

To Jon and Portia, it was obvious that their son was sick, and their goal was simple: to find him a cure.

They had immediately started looking into the available treatments, the ones that had credibility behind them, but felt instinctively that Dov's condition demanded an approach that went faster than the gradual, painstaking programs like TEACCH, and another known as "Floortime." It was developed by Maryland psychologist Stanley Greenspan, who recommended that parents literally get down on the floor with their children and follow their lead for a more immediate, responsive, and playful interaction with them. They also met personally with Ivar Lovaas at UCLA. Again, talking to him, they realized they were being offered an approach that would take years, with uncertain results. That demanded a patience they did not think matched Dov's situation. Already, the one conventional approach they'd tried, speech therapy, had gone poorly. After several months of it, the therapist had quit, telling Portia that, with her limited time, she felt obliged to work with children who had a real chance of making progress.

This was devastating to hear. But it also reinforced both parents' conviction that they were wasting Dov's time with these education-based therapies, when it seemed so evident that Dov's autism was intertwined with his physical ailments—the gastrointestinal problems, the sleep issues, the seizures, his hypersensitivity to most food. Jon and Portia were convinced that Dov was experiencing some sort of organic malfunction, one that clearly involved his brain.

But they could find no experts with whom to discuss Dov's autism at that level. The behavior analysts had nothing to offer in that regard. Neither did the psychiatrists and pediatricians. Though most experts now agreed that autism's roots were organic—that is, biologically based in the physical organism—no one had been trained to deliver any organic-focused treatments for autism. They were not taught in medical school, because they did not exist. Not outside of quack medicine, that is.

Portia began to understand this when, in her frustration, she boldly decided to wade into the medical literature, despite being a lifelong liberal-arts type. She set out to find the studies that looked at autism through the cross-sections of brain chemistry, nerve tissue, sleep patterns, and metabolic performance; began subscribing to scientific databases; and started haunting the UCLA medical school library. When she discovered—just as the Londons did in those binders of abstracts—that autism was no draw for biomedical researchers, she began pulling studies that she thought might shed some light on autism, even if their authors did not think so. Leaving UCLA with stacks of photocopies, she understood that she was well out of her depth, so she signed up to audit courses in molecular biology and neuroanatomy. She was not sure where all this would lead her, but she knew for sure the kind of knowledge she was after: anything that could shed light on Dov's autism as a medical condition—curable by medical treatment.

THE PROBLEM WAS, there was no career to be had in the biomedical research of autism. Scientists, like anyone else, needed to eat. They also had egos. New graduates choosing a field of scientific research approached the decision with, of course, a sense of native curiosity—probably the same thing that led them into science in the first place. But there were other considerations. They would want at least a minimal sense of assurance that the work they did would not lead them to a dead end. They also wanted to know that they had good odds to get their work funded, ideally for years to come. The matter of biomedical research into autism was stuck in self-reinforcing inertia. Young researchers were not looking at autism, because there was no prior work on it that suggested autism research held promise as a career. And funders were not demanding more research in that area, because little had been produced that made the investment seem worthwhile.

In New Jersey, Eric and Karen London understood what it would take to change the situation. Money. Eric would have the opportunity to test this proposition when he began attending scientific conventions. He strolled around the huge halls where researchers from around the world, by the hundreds, stood next to poster-sized displays of charts, data, and graphics illustrating the findings from their latest investigations. Such freewheeling "poster sessions" are a tradition at scientific gatherings and conferences, meant to encourage scientists to enjoy some spontaneous conversation and an open exchange of ideas. At one of these, a reconvening of the same neuroscience group where the three binders had come from, Eric again found that, among the thousands of posters, not one mentioned autism. Several, however, displayed work that suggested, to him at least, the possibility of being applicable to autism. Someone doing brain imaging or sensory research, for example, might pull from the autistic population for study subjects.

London was not surprised by the odd looks he received when he raised these possibilities with the researchers. Some of them needed to be reminded what autism was. None of them saw any point in bending their work to focus on an obscure disorder that, if anything, belonged to psychology. Some exhibitors became demonstrably impatient when London did not simply drop the subject.

But that changed the instant London informed the scientists that he had money in his pocket, and that he wanted to fund researchers looking at autism. Suddenly, he had the previously impatient scientists nodding, agreeing that, yes, in theory, there was no reason autism couldn't be brought into more focus in their research—what an interesting area of study!

Eric was not bluffing about having the money. In 1994, not long after Margaret Bauman called on him in front of everybody at her talk, he and Karen had launched the National Alliance for Autism Research (NAAR). Its mission, as spelled out in an early version of its website, was "funding and otherwise accelerating biomedical research" into autism. Since then, he and Karen, with help from other parents, had made rapid progress in building an organization. They were lucky to get some sizable donations within their first five months of existence, on the magnitude of tens of thousands of dollars, contributed by a small number of affluent donors. This initial success led them to believe that their vision might stand a chance of being realized, and that more money would follow.

These early donations also appeared to vindicate the strategy they had laid out. To ensure their credibility as a donation-worthy association, Eric and Karen insisted they should have the best people in the country associated with NAAR; autism had already seen more than its share of medical quackery. Eric, a scientist himself, was viscerally committed to sound scientific practice. They wanted that value reflected in the people with whom they worked. During those first months, pulling whatever strings they had and calling on friends of friends, he and Karen put together an advisory board composed of scientists with gold-plated credentials and a heavy sprinkling of Ivy League degrees. It was around this time that they rented the mailbox that gave them a Princeton address; they wanted to give autism research "establishment" credibility. To change the world for autism, and make biomedical research on the condition a mainstream matter, they intended to engage only serious scientific minds.

Jon Shestack, in his push to force science to focus on autism, had quickly coined a slogan for what he believed he and Portia had to do for Dov. They needed to "hurry up science." Jon's use of this phrase became as much a part of his activist repertoire as those times he pulled out Dov's photo. "Hurry up science" could have been the name of the organization he and Portia launched in March of 1995 with that goal in mind. But they chose another name, which captured the sentiment just as well. Cure Autism Now. Everyone called it "CAN"—as in, "can do."

CAN started out with less of a focus on a traditional scientific audience than the Londons' organization. Jon and Portia already believed that traditional science had let their son down. Neither of them was a trained scientist, and Jon, particularly, had no patience for boundaries. He wore Dov's autism as a wound, to justify an insistent, sometimes intimidating intensity when he pressed others to see why Dov's problem should be *their* problem. Some found this off-putting, but Shestack's relentlessness made him an unusually effective campaigner and fund-raiser.

Portia was the team's more placid partner, the more intellectual half of the pair. She was the one trying to understand the science. It was also through Portia that, in its early days, CAN started out by veering away from "establishment" science, allying itself with a man who, to his own detriment, had begun to lose the respect of much of the autism community.

At this time, Bernie Rimland, the "original" autism parent-activist, firebrand organizer, and slayer of the mother-blaming theory, was more passionate and dedicated than ever. He was still beloved by the parents whose calls he always returned, but he had nevertheless increasingly alienated himself in serious scientific circles. This was the result of his frequently dogmatic stands on certain pet theories of autism causation and treatment—like his insistence that courses of megavitamins could alleviate the symptoms of autism. The failure of these assertions to withstand scrutiny by sound scientific studies did not deter his commitment to them. Among some scientists, unkindly, the word "crackpot" began to be whispered about Rimland. By the mid-1990s, the time had passed when newspapers cited him as the world's authority on autism. In a world governed by peer review, the onetime hero of autism was headed for the margins.

This, however, did not deter Rimland. The outsider agitator who had once been right when all else were wrong—about refrigerator mothers—seemed comfortable believing that was still true. Besides, there were still members of the community who appreciated the outsiders, parents like Jon Shestack and Portia Iversen. And in 1994, they handed Rimland $25,000.

Right before the couple had started CAN, Portia had introduced herself to Rimland. She had read his science newsletter, discovering how much space he gave to studies detailing alternative therapies. The more they talked, the more she admired what she saw as his open-mindedness and his empathy for a mother who was frustrated by the lack of deeper research on the same kinds of biomedical therapies that intrigued him. Rimland had mentioned his ambition to hold a conference bringing together those kinds of researchers, but lamented that he lacked the funds to pull it together. Jon solved that problem in three weeks, with a passionate letter to several of his parents' well-connected friends around his hometown of Philadelphia.

Portia attended the conference, which was held in Dallas in January 1995. It was not a large gathering: six parents and twenty-seven medical doctors and PhDs. But Portia was impressed by the range of disciplines represented: genetics, immunology, psychiatry, biochemistry, neuroscience, pharmacology, endocrinology, gastroenterology, and toxicology. She also noted the nonjudgmental ground rules. A biochemist and autism parent named Jon Pangborn had decreed that, for the first day, no one who had the floor was to be challenged or questioned on his or her work or hypotheses. Everyone's idea was meant to land softly and have the benefit of germinating in an atmosphere where skepticism was temporarily suspended.

Thus, a wide range of hope-inducing, promising ideas were presented. They included special diets, more about supplements, and information about a procedure known as chelation, in which an individual is dosed with drugs that remove accumulated heavy metals from the body. The presenters fully understood that doctors representing such techniques, whose efficacy and safety were less than fully established, would be dabbling outside the usual cautious boundaries of science. But there was a consensus in the group that the "autism emergency" justified such measures. As remarked by Sid Baker, another physician participant, only some practitioners and parents "had the stomach for a risk/benefit relationship."

Portia and Jon had been talking about working with professionals who were comfortable with alternative thinking, so she was thrilled that she had found them in Dallas. She returned to Los Angeles excited.

The lack of follow-up over the ensuing months after the conference, however, disappointed her. Still in frequent touch with Rimland, she had expected that the members of the Dallas group would start pulling together fund-raisers and building a treasury to pay for formal studies. After all, they all wanted to build more solid evidence for their ideas in order to enhance their acceptance. But it didn't happen. Reluctantly, Portia concluded that, as much as she admired Rimland, she should stop counting on him to organize the sort of effort she had envisioned.

Her husband shared that frustration. None of the effort was helping Dov, and that was the priority. One night, as Jon lay spread out reading the newspaper, she sat at the foot of their bed folding laundry. Suddenly he looked up and announced, "We're going to have to start our own foundation."

Cure Autism Now launched in March 1995. In the space of a year, America had acquired two autism organizations, one in Princeton and one in Hollywood, devoted to precisely the same thing.

At the "merger" lunch, the argument had erupted when Eric London offered his opinion that, by calling their group "Cure Autism Now," the Hollywood pair was raising false hopes.

For a moment, Jon just looked at him.

The four of them were still new at this. They had only just learned about one another's existence. Neither couple had funded a single study yet. Karen, Eric's wife, was the most enthusiastic about joining forces, which could multiply both groups' influence and reduce competition for funding. She and Eric had already approached the Autism Society of America about working together but had been turned down. ASA had spurned a similar feeler from Jon and Portia. ASA at the time was not interested in funding biomedical research.

Merging seemed a real possibility, but then Jon and Eric got into their debate about hope. Five years could go by, Eric said to Jon, and there might still be no cure. What would Jon think then? he wanted to know.

"I'm going to think it's even *more* appropriate," Jon snapped.

Eric did not know it, but the "false hope" argument was one Jon heard all the time. He loathed it. "If you are a young parent," Jon went on, "and you don't have hope, you won't stay married. You won't keep living if you don't have something to live for."

Failure is not an option, Shestack insisted to the doctor across the table. To London, this made no sense; he knew that in science, failure was almost always part of the process.

And therein lay the important difference. In 1995, Jon and Portia wanted to "hurry up science" in time to cure their own son. Eric and Karen accepted Zach's autism as a fact, but wanted good science done now for the sake of future generations.

The meal ended after some further stilted conversation. Jon and Portia had made it clear by now that Cure Autism Now would go on being independent. As the two couples said goodbye, Eric threw out one last peace offering. He invited Jon and Portia to send him a fax if they changed their minds.

No fax ever came.

37

THE MAGIC MAN

HE WAS KNOWN IN MEDICAL CIRCLES AS THE "MAGIC MAN," and he wore his hair in a braid.

The year 1997 was his first on the house-call tour, when he journeyed all over California. Then, he struck out for the rest of America. In 2000, the magic man covered 2,500 miles and seven states in the first three weeks of January alone. Not fond of airplanes, he traveled by train, and then by rented car, driving alone surrounded by empty coffee cups and crumpled maps, a list of kids on the seat beside him. Back in the trunk, he had his specially designed suitcase packed full of glass vials to hold the blood.

Ed Berry was a phlebotomist—a professional collector of blood. He was called "magic" because of his rare gift for working with kids with autism—he could get the needle in and the blood out without the kids being traumatized. Berry had no gimmick. He simply went at it gently, smiling all the way, and the kids, for whatever reason, seemed to know they could trust him.

Berry's blood-drawing tour, with stops and starts, took seven years. He went into posh neighborhoods in New York and Chicago as well as suburban tracts in Virginia and Texas. He spent a good deal of time in rural America. Once, with Port Huron, Michigan, in his rearview mirror, he set out for a drive that turned out to take hours, down dirt roads, to a spot in the Michigan wilderness where one tiny, solitary house was home to triplets with autism. At least, for that effort, he came away with three sets of vials filled.

It had been more than twenty years since those parents in Washington had made that rushed, almost naïve attempt to probe autism's organics in only five days—hiring that van to race back and forth between the hotel and the clinic, running the kids through a gauntlet of tests in only forty-five minutes.

Doubtlessly, there was also something quaint in the prospect of a phlebotomist in the year 2000, renting a car to bounce all over the country, to pay visits to homes where more than one child with autism lived. The plan was to create a master library of genetic material, something that had never existed before. This "autism genetic resource exchange" would be used as a lure for scientists, to get them to start investigating autism as a story told in human DNA.

Unorthodox, improbable, and fraught with potential pitfalls, the scheme was cooked up by two autism parents, the Hollywood couple who believed that trying something like this—hiring Ed Berry and sending him on the road—would help them "hurry up science."

It was not until July 1996 that Eric and Karen London mailed out their first set of RFPs—requests for proposals—to several research institutions across the United States. These were the formal invitations to research scientists to encourage them to make a bid for NAAR funds by making attractive proposals for research. They set an October 15 deadline for responses.

In the two years since NAAR had been founded, the Londons had continued to assemble a top-caliber advisory board, and had begun putting together an honorary board of celebrities who would provide endorsements and glamour, such as NFL football player Dan Marino and jazz trumpeter Wynton Marsalis. The Londons also made continuous rounds of autism conferences and support groups, explaining NAAR's purpose and making their first appeals for donations.

At first, there was a trickle of small checks. But in December 1995, when the Manhattan chapter of the Autism Society of America decided to select NAAR for its Christmas appeal, money started arriving in larger chunks, starting with the $13,000 raised when Marsalis performed a small benefit concert for the cause. Then, two separate donations of $30,000 rolled in. By the end of 1996, a single anonymous contribution of half a million dollars had turned NAAR into a scientific powerhouse. The Londons were able to rent a real Princeton office, instead of just a mailbox, and hire their first staff members. Most important, they could begin giving away money to researchers.

Now they just had to wait to see what sort of responses would arrive in their new offices. The RFPs had been sent to dozens of centers conducting biomedical research all across the United States and the rest of the world. But that did not guarantee that anyone out there had any funding-worthy ideas for autism research—or the slightest interest in the subject. It would be a letdown if a lot of bad proposals came back, but it would be an embarrassment if none came back at all. And with only a few weeks to go before the October 15 deadline, that was how many had arrived in Princeton. None.

Hollywood connections would count for a lot for Cure Autism Now, especially during the organization's early days, when CAN was in a hurry to build up its bank account. In late 1995, Jon Shestack began calling up friends in the business to solicit dollar contributions and found quite a few ready to write hefty checks. One of them—actor Anthony Edwards—went further. Edwards had worked with Jon on the 1984 film *Revenge of the Nerds,* and he had just had his big breakout on television, playing an emergency room doctor on the hit TV medical drama *ER.* Because he played a trustworthy physician, Edwards often found himself chased by charities seeking his endorsement of their causes. Because Shestack was his friend, Edwards went with Cure Autism Now.

Though not an autism parent, he brought to CAN what Dan Marino and Wynton Marsalis brought to NAAR—a glitter factor, combined with real conviction. Edwards went out of his way to keep show-business contributions coming in, hosting fund-raising events and talking about autism to the Hollywood press. He was perfectly on message—the message of impatience. "The goal is to put ourselves out of business and cure autism," he once told *USA Today,* "not in a week or a month or whenever the scientists can get around to it—but NOW!"

As private donations poured in—beginning with an opening fund-raising event that netted $75,000—Jon Shestack also turned his energies to making taxpayer funds more available for autism research. It was in these years that Jon discovered his talent for political lobbying. It played to his gift for telling a story, while the energy and focus it required gave him a way to channel and vent his frustration over the fact that his son Dov was still a boy in need of a cure. Governors and legislators alike came to know Jon's unique passion. At one time or another, they all had the photo of Dov held in front of their eyes. Jon made it so difficult to say no to him that, years later, when Congress passed a bill authorizing nearly a billion dollars over five years for autism research—the landmark Combating Autism Act of 2006—a big part of the credit belonged to Jon Shestack.

Much earlier, Anthony Edwards had helped in another way—by turning Jon into the political persuader he became. Once, when US Senator Bill Frist was resisting a funding bill Jon wanted passed, Edwards intervened. He invited Frist, who happened to be visiting Los Angeles, to take a backstage tour of the *ER* set. Frist, who was a practicing surgeon before going into politics, was a big fan of the show. When he stepped into the fictional "residents' lounge," he found himself transported back to his own early days of training, where the chairs had been the same shabby, slashed specimens the set designers used for the *ER* set. Edwards could see the senator was enjoying himself. Thus warmed up, Frist was introduced to Jon, who was also on set and had brought along Dov. They all posed for pictures, and Jon made his pitch to get Frist to support the bill. Frist went one better than that and joined a group of senators leading the charge for its successful passage.

Such transactions, however, much like the fund-raising, ultimately required that Jon and Portia, and by extension CAN, be taken seriously—an assumption that could not be taken for granted. Indeed, the proposition that autism parents could conjure up a research field out of nothing but their own passion seemed implausible on its face. And the idea that parents would make key decisions about which scientific studies should be paid for with the money available—even if the parents raised it themselves—was easily dismissed as an amateur's pipe dream. The greatest threat to CAN's mission, in the beginning, was that it would merely be ignored. Indeed, some of the organization's early moves almost ensured that result.

Portia had continued putting her energy into mastering the scientific dimension of their operation. In addition to reading and trying to understand the books and papers she was studying, she also took on most of the task of creating CAN's organizational shape and filling its ranks. Like Eric and Karen London, she started with the idea of building a scientific advisory board, so she turned to people like those she had met in Dallas, scientists who had entranced her with their readiness to break the rules and to take risks on therapies even before the science on them was fully in. CAN's commitment to alternative therapies endeared them to parents who were frustrated with mainstream practice, though, to some eyes, this also ran the risk of making CAN appear close to the medical fringe.

Early on, Portia and Jon established a clear, nonnegotiable but highly unconventional guideline for any science that CAN would fund: it needed to be approved by nonscientists. At its founding, CAN established a second advisory board that would be made up almost entirely of parents, who would have final say on what research Cure Autism Now funded. This was an attempt to ensure that any research CAN funded had a "direct relevance to autism," as experienced by people who lived with autism. A study on sleep, for example, might not occur to a young lab researcher who had never spent a night in the home of a child with the condition, but almost any autism parent would be able to point out the close link between autism and sleep disturbances. CAN wanted the science to respond to the direct experiences of families and their insights about autism. It was CAN's rule that any project bear high odds for "concrete clinical findings that can make a direct impact on the lives of families." But this degree of parental control over scientific decision-making—which NAAR did not replicate—was likely to scare off many established scientists.

In 1995, Portia set out on a recruitment tour, traveling to cities all over the United States to make in-person appeals, mostly to younger scientists, not only to persuade them to see that autism was a fascinating and promising window into their specialties—whether it be genetics, molecular biology, neuroscience, or something else—but also to see whether they would be willing to play by CAN's rules.

Around this time, Portia was introduced to an assistant professor of neurology at UCLA named Daniel Geschwind. As a courtesy to a fellow faculty member who was raising two autistic children, Geschwind agreed to a half-hour chat in his lab's conference room. Three and a half hours later, the conversation was still going, and Geschwind was about to make the most momentous decision of his career. As he listened to Portia—this Hollywood art director who had somehow learned to talk the research "talk"—Geschwind felt himself getting pulled along. Portia was offering him a once-in-a-lifetime opportunity—even if it was a gamble—to be an early participant in a new and broad scientific endeavor. By the time they parted that day, Cure Autism Now had acquired a chairman for its scientific advisory board.

It was a turning point for Cure Autism Now. Geschwind was the perfect leader for an organization that hoped to leave behind its own adolescence. While he accepted CAN's rules about parental influence on funding, he believed that CAN needed to distance itself from the alternative-therapies crowd. Over the course of several months, the composition of its scientific advisory board underwent a transformation, losing several members whose viewpoints were less orthodox, while taking on scientists whose pedigrees came closer to those of the group that NAAR had put together, many of whom were still junior enough to take the same gamble Geschwind had.

BACK EAST, MEANWHILE, the Londons' New Jersey living room began to fill with boxes during the week before the October 15 deadline. Scientists from across the country were sending in proposals in response to NAAR's RFP letters. Each box represented one proposal, duplicated twenty times to be distributed among the members of NAAR's scientific advisory board.

When October 15 finally arrived, there was a total of twenty-seven boxes stacked up, waiting to be opened. Karen, who was Jewish, woke up finally understanding what a kid might feel like on Christmas morning. She and Eric sat on the living room floor, tore open the boxes, and dove into their contents. They were delighted to see that the proposals they were poring over were as solid as the places they came from were reputable. They heard from researchers at Duke University,

Johns Hopkins University School of Medicine, the Kennedy-Krieger Institute, the University of California at Irvine, and fifteen other leading universities. This was no longer a pipe dream. Every proposal validated the case they had been making for two years—that a parent-run organization could shape and drive serious scientific inquiry into autism. A few weeks later, the scientific advisory board the Londons had created met at a hotel near Harvard to pick the proposals to fund from among the twenty-seven applicants.

By that point, NAAR had raised nearly $850,000, and the goal was to disburse $150,000 in this first round of funding. The board divided it equally among five winners. Their studies ranged from using neuroimaging of the brain to explore the impact of high amounts of white brain matter seen in children with autism, to measuring the brain waves of kids with autism as they tried to speak, to the use of some new molecular detection methods to explore the possible role of a particular virus in provoking autistic behaviors.

All the work produced out of this first round of funding added substantively to the scientific understanding of autism and produced publishable findings. Within a year, two of NAAR's first grant recipients came to the attention of federal funders, who awarded them a combined $3.6 million to continue the investigations that NAAR's money had launched. This was the Londons' ideal scenario coming true. The "seed money" that had spread around to make autism appealing to researchers was catching the eye of other funders, who were also stepping up. It looked like the start of a virtuous cycle.

IN THE LATE spring of 1996, Jon Shestack had flown east to Washington to start lobbying Capitol Hill for increased spending on biomedical research. He was also headed for the National Institutes of Health, to share with scientists one of CAN's biggest ideas for "hurrying up the science." The particulars of the concept were so bold and radical that he had expected some excitement from the roomful of geneticists he was addressing. But as Shestack finished speaking that day, the chilly silence in the room told him otherwise. As the Hollywood autism dad looked around at the scientists' faces, he reached for his wallet. It was time, again, to get out the picture of Dov.

Cure Autism Now was ready to start spending money, and genetic research had moved into top place on its list of priorities. Once again, Dan Geschwind was making his influence felt. For months, he had been educating CAN's founders on both the promise and the challenges of investigating autism's genetic underpinnings. He told them that autism's complexity pointed to quite a large number of genes being involved, and an even greater number of combinations of genes. Each of these combinations, interacting with some yet-to-be determined environmental factors, might represent a distinct pathway to having the condition. In other words, there might be many kinds of autism with a wide range of causes. Diving into each pathway by following genetic footprints would be vital to sorting out these complexities and designing interventions.

Geschwind told CAN's founders that when they started spending money on research, gene research should be a primary target, but he also explained that the answers would not come by studying the DNA of one or two individuals with the condition. The subtle and multifarious differences among people with autism demanded that researchers have access to the DNA of, at a minimum, hundreds of individuals. Moreover, in order to derive the most meaningful genetic information, the DNA of siblings offered the best opportunity for discovery.

But there was one major obstacle: there was not a lab anywhere with that amount of genetic material from autistic siblings in its storage coolers. Because of the time and money it cost to find and analyze the DNA of just one set of donor siblings, most researchers had only a handful of specimens. Moreover, they all jealously guarded what little they had. Science was, after all, competitive. Glory and the ensuing financial reward came from being the "first and only" in making important discoveries. As a result, genetic researchers were loath to share their DNA specimens with one another, even though pooling their resources might lead to more meaningful discoveries faster.

Then Portia came up with a bold idea: CAN would create its own collection of DNA. It would make it big, and it would make it available to the scientific community at large. CAN would do this by leveraging one of its unique strengths as an organization: its intimate connection to families. In short, Portia wanted to call on CAN's network of parents to step up and volunteer their children as donors. CAN would do the recruiting, collect and store the DNA, and then make it available to any scientists who were committed to doing research on autism. It would be a massive "freebie" to the genetic labs of the world, because Cure Autism Now would be paying for everything.

As Shestack always told the story afterward, the NIH geneticists were cold to the idea when he first presented it. Perhaps they felt it would be too disruptive to the status quo and that it went against the prevailing ethos of competition among scientists. That may well have been true, but there were also sound scientific reasons for thinking that a parent-run DNA-collection program would be a disaster. Collecting genetic material was not for amateurs, but CAN's plan called for families to take their kids to a local doctor or clinic to draw blood, stick the sample in a mailer, and send it to CAN, who would then find a way to store it. Moreover, CAN had no reliable way to determine whether these kids actually merited a diagnosis of autism in the first place, nor would they know what specific combinations of autistic traits each child manifested. If it was to be presumed that different genetic patterns led to different "autisms," then this sort of information was crucial. All in all, the CAN plan was likely to produce scientific garbage.

And so, CAN adjusted its plan; Jon and Portia went out and hired "magic man" Ed Berry. CAN would now be sending out an expert to get blood drawn the right way: safely, consistently, professionally. They had met Berry when, in their long round of efforts to get Dov's medical treatments addressed, Dov had needed blood drawn, and the autism grapevine had informed them that Berry was the man to see.

Bringing Berry into CAN was only one of the steps Jon and Portia took, under Geschwind's guidance, to professionalize their concept. He schooled the couple on the absolute necessity of maximum consistency in the procedures used to get each sample, and in the way autistic traits were documented in each donating individual. He also explained that researchers would want detailed histories not only of the two or more children in a household with autism, but also of their family members, who shared most of the same DNA. Cure Autism Now's founders resigned themselves to spending a great deal more money than they initially intended.

They also hired Catherine Lord, PhD, who came with one of autism's more gold-plated résumés. She had degrees in psychology from UCLA and Harvard, had done her clinical internship with the famous TEACCH program at the University of North Carolina, and was renowned for helping to develop a new tool for identifying autism in children. The Autism Diagnostic Instrument (ADI) was a specialized questionnaire, directed at parents, to tease out recognition of behaviors in a child that were rare but indicative of autism. The ADI was recognized for its power to yield reliable and consistent results, regardless of the biases of the tester, as long as he or she was well trained in its use. With Cure Autism Now paying the cost, Lord began running workshops to turn a lot of bright, interested students into certified ADI "raters."

In 1997, just as their counterparts in New Jersey were handing out the first five NAAR grants, Jon and Portia finally launched the full DNA project, under the acronym AGRE—for the Autism Genetic Research Exchange. Scores of families signed up immediately, their imaginations captured by the possibility of cracking autism's genetic code. Each received a home visit from one of the new ADI raters, who spent hours interviewing the family. The results, along with audio- and videotapes made during the visit, went back to Los Angeles for analysis. Whenever an autism diagnosis was confirmed, Ed Berry showed up, dropping by after a long train ride and drive, to draw blood in his gentle way from the entire family. Next, Berry shipped the physical blood samples, packed against damage, east to the Rutgers University Cell Repository for perpetual preservation. Once there, each sample underwent genomic screening, as well as a process of "immortalization," in which copies of the blood's component cells were manufactured and multiplied to create an indefinite supply identical to the originals.

This was not a process that moved quickly. It took three years to get the first 150 families through it, at which point another 250 were already in the pipeline. The cost of sustaining the program eventually exceeded more than $1 million annually. But significant support arrived in the form of a multimillion-dollar grant from the National Institutes of Health, which was a major boost to Cure Autism Now. Getting outside money steered to autism had always been one of its goals, and getting that level of financial commitment also proved that it had conquered the quality-control challenge.

Certainly, the scientific community was convinced. As the collection slowly climbed, passing 540 samples collected in the 2005 edition of its online publication, *ADVANCES,* researchers from all over the world were calling on the library's resources regularly and had begun publishing papers crediting Cure Autism Now for their work on autism's genetics. By then, at least sixty-three authors had cited the database in their publications.

To be sure, these initial rounds of deeper research into the genomes of diagnosed individuals only confirmed that the "code" everyone wanted to crack was going to be even more complex than anticipated. But even that recognition represented a significant advance.

ON THE EAST COAST, as Karen and Eric London had hoped, getting real scientific results from the first round of NAAR-funded studies made it easier to raise funds for the next. Having more funds yielded still more quality research. The virtuous cycle continued. In 1998, the second year of its grant program, NAAR underwrote ten studies in the amount of half a million dollars. In 1999, when proposals came from as far away as Italy and Russia, sixteen recipients received $800,000 in grants and fellowships. The fellowships fulfilled a specific ambition of the Londons. Awarded in chunks of $100,000, split over two years, they were available to young researchers and MDs who were committed to making the biomedical dimension of autism the full-time focus of their developing careers. There was no shortage of applicants. Thanks to the Londons, a new kind of career path was being born as the new millennium began.

Then the Londons set out to build a library of biological material too. In NAAR's case, the goal was to create a bank of brain tissue, to permit anatomical research. In most cases, children with autism die unexpectedly—overwhelmingly by drowning or by seizures. NAAR created protocols for making sensitive yet timely approaches to grieving families, suggesting organ donation for the sake of future generations of kids. Over time, word of the tissue bank's existence spread among America's autism community and donations increased. Physically stored at the Harvard Brain Tissue Resource Center, the autism brain bank quickly caught the attention of researchers, launching many studies that might never have been undertaken otherwise.

To be sure, differences in style would continue to distinguish CAN and NAAR, along with nuances in philosophy. But in reality, as time passed, "Hollywood" and "Princeton" cooperated more than they competed. The two groups coordinated their calendars, so that they were not soliciting research proposals from the scientific community at the same time. They mentioned each other favorably in their respective newsletters and referred prospective researchers to each other when it seemed to be a better match. They scrupulously avoided criticizing each other's scientific choices in public.

The autism community had by this time grown accustomed to the idea that there were two organizations taking the lead in biomedical research, bringing about profound and enduring changes in the ways autism was investigated, perceived, and funded for research purposes. Working with nearly identical goals, these two groups inspired scientists from disparate and rarefied branches of research to embrace the mystery of autism as worthy of their time, their energy, and their own big ideas.

In 2001, NAAR and CAN jointly cosponsored the first International Meeting for Autism Research as an add-on to that year's conference of the Society of Neuroscience. Nicknamed IMFAR, it was a sign of how successfully the two groups had legitimized autism research that some two hundred scientists from the United States and Canada, who came for the main neuroscience conference, also made time for the autism meeting. This was the same pool of researchers among whom Eric London had strolled only a few years earlier, scanning their posters in vain for any sign of interest in autism and encountering impatience when he tried to bring it up. Now they were interested.

Those first two hundred scientists were only the start. Over the next few years, as IMFAR became a stand-alone event, researcher attendance doubled, then doubled again, as scientists traveled from six continents to be there. Even news organizations began sending representatives, looking for stories among the hundreds and hundreds of papers, posters, and presentations that scientists had now become eager to publicize.

For getting all this started—for creating this new scientific attention paid to autism, for getting money to move in that direction, for getting young researchers to make understanding autism the focus of their careers—the credit would always belong to the founders of CAN and NAAR. They pushed the boundaries—which had always existed, and always would, at the point where what was known for certain about autism collided with its persistent mystery. They were forever confounding, these boundaries—to where the experts could never decide for sure where autism's very outlines were to be found, and such that parents would continue to dream of leaping the mystery's own frontiers in one jump, as some once thought they could do, with fingers on a keyboard. But those four parents settled instead for the hard work of science. Largely because of what they started in the 1990s, the boundaries of knowledge would continue advancing while the mystery yielded, only little by little, but year by year, to inroads made by solid science.

But during these same years, and even as early as that first IMFAR conference the parents pulled together in 2001, there was another force in play, which trained a brighter spotlight on the subject of autism than ever before. It wasn't just scientists paying attention to the condition anymore. For the first time, a much larger public was learning what autism was about, but in ways that moved their response, in remarkably short order, from curiosity to fear.

PART VIII

HOW AUTISM BECAME FAMOUS

1980s–1990s

38

PUTTING AUTISM ON THE MAP

HEADS TURNED WHEN TEMPLE GRANDIN WALKED INTO the restaurant. She is a tall woman with a large face, and a voice that's almost always a little louder than necessary. In this case, she didn't have to say a word to get everyone's attention—her outfit did the job just fine: a brightly embroidered rodeo-style shirt, a western belt with a huge metal shield of a buckle, and, tied around her throat, a red kerchief straight out of an Old West film.

To Emily Gerson Saines, who was watching Grandin pound toward her table, it was like gazing upon a vision. By this time, in 2001, Gerson Saines had been an autism activist for eight years, long enough to know what everyone inside the closed world of autism knew—that Grandin was, if not a miracle, the greatest celebrity that world had known.

Even while pursuing her activism for autism, Gerson Saines had continued working as a manager for movie stars, and now she had a project in mind that would bring those two worlds together. She wanted to produce a movie about autism, and she wanted to base it on a book Grandin had written years earlier called *Thinking in Pictures*.

GRANDIN'S BOOK HAD special meaning for Gerson Saines. When it first came out, she had just become a member of the autism family herself. She was, at the time, in utter despair over her own son Dashiell's diagnosis. In those first months after getting the news, she had briefly held a copy of the book in her hands, sent to her by her mother. Still in shock over the diagnosis and rendered almost immobile by depression, Gerson Saines had tossed it aside.

In her Manhattan office, where she was a high-powered media executive, Gerson Saines always wore a poker face. But at home, in the suburban village of Larchmont, New York, she often felt like she was falling apart. Dashiell was a classic "runner"—a behavior that can bring even the strongest, most resilient parent to his or her knees. Given any opportunity, Dashiell would sprint outside and into the street, and the only way to avoid this, short of putting inside locks on all the doors, was to keep him constantly under watch.

There were other issues. Dashiell did not talk. He hardly slept. He did not like to eat. And, on one particularly bad day in 1996, he made an awful mess with his own feces, smearing it all over the walls and floor of the bathroom. When Gerson Saines saw this, she went down on her knees to clean it up, digging with a toothbrush to get at the grout, to scrub out the brown stain and the smell. *It's shit, everything is shit, I'm covered in shit, my life is shit,* she thought at that moment, and she began to cry. This was the side of her life that those in her office could never see.

Pulling herself together, she finished the cleanup, threw out the brush, and went upstairs to shower. On the way, she plunked Dashiell down in front of a video—something to distract him for the two minutes it would take her to step in and step out of the shower.

It was in the second minute that she heard the cars honking on the street outside. No, not that fast—it can't be him, she thought. Trailing water, she raced to an upstairs window and looked down. It *was* him. Dashiell had bolted, and there he was out in the middle of the road, dancing on the blacktop as cars from both directions stopped just short of him.

Gerson Saines ran to her closet to grab some clothes so she could go and rescue her child. She was reaching for the nearest shirt when a vicious stink hit her in the face. It was coming from the shirt, she realized in an instant. It was coming from her *entire wardrobe of clothes.* Somehow, Dashiell had been in there too, with his feces, and had smeared it on virtually every garment she owned.

In that same instant, she accepted the single option she had available. With the honking still going on outside, and voices starting to shout as well, she tore the shirt from its hanger and slipped it on, then ripped some soiled pants from another hanger and stepped into them. Seconds later, she rushed out into the street, strands of wet hair stuck to her forehead and shoulders, her clothes streaked brown, apologies to strangers bubbling up through her lips from a still remarkably coherent place inside her. Taking Dashiell by the hand, she marched him back into the house and closed the front door behind them, shutting out everything dangerous out there, out where everyone else got to live normally.

As she heard the cars drive away, and the softer suburban hush was restored, she leaned up against the door, let go of Dashiell's hand, and took stock. She knew it then. Of all the low points she had endured so far, this was the lowest.

But it was also in that moment, with her back to the door, that she made up her mind: Things are going to change around here. The first thing she did was to find some clean clothes. Then she called a locksmith, and, in short order, new locks were installed on the inside of every door in the house.

In time, Dashiell would grow into a handsome young adult who, after a great deal of work, acquired life skills sufficient to cope far better with the world around him. He even helped raise funds by taking part in autism walks. But that came much later. First, Temple Grandin entered his mother's life—not long after that discouraging day—when she finally picked up Grandin's book. She immediately became wrapped up in the message it conveyed: that autism was not an ending, nor was it a prison. Grandin and her story had served as a kind of lifeline. The book cracked her out of her inertia and launched her into activism. Indeed, one of the more energetic new autism organizations of the 1990s, the Autism Coalition for Research and Education, had Gerson Saines as a cofounder.

So, there she was, more than five years later, pitching Grandin on a movie about her life. She knew Grandin would make a great movie character in every way, her struggle and her triumph, not to mention the whole cowboy look she had worn to lunch that day. She was an authentically inspiring figure. Gerson Saines also knew, from *Thinking in Pictures,* that this was how Grandin had been dressing every day for at least thirty years. It was part of the legend, part of her celebrity.

As of 2001, the notion that autism had a "celebrity" made sense within the autism family, but outside of it, Grandin was not famous. In the language activists used, autism "awareness" was low, and the specific challenges faced by people who had autism—and their families—remained unknown to the public at large.

That, in fact, was part of Gerson Saines's reason for wanting to take Grandin's story to Hollywood. She hoped to inspire the autism community, but she also wanted to explain the condition to a wider public that was not paying any attention to autism. Because she understood that most people had much less incentive to think or feel much about the topic, one way or the other, she resolved to give them a good story so they had a reason to care. Temple Grandin's life didn't make for a good story; it made for a great one. Beyond that, she simply wanted to make a good film. A good film, about autism.

In 1969, in his last feature film, called *Change of Habit,* Elvis Presley played a doctor who falls in love with a nun while both are working with underprivileged children. When a young girl named Amanda, abandoned by her mother, arrives at the clinic refusing to speak, it is the nun, played by Mary Tyler Moore, who says, "I think she is autistic." Instantly, Presley confirms the diagnosis and goes right to the cure. Explaining to Moore that he was about to purge the girl's "autistic frustration," he wraps his arms around the child. Her frustration, it was implied, was the result of being deprived of her mother's love. Now Presley administered the antidote. Hugging the abandoned little girl tighter, he began murmuring to her in that famous Elvis voice. "You've got to start learning how to love people," he said. And then he began repeating, gently, the words that needed to be said: "I love you, Amanda. I love you. I love you."

Amanda had been wrestling against Presley's grasp, but suddenly, she stopped and found her voice. She uttered the word "mad." Then she said, "love." And with that, she was cured.

That was how the movies usually treated autism in the twentieth century, in the rare instances when it did: autism was a problem only solvable by love. It was the fundamental message of 1979's *Son-Rise,* whose subtitle was "A Miracle of Love." It told the story of real-life parents Suzy and Barry Kaufman, who claimed to have rescued their son from autism—which they traced to a lack of parental bonding—by showering their boy with attention, respecting his impulses, and mimicking his behaviors.

Back in the purely fictional category, 1993's *House of Cards* portrayed a young girl who, in response to her father's death, went silent, cold to human interaction. At the same time, she became adept at building elaborate towers out of playing cards and balancing in high places. Tommy Lee Jones, as a psychologist, diagnoses autism, but the mother, played by Kathleen Turner, refuses to accept the diagnosis, arguing defiantly that "all she needs is a little more attention from her mother." Working from some maternal instinct, the mother constructs her own tower out of plywood, higher than a house, mimicking her daughter's playing-card construction but on a much larger scale. The woman and the girl climb the tower together, and at that point, the child is cured.

Love was the answer, one way or the other, in each of these films, which did not veer far from the well-ingrained message, rooted in the era of mother blaming, that autism flourished where proper love was lacking.

On the other hand, an episode of the television medical drama *Marcus Welby, M.D.* showed its grandfatherly yet iconoclastic doctor practicing an early version of Lovaas-style applied behavioral analysis on a little boy named Paulie. Trying to get Paulie to look him in the eye, Welby rewards the boy with gumballs and a warm smile whenever he complies. When the boy resists, Welby shrieks at him, chasing the small child around the room, and finally slapping him hard across his cheek. When Paulie's mother objects, Welby turns to her with a stern reprimand: "You will see Paulie spanked," Welby lectures her. "You will learn to spank him yourself—or you'll see him in an institution for the rest of his life!"

In 1969, when this episode aired, autism parents viewed the broadcast of this episode as a positive—not so much because of the ABA message but because at this time, autism still barely registered in the public consciousness. Perhaps television's most beloved doctor would cause the public to finally pay attention. But it did not. Just as Welby, a week later, had moved on to some other malady, so too did viewers. That tended to be the pattern when Hollywood made forays into autism: it would create a blip of interest, but then most people stopped thinking about it.

Documentaries and the occasional print story also had little influence. Many of them depicted autism as exotic or as an intriguing puzzle. Magazine stories had headlines like: "The Trance Children," "The Strangers in Our Midst," "The Children of the Fairies," and "The Kids with the Faraway Eyes." Autistic children were cast as curiosities of nature, strange, mystical, and unreal. Another brand of story acknowledged the severity of autism and the strains it put on families by adopting a tone that was callously bleak. There was, for example, that notorious 1965 *LIFE* magazine headline that called the children "Far Gone Mental Cripples." Rather than describe autistic children as odd, such articles described children as too broken to be fully human.

It is true that around this time, narratives about real people with autism were becoming easier to find. As a rule, these were books written by parents about their children, a model that harkened back to the original mother's memoir of autism, *The Siege,* which had landed on shelves in 1967. Its author, Clara Claiborne Park, was an early autism activist who taught literature and writing at a New England college. Her story of the first eight years of raising her daughter Jessie—to whom she gave the name "Ellie" in the book—became assigned reading for young people training in special education during the 1970s, and inspired more than one student to specialize in autism. *The Siege* was also a persuasive counterweight to Bruno Bettelheim's *Empty Fortress,* which had appeared at about the same time and was positioned as the authoritative book about autism.

While a trickle of similar memoirs appeared in the 1970s and 1980s—notably 1973's *For the Love of Ann,* based on a father's diary, and 1989's *A Child Called Noah,* which inspired a story on *60 Minutes,* the readership for these books was always limited. Mostly, they were read by people who were already in the autism "family." The shared stories offered a sense of community, which softened the loneliness the families experienced, but they rarely told their readers anything about autism that they did not already know from firsthand experience.

Whether they were dramatic shows on television, or loving stories written by parents, or bleak articles published in magazines, the perceived rarity of autism gave the general public an excuse to keep thoughts of it at a comfortable distance. People could feel safe knowing autism had nothing to do with them and never would. It was a psychological novelty item, pushed out of mind when the channel was changed or the page was turned.

Then *Rain Man* was released, the first good movie about autism.

IN DECEMBER 1988, when *Rain Man* arrived in theaters, the effect was immediate. All over the United States and Britain, anyone with an intimate connection to autism suddenly began getting questions. They came from friends and family, and, in many cases, from reporters, all of whom were newly curious about this fascinating condition they had never given much thought to, or even heard of, before seeing the movie. Bernie Rimland himself took dozens of calls. He told the readers of his newsletter that "*Rain Man* has stimulated every newspaper and magazine in the country to run an article on autism." Ruth Sullivan, still the doyenne of autism activists, sat on the set of *The Oprah Winfrey Show* and declared, "*Rain Man* has advanced the field of autism by twenty-five years!" A headline in the *Orlando Sentinel,* appearing eight days after the movie's premiere, nailed what had just happened: "*Rain Man* Puts Autism on the Map."

Most people in the autism community agreed and were delighted by the film. Their sentiment was captured by the British autism researcher Uta Frith, who praised the movie for rendering "an outstanding portrayal" that "helped to lessen any feelings of fear and dread about autism."

Rain Man was not perfect, but it was nearly so—the first movie to get autism right, and to reach so many people while doing so. To be sure, lesser films about the subject had preceded *Rain Man,* and lesser films would follow it. But that only underscored *Rain Man*'s longstanding uniqueness as what it was: a good film about autism.

The first script for *Rain Man,* in fact, had nothing about autism in it. The original big idea was a story about a man who had what is called "savant syndrome." In 1983, screenwriter Barry Morrow bumped into such a person, thirty-two-year-old Kim Peek, at a conference of the Association of Retarded Citizens in Texas. Peek, too intellectually disabled to live on his own, lived with his father in Utah. He did not have autism. He did, however, have a phenomenal talent for ingesting and remembering information. He had memorized symphonic scores, the works of Shakespeare, and entire telephone directories. He was also a calendar calculator, able to name the day of the week for any calendar date going forward or backward for thousands of years. When he read books, he used his eyes independently, reading the left and the right page simultaneously.

Morrow was captivated. By October 1986, he had completed a draft script entitled *Rain Man,* about two brothers, one of whom had Peek's prodigious mental gifts. The younger brother, Raymond, is developmentally disabled and heir to a fortune. The older brother, Charlie, a sour soul who has only recently discovered Raymond's existence, just wants the money.

It was Dustin Hoffman who killed off that version of *Rain Man,* deciding that he wanted in on the project but that he did not want the part being offered—sour Charlie, the older brother. Instead, he wanted to play Raymond. He had seen a *60 Minutes* program in 1983 about a musical savant by the name of Leslie Lemke. Unable to speak or see, Lemke could play complex piano pieces nearly flawlessly after hearing them only once. Hoffman was deeply touched by Lemke's story. An associate producer, Gail Mutrux, was dispatched to learn more about savants. Savant syndrome was rare, she learned, and more likely to be present in people who were intellectually disabled than people with autism. At the same time, the producers became aware of actor Cliff Robertson's Academy Award–winning portrayal of an intellectually disabled adult in a 1968 movie called *Charly.* Nobody wanted merely to repeat that. And so it was settled: there had been no portrayal of an adult with *autism.* Raymond would be autistic.

Inevitably, Mutrux's search to learn more about autism quickly led her to Bernie Rimland, who was running his Autism Research Institute out of a storefront around the corner from his house in San Diego. When Mutrux reached Rimland by phone, he told her he would be happy to take a look at the script and share some information about autism.

A few days later, Mutrux drove down to San Diego to meet Rimland in person. He had an armload of books and articles waiting for her, and he regaled her with all the ways that autism was fascinating. Rimland wanted Raymond to be autistic; he could foresee the publicity a good Hollywood film would bring to the cause.

The project, meanwhile, picked up and lost a series of directors—Marty Brest, Steven Spielberg, Sydney Pollack—each coming aboard and then begging off for different reasons. Ultimately, the job went to Barry Levinson, who was fresh off directing 1987's *Good Morning, Vietnam.* Levinson and Hoffman were both attracted to the challenge of creating a character whose inner world would not be easy to identify with, and who, by the movie's end, would not experience the usual cathartic leap of self-discovery. Hoffman could not wait to get started. "When people look back on my career, I'll be remembered for two roles: Ratso Rizzo and Rain Man," Hoffman said at an early meeting. "I want to do this picture, and I want to do it fast."

Rimland was hired as a technical consultant, along with Darold Treffert, an authority on savants. Hoffman, of course, wanted to see what autism looked like, to try to get inside it. With help from Rimland, Mutrux dug out some documentaries, including two that were completed nearly twenty years apart but featured the same person—Joe Sullivan, Ruth Sullivan's son. It had only been a year or so since the second of these films, *Portrait of an Autistic Young Man,* had been completed and aired on PBS, so the outtakes were still available. Hoffman watched all fifteen-plus hours of them. When Hoffman eventually met Sullivan, he was eating cheese puffs the way he always did—one at a time with a toothpick. Hoffman took note. In the movie, Raymond would spear his food with a toothpick.

Bernie Rimland also brought his son Mark to a meeting with Hoffman and some of the producers. Mark, then in his early twenties, had grown up to get along at a relatively high level. He painted, and he helped his father out, running errands and sweeping up at the ARI office. It seems that he had also paid close attention to an autographed photo of Hoffman his dad hung up in the office after an earlier visit to Los Angeles, because that day, at lunch, it struck Mark that the movie star's hair had a lot more gray in it in real life. When he blurted this out in a loud monotone, his father cringed. Hoffman chuckled. He had officially seen autism in action.

It was Ruth Sullivan who steered Dustin Hoffman to a young man living independently in Princeton, New Jersey. Peter Guthrie, in his twenties, had a range of savant skills—calendar calculation, a phenomenal mind for statistics, and the ability to draw objects with near-perfect perspective and in minute detail. He also had autism. He read books with no sense of their meaning and was terrified of rain. He also had great difficulty conducting a conversation; he seemed better at collecting statistics about someone he was going to meet, and then talking about those when face-to-face with that person. Yet, of everyone Hoffman met in his research phase, Peter was the one he connected with best.

Peter had a caring and protective older brother, Kevin, who drove him into New York the first time Peter was invited to meet with the production team. It was Kevin's idea that Peter and Hoffman go bowling together, along with Tom Cruise. A real friendship got started that day. Over the coming months, Hoffman kept up with the Guthrie brothers, inviting them to his home, watching TV with them, and watching how they interacted. The posture, the voice, and the facial expression that Hoffman would wear throughout most of *Rain Man* were, to anyone who knew Peter Guthrie, more than familiar.

The plot of *Rain Man* was ultimately shaped, Levinson later said, by the characters of the two brothers. Charlie, a born manipulator, finds it impossible to manipulate Raymond. Instead, he has to figure out who Raymond is, and in doing so, enlarge his capacity for human connection. Raymond, for his part, does not reveal his inner self easily, not because he is deliberately evasive, but because of his autism. Little by little, more action-oriented plot points from the original script were dropped from the story, and *Rain Man* became a fresh, different kind of "relationship" movie.

But it was the film's sensitive and faithful depiction of autism that gave audiences something new to consider. One critical scene became known as the "toothpick moment." At a diner with Charlie, Raymond asks for toothpicks, so that he can use them to eat his pancakes. The waitress accidentally drops the box, spilling the toothpicks at Raymond's feet. Raymond glances down briefly, then softly mutters, "Eighty-two, eighty-two, eighty-two." He is counting, in increments of eighty-two, the number of toothpicks on the floor: 246. Charlie asks the waitress how many toothpicks come in the box. She checks, and responds, "250." Charlie scoffs, telling Raymond he was "pretty close." But then she looks inside the box and pauses. "There's four left," she tells Charlie quietly. The scene was breathtaking in how quickly and quietly it revealed the extraordinary gifts that Raymond possessed.

Hoffman, of course, was not just playing a savant. He was playing a man with autism, and the portrayal was flawless. Outside the walls of an institution for the first time, Raymond wears an expression that never changes: a slightly quizzical downward squint. His need for sameness—including a constant supply of toothpicks and underwear from Kmart—defined his journey. He has sensory issues and finds loud noises excruciating. He is naïve and literal-minded. He has a stiff gait and an obsession with sports statistics. When he is asked what it was like to be kissed for the first time, all he can say is "wet." Usually, being touched makes him wildly upset, and when he is anxious, he runs and reruns the dialogue from an old comedy bit, the Abbott and Costello "Who's on First?" routine. He has memorized it verbatim, without realizing that it is meant to be funny.

In the standard Hollywood ending, Raymond might have been cured of autism. Or he might have seen enough of the world to know he wanted to live outside those institution walls forever. Or perhaps he and his brother might have grown so close during their week of adventures and misadventures that they decide to move in together. But the ending of *Rain Man* does not follow the expected paths. Although younger brother Charlie is profoundly transformed, destined to be a nicer guy, Raymond's growth is less obvious. It takes some understanding of autism to appreciate how he has changed. Late in the film, for example, he gets a joke, for the first time. Two brief scenes later, he *makes* his first joke, which he has learned from being with Charlie.

And in the movie's final minutes—just for a moment—Raymond leans over and rests his forehead on Charlie's, newly at ease with the physical connection to a man he recognizes as family, a concept whose meaning seems to have deepened for him. It is a small gesture that represents a giant leap.

Yet there are no miracles. Raymond still has autism, to a debilitating degree. And because of that, he returns to the place where he feels safest. That happens to be an expensive institution that provides humane, round-the-clock care. It was an ending that spoke a real truth about autism, one that resonated for parents and people with autism: that autism is for always.

Rain Man had its official opening in New York City on December 12, 1988. Three months later, it won the Oscar for Best Picture, Best Director, and Best Original Screenplay, and Hoffman won for Best Actor.

There were, to be sure, some criticisms. *The New Yorker*'s Pauline Kael hated the movie and called it "wet kitsch." There was some degree of grumbling in the autism community too, from parents whose friends were suddenly curious about whether their children had memorized the phone book or were good at counting toothpicks.

At the same time, *Rain Man* solved a problem that had dogged parents since autism's earliest days, which was that autism was so hard to explain to outsiders. For so long, the parents of autistic children had felt unbearably alone, and finally the public had at least a rough understanding of the condition.

Ruth Sullivan was right, then. *Rain Man* changed the autism story for good. To be sure, it was still true that, for the vast majority of moviegoers, autism's real challenges remained exactly what they were before: someone else's emergency. But after 1988, most people at least grasped what the condition was, in some rough fashion, and also had a generally favorable view of what a person with autism might be like.

That was progress—even if the first celebrity produced by the autism universe, Raymond Babbitt, happened to be a fictional character. It would take a real-life celebrity with autism to carry the message even further.

Temple Grandin's first book, published when she was thirty-nine years old, in 1986, was considered groundbreaking. It was the first time that the experience of having autism was ever described in book form and in the first person, by someone who was actually living with it. Following a difficult childhood, during which her autistic traits were often disruptive and disabling, Grandin had emerged as an adult who had taken her place in the wider world. And yet, she still had autism. Her book's title, *Emergence: Labeled Autistic,* attempted to cover that sweep.

Its story was focused mostly on the 1950s and 1960s—years during which her mother's unwavering commitment to her daughter gave Grandin the opportunity to work with teachers and family who were invested in her success. As a young child, Grandin was incapable of speech and easily overwhelmed by sensory experiences that most people don't even notice. Once, on the way to a session with a speech therapist, her mother, Eustacia Cutler, had placed a hat on her head for the ride. To Grandin, the hat felt excruciatingly painful. Against her mother's instructions, she yanked it off and threw it out the driver's-side window of the car. Her mother, who was at the wheel, reached to catch it, but in doing so, she swerved into a tractor-trailer. In the stress of the moment, Grandin spoke some of her earliest words, saying the word "ice" over and over again, as the broken glass from the window rained down on her.

In *Emergence,* she wrote that she still saw this moment vividly, as she did with everything that had ever happened to her. She described herself as a "visual thinker," with a mind that uses pictures to recall the past and make calculations about the present and future.

Her mother's determination to avoid institutionalizing Grandin led to her attending a series of mainstream schools. This went well when she was in the younger grades but became more of a challenge during adolescence. She was expelled from high school for fighting. After that, she attended a Vermont boarding school for gifted children with emotional problems, where she met a science teacher named Dr. Carlock, who was able to make sense of how she thought. His encouragement changed her life. He saw the value in Grandin's different "fixations" and used them to help motivate her to study psychology and science.

Grandin went on to college and then moved to Arizona for graduate school, where she studied cattle's reaction to soothing pressure, a subject she had become fascinated by. Ultimately, her research laid the groundwork for more humane handling of livestock throughout the United States. This made Grandin, by the late 1970s, a known figure in the small universe of livestock management. Her name had appeared in its trade press many times, quoted on matters related to cattle handling, or in the bylines to her own published articles on the topic. Her autism, however, was never mentioned.

But word of Grandin's existence at some point began to trickle out into another small universe, the one comprised of autism parents, where her story was passed by word of mouth almost like a myth. People would hear whispers about a grown woman with a PhD who had autism, somewhere out west, working with cows. The details were always fuzzy, and the woman's identity was so vaguely known that even Ruth Sullivan, who knew everyone involved in autism in the United States in the mid-1980s, did not recognize Grandin when she bumped into her at an airport.

Both women had landed in Chicago on the same connecting flight from St. Louis, and then sat next to each other on the shuttle bus to the hotel, where both were attending an autism conference. Though neither was much for small talk, they chatted on the ride in, and Sullivan was impressed with how much this young woman seemed to know about autism. It was only on the conference's second or third day that Sullivan put it together—that the woman on the shuttle was the fabled PhD-holder. At that, she approached Grandin and asked her if she would be willing to speak at the following year's conference.

A year later, in 1987, a shy and awkward Grandin became the surprise hit of the annual conference of the National Society for Autistic Children. During an afternoon of workshops, Sullivan had slotted Grandin into a one-hour table session on "Adults with Autism," with ten chairs provided. The seats around the table filled immediately, and behind them, another dozen people stood leaning in to hear as Sullivan began the introduction. Soon the standing audience grew to four rows deep. Sullivan called for a time-out and quickly arranged for another room with more space and a raised stage.

Over the next sixty minutes, with Sullivan moderating, Grandin held her audience spellbound. To the parents, hearing her talk about her experience of autism was like suddenly finding an interpreter fluent in a language that had baffled them for years. Questions came fast. *Why does my son spin so much? Why does sound set him off? Why won't he look me in the eyes?* Grandin could not answer all of these questions, but she explained, with a pure firsthand perspective, what life felt like from her side of the autism experience. She talked about her own sensitivity to sound, saying that it was "like being tied up to the rail and the train's coming." She also explained her own extreme skin sensitivity, how some clothing felt so rough that it was actually excruciatingly painful. And she talked about her difficulties communicating what she felt and in understanding what other people felt.

It was an intensely intimate conversation, and some of the parents cried during it. This was a turning point in Grandin's life; that day, she became known as the most famous person with autism in the world. Soon autism groups all over the country were booking her for speaking engagements. In 1988, she was invited to join the board of the Autism Society of America (formerly NSAC), the first person with the diagnosis asked to serve. Sullivan observed that with each year, with more experience in public life, Grandin became remarkably comfortable with public speaking, even graduating to using humor effectively.

In the 1990s, Oliver Sacks, the British neurologist, included a profile of Grandin in a book of sketches of people with varying manifestations of atypical brain wiring. He was charmed by Grandin's remark, in a conversation with him, that she sometimes felt like "an anthropologist on Mars." He liked the phrase so much he made it the title of a piece about her in *The New Yorker,* and then used it later for his book.

In 1995, Grandin published her second book, *Thinking in Pictures.* Told in the first person, *Thinking in Pictures* was the true-life account of a girl with autism who, with a great deal of support from her mother, had grown up to become a scientist, a speaker, a writer, and an inspiration to anyone in the autism community who had ever heard of her.

When Emily Gerson Saines broached the topic of making a film about Grandin's story during their lunch together in 2001, Grandin did not need much convincing. She quite liked the idea of a movie about her life. She also was happy to hear that *Thinking in Pictures* had given Emily hope, which was something they both wanted to see spread around more. They wished to spread around something else as well—a better understanding of people with autism, along with more compassion for them. It was that kind of understanding and compassion that had made it possible for Grandin, a once-unspeaking girl, to take part in a proper business lunch in Manhattan, talking about a movie deal. That day, she and Gerson Saines came to an agreement, sealed with a handshake—together, they would make a film that would get people thinking about autism as never before, one that would have a true story at its heart.

It would take the rest of the decade to get it made. As it turned out, autism awareness would soar to unprecedented heights during that decade, but not because of anything Hollywood did. Instead, another driving force came into play early in the new millennium that produced a fundamentally new reality for autism's place in the public's imagination. Autism, a once-obscure condition, treated by the media as a curiosity, by politicians as a low priority, and by most of the research community as something of a career backwater, suddenly mutated into one of the most pressing matters of the day. By the end of the decade, it had become a media obsession, a political football, and the target for hundreds of millions of dollars' worth of scientific investigation.

The most profound change revolved around a new perception of who needed to worry about autism. Previously, the experience of autism had been limited to the families where it had already occurred. The condition was seen as so uncommon, that for everyone else, its relevance was close to nil.

But that complacency vanished with the introduction of a single word into the autism conversation.

"Epidemic."

39

SOCIETY'S EMERGENCY

When autism finally became truly "famous" in the United States, it was because people came to fear it. In the early 2000s, autism went from being something fascinating and uncommon to a threat that stalked the nation, one that might give pause to anyone raising children or even planning to. This momentous change in perception—when autism suddenly became society's emergency—rested on a commonsense observation. There just seemed to be more children with autism around than there used to be.

It appeared that autism had broken out of its old boundaries and was spreading fast. That was certainly how things appeared to a state senate official in California, who was the father of a boy with autism. Rick Rollens had served for twenty-four years as Secretary to the State Senate, but he resigned that position in 1996 in order to throw himself into autism activism, to help find his six-year-old a cure.

In 1997, shortly after leaving his statehouse job, Rollens sought out one of the Senate's most powerful members—Mike Thompson, the Democrat who chaired the Senate Budget Committee. They had become close friends over the years, and Rollens had a favor to ask. He wanted Thompson to insert some language into that year's budget bill. Thompson delivered. The language went in and was still there when the bill became law in 1998.

As a result, that year the state's Department of Disability Services (DDS) was required to undertake an internal study on the level of services being delivered to all people with developmental disabilities over an eleven-year span, dating back to the late 1980s. The services under review included all those offered in response to the full range of developmental disabilities, from cerebral palsy to epilepsy to autism.

Rollens, of course, was only interested in what numbers came up for autism, because he had a point he wanted to make about the condition. He was convinced that the department's records review would prove that, all of a sudden, in the mid-1990s, more young children had autism than ever before. It was disastrous, he thought, that this increase was being overlooked. The National Institutes of Health was expending more time and effort investigating sleep disorders than looking into anything related to autism.

True, Rollens lacked any statistical evidence of an increase, and he knew that; that's why he needed the DDS's numbers. But he could see with his own eyes that "busloads of kids" were showing up at the same schools and centers where his son Russell had started getting help several years earlier with far fewer children by his side. Meanwhile, through one of the organizations Rollens helped start—Families for Early Autism Treatment—parents he'd never met were reaching out to the organization via its new Internet newsletter. He seemed to be hearing a new diagnosis story every day.

At this time, the *DSM* still stated the standard assumption that autism occurred at the rate of 4 to 5 people in 10,000, which was a number derived largely from Victor Lotter's survey of a single British county more than thirty years earlier. Few follow-up studies on autism prevalence had been conducted in the interim, largely because the research community saw no need for one.

Rollens wanted the California records to fill this gap. As a tabulation of every person receiving services during the period under review—with autism diagnoses confirmed in each case by professionals—Rollens was confident that it would draw the trend line upward year by year and prove his theory right.

The DDS report was completed in the spring of 1999, and Rollens used contacts from his former life in the senate to get his hands on an early copy. What he read startled him. Between 1987 and 1998, according to the report's summary, there had been a 273 percent increase in the number of people availing themselves of state-provided services for autism. By "autism," the report meant only people with the "classic" sort of autism as spelled out in the *DSM*. As the state did not provide services to people diagnosed with Asperger's disorder or Pervasive Developmental Disorder Not Otherwise Specified, those conditions were not included in the report's count. Instead of 4.5 per 10,000 people with autism, the numbers of those getting services in California came closer to 60 per 10,000. The trend was far sharper than even he had suspected.

Rollens immediately leaked the report to the *Los Angeles Times*, which ran a story under what, to Rollens, was the perfect headline: "State Study Finds Sharp Rise in Autism Rate." Both the body of the piece and one of the sub-headlines used the word "epidemic."

The "California Study," as it came to be called, lit a match under a fire that did not go out for the next ten years, as the word "epidemic" became attached to autism with such frequency and with such force that the quotation marks around it soon fell away.

THE DISTURBING SPECTER of an autism epidemic became, by reluctant popular consensus, yet another one of the psychological stressors of the twenty-first century—another reason the world was a dangerous place for bringing up kids. *Child* magazine would capture this anxiety perfectly when it labeled autism the "Disorder That's Defining an Era."

The trope was seized on by advocacy groups of all stripes, as each recognized how much more persuasive their appeals for funding would be when autism could be framed as a terrifying national crisis. Leaders of these groups began citing the epidemic argument in every speech and press release, hammering home the urgency of their cause with two statistics: what the autism rate *used to be* and what it is *right now*. Different groups used different numbers, but no matter what, the statistics were all alarming.

The news media ran hard with the epidemic story. *Time* made it a cover story in 2002: "Inside the World of Autism: More Than One Million Americans May Have It, and the Number of New Cases Is Exploding." NBC News partnered with *Newsweek* in 2005 to produce a weeklong series of programs under the rubric "AUTISM: The Hidden Epidemic?"

Around this same time, in response to the public uproar, Congress held a series of hearings led by Republican representative Dan Burton. Burton took as his starting point the assumption that the nation was facing an epidemic that demanded investigation. "We have an epidemic on our hands," he declared in 2002, "and we in Congress need to make sure that the NIH and the CDC treat this condition like an epidemic." In coming elections, even candidates for the White House would be expected to have formulated positions on the epidemic question. Most took its reality as a given.

Corroboration for this came in the series of statistics reported throughout the decade by the Centers for Disease Control and Prevention. In 2004, the CDC published an alert for pediatricians reporting that autism in the United States affected 1 in 166 children. In 2007, the CDC announced a new number: 1 in 150. Two years later, it was 1 in 110. The same trend line that California had unearthed back in 1999 was now, according to the CDC, a nationwide concern.

It was clear—the numbers proved it. This thing was getting bigger all the time. Everyone had reason to be scared.

But as always, there were plenty of ways to count autism, and not all of them added up to the picture of an epidemic that Rick Rollens, Dan Burton, and the advocacy organizations projected. Indeed, it was the signal success of all those players that they kept the politicians, the public, and the media talking about an epidemic when, in the view of most social scientists who looked into the matter, the statistical case for any massive increase in the incidence of autism was highly dubious. Many of the experts suggested that the epidemic that had made everyone so scared actually might not exist at all.

The experts' misgivings began with the California numbers brought to light thanks to Rick Rollens's persistence. Those numbers seemed to tell an open-and-shut story: more children receiving state services for autism meant that autism was on the rise in the population. But that formulation assumed that calculating demand for services was the same thing as counting, one by one, all the kids in California with the condition. Not only were those not the same, but also, in practice, demand for services would never be a trustworthy yardstick for measuring the pace of autism's spread in the population.

For example, demand for anything—from drivers' licenses to public playgrounds—could be expected to go up when a population increase is under way. Indeed, during the years covered by California's autism report, the population did get significantly bigger, by roughly 16 percent. That was a factor that an epidemiologist would need to take into account and possibly subtract from any overall trend in whatever he was measuring. It is not a complicated adjustment to make, and indeed, the team that produced the California numbers purposefully did not count children who had moved into the state during the years they were examining.

But there were many other confounding factors that were not so easily corrected for, and none was more nettlesome than the lack of clarity about who should be counted in the first place. It was the same old problem that had hampered the original prevalence study—the one conducted by Victor Lotter in Britain in the mid-1960s, where he had confronted a lack of clear criteria for the condition he was trying to track.

Thirty-five years later, when the epidemic alarm revived efforts to figure out "true" prevalence, those efforts ran into the same kinds of obstacles Lotter had faced. Arguably, the problems were even worse in the late 1990s, given how frequently the *DSM* kept moving the goalposts for autism. People diagnosed with autism using the *DSM* in 1997, for example, might not have qualified for it using an earlier *DSM* in 1990 and vice versa.

Studies conducted later in the new millennium demonstrated that such outcomes were highly possible. Researchers in 2012, for example, revisited a set of excellent data that had been collected in Utah in the 1980s. UCLA's Ed Ritvo had spent four years—1982 to 1986—attempting to identify every single person in the state of Utah between three and twenty-five years of age who possibly had autism, whether officially diagnosed or not. A total of 379 individuals were located and examined, of whom 241 were deemed to have the condition. That left

138 who, though unusual in their behaviors, fell short of the diagnosis based on Ritvo's criteria, which he lifted from the 1980 edition of the *DSM.*

More than twenty-five years later, the same data was run again. Like Ritvo before them, the researchers wanted to identify autism in the exact same group of 379 individuals—but they wanted to see the effect of using a more up-to-date definition of autism. Fortunately for them, Ritvo had kept excellent records, which he readily shared. But in place of his criteria, the younger researchers substituted the autism checklist that arrived in the 2000 edition of the *DSM,* which had been through three revisions in the intervening two decades. When they did this, the results were striking. Suddenly, the group's autism "prevalence" shot up. The newer criteria had qualified an additional 64 individuals for the diagnosis, all of whom had fallen short of it in the 1980s. As a result, the portion of the original group that was considered to have autism was now roughly 25 percent bigger than a quarter century earlier. Clearly, this "increase" could never be used to claim that there had been a dramatic rise in the "true" prevalence of autism in Utah. Objectively, nothing had changed. Nothing, that is, except for the definition of autism.

These internal changes to the *DSM,* and the complications they created for studies of autism's prevalence, were the parts of the story that social scientists proved remarkably ineffective at explaining to the public. They made references to "loosened criteria," or a "broader autism phenotype," but such language was not nearly as evocative as the word "epidemic."

The same was true when they suggested that one of the factors adding to the impression of more autism than before was what they called increased surveillance and reporting. This referred to the possibility that more autism was being reported because more people were on the lookout for it. Such patterns were a recognized phenomenon throughout medical history. Prevalence rates for chlamydia or gonorrhea, for example, generally rose in places where screening programs for those diseases were put in place. "Surveillance," however, was not a word that conveyed this idea clearly.

Neither did the word "reporting" communicate how powerfully

prevalence could be affected by any particular authority's approach to collecting information. This became apparent in the early 1990s when, thanks to parental pressure, Congress began requiring states to specify the numbers for children with autism who were enrolled in special-education programs under the terms of the Individuals with Disabilities Education Act. Many of the children about to be counted were already in school by then, and some had been for several years. But previously, they had been lumped together into the category of "other health impairments," or perhaps other categories such as "mentally retarded" or "learning disabled."

Starting with the 1992–93 academic year, however, schools had to begin reviewing these children's evaluations to see if they should be moved into the new autism category. It took some years for each school district in each state to get this system up and running as local schools worked through their case files. The result was that, for several years running, state after state sent in numbers that, by themselves, leapt almost straight upward—which is what happens when any count starts from zero.

Illinois, for example, reported only 5 children receiving services under the autism category in the 1992–93 school year, the first year it was required to start looking for them, but in 2002–03, the number had reached 5,800. One advocacy group employed this statistic under the heading "Autism Increases DRAMATICALLY" in its online newsletter. It also did the math for its readers, revealing that the prevalence for autism in Illinois had increased by an astounding 101,500 percent in a decade. This outshone even the numbers Congressman Dan Burton cited when he chaired a 2000 House hearing. "Florida has reported a 571 percent increase in autism," he reported. "Maryland has reported a 513 percent increase between 1993 and 1998." He also mentioned the original 273 percent number from the California report.

This alarming string of numbers pointed to another odd aspect of the claimed national epidemic: its pace varied wildly from state to state. Even when states were next door to each other, their reported rates of autism prevalence were sometimes not even close. Thus, in 2002, according to federal data, Alabama had a prevalence rate of roughly 3 kids per 10,000, while Georgia's was more than twice that.

Not much separated these two states physically—just a river that does not even run the full length of their shared border. Minnesota and Iowa are merely separated by a straight line on the map, but in 2012, the reported prevalence rate in Minnesota was ten times higher than in its next-door neighbor.

Social scientists had a good idea why this was happening. The information that was being pored over had been gathered by educational authorities, not public health agencies. The Individuals with Disabilities Education Act had provided a standard definition of autism but had left it to each state's Department of Education to create its own criteria for determining eligibility for special-education services.

Each authority built its own checklist, which ranged from as few as five items long to as many as seventeen. Some states required strict adherence to some version of the *DSM* criteria, others to the IDEA definition, and several to both. Some required diagnosis by a board-eligible psychiatrist or licensed clinical psychologist, but others did not. In some cases, the decision to provide services—which was not at all the same thing as a clinical diagnosis—was left to a group including the parents, school principal, and special-education teachers. All these disparities led to researchers dealing with data that was anything but uniformly derived.

Moreover, rather than revealing "true" prevalence, these numbers represented what social scientists called "administrative" prevalence. Counting autism by counting the people receiving services was like counting vegetarians on an airplane by adding up orders for meat-free meals. Just as there would be all manner of ways to miss the true "prevalence" in that scenario, administrative prevalence of autism was subject to various distorting influences. These included simple clerical or arithmetic errors, as well as the inherent subjectivity of a diagnosis based on the observation of behavior.

Even when the same criteria were being referenced, autism was still a diagnosis determined by a nonobjective measure—the opinion of whoever was asked to do the evaluation. Research showed clear geographic and socioeconomic trends in this regard. Diagnoses were more likely in communities that offered more services overall, and they were more commonly given to white and more affluent Americans than to members of ethnic minorities or children from poor families. It was also possible for a child who was denied a diagnosis by one professional to receive it from another. Indeed, in some areas, parents shared lists of diagnosis-friendly evaluators who could be counted on to give an autism label to a child whose symptoms might be borderline.

Parents had a strong motive for such diagnosis shopping: thanks to their years of lobbying, schools had become much more responsive to the needs of children with an autism diagnosis than to those labeled with, for example, intellectual disability or some other kind of learning difficulty. Further, the autism label, again due to parent activism, had lost some of its stigma. It was known anecdotally that pediatricians and other professionals who held the power to label occasionally tilted the scale in the evaluations to ensure a child's access to better programs and state services.

In 2007, sociologist Richard Roy Grinker quoted a senior child psychiatrist at the National Institutes of Health as saying, "I'll call a kid a zebra if that will get him the educational services I think he needs." New York psychiatrist Isabelle Rapin, another prominent researcher in the field, was candid about this phenomenon. "I admit up front that I have contributed to the 'epidemic' in New York," she wrote in 2011, citing the example of a four-year-old patient she had diagnosed in the early 1990s as having "a severe developmental language disorder with serious behavioral problems." Years later, his father phoned, seeking an autism diagnosis for his son. Based on that conversation alone, and the leeway afforded by a newer, less restrictive definition of autism, Rapin agreed to provide the young man the label of autism.

This so-called diagnostic substitution could certainly account for some of the apparent increase in autism numbers. In the 1970s and 1980s, after the label "learning disabled" came into use, numbers for learning disabled children in school soared across the nation as, simultaneously, the numbers of students labeled "mentally retarded" dropped precipitously. This was due, in large measure, to children with mild intellectual disability being shifted into the category that carried less stigma.

The question of whether a similar dynamic was pushing up autism numbers fascinated a young social scientist in training named

Paul Shattuck in the early 2000s. Shattuck was a graduate student at the University of Wisconsin who was working toward a PhD in social welfare. He wanted to study "the relationship between the rising administrative prevalence of autism in US special education and changes in the use of other classification categories." Shattuck did not analyze or directly assess any children for his study. Instead, using data he collected from the US Department of Education, he looked at the annual state-by-state counts of children, aged six to eleven, with disabilities in special education.

Shattuck's results, which he published in 2006, were attention-getting and controversial for a number of reasons. Seen in aggregate, the data he reported showed that, in forty-four states, big upticks in "administrative" prevalence of autism went hand in hand with downticks in the numbers for children labeled "cognitively impaired" and "learning disabled." It was as if a group of children had walked from one end of a seesaw to the other. Shattuck's conclusion was that, at least in these states, diagnostic substitution appeared to account for much of the apparent increase in autism.

Shattuck's study had weaknesses, which he admitted and others pointed out as well. His reliance on school-based data, whose very credibility was so much in question, was a problem. He also did not dig down to the local level, much less to the even deeper level where he could track individual kids who had made the move from one category to the other. He also reported that a pattern of diagnostic substitution did not emerge in a handful of states, including California, and he had no explanation for this.

That said, his study—and even the criticisms of it—underscored an inescapable conclusion: no epidemic could be proven or disproven with the available numbers. The data was simply too much of a mess for anyone to be making either claim with even a hint of certainty. No credible scientist who looked at the numbers would disagree.

For a time in the mid-2000s, Australian TV viewers could see an emotional public service announcement in which a series of people spoke directly into the camera to describe the challenge of autism as it affected kids in Australia. At one point, a woman declares: "One out of every one hundred and sixty-six children born *will* have autism."

There was no place in that presentation to identify the 1 in 166 number for what it was—an American statistic, one that was often attributed to the CDC beginning in early 2004. As *Scientific American* put it three years later, the number had by then acquired a "familiar ring," a result of its ceaseless repetition by advocacy groups and media reports on autism. From India to Ireland to Argentina to South Africa, the 1 in 166 figure became the numerical expression of the epidemic story.

But the CDC never intended to make 1 in 166 the measure of the world's autism rate. The statistic burst into the spotlight only because of a skillful intervention by autism parent Peter Bell. The president of Cure Autism Now, Bell was one of several leaders seated around a table in Washington, DC, in 2003, at a meeting the CDC called to share information with the nation's various autism organizations. During the discussion, someone brought up the awkward fact that each group present, in discussing the prevalence of autism, was using a different number. This was confusing to the public and threatened to undermine the credibility of all of them. Despite the sometimes rancorous relations among the players, they agreed that consistency was of paramount importance when discussing the scale of the epidemic.

That day, the group heard a presentation by a CDC official named Marshalyn Yeargin-Allsopp. Together with the American Academy of Pediatrics, the CDC had been reviewing recent epidemiological studies in order to come up with a more accurate estimate of prevalence for pediatricians. But as Yeargin-Allsopp told Bell and the others, the numbers were all over the map. One study she had led looked at the population of metropolitan Atlanta and found autism in approximately 1 in 300 of the children. Yet another undertaken in Utah found a far lower rate: 1 in 500. Three other studies—one covering a single New Jersey town, one an English county, and the third, the state of Illinois—yielded much higher rates: approximately 1 in 166. The prevalence question still had no simple answer, no single unifying statistic.

When the presentation ended, Peter Bell, who had worked in

corporate marketing for a dozen years, turned to Yeargin-Allsopp with a question. Was she telling them that this broad range represented "the CDC's best estimate" of the prevalence of autism in the United States right then? Yeargin-Allsopp paused, looked around the room, and nodded. Yes, she confirmed, as of that date, the CDC had no better estimate. Now it was Bell who looked around the room, asking each person in turn whether his or her organization would agree to stick solely to one number, citing the CDC as their authority, in all future public discussion of the prevalence of autism. All agreed, and all rallied around the most alarming number in the range: 1 in 166. This became the number advertised by advocacy groups, and repeated by the news media. Soon it was widely accepted as hard fact.

Anyone visiting the CDC's website would discover that the agency did not endorse this. In fact, they made it clear that there was no single number, and that all of the studies employed were relatively small-scale. It stated clearly what few wanted to be told: "There is not a full population count of all individuals" with autism.

The American Academy of Pediatrics, on the other hand, dispensed with such nuance. The "Autism Alert" the AAP issued to pediatricians in the summer of 2004 delivered what most people were probably looking for anyway: a single number that made an immensely complicated story appear simple—and also, very frightening.

Within a few years, the 1 in 166 figure became obsolete. By 2007, the CDC was operating what had long been lacking—a government-funded system for tracking the prevalence rates of autism over time. At regular intervals—roughly two years apart—the agency would be reporting new rates based on its own monitoring. That year, the agency announced that the measured rate of prevalence was now 1 in 150. It was a marked increase and a major headline in a world now primed to find evidence of an autism epidemic. In all subsequent reports, the CDC number kept climbing, to the point where the rate it represented was more than double the old 1 in 166.

The CDC's new number was still not a "full population count" of people with autism. Such an effort would have been extraordinarily expensive and beyond any possibility of true quality control. The CDC's autism rate never had been, nor ever would be, an actual "autism census." Instead, the monitoring program relied, as does most epidemiology, on population sampling. Specifically, to get a "national" figure, the CDC picked approximately 60 counties out of the nation's 3,144, located in just ten states, plus all the counties in Arkansas. Rather than establish a scientifically representative sample of the nation as a whole, these sites were chosen because roughly 10 percent of the nation's population of eight-year-olds at any point in time lived in these communities. A panel of clinicians in Atlanta—all trained for the role by the CDC—got to know each of the eight-year-olds in these communities only on paper.

The obvious disadvantages inherent in long-distance diagnosis were somewhat balanced by the advantages of having all the evaluators applying a single, consistent set of criteria to the records of all the children from all eleven states. That way, local variations in how people viewed or diagnosed autism were less likely to skew the results. The CDC evaluators accessed school and health records and began searching through them for signs of autistic behaviors. In fact, they found themselves "diagnosing" autism, from their offices in Atlanta, in hundreds of eight-year-olds spread across the eleven states who had never been given an autism label in their lives.

And yet, in survey after survey, the CDC results still revealed major geographical inconsistencies in prevalence rates around the country. Its data for 2008 produced a higher-than-ever "national" rate of 1 in 88—the most alarming statistic ever used by autism advocates. But this ratio disguised a huge spread in state-by-state rates, because it was merely the average of all the local results. That year, for example, the number reported for New Jersey was 1 in 49, more than four times higher than Alabama's, which was 1 in 210. Moreover, Alabama seemed to be bucking the trend. Its reported prevalence in 2008 was 20 percent lower than in 2006—a fact few brought up amid all the talk of a worsening epidemic of autism.

Some saw the geographical disparities as a reflection of some sort of environmental contaminant in play, more active in some localities than in others. That could explain why a New Jersey address appeared to be a higher risk than one in Alabama. This could be considered a rough road map for investigating a possible environmental driver for autism—something that no scientist, even the "epidemic skeptics," would rule out: what is in New Jersey's air or water that is not in Alabama's?

Still, this approach would have to account for the role human behavior may have played in inflating the "epidemic" numbers. New Jersey, for example, had long been a magnet for autism families, who relocated there from surrounding states, adding to its prevalence rate moving van by moving van. The families were drawn by New Jersey's superior offerings in state-funded special education for autism, which were among the best in the nation. The same could not be said of Alabama.

A competing explanation held that the rising numbers throughout the 2000s, rather than marking an epidemic, were a case of epidemiology catching up with reality. In this view, autism, regardless of the specific criteria, was probably always a part of the human condition, but one that it took Leo Kanner to bring into focus, followed by several decades of fine-tuning the definition. It was not that autism was spreading to a larger percentage of the human race than in the past, but that society, prior to 1999, had made no intensive effort to go find the people who were already living with autism among them.

Beyond all that, all sorts of factors impeded the counting process: geographical biases in diagnosis, shifting definitions, racial and socioeconomic influences, and the sheer logistics of counting. The social scientists who argued this view took the rising CDC numbers as a positive sign that the epidemiology was missing fewer and fewer of the people who met autism's ever-expanding definition. This point of view further implied that, someday, the world would finally get the statistic that accurately captured all of the autism there was out there. Predictions varied as to what that figure might be, especially as it was always possible that the working definition of autism could be amended yet again.

The most extreme number proposed by credible investigators emerged from a 2011 study undertaken in South Korea, where the researchers looked at a population of more than 55,000 children and conducted face-to-face evaluations, including children who were not attending special-education classes. By going into regular classrooms, examining children who had never been given a diagnosis before, and using broad, inclusive criteria, the researchers came up with a prevalence rate of 1 in 38.

Time called it "likely . . . the most accurate estimate of autism prevalence in school-aged children to date." It was also the highest number ever produced by peer-reviewed researchers. The head researcher, Young-Shim Kim, disputed the idea that 1 in 38 was proof of an epidemic. "These children didn't just show up overnight. They have been there all along," she told *Time.* "We just didn't count them."

But that too was only a theory. At bottom, the case against a modern epidemic of autism—just like the case for one—was stopped by that same stream of statistical quicksand that ran through all the many, inconsistent, distortion-prone data sets produced over the years, whose inherent problems made comparison between past and present exercises in guesswork. Even when scientists were fairly convinced that diagnostic substitution and other extraneous factors could explain some, or even most, of the perceived increase, they did not deny that some portion of it remained inexplicable.

Furthermore, the lack of evidence of an epidemic was not evidence of *no* epidemic. Therefore, most refused to rule out that a true increase in incidence had occurred in their lifetimes. That's what it felt like, to autism families all over the world—that despite evidence for or against, there were more kids with autism around than ever before.

IN AUGUST 2010, a few months before the South Korean study would be published in *Time,* Emily Gerson Saines got dressed up to go to an awards program in Los Angeles with Temple Grandin. She wore a gown, while Grandin wore a black cowboy outfit. In the nine years since their lunch in Manhattan, Emily's film project about Grandin's life had churned forward, but slowly. This was not due to the usual money problems that get in the way of Hollywood dreams. In fact, HBO had bought into the idea early, and their support had never flagged. Emily had also met the single condition Grandin had requested before allowing the film to be made: that the producer get approval for it from her mother, Eustacia Cutler.

The real obstacle to a quick turnaround proved to be Gerson Saines herself. She was adamant that the movie get autism right, and she was particular about what she wanted the script to accomplish. She wanted audiences to learn some basic truths about the condition, to understand how the world looked to Temple Grandin, and how Grandin had faced numerous challenges but was simultaneously rewarded with insights that escape most people. Gerson Saines also wanted to get across how autism could affect a family, including the times when autism allowed for moments of joy and laughter. Getting all that into a good script, however, proved difficult. More than one screenwriter tried, and a series of directors also failed to hit the mark Gerson Saines was aiming for.

That changed when HBO brought British director Mick Jackson onto the project in the spring of 2008. Jackson took a new pass at the script. He and Gerson Saines were often at odds during the rewriting, but in the end, a version appeared that both were happy with. Filming began in 2008 in Texas. Actress Claire Danes was hired to play Grandin as a young woman. She spent an afternoon with Grandin in New York, which was the only time they met until filming was nearly complete, when Grandin flew to Texas to spend a couple of days watching herself be played by Danes.

Gerson Saines had one misgiving about this visit. She did not want the real Temple Grandin, at this late date in the production, to begin offering notes on Danes's performance or challenging any of the movie's other artistic choices. That, she thought, would be disastrous.

As she and Grandin sat down for dinner that night, it occurred to her that showing her guest some of the footage already shot would help Grandin get used to the experience of seeing someone else pretend to be her. She announced that they would skip dessert and would instead head back early to the hotel room to watch some of the movie.

A short time later, the pair sat perched on the edge of Gerson Saines's bed as scenes from the movie rolled. Grandin was delighted and amazed by what she saw.

"Claire Danes—she's me! I can't believe it!" she said.

But after a few more scenes had rolled, Gerson Saines heard an odd sound coming from her friend. Puzzled, she turned to look. Grandin was still staring at the screen, but this time she was crying. Gerson Saines assumed it was because of the scene they were watching, in which a horse had just died.

Instead, Grandin told Gerson Saines that she had been moved by one of the other characters in the film—her old teacher, Dr. Carlock, who was being played by David Strathairn. The real Carlock was deceased, and Grandin confessed that she had not thought of him in a while. The next day, the sadness had passed, and Grandin had a wonderful time on the set of the movie *Temple Grandin.* To Gerson Saines's relief, Grandin raised no objections to the way it told her story.

The critical reception was spectacularly good when the film premiered in early 2010 on HBO. Everything its producer had aspired to had been achieved. Reviewers hailed the movie as "brilliant," "triumphant," "daring," and "incredibly joyous and often humorous." Naturally, comparisons were drawn with the release of *Rain Man* more than two decades earlier—not just because of its quality, but also because of the power of the spotlight it cast on autism.

The difference in 2010, however, was that by then, there were not many people left in America—or many other places—who had not at least heard about autism. The many movie reviews did not have to waste words explaining that part of the story. Autism was now famous. If anything, the uplifting story of Temple Grandin's life served as an antidote to the general bleakness that tended to surround discussion of the condition—which was part of what Gerson Saines had set out to do.

Full confirmation came on the evening when she and Grandin, in her all-black cowboy attire, attended the Emmy Awards at the Nokia Theater in Los Angeles. As a television movie, *Temple Grandin* had been nominated for a total of fifteen Emmy Awards—only two short of the record. That night, it won seven, including the one that required Emily Gerson Saines to take the stage herself: Outstanding Made for Television Movie. In the excitement that followed the announcement,

Gerson Saines leapt to her feet and went up to collect the trophy, Temple Grandin and Claire Danes following her, along with others on the production team.

Handed the statuette, Gerson Saines began her acceptance speech. Her opening line was one that most everyone listening had heard before.

"Autism," she began, "has reached epidemic proportions."

PART IX

"EPIDEMIC"

1990s–2010

40

THE VACCINE SCARE

IF THERE WAS AN AUTISM EPIDEMIC UNDER WAY IN THE EARLIEST part of the twenty-first century, then it stood to reason that something had to have caused it. It would have to be something that had appeared on the landscape only a few years before the start of the new millennium, because that is when the numbers began to jump. It would also have to have been present in the lives of most children in the United States and the UK, since those were the epicenters of the phenomenon. Finally, it would have to be taking advantage of some as-yet-undetermined pathway into the bodies of these children, thus affecting their brains.

Recent. Everywhere. Invasive. Whatever the culprit, those would be its distinguishing characteristics.

In the winter of 1998, in London, a suspect was named. It was a vaccine.

THE FUROR OVER the so-called vaccine theory of autism was fueled by a widespread panic that children could get autism from a doctor's needle. Lasting for years, the fear was ignited at London's Royal Free Hospital on the morning of February 26, 1998. That day, the hospital's media department called in reporters for a preview of a paper by one of its star researchers, a young gastroenterologist named Andrew Wakefield. His paper, written with twelve coauthors, would be appearing in a few days in *The Lancet,* Britain's oldest medical journal, and one of its most respected. That association, and the hospital's name, bestowed instant credibility on Wakefield, which had a lot to do with how the world responded to what he said he had found.

Wakefield's paper described twelve children he had seen in the previous year or two as showing autistic behaviors paired with severe intestinal inflammation. Upon further examination, Wakefield reported, he had found something else in each of the children, who were between three and ten years old: traces of measles virus in their intestinal tracts. Based on this, Wakefield and his team speculated that this three-part combination—gut issues, autism, and measles virus—comprised the basis for a single syndrome. They touched briefly on the possibility of a "causal link," and then they named their candidate for what that causal link was: the vaccine known as MMR had been administered to eleven of the children, and not long before the stomach problems and autistic behaviors began.

MMR, a trio of vaccines delivered in a single shot, targeted three different diseases: measles, mumps, and rubella. According to the paper, eight of the twelve children had been developing normally, but then, within days of getting the injection, began to display classic symptoms of autism, including loss of speech. In one instance, the change occurred within a single day. In some cases, the authors reported, it was the parents who first suggested that the two events were linked by a "general association in time"—first the shot, followed soon after by a deterioration in behavior.

No one reading the paper could miss what its authors were getting at: that the live measles virus in the MMR vaccine might provoke inflammation in the gut, and that this inflammation might in turn cause the brain to become inflamed, resulting in autism. This was an intriguing idea, certainly, but it was still entirely speculative. The main evidence for it—the recollections of parents—was too thin to support strong scientific claims. Wakefield and his colleagues acknowledged that it was still only a hypothesis in their use of qualifiers throughout the paper: "might be," "possibly," "if," and even "did not prove an association."

The press conference was a debacle. The hospital's PR team had placed Wakefield at a table with four other doctors, including Arie Zuckerman, the dean of the medical school, who were there to reassure the public that the MMR vaccine was in fact safe. Wakefield, however, had copied Zuckerman on a letter four weeks earlier in which he stated that, if asked directly, he would acknowledge his doubts about MMR's safety. Of course the reporters egged on Wakefield to get specific about whether he saw the MMR as safe or not. As he had said he would, Wakefield replied that he had concerns about the MMR vaccine. In his view, he explained, its mixture of three kinds of live virus might be too much for some young children's immune systems. He was not opposed to the use of a measles-only vaccine for any child—including his own. But a three-in-one shot, he said, was something that parents might want to avoid in favor of splitting the vaccination into three separate shots spaced out over time.

"I do not think the long-term safety trials on MMR are sufficient," he said. Then he put an ethical frame around the issue. "One more case of this is too many," he declared.

Zuckerman, looking shocked, jumped to his feet. The reporters who were present remember him pounding on the lectern as he tried to erase the impact of the previous few minutes. "Hundreds of millions of doses of these vaccines have been given worldwide," he stated. "They've been shown to be absolutely safe."

For a moment, Wakefield seemed to read correctly that his boss wanted him to get back "on script." "I just want to say a couple of things," Wakefield broke in, "and that is to reassure you we are not at odds on our perception of the need for a measles vaccination. We are all agreed on that and that is extremely important." But in his next sentence, he was back off again. "I don't agree with Professor Zuckerman on the extent of the safety trials that have been conducted."

Remarkably, another doctor on the panel then began wondering aloud if perhaps the young gastroenterologist was on to something. "It does seem," he mused, "that this unique combination of having three viruses in the same injection may be an unnatural and unusual event." It went on like this for more than half an hour, after which Wakefield began giving one-on-one interviews, elaborating further on why his MMR discovery merited follow-up study, and, in the meantime, avoidance of the MMR vaccine. In the next few days, his most often quoted statement—a line he used in more than one interview following the news conference—was the one about his personal motivation for taking this stand: "It's a moral issue for me."

It was a rhetorical choice that would alter his career forever. Nearly every virologist, pediatrician, and public health official in the world knew the MMR vaccine to be a superb example of applied science and a lifesaver; it had driven all three of the targeted diseases into virtual oblivion. If Wakefield wanted to make this a moral issue, the science behind his claims had better be staggeringly persuasive.

But there was a second constituency that needed a good deal less persuasion. Britain had a storied history of vaccine skepticism, whose adherents had been at odds with the public health authorities since the late nineteenth century. By the late twentieth century, they were a fringe and not very successful force, given that the British public overwhelmingly supported the practice of vaccination. This was demonstrated with immunization rates above 90 percent for most vaccinations in the mid-1990s, even though Britain's program was not mandatory, the way it was for public school attendance in the United States. While some vaccine opponents flatly questioned the necessity of vaccines, suspecting pharmaceutical companies of scheming to make a market for themselves, others conceded vaccines' effectiveness but sought more evidence of their safety. Still others nurtured a philosophical hostility toward vaccines. They resented the state's forcing any person to submit to any invasive procedure, regarding it as an affront to individual liberty.

Of course, it could not be said that vaccines have never caused harm. Vaccines' most ardent supporters acknowledge that the minute risk exists, for any given individual, of an adverse reaction. This is true with any pharmaceutical product. Regardless of the precautions taken, there will always be individuals who, because of their unique biological makeup, will have a toxic reaction to a drug or a device that has generally been shown to be safe. These outcomes do not mean that the product is defective. Penicillin is not considered a defective antibiotic because a small subset of patients can have powerful, even fatal, allergic reactions to it. Such susceptibility cannot be predicted or screened for. Society accepts this imperfect situation because statistics show that penicillin does good for far more people than it will ever harm.

When an immunization program is launched, it is a given that some adverse effects will occur that were not discovered during clinical testing, because they are so rare and so specific to the individuals who suffer them. Public health professionals who promote mandatory universal immunization know this, but they believe that the minuscule risk is tolerable, as well as necessary. Not getting vaccinated exposes that same individual to the much more probable danger of contracting the disease the vaccine is targeting. Moreover, the more people who are vaccinated, the greater protection there is for the population as a whole.

But this logic offers no solace to those with the bad fortune to make it into the injured group, when the mandatory needle in the arm is the thing that makes a child blind, or deaf, or paralyzed for life. In those rare instances, a family's anguish is compounded by the fact that there is rarely proof that the injury is the direct result of a vaccine. Usually, the most convincing evidence, from the family's point of view, is timing: the observed fact that the first appearance of an affliction appears to coincide almost exactly with the administration of the vaccine—within days, or even hours. But coincidence does not prove causation. And that was all Wakefield had—"a general association in time"—to connect the MMR vaccine to the children's autistic behaviors.

Still, to the twelve families whose children took part in his study, the lack of convincing data to support Wakefield's claims was beside the point. They felt that Wakefield was the first scientist who had ever really listened to them. No one else had treated their ideas about the connection between the MMR shot and their children's illnesses as valid or meaningful. Moreover, Wakefield was a gastroenterologist. An extremely troubled digestive system was one of the two ailments common to all twelve of the children; the other was autism. As the families saw it, these two things had to be related, having started at about the same time.

It was a theory they could not get their own doctors to take seriously. Some parents felt scoffed at by the medical system. But this man in a lab coat—which Wakefield would don for some of his TV appearances—was telling the world that they were not crazy or naïve or ignorant. He was framing it as a matter of good and evil, right and wrong—on behalf of their children, whom the parents believed had been wronged for life. In that instant, under those TV lights at the Royal Free, a champion emerged from inside the medical world that had, until then, spurned their insights.

But now, there was the spectacle of the other doctors at the press conference pouncing on Wakefield's warning, falling over one another to vouch for the MMR vaccine's safety. Over the next couple of days, similar statements would be issued by a slew of British medical authorities, with vaccine experts in the United States joining them, and the World Health Organization declaring itself "frankly alarmed by suggestions there is a causal relationship."

To the families, to Wakefield, this phalanx of statements in support of MMR only proved what they were up against—a wall of well-entrenched interests, dead set against even entertaining the possibility that the MMR vaccine might have ill effects. Any critique of his work came to be seen as a villainous personal attack on a good man trying to do the moral thing. It was also an attack on the families, their children, and any future child who might receive the MMR vaccine. They circled protectively around this young rogue researcher. Now it was war.

And "vaccines cause autism" was their rallying cry.

Although Wakefield never actually spoke the words "Vaccines cause autism" in February 1998, that was what the public heard over the coming weeks and months. In a nation already jumpy about vaccines, headlines using words like "alert" and "ban" about the MMR vaccine triggered alarms that would never quite die down again. It was not that reporters bought into the theory as fact. All the stories pointed out that Wakefield was an outlier and that the measles vaccine had been a lifesaver. A report on Independent Television News (ITN) in the UK provided numbers as well as an animated graphic: compared with the 800,000 measles cases reported in 1950, there had been only 4,170 cases in 1997. A well-known immunization authority, Dr. Robert Aston, was also shown reminding viewers that "immunization is the best thing, bar none, that has come out of medical science."

But the autism parents who appeared in the same news reports, especially on television, were a lot more compelling than the experts and their numbers. The ITN coverage portrayed a number of attractive kids who had autism, whose mothers explained, with near certainty, that it was the "jab," in British parlance, that had made their children autistic. "It's Russian roulette," said one mother. "You take a child down for the jab, and which one's going to have the disorder?"

Wakefield's press conference had been at the end of February. By the middle of March, 1 out of 5 general practitioners in the UK had at least five families in their practice who either refused vaccination altogether or insisted on getting the measles vaccine separately. What was more, the *Guardian* reported, some doctors were starting to share the parents' doubts. A Dr. Nagle in North London was said to be "advising parents against the booster MMR given to children at about four years old."

It was a self-perpetuating cycle. The greater the number of parents who decided to refuse the MMR, the more the news media saw a valid trend story. By June, only four months after Wakefield published in *The Lancet,* MMR vaccinations had dropped almost 14 percent in South Wales.

It was a rare story that held the public in thrall not just for weeks or months, but for years. Through the rest of 1998 and into 1999, the groundswell of resistance to the MMR continued. While parents circulated petitions against the vaccine, Parliament debated its purported dangers. In 2001, the fear was still rampant, and Prime Minister Tony Blair stumbled into a political buzz saw. Having publicly encouraged parents to get the MMR for their kids, he then refused to say whether his twenty-month-old son had received his.

During this period, Wakefield's career went through its own tumult. He had continued with his research even as controversy bloomed all around him, parrying in print all the researchers who disputed him, and recording new cases of his syndrome—scores of them. By December 2001, nearly four years after the publication of the pivotal article on MMR, he had published nearly a dozen further studies on bowel disease, measles, and autism. These appeared in a broad range of well-regarded, peer-reviewed journals.

The vaccine scare made Andrew Wakefield famous and, in some circles, beloved. He was flooded with interview and speaking requests, and he traveled the world by invitation, more identified than ever with the idea that vaccines were the cause of autism. In 2000, he was brought to Washington to testify about his work on MMR before Congress. He appeared on CBS's *60 Minutes* to discuss his work that same year. Throughout, and though repeatedly challenged, he refused to rescind his recommendation that parents avoid the MMR pending proof of its safety.

His use of his increasingly high profile to spread the wrong message finally proved too much for Wakefield's employers. In November 2001, Wakefield resigned his position at the Royal Free Hospital, but only after being told he had no choice in the matter. "I can only assume," he told *The Lancet,* that his research "was politically incorrect." With the *Sunday Express,* he struck a now-familiar posture: "The medical establishment may not have the stomach for it, but I cannot abandon these children. . . . I'm not going to whinge, I am going to move on."

His departure from the Royal Free did nothing to set the public's mind at ease about vaccinations. On December 5, the *Guardian* reported that the MMR vaccination rate in London had fallen to 79 percent, when the ideal was 95 percent or above. Scotland's would fall to 86 percent by 2003, compared with 94 percent in 1995. "For now," wrote reporter Linda Steele, "a question mark still hangs over the safety of MMR."

Nor did Wakefield's dismissal damage his reputation in the eyes of his followers. After losing his job, he began spending more time in the United States, supporting his work and his family through private funding. His story, meanwhile, received the ultimate media accolade when it was made into a feature film for British TV in 2003, viewed by 1.6 million people. Wakefield was portrayed by the dignified, warmhearted Hugh Bonneville, who would later play the patriarch of the Crawley family on *Downton Abbey.* Titled *Hear the Silence,* the film depicted a dystopian medical universe in which most doctors and scientists are hidebound, cynical, cowardly, or scheming—with Wakefield as the pure-hearted, truth-seeking scientist-detective who went wherever the data led him. Asked early in the film whether he believed that the MMR caused autism, Bonneville as Wakefield paused, looked off into the middle distance, and responded, "I wish I knew." But the makers of the film made their views clear; the answer was an unqualified yes. Actress Juliet Stevenson was typically spectacular as the mother of a small boy with autism, who spent most of the film battling one doctor after another, each of whom coldly dismissed what she had to say. "Something happened to him!" she cried out in frustration to each. "That's what I know in my heart!" By the film's end, when Stevenson stood up to her pediatrician with the words "Fuck you!"—the second-to-last line in the movie—motherly instinct had been fully vindicated as the best kind of evidence there is.

The trouble was that mainstream medicine lacked a convincing rejoinder. Certainty requires data, and collecting data takes time. Until then, no one other than Wakefield had looked specifically at whether autism and the MMR were linked. In other words, the experts' best evidence for safety was the *lack* of evidence of a lack of safety. Unfortunately, that did not answer the question parents really wanted answered, which was, "Where's the evidence that MMR does *not* carry the risk suggested?"

The early lack of a convincing answer was a boon to Wakefield. It also gave a long head start in Britain to the popular nightmare that autism could be caught from a needle. Even Wakefield acknowledged the lack of scientific proof for such a link—but thanks to him, the British press, and human nature, the connection was held together by something else.

Fear.

In the years since Wakefield's initial press conference, that fear had long since spread to the other side of the Atlantic. Throughout 1999 and into the spring of 2000, the US Congress had held at least three hearings on vaccine safety. In the first couple of those, autism was mentioned only in passing. At the hearing held in April 2000, however, by the House Committee on Oversight and Government Reform, the epidemic story came into its own as a full-time political narrative, where it soon became rare in Washington for the words "autism" and "vaccines" *not* to be spoken in the same sentence together.

In that April hearing, the chief witness was Andrew Wakefield, making his American debut. It was a star turn. His British accent charmed, and the slides and data he brought along caused alarm. He reported finding still more cases of children with autism, stomach problems, and measles virus. "We have now investigated over one hundred and fifty children," he announced. He had found the syndrome in 146 of them. "The great majority had autism." In front of cameras and reporters from the nation's top networks, he spelled out what it all meant: "The story as told to us and which we have an obligation to report is that the majority of children regressed following a period of normal development in the face of MMR vaccination." As always, he added a footnote: "That does not mean it is the cause of the disease."

In June 2000, at yet another vaccine hearing held by Congress, a mother from Georgia named Lyn Redwood proved a superb witness. She spoke about her son Will, and how she believed vaccines had changed him. "He was a happy baby who ate and slept well, smiled, cooed, walked and talked, all by one year of age," she said. "Shortly after his first birthday, he experienced multiple infections, lost speech, eye contact and developed a very limited diet and suffered intermittent bouts of diarrhea." Redwood was certain vaccines were to blame.

It was dismally similar to the stories British parents had shared with the news media for the preceding two years. But Redwood's account differed from the British narrative in a crucial respect. It had nothing to do with the measles virus at the heart of Wakefield's theory. She never mentioned measles—or the MMR vaccine, for that matter. Instead, as Redwood explained it, an entirely different culprit was behind her son's injury.

That culprit was mercury. It was true: vaccines contained mercury, a known toxin. Since the 1930s, mercury had been added to many vaccines in order to guard against contamination. The bottles kept in hospitals and doctors' offices contained multiple doses and were corked with rubber stoppers. A syringe needle was inserted to siphon off a single dose each time a patient had to be given a shot. In theory, the needles were sterilized before each pull of vaccine. In practice, live microorganisms were sometimes able to get into the fluid, spoiling the whole bottle, and putting patients at risk of infection.

In the 1930s, to prevent this risk, Eli Lilly and Company began marketing a product called thimerosal, an antibacterial and antifungal powder designed to be used as a preservative, usually in solution. The second syllable of the word thimerosal—*mer*—was derived from one of its key components, mercury, which made up almost half its molecular weight. In minute measure—as little as .01 percent in solution—thimerosal proved so effective at preserving sterility that for decades it was a standard ingredient in a wide range of products, from nasal sprays to contact lens solution. But even after the manufacturers of those products switched to new preservatives, pharmaceutical firms stuck with thimerosal in vaccines. By the late 1990s, it had been used as an ingredient in more than thirty separate vaccines.

Mercury's presence inside the body does not necessarily warrant an alarm call. Virtually all humans have some amount of the compound known as methylmercury in their systems, a result of traces in the food they eat and in the air they breathe. Dosage matters. A typical six-ounce can of white tuna fish, for example, contains approximately 60 micrograms of methylmercury—approximately two-millionths of an ounce, which has never been grounds for a mass recall of tuna from the grocery store. At the same time, there are often warnings about tuna, at least for certain populations, like pregnant women and young children, reflecting the fact that precise risk levels for mercury in humans have always been a gray area. There is not much data, since experiments based on deliberately feeding people mercury would be ethically impossible.

Guesses have been made, however, by studying *accidentally* poisoned populations, such as the several thousand Iraqis who, in the early 1970s, ingested imported grain that had been treated with a methylmercury fungicide. Neurological damage was widespread, and included death. Afterward, scientists combed over the data from Iraq and a few other places with known high exposure. Out of this work, in 1999, the US Environmental Protection Agency produced a new so-called reference dose for mercury—the amount that humans can safely ingest every day without undue effect over time. But the EPA built in an extremely cautious—and therefore large—margin of safety. The number was 0.1 micrograms per kilogram of body weight per day, which deliberately "overstated" the statistically established risk by a factor of ten, to allow for scientific uncertainty. For a 170-pound man, that came to about 8 micrograms daily, or what he would get in about one-eighth of a can of white tuna. That was maybe three forkfuls, which demonstrated just how cautious the EPA wanted to be with its reference dose, in its uncertainty about how much trace mercury is too much. And yet, looked at another way, the EPA limit was not all *that* stringent. That 170-pound man could still eat a lot of tuna fish—47 cans a year—and stay within the reference dosage.

Vaccines made with thimerosal—like the ones Lyn Redwood went to Congress to sound the alarm about—contained 25 micrograms of mercury per shot. That seems small: less than half a tuna can's worth. Also, nobody is routinely given 47 shots a year, nor does the mercury compound used in the vaccine preservative break down in the body in the same manner, or linger as long there, as the mercury found in food. Nevertheless, it was only in 1998, in response to questions asked by Congress, that the scientists trusted with guiding US immunization policy even began to tally up how much mercury was getting into the bodies of young children by means of vaccinations. The result surprised them because it was more than they had realized.

In the mid-1980s, the DTP vaccine, which protected against diphtheria, was the only thimerosal-containing vaccine regularly given to infants. But soon, more shots were added to the recommended schedule. By 1991, it included the Hib vaccine, a defense primarily against influenza-induced meningitis, and the hepatitis B shot—with all three taking place, and followed up by boosters, during an infant's first six months. As a result, by 1999, a six-month-old infant's exposure to the mercury in thimerosal had reached 187 micrograms. Moreover, typically, there were days when an infant received multiple shots, delivering a mercury dose of more than 60 micrograms in the space of a few minutes. That was, to return to the tuna fish example, the equivalent of more than one can, fed to a 10-pound child. Of course, shots were not a daily occurrence. They were spaced months apart, with zero thimerosal exposure in between.

At a loss to know whether these levels represented a danger to children or not, the nation's top immunization experts decided to err on the side of caution. In July 1999, pushed especially hard by a Johns Hopkins pediatrician named Neal Halsey, the American Academy of Pediatrics (AAP) and the Public Health Service (PHS) released coordinated statements containing three recommendations: that pediatricians begin using thimerosal-free vaccines whenever possible; that vaccine manufacturers remove thimerosal from future formulations; and that the vaccine against hepatitis B, normally given at birth, be postponed in most cases to two to six months.

Bizarrely, the statement went on to say that none of these recommendations was actually justified by any known risk from thimerosal. It tried to sound unequivocally confident on this point, asserting that there was "no data or evidence of harm caused by the level of exposure." But much of the rest of the statement seemed to undermine that certainty, as it made repeated references to the "unknown and probably" quite small risk that something might be wrong with the vaccines—and gave as their reason for calling a retreat from thimerosal use the principle that "any potential risk is of concern."

On top of that, the AAP issued a press release containing remarks by the academy's president, Dr. Joel Alpert, which came out sounding less than reassuring, although the opposite effect was clearly intended. "The current levels of thimerosal will not hurt children," Alpert was quoted as saying. "But reducing the levels will make safe vaccines even safer." The two organizations' tangle of messages made for one of the most confusing public health announcements in US history. It was also among the most consequential.

IF NOT FOR the experts' strangely worded policy revision, Lyn Redwood might never have suspected a link between autism in her son and the mercury in vaccines.

But because the announcement seemed to point to a problem, it moved her to dig out her child's immunization records, and to calculate how much mercury he had been exposed to from vaccines in his first year of life. "My worst fears were confirmed," she later told Congress. "All of his early vaccines had contained thimerosal."

Around the United States, other autism parents, following the same impulse, were making similar discoveries. Some had been suspicious of vaccines already, as whispers of Wakefield's hypothesis about MMR vaccines started crossing the ocean. Cure Autism Now was soon demanding faster action by the government to get thimerosal out of vaccines. But for children who had shown signs of autism before ever receiving the MMR—and that included Redwood's son—it had to be something *else* about vaccines besides the measles virus that explained what had happened to their kids. For those parents, Redwood proved a superb spokesperson.

In late 1999, Redwood created a small website devoted to the topic of mercury in vaccines, which quickly became a crossroads for parents who stumbled online seeking counsel and company in their grief and certainty that thimerosal had caused autism in their kids. Through this spontaneously formed network, Redwood emerged as the most prominent of the "Mercury Moms," a moniker that stuck for a small circle of the most active mothers. Increasingly, it was how she was identified in the introductions to speeches she gave, and in TV interviews.

Redwood also had the advantage of presenting a consistent demeanor of calmness and composure. While there were times when parents blaming vaccines were depicted by critics as overwrought and ignorant, Redwood never fit that stereotype. Throughout all the adversarial discourse, she remained consistently even-tempered, earnest, and civil. Even those who thought her anti-thimerosal campaign was misguided had to acknowledge her professionalism, her preparedness, and her willingness to listen as well as speak. Like her husband, Tommy, an ER doctor, she was a medical professional—a nurse practitioner—who could engage in clinical discourse without drowning. Not only had she administered many vaccines herself in her career, but she continued to attest to the importance of vaccination as a public health priority. Her position that vaccines should be made "safer"—not eliminated—refuted the broad accusation made against the parents in her camp that they were all "anti-vaccine" extremists. Some were, to be sure, but the majority were not.

To many people, she made eminent sense in her July 2000 appearance before Congress, when she used the government's statement on thimerosal against it. "The statement that there is 'no evidence of harm,'" she said, "does not equate to *no* harm having occurred. The truth is that we have not adequately looked or we just refuse to see."

HAVING FOUND ONE ANOTHER, the parents who wanted thimerosal investigated—and someone made to pay for the harm they believed it caused—followed the path blazed by earlier generations of autism parents: they organized. In 2000, the group that had taken shape around Lyn Redwood formed a nonprofit called SafeMinds. Its founding members organized with sophistication, reflecting some of the leading activists' professional experience in law, health care, public relations, and management consulting. They were fluent in the use of the Internet, which was just then coming into its own as a vehicle for organizing and advocacy. And they were determined to arm themselves with arguments and data that would sell their message to a wider world.

Like other groups of parents before them, they immersed themselves in scientific literature, to where they could hold their own—up to a point—when challenging the pronouncements of established scientists with whom they disagreed. One group even produced a research-based paper laying out their hypothesis that autism was, as the paper's title put it, "A Novel Form of Mercury Poisoning." Deep with footnotes and tables of data, it nevertheless found no takers for publication, until it was accepted by a Scottish journal called *Medical Hypotheses.* That was not, however, the sort of ringing endorsement of their seriousness that the parents hoped for, since the journal's self-proclaimed mission was publication of "hypotheses where experimental support is yet fragmentary."

That revealed what would always be the vaccine activists' Achilles' heel—the lack of convincing scientific support for an unproven hypothesis that its adherents embraced as a given. Reversing the standard and time-honored traditions of science, they started with the conclusion that vaccines had hurt their children, and then went looking for the evidence that would prove them right. This was made explicit in a statement that appeared on the SafeMinds website in 2001, asserting that research "is expected to prove that thimerosal is a cause of autism." This mind-set was to the group's detriment, creating the impression for many that they were naïve about the ways of science. They readily embraced the full range of alternative therapies, with chelation still an option many employed. Chelation itself had toxic side effects, and even, in rare instances, caused death. Most radically of all, a Maryland doctor began injecting boys with Lupron, a drug that inhibits secretion of the so-called sex hormones—estrogen in women, and testosterone in men. Developed to slow the advance of prostate cancer and fibroids, it has also been administered to sex offenders as a form of "chemical castration." When injecting children with autism, the doctor posited that mercury-induced autism was accompanied and exacerbated by excessive levels of testosterone, which interfered with children's ability to excrete mercury. While many of the parents using these therapies reported seeing beneficial effects, none of the methods was supported by controlled research, and some were outright refuted by the scientific establishment.

Nevertheless, the mercury parents' political skills led to a significant win for them in the scientific arena in the second half of 2001. Responding to the fear they had fanned, Congress ordered the US government's medical think tank, the Institute of Medicine (IOM), to assess the state of the available research on thimerosal and autism. Several of the parents testified before the IOM commission assigned to the task. On October 1, the IOM panel issued its finding that "evidence to accept or reject" the parents' hypothesis of a causal relationship between thimerosal and autism was "inadequate." Moreover, the task force took the view that, pending further evidence to confirm or refute it, "the hypothesized relationship is biologically plausible."

To the parent-activists, this was a major win: validation from the top that their claim was not just some far-fetched fantasy. Encouraged, emboldened, they pressed forward with their case, evoking the autism parents of earlier generations in the sheer intensity of their efforts. In doing so, the mothers and fathers operating in this first half of the first decade of the new millennium had two huge advantages over their predecessors. One was the Internet, where a core group of users could log up to thousands of postings, leading to a sense of support and solidarity, if not an exaggerated sense of strength in numbers.

Their other advantage was the complete upending of the power balance between professionals and "consumers," which had occurred in the forty years since autism activism had been born. Gone was the habitual deference to expertise once expected of lay members of the public. Suspicion of authority, and the impulse to challenge it, had become familiar practice. The Mercury Moms never doubted their right to get in to see the top vaccine people at the FDA, the NIH, or the CDC. The officials at these agencies must have believed in this entitlement too, or at least found it politically wise, because they granted the parents the meetings. Parents were invited to question officials in open sessions and to present testimony at scientific hearings.

Once timid, almost "hat in hand" in their dealings with the expert class, autism parents of the 2000s assumed the right to hold the medical authorities' feet to the fire. One mother, who later was a guest on NBC's *Today* show, boasted in an online posting about joining fellow parents in disrupting a meeting at the NIH, where they had all been invited to be updated by some of the nation's leading autism researchers on their latest work. Irritated when the presenters began discussing studies that had nothing to do with "their" issues—vaccines, gastrointestinal issues, or food allergies—people in the audience began interrupting, grabbing the floor microphone, and hollering "We are not stupid!" and "Why are you wasting our time?" and "Listen to me: WE ARE NO LONGER SUSCEPTIBLE TO YOUR PROPAGANDA!" At one point, the mother who wrote the account tried to launch a mid-meeting boycott. "If the NIH is going to continue wasting our time," she declared, "then I am going to go have lunch." A section of the audience rose to follow her. Though she did not follow through, and later said she regretted behaving this way because it was "non-productive," she admitted that "to publicly humiliate those in power felt good."

So far had the pendulum swung that, at times, the bureaucrats in charge of the nation's public health came across as—if not humiliated—then thoroughly cowed by the fury of those who believed in the thimerosal link. Under powers Congress granted the people in the 1970s, the parents could now get copies of government scientists' internal emails, memos, and transcripts of meetings, which they perused for signs of a government cover-up of mercury's risks. One such transcript, fed to environmental lawyer Robert Kennedy Jr., was used by Kennedy in a 2005 *Rolling Stone* article called "Deadly Immunity," where he charged that the government and vaccine manufacturers had colluded "to hide the risks of thimerosal." He called it "a chilling case study of institutional arrogance, power and greed." Following the article's publication, the Senate launched a formal investigation into possible improprieties by government scientific officials, including financial conflicts of interest, where members of the nation's vaccine policy leadership were treated like defendants.

The year 2005 saw another landmark for the mercury theory. It was the year a writer named David Kirby published a potboiler-style account of the Mercury Moms' campaign called *Evidence of Harm.* Kirby adopted the posture of an impartial journalist, asserting that "there are two sides to every good story, and this one is no exception." But with Lyn Redwood as a leading player in the narrative, and one of its major sources, the book's sympathies were tilted unabashedly toward the activist parents who, Kirby wrote, "never abandoned their ambition to prove that mercury in vaccines is what pushed their children, most of them boys, into a hellish, lost world of autism."

For stoking fear and increasing awareness of autism, Kirby's book was unprecedented in its power. He was indefatigable in promoting it, appearing everywhere from the *Montel Williams Show* to NBC's *Meet the Press.* He gave talks all over the United States and was a frequent guest on a popular radio show whose host, Don Imus, was a complete believer in the thimerosal connection. The "Evidence of Harm" Yahoo! group drew first hundreds and then thousands of postings each month, taking over as the primary online meeting point of the mercury theorists.

With its overtones of the Erin Brockovich story, no one was surprised that Kirby's book, which became a *New York Times* bestseller, was quickly optioned for a Hollywood movie. Reading it made parents everywhere feel that there was a clear and present danger that their child could get autism. They became afraid, and no awareness campaign had ever been more powerful than fear.

More politicians began picking up on that fear. Lobbied by parents, and in particular by Cure Autism Now's Jon Shestack, the Senate in 2006 passed the Combating Autism Act without a single "no" vote. The act authorized a billion-dollar expenditure over five years, dedicated to meeting the needs of people with autism. President George W. Bush signed the revised bill into law in late December.

In addition to authorizing the billion dollars, the law overhauled the composition of a committee established to advise the federal government on how to spend the money. Called the Interagency Autism Coordinating Committee, it sounded like one more lifeless chunk of bureaucracy. But the reconstituted IACC was meant to have some real heat behind it, while reflecting the fact that autism had now become a political concern. This showed in the list of people asked to join the new IACC. It glittered with the names of experts, nearly all with MDs and PhDs, who represented the top ranks of the government services and health-research bureaucracy. But the law had also required the new IACC to include citizens it called "public members." There had to be at least six such members—people who were not part of any federal bureaucracy but who had a connection to autism. At least one had to be "a parent or legal guardian of an individual with an autism spectrum disorder."

In 2007, Lyn Redwood, by then president of SafeMinds, received a letter on official federal government stationery. Signed by Mike Leavitt, secretary of the Department of Health and Human Services, it informed her that she was being offered one of the six public slots.

To autism parents of earlier times, such an invitation would have been unthinkable. Redwood's appointment, in particular, represented a radical break. A Mercury Mom had acquired a top position in the hierarchy of autism policymaking in the United States, to sit among scientists. A direct outcome of the fear caused by the claim that vaccines had created an autism epidemic, it was a remarkable turn of events, and a signal indicator of the arrival of parents as a political force.

But another force had entered the autism arena by this time, an organization founded in 2005, whose dominance would soon, by design, have an influence on almost everything related to autism, from science to media attention to politics. The timing of its establishment—right in the midst of the epidemic scare—was critical, both to its purpose and to its strategy.

This group, however, was not founded by vaccine activists, or even by parents. This time, it was a pair of grandparents.

41

AUTISM SPEAKS

FOR FIVE DAYS IN LATE FEBRUARY 2005, THE NBC NETwork devoted some portion of every one of its news programs to the topic of autism. Under the rubric of "AUTISM: The Hidden Epidemic," the network's morning and evening news on each of those days presented autism as a national emergency that was being neglected. NBC's cable networks MSNBC and CNBC were also airing segments for the series. Four months in production, "The Hidden Epidemic" was a massive commitment to a single advocacy interest, which, as far as anyone could remember, was unprecedented for a network news division. NBC later reported that some 40 million people saw at least part of the series.

On the morning of its last day, viewers met the television executive who had put "The Hidden Epidemic" on the air. Appearing on the set of the *Today* show, NBC CEO Bob Wright, along with his wife, Suzanne, sat chatting on high stools with interviewer Matt Lauer. The subject was the problems faced by families trying to deal with autism's challenges. Wright pointed out that such families were "in most cases, exhausted and broke," with no way to advocate for more attention and money.

"Now, there are a lot of good organizations out there privately but—" Bob started to say, before Suzanne broke in.

"We need a national organization," she said.

With that, a few moments later, she folded back the lapel of her jacket, and pointed to the small pin she was wearing. It was blue and in the shape of a puzzle piece. It was the new logo of the new organization they announced that morning: Autism Speaks.

That winter, word had been circulating in autism circles that a couple with substantial wealth and power who lived in New York had a grandson who had just been diagnosed with autism. In fact, by the time the Wrights went on the *Today* show, and revealed themselves as those grandparents, the better part of a year had passed since doctors at New York–Presbyterian hospital had told them and their daughter Katie that they had no medical answer for the severe ailments of three-year-old Christian.

The doctors had diagnosed Christian with the mysterious, empty-sounding Pervasive Developmental Disorder—Not Otherwise Specified. It was, they knew, another way of saying that Christian had autism. His symptoms were unmissable. He no longer spoke, though he'd had a few words at one point. He made no eye contact with anyone, not even his mother. He barely ate and almost never slept. He was also one of those kids suffering repeated onslaughts of inflammation in his digestive system. His bottom was raw from constant diarrhea, and he kept getting staph infections, yeast infections, and eye infections. To the Wrights, it seemed apparent that whatever was wrong with Christian, it was a kind of sickness in his body.

Wright was stunned when the doctors told the family they had no fix for his condition. The doctors were surely aware that he held a seat on the board of directors of that hospital, which usually counts for something. But they had examined Christian for three days, and the boy's mother was taking him home with no medicine, no therapy, and no real answers. Wright was hurt, on his grandson's behalf—and his daughter's. He was also angry.

In the years that followed, many autism parents would say, with a note of grim gratitude, that the worst thing that ever happened to the Wright family, their grandson's diagnosis, was one of the best for their own families. It was an acknowledgment that Bob Wright's anger over the lack of answers for his grandson, and his and Suzanne's decision to go public with their story, had reordered the autism universe. Wright had clout, and he was willing to use all of it. The "Hidden Epidemic" series, when the full resources of a network news division were bent to address the subject, was only the first taste of that.

Its overall producer was a young NBC vice president named Alison Singer. Shortly after catching wind of Christian's diagnosis, she had emailed Bob and Suzanne offering her support in whatever way she might help, as a mother who knew some of what Wright's daughter was going through. Singer's own daughter, Jodie, then seven, was severely affected. Singer's adult brother, Steven, who had autism, was now under her guardianship as well. In fact, her mother was Rita Tepper, the woman who had once blamed herself for thinking that she might not have loved her infant son enough because of his temporary resemblance to a chicken.

A close bond soon formed between Wright and Singer. While he put her in charge of creating the "Hidden Epidemic" series—her biggest production assignment to date—she introduced him to Eric and Karen London, the parents who had started NAAR a decade earlier, and who were now more successful than ever in funding scientific research. Singer, who occasionally volunteered for NAAR, thought that hooking Wright as a donor could benefit NAAR immensely, given his passion for helping his grandson.

Wright did meet with the Londons. But he did not stop there. He went on to meet with the heads of many other autism organizations, as well as the directors of various autism education programs, university research centers, and government agencies. In all, he spent a good six months getting himself educated on autism, its leading thinkers and ideas, and on the responses that had been developed for it.

What he saw left him discouraged. Everywhere, he met people who impressed him, with their knowledge, and with their commitment, but it shocked him that the autism field was so fragmented, and so often at war with itself. It was not merely that there were so many different organizations, whose effectiveness was hampered by their small scale, and often pointless cold regard for one another. It was the very tenor of the discourse in the autism community. It had always had the tendency to be acrimonious. But by the mid-2000s, the vituperative tone had reached a new pitch. To anyone, like Wright, just discovering this for the first time, it was appalling how nasty the conversation had become and would continue to be in the years to come.

THAT WAS THE vaccine controversy. It was cutting up the community—and nowhere more so than online. On one side was a group of bloggers devoted to pressing the mercury thesis. On the other was a group of self-identified "skeptics," who devoted almost as much time to insulting and baiting the activists as they did to debunking their assertions about vaccines. For example, it was not unusual to see David Kirby, author of *Evidence of Harm,* described as "a real douche" and "an idiot." But the invective went the other way as well. One year, right after Thanksgiving, the *Age of Autism* site—which advertised itself as the "Daily Web Newspaper of the Autism Epidemic"—posted a parody of the classic Norman Rockwell painting *Freedom from Want.* The original showed a family sitting around a Thanksgiving feast, preparing to eat a turkey. But in this Photoshopped version, a live baby appeared where the turkey was supposed to be, while the faces of the dinner guests all belonged to leading figures in the NIH and the CDC, and others perceived as enemies. Among them was the face of Amy Wallace, a reporter for *Wired* magazine, who had only recently run afoul of the activists.

Wallace's sin was to have written favorably about the man who was most hated by adherents of the vaccine theory—a Philadelphia pediatrician by the name of Paul Offit. And Offit's sin was his readiness to challenge what he called the "wishful thinking" of parents who bought into the vaccine theory. Offit was one of the few well-credentialed critics of the vaccine camp to say, out loud, that it was time to end the pretense that parents' insights and instincts deserved as much weight as the findings of respected scientists. Offit's bluntness was a gift to the media, and, for a period of years, there was almost no big news report on vaccine safety that did *not* feature him as its leading voice, challenging with verve and vigor what parents were saying. He became the "go-to guy" without equal for the scientists' side of the story.

There was one wrinkle. In the 1990s, Offit had coinvented and patented a successful vaccine targeting the rotavirus, earning several million dollars at the time. In 2006, Offit's vaccine was made part of the recommended vaccine schedule, to be given in the second and fourth months of life. His parent foes pounced on this, arguing that Offit's true motive for attacking their beliefs was his desire to protect a large source of his income. As far as they were concerned, anytime Offit opened his mouth to opine on vaccine safety, whatever came out of it could be summed up in three words: *conflict of interest.*

The online vaccine activist community's obsession with Dr. Paul Offit became one of the wildest and longest-running sideshows of the controversy. Dubbed "Dr. All Profit," Offit emerged as the default demon in parents' long, wearying battle with unseen enemies in the government and medical establishment. But Offit was out there, visible, vocal. In posts on the *Age of Autism* site, he was called a "monster," a "scumbag," "one of the worst, most evil villains." Later, the site named him "Denialist of the Decade." Later still, J. B. Handley, founder of a group called Generation Rescue, wrote: "I will do everything within my power to ensure that Offit is remembered by history as one of the most sinister, dishonest, well-funded talking heads pharma ever produced." At various points, Offit received anonymous death threats, by phone and by email. Once, someone called his phone and reeled off the names of his kids. An emailer wrote him, "I will hang you by your neck until you're dead." For a time, he was accompanied by a security guard.

THIS WAS THE landscape Bob Wright surveyed when, prompted by his grandson's diagnosis, autism became something he cared about. The divisiveness offended his sensibilities, not because he was particularly delicate, but because he was a businessman, and a rather hard-nosed one at that. He was personable, witty, and loyal to those who showed him loyalty. But as a CEO interested in winning, he always figured out how to do exactly that, with an intensity that made him, in the corporate kingdom, rich, respected, and feared. At NBC, commanding vast resources, wielding unassailable executive power, he had transformed the network into a far bigger, more innovative, and more omnipresent media conglomerate than it had ever been before.

Now he set out to apply his skills, and seek similar gains, with regard to addressing the challenges of autism. Wright wanted to get all the smart people in the field to work together, as if under one "big tent," as he often put it. He wanted Autism Speaks streamlined for efficiency the way any business should be, with everyone in the enterprise synchronized, harmonized, and centralized under a single management team; a unifying logo; and a clear, consistent, and enforceable statement of the mission of confronting this epidemic. With a businessman's perspective, Wright brought in market research professionals, who came up with the name Autism Speaks, and refashioned the puzzle-piece logo that other autism groups had been using for forty years. He offered six-figure salaries to lure experienced nonprofit executives to run daily operations.

He had no intention of taking the slow-build, start-in-a-basement, one-dollar-at-a-time approach followed, through necessity, by the founders of virtually every other autism group in history. He wanted Autism Speaks big from its first day, and decided to lead personally, pulling whatever strings he could to get his organization started, funded, and recognized—and fast.

This paid off immediately, when his longtime friend Bernie Marcus donated $25 million over the first five years to get the organization up and running. Within months of starting up, Autism Speaks was throwing high-powered fund-raisers, like a concert that featured Jerry Seinfeld and Paul Simon, with former NBC anchorman Tom Brokaw as emcee—all friends of the Wrights. These were benchmarks that most nonprofit organizations could take years to achieve, and only few ever did.

Wright asked Alison Singer to serve as an interim CEO, and she accepted on the condition of flexible hours, because of the demands at home. With that, Singer's career as a television executive came to an end. Autism advocacy, and building Autism Speaks into a powerhouse as quickly as possible, became the new total focus of her professional life. Singer, given her personal connection to autism in her own home, grew closer to the Wrights, feeling almost like family as they worked together to build the "big tent" Bob saw as the way to end the pointless acrimony, and to make families' lives easier sooner.

In many ways, Autism Speaks met that goal. One of the organization's central priorities was "autism awareness," which simply meant getting people to know about and care about autism. On that score, the visibility the group achieved within its first year was worthy of envy in the overcrowded and always-struggling nonprofit sector. Of course, the vaccine scare had already let loose a wave of awareness propelled by fear, but Autism Speaks surfed the wave skillfully, sounding the epidemic alarm while presenting itself as an oasis of intelligent, professionally curated information delivered calmly and authoritatively. Parents of newly diagnosed children started to come to the Autism Speaks website first in their search for answers, while journalists seeking quotes and information put the Autism Speaks staff of experts at the top of their call lists. For the first time in its history, the Autism Society of America, the group founded by Bernard Rimland and Ruth Sullivan (originally the National Society for Autistic Children), was no longer the standard-bearer of the autism cause in the popular imagination. The ASA had served that cause nobly, and sometimes heroically, but it was now outshone by the star power and the energy embodied by the Wrights. As ambassadors for Autism Speaks, Bob and Suzanne seemed omnipresent, just like their blue puzzle logo. Celebrities were wearing it at award ceremonies. It showed up on 5 million Starbucks cups and at the checkout counter at every Modell's Sporting Goods store as a $1 pin for sale. Not then, or afterward, could any other advocacy organization claim as much credit for educating so many people so quickly.

A second Autism Speaks priority fell under the heading of "advocacy." Being perceived as a behemoth translated into immediate access to power for Autism Speaks lobbyists trying to effect changes in government policy. No politician wanted to say no to a meeting with Bob Wright or one of his emissaries. Over several years, this helped Autism Speaks ring up a string of victories by convincing state legislatures to pass laws requiring insurance companies to pay for autism treatment. Previously, families had been denied coverage, almost universally, on the grounds that autism was not a medical condition. Perhaps no other autism "reform" produced a more material benefit to families than the new insurance laws argued into existence by Autism Speaks.

And then there was scientific research. Autism Speaks wanted to "own" that area too.

But that was where things would become a lot more complicated.

Under Bob Wright's leadership, NBC television had quintupled in size, in terms of revenue, over the twenty years during which he held posts as president and CEO. Some of that growth came from the efficient nurturing of NBC's existing parts. But some also came from spotting valuable outside properties—companies that were already up and running and ideally making money—and then acquiring them, by purchase or some other arrangement. In this common business practice, known as mergers and acquisitions, growth happens at the stroke of a pen.

Autism Speaks, sprinting to bigness, borrowed from that approach. Prior to its founding, and during its first year of operation, Wright worked hard to bring the best of the best of autism nonprofits inside his big tent. Autism Speaks called these transactions "mergers," but it was always true that any outside organization brought in in this way immediately lost its identity behind the blue puzzle piece. It was clear that certain groups appealed to Autism Speaks for particular assets they possessed, including talented people. For example, the first announced merger, completed before the official launch, was with a group called the Autism Coalition for Research and Education (ACRE)—a group that excelled at organizing celebrity golf tournaments and other fund-raisers. One of its two cofounders was Emily Gerson Saines, the producer of the movie *Temple Grandin*. At the merger, ACRE's other cofounder, Kevin Murray, joined the Autism Speaks board, immediately delivering expertise in that kind of fund-raising, which Autism Speaks knew they wanted to pursue. ACRE had something else of value: its 501(c)(3) tax status. Its transfer to Autism Speaks allowed the new organization to begin accepting tax-deductible donations immediately.

It was inevitable, of course, that Bob Wright's eye would be caught early by the two most impressive parent-run organizations sponsoring scientific research. By the time Autism Speaks launched, NAAR—the creation of Eric and Karen London—and Cure Autism Now, founded and still run by Jon Shestack and Portia Iversen—represented two decades of combined experience, with long mailing lists and well-developed networks of scientists already in place. Moreover, NAAR had the brain-tissue bank, and CAN had its library of DNA. Both, which had taken years to build, were unique and precious. Even as Autism Speaks was launching in 2005, Wright knew he wanted these assets. He sent out Alison Singer to get the merger talks started.

For the first time, but not the last, Autism Speaks was about to hurt some feelings.

Jon Shestack was dead set against any kind of merger with Wright's group. His reasons were partly personal. He loved running Cure Autism Now. He loved giving everything he had to a cause that drew upon talents in him that he never knew he had, and that fed his passion as much as it exhausted his days. Moreover, it was his way to be *doing something* for his son Dov, which he found so much more conducive to his Hollywood producer's personality than doing nothing. He had no interest in giving any of that up to become part of a behemoth run out of New York.

Shestack also had a philosophical aversion to seeing CAN swallowed up. He had come to believe that it was a good thing for science when researchers had more, not fewer, places to turn for money. When a scientist was denied a grant from NAAR, for example, there was always CAN to try next, or vice versa. CAN and NAAR had reached a productive détente under which, despite a somewhat rivalrous relationship, the ground each group staked out for research was often non-overlapping. Shestack saw benefit in the existing arrangement, where no nonprofit group had monopoly power over the choice of avenues of autism science to explore.

That was why he saw Autism Speaks, which was also angling for NAAR—and at least one other smaller nonprofit—as a threat. Years earlier, he had turned down the chance to merge with NAAR, but after

Alison Singer called him for the first time, and told him of Bob Wright's interest in joining forces, Shestack immediately called the Londons in Princeton, and proposed that they all reconsider a marriage. A combined CAN-NAAR organization, Shestack argued, would serve as a counterweight to Autism Speaks, and that would be better for everyone.

But the Londons did not see it that way. They had been meeting with the Wrights, and had already concluded that combining with Autism Speaks could only leverage their work to a higher plane, with the increased funding and visibility that Wright's clout was proven to produce. Shestack pleaded with the Londons not to go ahead with it, but he had no idea how far along the Londons were in their talks with Singer and Wright. On November 30, 2005, Autism Speaks and NAAR issued a joint statement announcing "the consolidation of the two charities." Three members of NAAR's board, including Eric London, would sit on the board of Autism Speaks, but the NAAR name was gone. The "new structure," according to the press release, "will collectively be known as Autism Speaks, Inc."

Shestack was given a heads-up about the merger only on the day it occurred, and only a short time before it was publicly announced, when Singer, in New York, delayed her arrival for a meeting long enough to call his Los Angeles home from the sidewalk downstairs. Sitting herself down on someone's stoop on a side street off Madison Avenue, she braced herself for what she was about to do. Singer liked and respected Shestack, whom she had worked with when he had been interviewed for the "Hidden Epidemic" series. She also knew he would take the news hard. She wanted him to hear it from her.

Shestack was in the shower when she called, and asked her to call back a few minutes later. When she did, the expected happened. She heard Shestack let loose a string of curses, followed by a diatribe on why what Autism Speaks was trying to do was damaging to science. Singer heard him out but, still Wright's right hand in this matter, she had another message to deliver. As gently as she could, she made it clear to Shestack that if he chose to keep running CAN as an independent organization, he could expect no consideration from Autism Speaks in the competition for funding, media attention, or even the loyalty of Hollywood celebrities who, Singer pointed out, had every reason to want to curry favor with Bob Wright. Furthermore, Autism Speaks would soon be opening an office in Los Angeles, staging walks there, and taking out ad space in newspapers and on billboards. Shestack heard this message as *Join us or we will crush you.* Singer used no such language, but then, she did not feel it was necessary. She knew Shestack would get the point. She asked him to take some time, and to consider, please, whether a merger might not be the best thing for everyone.

Shestack, despondent, took the matter to one of his closest confidants at CAN, autism father Peter Bell, who was serving as its president. Bell was to Shestack what Singer was to Wright—a friend, and a dedicated activist, who, like Singer, had given up a successful career in another field—as a marketing executive in the pharmaceutical industry—to work full-time for Cure Autism Now. Bell had even relocated his family from New Jersey to Los Angeles. If anyone would have an idea for fending off what Shestack saw as a takeover threat, it would be Bell.

But Bell surprised Shestack. He told him that a fight against Bob Wright was not winnable. Moreover, like the Londons, he saw good reasons for being part of the bigger organization.

Some months later, Shestack learned that most of the board of Cure Autism Now felt the same way. Autism Speaks looked like the future, and it made no sense not to be part of it. When the matter was put to a vote, the proposal passed. Only two members voted against. Jon Shestack was one. Portia Iversen, his wife and cofounder, was the other.

On November 29, 2006, a joint statement announced the merger of Cure Autism Now and Autism Speaks. Once again, a name disappeared. "The consolidated organization," the statement read, "will be known as Autism Speaks, Inc." Peter Bell was immediately hired to serve as executive vice president of programs and services, and moved his family back east. Shestack and Iversen were given seats on the Autism Speaks board. When their terms ended three years later, neither was invited back.

AUTISM SPEAKS'S STEWARDSHIP of its research mission would prove to be controversial, to say the least. On the one hand, the money it began funneling into new scientific investigation quickly surpassed anything a private charity had ever contributed to autism science before. In 2006, the organization disbursed almost $14 million, which was 26 percent more than CAN and NAAR combined had given scientists in 2005. In 2007, Autism Speaks notched an even higher number: $24 million. In 2008, it jumped yet again, to $27 million. In addition, the organization now controlled both the DNA library and the brain-tissue bank. Eventually, Autism Speaks would start contributing to a global consortium of scientists set on sequencing the entire genomes of ten thousand individuals from families affected by autism.

Autism Speaks's political lobbying helped steer tens of millions of dollars of federal money into autism research, and its awareness programs also alerted more scientists than ever before to the possibilities and opportunities—for themselves—in the study of autism. Annually, scientists from more than forty countries were flocking to the annual meeting of the International Society for Autism Research, of which Autism Speaks became a lead sponsor and advertiser.

And yet, within a few short years, Autism Speaks's performance in the area of scientific research would come under question from all sides, and the group would yield leadership position in this realm to others, while Bob Wright's dream of a "big tent" organization—synchronized, harmonized, and centralized—would be seen sagging dangerously low, pulled down by the weight of too many irreconcilable viewpoints.

And all because Autism Speaks became entangled in the vaccine controversy, where the science on one side didn't add up, and never had.

42

A STORY UNRAVELS

ANDREW WAKEFIELD'S WORK HAD ALWAYS CONTAINED enough loose threads that critics could begin pulling it apart almost as soon as it was published in *The Lancet*, back in 1998. Richard Horton, *The Lancet*'s editor, had known the paper would spur controversy and had arranged for a rebuttal to appear in the very same issue.

Written by a pair of American vaccine researchers at the CDC, Robert Chen and Frank DeStefano, it was a preemptive broadside in which they argued that raising the question of a causal link between vaccines and autism was irresponsible, even dangerous. The facts, they had written, were grounds for reassurance about the MMR vaccine's safety. They cited its safe use in "hundreds of millions of people worldwide," with not a single report of anyone "developing either chronic bowel or behavioral problems." They cited the work of scientists who had attempted without success to reproduce Wakefield's findings "using more sensitive and specific assays." They pointed out that Wakefield's patients did not represent a random sampling, and that his reliance on parents' memories to pinpoint the onset of digestive and behavioral issues was problematic. They also showed that in several of the children, the behavioral problems had existed before the bowel problems.

Over the following year, the scientific evidence against Wakefield continued to mount. In June 1999, *The Lancet* had published an epidemiological investigation led by a Royal Free Hospital researcher named Brent Taylor. His team had examined vaccination records for nearly five hundred children who received diagnoses of autism over a span of years that included the introduction of the MMR in Britain. A causal link would be expected to show up as a sudden uptick in autism concurrent with MMR use. Taylor's team found none.

American researchers weighed in next, with a study out of California, published in early 2001, comparing trends in MMR vaccination and autism diagnosis among children born in California in 1980 and 1994. "Essentially no correlation was observed," the study authors reported in *The Journal of the American Medical Association.*

By 2006, the alleged link had been investigated by epidemiologists in Japan, Finland, the United States, Britain, Denmark, Canada, and elsewhere—more than a dozen times in total—and always the researchers found no meaningful association between MMR use and autism.

Other researchers, meanwhile, sought evidence of the proliferation of the measles virus that Wakefield had reported finding repeatedly in the intestines of children with autistic behaviors. But these studies too failed to replicate his findings.

The news media did not ignore this near-unanimous conclusion of scientists in half a dozen countries. The studies almost always made news, but they did so as part of a continuing narrative of competing truths—that of the scientists against that of the families. And somehow Wakefield continued to get the benefit of the doubt.

IT WAS A British freelance journalist who did the legwork that led to Wakefield's undoing. Brian Deer was an investigative reporter who often wrote for the *Sunday Times,* exposing malfeasance in the healthcare industry. In late 2003, the television movie about Wakefield and his theories, *Hear the Silence,* was getting a good deal of buzz just ahead of its premiere, and that buzz was giving fresh energy to public discussion of the MMR question. An editor at the *Sunday Times,* looking to catch that wave, thought to ask Deer to come up with "something big" on MMR.

Deer tackled the MMR story with a deep skepticism not yet demonstrated by most of his colleagues in the press. One of Deer's first calls was to a mother whose son had been part of the *Lancet* study. Deer did not give his real last name when he reached out to her, a maneuver he had cleared in advance with his editors. Instead, he used his middle name so that her guard would not go up if she were familiar with his reporting. Thus deceived, the woman spoke to Deer for several hours, answering his questions in ways that stunned him.

She told Deer, for example, that she had not noticed her son's first behavioral symptoms until months after he had been given the MMR injection—not within fourteen days, as Wakefield had reported. In a later interview with this mother, Deer also learned that it was no accident that she had chosen to have her child's intestinal problems treated at the Royal Free Hospital. As he would shortly discover, several of the families had consulted with a personal-injury lawyer who, in the late 1990s, was in the early stages of preparing a product-liability lawsuit against the manufacturers of MMR. It was the lawyer who guided several families to ask their family doctors for referrals to Wakefield. Yet Wakefield's *Lancet* paper had described all the families as "self-referred."

Deer also discovered that Wakefield and the attorney had previously corresponded about the possibility of establishing a causal link between the vaccine and autism sufficient to justify bringing suit. With the lawyer's intervention, it was arranged for Wakefield to receive roughly $80,000 to fund a pilot study—the very study that was later published in *The Lancet.* Moreover, Wakefield was passing along results of the *Lancet* study to the legal team before it was even in print.

When Deer asked Wakefield to respond to these discoveries, Wakefield tried to make them sound like a minor lapse in publishing etiquette. "I believe that this paper was conducted in good faith," he said. "It reported the findings." He wrote a letter to *The Lancet* denying any and all accusations of ethical wrongdoing. And in every interview, he reasserted his original findings.

But anyone who had ever conducted research, or relied on it, immediately grasped how damning Deer's story was. These included ten of Wakefield's twelve coauthors on the paper, who had been kept in the dark about Wakefield's involvement with lawyers. Embarrassed, they publicly retracted the part of the paper that raised a link between MMR and autism. *The Lancet*'s editor declared in writing: "If we had known the conflict of interest Dr. Wakefield had in his work, [the article] would have been rejected." Britain's chief medical officer publicly accused Wakefield of "mixing spin and science," and the health secretary called for Wakefield to be investigated as "a matter of urgency."

The British press, which had previously been a megaphone for Wakefield, helping to stir up the fear about MMR, now rushed to condemn him. "His credibility lies in ruins," wrote the *Sun.* "He has much to answer for." The *Independent* portrayed Wakefield as an "increasingly isolated man . . . led astray by the power of his own belief."

And yet, even as they turned on Wakefield, many media outlets remained reluctant to declare the death of his renegade hypothesis about MMR. Remarkably, a 2004 editorial in the *Independent* argued the opposite, insisting that "the urgent need now is for more real study of autism and MMR." The *Sun* pumped fresh oxygen into the controversy too, asserting it as "a fact that until the mysteries of autism are fully explained, MMR may never be fully accepted."

In short, fear of MMR lived on, and in some quarters, so did the conviction that Wakefield's science might still be right, even if he had broken a rule or two along the way. To some, his financial arrangements seemed beside the point. "He is not an accountant," one supportive mother told a reporter. "He is a doctor." If anything, the parents who stood by Wakefield became even more fervent in their affection for him.

As for Wakefield, he never flinched. He would always maintain that Deer's story was part of a smear campaign, a conspiracy designed to destroy him. By then, he was spending most of his time in the United States and he continued to practice medicine—treating American children, speaking to American audiences, and appearing, as ever, to relish the fight.

"I have absolutely nothing to hide," he told a reporter, with no note whatsoever of remorse, fear, or uncertainty. "There has been talk of an inquiry," he said. "I would welcome this."

Wakefield's claim of a conspiracy became a familiar part of the vaccine controversy. Often, whenever science did not support the vaccine activists' theories about how autism was caused by mercury or

MMR, this boosted their conviction that the negative results were part of a plot to hide the truth. That, of course, had been the thrust of Robert Kennedy's *Rolling Stone* portrait of a massive government cover-up of thimerosal's dangers. According to those who believed in the conspiracy, it had been under way for decades. The drug companies were in on it, along with American and British medical authorities, and, at a minimum, hundreds of scientists around the world, all of whom knew that vaccines were causing autism. Driving the plot, according to this view, were career ambitions and money. The pharmaceutical industry, it was said, was panicked by the prospect of product-liability lawsuits and had been buying off researchers, regulators, journalists, and perhaps a few politicians around the world. It had been going on since the 1930s. This was why science kept failing the vaccine theory. Among the institutions said to have been corrupted were the FDA, the NIH, the IOM, and of course the CDC.

The theory drew adherents from outside the autism community as well. To some on the far left politically, it fit well alongside narratives about the evils of large corporations. For those on the far right, it seemed another example of government bureaucrats colluding to take away people's rights to make their own choices about medical treatment.

But this too became a story that unraveled the more it was studied. Kennedy's article was found to contain enough nontrivial mistakes that both *Rolling Stone* and *Salon* issued corrections almost immediately after its publication. Later, critics faulted the article for taking quotations out of context, or editing them to heighten the apparent nefariousness of the officials being quoted. Eventually, *Salon* issued a full retraction of the article and pulled it from its website.

Perhaps the final blow for the conspiracy theorists came with the conclusion of the US Senate probe into the alleged plot. Led by Wyoming Republican Mike Enzi, a senator whom the vaccine activists considered an ally, investigators had subpoenaed thousands of pages of documents from the NIH, the IOM, and the CDC. For eighteen months, they pored over emails and meeting transcripts and interviewed officials from all three organizations. In the end, nothing incriminating was found. "Allegations of a cover-up are not substantiated," the final report would declare.

In the United States, the Mercury Moms also saw the story turn against them, beginning in 2004. That year, a new panel was convened by the Institute of Medicine to review the most recent research testing the allegation that thimerosal was causing autism. Three years earlier, a similar IOM panel had handed the moms a small win, when it conceded that the thimerosal link was "biologically plausible." But in 2004, there was much more data to examine. New epidemiological studies had been conducted in the United States, Britain, Sweden, and Denmark. Going back through several years of records, it was disappointing news for the vaccine camp: the IOM found no proof that autism was connected to thimerosal. Indeed, in Denmark, thimerosal had been removed from vaccines in 1992, yet autism was more prevalent than ever.

The IOM panelists listened respectfully to presentations by researchers allied with the Mercury Moms, but found these unimpressive. In one study, researchers had injected thimerosal into a strain of mice bred to be sensitive to mercury, who then showed signs of antisocial behaviors. However, even the researcher, a scientist at Columbia University who was partly funded by SafeMinds, acknowledged, "Of course, we need to determine the relevance of animal studies for human neural development." The panel politely judged the mouse work "difficult to assess."

In their 2004 report, the members of the IOM panel asserted, without ambiguity: "There is currently no evidence to support this hypothesis. The committee concludes that the evidence favors rejection of a causal relationship between thimerosal-containing vaccines and autism."

The IOM released its report on the morning of May 18, 2004. By the end of the day, activist groups, who had trusted the IOM's judgment when it matched their agenda, had already started a campaign to besmirch it. SafeMinds published a press release slamming the committee's thirteen expert members for having "compromised their integrity and independence" while acting under the "cartel's influence," and producing a report that was "a failure by any acceptable scientific standard." A year later, someone at SafeMinds would reveal that the release had been composed in advance of the IOM's release of the report—in case of an undesirable outcome. This admission only added to the impression that the activist parents would dismiss any and all data and conclusions that did not support their political agenda. It became increasingly difficult for them to claim that science—not evangelism—was at the heart of their argument about mercury.

IN LONDON, BRIAN DEER was not done with the Wakefield story. After his initial story ran in the *Sunday Times,* he had spent much of the rest of 2004 working on an hour-long television documentary based on his initial reporting, and whatever he could add to it by further investigation. This took him to the United States, where Wakefield was now employed by the Austin Surgical Hospital in Texas, treating children with autism at a facility called Thoughtful House.

When the documentary aired on November 18, Deer had a good deal more to report on Wakefield, none of it exculpatory. His major new discovery was that Wakefield, before his *Lancet* article was published in 1998, had already applied for a patent on a new type of measles vaccine that might appeal to parents seeking to avoid the MMR. The conflict of interest was stupefying: Wakefield would have had a direct financial stake in the public's being terrified of the MMR vaccine.

Deer also reported, for the first time, that massive problems with Wakefield's methodology had surfaced. Deer had tracked down a former student doctor, who'd since become a researcher, who had helped perform the studies on Wakefield's original twelve subjects. Assigned the task of looking for traces of measles virus in tissue taken from the children, the young man ran tests that came up negative in each and every instance. No measles virus. Though he reported these results to Wakefield—findings that undermined the very premise of the MMR-causation theory—Wakefield chose to omit them from his paper, and never mentioned them in interviews.

The climax of the film saw Deer tracking down Wakefield at a conference center in Indianapolis, where he had just finished a speech to the Autism Society of America. When Deer introduced himself,

Wakefield recognized the name instantly and, startled, reached over to cover the camera lens with his hand.

More than a year later, in an interview in Texas with a sympathetic reporter from the British newspaper *Express,* Wakefield told his public where he stood on the assault on his reputation. He casually batted away Deer's mounting findings as a lot of irrelevant and malicious interpretation of things that go on in the normal course of laboratory investigations.

"I'm not going away before this work is done," he said. "It's simply a job that needs to be done, to find the truth."

SCIENTIFIC TRUTH DERIVES from laboratories, not courtrooms. But at least the courtroom is a place where stories can be tested. And in 2004, a formal process was launched to give the vaccine theory of autism its day in court.

Lawyers had been lining up clients for some three years already, ever since the IOM's initial finding that the thimerosal theory was at least "biologically plausible." Most wanted to take on Eli Lilly, thimerosal's inventor, a target with deep pockets. Some firms advertised on TV for clients, while a notice circulating in online autism communities asked for families interested in "forcing the multi-billion dollar international pharmaceutical industry to pay." It urged parents to contact the Mercury Vaccine Alliance, a consortium of thirty-five law firms planning a state-by-state legal assault on Eli Lilly and several licensed producers of thimerosal.

The response was huge. Families who believed in the vaccine theory wanted to see justice done, and without question, they needed the money—the financial burden of their children's therapy and care was huge. By March 2002, families in at least twenty-five states had signed up, and the Mercury Vaccine Alliance had filed lawsuits in at least eleven states. Two more coalitions of lawyers had formed in the meantime. According to *The National Law Journal,* a group that included Dallas attorney Andrew Waters had already filed forty-five cases, with more to come. "We're considering about eight to nine hundred," Waters told the *Journal*'s Mary Cronin Fisk.

Lawyers told Fisk they saw the vaccine story "as one of the most enticing causes of action in recent memory" because the cases looked simultaneously very winnable and very lucrative. When the client is "a young child with his whole life ahead of him," Waters told Fisk, "the jury appeal is unparalleled." Moreover, as Fisk reported, "the potential damages could be astronomical"—in the range of $10 million to $30 million per case. The stage seemed set for one of the greatest product-liability sagas since the tobacco lawsuits of the 1990s.

But as it turned out, few of these cases would ever be tried in traditional courtrooms or in front of juries. Rather, they would be tried in the so-called vaccine court, a federal claims court in Washington, DC. Established in 1988 under the then-new National Vaccine Injury Compensation Program (NVICP), the vaccine court was intended to shield pharmaceutical companies from vaccine-injury lawsuits, so that they would not have an incentive to stop making vaccines altogether. The program barred individuals from suing manufacturers directly for vaccine-related injuries. Instead, claimants had to bring complaints first to the vaccine court and make the case for compensation from a federally controlled fund derived from a tax on every dose of vaccine sold in the United States. In vaccine court, where appointees known as special masters served as both judge and jury, and where the US government was effectively the defendant, mammoth dollar payouts were unlikely. The average award was about $650,000, with compensation in cases of death capped at $250,000. Claimants who lost their cases regained the right to sue the vaccine manufacturer in a conventional court, though in practice few individuals had the energy and resources to keep fighting.

Attorneys signing up clients to sue over thimerosal knew all this, but they believed they had found a loophole in the law that would allow plaintiffs to avoid vaccine court. They argued that because thimerosal was a preservative rather than a vaccine itself, NVICP strictures did not apply. It was a clever strategy that ultimately failed; civil court judges around the country sent plaintiffs away until they had first presented their cases in vaccine court. At the same time, Congress began wrestling over legislation to close the loophole, prompting parents to seize their day in vaccine court, where they faced tight deadlines to qualify for consideration. As a result, by 2003 the vast majority of thimerosal cases were being steered to the vaccine court—where the MMR cases were also heading.

But at the least the vaccine court offered the chance for vindication, and a form of due process, by which, if claimants could plausibly demonstrate that they had been hurt by a vaccine, they would be compensated. Indeed, the vaccine court already recognized certain kinds of injuries as sufficiently documented as to require no argument about the underlying biological mechanisms. It was common knowledge, for example, that the polio vaccine, in rare cases, actually *caused* polio, and that the DTP vaccine could cause anaphylactic shock. Autism, however, was not on the list of recognized adverse outcomes. This meant that lawyers seeking compensation for their clients would have to present a theory linking autism to a vaccine, back up the theory, and then make the argument that the children in question had autism because of the vaccination.

This was not an easy set of hurdles.

And then came another twist, when the judges at vaccine court found themselves overwhelmed by the sudden wave of new cases centered on autism. During its first decade or so, the court had been asked to adjudicate some 4,600 petitioned cases. Not one had alleged that a vaccine had caused autism until 1999, when a single such case was filed. No autism petitions were received the following year, but 18 were filed in 2001. From there, the caseload soared. During the first six months of 2002, 300 new autism filings hit the court. Six months later, that number had more than doubled. The following year, 2003, saw another 2,438 claims come in. Eventually, the total approached 5,000 autism-only cases waiting to be heard.

It was at this point that the judges announced a special approach to hearing these cases. Rather than working through them one at a time—a process that threatened to consume the rest of their working lives and delay resolution for thousands of families—they would cut through the logjam by putting the vaccines-cause-autism argument itself on trial. They would do this by taking a "test case" approach to the dispute. Lawyers for the families were invited to choose a few representative children and to use their medical histories, buttressed by scientific research, to illustrate the process by which vaccines gave them autism. If they succeeded, the remaining families could rely on that precedent for their claims. If the test cases failed, however, it would be the end of the road for claims about autism.

With billions of dollars in compensation in the balance, the stakes were huge. And now the families had a date to look forward to. The vaccine theory of autism was to go on trial in March 2004, with a verdict to be reached by that summer.

In Washington, DC, March 2004 came and went, and with it, so did the start date for the vaccine court to begin hearing arguments. The lawyers all found that they needed more time for the detailed research and discovery required for such a technically complex subject. In particular, the lawyers for the families admitted that they did not yet have sufficient evidence, and needed certain studies that were presently under way to reach completion. After several postponements over more than a year, a start date was set for well in the future: June 2007. In short, families would have to wait quite some time before this legal test of their story would even get started.

In the meantime, one more piece of bad news for the vaccine activists appeared in the form of an "own goal" scored against them by David Kirby, the author of *Evidence of Harm.* In 2005, in an exchange with a skeptical blogger, Kirby had recognized a simple benchmark test for the thimerosal theory: track the autism rate in California for a few years; if it goes down, the theory is correct. That would be because, in the early 2000s, vaccine manufacturers stopped using thimerosal in most vaccines given to children. It stood to reason that babies born in the new millennium would have a lower exposure to methylmercury via vaccines and therefore less autism would be reported. In an email to the blogger, who called himself Citizen Cain, Kirby conceded: "If the number of three- to five-year-olds diagnosed has not declined by 2007 that would deal a severe blow to the autism-thimerosal hypothesis."

In 2007, the deadline arrived, but the reported prevalence of autism in California did not decline. It went up. The year after that, it went up again.

This steady parade of setbacks for the vaccine argument slowly dismantled its proponents' main achievement: transforming what had always been a fringe tendency to mistrust vaccines into a mainstream cultural phenomenon. This transformation was abetted by the mainstream media, which often described the controversy as a "debate" in which scientists and the parents opposing them were granted equal stature. But that practice began to wane in 2007 and 2008, as the scientific data piled up, weakening the perception that the story had two sides. Somewhere in this period, too, the producers who optioned the movie rights to David Kirby's book, *Evidence of Harm,* must have seen the oxygen leaking from his story of parents struggling to get at the truth. The movie was never made.

And yet, even as it was losing momentum, the campaign blaming vaccines received one last jolt of fresh energy, in the person of reality-TV star, comedienne, and former *Playboy* model Jenny McCarthy. McCarthy's son had been diagnosed with autism in 2005, so she came relatively late to the autism conversation, in 2007. But she was glamorous, confident, and highly visible. For years to come, McCarthy's face and name would be identified with the controversy, and she would be known for her defiance of experts. Claiming that her son's autism was the result of vaccination, and that she had figured out how to "heal" him using alternative remedies, she chose to advertise her complete lack of formal education in medicine, psychology, nutrition—or anything related to science—as an asset. "The University of Google is where I got my degree from," she famously said on *The Oprah Winfrey Show,* a line that was met with warm applause.

Clearly, in some circles, the story still held.

43

THE GREATEST FRAUD

By the summer of 2007, nearly five thousand families had been waiting—in some cases, up to five years—for the vaccine court in Washington, DC, to begin hearing evidence for and against their claim that vaccines caused autism in their children. On June 11, their wait ended. At nine o'clock that morning, three special masters took their seats in a modern, unadorned courtroom a two-minute stroll from the White House. The gallery was filled largely with lawyers, but arrangements had been made to let families dial in to listen to the proceedings by telephone. Hundreds did so.

For those families, winning compensation would depend on showing a biologically plausible explanation for how a vaccine had caused each child's autism. The existence of two hypotheses—one based on measles, the other on mercury—complicated the picture. But lawyers for the families had banded together, forming a legal committee that agreed to present both hypotheses, one at a time, plus a third: that sometimes autism results from the measles virus and mercury acting in concert. All three hypotheses would be challenged by lawyers representing the federal government.

Among those physically present on the first day of the hearings were the parents of twelve-year-old Michelle Cedillo, of Yuma, Arizona, who was to be the first test case for the third hypothesis. Michelle sat belted into a wheelchair, wearing a noise-muffling headset similar to what a ground crew member wears on the tarmac at airports. Diagnosed with autism, Michelle was profoundly disabled in other ways as well. According to her parents, she had developed normally as an infant but had suffered a barrage of illnesses after getting her MMR vaccination at sixteen months.

For them to win compensation, it was critical to establish that there had once been a "before" Michelle—a healthy, normally developing child who would have been fine had she never been vaccinated. Here, her mother, Theresa, provided moving testimony, offering a vivid account of a child who had laughed and played and said words like "apple," and "Mama," and even "Jesus," because, Theresa explained, "my mom had shown her a crucifix in her house every day, [telling Michelle] 'Jesus loves you.'" Then, as excerpts from home videos were played, Theresa offered commentary on her daughter's first fifteen months or so of life. The tapes showed a smiling baby—playing with toys, laughing with adults, enjoying a bath in the kitchen sink.

The contrast with the Michelle sitting before the panel was stark. She was now a severely ill twelve-year-old girl. She was losing her sight, suffered seizures, could not use words, and endured arthritis and extreme abdominal irritation. When she was eleven, she had fallen during a seizure and broken her leg.

Throughout the morning testimony, Michelle grunted and hit herself repeatedly. Eventually, her parents took her outside. The point had been made: the stakes were huge for the families. So were their needs. Special Master George Hastings affirmed this when he looked at the small audience before him, largely composed of lawyers, and said: "Clearly, the story of Michelle's life is a tragic one."

The hearings specific to Michelle's life and difficulties lasted twelve days. Then Hastings had to rule. But first he had to read more than 3,000 pages of testimony, as well as thousands of pages of Michelle's medical records, some twenty experts' reports, and approximately 800 academic studies. He was not going to be done with this in just a few months.

On June 18, 2007, just as the public hearing on Michelle Cedillo's case reached its midpoint, the *New York Times* published a front-page story with the headline "Autism Debate Strains a Family and Its Charity." Embarrassing in its details, the piece exposed a bitter quarrel that had cut through a family of autism activists: the family of Bob, Suzanne, and Katie Wright.

Painful enough in what it said about them, it also made it obvious that the vaccine controversy was wreaking havoc at Autism Speaks.

For some weeks prior to the *Times* story, Katie Wright, Bob and Suzanne's daughter, had been sharing with the autism community online her growing belief that it was a vaccine that had made her son sick. She repeated this opinion in a videotaped interview with David Kirby. Then she went on an episode of *The Oprah Winfrey Show* devoted to autism, where she described Christian as having experienced a horrible reaction to multiple vaccines.

This was decidedly awkward, given that Autism Speaks had always sought to remain scrupulously impartial in the vaccine controversy. This irked people on both sides of the issue: those who wanted the organization to disavow the theory, and those who wanted it embraced. During the Kirby interview, Katie Wright indicated which side she was on when she shared her view that some members of Autism Speaks were "resistant to change" and "afraid to offend government officials." It was understood that she was talking about some of the older generation of autism parents, at least one of whom—NAAR founder Eric London—now sat on the Autism Speaks board. "A lot of these people," Wright said, "their children are adults now. And I think it's time to step aside."

Even though Wright was always careful to point out that she was speaking for herself, and not for her parents' organization, the distinction was overshadowed by the fact that she was, after all, the boss's daughter.

A terse statement from Bob and Suzanne quickly appeared on the Autism Speaks website. "Katie Wright is not a spokesperson for Autism Speaks," it said. "Our daughter's personal views differ from ours and do not represent or reflect the ongoing mission of Autism Speaks. . . . Her appearance with David Kirby was done without the knowledge or consent of Autism Speaks." They also addressed the many people Katie might have insulted, insisting that their efforts were appreciated, regardless of which generation of activist they belonged to. The last line said this: "We apologize to our valued volunteers who were led to believe otherwise by our daughter's statement."

The *Times* story reported that parents and daughter were not on speaking terms. But Katie, an active blogger, had continued communicating with her online public. "I am terribly sorry if statements reflecting my frustration with the pace and scope of autism research offended . . ." she wrote to parents and volunteers. At the same time, she affirmed her animosity toward the "scientists at the CDC, NIH and elsewhere, who have discounted and obfuscated the autism/environment connection for far too long." And she addressed the tough statement her parents posted: "I do not understand why such a personal denouncement of me was necessary." In fact, her mother and father seemed to rethink the tone of their post, later adding: "She is our daughter, and we love her very much."

None of the Wrights wanted this feud perpetuated. The need to look out for Christian connected them all. Katie and her parents reconciled soon after the *Times* story.

The story blew over, but not its unsettling effect on Autism Speaks's aspiration to remain above the fray in the vaccine debate. The public could now easily wonder whether the organization would bow to activist pressures to take the vaccine theory more seriously in order to keep the peace in the Wright family. At the same time, the episode spurred at least one Autism Speaks executive to begin lobbying internally for the group to take the opposite step, and explicitly disavow any adherence to the belief that vaccines cause autism.

That executive was Alison Singer, one of Bob Wright's most trusted lieutenants. By 2007, the year of the article, and the start of the vaccine trials, Singer—who at one time believed the vaccine theory had merit—had changed her mind. She had the IOM reports, and other studies, and felt that the data had answered the question convincingly. Indeed, she would always say that, had the studies gone the other way, then of course her opinion would be different. In making the case inside Autism Speaks, however, she was up against an uncomfortable reality: the boss's daughter was an autism mom who still believed that vaccines caused autism, and the boss himself was committed to a philosophy of inclusiveness that required not alienating those in the autism community who hewed to the vaccine theory.

Singer knew that Wright trusted her. She could talk to him about these concerns behind closed doors and always get a respectful hearing. She often heard him finish these conversations by saying, "Alison, I know you'll do the right thing." Singer understood what was expected of her. Because she still believed in the larger mission, she complied, keeping her misgivings to herself when representing Autism Speaks.

But in the period that followed the *Times* story, Singer found that going along was becoming harder to do, as she also came to believe that the vaccine controversy was draining away years of research funding and energy that could have been put to better use. Moreover, reports had started coming in of disease outbreaks that could be plausibly—though not decisively—linked to parents refusing to have their children vaccinated. In 2004, and again in 2005, cases of pertussis, or whooping cough, suddenly tripled to more than 25,000. (The trend did not stop there: in California, the hardest-hit state, whooping cough killed 10 infants in 2010, while racking up 9,000 reported cases overall—the highest state tally since 1947. Meanwhile, measles was becoming active again in the United States, with reported infections reaching a twenty-year high in 2014.)

Singer saw a nightmare scenario: one where Autism Speaks was someday blamed for children getting sick and dying because it failed to use its moral authority to set the record straight on what the science said: that vaccines do not cause autism. She was not sure how much longer she could continue to remain publicly silent on the matter. Then, a single email led her to an answer.

It came in late January 2009, as Singer was putting chicken nuggets in the oven for her daughter's dinner. Popping up on her open laptop on the kitchen counter, the email's author, Singer could see, was Lyn Redwood. Still president of the anti-thimerosal organization SafeMinds, Redwood had continued to serve on the federal Interagency Autism Coordinating Committee. But Singer held a seat there too, named to the committee because of her position at Autism Speaks. Each month, she and Redwood sat at the same table, two of the IACC's six "public members," casting their votes on the nation's autism policies.

Redwood's email was distributed to all IACC members, urging

them to insert new language in a draft of research recommendations that had been approved during the prior session. The timing was important. The full committee was due to meet the next day, to finalize the draft, which Autism Speaks had already endorsed publicly. It contained two new research initiatives centered on vaccines, but Redwood was asking that the document add an explicit statement of principle "to leave no stone unturned in these investigations, including the potential role of vaccines and vaccine components." She proposed several other edits to the draft, which would have the net effect of aligning the strategic plan more closely with the priorities of the vaccine activists.

Something shifted in Singer when she saw this. She asked her husband to take over the kitchen duties, then went downstairs to their basement to phone Bob Wright. She told him that she could not bring herself to vote in favor of Redwood's changes. What's more, she could no longer support the two vaccine-focused studies that had already been approved, because she did not believe they were scientifically justified. Wright heard her out sympathetically, but he told her that he and Suzanne still believed that a vote for more vaccine-centered research was in the best interests of all.

It was a warm conversation, at the end of which Wright told Singer that he trusted her judgment, and was counting on her, once more, to "do the right thing."

Late that night, Singer emailed Wright her letter of resignation. In it, she praised Bob and Suzanne, and expressed gratitude for being part of what they had built at Autism Speaks. Together, she wrote, they had "elevated 'autism' to the global vocabulary." However, she explained, "as a matter of personal conscience, I cannot vote in favor of dedicating more funds to vaccine research that has already been undertaken and which I and many others find conclusive."

The news shocked the autism world the next morning, in part because Singer was so identified with Autism Speaks. She had appeared in the organization's videos, helped write its policy positions, and served as its executive vice president. She had been the Wrights' lieutenant, their enforcer, their confidante, and their friend.

This was reflected in Bob Wright's generous response, which arrived before sunrise. "Alison," it began, "I respect your decision. I am surprised but I do want to thank you for all your contributions to AS. We would not have built this organization without your talent and efforts."

That day, when Singer took her seat at the IACC meeting, she was no longer there as a representative of Autism Speaks. She voted to reject Lyn Redwood's proposed language. And when the committee unexpectedly revisited the parts of the strategic plan that already called for further investigations of vaccines, she joined the majority in voting to strike those recommendations.

Autism Speaks's official response to Singer's vote was a great deal less warm than Wright's email to her had been. A statement quoted Wright as saying, "We are angered and disappointed by this last-minute deviation in the painstaking process of approving the Strategic Plan." As a result, the statement announced, "Autism Speaks is withdrawing its support for the Strategic Plan."

Next came a full paragraph devoted to Singer. It said nothing about her years of service. Confirming that she was "no longer . . . a representative" of the group, it made a point of saying that, when she submitted her resignation, "it was accepted." This immediately let loose a wave of speculation by bloggers as to whether Singer had been pushed out the door of AS. Some used the word "fired."

But the drama of Singer's split from Autism Speaks also galvanized a good many autism parents who had not previously spoken up in favor of the stand she had taken. Her supporters included mothers and fathers who had grown weary of seeing the vaccine controversy steal the limelight when there was so much else to talk about. Like Singer, these parents believed that science had answered the questions about MMR and thimerosal and that it was time to move on.

Losing Singer was disruptive for Autism Speaks, and not only because she had contributed so much to its establishment and growth. Her departure was a direct and public challenge to the organization's commitment to serious science. A second blow came a few months after Singer's resignation, when Eric London also quit Autism Speaks. On his way out, London, who sat on the group's scientific advisory board, took a direct shot at that aspect of the organization's work. "After three years of great hopes for Autism Speaks being the optimal vehicle to advance autism science and treatment," he wrote in his letter of resignation, he now felt that the choices made by Autism Speaks "have adversely impacted autism research." These developments had consequences. The energy Autism Speaks would exert to defend its reputation on the science front became a distraction from its runaway success in its other mission: getting the world to care about autism.

With the vaccine debate, Autism Speaks had run afoul of its own well-intentioned determination not to leave anybody out in the cold. Attempting to bridge the chasm between two polarized constituencies, the organization had been forced into rhetorical somersaults, with a policy statement that endorsed the "proven benefits" of vaccination, but at the same time pledged to investigate the possibility that vaccines might be harmful. Phrased so as not to alienate either side, it alienated both.

The Wrights were caught in the middle. They gave copious amounts of their personal time to helping families, only to be rewarded with disparagement and disdain from both factions of the vaccine debate. As the most prominent face of the organization, Bob Wright in particular was often called upon to declare himself for one side or the other. As he continued to try to straddle a middle ground, and to shift attention to other important issues, he and his wife were sometimes nastily maligned, especially by believers in conspiracies, for their "silence."

Meanwhile, Autism Speaks's financial contribution to autism research declined steeply from its peak. In 2009, the group's direct investment in science dropped to just over $11 million, less than half the 2008 figure, which had marked a high point. Over the next few years, that number seesawed but never came close again to the 2008 level. In some years, the total grant amount was not much higher than what CAN and NAAR together had been giving out before the merger with Autism Speaks, with its promised synergy.

Soon after her departure, Alison Singer started the Autism Science Foundation (ASF), also with the mission of funding autism research, though not into the potential dangers of vaccines. That gave the ASF the aura of being a counterweight to Autism Speaks, albeit a small one. More significantly, in terms of money and prestige, an endeavor called the Simons Foundation Autism Research Initiative (SFARI) entered the arena in 2007, awarding an average of $45 million per year in grants, eclipsing Autism Speaks and every other autism nonprofit. SFARI, which maintained a deliberately low profile—no television ads, no walks, no lobbying—was funded through the generosity of a single family, whose sole goal was moving forward the science on autism. Truly above the fray, with no public to answer to, SFARI steered completely clear of the vaccine controversy and was respected all the more for that. Without question still the brand name among autism nonprofits, justifiably credited with advancing the cause in many ways, Autism Speaks was no longer the leader in the area of scientific research—partly as a result of the schisms the vaccine debate had created.

Eventually, Autism Speaks did choose sides. In 2015, it quietly deleted its online policy statement about vaccines and replaced it with one that said: "Over the last two decades, extensive research has asked whether there is any link between childhood vaccinations and autism. The results of this research are clear: Vaccines do not cause autism. We urge that all children be vaccinated." Posted without fanfare, it felt like a footnote.

When Alison Singer resigned from Autism Speaks in the winter of 2009, the family of Michelle Cedillo was still waiting for the vaccine court to rule. Seventeen months had gone by, during which the remaining set of test cases had proceeded. Two of them featured children like Michelle, whose parents were claiming injury by MMR and thimerosal acting in combination. A second series of three cases attempted to document thimerosal acting alone. A third series of cases focusing on MMR acting alone was canceled. The first set of cases had explained the mechanisms well enough.

On February 12, 2009, in a 174-page decision, Special Master Hastings issued a stark ruling against Michelle Cedillo's claim for compensation. Using italics, he declared it "*extremely unlikely* that any of Michelle's disorders were in any way causally connected to her MMR vaccination, or any other vaccination." This decision was not out of any lack of sympathy for her or her parents. Indeed, Hastings praised them as having a "very loving, caring and courageous nature." But in his capacity as a special master, he found no grounds for saying that their daughter's autism was caused by vaccines.

To the contrary, Hastings said, the bulk of the evidence was "overwhelmingly contrary" to the parents' claims, "concerning virtually all aspects of their causation theories." So "one-sided" was the case that, in the end, the decision he had to make was "not a close call."

This was devastating enough to those who believed in the merits of the vaccine theory and those who had spent years promoting it. But then, most unusually, Hastings devoted a sentence or two to scolding those who had helped convince families like the Cedillos to buy into the theory. They had trusted doctors and other specialists whose advice, he wrote, using italics again, had been "*very wrong.*" "The Cedillos have been misled," he said—misled "by physicians who are guilty, in my view, of gross medical misjudgment."

It was as harsh as it was blunt. The vaccine theory had failed once again.

One by one, the rest of the test cases also failed. After that, appeals were filed, but they went nowhere. In the summer of 2010, the last of these appeals—brought by the parents of Michelle Cedillo—was denied. Soon the lawyers who had encouraged the parents to sue lost interest, seeing that there would never be a payday. The science simply wasn't on their side.

The year 2010 was a bad one for Andrew Wakefield as well, probably the worst of his career. He had been waiting since the middle of 2007 for the General Medical Council, the UK's physician licensing authority, to rule on his "fitness to practice." The investigation had turned out to be the longest in the GMC's history, requiring a combined 217 days of hearings, filings, and deliberations, and costing approximately $9 million.

On January 28, 2010, the five-member panel found against him in overwhelming fashion. Three dozen charges against him were upheld. The ruling repeatedly branded Wakefield's behavior with words like "dishonest," "irresponsible," "unethical," and "misleading."

In February, *The Lancet* finally fully retracted his 1998 article. "I feel I was deceived," complained its editor, Richard Horton, who said it was now "utterly clear" that the paper's claims were "utterly false."

In May, at the equivalent of a "sentencing" hearing, the GMC panel found Wakefield not "fit to practice" and ordered him "struck off the medical register." This stripped him of his medical license; he would never again work as a physician in the UK.

These two events had a decisive effect on the conversation about vaccines, especially among the vast majority of the public that did not devote hours of study to understanding the details. It was enough to say that the doctor who said vaccines were dangerous had been stripped of his license, and that the research he published had been retracted, to make it clear to most people that the whole episode had been one long, confusing, acrimonious misadventure.

Like the MMR scare he had created fifteen years earlier, the story of Wakefield's downfall crossed the globe. The news was reported not only in the UK, but on the major American news networks and in newspapers as far away as Australia. Weighing Wakefield's reported transgressions on the day the GMC panel issued its findings, the *New York Daily News* opined, "Hippocrates Would Puke."

After 2010, the mainstream news media virtually abandoned any slant of its own that tended to support the vaccine hypothesis. In most coverage, the word "discredited" became the default adjective. *Time* magazine took this idea to its carnivalesque limit in a 2012 issue listing history's "great science frauds." In the number one position: Andrew Wakefield.

He was now as infamous as autism itself was famous—two outcomes that were undeniably intertwined. And while the controversy Wakefield ignited eventually cooled, it left a third outcome in its aftermath: the lasting push it gave to a new set of voices, rarely heard from before, with a fresh perspective on what it means to have autism. Offended by the vaccine activists' fundamental premise that autism was a kind of sickness and a tragedy, they would turn that proposition on its head, celebrating "being autistic," and declaring "cure" a dirty word.

As they launched autism's latest great debate, they would also claim a unique authority to speak on the matter: they were autistic themselves.

PART X

TODAY

44

FINDING A VOICE

"THIS CAME FOR YOU."

In the summer of 2013, on a Los Angeles soundstage, Alex Plank spoke his first line as a television actor. For months, he had been working as a script consultant for a crime series called *The Bridge.* During that time, he had endeared himself to everybody on the set with his easygoing manner. True, he did keep asking for an on-camera part, but he kept the lobbying lighthearted—as if he knew that this ambition of his would never be fulfilled.

But that summer, an actor was needed on short notice for a walk-on character—"the intern"—who would deliver an envelope to some reporters. After a table read, the producer turned to the casting director and suggested that Alex should get the part, maybe even a line.

Alex's time on-screen ran eleven seconds. On cue, he strode into the frame, approached the series regulars, and stuck out the envelope. He delivered his line cleanly, then pivoted and made to leave the newsroom.

At that moment, one of the other actors ad-libbed a line.

"Thanks, Alex."

The young script consultant was touched that, when the show aired, the ad-lib stayed in.

Plank had just turned twenty-seven when he got the intern role. By that time, he had already achieved a good deal beyond talking his way onto a well-regarded cop show. Before he was out of his teens, he had founded a groundbreaking website and launched an Internet television program. Later, he produced and directed documentary films and traveled all over the country on the speakers' circuit.

And it had all come his way, because, when he was nine, a doctor had diagnosed him with Asperger's.

ALEX GREW UP healthy, loved, and safe, but his childhood outside the home was a social torment. Born in 1986 and raised in Charlottesville, Virginia, he seemed ill at ease with his environment even in infancy. He startled easily. He never relaxed into his mother's arms; it was as if he could not find a comfortable position there. He had no patience for being read to, or for snuggling. There were times when, with his body perfectly rigid, he would scream for hours.

When he was a few years older, more obviously odd behaviors began. Spinning was a major one. Alex twirled and twirled and never seemed to get dizzy. He flapped his hands when he was excited. He covered his ears to shut out sound. At a playgroup his parents put him in, and then in kindergarten, he stood apart from the other children. He appeared to despise group activities, none more so than the game that involved leaping under and over a flapping parachute, which terrified him.

At the same time, though, Alex was hitting all the expected milestones for intellectual development. He started speaking around the normal time, and as a kindergartner, he could count and do some simple addition. When he was later given an intelligence test, the school principal was stunned. She called Alex's mother to tell her he had recorded the highest score in his school's history. Still, because of his social challenges, his parents decided to have him start first grade a year later than usual, so he was seven when he started elementary school.

The price for being socially out of step in elementary school was high. Other kids started noticing that he was different and began making fun of him, or bullying him, or, at best, having nothing to do with him. The painful irony was that, by this point, Alex was beginning to *want* to have friends. The shunning, however, was total; friendships and shared interests divided his class and his neighborhood into groups that Alex was left out of. One year, a single boy accepted the invitation to come celebrate Alex's birthday. He happened to be a boy with his own challenges, as he suffered from severe allergies. Alex's mother baked a peanut-free cake to accommodate this one potential friend. On the morning of the celebration, however, the boy's father phoned to apologize. His son would not be coming after all. Something had "come up."

Through these years, Alex amazed his parents with his emotional resilience. He weathered the birthday snub by going on a hike with his dad and brother and having a great day despite what had happened. When he failed to find companionship among kids, he found ways to connect instead with adults. He grew especially close to his grandparents, who lived near Washington, DC, and often had Alex over as a guest. Both they and his parents took note of some of Alex's marked strengths, including an unusual ability to stay focused where other kids grew restless. They could take him to concerts, for example, and Alex, even as a young boy, proved able to sit perfectly still, his attention focused intently on the sounds the orchestra was making.

Music was important to Alex's family. Both his parents and his younger brother and sister were accomplished musicians. Alex, too, learned to play some piano and clarinet, but his path was atypical. He seemed enamored of playing musical scales over and over, to where he could make them sound beautiful, almost like songs themselves. As for actual songs, he worked them by ear and memorized them, because he couldn't simultaneously read and play music, which required some feat of hand-eye coordination that was simply out of reach for him.

He had the same problem in sports—he could not master the fluidity and finesse required for any game involving a moving ball. In basketball, for example, he seemed unable to figure out the mechanics of timing needed to interact with other players, in throwing or catching passes, or for building a coordinated play toward the basket. Swimming, on the other hand, suited him—even competitive swimming. Here again, his resilience and determination gave him an advantage, as he put in more hours practicing than anyone else on his team. The physical complexities of the butterfly, the backstroke, and the breaststroke were beyond him. But freestyle, he mastered, and it was enough. When he was in the water, facedown and sprinting, his inability to understand jokes on dry land was no drag on his speed toward the other end of the pool.

Academically, he was competent and, sometimes, creative. To mark Black History Month in his first-grade class, the kids were asked to pick a historical figure, draw that person's shape onto a life-size piece of construction paper, and then fill in the details, for mounting on the classroom walls. Alex produced a figure that had no face, and he insisted that it be hung on the wall upside down. This was his depiction of Guion Bluford, the first African American astronaut, floating in space, wearing a helmet, seen from behind. That year, he had an understanding teacher.

Other years, teachers found him exasperating. Alex lacked tact and could not stop himself from declaring teachers wrong on this or that point when he was sure he was right. They did not find this trait endearing. One teacher gave him a time-out for challenging her, even though he was correct on the point. Others had a tendency to see most of his social problems at school as avoidable if he would only make more of an effort to be "normal." A physical-education teacher, genuinely troubled at seeing Alex bullied so often, suggested to his mother, Mary, that she show Alex how to hold his mouth and lips differently, because the way he did it currently was the cause of ridicule. Another time, the school principal sat Alex down with seven boys who had been picking on him, and apparently aiming for some conflict resolution, she went around the circle asking each child to discuss his grievances. While Alex listened, the seven boys took turns complaining to the principal about how weird and annoying he was.

This infuriated Alex's parents and led to a change of schools. But at some level, they recognized that both the teachers and the kids were responding to aspects of Alex's personality that were, in fact, socially disruptive. His approach to making friends was awkward: he would simply walk up to people and ask to be friends. His correcting of teachers reflected, his mother would say, an inability to "see other people's discomfort." Moreover, when asked a question, he was unable to see where the teacher was leading, as other kids might, because he seemed to lack any insight into another person's thought process. His difficulty making eye contact, meanwhile, degraded the quality of the give-and-take he could achieve with whomever he was trying to engage in conversation.

None of these social ineptitudes—any more than his physical clumsiness—were Alex's fault. They did not arise because he was not trying hard enough to be more "normal." In truth, he would have had no idea how to do that. Neither did they stem from his parents' failure to make Alex "measure up"—something that was hinted at from time to time by school authorities. But they were liabilities that detracted from his obvious strengths: his high intelligence, his creativity, his resilience, and his determination.

By the third grade, Alex's parents had brought him to several specialists for evaluation. Once, this produced a diagnosis of a communication disorder. Another time, his parents were told he had ADHD—attention deficit hyperactivity disorder. Obsessive-compulsive disorder was also diagnosed. To his mother and father, none of these captured what it was that made Alex different. Not one explained why his young life was such a social obstacle course. If "it" had a name, they still did not know what it was.

The first time they heard the term *Asperger's syndrome* was from a psychiatrist in Charlottesville in 1995. They were reluctant to see their son placed too neatly "in a box," as Mary thought of it. At the same time, they had to admit that the diagnosis, which had just appeared in the *DSM* the year before, captured Alex's mix of behaviors quite well.

The weight of the word "diagnosis" hit the nine-year-old Alex hard, as he had a child's sense of its meaning. To him, it said "defective." It felt shameful.

It also made him feel further isolated. This was a feeling his parents also experienced when the diagnosis came in. ADHD and OCD were at least familiar; they were conditions that were reported about on television and in magazine stories. But this diagnosis was different. *Asperger's* had such a mysterious ring to it, so foreign and yet simultaneously so particular. They knew of no other children with the label. There were no books about it in the library. In the academic literature, most of the studies treated the condition as preciously exotic or hopelessly arcane, reports with titles like "Asperger's Syndrome: A Report of Two Cases from Malaysia," or "Possible Asperger's Syndrome in a Mentally Handicapped Transvestite Offender," or "Corticocallosal Anomalies in Asperger's Syndrome."

A mother in Delaware named Barbara Kirby went through the same thing when her son received the diagnosis in 1993. Her pediatrician didn't know anything about Asperger's, and her local autism group, when she inquired, had only "heard of it" and did not have any further information. She even called doctors at local hospitals, all of whom said they had never seen a case. In frustration, Kirby went online in the hopes of connecting with anyone who might have experience with Asperger's. In late 1995, she set up the first online discussion group devoted to the subject, which she named OASIS. Its plain-speaking approach to the topic and its supportive atmosphere filled a previously invisible need. Traffic climbed quickly, as five thousand families signed up as members. By 2001, visits to the site had hit 1 million. That year, Kirby described OASIS as "the central meeting place for families whose children were diagnosed with Asperger Syndrome."

That remained true for some years. But in 2004, an Asperger's site appeared that broke new ground in cyberspace by taking off as a gathering place for people who had—or thought they had—the syndrome. So successful and visible was the startup that it helped effect a dramatic change in the way Asperger's—and autism in general—were talked about and perceived. The site was the work of a teenager: the seventeen-year-old Alex Plank, who came up with a clever name for his new media venture: Wrong Planet—also known as wrongplanet.net.

He built it for one reason: he wanted company.

By his late teens, Alex had come to terms with his diagnosis. He was finally in a high school that was more accommodating to his differences, and he was happier overall. When he landed a part in the school production of *West Side Story,* he found that he loved this sort of structured collaboration, as well as the spotlight. Typically, for some people with Asperger's, he was also drawn to computers. He spent hours teaching himself to program and was an avid contributor to

Wikipedia as one of their volunteer fact-checkers. He made corrections to thousands of its entries.

But none of these activities addressed his sense that he was the only person he knew with Asperger's syndrome. He had hoped that going online would help him find others like himself, with whom he could interact and swap perspectives of what it meant to live life with the Asperger's label. He found plenty of sites devoted to Asperger's filled with the parent perspective, but he wasn't finding other people with Asperger's anywhere.

Then he had his big idea. During the early summer of 2004, in the midst of one of his periodic stays with his grandparents near Washington, he hit on the idea of a website that would pull other people with Asperger's toward one another. For a month, he biked to the local library, because there was no Internet at his grandparents' house, and set up the basic infrastructure for Wrong Planet using his budding programming skills. The site went live in July 2004, billing itself as "a web community designed for individuals with Asperger's Syndrome."

By July 20, a little over a month later, it already had 328 members. By November, it had 694. The following March, it passed 1,000. And by January 2007, 8,156 people had joined. As its forums filled with thousands and then hundreds of thousands of postings—on topics ranging from school to bullying to dating to computers—the site was discovered by the *Washington Post,* which ran a profile on Alex in 2005. TV appearances on *Good Morning America* and Fox News would follow the next year. Alex was initially overwhelmed by how quickly things were moving. He had never expected Wrong Planet to be much more than a small support group. But the *Post* was crediting him with "creating an Asperger's community," one with its own personality—and personalities. Cliques formed at Wrong Planet. Feuds were fought. Romantic relationships were sparked. Some marriages were recorded. That in itself was remarkable, since so many of the consistent themes in its forum pages came in postings that reflected their writers' despair over ever having a romantic relationship.

In 2005, pondering why Wrong Planet proved so appealing to its audience so quickly, Alex explained to the *Post* that "chatting online allows people [with Asperger's] not to be worried" by others' judgment of their speech or mannerisms. The social pressure was off.

But something even more fundamental was in play, which related to having Asperger's: online, eye contact didn't matter. Or any of the other ephemeral aspects of nonverbal speech—the eyebrow raises, the subtle changes in intonation that were part of conversation in the real world and that had always caused trouble for Alex and his community. Pure communication by text, however—the idiom of the Internet circa 2005—liberated Wrong Planet's users from that burden. Overall, for anyone who struggled with facial and vocal cues, the Internet was an equalizer, because in a chat room, no one knew you had Asperger's.

Alex Plank, then, facilitated the emergence of a new set of voices in the global conversation about autism—and just at the time when that conversation was getting the attention of a much wider public. After 2000 or so, because of the vaccine scare, curiosity about autism continued to grow. To the news media, the phenomenon of individuals who could talk about autism from firsthand experience was fodder for endless reportage. *Wired* magazine's Steve Silberman wrote a celebrated article, "The Geek Syndrome," featuring a number of such people, while suggesting they made up a significant percentage of the tech industry population in Silicon Valley. A British author, Mark Haddon, published a bestselling novel, *The Curious Incident of the Dog in the Night-Time,* whose narrator was a fifteen-year-old boy with all the hallmarks of Asperger's syndrome. The book proved so popular it was eventually made into an award-winning play running on Broadway and London's West End.

Alex was part of this growing recognition of Asperger's. He continued running Wrong Planet while attending George Mason University from 2005 to 2009. During those years, he was getting invitations to talk shows and conferences. After graduating, he set out to make documentaries, such as the short film *autism reality,* which found audiences at autism gatherings, at general-interest film festivals, and on YouTube. Eventually, it was Alex's growing celebrity as a first-person narrator of the Asperger's "experience" that led to his being hired to work as a script consultant. The protagonist of *The Bridge* was a brilliant police detective with autistic traits. Alex was there to make sure the writers got autism "right." The actress playing the detective, Diane Kruger, publicly credited Alex with keeping her honest in her portrayal of the condition.

Before that, however, Alex had already acquired a video platform of his own called *Autism Talk TV,* a series of videos he hosted with two friends who also identified as being "on the spectrum." Produced over multiple years, and appearing on the websites of both Wrong Planet and Autism Speaks, the videos had a wry, self-aware, and "Aspergian" sensibility to them. There were a lot of insider jokes about the highlights and pitfalls of life lived with Asperger's, and a good deal of advice for navigating a world where, despite rising awareness, the hosts and their presumed audience were still the odd people out. One episode was called "How to Flirt and Get a Date," in which, at the beginning, the presenter announced, with a twinkle in her eye, "In this episode, Alex learns to flirt, and Alex will be flirting with a *real girl.*"

These videos received tens of thousands of clicks, presumably by many of the people they were aimed at. It was their lives Alex's videos were talking about. Their stories, being told by one of their own. Suddenly, people "on the spectrum" were speaking for themselves, and in a way that could not be ignored. That changed everything.

Once, there was only one famous person known to be capable of talking about autism from the inside: Temple Grandin. When she was first "discovered" in the 1980s, she startled and fascinated the activist autism community, which was then made up almost entirely of parents, along with a few researchers and educators. She was cherished and regarded as an anomaly for her ability to converse in detail about how the world might be experienced by their own children, the overwhelming majority of whom could never hold such a conversation.

Suddenly, there were thousands of people like Temple Grandin, all joining in that conversation, congregating at Wrong Planet and other sites, as well as at Asperger's meet-ups and conferences. Some who took part, however, had never actually been given an Asperger's diagnosis. Instead, some had been labeled, at some point, as "HFA," which stood for "high-functioning autism." This term, never a *DSM* diagnosis but popular with clinicians, pre-dated the popularization of Asperger's and was epitomized by Temple Grandin, who describes herself that way on her own website. "High-functioning" was used for individuals who had definite autistic traits but who were also at least average, and often above average, in verbal skills and IQ scores. This made HFA sound a lot like Asperger's, and in fact, one of autism's most intense debates at one time focused on whether any meaningful difference existed between HFA and Asperger's.

For many, discovering they had Asperger's was like being handed the missing piece that completed the puzzle of their own lives. Their families saw it that way too. Lorna Wing spoke of husbands who showed up at her clinic to be evaluated for Asperger's, bringing along their wives, who had just as much of a stake in the outcome. "Both have felt happier and closer to each other once they know the reasons for their past problems," Wing wrote.

As Wrong Planet's subscriber base surged, an identity constructed around Asperger's was already a well-established cultural phenomenon—from its expression in the arenas of policy and politics to Hollywood taking chances on shows with "Aspergian" characters to the online swag shops selling coffee mugs, hairbands, curtains, tote bags, and T-shirts with an "Aspie Pride" theme to them. One popular T-shirt read: SOCIALLY AWKWARD, INTELLECTUALLY ADVANCED.

"Surely everyone is a little bit autistic on occasion?" Uta Frith asked. "I too would sometimes like to claim a dash of autism for myself." Indeed, it became popular to see Asperger's as sometimes shading so close to "normal" that the distinction seemed at risk of losing much of its importance. This idea had all kinds of appeal. Potentially, anyone could dip a toe into spectrum waters from time to time: anyone who never got the jokes everyone else found funny; anyone who got ribbed for being a stickler for the rules; or anyone who just had a difficult time making and keeping friends. There was respite, and some satisfaction, in being able to tie these occasional traits to a *DSM*-sanctioned diagnosis.

This was even more true as some "Aspies" began to claim a certain superiority for themselves, turning the disability prototype upside down. Temple Grandin liked to say that the first stone spear "was probably invented by an Aspie who chipped away at rocks while the other people socialized." She was far from the only person reporting from the spectrum who made the case for a touch of autism being a good thing.

In this view, the autistic brain was uniquely capable of original thought and had the perseverance needed to develop world-changing ideas. It became something of a parlor game for people identifying as Aspies to compose lists of historical figures whose contributions to knowledge and culture they credited to the supposed presence of autism. Some of the more illustrious names included Albert Einstein, Isaac Newton, Emily Dickinson, Abraham Lincoln, Michelangelo, Mozart, and Van Gogh. An entire book, Norm Ledgin's *Diagnosing Jefferson,* which had a foreword by Temple Grandin, was devoted to attempting to prove that America's third president had Asperger's syndrome, and that this was "the only explanation for the full range of Jefferson's idiosyncrasies."

"Now it's almost cool to have Asperger's," Tom Hibben, the father of a boy with Asperger's, would tell *Slate.* On his own blog, called *Adventures in Aspergers,* Hibben wrote about TV sitcoms such as *Parenthood* and *The Big Bang Theory,* whose casts had characters with autistic traits and were "showing the masses that these kind[s] of people are not only productive members of society but they are awesome!" As early as 2001, *Wired* was inviting readers to "Take the AQ Test," offering a fifty-item questionnaire, based on one used by leading researcher Simon Baron-Cohen, "as a measure of the extent of autistic traits in adults." Item 13 read: "I would rather go to a library than a party." *Wired* included the necessary warning that "the test is not the means for making a diagnosis."

In fact, amateur diagnosis of autism became something of a trend. The writer Nora Ephron was quoted posthumously in *New York* magazine in 2012 telling a friend in an email, "I notice that at least three times a week I am told (or I tell someone) that some man or other is on the spectrum." The article's author, Benjamin Wallace, suggested Asperger's syndrome—which he believed to represent a truly disabling set of behaviors in some people—was being trivialized into "common slang, a conceptual gadget for processing the modern world." As

Wallace argued, standards of stringency in diagnosis seemed to be slipping in how the label was becoming "shorthand for the jerky husband, the socially inept plutocrat, the tactless boss, the child prodigy with no friends, the remorseless criminal."

Wrong Planet, meanwhile, hosted a thread devoted to self-diagnosis, where members explained why they were declaring themselves, without a professional evaluation, to "have Asperger's." *New York*'s Wallace took a skeptical view of this trend in the 2000s. "The self-diagnosis boom," he wrote, "has been accompanied by self-diagnoses that can be bracing in their un-persuasiveness."

Put another way, not everyone wearing the Asperger's label appeared to be held back in life by an undue dose of social clumsiness. It would be easy for a general audience to watch Alex Plank, articulate, witty, and relaxed, discussing disability on *Good Morning America,* then come away asking themselves, "What disability?" In that blur where autistic meets "normal," Plank would impress a lot of people as fitting the "normal" category, where, if anything, his string of successes as an Internet entrepreneur, video host, and motivational speaker would suggest he possessed, on the contrary, rather well-developed social skills.

Had Alex been born just one generation earlier, the chances of his success story being associated with the word "autism" would have been virtually nil. Indeed, it is hard to imagine that a clinician examining someone as talkative, innovative, and driven as Alex in 1975 would even have entertained a diagnosis of autism. At that time, the diagnosis was reserved for people facing much greater challenges than Alex or others of his generation who would be given the Asperger's label. Put another way, before the spectrum, saying that Alex had autism might have seemed a bit like saying that a person who is color blind and a person who cannot see at all should both be described as "visually impaired." While technically true, it would not have been entirely helpful to group them together.

But Alex was born in the era of the spectrum. And, even though he was high-functioning, his struggles were real. That combination empowered him to declare, with a mixture of pride and defiance, and with affirmation from many, "I have autism." Those who saw no evidence of impairment in Alex's performances in front of big audiences were likely not aware of what his childhood was like, or of how much his hit-the-jackpot success with Wrong Planet had boosted his self-confidence. His social savoir faire as an adult was the result of assiduous effort and practice he put in during his teen years, when he actively studied the behaviors of other people—their expressions, their tones of voice in given situations—and then memorized them, note by note, like those songs he learned to play on the piano as a kid. In his 2009 documentary, *autism reality,* the twenty-three-year-old Alex appears behind the wheel of a car (he had only just learned to drive) and explains how hard he has to work every moment of every day to "pass" for "normal."

"I don't think anyone realizes how much I struggle on a day-to-day basis just with normal social situations," he says, lifting his hands from the steering wheel momentarily to mark "normal" with air quotes. "It takes a great expenditure of mental energy."

ANOTHER PROMINENT ASPIE, Michael John Carley, met his social challenges so successfully that his disability also appeared almost invisible. In fact, he thought of himself as different, rather than disabled. Like Alex, he became known for establishing a place where people with Asperger's could congregate, but his was mainly offline. In 2003, Carley founded an organization called GRASP—the Global and Regional Asperger Syndrome Partnership—which sponsored in-person support groups for adults with Asperger's. At this time, many adults were being newly diagnosed, and Carley was one of them. He was thirty-six in 2000 when his young son was diagnosed, and then, days later, he was told that he too qualified for a diagnosis.

Carley was a gifted writer, a produced playwright, and a competent guitarist who sometimes performed in clubs, and he had also worked for a series of nonprofits and participated in aid projects overseas. But when he got the label, it felt right to him, and he embraced it. "I'd always suspected," he told radio interviewer Terry Gross in 2004, "that I really didn't have the sense of shared experience with other people that I had wanted and yearned for in my life." He also said that he was not good at small talk, and was too given to telling people what he really thought.

It was Carley's recognition that others with Asperger's struggled more than he did that inspired him to start an organization to represent their interests. GRASP soon grew to include thirty chapters around the United States. As its leader, Carley devoted himself especially to fighting back against stigmatization, and to standing by people when their Aspergian tendencies got them in trouble. He befriended the notorious subway hijacker Darius McCollum, a man who was arrested repeatedly for faking his way into the driver's cabs of New York City subway trains and then hauling the trains across New York's boroughs with unwitting passengers on board. Truly an expert on the inner workings of the New York subways—their routes, regulations, vehicle numbers, schedules, and signals, which he had studied obsessively since he was a young boy—McCollum never hurt anyone. Whenever he hijacked a train, it still made its scheduled stops. He took off with a few buses here and there too. By 2013, when he was forty-nine, he had been arrested twenty-nine times and spent nearly a third of his life in jail. Treated relatively leniently at first, he began getting tougher sentences in later years. Judges weren't buying his new defense: that he had Asperger's syndrome, and that his compulsive train thievery grew out of an Aspergian obsession that was nearly impossible for him to resist.

During one of his few interludes of freedom, McCollum had dropped in once or twice at support-group meetings at the Manhattan chapter of GRASP. That was where he and Carley got to know each other. When, inevitably, McCollum was rearrested, Carley began visiting him in jail on Rikers Island. As they sat on steel benches on opposite sides of a low wall, Carley mixed solace, understanding, and bear hugs with a kind of older-brother scolding. *What the fuck did you do this time?*—was Carley's greeting on one of these visits. He repeatedly warned McCollum that he needed to learn to put distance between himself and the temptation that was ruining his life.

On the outside, however, Carley did everything he could to portray the subway obsessive as a victim of his own brain wiring. "We haven't created anything for him to go to," Carley told the *Huffington Post.* "People take one look at him, at his demeanor and his smarts, and they think he should know better. They don't understand because the disorder isn't really understood in this context."

In December 2012, Carley acted quickly when a twenty-year-old named Adam Lanza carried out a massacre by gunfire in an elementary school in Newtown, Connecticut. Within hours, news media outlets were reporting that Lanza, who had killed himself, had a diagnosis of Asperger's. Alarm spread in the autism community; they feared a renewed narrative that saw people on the spectrum as a risk to public safety. On this occasion, the entire autism community set aside its internal squabbles as one group after another issued statements explaining why the facts did not sustain a connection between Asperger's and violence against others.

Carley's contribution stood out, as his often did, for its elegance and power. "We ask that everyone please steer away from getting too caught up in the spectrum angle," he said in a statement released within hours of the shootings. "Let us focus instead on mourning; lamenting through grief that such a terrible and tragic event befell us all on this awful, awful day."

Carley's diagnosis was Asperger's. But he could hit an emotional note better than most people. In that way, he was like Alex Plank and so many other people who acquired the Asperger's label in the 1990s and 2000s—people who exuded competence and a fair degree of confidence as well. Even if he and Plank were constantly working to compensate for social deficits, their success and eloquence only showed that the effort was paying off. By being able to "pass" so often for "normal"—and more important, by exhibiting pride in their difference at the same time—they were in fact "normalizing" autism in the popular imagination. Their ability to get along in the real world demystified and destigmatized the concept.

But their presence in the autism conversation also upset what had been one of its ongoing assumptions. This was the solid consensus among experts, dating back to the 1960s, that most people with autism were also intellectually disabled. This was a data-based finding, reported in several studies, which found that somewhere between 70 and 80 percent of all people diagnosed with autism also fell into the "below average" range for intelligence.

But then, that was before there was an autism spectrum, back when definitions were different. By 2010, the scale had tipped dramatically in the opposite direction. That year, the CDC reported that almost half of the diagnosed autism population hit the upper ranges for intelligence. This "demographic shift," driven by a combination of the autism spectrum's greater inclusiveness, which also helped push prevalence rates higher, would have profound social consequences. This recognition of more so-called high-functioning people certainly altered the kinds of services society was called upon to provide for them, which became a new arena for activism. But when the shift took place, something even more radical occurred, which changed the politics of autism for good.

It was the birth of a new philosophy called "neurodiversity," which was welcomed by many in the autism community. But at the same time, some autism parents in that community discovered a new adversary in the arena: people with autism themselves.

45

NEURODIVERSITY

During the second week of December 2007, word spread through certain Internet sites of a new ad campaign, already hitting billboards and soon to appear in the pages of *Newsweek* and *New York* magazine. The content, in the view of many, was outrageous, although the ads comprised nothing but words on a page. But those who saw images of the ads, usually as an attachment forwarded by an upset friend or acquaintance, instantly grasped what they referred to. A ransom note. The kind kidnappers type out on beat-up, untraceable old typewriters. One read:

> We have your son.
> We will make sure he will
> not be able to care for
> himself or interact socially
> as long as he lives.
> This is only the beginning.
> Autism

It was the launch date of New York University Child Study Center's long-planned "Ransom Notes" campaign. An ad agency had a whole series of other make-believe ransom letters ready to go, including one penned in block letters: **WE HAVE YOUR SON. WE ARE DESTROYING HIS ABILITY FOR SOCIAL INTERACTION.** This note was signed: **ASPERGER'S SYNDROME.**

Months in its design, the ransom notes campaign was intended, according to one of the ad men, to act as "a wake-up call to families, educators and healthcare professionals, and spark dialogue so children can get the help they need." The mock notes were being rolled out first in New York City, on eleven billboards and two hundred kiosks. After that, the campaign would be expanding to hit newspapers in a total of five major markets, over a period lasting at least sixteen weeks. The initial launch, according to an NYU press release, was "expected to net over 700 million impressions," which sounded like a huge number.

Eighteen days after it was announced, however, the campaign was dead.

It had run afoul of the neurodiversity movement. And the movement had won.

THE BEGINNINGS OF the neurodiversity movement are usually traced to the day in July 1993, when a thirty-one-year-old man named Jim Sinclair stood in front of an audience of parents at an autism conference in Toronto and identified himself as a person with autism. Then he delivered a manifesto. He proclaimed that for people like him, autism parents were part of the problem. For too long, he argued, fathers and mothers had made the mistake of believing that their children—by having autism—had been dealt some terrible blow by fate. But this was not true, Sinclair insisted. "Don't mourn for us," he said, because grief was not called for and never had been.

Later, Sinclair published an online essay based on the talk, in which he fleshed out his critique of the parent advocacy movement. The thrust of his argument was this: rather than always making life better for their children, they had insulted their children's humanity and undermined their dignity.

"When parents say, 'I wish my child did not have autism,'" Sinclair wrote, "what they're really saying is, 'I wish the autistic child I have did not exist.'"

It was jarringly reminiscent of Bruno Bettelheim's discredited claim from the 1960s that mothers harbored a secret wish "that it would be much better if the child wouldn't live," thus causing autism in their children. In 1993, in a distant echo of mother blaming, Sinclair was attributing a parallel impulse to parents coping with autism in their kids.

"Read that again," Sinclair continued. "This is what we hear when you mourn over our existence. This is what we hear when you pray for a cure."

Sinclair was not a father. He had been driving himself to autism conferences for several years, speaking at many. But he had never delivered a message like this one, to parents whose children were, in many cases, disabled in the extreme. To Sinclair, that was beside the point.

"You try to relate to your autistic child," he said, "and the child doesn't respond . . . there's no getting through. That's the hardest thing to deal with, isn't it?

"The only thing is, it isn't true."

He chided the parents for not trying hard enough to relate to their autistic children. "It takes more work to communicate with someone whose native language isn't the same as yours," he said.

As for the parents' feelings of loss over the future their children would never have, Sinclair suggested that "the best place to address these issues is not in organizations devoted to autism, but in parental bereavement counseling and support groups."

"Go do whatever grieving you have to do," he urged, but don't do it in front of the autistic child. Then, he counseled, "start learning to let go."

In the history of the neurodiversity movement, Sinclair's essay became known as the "Don't Mourn for Us" statement.

For forty years, from the 1960s onward, the work of autism advocacy had been a mission carried out almost entirely by mothers and fathers dedicated to making the world better for their kids. Theirs were the voices heard, speaking for people who could not speak for themselves. On behalf of their children, they had changed the world.

But Sinclair, speaking in 1993, was largely correct that the image of autism projected by the parents' movement was often layered with sorrow, and rested on the premise that autism represented something gone wrong in the life of a child. This did not mean parents were lacking love for their children. Their irrefutable dedication to making their kids' lives better proved the opposite. Mothers and fathers celebrated their children's triumphs and laughed along with their quirks.

But in the three decades of activism before 1993, and certainly through the years following it, the predominant opinion was, very simply, that autism was a bad thing. The activist rhetoric so often portrayed the condition as an alien invader, a parasite, an epidemic, an enemy. This sentiment was captured precisely in the description of autism given to *Newsweek* by Portia Iversen, one of the parent-founders of Cure Autism Now. "It's like 'The Village of the Damned,'" Iversen said. "It's as if someone has stolen into your house during the night and left your child's bewildered body behind."

Organizations had been picking names like Defeat Autism Now!, and books had titles like *Targeting Autism*. The greatest legislative triumph ever achieved by parent advocacy was called the Combating Autism Act, and the vaccine activists had seen autism as a criminally inflicted injury. They wanted the damage reversed and heads to roll. The largest and most prominent advocacy organization in autism in the early 2000s, Autism Speaks, had launched with a website that declared: "This disease has taken our children away. It's time to take them back."

It was exactly such thinking that Jim Sinclair and others attempted to refute by expounding on a philosophy they called neurodiversity. Its central tenet was that having autism—or "being autistic," the phrase preferred by its adherents—was but one more way of being human. Framed in such a way, the idea sounded wholesome and wholly uncontentious. But its logical next step was a far more controversial assertion: Since being human required no cure, autism didn't need a cure either. People with autism didn't need to be rescued from their autism. And no effort should be put forth to make autism disappear.

The coinage "neurodiversity" is credited to an Australian sociologist, Judy Singer, who was on the spectrum herself, and who used the term in an honors thesis sometime in the 1990s. It took many years before the word was heard by a broader audience. Jim Sinclair, who was still talking about it, had set up an online organization for discussion of the idea about a year after his Toronto speech. The site, called Autism Network International (ANI), did not do much to popularize the neurodiversity point of view, perhaps because its small group of regulars tended to come across as hostile to site visitors who did not identify as autistic. There was not much love at ANI for "neurotypicals"—the term the neurodiversity camp used for anybody who did not have autism.

In 1998, an autistic woman known as Muskie had some fun with this when she set up a mock website for a fake organization she called the Institute for the Study of the Neurologically Typical. Muskie had her ISNT "experts" present the facts behind the disorder she referred to as "Neurotypical Syndrome."

> **WHAT IS NT?** Neurotypical Syndrome is a neurobiological disorder characterized by preoccupation with social concerns, delusions of superiority, and obsession with conformity.
>
> **HOW COMMON IS IT?** Tragically, as many as 9625 out of every 10,000 individuals may be neurotypical.
>
> **ARE THERE ANY TREATMENTS FOR NT?** There is no known cure for neurotypical syndrome.

Neurodiversity made a fleeting appearance in the mainstream media in 1998, when *The Atlantic*'s Harvey Blume made the provocative suggestion that, for the coming Information Age, "neurodiversity may be every bit as crucial for the human race as biodiversity is for life in general."

Echoes of the neurodiversity perspective were heard again in a court proceeding in Canada a few years later, when families who had been denied funding for ABA treatment brought suit against the government of British Columbia. Eventually, in 2004, the Supreme Court of Canada agreed to hear the case. That was when a woman with autism named Michelle Dawson filed an "intervener's factum" (similar to an amicus brief in the United States), in which she rejected the idea "that without 'effective treatment,' autistics are doomed"—the premise she believed both sides in the case were guilty of taking for granted. Dawson, who had been given an autism diagnosis as an adult and worked as an autism researcher, objected that "not one Canadian autistic was either heard or consulted" in the case, and declared the entire proceeding "gravely flawed in the gross stereotyping of and the denial of the basic humanity of autistic individuals." Although it is impossible to say to what degree Dawson's statement influenced the judges, the court ultimately ruled against the parents.

But those were pinprick impressions. By 2006, with fear spreading, autism had become a public concern, and Autism Speaks was in its second year of promoting awareness of the condition as a national emergency. Even so, almost no one in the general public, or even in most autism circles, had ever heard of neurodiversity. This was frustrating, and even alarming, to those who saw autism not as an emergency, but as central to their identities—and at the core of who they were as humans.

Then one of them, a teenager at the University of Maryland in Baltimore, decided to change the story line.

ARI NE'EMAN WAS five years old when "Don't Mourn for Us" was composed. Fourteen years later, as a college sophomore from New Jersey, he founded the Autistic Self-Advocacy Network (ASAN). Its motto, borrowed from disability-rights campaigns of the 1990s, was "Nothing About Us, Without Us." ASAN's mission—ensuring that the voices of autistic people were heard in policy debates and the halls of power—was another iteration of the neurodiversity movement. It was a large ambition for a campaign with no paid staff that was run out of a dorm room.

Ne'eman, who, even in college, was usually seen wearing a necktie and lugging around a briefcase, was diagnosed with Asperger's at the age of twelve. He was sent for a while to a special school, which he disliked. He was reticent with reporters who asked about his past beyond that. In Troy, New York, in 2013, he gave a sympathetic newspaper reporter a typically vague answer to the question: "My experience growing up was similar to most autistic people," he said. "We struggle socially. I had very strong interests in particular topics." The reporter seemed to take the cue. That was all Ne'eman wanted to say about the subject.

Ne'eman was not at all bashful, however, in his choice of words when he began speaking out against those he believed were attacking him. As a man who prized his autistic identity, he despised the messaging of Autism Speaks, whose influence was unrivaled and whose puzzle-piece logo was everywhere he looked. After founding ASAN in 2006, Ne'eman began writing and speaking against the group's "continued dehumanizing advertising," accusing it of "encouraging a lesser value for autistic life." In 2007, after the attempted murder of an autistic girl by her own mother, Ne'eman went so far as to charge that Autism Speaks was "morally complicit" in the crime. He linked the murder attempt to a recently released Autism Speaks video in which Alison Singer confessed to having days when she considered driving herself and her daughter off a bridge. Ne'eman made the "morally complicit" comment in a prepared statement before the federal Interagency Autism Coordinating Committee, on which Singer sat. The IACC censored those words from its online transcript of the session.

Ne'eman also opposed many of the avenues of scientific investigation Autism Speaks endorsed and funded. On one hand, he was not opposed to research "on issues related to the quality of life of autistic people." He had nothing against epidemiological studies or the development of diagnostic tools that helped identify populations who should be counted as belonging on the spectrum. He also favored research on more innovative assistive technology for people whose autistic traits caused them difficulty functioning, such as tools to help the non-speaking to communicate. But Ne'eman adamantly opposed further development of any methodologies that, in his view, forced people to stifle their autistic personalities in order to seem more "normal." This included some drug development, and it definitely included Lovaas-style ABA. "To pursue normalization" by use of such methods, Ne'eman wrote, "forces us into a struggle against ourselves." Above all, Ne'eman, and the neurodiversity movement as a whole, rejected any scientific endeavor whose ultimate target was finding a "cure" for autism.

But by 2007, a search for a cure was already the well-established thrust of much of the research already under way. In labs from New York's Mount Sinai Hospital and Columbia University to the National Institutes of Health outside Washington and the Mind Institute in Davis, California, autism research was now so hot that it seemed virtually any study in any field improved its chances for funding by having the word "autism" appear in the grant proposal. The word "cure" was not mentioned, but then, it did not have to be.

Some fascinating discoveries and some amazing developments had been made in the decade or so since parent pressure had kick-started the process. Scientists had uncovered all kinds of ways in which people with autism were organically distinctive. They had found that actual brain size in kids with autism is 20 percent larger than in other children; that dopamine, the brain chemical that spikes in response to pleasure, does not flow as usual in autistic brains in response to hearing a human voice; and that when an autistic person is asked to perform a visual task with an emotional component, such as remembering a face, blood flow to the front and rear parts of the brain appears to be out of sync. Eye-tracking technology was developed that could identify babies as young as two months old who were at risk of developing autism. And a discovery was made about the sleep of autistic children: rapid eye movement—which tends to coincide with dreaming—occurs one-third less often than in other kids. It was also established that children with autism get an hour less sleep per night than other children. It was found that older fathers have an increased chance of having a child with autism, and that mothers who take folic acid before becoming pregnant show a 40 percent reduced risk of having a child with autism. Prenatal studies were also launched based on the finding that the risk of autism was higher when mothers fell ill during the first trimester of pregnancy.

Leads came from some unexpected areas, one of which involved fevers. Parents had been reporting a "fever effect" since at least the 1980s, where their kids' autistic symptoms improved dramatically when they were experiencing high fevers. This became the starting point for several fever studies. Meanwhile, certain substances were found to mitigate symptoms. Melatonin helped some children sleep better. Risperidone and other antipsychotics helped reduce repetitive and hyperactive behaviors in some children.

As with behaviorism, the biomedical researchers were also learning by studying nonhumans. At the National Institutes of Health, the DNA of mice was being modified by researcher Jacqueline Crawley to produce new rodents exhibiting a theoretical "mouse version" of autism. The result was mice who were excessively antisocial, or obsessively given to repetitive self-grooming. Far from perfect analogies for the human organism, these "transgenic" mice did, however, allow for experiments involving injections of chemicals. The neural wiring of the fruit fly also yielded new insights when researchers found that these insects, when faced with overwhelmingly intense odors, have the ability to dial back their sensitivity—almost tuning the odor out—something some people with autism seem unable to do in the face of loud noises, bright lights, or tactile experiences that they find unpleasant.

As ingenious and wide-ranging as these findings and investigations were, nearly all of them were motivated by the same end goal—and the one that troubled the neurodiversity movement: preventing autism before it happened, or making it go away if it did.

That was why, in Ne'eman's opinion, nothing was more terrifying than the search under way to unravel autism's complex genetic underpinnings. Enormous effort was being made to identify "risk" genes, which would become targets for future treatment if, as expected, the gene research ultimately pointed to multiple paths to autism, or to many different *autisms.* But Ne'eman dreaded the day any of those became so clearly marked that a genetic test for autism would result from it. Then, wrote Ne'eman, "the most likely form of prevention would be that of eugenic abortion." He pointed out that this was already happening with Down syndrome, where a prenatal test had been available since the 1980s, after which 92 percent of pregnancies that tested positive for the chromosomal abnormality responsible for Down's were being terminated across a range of countries, including the United States, the UK, New Zealand, France, and Singapore. "Most of us on the autism spectrum do not wake up in the morning," he wrote, "and wish that we had never been born."

That was not much different from what Temple Grandin had said to Oliver Sacks in *The New Yorker* years earlier. "If I could snap my fingers and be nonautistic, I would not," she said in that 1993 interview. "Autism is part of what I am." But Grandin had always charmed the audience of autism parents, while Ne'eman, like Sinclair before him, turned a large part of that audience off. For many mothers and fathers, it was galling to be lectured to by perfectly verbal, automobile-driving, college-attending grown-ups whose supposed autism-produced disability appeared minuscule in comparison to what their own kids were facing.

Of course, no parent took issue with the part of Ne'eman's argument that said that people on the spectrum were owed respect, dignity, safety, and as much say over their own lives as possible—values that society had embraced, at least in theory, when it shut down the mental institutions a quarter of a century earlier. But it was neurodiversity's more radical proposition—that a child with severe autism was not, in some fashion, sick—that was not getting much of a hearing as of 2007. Many parents who were alienated by Ne'eman questioned whether he even had autism—of any kind. Some, however, thought they recognized such a dramatic failure of empathy in his pronouncements about them as parents, or at least a failure of tact, that they took it as evidence that he did, after all, match the stereotype of Asperger's. Either way, he was a just a college kid—easy to ignore.

Then those "Ransom Notes" billboards began to appear.

WE HAVE YOUR SON.

The stark fearmongering insensitivity stunned many in the autism community. But when Ari Ne'eman heard about it, he saw an opportunity. He was walking across the University of Maryland–Baltimore campus when his phone received a burst of emails from members of his organization who were alarmed about what was happening in New York. The campaign was only a few days old when several neurodiversity bloggers became aware of it and alerted several others. It had become a storm, but only inside their small circle.

Ne'eman moved rapidly. He immediately put out an action alert to ASAN's members, urging them to email and call the NYU Child Study Center without delay. The alert provided names of actual people to ask for at NYU, as well as at the ad agency and the billboard company that had donated their time and space. A petition was started. The New York newspapers were called. And, most critically, Ne'eman solicited support from other, more recognized, disability organizations, whose credibility he hoped would elevate his own protest above the level implied by a mere college student rallying a bunch of bloggers.

Out of this came a letter signed by fourteen veteran organizations. News coverage followed. Within days, the ad campaign—and the campaign against the ad campaign—had attracted coverage from the *New York Times* and the *New York Daily News.* Reached by reporters, the director of the Study Center, Harold Koplewicz, appeared not to recognize the damage. He stated he was satisfied that the campaign was serving its purpose, which was to bring attention to autism. He had already decided, he told the *Times,* that despite the upset, for which he was sorry, "we should stick with it and ride out the storm."

But the storm widened. Altogether, more than three thousand people contacted NYU, the vast majority of them unhappy with the campaign, including many parents. "Dear Autism," one mother wrote in an email to NYU, in mockery of the campaign, "You don't have my son. I do. I will make sure that he is never defined by his autism alone . . . I will make sure that we celebrate his gifts." Soon NYU was also getting calls from the *Washington Post* and the *Wall Street Journal.*

Two weeks after sending the action alert, Ne'eman was in his dorm room when a reporter from the *Post* called. He was seeking a reaction to the announcement just made in New York City: NYU was killing the ad campaign. Ne'eman asked the reporter to hold a moment, placed his phone on mute, punched the air as hard he could, then returned to the call. "These ads reflect some very old and damaging stereotypes," Ne'eman said, sounding like an activist who had been doing this work for years.

It was a turning point—for neurodiversity, for the Autistic Self-Advocacy Network, and for its founder, Ari Ne'eman. Emboldened, and—just as important—no longer a bit player in the autism conversation, Ne'eman became someone reporters turned to for quotes, and ASAN saw its membership swell. In the next few years, Ne'eman continued using action alerts to rally his followers against those he saw as enemies. Autism Speaks remained a preferred target. In

Columbus, Ohio, an Autism Speaks awareness-raising "walk" was met by a counter-walk organized by local ASAN members. In 2009, ASAN helped organize a web-wide protest that led to the removal of an Autism Speaks video called *I Am Autism*—which again personified autism as an evil thief that steals children.

Meanwhile, in recognition of neurodiversity's rising profile, Ne'eman, as its most visible representative, was chosen by the White House in 2009 to serve on the National Council on Disability. In 2010, he was named to the federal Interagency Autism Coordinating Committee, the board that sets priorities for the federal government on autism research and services, which autism parents Lyn Redwood and Alison Singer had both served on. His presence on the committee helped it fulfill its legal mandate to include at least one person who was on the spectrum.

Being on the spectrum offered Ne'eman a distinct political advantage over those he saw as adversaries. It was this: there were few people who wanted to take him on in public. Although Ne'eman himself did not shrink from engagement, there was little upside for anyone to be seen arguing with a man who wore his autism as a badge of honor, depicting himself and his cohorts as targets of bigotry. In that regard, Ne'eman had launched ASAN at the exact right moment. The organization's assertion that being autistic should be seen not merely as a developmental disability, but as a neurological variation—one that makes "all Autistics as unique as any other human being"—resonated in a culture on the cusp of accepting wider variations in gender identity. Supporters of the neurodiversity viewpoint in fact often invoked the campaign for LGBT rights, pointing out parallels to their own campaign, and referring to Ne'eman and other outspoken advocates as being "openly autistic." The implication was that anyone challenging Ne'eman's arguments was narrow-minded and intolerant of difference. This was why Ne'eman often ended up in a one-sided debate. No respectable organization wanted to risk coming off as unenlightened by getting into an argument with him. True, he had plenty of detractors in chat rooms and on blogs, but Ne'eman's biggest target, Autism Speaks, more or less gave him a pass to say what he wanted to say without retort.

And so, in 2012, Autism Speaks turned the other cheek when one of its own executives was named to a prestigious post by the White House, and Ari Ne'eman's organization put out a statement condemning both the executive and the decision to appoint him. The post was a slot on the President's Committee for People with Intellectual Disabilities, and the appointee was Peter Bell, Autism Speaks's executive vice president. Bell had entered autism advocacy in the late 1990s as president of that group whose name—Cure Autism Now—was anathema to everything Ne'eman believed. Calling the appointment "disappointing and ill-advised," the statement charged that "Peter Bell has a long history of supporting fringe, anti-vaccine positions widely discredited in the scientific community," while Autism Speaks had its own "checkered and controversial history." Like his employers, Bell was constrained by his position when this attack came. He left it unanswered.

It turned out, however, that Bell's wife, Liz, had once given Ne'eman a piece of her mind. Three years earlier, in April 2009, she and Ne'eman happened to attend the same public forum, which had brought together a group of autism "stakeholders" for a conversation with New Jersey governor Jon Corzine. When Ne'eman was called on, he stood, faced the governor, and made his familiar two-prong argument—that people with autism did require supports, which should be provided, but that did not justify any attempts at treatment, or cure, or any other response that would make an autistic person any less autistic.

To Liz Bell, who had never heard Ne'eman speak before, the first part of his argument sounded completely reasonable. Acceptance by the community, work opportunities, self-determination to the maximum degree possible—these were values she and her husband and virtually every autism parent she knew believed in and had spent years fighting for. If this was neurodiversity, Liz Bell was all for it.

But the other part of his message—*don't cure*—was one Bell hoped would make no strong impression on this audience, especially on an outsider with real power like the governor. She didn't want him mistaking this impressive college student for the face of all autism. Indeed, the more activists like Ne'eman—talented, articulate, persuasive—proudly asserted their autistic identities, the more people seemed to forget about those with autism who had severe impairments. Bell had in mind those who would never speak, who had to be watched round-the-clock so that they didn't wander out at night and drown in a river or a swimming pool, who needed their diapers changed at least twice a day, even as adults. Unable to give interviews, these members of the autism community rarely had their stories told on the evening news, leaving the public with a skewed understanding of just how debilitating it could be, and how much it undermined opportunities for a life well lived, to have what some families privately called, in defiance of the neurodiversity movement's argument, "real autism."

Bell's son, Tyler, age sixteen, had the kind of autism the cameras rarely turned to. He had an IQ far lower than Ari's, little ability to speak, and extreme difficulty with such basic skills as taking a shower, shaving, or dressing himself. Like about a quarter of individuals with "classic" autism, Tyler also suffered seizures. He was frequently in intense pain from digestive problems.

Listening to Ne'eman addressing the governor, Bell understood that he meant Tyler no harm. But he had never lived with anyone like Tyler. Or cared for anyone like him, day after day. And despite the insinuation in Jim Sinclair's "Don't Mourn for Us" manifesto that parents like her wished their kids did not exist and just weren't trying hard enough to understand them, Bell believed that no one in Tyler's life understood him better than she did—whether he was communicating with words or not. At times, she despaired for what might happen to him after she was gone, when there might be no one left who could make sense of his wants and needs. That too was a problem neither Ari Ne'eman—nor Ari Ne'eman's mother—would have to address.

As the event broke up, Bell could not help herself. She wanted to say all of this to Ne'eman's face. A friend escorted her over to the office of the director of the center hosting the forum and dropped her off in front of Ne'eman, introducing her as "Liz, Peter Bell's wife." Noting both Bells' past association with Cure Autism Now and current position with Autism Speaks, Ne'eman could not help himself either. He launched into his talking points about what was wrong with any group fighting for a cure. Liz Bell pushed back, describing her own son and what his life was like. She talked about the constant diarrhea. About how Tyler had been talking at two and then started losing language. About how he also lost the ability to sleep through the night, which he had also been doing until the age of three. About the pain he was often in now. About his seizures. Put all that together, she said, and that was not "another way of being human." That was being sick.

As for Ne'eman's distaste for the word "cure," Bell told him: "If someday, Ari, my son and I can argue like you and I are arguing now, and he can make the case you're making against cures—then, yeah, I will be saying he was cured."

Ne'eman listened respectfully, but he stood his ground. He also left Bell with an insight about him she had not anticipated. His determination and his integrity as a campaigner were unassailable. He refused to mince words, fudge facts, or make plays for the affection of his audience. Even face-to-face with an autism mom, whose total love for her child and despair over his future should have been evident, Ne'eman was unyielding. He did not flinch, offer sympathy, or soften his tone. Experiencing that, Bell went home thinking that people who still seriously doubted that Ne'eman had true autistic impairments were wrong. The total imperviousness she had witnessed appeared to her to reflect not simply Ne'eman's convictions, but also an inability to take on a point of view other than his own. This, she knew, was considered a classic autistic trait—one that Simon Baron-Cohen had referred to as "mindblindness."

A corollary theory, also put forth by Baron-Cohen, held that this cognitive style interferes with the experience of feeling empathy. The idea was controversial and insulting to some people with Asperger's syndrome, who pointed to studies suggesting the empathy "deficit" in Asperger's was overstated. But others reluctantly accepted impairment in this area as something real, part of what made Asperger's so challenging to live with in a world of "neurotypicals."

Ari Ne'eman was definitely on the spectrum, Liz Bell told herself as she headed for her car that day. And yes, it was integral to who he was. But she didn't want him speaking for her son, Tyler. His condition, and Ari's, had nothing in common.

THE NEURODIVERSITY ARGUMENT, which continued to gain adherents, owed its existence to the recognition of Asperger's syndrome in the latter part of the twentieth century. When Lorna Wing had used Asperger's to make her argument that autism was a big, wide, deep, and blurry spectrum, and the *DSM* recognized the diagnosis in its 1994 edition, the *DSM-IV,* the boundaries around the condition grew exponentially. Without both these developments, it seems unlikely that the notion of autism that Leo Kanner coined in 1943 could legitimately be stretched to include large numbers of people as intelligent, talented, and independent as Alex Plank, Michael John Carley, and Ari Ne'eman in 2010. Asperger's was their ticket onto the spectrum—theirs and many others, and it gave the neurodiversity argument its most effective debaters and promoters.

Then, in 2013, Asperger's as a diagnosis was killed off by the American Psychiatric Association—dropped from the *DSM.* The turnabout had nothing to do with the discoveries reported three years earlier by Austrian historian Herwig Czech, suggesting that Asperger may have cooperated with the Nazis' program of killing disabled children. Because Czech had made his presentation in German, to a mostly local audience, his findings had made no impression in the English-speaking world, where awareness of Asperger's predominated.

Rather, the move by the American Psychiatric Association, which had been a long time coming, was the result of continuing doubts about the usefulness of the concept of Asperger's. This was evident in the medical literature as early as 2001. "Does *DSM-IV* Asperger's Disorder Exist?" asked the title of an article that year in the *Journal of Abnormal Child Psychiatry.*

More such papers followed, asking similar questions, and most of them were answered in the negative. Twelve years later, a paper in *Health* was still noting that, "in scientific terms, [Asperger's Disorder] has proved to be rather an elusive category."

To tens of thousands of people with the diagnosis, this seemed an absurd discussion. Of course Asperger's existed—because they existed. And so did Asperger's organizations, support groups, and clinics specializing in it, operating all over the United States and elsewhere, especially in Britain and Australia. But professionals who studied Asperger's knew what some wearers of the label did not: from a scientific perspective, Asperger's syndrome constituted a diagnostic malfunction. From the start, it had failed to meet a basic requirement: to mean the same thing every time it was used.

It was the same problem that had plagued the understanding of autistic traits from the beginning—a lack of agreement on whether everyone was even talking about the same thing. Hans Asperger had described the first cases of the syndrome named for him, but he never drew up a strict list of criteria. Lorna Wing attempted to do so when she brought Asperger's to the world's attention, as did Sweden's Christopher Gillberg, whose criteria were adopted for many, but by no means all, research studies elsewhere. The *DSM-IV* committee, back in 1994, tried to define the diagnosis as well, as did plenty of others. But none of these varied lists of criteria was quite the same as any other. For example, different theorists weighed language development and intelligence differently. There was also disagreement about how to label a person whose behavior changed over time—someone who might seem more "Aspergian" later in life than he or she had in early childhood.

As ever, clinicians giving out labels were making judgments based on their personal experience and understanding of what Asperger's should look like. And as usual, objectivity suffered in the process. One much-publicized study discovered that among twelve different American research centers, the likelihood of a person being diagnosed with Asperger's depended less on his or her actual traits than on which of the twelve centers he or she went to for evaluation. In another study, researchers found that, using the *DSM-IV* criteria, even Hans Asperger's own original four cases would not qualify for an Asperger's diagnosis. The authors who asked "Does *DSM-IV* Asperger's Disorder Exist?" published data suggesting to them that clinicians were simply ignoring the *DSM* definition and instead were diagnosing with "definitions influenced by the literature and popular belief."

"Asperger's means a lot of different things to different people," researcher Catherine Lord told the *New York Times* in 2009. "It's confusing and not terribly useful."

As Lord spoke, yet another new version of the *DSM* was in the planning stages. She was in the working group assigned to figure out what to do about Asperger's and the three other diagnoses based on autistic traits: Autistic Disorder (the "classic" autism), childhood disintegrative disorder, and the catchall PDD-NOS. In February 2010, the group published a draft version of its likely solution. Its plan was to collapse all four diagnoses into one, all-encompassing diagnosis, to be known as Autistic Spectrum Disorder. It would still include a way to distinguish among various presentations of autistic traits, by introducing a scale for specifying severity of the key symptoms. This would mean that a person previously diagnosed with Asperger's would most likely be recognized, for future *DSM* purposes, as having autism, but without accompanying intellectual or language impairment. It would also be the end of the line for Asperger's. The name, and the diagnosis, would be departing the pages of the *DSM* forever.

Opposition came from all over the autism community. Fred Volkmar of Yale resigned from the working group when he could not prevail upon his colleagues to keep Asperger's alive. Temple Grandin weighed in, citing the size and vocal strength of the Asperger's community as a reason to retain the category. "PDD-NOS, I'd throw in the garbage can," she told the *Times*. "But I'd keep Asperger's."

A New York State lawmaker, an autism dad, tried to stop the clock with a bill that would officially establish the outgoing *DSM* language as the state's "definition" of autism. It drew 44 cosponsors in the legislature's two houses. Some 9,000 people signed an online petition, written by Michael John Carley, opposing the changes. Another 5,400 signed a petition sponsored by the Asperger's Association of New England, demanding that the *DSM* retain Asperger's "to help ensure clinical continuity and the established sense of community precious to already diagnosed individuals and families, and to maintain the hard won understanding of the label in the population at large."

Discussions erupted on the forums of Wrong Planet. One thread, entitled "DSM-5 is taking away our identity," laid out one of the key fears heard in the Asperger's community. The opening post argued that the merging of Asperger's syndrome with autism "would do great damage to the small amount of Asperger's awareness we have worked our A$$es off for in the past fifteen years. Autism has many negative connotations, which are not exactly unwarranted, but to be lumped into such a broad group will set us back 20 years."

A second concern raised by the new definition appeared in a *New York Times* headline in early 2012: "New Definition of Autism Will Exclude Many, Study Suggests." This touched off a whole new furor. At Yale, three researchers, including Fred Volkmar, had run some old case data through the parameters set by the proposed new definition. Their results showed that of all those in a 1993 group who had been given any of the four soon-to-be-obsolete autism diagnoses, almost 40 percent would now not qualify for the new *DSM-5* autism category. Fear spread throughout the autism community that, under the new definition, people would lose their access to government services and support.

Responding to the panic, the *DSM* working group itself issued assurances that the risk of people losing their diagnoses was an overblown concern, and that the new definition could well include people whose autism had been overlooked in the past. Before long, studies appeared supporting this prediction.

Interestingly, some of the posters at Wrong Planet made the same argument. And Ari Ne'eman began writing papers proposing that an all-in-one diagnosis should appeal to people on the spectrum because it in fact recognized the validity of the spectrum, which was a concept the neurodiversity movement cherished. Ne'eman and UCLA's Steven Kapp coauthored a paper that praised the reconceived disorder as "a positive development both from the standpoint of expanding access to service provisions and as a means of showing fidelity to the research literature." As a philosophical matter, as well, Ne'eman favored the erasure of division of the autism population into so-called high-functioning and low-functioning groups, which the neurodiversity movement saw as a false division based on "neurotypical" dictates of what constituted "functioning" in the first place.

In the end, after six years of tweaking the definition of autism based on continuing research, the working group and the editors of *DSM-5* approved Autistic Spectrum Disorder—the new, all-encompassing definition of autism, which became effective in May 2013. Asperger's syndrome was gone, although, in the words of Francesca Happé, another member of the working group, it had made a valuable contribution while it lasted. "Asperger disorder . . . did a great service in raising awareness that some people on the autism spectrum have high IQ and good language," Happé wrote. But with that purpose served, it was also time, as Lorna Wing had been arguing for decades, that autism—whatever it was, however many ways it manifested—be recognized as something that existed across a spectrum.

At last, that was the triumphant idea.

For the time being.

THAT IS PROBABLY autism's single certainty: that the story is far from over. The mystery remains complex. Attempts to investigate its nature continue to bring new questions to the surface. The boundary lines set by professionals can, and should be expected to, move yet again.

In that uncertainty lies much of the explanation for why, over a span of eighty years, the story of autism has been so uniquely riven with division and dispute. The concept's inherent elusiveness, the vagueness in how it has been described, and the variety in how it presents itself—to a degree that hints at infinity—has meant that anyone could say anything about autism, and eventually probably would. This effect was seen repeatedly, in the latching on to the word "autism" by all manner of theories, therapies, claims, interpretations, and controversies—from the scientific to the social to the legal to the nearly religious.

While only some of this helped shed light on what autism is, *all* of it served as a mirror for the societies that recognized autism as something real. Not everything revealed in that mirror was flattering: not the blaming that autism inspired, or the vituperation, or the exploitation, or the grandstanding, or the outright and sometimes willful neglect of the vulnerable.

At the same time, however, that mirror showed how, in the search for treatments and services, for recognition and understanding, some good and admirable qualities came into play over the decades, on the part of many people. They demonstrated talents for organization, self-sacrifice, the expansion of knowledge through solid science, and for channeling love into pure, inexhaustible energy. This was most true of parental love. To be sure, that love could run awry at times, and be fierce to a fault, but it was one element in the whole long saga that was always, unquestionably, pure.

Indeed, the fact is that even with all the contentiousness attached to the word "autism," the momentum pushing all the argument has also, over time, pushed all the societies that have tried to deal with autism in the most commendable direction, which is toward ever greater recognition of the dignity of individuals who are different by virtue of fitting the label in some way. It is this interpretation of autism that has come to be shared by the bitterest foes and the most casual bystanders: that having autism—being autistic—represents but one more wrinkle in the fabric of humanity, and that no one among us is living a life "unwrinkled."

46

A HAPPY MAN

In September 2013, Donald Triplett's friends and family took over an art gallery in Forest, Mississippi, to throw him a party. Everyone in the room was from town, and pretty much all the guests had known him most of their lives. Three years earlier, an article in *The Atlantic* had told the story of his role in the early history of autism—something most of them had not heard before. It added a mild luster of celebrity to their well-loved neighbor, of whom they were also proud. More than one hundred people showed up that day, including many of Forest's business and political notables. There was wine and cheese, toasts in Donald's honor, a cake with eighty candles, and a boisterous rendition of "Happy Birthday."

It had been Mary Triplett's most heartfelt wish that life would turn out well for her baffling, complicated son.

That wish came true in almost every way his mother had hoped for, the local boy made good.

Donald learned how to drive when he was twenty-seven, in 1960. After that, the road was his whenever he wanted.

It was Mary who handed Donald the car keys that September. He was living with both his parents then, in the house that would be his home for the rest of his life. His younger brother, Oliver, had left for college four years earlier, and then gone to law school at Ole Miss. Within two years, Oliver would marry and start a family.

The Ford Fairlane, a big boat of a car, was parked as always beneath the tall tree that shaded the gravel driveway just off the side entrance to the house. Mary took on the role of driving instructor. It made sense; she had been Donald's teacher for so many years now. With the engine off, she talked him through it: how to adjust the mirrors, where to place his hands on the steering wheel, how the brake and accelerator worked. Then she told him to put the key into the ignition and turn it.

No doubt, when the Ford hopped alive, Donald tensed a bit, and his hands slid toward the top of the steering wheel, pulling him forward so that his chin almost touched it. From then on, that would be his preferred pose in the driver's seat. His mother had instructed him to let up on the gas with his right foot and use the same foot for braking, but Donald didn't get that part right. As the car moved slowly away from the house and out toward the paved road, he was using both feet, left on the brake, right on the gas. It was a little rough, as the car jolted forward in small surges and hiccups. But it worked well enough that Donald could never be talked out of it. He would remain a two-footed pedal man for the rest of his driving life.

That first day, though, he was still a tentative driving student turning onto the road for the first time. Maybe it occurred then to Mary that this was the same road she had obsessively worried about throughout Donald's early childhood, fearing that he would run out into it and get himself killed. That was back when her little boy seemed incapable of recognizing danger. But this was one of many things about Donald that had changed. Once she had thought him hopelessly insane, lost to the world. But as the pair of them advanced in fits and starts up and down the road between the pines, she realized how incredibly far he had come.

BACK IN 1953, as he finished high school, Donald had scrawled that one-sentence note to himself beside his picture in the yearbook: "*I wish myself luck.*" At the time, luck was already rolling his way, setting the tone for the next several decades of his life. A pattern was already in place. One after another, he met the milestones of growing up—finishing high school, going to college, starting a job, learning to drive. To be sure, he did all these things "behind schedule," often years after his peers. But with help from others, he kept on hitting the marks, in his own way and in his own time.

JOHN RUSHING, the teenage football star who had been one of Donald's protectors at Forest High School, was home packing for college in the late summer of 1953 when the phone rang. It was Beamon Triplett, offering him a ride with the Tripletts when they drove Donald to college in a few days. Both Donald and John were starting at East Central Community College, about forty minutes by car from Forest. Beamon also asked a favor. It would mean a great deal to the family, he said, if Rushing could keep an eye out for Donald at school. Rushing was a little taken aback, honored to be confided in by one of the most important men in town. He accepted the ride and the role, giving Beamon his word that he would allow no harm to come Donald's way.

In fact, Donald and East Central clicked so well that Rushing's unofficial guardianship was never put to the test. This might have had something to do with Donald's new, unbridled enthusiasm for joining clubs. During his two years at East Central, a more socially engaged side of Donald began to emerge as he packed his days and weekends outside the classrooms with group activity. According to the school yearbook, Donald was treasurer of his freshman class, song leader of the Young Men's Christian Association, member of the Student Christian Association, member of the Drama Club—and that was only half the list. He was earning mediocre grades—mostly B's and C's—but his social life was exploding.

Yet he retained all his quirks: not looking people in the eye, an odd way of walking, abrupt exits from conversations—if they could even be called conversations. He began every utterance with the two-syllable warm-up "Uh, uh—" followed with a single sentence, at most two, and then lapsed into silence. If he was ever curious to know the thoughts or feelings of the person trying to speak with him, he never let it show in a conventional way. He wrote his mother often from East Central, sharing details of activities like coursework or shopping, but never about what he was thinking or feeling.

Donald still had autism. His fellow students at East Central were reminded of that during a pep rally held before a key game against a longtime basketball rival. As the cheers and speeches went on, the crowd chanted for Donald to be summoned from the stands and onto the gym floor, where he was handed a microphone and asked to predict the outcome.

"Uh, uh! I think East Central will lose that game!" Donald declared, literal-minded and truthful to a fault.

This produced a stunned silence, followed immediately by an explosion of booing and catcalls. The reaction threw Donald off balance. He understood what booing signified, but he did not grasp what he had done to provoke it—it had to be explained to him. The razzing was, in fact, good-natured, but Donald was unable to tell that he was still liked by the people in the stands—that they understood that he was different, and that they accepted him.

On a Friday night in September 1955, close to the dinner hour, the brothers of Alpha Lambda Chi—a fraternity at Millsaps College in Jackson, Mississippi—gathered in their redbrick chapter house to perform a solemn ritual. Clean-cut and conservatively attired, the young men worked down a list of fifty-four Millsaps men seeking to join their exclusive membership. That night, the brothers were generous in their judgments. Only four men were turned away. Fifty were invited to join. One of them was Donald, who was then a twenty-two-year-old junior.

Donald's years at Millsaps College were one of the best things to happen in his life. As with everything else, he ambled into this phase belatedly. At twenty-two, most students have already graduated or soon will. But Donald had only just arrived at Millsaps, after two years at East Central Community College, where he earned his associate degree in liberal arts. At Millsaps, his grades were again middling, but his social understanding continued to flourish, enhanced by his fraternity brothers' willingness to roll with his oddities. He was befriended by a nineteen-year-old named Brister Ware, a freshman from Jackson who came from a family of doctors and had an instinct for protecting vulnerable people. When he met Donald, Ware saw a decent, guileless, honest young man who could perhaps use some help in parts of his life where his skills were poorly developed. He was concerned that Donald's speech, perpetually flat-toned and stiff, might prove a detriment to his success, and he began pushing his friend to pump more variety and energy into his conversation. He tried to teach him bits of slang. And when he learned that no one had ever taught Donald to swim, he hauled him to the nearby Pearl River, where for forty-five minutes they floundered through the muddy water. This effort flopped; Donald was too uncoordinated to get the hang of it. But Ware kept looking for other ways to help Donald. This was not charity, at least not in Ware's eyes. He felt grateful to have Donald as a friend.

While at Millsaps, Donald once again moved at his own slower pace, taking three years to graduate instead of two. He majored in French, an ironic choice given his inability to hold a true conversation. He survived in part by scoring well on the vocabulary portion of his exams, where he could count on rote memory to get himself through.

In November 1955, a school dance appeared on the calendar, and Donald wrote his mother about going out to buy a tuxedo "and things that go along with it." In the same note, he informed her, "The Lambda Chis are expected to bring dates, so I will be taking some girl."

Donald did not sound enthusiastic about the prospect. Whether that date ever took place is unknown; Donald did not write to his mother about it. But it was known that Donald did not have a girlfriend while at college or afterward. Well into his twenties and thirties, his deepest relationship with a woman—with anyone—continued to be the one he had with his mother. Mary seemed unperturbed by this. She reported in a letter around this time: "He takes very little part in social conversation, and shows no interest in the opposite sex."

Donald's family had close ties to Millsaps College. Beamon was a star graduate, and president of the alumni association while Donald was a student there. And the college's founder, a Major Millsaps, was once business partners with Mary's grandfather. That may or may not have facilitated Donald's admission to the school, especially with the less-than-stellar grades he'd earned at East Central. However, his family connections were unambiguously helpful in securing a job for him after graduation. Donald returned to Forest, where he went to work as a teller in the family-owned bank.

Donald's mother and father were committed to securing their son a place in the world, and the family business was the vehicle for doing so. He was allowed to make mistakes—more than any other employee—and some were notorious. When handling customer phone calls, he had been known to put the phone down on a counter while the customer was still talking and walk away to work on some other task. For a while, he also fell into greeting bank customers by their account numbers, which, for some people, was off-putting. Over the years, as one job or another proved too much for him, he found himself doing more clerical work, which required less face-to-face interaction with customers. As long as the Tripletts controlled the bank, no matter how erratic his performance, Donald had lifelong tenure.

Thus ensconced in work, his family, and the bedroom he had known since childhood, Donald moved through life protected from the hardships faced by so many other people with autism. In 1956, he discovered golf and became somewhat obsessed. Throughout the 1960s, the 1970s, and on into middle age and then late middle age, it was a given that, whenever Donald was in town, there was only one place to find him in the afternoon. Golf was a lifelong pleasure he could never explain in words.

Donald was a sight to see on the golf course of the Forest Country Club, noticeable even from the rockers on the clubhouse porch. His stroke was stodgy, stiff, and awkward, but it was consistent, highly choreographed, and entirely his own. It began with his thumbs. While standing a little too far from the ball, his legs in a wide A-frame, Donald would lick the pad of each thumb in turn—first right, then left—before taking his full grip on the club handle. That done, he would lift the club entirely over his head, until he had his arms nearly straight up in the air, like someone holding a sign on a pole. He would hold that pose a moment and then commence a full rehearsal of the downstroke, heaving the club head in an arc back to earth until it landed between his feet, in the general vicinity of the ball. After a beat, he would yank the club back up into the pole position, pause, and then bring it down again—just as before, only faster this time. Then a third round of up and down. At this point, with the club head approaching full swing velocity, he would inch forward, his eyes fixed on the ball, his body bending toward it, his wrists rolling the right way. When he finally made contact, Donald could almost always get a good crisp *thwack!* out of it as the ball took off, generally in the right direction.

His follow-through after hitting the ball was also one of a kind. Rather than let his club and body twist, lose momentum, and come to a stop on their own, he came to a shuddering stop the minute he made contact, and then immediately began to bounce up and down at the knees, scanning the sky for his ball. Only when he spotted it did he truly come to rest. Then he headed for his golf cart and his next swing.

Despite his rituals—or perhaps because of them—Donald's golf game was not half bad. He had no trouble getting around the course, could handle the different kinds of clubs, and sank putts from ten or fifteen feet out now and then. It probably helped that proficiency in golf hinges on a certain mechanical repetitiveness. He was a man who was, more than anything, comfortable with sameness, and there are plenty of things about golf that never vary. The basic swing stays the same. And the ball is always sitting still at the moment the golfer has to do anything about it. And while golf is generally seen as a social game, it always comes down to the golfer against the course. If Donald wanted to, he could simply play alone.

And that was what he did. He almost always went golfing by himself, and was content to do so.

TO HIS MOTHER, part of Donald would always be a mystery. "I wish I knew what his inner feelings really are," Mary wrote in her last letter to Kanner, when Donald was thirty-six. But the letter was also full of optimism. All in all, Mary wrote, things for Donald had turned out "so much better than we had hoped for." She had attained the goal every parent dreams of—to raise a child who would be just fine when she was gone from this world. "If he can maintain status quo," she said, "I think he has adjusted sufficiently to take care of himself. For this much progress, we are truly grateful."

Mary was a few months short of sixty-six then. She became a widow ten years later, when Beamon was killed in a car accident. She died five years after that, at the age of eighty, of heart failure. At neither funeral did Donald show any particular emotion. He later said, in answer to a direct question about losing his mother: "It was rather expected. I wasn't really downhearted or weeping or anything like that."

Yet when Donald was truly happy, it showed. His contentment registered in the smile that often lit up his face. Though he remained an enigma to his mother, she and anyone else who knew him could say with certainty that Donald was a happy man.

And how that came about is not much of a mystery, actually. Much of it was because of where he lived—Forest, Mississippi.

For a man with autism, life in a small community in Mississippi offered a number of gifts: familiarity, predictability, tranquillity, and safety. Forest was a place where the pace was slow, the noise level low, and where Donald could be confident that one day would be much like the next. There was also the embracing web of relationships endemic to small-town living, where everyone knows more than a little about everyone else.

Not that Forest was a paradise. The town was never without poverty, substance abuse, political disputes, or crime, including the rare murder every few years. It enforced segregation into the 1960s, and saw most of its once-charming downtown die a slow death in the 1970s. But Donald didn't need to live in paradise to be happy. In Forest, he lived within a circle of Mississippians who were simply not bothered by the ways in which he was different. They were unbothered, hence he was unbothered, by fear, by ridicule, or by cruelty. And the more his social deficits were overlooked, the more they lost their relevance, while his strengths and abilities continued to develop and expand.

Yes, his family had money, which had a lot to do with his

circumstances and the way he was received. As a Mississippi newspaperman observed, in relation to how Forest responded to Donald: "In a small southern town, if you're odd and poor, you're crazy. But if you're odd and rich, all you are is a little eccentric."

But there was another part to it, where Donald was concerned. People just liked him. As he approached old age, it was fair to say that, in his little community, he was beloved.

CELESTE SLAY, A regular congregant at the First Presbyterian Church of Forest, sat prayerfully among her fellow worshippers, attending to the minister's parting words, her husband, Mervyn, at her side. Suddenly, she was stung in the back of the neck by a rubber band.

Celeste turned around, but she already knew who did it. Donald Triplett, from some rear pew, had just zipped a "howdy" through holy space, aimed at one of the ladies he liked. It was not the first time, and it was not just her. There was a small group of people in Forest—fewer than a dozen—whom Donald, in his seventies, had taken to pinging by rubber band, whenever and wherever they went. Some had been hit in church, some high up in the stands at a Forest High football game, some while turning the corner of an aisle at Walmart.

Donald's rubber-band stunt was his way of flirting. Mary had misread him all those years ago, when she said that he took no interest in the opposite sex. Either that, or Donald had changed. Because when he was well past his middle years, he had begun, in a rather naïve way, to let women know when he liked them. Because it was Forest, where everyone knew him, no one's feelings were hurt, and no one was offended. The women Donald tended to plink with rubber bands—all employees of the bank, and all middle-aged—knew what they were dealing with: a friend who was working out a mild sort of crush. They were charmed by the nicknames he came up with for each of them. Jan Nester—one of his favorites—was "Jan with a Plan." Celeste Slay, the woman in the church, was "Celestial Celeste." There were presents too. Donald would show up at one of their desks with a clumsily wrapped trinket of some sort—a refrigerator magnet or a spatula. Often the items carried their original price tags. Sometimes he would give the gift, and then request immediate cash reimbursement for it. Some steps in this dance he would never master.

Still, in return for his exertions, Donald received something real: attention, which he had come to prize. The women mothered him, called him "Don darling," and made him feel welcome and needed at the bank, where he dropped in every afternoon. By the early 2000s, he had not officially worked there for many years. In fact, Mary's family no longer ran it. After the bank encountered financial difficulties in the 1980s, day-to-day control passed to a twenty-seven-year-old named Gene Walker, who gave his word to the family that he would always find something in the bank for Donald to do. For the next thirty years, Walker kept his word. He saw to it that new employees were briefed on Donald's status in the office, and ensured that Donald never encountered anything but full respect. Though his job responsibilities grew smaller with the years, and income from a trust fund replaced a paycheck from the bank, Donald never stopped having a place at the Bank of Forest. In his seventies, he began referring to himself as "retired," but he still came by daily to see his bank friends, who were nearly family to him in his later years.

When Donald was about seventy-nine, Jan Nester from the bank insisted that he get a cell phone, and she showed him how to send text messages. Donald was hooked. It was as if some sort of interior barrier fell. Suddenly, he was tapping out words constantly, communicating with real fluency for the first time in his life. Nonverbal children with autism experienced a similar breakthrough when the iPad was introduced in 2010. By manipulating images and characters on the screen, some were able to express themselves without relying on words and grammar, which had always been obstacles. Likewise, when Donald texted, he could forget about the complex visual and physical requirements of spoken language, such as eye contact, facial expressions, and the neurological gymnastics of turning thought into sound. While texting, he "spoke" in a different voice.

Most of his texts were directed at his rubber-band friends. Once, in 2014, Donald texted Celeste from Texas:

Donald: Is it pretty in MS like it is in TX, Celestial Celeste?
Celeste: It is sunny and 80 degrees. Very pretty. Glad you made it safe . . .
Donald: See u on June 16
Celeste: Have fun and be careful Don!!
Donald: I shoot u with a rubber band Sunday

Sunday meant church, which Donald never missed unless he was out of town.

In fact, Donald was out of town a lot—probably more than anyone else in Forest—the result of a streak of wanderlust he had developed in his thirties. It was then that world travel became one of his two full-time hobbies, alongside golf.

Donald never went anywhere for long. The maximum length of his trips was usually six days, because he tried to be back in Forest for Bible class on Sundays at Forest Presbyterian. But at least a dozen times a year, he left town for points elsewhere. Traveling via highway, air, rail, river, and sea, by the time he was in his late seventies, he had been to at least twenty-eight American states—including Hawaii more than fifteen times—and more than thirty-six places abroad, including Germany, Tunisia, Hungary, Dubai, Spain, Portugal, France, Bulgaria, and Colombia. He took snapshots of the pyramids, went on safari in Africa, and wore a muumuu to dance opposite a belly dancer on a cruise ship off the coast of Morocco. Wherever he went, he went solo.

Notably, Donald made no friends while traveling. Doing so would have required small talk, for which he had no talent or interest. Rather, he appeared to travel with the aim of making contact with *things*—with all the iconic structures and statues and mountaintops he had seen in books, on the Internet, and on TV. When he got home from his trips, he organized all of his photos in thick albums, until his bookshelves were crammed with dozens of them. In the late 1990s, after he learned to use a computer, he went back through them all, assigning numbers to each of his trips, and creating a database and an index that made it easier to find specific photos. That was how he tended to his memories. As he approached eighty, he was still on the road several times a year, collecting more of them.

Whenever, during his later years, Donald needed to be well dressed for an event, Jan Nester, from the bank, took him shopping for clothes. He needed the help. Without any intervention, he would wear his pants extremely low, beneath his protruding belly. To keep them from falling down, he cinched his belt as tightly as possible. Because this often proved insufficient for the task, Donald usually went around with one hand reaching around to his backside, fidgeting with and tugging at his belt. Now and then, he wore suspenders, which solved that problem. But when he did wear suspenders, often as not, they were twisted in the back.

As for colors and patterns, Donald seemed indifferent to how they played together, and even choosing the right size was a hit-or-miss affair. Once he put on a particular shirt and pair of pants, he was as likely as not to keep wearing the same outfit for several days running. He was oblivious to staining, tattering, or accidental rips. Usually, it took a gentle suggestion from Jan to get him to realize that a well-used polo shirt, or a pair of Bermuda shorts, were too dingy to be worn in public. "Don, darling," she would say, "you really do not need to wear that shirt anymore."

Usually she took him to Burns Clothing, in Forest's downtown. Burns happened to adjoin the building that housed Donald's dad's old law office, where Beamon wrote his letter to Leo Kanner in 1938. And it stood on the same courthouse square where Donald had once made the rounds memorizing license plates. Tom and Margaret Burns, the mom and pop of Burns Clothing, had hung on, even as most of the businesses around them had been shuttered. They were still thriving, thanks to their knowing how to cater to customers' particular preferences.

Tom Burns was, for example, well acquainted with Donald's low-belt situation, and took that into account when he positioned Donald in front of the double mirrors and knelt to get a waistline-to-shoe measurement. Burns knew that whatever trousers this customer bought, he would have to remake them, taking in the waist, cutting off the cuffs, and hemming the bottoms. But he was happy to do it for Donald. And happy to help him get ready to celebrate his eightieth birthday that coming Friday.

It was a late-afternoon event. Everyone from the bank was there. And his brother, Oliver, and Oliver's son's family. And a good many people from the country club.

Donald smiled throughout the gathering, but as ever, he gave no speech. "I'm just glad I made it to eighty," he told a newspaper reporter who covered the event. If the reporter was hoping for something more emotional, Donald disappointed. Of course, since it was a daytime party, Donald was missing that day's golf. But he did not seem to mind. As he put it to the reporter: "The reception was a good idea . . . I sure thought a lot of everyone who put it together." For Donald, that was a lot of sentiment.

Besides, he knew that on the next day, and the days to follow, he would be back on the course again, back on schedule, playing through the dwindling light of those September afternoons. Donald was embarking on his ninth decade. And as that autumn advanced, and on those days and hours when the sun dipped behind the pines along the fairways, and his shadow on the greens lengthened, it would be easy for anyone watching from the rocking chairs on the clubhouse porch to guess who was out there, in the dusk, playing golf by himself. It was autism's first child, using the remaining light given him to get in a few last holes before dinner.

EPILOGUE

ONE DAY IN 2007, A THOUSAND MILES FROM MISSISSIPPI, TWO men on a bus noticed a teenager sitting alone, one row in front of them, rocking and grunting and making strange, repetitive movements with his fingers in front of his eyes. As the bus made its regular afternoon run through Caldwell, New Jersey, the men began to mock the young man's "weirdo" behavior, in voices deliberately loud enough to be overheard by other passengers, whose heads turned in the direction of the noisy riders. The young man himself seemed oblivious to the commentary. He did not stop rocking. If anything, his movements and vocalizations became more intense, which made the men behind him angry. One leaned forward, close to the young man's ear, and asked, sharply, "Hey, what's your problem, man?" An altercation seemed imminent.

This brought a passenger in a rear seat to his feet. Pete Gerhardt, a psychologist specializing in adolescent and adult autism, had heard everything happening up front via the Bluetooth headset he wore, which matched a headset worn by the teenager. Gerhardt and Nicholas, the teenager, had been riding the route together for weeks, as Gerhardt taught the teen the ins and outs of getting around by bus. They had started out sitting side by side, but gradually, the teacher put some distance between them, relying on the headsets to stay in contact. Gerhardt spoke as little as possible, just whispering encouragement from time to time, or calmly talking Nicholas through unexpected events that are part of anyone's bus-traveling experience, like getting stuck in heavy traffic, or missing a stop.

But getting harassed by passengers was not supposed to be part of that experience.

Gerhardt headed for the front.

Not every place is Forest, Mississippi. And not every adult with autism has the advantages Donald Triplett enjoyed through more than eight decades. The Triplett family's wealth and influence undoubtedly played a critical part in his being accepted, even embraced, by the community. Those same advantages supported a fulfilled life, with a network of people watching out for him, and the chance to live independently, in a home of his own. To be sure, Donald's own inherent capabilities—his native intelligence and his learned adaptability—were also crucial. But it is hard to believe he would have fulfilled his potential had he spent his life inside an institution, or in a community hostile to his differences and indifferent to his circumstances. Outside of Forest, it is easy to picture Donald being treated like that teenager on the bus.

Having been driven by parents for so long, the global conversation on autism has tended to focus on children. Beginning with Leo Kanner's original name for the condition, "infantile autism," moving throughout Ivar Lovaas's ABA therapy, the battle for public schooling, and the storm around vaccines, autism as a childhood condition has almost always held the spotlight. There have been exceptions, of course—*Rain Man*'s Raymond and Temple Grandin gave us a compelling view of adults with autism—but when society thinks about autism, it usually thinks about kids. Pete Gerhardt always joked that it was only because he faced so little professional competition at the "grown-up" end of the spectrum that he became so prominent an expert in adult autism. He understood his colleagues' preference for working with children. The kids, he would say, are cuter than the adults, who, because of their physical size and set ways, are also harder to help. Choosing to specialize in adults, Gerhardt said, was not seen as "a career move."

The bias toward helping children with autism was evident also in advocacy messaging, which depicted kids as the protagonists (and sometimes the victims) in the autism story. Adults were rarely seen in fund-raising ads. Even biomedical and psychological research was heavily slanted toward autism in childhood, judging by scientists' preference to recruit children when they had need for human study subjects. Research on adults with the condition lagged dramatically by comparison.

All this means that, on their twenty-first birthdays, at the age when their "neurotypical" peers are expected to launch themselves out into the world, individuals with autism, especially those with more severe symptoms, find themselves struggling to stay engaged in the world at all. Those who require significant support to get through school—and had it in the form of state-funded aides—suddenly lose it. To be sure, pockets of excellence do exist, though they are scattered around the United States. Headquartered in Phoenix, the Southwest Autism Research & Resource Center offers a broad range of services that cover the full life span of an individual with autism and is widely admired. So is the Extraordinary Ventures program, based in Chapel Hill, North Carolina, which focuses exclusively on employment for adults. But in much of the country, there are not enough solutions like these. For most adults whose independence is challenged by autism, there are few opportunities to work, or to continue their education, or even to live in a setting consonant with the concept of adulthood. Most literally go on living in their childhood bedrooms, as long as their parents are alive.

If that isn't possible, and if state support can be procured, they are likely to be funneled into one of the small group homes that have become the default living arrangement for the disabled since the large institutions were shut down. These places, while called "homes," are closer to dormitories, albeit with no college attached, and nothing to do all day but watch TV, go online, or go on sporadic group outings. Residents have no say in who their housemates are, or even, sometimes, when and what to eat. Minimal support staff is present, and those hired, generally at minimum wage, often have minimal training. As Gerhardt pointed out, a manicurist's job pays about as well, but comes with tougher licensing requirements.

It is difficult to pinpoint the number of Americans vulnerable to such a fate, in part because statistics derived from the spectrum concept often lump people with reasonably well-developed life skills together with those who are not close to independence. Obviously, they will not all need help. But tens of thousands, at least, will lead wilting lives without it. A 2013 study found that approximately 50,000 adolescents with autism were turning eighteen that year. This suggests that we might see half a million people joining the adult autistic population by 2023. Of those who had already reached young adulthood, more than half had never held a job for pay, and only 12 percent of the more severely impaired had ever been employed in any capacity. Eight out of ten in this group were still living at home, with aging parents.

The invisibility of adults with the more severe variants of autism is one of the main reasons this is happening. Outside their own families, they have few advocates, and it does not help that, as Gerhardt pointed out, they are no longer cute. That said, however, there is at least a scattering of efforts under way to address this situation, some of them very creative.

A Danish father named Thorkil Sonne, for example, took out a second mortgage in 2003 in order to start a company staffed almost exclusively with people who have autism. Sonne's gamble was that his company's service—software testing—would play to the strengths of many on the spectrum, such as superior memory and the ability to tolerate repetitive detail without getting bored or losing focus. Knowing that people on the spectrum would struggle in traditional job interviews, Sonne developed a series of programming and LEGO robot-building tasks to evaluate potential hires. His firm, called Specialisterne, or "The Specialists," has consistently turned a profit in Denmark. He has since undertaken the challenge of exporting the model to other countries, including the United States.

In late 2015, a New York mother named Ilene Lainer, cofounder with Laura Slatkin of the country's first public charter school for children with autism, as well as an autism services agency called New York Collaborates for Autism, launched a pilot housing program intended as a better alternative to the group-home model. Based on a Kansas City program for people with developmental disabilities, Lainer's program uses state funding to compensate families that agree to provide room, board, and an inclusive embrace to individuals not quite capable of living on their own. It is, in essence, a "foster family" model, requiring no new construction and offering both a means of oversight and the possibility that adults with autism will form close and enduring relationships with surrogate families.

In 2013, Connie and Harvey Lapin—who in their late seventies were still autism activists—pushed through the California legislature a mandate blocking the state from imposing one-size-fits-all housing solutions. Instead, the Self-Determination Program they created allowed individuals and families choices, ranging from solo living to group living arrangements for individuals whose severe impairment required greater support.

These and other efforts to change the fate of autistic adults tend to have at least two things in common: all are still small-scale and experimental; and all were initiated by parents, who worry about how their aging children will fare after they die, and who remain their prime advocates.

Still, that may not always be the case. As awareness of autistic difference continues to spread, a broader sense of shared responsibility may come with it, inspiring communities to work harder to make room for people with autism, and not only those with language, and the gifts and skills that attract the most media coverage. In this regard, it was a remarkable development when, in 2014, the College of William & Mary introduced a course on neurodiversity, taught in part by John Elder Robison, a man whose own diagnosis of Asperger's syndrome as an adult changed his life for the better. Robison has always tried to play a conciliatory role among the various factions in the neurodiversity discussion, urging "neurotypicals" to appreciate the perspectives of "spectrumites," and vice versa. Courses like Robison's advance the cause of acceptance of people on the spectrum, and may even inspire a desire to be part of the solution to the problems faced by adults.

Pete Gerhardt, for one, has long argued that the mission of advocacy for adults with autism ought to be shared by a community larger than that of aging parents. In his ideal world, acceptance of individuals' autistic differences would become so widespread and automatic that, in virtually any setting—at our jobs, at the local diner on Saturday mornings, on the bench that gets the afternoon shade in the park, or anyplace where the same people tend to bump into one another, again and again, even among strangers—we would recognize, and take steps to welcome and protect, the odd man out.

Hey, what's your problem, man?

To Gerhardt, the words sounded threatening. Now he was moving toward the front of the bus, trying to reach Nicholas before the situation flew out of control.

Suddenly, a different passenger stood up, blocking the way. Gerhardt didn't know him, but after all these weeks spent riding around with Nicholas, he realized he had seen him before. The man approached the bullying passengers, and, according to Gerhardt, he said to them: "What's his problem? He's got autism. So what's *your* problem? How about you shut up?"

There was a tense silence and a whiff of threatened violence in the air. But the bullies must have sensed that everyone else on the bus had just lined up behind Nicholas. They shrugged. And then they left him alone.

Gerhardt was stunned. He was also elated. That bus, on that route, he realized, had become one of those impromptu communities he had in mind. No introductions had been made, but a familiarity had arisen among the regulars, the dozen or so passengers who took that same route at the same time every day. As in Forest, Mississippi, a neighbor had decided that the odd man out was, in fact, "one of us," simply part of the group.

It happened on a bus in New Jersey. It can be that way anywhere.

AUTISM TIMELINE

This is actually two timelines. One is made up of political, scientific, and other public milestones. The other, in italics, shows personal milestones in the lives of several of the parents and young people with autism who are profiled in this book. The combination, we hope, helps to illuminate how changes in laws and attitudes affected individuals.

1848

Samuel Gridley Howe, an educator and advocate, reports to the Massachusetts legislature on his investigation into conditions of the intellectually disabled statewide. Several of the individuals then categorized as "idiots" would likely be diagnosed with autism today.

1910

Eugen Bleuler, a Swiss psychiatrist, coins the term *autistic thinking* to describe the thought patterns of some of his schizophrenic patients.

1919

Archie Casto, age five, from a family of six in Huntington, West Virginia, is sent to live at the Huntington State Hospital for the Insane.

1933

On September 9, Donald Triplett is born to Mary and Beamon Triplett of Forest, Mississippi.

1937

On advice from their doctors, Mary and Beamon Triplett place Donald in the Preventorium, an institution to prevent children from contracting tuberculosis in Sanatorium, Mississippi.

1938

Beamon Triplett writes a thirty-three-page account of his four-year-old son Donald's unusual behaviors and sends it to child psychiatrist Leo Kanner, head of the department of child psychiatry at Johns Hopkins Hospital.

Hans Asperger, an Austrian pediatrician, delivers a talk at Vienna's University Hospital describing boys seen in his clinic who exhibit social deficits combined with strong intelligence. Influenced by Bleuler's use of *autistic,* he borrows the term to identify a syndrome he calls *autistic psychopathy.* It is the first time it is used in its modern sense.

Mary and Beamon Triplett take Donald, now five, to meet with Kanner.

1942

In a letter to Mary Triplett, Leo Kanner theorizes that Donald and several other children with similar behaviors have a disorder not previously recognized. Like Asperger, he too borrows the word "autistic" from Bleuler, calling this new disorder "Autistic Disturbances of Affective Contact."

1943

Leo Kanner publishes "Autistic Disturbances of Affective Contact," the clinical account of eleven children that will lead to the recognition of autism as a distinct syndrome.

Donald Triplett goes to live with Ernest and Josephine Lewis on a farm outside Forest, Mississippi.

1944

Hans Asperger publishes his postgraduate thesis, "Die 'Autistischen Psychopathen' Im Kindesalter." Largely overlooked for most of the next four decades, it will lead to the recognition of Asperger's syndrome.

1947

Donald Triplett is hospitalized with juvenile rheumatoid arthritis.

1948

In an article in *Time* magazine, Kanner describes children with autism as being "kept neatly in a refrigerator which didn't defrost" by their withholding parents. His metaphor will give rise to the phrase "refrigerator mother"—a mother whose cold and rejecting behavior was said to have caused her child's autism.

1959

Researchers conduct experiments in which they administer LSD to children with autism, partly in the hope of facilitating speech. The experiments are unsuccessful, and the research is later abandoned, as LSD becomes stigmatized and hard to obtain.

Psychiatrist Lorna Wing's three-year-old daughter is diagnosed with autism.

1960

Donald Triplett, now twenty-seven, learns to drive.

1961

British child psychiatrist Mildred Creak publishes "Nine Points," an attempt to define the criteria for diagnosing "Schizophrenic Syndrome in Childhood," one of many competing descriptions for clusters of autistic traits.

1962

A group of parents in Britain founds what will become the National Autistic Society, the first autism organization.

1963

British psychologists Beate Hermelin and Neil O'Connor conduct experiments, the results of which strongly suggest a biological rather than a psychogenic basis to autism. They will continue this research through 1970.

Ruth and William Sullivan's son Joseph is diagnosed with autism.

1964

Bernard Rimland, a psychologist and parent of a son with autism, publishes *Infantile Autism: The Syndrome and Its Implications for a Neural Theory of Behavior.* Its attack on the theory of the refrigerator mother proves decisive.

Parent activist Ruth Sullivan organizes a small group of autism mothers to campaign for their children's access to public education.

An early successful use of applied behavior analysis (ABA)—known as the Dicky study—conducted by Montrose Wolf, Todd Risley, and Hayden Mees, prevents a child with severe autism from losing his sight.

O. Ivar Lovaas, a psychologist, begins experiments using ABA at UCLA with severely affected children as his subjects. As part of his attempt to modify autistic behaviors, he administers electrical shocks.

1965

LIFE magazine publishes an article introducing the public to Lovaas's controversial treatment.

A group of parents founds the National Society for Autistic Children (NSAC), the first organization in the United States to campaign for the rights of children with autism. Bernard Rimland and Ruth Sullivan are prime movers.

Educator Sybil Elgar opens the first school for autistic children in the United Kingdom.

1966

South African psychologist Victor Lotter publishes the first prevalence study on autism, based on his survey of eight- to ten-year-olds in Middlesex County, England. His finding of 4.5 cases per 10,000 children will become the baseline for all subsequent prevalence reports.

Psychologists Eric Schopler and Robert Reichler launch a pilot program at the University of North Carolina that will lead to the establishment of TEACCH (Treatment and Education of Autistic and Related Communication Handicapped Children).

1967

Bruno Bettelheim, director of the Orthogenic School at the University of Chicago, publishes *The Empty Fortress: Infantile Autism and the Birth of the Self* and it becomes a bestseller. The book blames autism on psychological trauma, usually inflicted by mothers during childhood.

Burton Blatt, an educator, and Fred Kaplan, a photographer, publish *Christmas in Purgatory,* a graphic exposé of the "hell on earth" they discovered inside several American institutions for the intellectually disabled.

Rita and Jerry Tepper's son Steven is diagnosed with autism.

1969

At the annual meeting of the National Society for Autism, Kanner gives a speech in which he "exonerates" parents of responsibility for their children's autism.

1970

Lorna Wing, psychiatrist and mother of a daughter with autism, publishes the first book aimed at parents about the challenges of raising a child with autism: *Autistic Children: A Guide for Parents and Professionals.*

Alice and George Barton adopt Frankie, a six-year-old boy with severe autism, from an orphanage in California.

1971

Tom Gilhool, an activist and lawyer, represents the Pennsylvania Association for Retarded Children in a lawsuit demanding access to public education for children with developmental disabilities. Gilhool wins, after which many other states follow Pennsylvania's lead in changing their laws to accommodate such students.

Activist parents Mary Lou "Bobo" Warren and Betty Camp succeed in getting the North Carolina State Legislature to pass a bill funding TEACCH, which will become one of the most influential and widespread educational programs for children with autism.

In California, Alec Gibson kills his thirteen-year-old son with autism, thinking that he is saving him from the world's cruelties. He confesses immediately and is given a life sentence.

1972

Geraldo Rivera, a television news reporter, exposes horrendous conditions at the Willowbrook State School, an institution for the mentally disabled in Staten Island, whose population includes many children and adults with autism. The scandal leads to the closing of Willowbrook and increased pressure to close similar institutions.

1974

California governor Ronald Reagan signs into law a bill committing the state to educate all children, regardless of handicap.

Shawn Lapin, a six-year-old boy with autism, is prominently featured in a Newsweek *cover story titled "The Troubled Child."*

1975

The Federal Education for All Handicapped Children Act is passed, later to be renamed the Individuals with Disabilities Education Act.

1977

British psychiatrist Michael Rutter and American psychologist Susan Folstein publish their "twin study," significantly bolstering the understanding of autism as a condition with a strong genetic component.

1979

Lorna Wing and psychologist Judith Gould publish data that supports their argument that autism should be described as a "spectrum."

1980

Rosemary Crossley and Annie McDonald publish *Annie's Coming Out,* an account of how Crossley used "facilitated communication" to enable Annie, who is severely physically disabled, to communicate.

Autism is listed as a mental disorder for the first time in the *DSM (Diagnostic and Statistical Manual of Mental Disorders).*

1981

Lorna Wing publishes her paper "Asperger's Syndrome: A Clinical Account," introducing Hans Asperger to the English-speaking world.

Ivar Lovaas publishes *Teaching Developmentally Disabled Children: The ME Book,* the first hands-on guide for parents and professionals on the use of ABA to treat children with autism.

1985

Psychologists Simon Baron-Cohen, Alan Leslie, and Uta Frith publish a landmark study on autism and "Theory of Mind," the idea that individuals are aware that others possess mental states distinct from their own. People with autism, they find, often fail to employ a Theory of Mind.

1986

Temple Grandin publishes *Emergence: Labeled Autistic,* her first book about the experience of having autism.

1987

Ivar Lovaas publishes a study asserting that 47 percent of the children he is treating have achieved "recovery" from autism due to his program of ABA. Controversy erupts over the validity of his results.

1988

Dustin Hoffman stars in the movie *Rain Man,* which puts autism on the map as never before.

Archie Casto is released from Spencer State Hospital after six decades of institutionalization.

1990

Having learned about facilitated communication (FC) at Rosemary Crossley's lab in Australia, Douglas Biklen, an educator at Syracuse University, publishes his findings about it in the *Harvard Educational Review.* Professionals working with autistic children rapidly adopt FC.

The US Congress passes the Individuals with Disabilities Education Act. For the first time, autism is classified as a disability for purposes of entitlements.

Alison Tepper Singer's daughter, Jodie, two years and eight months old, is diagnosed with autism.

1993

Working with speech clinician Janyce Boynton, Betsy Wheaton, a nonverbal sixteen-year-old girl with severe autism, uses FC to accuse her family of sexual abuse. Harvard speech pathologist Howard Shane stages a rigorous experiment revealing that Boynton is herself responsible for Betsy's communications, and that no abuse occurred. Enrollment in FC training courses plummets.

Self-advocate Jim Sinclair delivers a speech titled "Don't Mourn for Us," marking the birth of a movement for self-advocacy by people with autism. The speech lays the foundation for a philosophy that opposes attempts to cure autism, later dubbed "neurodiversity."

Catherine Maurice, the mother of two children with autism, publishes *Let Me Hear Your Voice,* an account of her children's recovery from autism using ABA. Demand for ABA explodes.

Karen and Eric London's son, Zachary, almost two years old, is diagnosed with autism.

1994

The American Psychiatric Association adds Asperger's disorder to the *DSM.*

Karen and Eric London, the parents of a child with autism, found the National Alliance for Autism Research (NAAR). It is the first organization to fund biomedical research of autism.

1995

Bernie Rimland founds Defeat Autism Now! (DAN), an offshoot of his Autism Research Institute, to promote nontraditional, biomedical treatments for autism.

Portia Iversen and Jon Shestack, the parents of a child with autism, found Cure Autism Now (CAN), the second organization to raise money to fund biomedical research. Like NAAR, they also lobby for support services for people with autism.

Portia Iversen and Jon Shestack's son Dov is diagnosed with Pervasive Developmental Disorder. He will later be diagnosed with autism.

Alex Plank, age nine, is diagnosed with Asperger's syndrome.

1996

Australian sociologist Judy Singer, herself on the spectrum, coins the term *neurodiversity* and speaks of a neurodiversity movement in her dissertation.

Gary Mayerson initiates legal action to compel the Westchester County Department of Health to pay for his son's ABA therapy. Mayerson prevails.

1997

NAAR awards its first grants, totaling $150,000, to five scientists researching autism.

CAN launches the Autism Genetic Research Exchange, a bank of DNA samples from families who have children with autism that is made available to all autism researchers.

1998

Andrew Wakefield, a British gastroenterologist, publishes a paper in *The Lancet* reporting an association between the MMR vaccine, autism, and bowel disease.

Harvey Blume writes about neurodiversity in *The Atlantic,* arguing that it "may be every bit as crucial for the human race as biodiversity is for life in general." It is the first time the term has appeared in a mainstream publication.

1999

NAAR establishes a bank of brain tissue from children with autism for the purposes of anatomical research.

The California Department of Disability Services reports that the number of people receiving autism services has increased by 273 percent since 1987. The numbers spark fears of an autism epidemic.

The American Academy of Pediatrics and the Public Health Service recommend that thimerosal be removed from vaccines, and that pediatricians begin using thimerosal-free vaccines whenever possible. At the same time, the two organizations assert the lack of evidence that thimerosal is harmful. The move causes confusion and increases public fears about vaccines.

2000

A group of parents found SafeMinds, an organization demanding more research into vaccine safety.

Republican representative Dan Burton, chairman of the Government Reform Committee, holds hearings investigating the link between vaccines and autism. He urges the National Institutes of Health and the Centers for Disease Control to treat autism as an epidemic.

2001

NAAR and CAN cosponsor the first International Meeting for Autism Research, an event that draws autism researchers from around the world. The annual event grows to become the largest of its kind.

As a result of the controversy his work is causing, Andrew Wakefield is made to resign his position at the Royal Free Hospital.

2003

Activist Michael John Carley, diagnosed with Asperger's syndrome shortly after his son receives the diagnosis, forms the Global and Regional Asperger Syndrome Partnership organization (GRASP) to support people on the spectrum and fight the stigma surrounding autism.

2004

Major autism organizations begin publicizing 1 in 166 as the prevalence rate of autism.

The Institute of Medicine issues a report finding that the evidence does not support a causal relationship between thimerosal in vaccines and autism.

Investigative reporter Brian Deer publishes his first exposé of financial conflicts of interest surrounding the work described in Andrew Wakefield's *Lancet* paper. He will pursue the story for the next seven years.

High-schooler Alex Plank, diagnosed with Asperger's syndrome as a child, creates Wrong Planet, an online resource and community for people with autism and Asperger's.

2005

Journalist David Kirby's *Evidence of Harm* is published. The book is a dramatic account sympathetic to the parents fighting to prove a link between vaccines and autism.

Bob and Suzanne Wright announce the formation of Autism Speaks, which aims to educate the public, fund research, increase government involvement, and help find a cure for autism. NAAR merges with the new organization.

2006

CAN merges with Autism Speaks.

The Combating Autism Act is passed, authorizing a billion dollars for autism research.

Activist Ari Ne'eman, who himself has Asperger's, founds the Autistic Self-Advocacy Network to ensure that the voices of people on the autism spectrum are heard in policy debates.

2007

The "vaccine trials" begin in the US Court of Federal Claims. Nearly five thousand families seek compensation for alleged injuries to their children. They argue that their children's autism was caused by vaccines.

The New York University Child Study Center launches its "Ransom Notes" campaign, depicting autism as a kidnapper of children, in New York City. Ari Ne'eman leads a successful fight to get the campaign pulled.

2009

Alison Singer, executive vice president of Autism Speaks, resigns over the group's continued support of research into whether vaccines can be linked to autism. She establishes the Autism Science Foundation to pursue biomedical research into possible causes and medical treatments for autism.

Eric London, founder of NAAR, resigns from the board of Autism Speaks, also at odds with the group's position on research into autism.

In the US Court of Federal Claims, the special masters rule in the case brought by the family of Michelle Cedillo. In this first of a series of test cases of the vaccine theory, they find no connection between vaccines and autism. The result will be the same for all subsequent cases.

2010

The Lancet retracts Andrew Wakefield's 1998 article, following years of investigation that point to fraud on Wakefield's part. Wakefield is stripped of his medical license.

At a conference to honor Hans Asperger, Herwig Czech, an Austrian historian, surprises those assembled by revealing that Asperger likely had a role in sending disabled children to the Spiegelgrund facility during World War II, where they were murdered. The news does not travel to the English-speaking world.

HBO's movie *Temple Grandin* wins seven Emmy Awards.

2013

Asperger's disorder is dropped from the *DSM-5*. All recognized clusters of autistic behaviors, including those previously attributed to Asperger's, are now subsumed under the heading Autism Spectrum Disorder.

Donald Triplett, the first person diagnosed with autism, turns eighty.

NOTES

Chapter 1: Donald

3 **In 1935, five Canadian:** This and other details about the Quintland phenomenon are from Pierre Berton, "The Dionne Years," *New York Times Magazine,* April 23, 1978.

4 **"Annette and Cecile make purple":** Leo Kanner, "Autistic Disturbances of Affective Contact," *Nervous Child* 2 (1943): 220. Donald's early childhood behaviors were recorded by clinicians and by his parents and relayed by Kanner.

5 **"Semicolon, capital, twelve":** Ibid., 221.

6 **"hopelessly insane":** Letter from Leo Kanner to Mary Triplett, September 17, 1939, Johns Hopkins Hospital medical archives. The records were given to the Triplett family in December 2007.

7 **raised to get the best out of life:** Biographical information on Mary and Beamon Triplett was provided in author interviews with the Triplett family. A thumbnail account of their ancestry, education, and civic activities can also be found scattered through the social pages of the *Scott County Times* in the 1950s. See Scott County History Book Committee, *History of Scott County, Missouri: History & Families* (Paducah, KY: Turner, 2003).

8 **"The Star Spangled Banner":** Pat Putnam, "Sports Scrapbook," *Sarasota Journal,* September 13, 1957; Angela Christine Stuesse, "Globalization 'Southern Style': Transnational Migration, the Poultry Industry, and Implications for Organizing Workers Across Difference," PhD diss., University of Texas at Austin, 2008.

9 **he was the former mayor's son:** Scott County History Book Committee, *History of Scott County, Missouri,* Paducah, KY: Turner, 2003.

9 **talked a little early:** Hospital records of Donald Grey Triplett, the Harriet Lane Home for Invalid Children at the Johns Hopkins Hospital, provided to the authors by the Triplett family. (Note that the Harriet Lane Home closed in 1972.) Summary report from Dr. Leo Kanner.

9 **could not feed himself:** Kanner summary report.

10 **memorized the twenty-five questions:** Kanner, "Autistic Disturbances," 217.

10 **"Say 'Eat it or I won't'":** Ibid., 219.

11 **facility known as the Preventorium:** The Preventorium building still stands today, serving as a storage facility on the grounds of what is now the Boswell

Regional Health Center. Our account of its operation and the texture of life inside its walls comes from *The Mississippi State Sanatorium: A Book of Information About Tuberculosis and Its Treatment in Mississippi,* 1939, located at the Department of Archives and History, Jackson, Mississippi; author interview with former child resident Cecile Snider, who lived in the Preventorium in the early 1930s; and author interview with David Tedford, director of vocational services at the Boswell Regional site.

Chapter 2: A Menace to Society

13 ***You have overstimulated him:*** A summary medical history of Donald that was discovered in the archives at Johns Hopkins and obtained by the Triplett family cites the opinion of the Triplett family doctor, who "felt the family had overstimulated the child" and advised change of environment.

13 **Donald stopped eating:** Ibid.

14 **resident of the Preventorium:** Although the minimum age of the Preventorium was four, Donald was permitted to enter at the age of three. He remained at the Preventorium three to four times as long as the average resident.

14 **were designated, in 1902:** "Report of Committee on Classification of Feeble-Minded," *Journal of Psycho-Asthenics* 15 (1910): 61.

15 **five name changes in its history:** "Brief History of the Association," Approved Board of Directors, *AAID Chapter Leadership Manual,* October 12, 2011, 1. The AAID explains its historical evolution at http://aaidd.org/intellectual-disability.

15 **bestselling book on parenting:** Benjamin Spock, *The Common Sense Book of Baby and Child Care* (New York: Duell, Sloan, and Pearce, 1946), 502.

17 **"long years of suffering":** This and all other details of Petey Frank's life are from his father's account, John P. Frank, *My Son's Story* (London: Sidgwick & Jackson, 1952).

17 **"cast a blight":** Ibid., 100.

17 **Petey died there in 2010:** John Peter Frank obituary, ObitsForLife, http://www.obitsforlife.com/obituary/52773/Frank-John.php.

17 **"happier if he stays at home":** Spock, *Common Sense Book,* 503.

18 **"faded away physically":** This and other details of Donald's decline come from Donald Triplett's hospital records, the Harriet Lane Home for Invalid Children and Johns Hopkins, provided to authors by the Triplett family.

18 **"not paying attention to anything":** Ibid.

18 **"he had there his worst phase":** Ibid.

20 **"KELLEYS WIN IN 'FITTER FAMILIES' CONTEST":** *Savannah Press,* November 6, 1924.

20 **"testing the Joneses, Smiths and the Johnsons":** As quoted in Jonathan Peter Spiro, *Defending the Master Race: Conservation, Eugenics and the Legacy of Madison Grant* (Burlington: University of Vermont Press, 2008), 185.

21 **examined by an expert team:** Details of the testing criteria available from images of scorecards viewable in "Fitter Family Contests," Image Archive on

the American Eugenics Movement, http://www.eugenicsarchive.org/eugenics/list2.pl. The text of the three signs can also be read here in original photographs of the Fitter Family contests.

22 **for the good of society:** "Fitter Families for Future Firesides: A Report of the Eugenics Department of the Kansas Free Fair, 1920–1924," prepared by the Kansas Bureau of Child Research (Eugenics Committee of the United States of America, 1924), http://www.eugenicsarchive.org/html/eugenics/essay_6_fs.html.

22 **a scientific, political, and philosophical movement:** Our discussion of the pervasiveness and respectability achieved by the eugenics movement in America's upper classes rests largely on the superb account of this period provided by Spiro, *Defending the Master Race.*

22 **a brand-new science:** Madison Grant, *The Passing of the Great Race* (Abergele, UK: Wermod and Wermod Publishing Group, 2012).

23 **"the broken, the mentally crippled":** Ibid., 77.

23 **"facts our people most need":** Theodore Roosevelt commends Madison Grant's book, *The Passing of the Great Race* (New York: Scribner's, 1916).

23 **His name was Adolf Hitler:** Spiro, *Defending the Master Race,* 372.

23 **"increasing race of morons":** Ibid., 192.

23 **Mississippi's sterilization law:** The 1933 sterilization figures for Mississippi, Virginia, and California are from "Sterilization Laws," Image Archive on the American Eugenics Movement, http://www.eugenicsarchive.org/eugenics/list2.pl.

23 **"insanity, feeblemindedness":** Image no. 948, "Sterilization Laws," Image Archive on the American Eugenics Movement, http://www.eugenicsarchive.org/eugenics/list2.pl.

23 **bother an editorial writer:** Unsigned editorial, *Delta Democrat Times,* Greenville, Mississippi, January 11, 1939.

24 **"the agony of living":** Foster Kennedy, "The Problem of Social Control of the Congenital Defective: Education, Sterilization, Euthanasia," *American Journal of Psychiatry* 99 (July 1942): 13–16.

24 **"we thus exonerate ourselves":** Leo Kanner, "Exoneration of the Feebleminded," *American Journal of Psychiatry* 99 (July 1942): 17–22.

Chapter 3: Case 1

25 **top child psychiatrist:** This and the subsequent biographical details about Kanner's early years are from Eric Schopler, Stella Chess, and Leon Eisenberg, "Our Memorial to Leo Kanner," *Journal of Autism and Developmental Disorders* 11, no. 3 (1981): 257–69.

25 **since psychiatry had discovered childhood:** Kanner covered the early history of his field succinctly in a talk later published as "Historical Perspective on Developmental Deviations" in *Psychopathology and Child Development* (New York: Springer, 1976), 7–17.

26 **hit by a train:** "Doctor Misses Death," *Halifax Herald,* September 6, 1937.

27 **learned the specialty:** James W. Trent, *Inventing the Feeble Mind: A History*

of Mental Retardation in the United States (Berkeley: University of California Press, 1994).

28 **He also worked for years:** Leo Kanner, unpublished autobiography, American Psychiatric Association Archives, Arlington, Virginia.

28 **Kanner blew the whistle:** "Charge of Freeing Insane Is Repeated, Hopkins Doctor Says Girls Were Let Go to Provide Fees and Cheap Labor," *Baltimore Sun,* May 14, 1937.

29 **"a comparison of the Negro":** Letter from James Lamphier to Leo Kanner, June 16, 1938, American Psychiatric Association Archives.

29 **"The fact that a child":** Letter from Leo Kanner to James Lamphier, June 23, 1938, American Psychiatric Association Archives.

29 **"a desirable procedure":** Leo Kanner, "Exoneration of the Feebleminded," *American Journal of Psychiatry* 99, no. 1 (July 1942): 17–22.

30 **filled her notepad with shorthand:** Author interview with Oliver Triplett.

30 **"He never seems glad":** The contents of Beamon Triplett's letter are preserved only in the form of excerpts quoted by Leo Kanner in "Autistic Disturbances of Affective Contact," *Nervous Child* 2 (1943), 217–22.

31 **experiment was deemed a failure:** Jimmy was not, after all, returned to the orphanage. He was adopted by acquaintances of the Tripletts, who bonded with him immediately upon seeing him. He lived in Forest the rest of his life.

32 **"let him alone":** Leo Kanner, "Follow-up Study of Eleven Autistic Children Originally Reported in 1943," *Journal of Autism and Childhood Schizophrenia* 1, no. 2 (1971): 120.

33 **"glandular disease":** Ibid., 121.

34 **"referring to the foot on the block as 'umbrella'":** Kanner, "Autistic Disturbances," 220.

34 **"He wandered about smiling":** Ibid., 219.

35 **"a hopelessly insane child":** Letter from Leo Kanner to Mary Triplett, September 17, 1939, Johns Hopkins Hospital medical archives. The records were given to the Triplett family in December 2007.

36 **"the good sense you are using":** Ibid.

36 **Kanner wrote back to reassure her:** Letter from Leo Kanner to Mary Triplett, September 28, 1942, Johns Hopkins Hospital medical archives.

37 **Kanner's first recorded use of "autistic":** As this book was nearing publication, journalist Steve Silberman published his book *Neurotribes.* In it he reported his original finding that a Czech diagnostician named Georg Frankl, who worked under Kanner in Baltimore in this period, had previously worked alongside the Austrian pediatrician Hans Asperger in Vienna. Silberman contends that through Frankl, and through Kanner's own reading of German-language medical journals, Kanner would have known that Asperger had already used the term *autistic* as early as 1938. We find Silberman's discovery of Frankl's connection to both men intriguing. Moreover, his theory that Kanner built aspects of Asperger's thinking into his own model of autism, without

crediting him, cannot be ruled out as a possibility. However, it seems just as plausible that Kanner, like Asperger, borrowed the term *autistic* from Swiss psychiatrist Eugen Bleuler, who famously used it in 1911 to describe behaviors he saw in schizophrenia. In a 1965 lecture, Kanner said exactly that. In addition, while both men called the cases they studied "autistic," they focused on different populations of children, and the conditions they described diverged in several important respects.

In either case, it was Kanner's use of the term *autistic*—not Asperger's, which was little known outside the German-speaking world—that set off the complex chain of events that comprise the story of autism as it was lived and understood by thousands of families for decades to come. That is the story we tell.

In addition, as will become clear in chapters 31 and 32, our assessment of Asperger's work and character differs from Silberman's in significant ways.

Chapter 4: Wild Children and Holy Fools

38 **"It was there before":** Leo Kanner, speech given at the annual National Society for Autism Meeting, Washington, DC, July 17, 1969. A transcription is available from the American Psychiatric Association.

40 **Around 1910, Bleuler:** Uta Frith, ed., *Autism and Asperger Syndrome* (Cambridge, UK: Cambridge University Press, 1991), 38.

42 **Half a millennium ago:** Natalia Challis and Horace W. Dewey, *The Blessed Fools of Old Russia* (Ann Arbor: University of Michigan; Franz Steiner Verlag, 1974), 1–11.

42 **a pair of Russian-speaking scholars:** Natalia Challis and Horace W. Dewey, "Basil the Blessed. Holy Fool of Moscow," *Russian History* 14, no. 1 (1987): 47–59.

43 **Hugh Blair of Borgue:** Rab Houston and Uta Frith, *Autism in History: The Case of Hugh Blair of Borgue* (Oxford: Blackwell, 2000).

44 **"The available evidence":** Ibid., 149.

46 **The so-called Wild Boy:** Jean-Marc-Gaspard Itard, *The Wild Boy of Aveyron,* trans. George and Muriel Humphrey (Englewood Cliffs, NJ: Prentice-Hall, 1962).

48 **"Seeing that my efforts":** Ibid.

49 **"to respect humanity in every form":** Samuel Gridley Howe, *The Servant of Humanity* (Boston: Dana Estes & Co., 1909), 204.

49 **"its moral character":** Ibid., 204.

49 **The result of Howe's outrage:** Samuel G. Howe, *Report Made to the Legislature of Massachusetts upon Idiocy* (Boston, 1848), 8–17, 51–53.

49 **"Science has not yet":** Ibid., 7.

51 **the Idiot's Cage:** Catherine Slater, "Idiots, Imbeciles and Intellectual Impairment," Langdon Down Museum of Learning Disability, http://langdondownmuseum.org.uk/the-history-of-learning-disability/idiots-imbeciles-and-intellectual-impairment/.

Chapter 5: Doubly Loved and Protected

52 **In the late summer of 1939:** Except where otherwise specified, the details of Donald's life during the years 1939–1945 are from Leo Kanner, "Autistic Disturbances of Affective Contact," *Nervous Child* 2 (1943), and Leo Kanner, "Follow-up Study of Eleven Autistic Children Originally Reported in 1943," *Journal of Autism and Childhood Schizophrenia* 1, no. 2 (1971).

55 **publication dates of *Time* magazine:** Author interview with Donald and Oliver Triplett.

55 **an obsession with calendars:** Author interview with James Rushing.

55 **It was not an institution:** Authors' visit to Lewis home; interview with Oliver Triplett.

56 **"Mr. & Mrs. Lewis are":** Letter from Donald Triplett's grandfather, William McCravey, June 22, 1943, provided to the authors by Oliver Triplett.

Chapter 6: Some Kind of Genius

60 **When Donald was fourteen:** In 2005, a UPI journalist named Dan Olmsted, later a founder of the website AgeofAutism.com, theorized that mercury was the cause of Donald's autism. He built his case partly on the fact that Donald seemed to have improved after doctors at the Campbell Clinic gave him a compound known as "gold salts," which was then a standard treatment for rheumatoid arthritis. Olmsted proposed that the gold salts had accelerated the removal of mercury from Donald's body. In a book arguing that autistic behaviors in a child may often be the result of an environment contaminated by mercury, Olmsted elaborated on how mercury might have reached Donald's developing brain. The lumber used in the construction of the Triplett home, he suggested, might have been treated with a mercury-based fungicide, which might in turn have leached into the air inside the house, where Mary Triplett would have inhaled it while pregnant with Donald.

In his initial reporting, Olmsted went so far as to suggest gold salts had cured Donald's autism. He quoted Donald's brother, Oliver Triplett, saying that Donald's "proclivity to excitability and extreme nervousness had all but cleared up." He also quoted a doctor—clearly one who had not examined Donald—who said, "It sounds like he moved right off the spectrum."

The theory has several weaknesses, most notably the lack of any evidence that the wood in the walls of the Triplett home contained mercury, or that Mary Triplett was ever exposed to toxic levels of mercury. Also, as is clear to anyone who has ever met Donald, he continues to this day to be a person with autism. He did not "move off the spectrum." Moreover, a 1956 write-up on Donald by Kanner's deputy, Leon Eisenberg ("The Autistic Child in Adolescence," *American Journal of Psychiatry* 112, 8 [Feb. 1956]: 607–12), reported that the moderation of his autistic behaviors had started *before* he became sick. True, Eisenberg noted that Donald's improvement had apparently continued during the illness and afterward, when it even accelerated, but this perception could easily have been the natural result of watching a boy in terrible pain returning to himself as the pain receded.

In a 2007 interview, his brother Oliver told us that neither of Donald's parents traced the lessening of his "nervousness" to the gold salts he was given at Campbell. Rather, according to Oliver, his mother believed that it was the high fevers Donald experienced that had improved his behavior. While her hunch is just as speculative as Olmsted's gold salts theory, it dovetails intriguingly with recent research indicating that high fevers have a moderating effect on certain autistic behaviors. See, for example, Curran et al., "Behaviors Associated with Fever in Children with Autism Spectrum Disorders," *Pediatrics* 120, no. 6 (December 1, 2007): e1386–e1392.

61 **about the bricks:** Author interview with Oliver and Donald Triplett.

62 **They simply let him be:** Author interviews with Janelle Brown, John Rushing, and Celeste Graham.

63 **and piano recitals:** Mary Triplett's activities were often noted in the *Scott County Times,* the local newspaper, published in Forest, Mississippi, from 1950 to 1951.

64 **Fortunately for Donald:** Janelle Brown interview.

64 **blend in themselves:** Celeste Graham interview.

65 **Donald *was* a numbers whiz:** Author interview with Buddy Lovett.

66 **then a senior, approached her:** Janelle Brown interview.

66 **Donald continued doing this:** Buddy Lovett interview.

66 **One classmate, John:** John Rushing interview.

67 **This was a landmark:** Scott County History Book Committee, *History of Scott County, Missouri: History & Families* (Paducah, KY: Turner, 2003).

68 **"Billy Bob Hefferfield":** Author interviews with Donald and Oliver Triplett.

68 **When he graduated:** Donald Triplett shared his Forest High School yearbooks with the authors.

Chapter 7: The Refrigerator Mother

73 **"You have a major problem":** This and other details about Rita Tepper's experience from an author interview with Tepper.

79 **"diaper-aged schizoids":** "Medicine: Frosted Children," *Time,* April 26, 1948.

80 **"kept neatly in a refrigerator":** Ibid.

Chapter 8: Prisoner 15209

81 **He was called *Dr.* Bruno Bettelheim:** Except where otherwise specified, details of Bruno Bettelheim's life are from Richard Pollak, *The Creation of Doctor B: A Biography of Bruno Bettelheim* (New York: Simon & Schuster, 1997), and Bruno Bettelheim, "Individual and Mass Behavior in Extreme Situations," *Journal of Abnormal and Social Psychology* 38, no. 4 (1943): 417–52.

83 **Bettelheim, upon his release:** Theron Raines, *Rising to the Light: A Portrait of Bruno Bettelheim* (New York: Knopf, 2002), 124.

85 **"From these children":** Grant application to Ford Foundation submitted by the Shankman Orthogenic School of the University of Chicago and Bruno Bettelheim, August 9, 1955, 4, Rockefeller Archive Center, Sleepy Hollow, NY. The files include Bruno Bettelheim's proposals and responses to the Ford Foundation.

86 **"From what we know":** Bruno Bettelheim, *The Empty Fortress: Infantile Autism and the Birth of the Self* (Glencoe, NY: Free Press, 1976), 60.

86 **Critics were awed:** Robert Coles, "A Hero of Our Time," *New Republic*, March 4, 1967.

86 **"as much a philosophical":** Eliot Fremont-Smith, "Children Without an I," *New York Times Book Review*, March 10, 1967.

86 **"She studied it with intense":** Bettelheim, *Empty Fortress*, 163.

86 **"completely ignored":** Bruno Bettelheim, "Joey, a Mechanical Boy," *Scientific American*, March 1959, 131.

88 **"This is essentially the same":** Bettelheim, *Empty Fortress*, 67.

Chapter 9: Kanner's Fault?

89 **Kanner's Fault?:** In the hardcover edition of this book, there is no question mark in the title of this chapter, since at the time of original publication we believed that Leo Kanner did, for a period of several years, abandon his conviction that autism was innate and turn to blaming parents. The evidence supporting that critical portrait of Kanner was, and remains, compelling.

However, following publication of the hardcover edition, and partially in response to it, a detailed defense of Kanner appeared in *The Journal of the American Academy of Child and Adolescent Psychiatry*. A second defense was published on the well-regarded SpectrumNews website. These challenges were brought by psychologists whose credibility we hold in high regard, not only because of their stature in the field, but because they knew Kanner personally. While it is possible that their close working relationships with Kanner render them less impartial, we find their alternate interpretation of the evidence—that Kanner's writing about parents was misunderstood, and that it built upon, but did not contradict, his belief that autism was innate—persuasive enough to merit serious consideration in the conversation about Kanner and mother blaming. Accordingly, and in fairness to Kanner, we have revised the chapter to account for this point of view, and added that question mark to the title.

89 **In 1949, Leo Kanner:** Leo Kanner, "Problems of Nosology and Psychodynamics in Early Infantile Autism," *American Journal of Orthopsychiatry* 19, no. 3 (1949): 416–26.

90 **"For here we seem":** Leo Kanner, "Autistic Disturbances of Affective Contact," *Nervous Child* 2 (1943): 250.

91 **"almost word-for-word":** Letter from Louise Despert to Leo Kanner, July 12, 1942, American Psychiatric Association Archives, Arlington, Virginia.

92 **as successfully autistic adults:** Kanner, Leo. "Constitutional Inadequacies,"

Genetics and the Inheritance of Integrated and Neurological and Psychiatric Patterns, ed. D. Hooker and C.C. Hare (Williams & Wilkins, 1954): 378–85.

92 **innate as well as experiential factors:** "Early Infantile Autism, 1943–1955," *American Journal of Orthopsychiatry* 26 (1956): 55–65.

92 **"When Kanner coined":** Leon Eisenberg, "The Past 50 Years of Child and Adolescent Psychiatry: A Personal Memoir," *Journal of the American Academy of Child and Adolescent Psychiatry* 40, no. 7 (July 2001): 743–48.

92 **Some fifty-two articles:** Leo Kanner, "Infantile Autism and the Schizophrenias," *Behavioral Science* 4 (1965): 412–20.

93 **"I need not mention":** Leo Kanner, speech given at the annual National Society for Autism Meeting, Washington, DC, July 17, 1969. A transcription is available from the American Psychiatric Association.

94 **moment as "thrilling":** Author interview with Ruth Sullivan.

94 **a guest on *The Dick Cavett Show*:** Dick Cavett interview with Bruno Bettelheim, *The Dick Cavett Show,* ABC, original airdate June 2, 1971.

Chapter 10: Biting Her Tongue

95 **It was winter 1964:** The story of Audrey and Melissa Flack, and the events that took place at Lenox Hill Hospital, were told in author interviews with Audrey Flack.

96 **The term used by the team was *psychogenic factors:*** Unless otherwise noted, all information about this study is from Katharine F. Woodward, Norma Jaffe, and Dorothy Brown, "Psychiatric Program for Very Young Retarded Children," *American Journal of Diseases for Children* 108 (1964): 221–29.

96 **"any organic basis":** Ibid.

97 **mandatory "casework treatment":** Ibid.

100 **In 1978, her painting of Anwar:** "Anwar Sadat, Man of the Year," *Time,* January 2, 1978.

100 **"Doctor, do you think":** Audrey Flack, *Audrey Flack, Art and Other Miracles,* unpublished manuscript shared with the authors by Audrey Flack.

104 **"renowned figure in":** James Warren, "Another Opinion: Chicago Adds to Doubts Raised About Bettelheim's Methods, Personality," *Chicago Tribune,* July 25, 1991; Shari Roan, "A Quiet Advocate for the Child: Psychology: The Late Bruno Bettelheim Rewrote the Code of Treatment for Emotionally Disturbed Children," *Los Angeles Times,* March 16, 1990.

104 **"The point of view":** Daniel Goleman, "Bruno Bettelheim Dies at 86—Psychoanalyst of Vast Impact," *New York Times,* March 14, 1990.

Chapter 11: Mothers-in-Arms

105 **Ruth Sullivan had no patience:** Author interview with Ruth Sullivan.

106 **"He will always be a little odd":** Ibid.

110 **"ready for school":** John Machacek, "No School for Bright Boy Suffering from Autism," *Knickerbocker News,* February 22, 1966.

111 **she would write up a set of guidelines:** Ruth Sullivan, "Parents As Trainers

of Legislators, Other Parents, and Researchers," in *The Effects of Autism on the Family,* ed. Eric Schopler and Gary Mesibov (New York: Plenum Press, 1984).
111 **"poignant beauty":** Ibid., 235.
111 **"one of the most sensitive":** Ibid.
111 **"reading reports, budgets, studies":** Ibid., 237.
111 **families in Suffolk County:** In the United States, the first schools parents started on their own were: the May Institute, originally called the Parents' School for Atypical Children, started by Jacques and Marie May in 1955 on Cape Cod; the Developmental Disabilities Institute, originally called the Suffolk Center for Emotionally Disturbed Children, in Suffolk County, Massachusetts; and the Center for Developmental Disabilities, originally called the Nassau Center for Emotionally Disturbed Children, in Woodbury, New York. See http://198.173.67.27/dramatic_progress_in_the_past.htm.

Chapter 12: The Agitator

113 **he was famously happy:** Author interview with Jon Panghorn.
113 **Bernie's own parents were:** This and other details of Bernard Rimland's life are from an author interview with Gloria Rimland, his wife, and Stephen Edelson.
114 **"a perfectly normal-looking infant":** *Autism: Present Challenges, Future Needs—Why the Increased Rates? Hearing Before the House Committee on Government Reform,* 106th Congress, statement by Bernard Rimland, PhD, Autism Research Institute, 2000.
118 **"Only Churchill comes to mind":** Letter from Bernard Rimland, PhD, to Leo Kanner, MD, c. 1960, American Psychiatric Association Archives.
118 **encouraged Rimland to keep going:** Letter from Bernard Rimland, PhD, to Leo Kanner, MD, c. 1960, American Psychiatric Association Archives.
119 **Rimland's first letter to Bettelheim:** Letter from Bernard Rimland to Bruno Bettelheim, March 22, 1965, Bettelheim papers, University of Chicago.
119 **"I . . . shall give you no help":** Letter from Bruno Bettelheim to Bernard Rimland, March 25, 1965, Bettelheim papers, University of Chicago.
119 **"any reprints, reports or references":** Letter from Bernard Rimland to Bruno Bettelheim, April 5, 1966, Bettelheim papers, University of Chicago.
119 **"You see, feelings are":** Letter from Bruno Bettelheim to Bernard Rimland, March 25, 1965, Bettelheim papers, University of Chicago.
121 **"father of autism":** Leo Kanner, foreword in Bernard Rimland, *Infantile Autism: The Syndrome and Its Implications for a Neural Theory of Behavior* (New York: Appleton-Century-Crofts, Educational Division, Meredith Publishing, 1964), 21.
121 **parents were actually stealing:** Edelson interview.
121 **a "diagnostic checklist":** Rimland, *Infantile Autism,* 278.
123 **calling his Baltimore clinic:** Leo Kanner, "The Specificity of Early Infantile Autism," *Acta Paedopsychiatrica* 25 (1958): 108–13.
123 **"one of the nation's leading authorities":** William G. Patrick, "Bizarre Withdrawal Symptoms Mark Infantile Autism Cases," *Salt Lake City Tribune,* March 17, 1967.

123 **"a recognized authority":** "Autism Film Screened Tonight," *Oxnard Press Courier,* May 8, 1969.

123 **"two major schools of thought":** Ellen Hoffman, *Washington Post,* July 1969.

124 **Robert Crean was a playwright:** Robert J. Crean papers, 1947–1971, Wisconsin Historical Society Archives, Wisconsin Center for Film and Theater Research, http://digital.library.wisc.edu/1711.dl/wiarchives.uw-whs-us0095an.

124 **The episode was called "Conall":** TV listings, *Herald Statesman,* February 6, 1965.

124 **The program aired:** Author interview with Christopher Crean. Crean provided the authors a copy of the original show his father produced in 1965, "Directions '65: 'Conall.'"

125 **referring to the "Rimland book":** Author interview with Ruth Sullivan.

125 **The National Society for Autistic Children:** Interviews with Ruth Sullivan and Ellen Rampell, daughter of Herbert and Roslyn Kahn; Frank Warren, "The Role of the National Society in Working with Families," in *The Effects of Autism on the Family,* ed. Eric Schopler and Gary Mesibov (New York: Plenum Press, 1984).

Chapter 13: Home on a Monday Afternoon

128 **"Blind Child Slow Learner":** This and other recollections about Frankie Barton are from an author interview with Alice and George Barton.

132 **Wouldn't that be a relief?:** Author interview with Lorenzo Dall' Armi, superintendent of the Santa Barbara school system.

133 **election was held to replace her:** Mooza V. P. Grant, "The President Reports," *National Society for Autistic Children, Inc., Newsletter,* Summer 1968.

133 **legal action to prevent Grant:** Author interview with Ruth Sullivan.

134 **lost his trust in psychiatry:** The story of the psychiatry crisis is well told in Edward Shorter, *A History of Psychiatry: From the Asylum to the Age of Prozac* (New York: John Wiley & Sons, 1997).

134 **established the Santa Barbara:** Author interview with Mary Ellen Nava.

136 **Then Dougie was diagnosed with autism:** This and other recollections of life in the Gibson household are from an author interview with Junie Gibson.

139 **"I have done a terrible thing":** "Retarded Son Is Dead: Father Calls Police to Say He Shot Boy," *Santa Barbara Press,* January 6, 1971.

140 **"schizophrenic reaction, childhood type":** Ibid.

140 **a letter to the editor appeared:** Mary Ellen Nava, "Readers Comments," *Santa Barbara Press,* January 9, 1971.

140 **"mercy killing":** Mary Ellen Nava interview.

140 **At the trial, a sympathetic psychiatrist:** *The People of the State of California, Plaintiff, v. Alexander Gibson, Defendant,* Original Reporter's Transcript of Grand Jury Proceedings, January 12, 1971, Superior Court of the State of California for the County of Santa Barbara.

142 **given a life sentence:** Ibid.

142 **understood what Alec had been up against:** Mary Ellen Nava interview.

142 **"what future does my boy have?":** Nava, "Readers Comments."

143 **officials from the California Department of Education:** Author interview with Mary Ellen Nava. As president of the Santa Barbara Society for Autistic Children, Mary Ellen Nava was interviewed by officials from the California Department of Education. She and Alice Barton were part of the pilot program Dr. Koegel launched for children with autism in response to the death of Dougie Gibson.

144 **"are cooperating on a model program for autistic":** Ursula Vil, "Mother of Slain Autistic Child Describes an Odyssey of Grief," *Los Angeles Times,* March 26, 1972.

144 **a model that persisted, evolved, and expanded:** Author interview with Robert and Lynn Koegel.

144 **"probably would not have been":** *A Minority of One,* directed by Mike Gavin, KNBC, original airdate May 11, 1975.

Chapter 14: "Behind the Walls of the World's Indifference"

147 **Archie Casto's parents moved him:** Unless otherwise noted, details about Archie Casto's adult life are from an author interview with Ruth Sullivan and Harriet Casto, "Archie, Autism and Another Time," *ADVOCATE: Autism Society of America Newsletter,* Fall 1991.

148 **first eleven children Kanner wrote about:** Leo Kanner, *Childhood Psychosis: Initial Studies and New Insights* (New York: Winston/Wiley, 1973), 161–87.

148 **"in empty hopelessness":** Bernard Rimland, *Infantile Autism: The Syndrome and Its Implications for a Neural Theory of Behavior* (New York: Appleton-Century-Crofts, Educational Division, Meredith Publishing, 1964), 10.

149 **A 1967 British study:** Michael Rutter and Linda Lockyer, "A Five to Fifteen Year Follow-up Study of Infantile Psychosis," *British Journal of Psychiatry* 113 (1967), 1169–82.

149 **As late as 1982, another British:** A. Shah, N. Holmes, and L. Wing, "Prevalence of Autism and Related Conditions in Adults in a Mental Handicap Hospital," *Applied Research in Mental Retardation* 3, no. 3 (1982): 303–17.

150 **Home for Incurables:** Ed Prichard, "The Huntington State Mental Hospital," Doors to the Past, January 4, 2008, http://www.rootsweb.ancestry.com/~wvcccfhr/history/hospital.htm.

151 **The 1920 census:** United States Federal Census 1920, Census Place: Huntington Ward 7, Cabell, West Virginia; Roll: T625_1951; Page: 1B; Enumeration District: 193; Image: 504, Ancestry.com.

152 **"kicking and beating patients":** "Cruelty to Lunatics: Serious Charges Against a Pennsylvania Asylum," *New York Times,* March 31, 1890.

152 **It was a scandal again:** "Nurses Tell of Cruelty," *San Bernardino Daily Sun,* August 11, 1903.

152 **"relics of the dark ages":** Albert Maisel, "Bedlam," *LIFE,* May 6, 1946.

153 **Armentrout snuck into:** Charles Armentrout, "Mentally Ill Tots Crying for Love and Attention," *Charleston Gazette,* January 31, 1949.

154 **Lena Wentz—was only eleven:** Charles Armentrout, "Huntington Hospital Fire Kills 14 Patients," *Charleston Gazette,* November 27, 1952.

154 **exposing the appalling treatment:** Burton Blatt, "The Tragedy and Hope of Retarded Children," *Look,* October 31, 1967.

155 **"It smelled of disease":** Clip from *Willowbrook: The Last Great Disgrace,* produced by Albert T. Primo (1972), https://www.youtube.com/watch?v=k_sYn8DnlH4.

Chapter 15: The Right to Education

159 **"beautiful and well-formed":** Bernard Rimland, *Infantile Autism: The Syndrome and Its Implications for a Neural Theory of Behavior* (Appleton-Century-Crofts, Educational Division, Meredith Publishing, 1964), 80.

159 **"I'm going to have to teach you":** Fred Pelka, *What We Have Done: An Oral History of the Disability Rights Movement* (Amherst: University of Massachusetts Press, 2012), 136.

159 **"because my brother is retarded":** Ibid., 136.

160 **against keeping Bob in an institution:** Author interview with Tom Gilhool.

161 **"Well, these things happen":** Pelka, *What We Have Done,* 137.

161 **"I can do this":** Ibid., 138.

161 **equal protection under the law:** Leopold Lippman and I. Ignacy Goldberg, *Right to Education: Anatomy of the Pennsylvania Case and Its Implications for Exceptional Children* (New York: Teachers College Press, 1973).

162 **"Your Honors, we surrender":** Gilhool interview.

162 **"an intelligent response":** *The Pennsylvania Association for Retarded Children et al., Plaintiffs, v. Commonwealth of Pennsylvania, et al., Defendants,* US District Court, E.D. of Pennsylvania, May 5, 1972, 11. Text available at http://www.pilcop.org/wp-content/uploads/2012/04/PARC-Consent-Decree.pdf.

163 **"appropriate to his learning capacities":** Thomas K. Gilhool, "The Uses of Litigation: The Right of Retarded Citizens to a Free Public Education," US Department of Health, Education, and Welfare, 1972, http://mn.gov/mnddc/parallels2/pdf/70s/72/72-CII-USD.pdf.

163 **"placement in a regular public school":** *Pennsylvania Association for Retarded Children,* 25.

163 **thirty federal court decisions had affirmed:** Lippman and Goldberg, *Right to Education,* 44.

Chapter 16: Getting on the Bus

165 **"The Troubled Child":** Matt Clark, "The Troubled Child," *Newsweek,* April 8, 1974.

166 **he suddenly tuned out:** This and other recollections of life with Shawn Lapin are from an author interview with Connie and Harvey Lapin.

167 **they could and did say, "Go away":** IDEA ensures access to public education for students with disabilities, policies that were not required in all states prior to 1975.

171 **"All the children who come to us":** Harry Nelson, "New Help Seen in the Child Care Practitioner," *Geneva Times,* May 10, 1971.

176 **the Lapins sued:** Connie and Harvey Lapin dropped their lawsuit in September 1974 after Ronald Reagan signed the Education Bill into law. Further information on the Lapins' activism can be found on their website, Autism & Activism: http://autismandactivism.com/policy-legislation/ and Harvey and Connie Lapin Collection, Special Collections and Archives, Oviatt Library, California State University, Northridge, http://www.oac.cdlib.org/findaid/ark:/13030/c80p1286/entire_text/.

177 **The NSAC June 1974 newsletter:** *National Society for Autistic Children, Inc., Newsletter,* June 1974.

178 **bill had passed both houses:** Author interview with Kimberly Gund.

179 **told his son's story to Ursula Vils:** Ursula Vils, "Lloyd Nolan Recalls Tragedy of Autism," *Los Angeles Times,* March 11, 1973.

179 **he narrated a televised documentary on autism:** *A Minority of One,* directed by Mike Gavin, KNBC, original airdate May 11, 1975.

Chapter 17: Seeing the Ocean for the First Time

182 **peak for that age group:** Gil Eyal, *The Autism Matrix* (Cambridge, UK: Polity Press, 2010), 101–102.

183 **autism information and referral service:** The Autism Services Center was founded by Ruth Sullivan and began in her home in 1979. It is a nonprofit behavioral health center created to provide services in Cagell, Wayne, Lincoln, and Mason counties in West Virginia. Information about the creation of the ASC is from an author interview with Ruth Sullivan.

185 **When Harriet heard that:** This and other details about Archie Casto's adult life are from an author interview with Ruth Sullivan and Harriet Casto, "Archie, Autism and Another Time," *ADVOCATE: Autism Society of America Newsletter,* Fall 1991.

187 **home to a Walmart superstore:** "Spencer State Hospital," Kirkbride Buildings, http://www.kirkbridebuildings.com/buildings/spencer/.

Chapter 18: The Behaviorist

191 **got high on it completely by accident:** Andy Roberts, *Albion Dreaming: A Popular History of LSD in Britain* (Singapore: Marshall Cavendish, 2008), 12–14.

192 **in hopes of getting him to talk:** A. M. Freedman and E. V. Ebin, "Autistic Schizophrenic Children. An Experiment in the Use of D-Lysergic Acid Diethylamide (LSD-25)," *Archives of General Psychiatry* 6 (1962): 203–13; the League School was identified as the site of Freedman's LSD experiment by L. Bender, G. Faretra, and L. Cobrinik, "LSD and UML Treatment of Hospitalized Disturbed Children," *Recent Advances in Biological Psychology* 5 (1963): 84.

192 **"who had been mute for some years":** As quoted in Freedman and Ebin, "Autistic Schizophrenic Children," 205.

192 **"since Mr. G. never spoke":** Ibid., 205.
193 **"depressed, but relaxed":** Ibid., 211.
193 **"The hoped-for change":** Ibid., 212.
193 **symptoms that today would fit neatly:** L. Bender, L. Goldschmidt, and D. V. Siva Sankar, "Treatment of Autistic Schizophrenic Children with LSD-25 and UML-491," in *Recent Advances in Biological Psychiatry,* ed. J. Wortis (New York: Springer, 1962), 170.
193 **"even obtaining parents' consent":** Bender, Faretra, and Cobrinik, "LSD and UML Treatment of Hospitalized Disturbed Children," 85.
193 **having experimented on a total of eighty-nine children:** L. Bender, "Children's Reactions to Psychotomimetic Drugs," in *Psychotomimetic Drugs,* ed. D. H. Efron (New York: Raven Press, 1970), 265–73.
193 **Similar work was taking place at UCLA:** J. Q. Simmons, D. Benor, and D. Daniel, "The Variable Effects of LSD-25 on the Behavior of a Heterogeneous Group of Childhood Schizophrenics," *Behavioral Neuropsychiatry* 4, no. 1–2 (1972): 10–16.
194 **"new hope":** Harold A. Abramson, "The Use of LSD-25 in the Therapy of Children (A Brief Review)," *Journal of Asthma Research* 5 (1967): 139–43.
194 **done anything good at all for children with autism:** See for example, E. M. Ornitz, "Childhood Autism: A Review of the Clinical and Experimental Literature," *California Medicine* 118 (1973): 21–47; and Simmons, Benor, and Daniel, "Variable Effects," *Behavioral Neuropsychiatry* 4, no. 1–2 (1972): 10–16, where Simmons concludes, "Findings cast some doubt on the value of LSD as a therapy in itself or as a therapeutic adjunct."
194 **used again by a UCLA psychologist:** "It is important to note, in view of the moral and ethical arguments which might preclude the use of electric shock, that their future was certain institutionalization. They had been intensively treated in a residential setting by conventional psychiatric techniques for one year prior to the present study without any observable modification in their behaviors. This failure in treatment is consistent with reports of other similar efforts with such children." From O. Ivar Lovaas, Benson Schaeffer, and James Q. Simmons, "Building Social Behavior in Autistic Children by Use of Electric Shock," *Journal of Experimental Research in Personality* 1 (1965): 100.
194 **on a music scholarship:** Laura Schreibman, "Memories of Ole Ivar Lovaas, 'Never, Ever Dull,'" *Observer* (Association for Psychological Science), November 2010, 23.
195 **and had been disappointed:** J. Q. Simmons et al., "Modification of Autistic Behavior with LSD-25," *American Journal of Psychiatry* 122, no. 11 (1966): 1201–11.
195 **his initial experiments:** Lovaas, Schaeffer, and Simmons, "Building Social Behavior," 99–105.
195 **Mike and Marty:** The boys' first names are paired in a list of names appearing in the dedication to Lovaas's *Teaching Developmentally Disabled Children: The ME Book* (Baltimore: University Park Press, 1981), xii.

196 **delivered 1,400 volts:** O. Ivar Lovaas and James Q. Simmons, "Manipulation of Self-Destruction in Three Retarded Children," *Journal of Applied Behavior Analysis* 2, no. 3 (1969): 143–57.

196 **tried it on himself:** Lovaas wrote, "It was definitely painful to the experimenter" (ibid., 149). We have made the assumption that Lovaas, both as lead author on the study and as a matter of principle, would have subjected himself to a taste of the Hot-Shot, and was therefore speaking of himself when he referred to "the experimenter." Similarly, we assume that Lovaas was referring to himself when he identified "Experimenter 1" as the person who dealt shocks to the boy named John. Again, as lead author, Lovaas would almost certainly have given himself that designation.

200 **"John was effectively freed":** Ibid., 150.

201 **"Male Chauvinist Pig Award":** Schreibman, "Memories of Ole Ivar Lovaas," 23.

201 **"more brains in this salad":** Paul Chance, "A Conversation with Ivar Lovaas About Self-Mutilating Children and How Their Parents Make It Worse," *Psychology Today,* January 1974, 78.

201 **"They are little monsters":** Ibid., 76, 79.

201 **"If I had gotten Hitler here":** Robert Ito, "The Phantom Chaser: For Ivar Lovaas, UCLA's Controversial Autism Pioneer, a Life's Work Is Now Facing a Crucial Test," *Los Angeles Magazine,* April 2004, 50.

Chapter 19: "Screams, Slaps, and Love"

203 **"far-gone mental cripples":** Dan Moser and photographer Alan Grant, "Screams, Slaps & Love: A Surprising, Shocking Treatment Helps Far-Gone Mental Cripples," *LIFE,* May 7, 1965.

204 **Ivan Pavlov, a physiologist:** Ivan Pavlov, "Physiology of Digestion," in *Nobel Lectures: Physiology or Medicine 1901–1921* (Singapore: World Scientific, 1999).

205 **"wrapped in darkness":** Ibid., 154.

205 **"between man and brute":** John B. Watson, "Psychology as the Behaviorist Views It," *Psychological Review* 101, no. 2 (1994): 248–53. Published from a lecture given at Columbia on February 24, 1913.

206 **with only ninety seconds of conditioning:** A demonstration of this feat by Skinner can be seen at https://www.youtube.com/watch?v=TtfQlkGwE2U.

207 **Bijou was contacted:** Amber E. Mendres and Michelle A. Frank-Crawford, "A Tribute to Sidney W. Bijou, Pioneer in Behavior Analysis and Child Development: Key Works That Have Transformed Behavior Analysis in Practice," *Behavior Analysis in Practice* 2, no. 2 (2009): 4–10; Sidney Bijou, "Reflections on Some Early Events Related to Behavior Analysis of Child Development," *Behavior Analyst* 1, no. 19 (1996): 49–60.

207 **The "Dicky study":** M. Risley and T. Mees, "Application of Operant Conditioning Procedures to the Behaviour Problems of an Autistic Child," *Behavior Research and Therapy* 1 (1964): 305–12.

Chapter 20: The Aversion to Aversives

216 **Lovaas had squeezed everything:** O. Ivar Lovaas, *Teaching Developmentally Disabled Children: The ME Book* (Baltimore: University Park Press, 1981).

216 **returned to the institutions where they lived:** O. Ivar Lovaas, Robert Koegel, James Q. Simmons, and Judith Stevens Long, "Generalization and Follow-up Measures on Autistic Children in Behavior Therapy," *Journal of Applied Behavior Analysis* 6, no. 1 (1973): 131–66.

218 **"justification for using aversives":** Lovaas, *Teaching Developmentally Disabled Children,* 16.

218 **The year of its publication:** "Resolution on Intrusive Interventions," reported in Susan Lehr and Robert Lehr, "Why Is My Child Hurting? Positive Approaches to Dealing with Difficult Behaviors. A Monograph for Parents of Children with Disabilities," 25, http://eric.ed.gov/?id=ED334728.

218 **"perhaps the single most frequently":** As quoted in C. Holden, "What's Holding Up 'Aversives' Report?" *Science* 249, no. 4972 (1990): 980.

219 **"chewing off both thumbs":** Bernard Rimland, "Aversives for People with Autism," *Autism Research Review International* 2, no. 3 (1988): 3.

219 **"couldn't envision sitting with roses":** "Autistic Child Brings Years of Toil as Loving Parents Strive to Help," *Daily Herald,* June 19, 1973.

219 **within days of the helmet:** Brian A. Iwata, "The Development and Adoption of Controversial Default Technologies," *Behavior Analyst* 11, no. 2 (1988): 149–57.

220 **a position against "aversive techniques":** Eric Schopler and Gary B. Mesibov, eds., *Behavioral Issues in Autism* (New York: Plenum Press, 1994), 18.

221 **"and ignoring a nuclear holocaust":** Robert S. P. Jones, *Challenging Behaviour and Intellectual Disability: A Psychological Perspective* (Clevedon, UK: BILD Publications, 1993), 101.

221 **Donnellan likened this paper:** Anne Donnellan and Gary LaVigna, "Myths About Punishment," in *Perspectives on the Use of Nonaversive and Aversive Interventions for Persons with Developmental Disabilities,* ed. A. C. Repp and N. N. Singh (Belmont, CA: Wadsworth, 1993), 33–57.

221 **"political correctness":** John W. Jacobson, Richard M. Foxx, and James A. Mulick, *Controversial Therapies for Developmental Disabilities: Fad, Fashion, and Science in Professional Practice* (New York: CRC Press, 2005), 295.

222 **"would not deign to provide treatment":** Jacobson et al., *Controversial Therapies for Developmental Disabilities,* 296.

222 **"Often the happiest people":** Lovaas, *Teaching Developmentally Disabled Children,* 3.

Chapter 21: The "Anti-Bettelheim"

224 **Eric Schopler stomped into his offices:** Many of the details about Eric Schopler were provided in author interviews with Gary Mesibov, Lee Marcus, and Brenda Denzler.

224 **kept bees, chickens:** Schopler to E. B. White, February 27, 1977, TEACCH Files, University of North Carolina.

224 **mothers, far from being blamed:** Eric Schopler, "Parents of Psychotic Children as Scapegoats," *Journal of Contemporary Psychotherapy* 4, no. 1 (1971): 17–22.

224 **"when Eric Schopler was our main defense":** Richard Pollak, *The Creation of Doctor B: A Biography of Bruno Bettelheim* (New York: Simon & Schuster, 1997), 282.

225 **chief psychiatric social worker:** Eric Schopler, "Recollections of My Professional Development," presentation for the Emma P. Bradley Symposium, "What Future for the Helping Professional," October 22, 1971.

225 **perfect opening to bring:** Schopler related this anecdote in Eric Schopler, "The Anatomy of a Negative Role Model," in *The Undaunted Psychologist: Adventures in Research,* ed. Gary Brannigan and Matthew Merrens (Philadelphia: Temple University Press, 1993), 173–86.

225 **"I am only the doctor prescribing":** Schopler, "Anatomy of a Negative Role Model," 177.

225 **"identifying with the disease!":** Pollak, *Creation of Doctor B,* 228.

226 **as he was later accused of doing:** Pollak, *Creation of Doctor B,* 198–99, 207–8.

226 **Schopler began work on a doctoral degree:** Schopler's work turned into a published paper, "The Development of Body Image and Symbol Formation Through Bodily Contact with an Autistic Child," *Journal of Child Psychology and Psychiatry* 3, no. 3–4 (1962): 191–202.

227 **"Why is it you scientists always try":** Schopler archival interview with Brenda Denzler, Carrboro, North Carolina, in his TEACCH office, December 17, 2001.

227 **Schopler arrived in North Carolina:** Eric Schopler's and Robert Reichler's recollections of their experiences come from "Recollections of My Professional Development," Schopler presentation for the Emma P. Bradley Symposium, October 22, 1971; Gary Mesibov interview with Eric Schopler, June 18, 1988, provided by TEACCH; Schopler archival interview with Brenda Denzler; and author interview with Robert Reichler.

227 **"Psychotic Children's Group":** This experiment is described in Rex W. Speers and Cornelius Lansing, *Group Therapy in Childhood Psychosis* (Chapel Hill: University of North Carolina Press, 1965).

229 **a mother named Mardy:** In the interest of privacy preferences, the surname is omitted in this case.

231 **videotapes of his sessions:** The tapes were edited into the film *Conjoint Parent-Therapist Teaching of a Pre-School Psychotic Child, Child Research Project,* University of North Carolina, 1967.

232 **"than as having caused them":** Eric Schopler and Robert Reichler, "Parents as Co-therapists in the Treatment of Psychotic Children," *Journal of Autism and Childhood Schizophrenia* 1, no. 1 (1971): 87–102.

232 **Betty was a special-education teacher:** Author interview with Betty and Norman Camp.

233 **One of her most vivid memories:** Author interview with Mary Lou Warren.

236 **George had just attempted to feed grits:** Mary Lou "Bobo" Warren, *My Humpty-Dumpty: A Mother's View,* unpublished manuscript given to authors by Mary Lou Warren.

237 **"not to rest until something":** Warren, *My Humpty-Dumpty.*

Chapter 22: 47 Percent

239 **On March 10, 1987:** Daniel Goleman, "Researcher Reports Progress Against Autism," *New York Times Magazine,* March 10, 1987.

239 **"to transform a large proportion":** Ibid.

239 **"If you met them now":** Ibid.

240 **All nine achieved "normal functioning":** O. Ivar Lovaas, "Behavioral Treatment and Normal Educational and Intellectual Functioning in Young Autistic Children," *Journal of Consulting and Clinical Psychology* 55, no. 1 (1955): 3–9.

241 **"The Lovaas study":** Bernard Rimland, "In Defense of Ivar Lovaas," editor's column, in *Autism Research Review International* 1, no. 1 (1987): 3.

242 **"having neurological problems":** Gary Mesibov interview with Eric Schopler, June 18, 1988, provided by TEACCH.

242 **"with a different woman":** Ibid.

242 **"dismayed to read":** Eric Schopler, "Lovaas Study Questioned," letters to the editor, in *Autism Research Review International* 1, no. 3 (1987): 6.

244 **"improvement":** Eric Schopler and Gary B. Mesibov, *Diagnosis and Assessment in Autism* (New York: Plenum Press, 1988), 6.

244 **threatened a libel suit:** Mesibov interview with Schopler.

244 **"widely and untrue":** Ivar Lovaas, "Clarifying Comments on the UCLA Young Autism Project," University of California, Los Angeles, Department of Psychology, August 2, 2000.

244 **"from prevailing theories":** Ibid.

245 **"and educational functioning":** John J. McEachin, Tristram Smith, and O. Ivar Lovaas, "Long-Term Outcome for Children with Autism Who Received Early Intensive Behavioral Treatment," *American Journal on Mental Retardation* 97, no. 4 (1993): 360.

245 **"a kind of scientific limbo":** R. M. Foxx, "Commentaries on McEachin, Smith and Lovaas: Rapid Effects Awaiting Independent Replication," *American Journal of Mental Retardation* 97, no. 3 (1993): 375.

246 **"implemented throughout":** Tristram Smith, "Outcome of Early Intervention for Children with Autism," *Clinical Psychology: Science and Practice* 6 (1999): 40.

Chapter 23: Look at Me

247 **"It's hanging in the job placement office":** Unless otherwise noted, this and all subsequent quotations attributed to Bridget Taylor are derived from several author interviews with Taylor. Details of her work with the Maurice children come from the same interviews, and from Catherine Maurice, *Let Me Hear Your Voice* (New York: Knopf, 1993).

254 **Bruno Bettelheim had told:** Bruno Bettelheim, *The Empty Fortress: Infantile Autism and the Birth of the Self* (Glencoe, NY: Free Press, 1976).

254 **Bernard Rimland's book:** Bernard Rimland, *Infantile Autism: The Syndrome and Its Implications for a Neural Theory of Behavior* (Appleton-Century-Crofts, Educational Division, Meredith Publishing, 1964).

254 **Clara Park's 1966 *The Siege*:** Clara Claiborne Park, *The Siege* (New York: Harcourt, Brace & World, 1967).

Chapter 24: From Courtroom to Classroom

256 **"immediate and intense intervention":** Unless otherwise noted, recollections about the Mayersons' experience are from an author interview with Gary Mayerson.

257 **"despicable":** Author interview with SueAnn Galante.

257 **But in the 1990s:** Perry A. Zirkel, "The Autism Case Law: Administrative and Judicial Rulings," *Focus on Autism and Other Developmental Disabilities* 17, no. 2 (2002): 84–93.

257 **"a legally hot topic":** Ibid., 84.

258 **ten times the actual proportion:** Perry A. Zirkel, "Autism Litigation Under the IDEA: A New Meaning of 'Diproportionality'?" *Journal of Special Education Leadership* 24, no. 2 (2011): 93–102.

258 **employed an expert witness:** Memorandum Decision and Order Granting Plaintiffs' Motion for Attorneys' Fees, *BD, et al., Plaintiffs, v. Barbara A. Debuono, et al.,* United States District Court, Southern District of New York, November 14, 2001.

258 **to get ABA funding:** Janet Gramza, "Families Struggle with Schools, Governments," *Post-Standard* (Syracuse, New York), April 14, 1997.

258 **"is proven effective":** Beverley Sharp, "Autism and Discrimination in British Columbia," speech given at the British Columbia Woman's Rights Committee, December 8, 1997.

259 **$50,000 per child:** Glen Sallows and Tamlynn Graupner, "Intensive Behavioral Treatment for Children with Autism: Four-Year Outcome and Predictors," *American Journal on Mental Retardation* 110, no. 6 (2005): 417–38.

260 **Before 1996, they:** *Special Education: Is IDEA Working as Congress Intended? Hearing Before the House Committee on Government Reform,* 107th Cong. (2001).

260 **In Monroe County, New York:** Gramza, "Families Struggle with Schools, Governments."

260 **who was furiously taking notes:** Galante interview.

261 **Kaplan decided to contact:** Author interview with Suzanne Kaplan.

261 **"a law alert":** Galante interview.

262 **talking to Professor Janet Twyman:** Author interview with Janet Twyman.

264 **"a policy that limits":** Transcription of minutes from hearing between Gary Mayerson and the State Department of Health, in the Matter of GSM Petition on behalf of "MM" child. Hearings began October 2, 1996, and concluded December 30, 1996, at the New York State Department of Health,

Mamaroneck, New York. Transcription was provided to the authors by Gary Mayerson.

264 **"meaningful educational benefit":** The IDEA includes two fundamental requirements: (1) that the child will receive a free, appropriate public education in the least restrictive environment; (2) that children are placed in settings that will provide them with a meaningful educational benefit. See Pete Wright and Pamela Wright, *Wrightslaw: Special Education Law,* Second Edition (Hartford, VA: Harbor House Law Press, 2007), www.wrightslaw.com/advoc/articles/idea.lre.fape.htm.

264 **adequately for each different child:** Mitchell L. Yell and Erik Drasgow, "Litigating a Free Appropriate Public Education: The Lovaas Hearings and Cases," *Journal of Special Education* 33 (2000): 205.

265 **"I am *trying* to answer":** The following facts are related in an April 3, 1997, decision on *In the Matter of Gary S. Mayerson & Lilli Z. Mayerson, Petitioners, on behalf of MM, Child,* following a hearing in front of New York Department of Health Administrative Law Judge G. Liepshutz, September 5, 1996.

266 **"We look at it as a way of beginning":** Kaplan interview.

268 **"Clinical Practice Guidelines":** "Quick Reference Guide for Parents and Professionals: Autism/Pervasive Developmental Disorders," New York State Department of Health, 1999, http://www.health.ny.gov/publications/4216.pdf.

268 **"thirty years of research":** "Mental Health: A Report of the Surgeon General," National Institutes of Health, 1999, http://profiles.nlm.nih.gov/ps/access/NNBBHS.pdf.

268 **But not all schools had:** Information on Melinda Baird and her strategy, including "Building a Blueprint for an Appropriate and Defensible Autism Program," were entered into the court records by Gary Mayerson during the trial.

269 **use an "eclectic approach":** Author interviews with a wide range of experts in the field of autism and studies on eclectic behavior approaches were the basis for this information. See also J. S. Howard et al., "A Comparison of Intensive Behavior Analytic and Eclectic Treatments for Young Children with Autism," *Research in Developmental Disabilities* 26, no. 4 (2005), 359–83.

270 **In 2005, Glen Sallows:** Sallows and Graupner, "Intensive Behavioral Treatment."

Chapter 25: The Questions Asked

274 **copied again and again:** Helen Green Allison in *Aspects of Autism: Biological Research,* ed. Lorna Wing (London: Gaskell Psychiatry, 1988), 18–20.

274 **teacher named Sybil Elgar:** Lawrence Goldman, ed., "Elgar, Sybil Lillian," *Oxford Dictionary of National Biography 2005–2008* (Oxford University Press, 2013), 344.

275 **Helen Green Allison was:** Micah Buis, "Educating About Autism," *Vassar, the Alumnae/i Quarterly,* Fall 2006.

276 **Through Mencap, Baron:** Email correspondence between Baron and the authors.

277 **children with autism could be taught:** Goldman, "Elgar, Sybil Lillian," 344.

278 **to ask these questions:** Uta Frith, "Looking Back: The Avengers of Psychology," *Psychologist* (British Psychological Society), August 2009.

279 **The inside of the box:** Neil O'Connor and Beate Hermelin, "Auditory and Visual Memory in Autistic and Normal Children," *Journal of Mental Deficiency Research* 11, no. 2 (1967): 126–31.

Chapter 26: Who Counts?

281 **Victor Lotter left South Africa:** Details of Lotter's early life and hiring in London are from an author interview with Grace Lotter, his wife.

281 **an epidemiological study:** Victor Lotter, "Epidemiology of Autistic Conditions in Young Children," *Social Psychiatry* 1, no. 3 (1966): 124–35.

282 **"It is by no means clear":** Michael Rutter, "Concepts of Autism: A Review of Research," *Journal of Child Psychology and Psychiatry* 9 (1968): 1.

282 **"one or another isolated symptom":** Leo Kanner, "Infantile Autism and the Schizophrenias," *Behavioral Science* 10, no. 4 (1965), 413.

284 **preservation of sameness:** Leo Kanner and Leon Eisenberg, "Childhood Schizophrenia: Symposium, 1955: 6. Early Infantile Autism, 1943–55," *American Journal of Orthopsychiatry* 26, no. 3 (1956): 556–66.

284 **"Creak's Nine Points":** Mildred Creak, "Schizophrenic Syndrome in Childhood: Further Progress Report of a Working Party," *Developmental Medicine and Child Neurology* 6 (1964): 530–35.

286 **"The point where a line is drawn":** Lotter, "Epidemiology," 132.

286 **"'True' prevalence may not be":** Ibid., 132.

Chapter 27: Words Unstrung

288 **be replaced by "autistic":** Dorothy V. M. Bishop, "Forty Years On: Uta Frith's Contribution to Research on Autism and Dyslexia, 1966–2006," *Quarterly Journal of Experimental Psychology* 61, no. 1 (1988): 16–26.

290 **teaching methods were shaped:** B. Hermelin and N. O'Connor, "Remembering of Words by Psychotic and Normal Children," *British Journal of Psychiatry* (1967): 213–18.

290 **"collaboration with the authors":** N. O'Connor and B. Hermelin, "Auditory and Visual Memory in Autistic and Normal Children," *Journal of Mental Deficiency Research* 11, no. 2 (1967): 126–31.

290 **biggest names in the field:** See Bishop, "Forty Years On."

290 **Her book, *Autism, Explaining:*** Uta Firth, *Autism: Explaining the Enigma* (Oxford, UK: Basil Blackwell, 1989).

Chapter 28: The Great Twin Chase

292 **"any doctor knowing":** M. P. Carter, "Twins with Early Childhood Autism," *Journal of Pediatrics* 71, no. 2 (1967): 303.

292 **the names came to be given:** Author interview with Sir Michael Rutter.

293 **"the possibility of genetic contributions":** As quoted in Leon Eisenberg,

"Why Has the Relationship Between Psychiatry and Genetics Been So Contentious?" *Genetics in Medicine* 3 (2001): 377.

294 **"become an expert in something":** This and other recollections from work on autism in twins are from an author interview with Susan Folstein.

296 **Twenty-one sets of twins:** Susan Folstein and Michael Rutter, "Genetic Influences and Infantile Autism," *Nature* 265, no. 5596 (1977): 726–28.

Chapter 29: Finding Their Marbles

299 **school called Family Tree:** Author interview with Simon Baron-Cohen.

299 **a concept called Theory of Mind:** Heinz Wimmer and Josef Perner, "Beliefs About Beliefs: Representation and Constraining Function of Wrong Beliefs in Young Children's Understanding of Deception," *Cognition* 13, no. 1 (1983): 103–28.

300 **became an instant classic:** David Premack and Guy Woodruff, "Does the Chimpanzee Have a Theory of Mind?" *Behavioral and Brain Sciences* 4 (1978): S15–S26.

301 **"passed the false belief test":** Wimmer and Perner, "Beliefs About Beliefs," 113.

301 **"This is Sally":** Details of the experimental framework are from an author interview with Simon Baron-Cohen. In addition, we received a video re-creation of the "Sally-Ann Experiment" from Simon Baron-Cohen, produced by Hugh Phillips and academic consultant Ilona Roth for the Open University, UK, 1990.

303 **field's landmark papers:** Simon Baron-Cohen, Alan M. Leslie, and Uta Frith, "Does the Autistic Child Have a 'Theory of Mind'?" *Cognition* 21 (1985): 37–46.

303 **"strongly support the hypothesis":** Ibid., 43.

303 **debated for years:** See, for example, S. Fisch, "Autism and Epistemology IV: Does Autism Need a Theory of Mind?" *American Journal of Medical Genetics Part A* 161A, no. 10 (2013): 2464–80.

303 **"weak central coherence":** Amitta Shah and Uta Frith, "Why Do Autistic Individuals Show Superior Performance on the Block Design Task?" *Journal of Child Psychology and Psychiatry* 34, no. 8 (1993): 1351–64; and Francesca Happé and Uta Frith, "The Weak Coherence Account: Detail-focused Cognitive Style in Autism Spectrum Disorders," *Journal of Autism and Developmental Disorders* 36, no. 1 (2006): 5–25.

304 **"an extreme male brain":** Simon Baron-Cohen, *The Essential Difference: Male and Female Brains and the Truth About Autism* (New York: Basic Books, 2004), 133–54.

Chapter 30: The Autism Spectrum

307 **"a concept of considerable complexity":** Lorna Wing, "The Continuum of Autistic Characteristics," in *Diagnosis and Assessment in Autism,* ed. Eric Schopler and Gary Mesibov (New York: Plenum Press, 1988), 92.

308 **Wing later recalled:** Unless otherwise noted, biographical information about Lorna Wing is from Giulia Rhodes, "Autism: A Mother's Labour of Love," *Guardian,* May 24, 2011; "Lorna Wing; Psychiatrist Whose Work Did Much to Improve the Understanding of Autism After Her Only Child Had the Condition Diagnosed," *Times* (London), June 12, 2014; and "Lorna Wing—Obituary," *Daily Telegraph,* June 9, 2014.

308 **became its director:** Traolach S. Brugha, Lorna Wing, John Cooper, and Norman Sartorius, "Contribution and Legacy of John Wing, 1923–2010," *British Medical Journal* 198, no. 3 (2011): 176.

308 **Lotter's landmark study:** Victor Lotter, "Epidemiology of Autistic Conditions in Young Children," *Social Psychiatry* 1, no. 4 (1967): 163–73.

309 **the dominant personality in parent advocacy:** "Dr Lorna Wing OBE—1928–2014," National Autistic Society, June 13, 2014, http://web.archive.org/web/20150315024118/http://www.autism.org.uk/news-and-events/news-from-the-nas/dr-wing-obe-1928-2014.aspx.

309 **start Britain's National Society:** Frank Warren, "The Role of the National Society in Working with Families," in *The Effects of Autism on the Family,* Eric Schopler and Gary Mesibov, eds. (New York: Plenum Press, 1984), 102.

309 **that chose Sybil Elgar to run:** Adam Feinstein, *A History of Autism: Conversations with the Pioneers* (Malden, MA: Wiley-Blackwell, 2010), 88.

309 **an overwrought parent:** It was different when Rimland's audience was comprised of other parents, legislators, and media. In those situations, he alluded to his status as a parent without hesitation.

309 **"the child's name should always be used":** Lorna Wing, *Autistic Children: A Guide for Parents* (New York: Brunner/Mazel, 1972), 90.

310 **the Camberwell Register:** Camberwell psychiatric case register records, available at http://www.kingscollections.org/catalogues/kclca/collection/i/10in7050/.

310 **a database for psychiatric research:** Lorna Wing, Christine Bramley, Anthea Hailey, and J. K. Wing, "Camberwell Cumulative Psychiatric Case Register Part I: Aims and Methods," *Social Psychiatry* 3, no. 3 (1968): 116–23.

311 **did not meet the full set:** Author interviews with Susan Folstein and Sir Michael Rutter.

311 **she was hired:** Author interview with Judith Gould.

312 **"the effect of excluding those":** Fred Volkmar, Rhea Paul, Ami Klin, and Donald Cohen, *Handbook of Autism and Pervasive Developmental Disorders, Diagnosis, Development Neurobiology, and Behavior* (Hoboken, NJ: John Wiley & Sons, 2005), 599.

313 **"triad of impairment":** Wing and Gould's three-part concept of autism was reminiscent of, and likely informed by, Rutter's much earlier proposal that autism manifested in three "domains." But they introduced deficit of "imagination" to the mix and, more important, emphasized the relative looseness and flexibility of their triad.

313 **"borderline of normality":** Volkmar et al., *Handbook of Autism,* 599.

313 **"Nature never draws a line":** Lorna Wing, "Reflections on Opening Pandora's Box," *Journal of Autism and Developmental Disorders* 35, no. 2 (2005): 202.

313 **She kept writing about it:** See, for example, M. B. Denckla, "New Diagnostic Criteria for Autism and Related Behavioral Disorders—Guidelines for Research Protocols," *Journal of the American Academy of Child Psychiatry* 25, no. 2 (1986): 221–24.

313 **revised her classic parent handbook:** Lorna Wing, *The Autistic Spectrum: A Guide for Parents and Professionals* (London: Constable, 1996).

Chapter 31: The Austrian

317 **the "Wandering Scholars":** Maria Felder Asperger, "Hans Asperger (1906–1980) Leben und Werk," in *Hundert Janfre Kind-in Jugendpsychiatries,* ed. R. Castell (Germany: V&R Unipress, 2008), p. 100.

317 **There is no record:** At the time of the writing of this book, Herwig had submitted for publication his paper "'The Child Must Be an Unbearable Burden to Her Mother': Hans Asperger, National Socialism, and 'Race Hygiene' in World War II Vienna," to *Molecular Autism.*

317 **father of five:** V. Lyons and M. Fitzgerald, "Did Hans Asperger (1906–1980) Have Asperger Syndrome?" *Journal of Autism and Developmental Disorders* 37 (2007): 2020–21.

319 **a medical weekly:** Hans Asperger, "Das psychisch abnormale Kind," *Wiener Klinische Wochenschrift* 51 (1938): 1314–17. The authors thank Jeremiah Riemer for his assistance in translating all of Asperger's writings quoted in this book. For the sake of readability, we made occasional modifications to his language, such that the responsibility for the translations is ours alone.

319 **postgraduate thesis:** Hans Asperger, "Die 'Autistischen Psychopathen' im Kindesalter," *Archiv fur Psychiatrie und Nervenkrankheiten* 117 (1944): 76–136.

320 **"malevolent light":** Hans Asperger, "Autistic Psychopathy in Childhood," in *Autism and Asperger Syndrome,* ed. Uta Frith (Cambridge, UK: Cambridge University Press, 1991), 79.

321 **he was named a lecturer at:** Frith, *Autism and Asperger,* xii.

321 **published more than three hundred times:** Ibid., 208.

321 **continued lecturing past:** Feinstein, *History of Autism,* 18.

322 **Asperger's name once:** Bernard Rimland, *Infantile Autism: The Syndrome and Its Implications for a Neural Theory of Behavior* (Appleton-Century-Crofts, Educational Division, Meredith Publishing, 1964), 54.

322 **"I do not understand":** Letter from Bernard Rimland to Dr. Joshua Lederberg, July 31, 1964, the Joshua Lederberg Papers, National Library of Medicine, http://profiles.nlm.nih.gov/ps/retrieve/ResourceMetadata/BBALQA.

322 **Leo Kanner made a passing:** Gil Eyal, *The Autism Matrix* (Cambridge, UK: Polity Press, 2010), 216.

322 **Krevelen, an early autism researcher:** D. Arn Van Krevelen, "Early Infantile Autism and Autistic Psychopathy," *Journal of Autism and Childhood Schizophrenia* 1, no. 1 (1971): 82–86.

322 **did not trouble him much:** In a talk by Asperger in German in 1977, before the Congress of the Swiss Association of the Parents of Autistic Children, he shrugged off his relative obscurity in the autism world vis-à-vis Leo Kanner

with a joke: "Americans don't read German papers." In context, it reads as more resigned than resentful. *Communication* 13, no. 3 (1979): 45–52.

322 **Wing's husband who first stumbled:** "Lorna Wing—Obituary," *Daily Telegraph,* June 9, 2014.

323 **Wing published "Asperger's Syndrome":** Lorna Wing, "Asperger's Syndrome: A Clinical Account," *Psychological Medicine* 11, no. 1 (1981): 115–29.

323 **"the neutral term":** Ibid., 115.

323 **"no clear boundaries":** Lorna Wing, "Past and Future of Research on Asperger Syndrome," in *Asperger Syndrome,* ed. Ami Klin, Red R. Volkmar, and Sara S. Sparrow (New York: Guilford Press, 2000).

323 **"Identification of any of the eponymous":** Lorna Wing, "The Relationship Between Asperger's Syndrome and Kanner's Syndrome," in Frith, *Autism and Asperger,* 116.

323 **"who often cannot believe":** Ibid.

324 **"Asperger, despite listing numerous":** Lorna Wing, "Reflections on Opening Pandora's Box." *Journal of Autism and Developmental Disorders* 35, no. 2 (2005): 198. The scene of Lorna Wing and Hans Asperger meeting is also recounted in Adam Feinstein's *The History of Autism.*

324 **"We cordially agreed to differ":** Ibid.

324 **a 1968 paper:** Hans Asperger, "Zur Differentialdiagnose des Kindlichen Autismus," *Acta Paedopsychiatrica* 35 (1968): 136–45.

324 **"complete agreement in some":** Hans Asperger, "Problems of Infantile Autism (A Talk)," *Communication* (1979): 45–52.

324 **"psychotic or near psychotic state":** Ibid.

325 **"Asperger's typical cases":** It is not clear whether Asperger used the third person in this instance or whether that was a translator's choice. The original German was not available to the authors.

Chapter 32: The Signature

327 ***Was Hans Asperger, as a young man:*** The account of the Wing-Volkmar conversation in this chapter is from an author interview with Fred Volkmar. It represents Volkmar's best recollection of the call, with a high degree of confidence in its accuracy, but should not be regarded as excerpts from a strict verbatim transcript of the phone call, which does not exist.

327 **a research request for volunteers:** Ami Klin, Fred R. Volkmar, and Sara S. Sparrow, *Asperger Syndrome* (New York: Guilford Press, 2000), 2.

328 **"The seeds for our current syndrome":** Eric Schopler, "Premature Popularization of Asperger Syndrome," in *Asperger Syndrome or High-Functioning Autism?,* ed. Eric Schopler, Gary B. Mesibov, and Linda J. Kunce (New York: Plenum Press, 1998), 386.

328 **guilt by association:** Account of Schopler's suspicions of Asperger corroborated in author interview with Gary Mesibov, Schopler's longtime collaborator at TEACCH.

328 **"longstanding interest":** Eric Schopler, "Ask the Editor: Are Autism and

Asperger Syndrome Different Labels or Different Disabilities," *Journal of Autism and Developmental Disorders* 26, no. 1 (1996): 109.

329 **Volkmar, for example, did not hear:** Details of the conversation between Fred Volkmar and Lorna Wing are from author interview with Fred Volkmar.

329 **As a psychology PhD:** Ami Klin, "Young Autistic Children's Listening Preferences in Regard to Speech: A Possible Characterization of the Symptom of Social Withdrawal," *Journal of Autism and Developmental Disorders* 21, no. 1 (1991): 29–42.

329 **The question the two men:** Account of Cohen-Klin conversations from author interview with Ami Klin.

329 **"If you are going to kill":** As quoted by D. Konziella, "Thirty Neurological Eponyms Associated with the Nazi Era," *European Neurology* 62 (2009): 56–64.

330 **"Hans Asperger, a Nazi?":** Author interview with Fred Volkmar.

330 **"We would like to be able":** The details of Ami Klin's correspondence with Michael Hubenstorf come from author interviews with Klin and letters he shared with the authors.

331 **she wrote that her father had been at odds:** Maria Asperger, foreword to *Asperger Syndrome,* Klin et al., xiii.

332 **"Far from despising":** Hans Asperger, "Autistic Psychopathy in Childhood" in *Autism and Asperger Syndrome,* ed. Uta Frith (Cambridge, UK: Cambridge University Press, 1991), 37–92.

332 **"humanity and his courageous":** Brita Schirmer, "Autismus und NS-Rassengesetze in Österreich 1938: Hans Aspergers Verteidigung der 'Autistischen Psychopathen' gegen die NS-Eugenik," *Die neue Sonderschule* 47, no. 6 (2002): 460–64.

332 **"tried to protect these":** Viktoria Lyons and Michael Fitzgerald, "Did Hans Asperger (1906–1980) Have Asperger Syndrome?" *Journal of Autism and Developmental Disorders* 37 (2007), 2020–21.

332 **"The very opposite is more likely":** Feinstein, *History of Autism,* 15. Hans Asperger's diary is cited in Maria Feldner Asperger, *Zum Sehen geboren, zum Schauen bestellt.*

332 **"An entire nation goes in a single":** Hans Asperger, diary, 1934, in Maria Asperger Feldner, *Zum Sehen Geboren, zum Schauen Bestellt.*

332 **His Catholic faith:** Steve Silberman, *NeuroTribes: The Legacy of Autism and the Future of Neurodiversity* (New York: Avery, 2015), 121.

333 **Allies' "denazification" policy:** The phenomenon of Nazi Party members trying to rewrite their pasts during the denazification period is well illustrated in a case history by Herwig Czech and Lawrence A. Zeidman, "Walther Birkmayer, Co-describer of LDopa, and His Nazi Connections: Victim or Perpetrator?," *Journal of the History of the Neurosciences: Basic and Clinical Perspectives* (April 3, 2014): 19.

333 **a *persilschein,* or "Persil certificate":** Ernst Klee, *Persilscheine und falsche Passe. Wie die Kirchen den Nazis halfen* ("Persil Certificates and False Passports:

How the Church Aided the Nazis") (Frankfurt, Germany: Fischer Taschenbuch-Verlag, 1991).

334 **in a 1962 talk:** Excerpts from both Hans Asperger's 1962 talk and his 1974 radio appearance are from Hans Asperger, "Ecce Infans. Zur Ganzheitsproblematik in der modernen Pädiatrie," Wiener Antrittsvorlesung, 1962, in *Wiener klinische Wochenschrift* 74, 936–41. Austrian historian Herwig Czech discovered and shared this material with the authors.

334 **While ardently pro-Catholic:** John Connelly, *From Enemy to Brother: The Revolution in Catholic Teaching on the Jews, 1933–1965* (Cambridge: Harvard University Press, 2012).

334 **"excessive Jewish influence":** An example of Bund Neuland's political and philosophical leanings can be found in L.Z., "Die Juden Wiens," 1935, in *Neuland. Blätter jungkatholischer Erneuerungsbewegung,* 19–21. This information was shared with the authors by Herwig Czech.

335 **"We stand in the midst":** Hans Asperger, "Das Psychisch Abnorme Kind" *Wiener Klinische Wochenschrift* (1938): 1314–17.

335 **A review of other medical talks:** A review of the talks and other journals and papers was shared with the authors by Herwig Czech.

335 **"deft chess move":** Brita Schirmer, "Autismus und NS-Rassengesetze in Österreich 1938: Hans Aspergers Verteidigung der 'Autistischen Psychopathen' gegen die NS-Eugenik," *Die neue Sonderschule* 47, no. 6 (2002): 460–64.

336 **what he called "social worth":** Hans Asperger, "Die 'Autistischen Psychopathen' im Kindersalter," *Archiv fur Psychiatrie und Nervenkrankheiten* 117 (1944): 76–136; ibid.

336 **That turns out to be a myth:** Swedish psychologist Chris Gillberg, who popularized the term "Little Professors" in a widely read 1991 book, confirmed to the authors in 2015 that he coined it himself, to capture the essence of the boys Asperger studied. Although historian Herwig Czech notes that Asperger described one child's manner of speaking as "professorial" in a 1939 paper, the phrase "Little Professors," frequently attributed to Asperger, cannot be found anywhere in his writings.

336 **"thought it more rewarding":** Hans Asperger, "Das Psychisch Abnorme Kind."

336 **autistic traits were more often a detriment:** In Asperger's 1944 paper, "Die 'Autistischen Psychopathen' im Kindersalter," page 118, he wrote: *"Leider überwiegt nicht in allen, nicht einmal in den meisten Fällen das Positive, Zukunftweisende der autistischen Wesenszüge."* The translation: "Unfortunately, the things that are positive and promising [more literally, 'forward-looking'] about autistic traits are not their overriding features in all cases, and not even in most."

337 **"pronounced intellectual inferiority":** Ibid

339 **"When at home, this child must":** Based on documents shared with the authors by Herwig Czech. See also Herwig Czech, "'The Child Must Be an Unbearable Burden to Her Mother': Hans Asperger, National Socialism, and

'Race Hygiene' in World War II Vienna," unpublished paper submitted in 2016 to *Molecular Autism.*

340 **"conforms to the principles of the policy of racial hygiene":** Ibid.

341 **"his Nazi credibility":** Ibid.

341 **the director of the clinic:** Author interview with Arnold Pollak.

Chapter 33: The Dream of Language

345 **the civil rights of people with disabilities:** Unless otherwise noted, this and other details about Chris Borthwick and Douglas Biklen are from an author interview with Biklen and a letter from Borthwick to Biklen, April 15, 1987, provided to the authors by Biklen.

346 **Biklen was well-known:** Steven J. Taylor and Douglas Biklen, *Understanding the Law: An Advocates Guide to the Law and Developmental Disabilities* (Syracuse, NY: Human Policy Press, 1980); author interview with Douglas Biklen.

346 **The inherent merit of his argument:** Biklen interview.

347 **Rosemary Crossley was a celebrity:** Rosemary Crossley and Anne McDonald, *Annie's Coming Out* (Melbourne: Deal Books, Penguin Books Australia, 1980).

347 **"Excuse me. Get Mommy":** Douglas Biklen, "Communication Unbound: Autism and Praxis," *Harvard Educational Review* 60, no. 3 (1990).

349 **"What really does integration":** Ibid.

349 **"installed a 'talking typewriter'":** Irene Mozolewski, "Dr. Goodwin to Be Seen on British TV," *Oneonta Star,* June 7, 1966.

350 **"learning . . . a successful, enjoyable":** Barbara A. Sanderson and Daniel W. Kratchvil, "The Edison Responsive Environment Learning System or the Talking Typewriter Developed by Thomas A. Edison Laboratory, a Subsidiary of McGraw Edison Company," American Institutes for Research in the Behavioral Sciences, Palo Alto, California, January 1972.

350 **likely seen in ads:** Shirley Cohen, *Targeting Autism: What We Know, Don't Know, and Can Do to Help Young Children with Autism Spectrum Disorders* (Berkeley: University of California Press, 2006): 168–69.

350 **Also in the 1960s:** Rosalind Oppenheim, "They Said Our Child Was Hopeless," *Saturday Evening Post,* June 17, 1961.

351 **Simple and effective:** Developed by Andrew S. Bondy, PhD, and Lori Frost, MS, CCC/SLP, 1985 Picture Exchange Communication System, PECS Pyramid Educational Consultants, Inc., http://www.pecsusa.com/pecs.php; Jennifer B. Ganz, Richard L. Simpson, and Emily M. Lund, "The Picture Exchange Communication System (PECS): A Promising Method for Improving Communication Skills of Learners with Autism Spectrum Disorders," *Education and Training in Autism and Developmental Disabilities* 47, no. 2 (2012): 176–86.

352 **"Tell my mother":** Letter to the editor by Jacqueline J. Kingon and Alfred H. Kingon, "The Words They Can't Say," *New York Times Magazine,* November 3, 1991.

352 **workshops were being offered:** Daniel Gonzales, "Critics Call It a Hoax but 100 Teachers Soon Will Gather to Learn More," *Syracuse Herald-Journal,* February 22, 1994.

352 **"Knowledge of augmentative":** "Special Education Teacher Vacancies," *Syracuse-Herald Journal,* Cayuga-Onondaga BOCES, July 20, 1991.

Chapter 34: The Child Within

353 **Janyce Boynton blamed herself:** Unless otherwise noted, details about Janyce Boynton's facilitated communication experience are from an author interview with Boynton and from Janyce Boynton, "Facilitated Communication—What Harm It Can Do: Confessions of a Former Facilitator," *Evidence-Based Communication Assessment and Intervention* 6, no. 1 (2012): 3–13.

354 **typed out, "t-h-e-s-o-n-o-f-a-b-i-t-c-h":** Betsy's FC responses as reported throughout this chapter are from papers shared with the authors by Phil Worden, who acted as guardian ad litem for Betsy and Jamie Wheaton. Worden collected all files, papers, and written communications applicable to the Validity Testing on Facilitated Communications for Fifth District Court & Maine Dept. of Human Services, January 1993.

354 **"all [were] unquestionably endowed":** Leo Kanner, "Autistic Disturbances of Affective Contact," *Nervous Child* 2 (1943): 247.

355 ***"Last night, I dreamed":*** "What I Imagine He Sounds Like," *Short Bus Diaries,* September 26, 2012, http://shortbusdiaries.com/what-i-imagine-he-sounds-like/.

355 **rid the body of evil spirits:** Author interviews with traditional and faith healers in South Africa.

355 **Parents signed up for "holding therapy":** Jan Mason, "Child of Silence: Retrieved from the Shadow World of Autism: Katy Finds Her Voice," *LIFE,* September 15, 1987.

356 **parents tried "packing therapy":** L. Spinney, "Therapy for Autistic Children Causes Outcry in France," *Lancet* 370 (2007): 645–46.

356 **had drastically improved:** Author interview with Victoria Beck.

356 **shot up as high as $8,000:** Laura Johannes, "New Hampshire Mother Overrode Doubts on New Use of Old Drug," *Wall Street Journal,* March 10, 1999.

358 **These cases, nearly all:** Lawrence Wright, "Child-Care Demons," *New Yorker,* October 3, 1994.

358 **She looked at her and said, simply, "Hi":** Transcription of interview with police, DHS investigator, and all other relevant documents pertaining to proceedings of FC testing provided to authors by Phil Worden.

360 **they waived their right to an attorney:** Author interview with Suzette and Jim Wheaton.

360 **Boynton also impressed him as honest:** This and other recollections of interactions between Phil Worden and Janyce Boynton are from author interviews with Worden and Boynton.

362 **Soon he was on the phone with Rimland:** Worden interview.

363 **he believed in technology, not FC:** Author interview with Howard Shane.

364 **"That student is lucky to have you in her life":** Author interview with Boynton.

365 **reenacted, nearly verbatim, the experiment:** "Prisoners of Silence," *Frontline,* produced by John Palfreman, PBS, October 19, 1993, transcript available at http://www.pbs.org/wgbh/pages/frontline/programs/transcripts/1202.html.

366 **"is not the same as having nothing to say":** Nancy Shulins, "Debate Over Autism Communication Rages On," *Chicago Daily Herald,* May 16, 1994.

366 **"the controversy about facilitated communication":** Chancellor Nancy Cantor, "Imagining America; Imagining Universities: Who and What?" welcome address for the Imagining America Annual Conference at Syracuse University, September 7, 2007, http://www.syr.edu/chancellor/speeches/ImaginingAmericaAnnualConferenceRemarks090707.pdf.

367 **Betsy's younger brother, Jamie, committed suicide:** Bill Trotter, "Deaths Motive Unknown; Recently Wed Woman Stabbed, Man Shot on Swans Island," *Bangor Daily News,* July 24, 2001, http://archive.bangordailynews.com/2001/07/24/deaths-motive-unknown-recently-wed-woman-stabbed-man-shot-on-swans-island.

368 **Julian and Tal Wendrow, Aislinn's parents:** Author interviews with Tal and Julian Wendrow.

369 **he was forced to abandon:** Julian Wendrow interview.

Chapter 35: An Elusive Definition

370 **"It forced me to redefine autism":** Douglas Biklen, "Communication Unbound: Autism and Praxis," *Harvard Educational Review* 60, no. 3 (1990): 291–315.

370 **"the received knowledge":** Robert Cummins and Margot Prior, "Further Comment: Autism and Assisted Communication: A Response to Biklen," *Harvard Educational Review* 62, no. 2 (1992): 228–42.

370 **an "ideologue":** Eric Schopler, in "Editor's Note" to Margot Prior and Robert Cummins, "Questions About Facilitated Communication and Autism," *Journal of Autism and Developmental Disorders* 22, no. 3 (1992): 331.

371 **"hopelessly confused state":** Michael Rutter, "Concepts of Autism: A Review of Research," *Journal of Child Psychology and Psychiatry* 9, no. 1 (1968).

371 **"because criteria for diagnosis are different":** Eric Schopler, "On Confusion in the Diagnosis of Autism," *Journal of Autism and Childhood Schizophrenia* 8, no. 2 (1978): 137–38.

371 **"long and controversial history":** Fred R. Volkmar and Donald J. Cohen, "Classification and Diagnosis of Childhood Autism," in *Diagnosis and Assessment in Autism,* ed. Eric Schopler and Gary Mesibov (New York: Plenum Press, 1988), 72.

371 **"the confusion and the plethora":** Fred R. Volkmar and Ami Klin, "Asperger Syndrome and Nonverbal Learning Disabilities," in ibid., 107.

372 **bring order to chaos in 1961:** Mildred Creak, "Schizophrenic Syndrome in

Childhood: Progress Report of a Working Party" (April 1961), *British Medical Journal* (September 1961): 889.

372 **"to the wolves":** Mildred Creak, "Schizophrenic Syndrome in Childhood: Further Progress Report of a Working Party," *Developmental Medicine and Child Neurology* 6 (1964): 530.

372 **"politely and respectfully":** Michael Rutter, "Childhood Schizophrenia Reconsidered," *Journal of Autism and Childhood Schizophrenia* 2, no. 3 (1972): 315.

372 **"Rutter criteria":** This was not Rutter's term, but was commonly used by researchers who employed his criteria. See, for example, R. J. McClelland, D. G. Eyre, O. Watson, G. J. Calvert, and Eileen Sherrard, "Central Conduction Time in Childhood Autism," *British Journal of Psychiatry* 160, no. 5 (1992): 659–63.

372 **the criteria specified:** A description of the Rutter criteria can be found in Michael Rutter's "Diagnosis and Definition," in *Autism: A Reappraisal of Concepts and Treatment,* ed. Michael Rutter and Eric Schopler (New York: Plenum Press, 1978), 1–25.

372 **"The question was not how to differentiate":** Michael Rutter, "The Emanuel Miller Memorial Lecture 1998, Autism: Two-Way Interplay Between Research and Clinical Work," *Journal of Child Psychology and Psychiatry* 40, no. 2 (1999): 170.

373 **National Society for Autistic Children:** After 1987, the name was changed to the Autism Society of America.

373 **"abnormal responses to sensations":** Edward Ritvo and B. J. Freeman, "National Society for Autistic Children Definition of the Syndrome of Autism," *Journal of Pediatric Psychology* 2, no. 4 (1977): 146.

373 **the American Psychiatric Association's *DSM*:** The discussion of changes in the *DSM* between 1980 and 2013 are based on the actual text in the *Diagnostic and Statistical Manual of Mental Disorders,* by the American Psychiatric Association, Washington, DC: *DSM III* (1980), *DSM III-R* (1987), *DSM-IV* (1994), and *DSM-5* (2013).

374 **more than two thousand:** Fred Volkmar and Brian Reichow, "Autism in *DSM-5:* Progress and Challenges," *Molecular Autism* 4 (2013): 13.

Chapter 36: Meeting of the Minds

377 **so much in common:** Anecdotes pertaining to the founding and running of CAN are from author interviews with Jon Shestack and Portia Iversen. Lisa Lewis was the conduit for the Princeton meeting: she attended the DAN conference as an autism parent alongside Portia, and also knew the Londons from the "autism community."

377 **focused on autism:** Anecdotes pertaining to the founding and running of NAAR are from an author interview with Karen and Eric London.

377 **Eleven hits, out of eleven thousand:** Author interview with Karen and Eric London; author interview with researcher at Society of Neuroscience (http://www.sfn.org/).

378 **The biologically based observations:** Mary Coleman, ed., *The Autistic Syndromes* (Amsterdam: North-Holland Publishing Co., 1976).

378 **Bauman, a pediatric neurologist:** See, for example, Margaret L. Bauman, "Brief Report: Neuroanatomic Observations of the Brain in Pervasive Development Disorders," *Journal of Autism & Developmental Disorders* 26, no. 2 (1996): 199–203.

379 **London excused himself:** London interview.

381 **Stanley Greenspan, who recommended:** More information of Dr. Greenspan's Floortime can be found on his website: http://www.stanleygreenspan.com.

383 **"accelerating biomedical research":** The NAAR website no longer exists, but some material from their newsletter, the *NAARative,* can be found on the Autism Speaks website, https://www.autismspeaks.org/news/news-item/naarative.

385 **courses of megavitamins:** Bernard Rimland, "Megavitamin B6 and Magnesium in the Treatment of Autistic Children and Adults," *Neurobiological Issues in Autism, Current Issues in Autism* (1987): 389–405.

385 **the onetime hero of autism:** Sid Baker, "Learning About Autism," *Global Advances in Health and Medicine* 2, no. 6 (2013): 38–46; author interview with Sid Baker.

385 **they handed Rimland $25,000:** Shestack and Iversen interview.

385 **Jon solved that problem:** Others, in addition to Jon and Portia, contributed to the costs of funding the conference.

386 **"had the stomach for a risk/benefit relationship":** Baker interview.

386 **the Dallas group:** DAN! (Defeat Autism Now!) represented a loose network of medical doctors and other practitioners who remained open to the use of several of the alternative biomedical therapies discussed at the meeting. The "DAN protocol" of alternative treatments gained a following, especially among parents who believed that their children's autism was the result of injury from vaccination. The network disbanded in 2011.

386 **"start our own foundation":** Portia Iversen, *Strange Son: Two Mothers, Two Sons, and the Quest to Unlock the Hidden World of Autism* (New York: Riverhead, 2006), 30.

387 **not interested in funding biomedical research:** Although ASA did not want to join forces with either biomedical research group, from very early on they supported and contributed to CAN and NAAR's research.

387 **Jon and Eric got into their debate:** Recollections from this conversation are from the Shestack interview.

Chapter 37: The Magic Man

388 **in medical circles as the "magic man":** Author interview with Ed Berry.

389 **their first set of RFPs:** Copy of original RFP sent to potential researchers from NAAR, July 1996, provided to the authors by Karen London.

390 **"The goal is":** John Morgan, "*ER*'s Anthony Edwards Curing Autism Now," *USA Today,* October 12, 2000.

390 **netted $75,000:** Author interview with Jon Shestack.
391 **belonged to Jon Shestack:** Combating Autism Act of 2006, S. 843, 109th Cong. (2006).
392 **"concrete clinical findings":** Cure Autism Now, *ADVANCES: Hope, Partnership, and Action to Accelerate the Pace of Biomedical Research in Autism and Related Disorders,* 10th Anniversary Edition, Fall 2005.
393 **composition of its scientific advisory board:** Author interview with Daniel Geschwind.
394 **NAAR had raised nearly $850,000:** Author interview with Karen and Eric London; documents shared with authors by Karen London.
397 **They also hired Catherine:** Author interview with Catherine Lord.
397 **The ADI was recognized:** Michael Rutter, Anne Le Couteur, and Catherine Lord, "ADI–R, Autism Diagnostic Interview—Revised." Details on the ADI and how it can be implemented can be found at http://nyp.org/services/cadb-adir-diagnostic-instrument.html.
398 **sixty-three authors had cited:** Ibid.
399 **by drowning or by seizures:** J. Pickett, E. Xiu, R. Tuchman, G. Dawson, and C. Lajonchere, "Mortality in Individuals with Autism, with and Without Epilepsy," *Journal of Child Neurology* 8 (2011): 932–39; Lori McIlwain, "Autism & Wandering: A Guide for Educators," National Autism Association, April 20, 2015, http://nationalautismassociation.org/autism-wandering-a-guide-for-educators/.
399 **generations of kids:** London interview.

Chapter 38: Putting Autism on the Map

403 **the greatest celebrity:** The anecdotes surrounding the production of *Temple Grandin* for HBO are from an author interview with Emily Gerson Saines.
405 **The book cracked:** Temple Grandin, *Thinking in Pictures: My Life with Autism* (New York: Vintage, 1995).
406 **"I think she is autistic":** *Change of Habit,* directed by William Graham, produced by Joe Connelly, 1969.
407 **"A Miracle of Love":** Barry Kaufman published the book *Son-Rise* in 1976, a story about his son Ryan. The book became a docudrama that aired on NBC in 1979.
407 **"You will learn to spank":** *Marcus Welby, M.D.,* Daniel Petrie, ABC. Season 1, Episode 2: "The Foal," September 30, 1969.
408 **"The Strangers in Our Midst":** M. Ballin, "Autistic Children: The Strangers in Our Midst," *McCall's* (101), November 1973.
408 **"The Children of the Fairies,":** *Ha'aretz* daily newspaper, 1973.
408 **"The Kids with the Faraway Eyes":** D. R. Katz, "Kids with the Faraway Eyes," *Rolling Stone,* March 8, 1979, 48–53.
408 **"Far Gone Mental Cripples":** Dan Moser and photographer Alan Grant, "Screams, Slaps & Love: A Surprising, Shocking Treatment Helps Far-Gone Mental Cripples," *LIFE,* May 7, 1965.

408 **the original mother's memoir:** Clara Claiborne Park, *The Siege* (Boston: Back Bay Books, 1967).

408 **on a father's diary:** James Copeland, based on a diary by Jack Hodges, *For the Love of Ann* (London: Random House, 1973).

408 **which inspired a story on *60 Minutes:*** Josh Greenfield, *A Child Called Noah: A Family Journey* (New York: Holt, Rinehart and Winston, 1989).

409 **"to run an article on autism":** Bernard Rimland, "*Rain Man* and the Savant Secrets," *Editors Notebook, Autism Research International Newsletter* 3, no. 1 (1989): 3; http://www.ariconference.com/ari/newsletter/031/page3.pdf.

409 **"*Rain Man* has advanced the field of autism":** Ibid. for Sullivan quotes on *The Oprah Winfrey Show.* See also Darold Treffert's website at http://www.daroldtreffert.com/.

409 **eight days after the movie's premiere:** Agnes Torres Al-Shibibi, "'Rain Man' Puts Autism on the Map," *Orlando Sentinel,* December 22, 1988.

409 **"an outstanding portrayal":** Lance Workman, "From Art to Autism: A Q&A with Uta Frith," *Psychologist* (British Psychological Society), December 2013.

410 **prodigious mental gifts:** Fran Peek, *The Real Rain Man* (Salt Lake City: Harkness Publishing Consultants, 1996).

410 **An associate producer, Gail:** Author interview with Gail Mutrux.

410 **Raymond would be autistic:** Author interview with Barry Levinson.

411 **Rimland wanted Raymond:** Author interview with Steve Edelson.

411 **"want to do it fast":** David Ansen, Michael Reese, Sarah Crichton, and Jennifer Foote, "Who's on First?" *Newsweek,* January 16, 1989, 52.

411 **authority on savants:** "Savant Syndrome: Islands of Genius," Wisconsin Medical Society, https://www.wisconsinmedicalsociety.org/professional/savant-syndrome/.

411 **Bernie Rimland also brought his son:** Edelson interview; author interview with Gloria and Mark Rimland.

412 **The posture, the voice:** Sherri Dalphonse, "Dustin and Me," *Washingtonian,* July 1992.

414 **"wet kitsch":** Matt Patches, "Remembering 'Rain Man': The $350 Million Movie That Hollywood Wouldn't Touch Today," *Grantland,* January 9, 2014.

415 **the present and future:** Temple Grandin and Margaret M. Scariano, *Emergence: Labeled Autistic* (New York: Grand Central Publishing, 1996).

417 **"like being tied up to the rail":** Ruth Sullivan, foreword to Temple Grandin's *The Way I See It: A Personal Look at Autism and Asperger's* (Arlington, TX: Future Horizons, 2008), xiv.

417 **"an anthropologist on Mars":** Oliver Sacks, *An Anthropologist on Mars: Seven Paradoxical Tales* (New York: Picador, 1995), 244

Chapter 39: Society's Emergency

419 **his six-year-old:** This and other anecdotes in this chapter about Russell Rollens are from an author interview with Rick Rollens.

420 **investigating sleep disorders:** Martha U. Gillette, Thomas Roth, and James

P. Kiley, "NIH Funding of Sleep Research: A Prospective and Retrospective View," *SLEEP* 22, no. 7 (1999): 956–58.

420 **4 to 5 people in 10,000:** Victor Lotter, "Epidemiology of Autistic Conditions in Young Children," *Social Psychiatry* 1, no. 3 (1966): 124–35.

420 **The DDS report was completed:** *Changes in the Population of Persons with Autism and Pervasive Developmental Disorders in California's Developmental Services System: 1987 Through 1998,* Report to the Legislature by the Department of Developmental Services, March 1, 1999. Text available at http://www.dds.ca.gov/Autism/docs/autism_report_1999.pdf.

421 **"State Study Finds":** Thomas H. Maugh, "State Study Finds Sharp Rise in Autism Rate," *Los Angeles Times,* April 16, 1999.

421 **"Defining an Era":** Tracy Mayor, "A Disorder That's Defining an Era," *Child,* December 2005.

421 ***Time* made it a cover story:** J. Madeleine Nash and Amy Bonesteel, "The Secrets of Autism," *Time,* May 6, 2002.

422 **"We have an epidemic":** *The Autism Epidemic—Is the NIH and CDC Response Adequate? Hearing Before the House Committee on Government Reform,* 107th Cong. (2002), statement of Dan Burton, Chairman of the Committee.

422 **1 in 166 children:** Unless otherwise noted, statistics on autism prevalence in this chapter are from *Prevalence of the Autism Spectrum Disorders (ASDs) in Multiple Areas of the United States, 2000 and 2002,* Community Report from the Autism and Developmental Disabilities Monitoring (ADDM) Network, available at http://www.cdc.gov/ncbddd/autism/documents/AutismCommunityReport.pdf; and *Prevalence of the Autism Spectrum Disorders (ASDs) in Multiple Areas of the United States, 2008,* Community Report from the Autism and Developmental Disabilities Monitoring (ADDM) Network, available at http://www.cdc.gov/ncbddd/autism/documents/ADDM-2012-Community-Report.pdf.

423 **Researchers in 2012:** Eric Fombonne, Judith S. Miller, et al., "Autism Spectrum Disorder Reclassified: A Second Look at the 1980s Utah/UCLA Autism Epidemiologic Study," *Journal of Autism and Developmental Disorders* 43, no. 1 (2012): 200–210.

424 **based on Ritvo's criteria:** E. R. Ritvo et al., "The UCLA–University of Utah Epidemiologic Survey of Autism: Prevalence," *American Journal of Psychiatry* 146, no. 2 (1989): 194–99.

424 **increased surveillance:** Eric Fombonne, "Epidemiology of Pervasive Developmental Disorders," *Pediatric Research* 65, no. 6, 591–98.

425 **any count starts from zero:** Author interview with Paul Shattuck.

425 **"Autism Increases DRAMATICALLY":** Post by "Orac," "Well, That Didn't Take Long," Respectful Insolence (Science Blogs), April 5, 2006, http://scienceblogs.com/insolence/2006/04/05/well-that-didnt-take-long-the.

425 **"Florida has reported":** *Autism: Present Challenges, Future Needs—Why the Increased Rates? Hearing Before the House Committee on Government Reform,* 106th Cong. (2000), statement of Dan Burton, Chairman of the Committee.

425 **according to federal data:** *Prevalence of the Autism Spectrum Disorders (ASDs) in Multiple Areas of the United States, 2008,* 8–23.

426 **Minnesota and Iowa:** Doug Smith, "Autism Rates by State," *Los Angeles Times,* December 9, 2011.

427 **"I'll call a kid a zebra":** Arthur Allen, "The Autism Numbers, Why There's No Epidemic," *Slate,* January 15, 2007.

427 **"I admit up front that":** David Amaral, Daniel Geschwind, and Geraldine Dawson, *Autism Spectrum Disorders* (Oxford University Press, 2011), 4.

427 **"mentally retarded" dropped precipitously:** Paul T. Shattuck, "Prevalence of Autism in US Special Education: The Contribution of Diagnostic Substitution to the Growing Administrative Prevalence of Autism in US Special Education," *Pediatrics* 117 (2006): 1029. Shattuck's data was compiled from the 1984–2003 annual special-education counts published by the US Department of Education.

428 **"the relationship between the rising":** Ibid., 1028.

429 **"*will* have autism":** Autism Awareness Commercial, "Autism Awareness," https://www.youtube.com/watch?v=y7t3daKTQMg.

429 **"familiar ring":** Hal Arkowitz and Scott O. Lilienfeld, "Is There Really an Autism Epidemic?" *Scientific American,* December 6, 2007.

429 **The statistic burst:** Author interview with Peter Bell.

430 **"There is not a full population count":** *Prevalence of the Autism Spectrum Disorders (ASDs) in Multiple Areas of the United States, 2000 and 2002,* 31.

431 **in just ten states:** The number of states and counties often changes from one year to another, and from one report to another. For example, in 2008 Alabama, Arizona, Arkansas, Colorado, Florida, Georgia, Maryland, Missouri, New Jersey, North Carolina, Pennsylvania, South Carolina, Utah, and Wisconsin participated in the ADDM Network. In 2010, however, South Carolina was not a participant; these differences can significantly alter the prevalence numbers.

432 **The most extreme number:** A new study released by P. C. Pantelis and D. P. Kennedy in *Autism* (June 2015) reports that the prevalence rate found in the South Korean 2011 study was based on flawed assumptions. Pantelis and Kennedy conclude that had the South Korean researchers compensated for the uncertainty built into their study design, the range of their results would have been almost twice as large as originally reported, making their conclusions questionable.

433 **prevalence rate of 1 in 38:** Y. S. Kim et al., "Prevalence of Autism Spectrum Disorders in a Total Population Sample," *American Journal of Psychiatry* 168, no. 9 (2011): 904–12.

433 **"We just didn't count them":** Alice Park, "South Korean Study Suggests Rates of Autism May Be Underestimated," *Time,* May 9, 2011.

434 **her mother, Eustacia Cutler:** Author interview with Emily Gerson Saines.

436 **"reached epidemic proportions":** Speech given by Emily Gerson Saines after winning an Emmy as producer of *Temple Grandin,* 2010.

Chapter 40: The Vaccine Scare

439 **the fear was ignited:** Prior to the press conference, the Royal Free Hospital issued a press release—"New Research Links Autism and Bowel Disease"—and distributed a twenty-minute video news release, both promoting *The Lancet*'s upcoming study.

440 **Wakefield's paper described twelve children:** A. J. Wakefield et al., "Ileal-Lymphoid-Nodular Hyperplasia, Non-Specific Colitis, and Pervasive Developmental Disorder in Children," *Lancet* 351 (1998): 637–41. All details of the study relayed in this chapter are sourced from this paper.

441 **copied Zuckerman on a letter:** Wakefield presents the letter in Andrew Wakefield, *Callous Disregard: Autism and Vaccines—The Truth Behind a Tragedy* (New York: Skyhorse Publishing, 2010), 96–99.

441 **"MMR are sufficient":** Rebecca Smith, "Andrew Wakefield—The Man Behind the MMR Controversy," *Telegraph,* January 29, 2010.

441 **"One more case of this":** Partial transcript of February 26, 1998, Royal Free Press Conference. This and all quotations from the press conference appear in transcript of General Medical Council, Fitness to Practice Panel, in cases of Dr. Andrew Wakefield, Professor John Walker-Smith, Professor Simon Murch. Chairman: Dr. Surendra Kumar. April 7, 2008. Available at http://wakefieldgmctranscripts.blogspot.com/2012/02/day-17.html.

441 **pounding on the lectern:** The scene was vividly recalled by *Independent* journalist Jeremy Laurance, in interview with authors, and in Jeremy Laurance, "I Was There When Wakefield Dropped His Bombshell," *Independent,* January 29, 2010.

442 **"It's a moral issue for me":** Jeremy Laurance, "Health: Not Immune to How Research Can Hurt; Jeremy Laurance Talks to the Man at the Centre of the Controversy over the MMR Vaccine," *Independent,* March 3, 1998.

442 **storied history of vaccine skepticism:** In 1885, for example, 100,000 people marched against a mandatory program of vaccination for smallpox in the city of Leicester.

442 **they were a fringe:** A systematic survey published in 2007 discovered a scattering of small "vaccine skeptical" organizations, with membership enrollments as small as 60 people, and none larger than 2,000. See P. Hobson-West, "'Trusting Blindly Can Be the Biggest Risk of All': Organised Resistance to Childhood Vaccination in the UK," *Sociology of Health and Illness* 29, no. 2 (2007): 198–215.

442 **immunization rates above 90 percent:** See Figure 2 in Dan Anderberg, Arnaud Chevaliera, and Jonathan Wadsworth, "Anatomy of a Health Scare: Education, Income and the MMR Controversy in the UK," *Journal of Health Economics* 30, no. 3 (2011): 520.

442 **Britain's program was not mandatory:** G. L. Freed, "Vaccine Policies Across the Pond: Looking at the U.K. And U.S. Systems," *Health Affairs* 24, no. 3 (2005): 755–57.

442 **most ardent supporters acknowledge:** See, for example, the statement "Vaccines can and do cause harm" in G. A. Poland and R. M. Jacobson,

"Understanding Those Who Do Not Understand: A Brief Review of the Anti-Vaccine Movement," *Vaccine* 19, no. 17–19 (2001): 2440–45.

443 **some adverse effects will occur:** An excellent discussion of complex practicalities and politics of this cost-benefit balance can be found in Arthur Allen, *Vaccine* (New York: W. W. Norton & Company, 2008).

443 **ever really listened to them:** More than a decade later, the families still made this assertion. See, for example, Fiona Macrae and David Wilkes, "Damning Verdict on MMR Doctor: Anger as GMC Attacks 'Callous Disregard' for Sick Children," *Daily Mail,* January 29, 2010.

444 **"frankly alarmed by suggestions":** Sarah Boseley, "Jab Warning 'Wrong; WHO Chief Attacks Doctors over Claim of Vaccine Link with Autism," *Guardian,* March 12, 1998.

444 **provided numbers as well as an animated graphic:** ITN report, Independent Television News, "MMR Vaccine: Autism Link Story," February 26, 1998, reference number BSP270298055, www.itn.source.com.

445 **"advising parents against":** Sarah Boseley, "MMR Vaccination Fears 'Not Justified'; No Evidence of Link to Autism or Bowel Disease, Scientists Say," *Guardian,* March 25, 1998.

445 **Tony Blair stumbled:** Sarah Womack, "Blair Silent over Leo's MMR Jab," *Telegraph,* December 21, 2001.

445 **scores of them:** See, for example, A. J. Wakefield, "Enterocolitis in Children with Developmental Disorders," *American Journal of Gastroenterology* 95, no. 9 (2000): 2285–95.

446 **Wakefield resigned his position:** Lorraine Fraiser, "Anti-MMR Doctor Is Forced Out," *Telegraph,* December 2, 2001.

446 **he told *The Lancet:*** Sarah Ramsay, "Controversial MMR-Autism Investigator Resigns from Research Post," *Lancet* 358, no. 9297 (December 8, 2001): 1972.

446 **"I'm not going to whinge":** Lucy Johnston, "US Research on Controversial Vaccine May Vindicate Consultant Who Was Forced to Resign; New Tests Back Expert Who Sounded Alarm over Triple Jab for Children," *Sunday Express,* December 9, 2001.

446 **fallen to 79 percent:** Maxine Frith, "Measles Alert in MMR Crisis," *Evening Standard,* July 3, 2002.

446 **"a question mark still hangs":** Linda Steel, "Parents: 'It Is Not About the Science. It's About Belief': Andrew Wakefield—the Doctor Who First Linked MMR and Autism—Has Resigned. But Does That Mean He Was Wrong About the Vaccine?" *Guardian,* December 5, 2001.

446 **made into a feature film:** *Hear the Silence,* directed by Tim Fywell, Channel 5 (UK), original airdate December 9, 2002.

448 **chief witness was Andrew Wakefield:** Wakefield's testimony in "Autism: Present Challenges, Future Needs—Why the Increased Rates?" *Hearing Before the Committee on Government Reform,* House of Representatives, April 6, 2000.

448 **at yet another vaccine hearing:** "Mercury in Medicine—Are We Taking

Unnecessary Risks?" *Hearing Before the Committee on Government Reform,* House of Representatives, July 18, 2000.

448 **Since the 1930s, mercury had been added:** These accounts of the history of the development of thimerosal can be found in the July 18, 2000, committee report cited above, and in Paul Offit, *Autism's False Prophets: Bad Science, Risky Medicine, and the Search for a Cure* (New York: Columbia University Press, 2008), 96–97.

449 **more than thirty separate vaccines:** Anne M. Hurley, Mina Tadrous, and Elizabeth S. Miller. "Thimerosal-Containing Vaccines and Autism: A Review of Recent Epidemiologic Studies," *Journal of Pediatric Pharmacology and Therapeutics* 15, no. 3 (July–September 2010): 173.

449 **warrant an alarm call:** The US Food and Drug Administration makes this point, in publishing and updating guidelines on safe levels of mercury in food consumed. See, for example, the pamphlet "Mercury in Fish: Cause for Concern?" 1995, Food and Drug Administration, downloadable at http://www.fda.gov/OHRMS/DOCKETS/ac/02/briefing/3872_Advisory%207.pdf.

449 **60 micrograms of methylmercury:** Calculation based on mean amount of methylmercury—0.035 ppm—reported in canned albacore tuna by the US Food and Drug Administration for the years 1990–2010, in the online publication "Mercury Levels in Commercial Fish and Shellfish (1990–2010)," www.fda.gov.

449 **warnings about tuna:** See, for example: "Fish: What Pregnant Women and Parents Should Know," draft updated June 2014, FDA and EPA, http://www.fda.gov/Food/FoodborneIllnessContaminants/Metals/ucm393070.htm.

449 **several thousand Iraqis:** F. Bakir et al., "Methylmercury Poisoning in Iraq," *Science* 181, no. 4096 (July 1973): 230–41.

450 **0.1 micrograms per kilogram:** "How People Are Exposed to Mercury," United States Environmental Protection Agency online circular, December 29, 2014, http://www.epa.gov/mercury/exposure.htm.

450 **25 micrograms of mercury:** "Uproar over a Little-Known Preservative, Thimerosal, Jostles U.S. Hepatitis B Vaccination Policy," Hepatitis Control Report, Summer 1999, 4:2. http://www.hepatitiscontrolreport.com/articles.html.

450 **as the mercury found in food:** The methylmercury found in the food chain is molecularly different from the ethylmercury produced when thimerosal is metabolized by the body. A Centers for Disease Control online guide explains: "Ethylmercury is formed when the body breaks down thimerosal. The body uses ethylmercury differently than methylmercury; ethylmercury is broken down and clears out of the blood more quickly." http://www.cdc.gov/vaccinesafety/Concerns/thimerosal/thimerosal_faqs.html#b.

450 **began to tally up:** Hepatitis Control Report, op. cit.

450 **soon, more shots were added:** Ibid.

450 **187 micrograms:** Ibid.

451 **immunization experts decided:** An account of the scientists' reasoning and actions can be found in Arthur Allen, "The Not-So-Crackpot Autism Theory," *New York Times Magazine,* November 10, 2002.

451 **released coordinated statements:** Statement by Public Health Service carried in "Notice to Readers: Thimerosal in Vaccines: A Joint Statement of the American Academy of Pediatrics and the Public Health Service," *Morbidity and Mortality Weekly Report,* Centers for Disease Control, July 9, 1999, 48(26): 563–65.

451 **remarks by the academy's president:** "Press Release: AAP Address FDA Review of Vaccines," July 14, 1999. Accessed at: http://www.aap.org/advocacy/archives/julvacc.htm.

451 **Lyn Redwood might never have suspected:** Author interview with Lyn Redwood. A detailed account of Redwood's journey can also be found as a main story line in David Kirby, *Evidence of Harm: Mercury in Vaccines and the Autism Epidemic: A Medical Controversy* (New York: St. Martin's Press, 2005).

452 **"My worst fears":** Redwood testimony before House Government Reform Committee Hearing, July 18, 2000.

452 **demanding faster action:** "Cure Autism Now Calls for Removal of Mercury-Based Preservative in Children's Vaccinations," PR Newswire, July 17, 2001.

453 **nonprofit called SafeMinds:** The name is an acronym for "Sensible Action for Ending Mercury-Induced Neurological Disorders."

454 **the full range of alternative therapies:** Such therapies were and remain widely advertised online, especially on sites that promote the vaccine theory of autism. A critical but accessible assessment of these approaches can be found in Trine Tsouderos and Patricia Callahan, "Risky Alternative Therapies for Autism Have Little Basis in Science," *Chicago Tribune,* November 22, 2009.

454 **injecting boys with Lupron:** A blogger/investigator's exhaustive and critical report on this practice can be found in Kathleen Seidel, "Autism and Lupron: Playing with Fire," Neurodiversity.com, February 19, 2006, http://web.archive.org/web/20120204153600/http://neurodiversity.com/weblog/article/83/autism-testosterone-lupron-playing-with-fire.

454 **state of the available research:** The background and findings of the IOM review can be found in *Immunization Safety Review: Thimerosal-Containing Vaccines and Neurodevelopmental Disorders* (Washington, DC: National Academy Press, 2001).

455 **Mercury Moms never doubted:** Lyn Redwood interview. In addition, Kirby's *Evidence of Harm* depicts multiple scenes where parents are afforded direct access to top policymakers.

455 **boasted in an online posting:** The account of this confrontation appears in Kirby, *Evidence of Harm,* 104.

456 **"to hide the risks":** Robert Kennedy Jr., "Deadly Immunity," *Rolling Stone,* July 14, 2005, and Salon.com, June 16, 2005, http://www.rollingstone.com/politics/news/deadly-immunity-20110209.

456 **"two sides to every good story":** Kirby, *Evidence of Harm,* xii.

456 **"hellish, lost world":** Ibid.

456 **"Evidence of Harm" Yahoo! group:** The "Evidence of Harm" group subsequently evolved into one called "Environment of Harm," with a restricted membership: https://groups.yahoo.com/neo/groups/EOHarm/info.

456 **optioned for a Hollywood movie:** Per EvidenceOfHarm.com (now defunct), https://web.archive.org/web/20060815043144/http://www.evidenceofharm.com/.

457 **Combating Autism Act:** The text and legislative history of the law can be found at https://www.congress.gov/bill/109th-congress/senate-bill/843.

457 **glittered with the names of experts:** "HHS Secretary Leavitt Announces Members of the New Interagency Autism Coordinating Committee," News Release, US Department of Health and Human Services, November 27, 2007.

Chapter 41: Autism Speaks

459 **the NBC network devoted:** An NBC press release stated: " 'Autism: The Hidden Epidemic?' is part of a weeklong series of special autism coverage airing across the various networks of NBC News during the week of February 21. 'Today,' 'Nightly News with Brian Williams,' CNBC, MSNBC, Telemundo and MSNBC.com will all provide extensive information and reports on the disorder." Source: PRNewswire, "NBC 10 to Air One-Hour Special 'Autism: The Hidden Epidemic?' " February 16, 2005.

459 **some 40 million people:** Autism Speaks Website, "About Us: 2005 Highlights," www.autismspeaks.org/about-us/annual-reports/2005-highlights.

459 **"in most cases, exhausted and broke":** Video of the *Today* show appearance, titled "Bob Wright: I Want My Grandson Back," available at http://www.today.com/id/7024923/ns/today/t/bob-wright-i-want-my-grandson-back/#.VZ0la_kgkqM.

460 **The doctors had diagnosed Christian:** Details of the Wright family's experiences of autism and the founding of Autism Speaks are from authors' interview with Bob and Suzanne Wright.

461 **she had emailed Bob and Suzanne:** Details of Singer's experiences and work with Autism Speaks are from authors' interview with Alison Singer.

462 **Photoshopped version:** Titled "Pass the Maalox: An AoA Thanksgiving Nightmare," the image was taken down from the site after prompting criticism. The incident, which dates to late 2009, was chosen by the authors to illustrate an antagonism in the discourse that was well under way in 2005, and persists to the present day.

462 **to have written favorably:** Amy Wallace, "An Epidemic of Fear: How Panicked Parents Skipping Shots Endanger Us All," *Wired,* October 19, 2009.

464 **offered six-figure salaries:** Per Autism Speaks filing of Internal Revenue Service Form 990, for 2006 and 2007.

464 **Marcus donated $25 million:** "About Us," Autism Speaks, www.autismspeaks.org/about-us.

464 **concert that featured Jerry Seinfeld:** Lawrence Van Gelder, "Arts, Briefly," *New York Times,* August 5, 2005.

465 **sounding the epidemic alarm:** See, for example, Autism Speaks's later press release, "Autism Speaks Demands an Urgent, New Response to the Autism Epidemic as CDC Updates Prevalence Estimates," March 29, 2012.

465 **Bob and Suzanne seemed omnipresent:** For much of the next decade, the

Wrights traveled the United States and the world to promote Autism Speaks, speaking at conferences, and appearing on magazine covers and on radio and television.

465 **5 million Starbucks cups:** Autism Speaks Annual Report, 2007, and Annual Report "Highlights," at https://www.autismspeaks.org/about-us/annual-reports/2007-highlights.

466 **Under Bob Wright's leadership:** Marc Gunther and Henry Goldblatt, "How GE Made NBC No. 1 When He Became NBC'S CEO," *Fortune,* February 3, 1997.

466 **borrowed from that approach:** Giacinta Pace, "Philanthropist Wages Fight to Cure Autism, Suzanne Wright's Foundation Raises Money to Fund Research on Disorder," NBC News, November 12, 2009, www.nbcnews.com/id/33868343/ns/us_news-giving/t/philanthropist-wages-fight-cure-autism/#.VZ1HY_kgkqM.

467 **Jon Shestack was dead set against:** Shestack's recollections of CAN relationship with Autism Speaks are from authors' interview with Jon Shestack.

468 **the Londons did not see it that way:** The Londons' recollections of NAAR's relationship with Autism Speaks are from authors' interview with Eric and Karen London.

468 **"the consolidation of the two charities":** Autism Speaks, "Autism Speaks and the National Alliance for Autism Research (NAAR) Announce Plans to Combine Operations," press release, November 30, 2005, https://www.autismspeaks.org/about-us/press-releases/autism-speaks-and-national-alliance-autism-research-naar-announce-plans-comb.

468 **Shestack was given a heads-up:** Singer and Shestack interviews.

469 **announced the merger of Cure Autism Now:** Autism Speaks, "Autism Speaks and the National Alliance for Autism Research."

470 **surpassed anything a private charity:** Grant statistics from Autism Speaks annual reports available at autismspeaks.org.

Chapter 42: A Story Unravels

471 **Written by a pair of American vaccine researchers:** Robert T. Chen and Frank DeStefano, "Vaccine Adverse Events: Causal or Coincidental?" *Lancet* 351 (1998): 611–12.

471 **researcher named Brent Taylor:** Brent Taylor et al., "Autism and Measles, Mumps, and Rubella Vaccine: No Epidemiological Evidence for a Causal Association," *Lancet* 353 (1999): 2026–29.

472 **a study out of California:** L. Dales, S. J. Hammer, and N. J. Smith, "Time Trends in Autism and in MMR Immunization Coverage in California," *Journal of the American Medical Association* 285, no. 9 (2001): 1183–85.

472 **Brian Deer was an investigative reporter:** A significant portion of Deer's work can be found online at briandeer.com.

472 **thought to ask Deer:** Author interview with Brian Deer. Our account of Deer's legwork also draws upon Deer's own detailed account submitted for legal purposes when he was named a defendant in a libel suit, ultimately dismissed, brought by Andrew Wakefield. Titled "Amended Declaration of Brian

Deer in Support of Defendants' Anti-Slapp Motion to Dismiss," it can be found online at http://briandeer.com/solved/slapp-amended-declaration.pdf.

473 **"I believe that this paper":** Brian Deer, "Revealed: MMR Research Scandal," *Sunday Times,* February 22, 2004.

473 **they publicly retracted:** Simon H. Murch et al., "Retraction of an Interpretation," *Lancet* 363, no. 9411 (2004): 750.

473 ***The Lancet*'s editor declared:** Quoted by Brian Deer, "MMR: The Truth Behind the Crisis," *Sunday Times,* February 22, 2004.

474 **"mixing spin and science":** Fiona Macrae and David Wilkes, "Damning Verdict on MMR Doctor: Anger as GMC Attacks 'Callous Disregard' for Sick Children," *Daily Mail,* January 29, 2010.

474 **"matter of urgency":** David Hughes and Jenny Hope, "MMR: The Betrayal of These Tragic Parents," *Daily Mail,* February 24, 2004.

474 **"His credibility lies in ruins":** Editorial Board, "Doctor's Secret," *Sun,* February 23, 2004.

474 **"increasingly isolated man":** Jeremy Laurance, "A Doctor, the Distinguished Journal, and a Scare That Need Never Have Happened," *Independent on Sunday,* February 22, 2004.

474 **"urgent need now is for more real study":** "This Carefully Orchestrated Campaign Must Not Be Allowed to Stifle Real Debate on MMR," *Independent,* February 24, 2004.

474 **"until the mysteries of autism are fully explained":** "Doctor's Secret."

474 **"He is not an accountant":** "Another New Twist in MMR Controversy," *Bath Chronicle,* February 24, 2004.

474 **"There has been talk of an inquiry":** Liam Mcdougall, "MMR: Wakefield Welcomes Probe," *Sunday Herald,* February 22, 2004.

475 **critics faulted the article:** See, for example, Seth Mnookin, *The Panic Virus: The True Story Behind the Vaccine-Autism Controversy* (New York: Simon & Schuster, 2011).

475 ***Salon* issued a full retraction:** *Salon*'s explanation for retracting can be found at www.salon.com/2011/01/16/dangerous_immunity/.

475 **Senate probe into the alleged plot:** US Senate Committee on Health, Education, Labor and Pensions, "Thimerosal and Autism Spectrum Disorders: Alleged Misconduct by Government Agencies and Private Entities," Executive Summary, September 2007.

476 **a new panel was convened:** *Immunization Safety Review: Vaccines and Autism* (Washington, DC: National Academy Press, 2004).

476 **SafeMinds published a press release:** SafeMinds, "SafeMinds Outraged That IOM Report Fails American Public," press release, May 18, 2004, http://www.prnewswire.com/news-releases/safeminds-outraged-that-iom-report-fails-american-public-74103762.html.

477 **composed in advance:** David Kirby, *Evidence of Harm: Mercury in Vaccines and the Autism Epidemic: A Medical Controversy* (New York: St. Martin's Press, 2005), 376–77.

477 **an hour-long television documentary:** *"MMR: What They Didn't Tell You," Dispatches,* Channel 4 (UK), original airdate November 18, 2004.

478 **in an interview in Texas:** Bonnie Estridge, "I Demand the Right to Clear My Name," *Express,* July 17, 2006.

478 **firms advertised on TV:** Margaret Cronin Fisk, "Mercury's Legal Morass: A Surge of Lawsuits Allege That Vaccinations Triggered Autism," *National Law Journal,* March 20, 2002.

478 **"forcing the multi-billion dollar":** The notice was a press release attributed by PRNewswire to the Portland, Oregon, firm Williams, Dailey, O'Leary, Craine & Love.

478 **The response was huge:** Fisk, "Mercury's Legal Morass."

479 **a federal claims court in Washington, DC:** "About the National Vaccine Injury Compensation Program," US Department of Health and Human Services. Online at: http://www.hrsa.gov/vaccinecompensation/about/index.html.

479 **The average award:** National Vaccine Injury Compensation Program Monthly Statistics Report at http://www.hrsa.gov/vaccinecompensation/data/statistics report.pdf.

481 **in an exchange with a skeptical blogger:** Citizen Cain's report of their exchange can be found at "Slouching Toward Truth—Autism and Mercury," November 30, 2005, http://citizencain.blogspot.com/2005/11/slouching-toward-truth-autism-and_30.html.

481 **It went up:** R. Schechter and J. K. Grether, "Continuing Increases in Autism Reported to California's Developmental Services System: Mercury in Retrograde," *Archives of General Psychiatry* 65, no. 1 (2008): 19–24.

482 **the story still held:** McCarthy's first book on the subject, *Louder Than Words: A Mother's Journey in Healing Autism* (New York: Dutton, 2007), became a New York Times bestseller.

Chapter 43: The Greatest Fraud

483 **three special masters took their seats:** Gardiner Harris, "Opening Statements in Case on Autism and Vaccinations," *New York Times,* June 12, 2007.

483 **Hundreds did so:** As reported in "Autism Update," July 12, 2007, filing, "In Re: Claims for Vaccine Injuries Resulting in Autism Spectrum Disorder or a Similar Neurodevelopmental Disorder," Office of Special Masters. All such updates issued in the case are available online at http://www.uscfc.uscourts.gov/docket-omnibus-autism-proceeding.

483 **wearing a noise-muffling headset:** See Harris, "Opening Statements," for this and other details of courtroom events not evident in the transcript.

484 **Theresa, provided moving testimony:** Full transcript at http://www.uscfc.uscourts.gov/cedillo-v-secretary-health-and-human-services-case-no-98916v-concluded-june-26-2007.

484 **a front-page story:** Jane Gross and Stephanie Strom, "Autism Debate Strains a Family," *New York Times,* June 18, 2007.

485 **sharing with the autism community:** Excerpts of Katie Wright's postings

to the EOH Yahoo! group (which has since become a restricted group) were detailed in Seth Mnookin, *The Panic Virus* (New York: Simon & Schuster, 2012), 239–42.

485 **videotaped interview with David Kirby:** "David Kirby Interviews Katie Wright," April 19, 2007, available at http://www.autismmedia.org/media15.html.

485 **A terse statement:** "Statement from Bob and Suzanne Wright, Co-founders of Autism Speaks," retrieved via web.archive.org/web/20070806215254/http://www.autismspeaks.org/wrights_statement.php.

486 **continued communicating with her online public:** "Statement on Autism Speaks from Katie Wright," Adventures in Autism, June 15, 2007, web.archive.org/web/20150322050800/http://adventuresinautism.blogspot.com/2007/06/statement-on-autism-speaks-from-katie.html.

486 **That executive was Alison Singer:** Author interview with Alison Singer.

487 **tripled to more than 25,000:** Jessica Atwell et al., "Nonmedical Vaccine Exemptions and Pertussis in California, 2010," *Pediatrics,* published online September 30, 2013, http://pediatrics.aappublications.org/content/early/2013/09/24/peds.2013-0878.full.pdf+html.

487 **a twenty-year high in 2014:** Gary Baum, "Hollywood's Vaccine Wars: L.A.'s 'Entitled' Westsiders Behind City's Epidemic," *Hollywood Reporter,* September 12, 2014. Reporting on parents seeking exemptions for their children's vaccinations, the paper found the exemption rate was highest for the children of Hollywood's elite, "particularly those attending exclusive, entertainment-industry-favored child care centers, preschools, and kindergartens." At one school, the opt-out figure was 57 percent; at another, 62 percent. The paper pointed out that "such numbers are in line with immunization rates in developing countries like Chad and South Sudan."

487 **a single email led her to an answer:** Copy of the email provided to authors by Alison Singer.

488 **"leave no stone unturned":** Proposed text changes contained in memo attached to email: "Intro draft provisions & priorities-revised 1-13-09."

488 **Singer emailed Wright:** Copy of the email provided to authors by Alison Singer.

488 **Wright's generous response:** Copy of the response email provided to authors by Alison Singer.

489 **She voted to reject:** Interagency Autism Coordinating Committee, Full Committee Meeting, January 14, 2009. Transcript available at https://iacc.hhs.gov/events/.

489 **Autism Speaks's official response:** Autism Speaks, "Autism Speaks Withdraws Support for Strategic Plan for Autism Research, Decries Unexpected Change in Final Approval Process," press release, January 15, 2009, https://www.autismspeaks.org/about-us/press-releases/autism-speaks-withdraws-support-strategic-plan-autism-research-decries-unexp.

489 **took a direct shot:** "NAAR Founder Eric London Resigns from Autism Speaks Citing Disagreement over Vaccine Research," Autism Science Foundation,

June 30, 2009, autismsciencefoundation.wordpress.com/2009/06/30/naar-founder-eric-london-resigns-from-autism-speaks-citing-disagreement-over-autismvaccine-research/.

490 **policy statement that endorsed:** "Information About Vaccines and Autism," Autism Speaks, January 3, 2010, https://web.archive.org/web/20110620215135/http://www.autismspeaks.org/science/policy-statements/information-about-vaccines-and-autism.

490 **for their "silence":** See, for example, John Stone, "Bob and Suzanne Wright, Why Won't Autism Speaks Address the Vaccine Issue?" *Age of Autism,* February 22, 2011, http://www.ageofautism.com/2011/02/bob-and-suzanne-wright-why-wont-autism-speaks-address-the-vaccine-issue.html.

490 **Autism Speaks's financial contribution:** Financial data from Autism Speaks annual reports, available at https://www.autismspeaks.org/about-us/annual-reports.

490 **amount was not much higher:** In 2013, for example, the organization's total operating expenses for the year stood at $120 million, most of which was spent on advocacy, awareness, and overhead, with approximately $15 million going to scientists as grants. In 2005, NAAR distributed grants totaling $6.9 million, and CAN gave out $4.1 million ($11 million combined).

490 **potential dangers of vaccines:** Meredith Wadman, "Autism's Fight for Facts: A Voice for Science," *Nature* 479 (2001): 28–31.

491 **average of $45 million per year:** "About SFARI," Simons Foundation Autism Research Initiative, https://sfari.org/about-sfari.

491 **Eventually, Autism Speaks did choose sides:** Rob Ring and Bob Wright, "Vaccines and Autism," updated statement, https://www.autismspeaks.org/science/policy-statements/information-about-vaccines-and-autism.

491 **a 174-page decision:** Decision, Office of Special Masters, No. 98-916V, filed February 12, 2009.

492 **the longest in the GMC's history:** History of case and ruling contained in General Medical Counsel, Fitness to Practice Hearing, www.nhs.uk/news/2010/01january/documents/facts%20wwsm%20280110%20final%20complete%20corrected.pdf.

493 ***The Lancet* finally fully retracted:** "RETRACTED: Ileal-Lymphoid-Nodular Hyperplasia, Non-Specific Colitis, and Pervasive Developmental Disorder in Children," *Lancet* 351, no. 9103 (1998): 637–41.

493 **"I feel I was deceived":** Sarah Boseley, "*Lancet* Retracts 'Utterly False' MMR Paper," *Guardian,* February 2, 2010.

493 **"struck off the medical register":** Sarah Boseley, "Andrew Wakefield Struck Off Register by General Medical Council," *Guardian,* May 24, 2010.

493 **"Hippocrates Would Puke":** Editorial, "Hippocrates Would Puke: Doctor Hoaxed Parents into Denying Kids Vaccine," *New York Daily News,* February 5, 2010.

493 ***Time* magazine took this idea:** "Great Science Frauds," *Time,* January 12, 2012.

Chapter 44: Finding a Voice

497 **ad-libbed a line:** Author interview with Alex Plank.

497 **directed documentary films:** *autism reality,* produced and directed by Alex Plank for Wrong Planet, https://www.youtube.com/watch?v=jLOCYubVc7g.

498 **ill at ease with his environment:** Details of Alex Plank's childhood from author interviews with Alex Plank and his parents, Mary and Doug.

501 **hopelessly arcane:** See K. Kasmini and S. Zasmani, "Asperger's Syndrome: A Report of Two Cases from Malaysia," *Singapore Medical Journal* 36, no. 6 (1995): 641–43; S. A. Cooper, W. N. Mohamed, and R. A. Collacott, "Possible Asperger's Syndrome in a Mentally Handicapped Transvestite Offender," *Journal of Intellectual Disability Research* 37 (1993): 189–94; and M. L. Berthier, "Corticocallosal Anomalies in Asperger's Syndrome," *American Journal of Roentgenology* 162, no. 1 (1994): 236–37.

502 **she named OASIS:** Patricia Romanowski Bashe and Barbara L. Kirby, *The Oasis Guide to Asperger Syndrome* (New York: Crown, 2001), 2–4.

502 **hit 1 million:** Ibid., 4.

503 **"a web community":** Wrong Planet, http://wrongplanet.net/.

503 **it already had 328:** These numbers were derived using web.archive.org to spot-check during the time periods cited.

503 **"chatting online allows":** Samantha Sordyl, "Creating an Asperger's Community," *Washington Post,* December 20, 2005.

504 ***Wired* magazine's Steve Silberman wrote:** Steve Silberman, "The Geek Syndrome: Autism—and Its Milder Cousin Asperger's Syndrome—Is Surging Among the Children of Silicon Valley. Are Math-and-Tech Genes to Blame?" *Wired,* December 2001.

504 **narrator was a fifteen-year-old boy:** Mark Haddon, *The Curious Incident of the Dog in the Night-Time* (New York: Vintage, 2004).

505 **"a *real girl*":** Autism Talk TV, https://www.youtube.com/watch?v=eIqFrbgBEQY.

505 **only one famous person:** To be sure, there were less-well-known figures, several of whom were invited to speak to parents by the National Association for Autistic Children. These included William Donovan, who gave a talk in 1970, and Jerry Alter, who gave a talk in 1972, at the age of twenty-one.

506 **describes herself that way:** Temple Grandin, http://www.templegrandin.com/.

506 **"reasons for their past problems":** Lorna Wing, "Past and Future of Research on Asperger Syndrome," in *Asperger Syndrome,* ed. Ami Klin, Fred R. Volkmar, and Sara S. Sparrow (New York: Guilford Press, 2000), 419.

506 **well-established cultural phenomenon:** David C Giles, "'*DSM-5* Is Taking Away Our Identity': The Reaction of the Online Community to the Proposed Changes in the Diagnosis of Asperger's Disorder," *Health* 18, no. 2 (2014): 179–95.

506 **"dash of autism for myself":** Uta Frith, ed., *Autism and Asperger Syndrome* (Cambridge, UK: Cambridge University Press, 1991), 26.

507 **"while the other people socialized":** Temple Grandin, *Thinking in Pictures: My Life with Autism,* Expanded Edition (New York: Vintage, 2006), 122.

507 **"the only explanation for the full range":** Norm Ledgin, *Diagnosing Jefferson: Evidence of a Condition That Guided His Beliefs, Behavior, and Personal Associations* (Arlington, TX: Future Horizons, 2000), 2.

507 **"Now it's almost cool":** Amy S. F. Lutz, "You Do Not Have Asperger's," *Slate,* May 22, 2013, http://www.slate.com/articles/health_and_science/medical_examiner/2013/05/autism_spectrum_diagnoses_the_dsm_5_eliminates_asperger_s_and_pdd_nos.html.

507 **On his own blog:** Tom Hobben, *Adventures in Aspergers: The Side Effects of Parenthood,* http://theaspieadventures.blogspot.com/.

507 **"means for making a diagnosis":** "Take the AQ Test," *Wired,* December 12, 2001, http://archive.wired.com/wired/archive/9.12/aqtest.html.

507 **"a conceptual gadget":** Benjamin Wallace, "Is Everyone on the Autism Spectrum?" *New York Magazine,* October 28, 2012.

508 **"The self-diagnosis boom":** Wallace, "Is Everyone on the Autism Spectrum?"

509 **"a great expenditure of mental energy":** Plank, as quoted in *autism reality.*

509 **founded an organization called GRASP:** Author interview with Michael John Carley.

510 **spent nearly a third of his life:** Cara Buckley, "Man Obsessed with Trains Again Runs Afoul of Law," *New York Times,* November 11, 2006.

510 **"People take one look at him":** Colleen Long, "Darius McCollum, Serial Transit Impostor, Arrested 29 Times for Stealing Trains and Buses," *Huffington Post,* August 12, 2013, http://www.huffingtonpost.com/2013/08/12/darius-mccollum_n_3742778.html.

511 **"Let us focus instead on mourning":** Statement from Michael John Carley on the Newtown, Connecticut, shootings, December 14, 2012, available at https://web.archive.org/web/20121218041020/http://grasp.org/profiles/blogs/statement-from-michael-john-carley-on-the-newtown-ct-shootings.

511 **This was a data-based finding:** Peter Szatmari and Marshall B. Jones, "IQ and the Genetics of Autism," *Journal of Child Psychology and Psychiatry* 32, no. 6 (1991): 897–908.

512 **That year, the CDC:** Centers for Disease Control and Prevention, *Morbidity and Mortality Weekly Report* 63, no. 2, Surveillance Summaries, March 28, 2014.

Chapter 45: Neurodiversity

513 **"a wake-up call to families":** NYU Child Study Center, "Millions of Children Held Hostage by Psychiatric Disorders," press release, December 3, 2007.

514 **"Don't mourn for us":** Jim Sinclair, "Don't Mourn for Us," originally posted November 3, 1993, at http://www.autreat.com/dont_mourn.html.

514 **"that it would be much better":** Dick Cavett interview with Bruno Bettelheim, *The Dick Cavett Show,* ABC, original airdate June 2, 1971.

516 **"left your child's bewildered body behind":** Geoffrey Cowley, "Understanding Autism," *Newsweek,* July 30, 2000.

516 **"This disease has taken":** Autism Speaks, "Founders' Message. A Message from

Suzanne and Bob Wright: Co-founders," 2006, available at https://web.archive.org/web/20060209121732/http://www.autismspeaks.org/founders.php.

516 **an Australian sociologist:** Judy Singer, "Odd People In: The Birth of Community Amongst People on the 'Autistic Spectrum,'" BA diss., University of Technology, Sydney, 1998.

517 **"Neurotypical Syndrome":** Institute for the Study of the Neurologically Typical, March 18, 2002, http://autisticadvocacy.org/.

517 **"neurodiversity may be":** Harvey Blume, "Neurodiversity: On the Neurological Underpinnings of Geekdom," *Atlantic,* September 1998, http://www.theatlantic.com/past/docs/unbound/citation/wc980930.htm.

517 **Dawson filed an "intervener's factum":** "An Autistic at the Supreme Court: The Auton Case: The Intervener's Factum." Online at http://www.sentex.net/~nexus23/naa_fac.html.

518 **"Nothing About Us, Without Us":** Autistic Self Advocacy Network, http://autisticadvocacy.org/.

518 **"We struggle socially":** Mike Ervin, "Autism Group Founder: It's Time to Listen to What We Have to Say," *Independence Today,* June 13, 2013, http://www.itodaynews.com/2013-issues/june13/asan-cover.htm.

519 **"continued dehumanizing advertising":** Ari Ne'eman, "Comments at November 30, 2007 IACC Meeting," Autistic Self Advocacy Network, December 8, 2007, http://autisticadvocacy.org/2007/12/comments-at-november-30-2007-iacc-meeting/.

519 **"on issues related to the quality of life":** Ari Ne'eman, "The Future (and the Past) of Autism Advocacy, Or Why the ASA's Magazine, *The Advocate,* Wouldn't Publish This Piece," *Disability Studies Quarterly* 30, no. 1 (2010). Text available at http://dsq-sds.org/article/view/1059/1244.

519 **"To pursue normalization":** Ibid.

520 **They had found that actual brain size:** "Autism: What We Know. What Is Next?" Simons Foundation Research Initiative, May 2014, http://simonsfoundation.s3.amazonaws.com/share/sfari-specials/2014/whatweknow/20140501whatWeKnow.pdf.

520 **that dopamine, the brain chemical:** Nicholette Zeliadt, "Diverse Dopamine Defects Found in People with Autism," Simons Foundation Autism Research Initiative, November 19, 2014, http://sfari.org/news-and-opinion/conference-news/2014/society-for-neuroscience-2014/diverse-dopamine-defects-found-in-people-with-autism.

520 **Eye-tracking technology:** W. Jones and A. Klin, "Attention to Eyes Is Present but in Decline in 2–6-Month-Old Infants Later Diagnosed with Autism," *Nature* 504, no. 7480 (2013): 427–31.

520 **the sleep of autistic children:** K. A. Schreck and J. A. Mulick, "Parental Report of Sleep Problems in Children with Autism," *Journal of Autism and Developmental Disorders* 30, no. 2 (2000): 127–35.

520 **older fathers have an increased chance:** Emma M. Frans et al., "Autism Risk Across Generations: A Population Based Study of Advancing Grandpaternal and Paternal Age," *JAMA Psychiatry* 70, no. 5 (2013): 516–21.

520 **mothers who take folic acid:** R. J. Schmidt, R. L. Hansen, and I. Hertz-Picciotto, "Maternal Periconceptional Folic Acid Intake and Risk for Autism Spectrum Disorders in the CHARGE Case-Control Study," *American Journal of Clinical Nutrition* 96, no. 1 (2012): 80–89.

520 **Prenatal studies were also:** Brian Lee et al., "Maternal Hospitalization with Infection During Pregnancy and Risk of Autism Spectrum Disorders," *Brain, Behavior, and Immunity* 44 (2015): 100–105.

520 **experiencing high fevers:** Lauren P. Curran et al., "Behaviors Associated with Fever in Children with Autism Spectrum Disorders," *Pediatrics* 120, no. 6 (2007): 1386–92.

520 **Melatonin helped some children:** Beth A. Malow et al., "Melatonin for Sleep in Children with Autism: A Controlled Trial Examining Dose, Tolerability, and Outcomes," *Journal of Autism and Developmental Disorders* 42, no. 8 (2012): 1729–37.

520 **Risperidone and other antipsychotics:** C. J. McDougle et al., "Risperidone for the Core Symptom Domains of Autism: Results from the Study by the Autism Network of the Research Units on Pediatric Psychopharmacology," *American Journal of Psychiatry* 162, no. 6 (2005): 1142–48.

520 **At the National Institutes of Health, the DNA:** Jill L. Silverman, Mu Yang, Catherine Lord, and Jacqueline N. Crawley, "Behavioural Phenotyping Assays for Mouse Models of Autism," *Nature Reviews Neuroscience* 11 (2010): 490–502.

521 **neural wiring of the fruit fly:** Ralph Greenspan, "Using Fruit Flies to Map the Network of Autism-Associated Genes," Simons Foundation Autism Research Initiative, January 2011, https://sfari.org/funding/grants/abstracts/using-fruit-flies-to-map-the-network-of-autism-associated-genes.

521 **"that of eugenic abortion":** Ne'eman, "Future (and the Past) of Autism Advocacy."

521 **"Autism is part of what I am":** Oliver Sacks, "A Neurologist's Notebook: An Anthropologist on Mars," *New Yorker,* December 27, 1993.

522 **call the NYU Child Study Center:** "An Urgent Call to Action: Tell NYU Child Study Center to Abandon Stereotypes Against People with Disabilities," Autistic Self Advocacy Network, December 8, 2007, http://autisticadvocacy.org/2007/12/tell-nyu-child-study-center-to-abandon-stereotypes/.

522 **other, more recognized, disability organizations:** Ne'eman's recollections on ASAN and his campaign for neurodiversity are from an author interview.

523 **had attracted coverage from:** Christina Boyle, "Psych Groups' Fury over 'Ransom' Ads," *New York Daily News,* December 13, 2007.

523 **"ride out the storm":** Joanne Kaufman, "Campaign on Childhood Mental Illness Succeeds at Being Provocative," *New York Times,* December 14, 2007.

523 **"You don't have my son":** "Ransom Notes and Love Letters," MOM–Not Otherwise Specified Blog, December 10, 2007, http://momnos.blogspot.com/2007/12/ransom-notes-and-love-letters.html.

523 **"These ads reflect":** Ari Ne'eman interview.

524 **Autism Speaks awareness-raising "walk":** "Locally-Founded Autism Group

Protests D.C. Walk for Autism," WAMU American University Radio, Washington, DC, November 2, 2009.

524 **video called *I Am Autism:*** Claudia Wallis, "'I Am Autism': An Advocacy Video Sparks Protest," *Time,* November 6, 2009.

524 **few people who wanted to take him on:** Jon Shestack was an exception, who publicly challenged Ne'eman's argument multiple times.

525 **"disappointing and ill-advised":** "ASAN Condemns Presidential Appointment of Anti-Vaccine Activist Peter Bell," Autistic Self Advocacy Network, January 12, 2012, autisticadvocacy.org/2012/01/asan-condemns-presidential-appointment-of-anti-vaccine-activist-peter-bell/.

525 **an autistic person any less autistic:** Liz Bell's recollections of her meeting with Ari Ne'eman are from an interview with the authors.

527 **"mindblindness":** Simon Baron-Cohen, *Mindblindness: An Essay on Autism and Theory of Mind* (Boston: MIT Press/Bradford Books, 1995).

527 **A corollary theory:** Simon Baron-Cohen, *The Essential Difference: Male and Female Brains and the Truth About Autism* (New York: Basic Books, 2003), 37–44.

528 **"rather an elusive category":** David C. Gile, "'*DSM-5* Is Taking Away Our Identity': The Reaction of the Online Community to the Proposed Changes in the Diagnosis of Asperger's Disorder," *Health* 18, no. 2 (2014): 179–95.

529 **twelve different American research centers:** C. E. Lord et al., "Multi-Site Study of the Clinical Diagnosis of Different Autism Spectrum Disorders," *Archives of General Psychiatry* 69, no. 3 (2012): 306–13.

529 **would not qualify for an Asperger's diagnosis:** J. Miller and S. Ozonoff, "Did Asperger's Cases Have Asperger Disorder? A Research Note," *Journal of Child Psychology and Psychiatry* 38, no. 2 (1997): 247–51.

529 **"definitions influenced by the literature":** Susan Dickerson Mayes, Susan L. Calhoun, and Dana L. Crites, "Does *DSM-IV* Asperger's Disorder Exist?" *Journal of Abnormal Child Psychology* 29, no. 3 (2001): 263–71.

529 **"It's confusing and not terribly useful":** Claudia Wallis, "A Powerful Identity, a Vanishing Diagnosis," *New York Times,* November 2, 2009.

530 **Fred Volkmar of Yale resigned:** Author interview with Fred Volkmar.

530 **"But I'd keep Asperger's":** Wallis, "A Powerful Identity, a Vanishing Diagnosis."

530 **"to help ensure clinical continuity":** Michael John Carley, "Improve *DSM-5* Diagnostic Criteria for Autism," petition on change.org, https://www.change.org/p/american-psychiatric-association-dsm-5-task-force-and-work-group-improve-dsm-5-diagnostic-criteria-for-autism.

530 **"taking away our identity":** Thread on wrongplanet.net, beginning July 17, 2010, "*DSM-5* Is Taking Away Our Identity Soapbox Alert," http://www.wrongplanet.net/forums/viewtopic.php?p=2923037.

531 **"New Definition of Autism Will Exclude":** Benedict Carey, "New Definition of Autism Will Exclude Many, Study Suggests," *New York Times,* January 19, 2012.

531 **"showing fidelity to the research":** Steven Kapp and Ari Ne'eman, "ASD in *DSM-5:* What the Research Shows and Recommendations for Change," ASAN Policy Brief, June 2012, http://autisticadvocacy.org/wp-content/uploads/2012/06/ASAN_DSM-5_2_final.pdf.

532 **"did a great service in raising awareness":** Francesca Happé, "Why Fold Asperger Syndrome into Autism Spectrum Disorder in the *DSM-5*?" View—Simons Foundation Autism Research Initiative, March 29, 2011, http://sfari.org/news-and-opinion/viewpoint/2011/why-fold-asperger-syndrome-into-autism-spectrum-disorder-in-the-dsm-5.

Chapter 46: A Happy Man

534 **had not heard before:** Donald's first media contact from outside Mississippi was with French documentarian Anne Georget, who featured him in her 2000 French-language film *Histoire, histoires d'autisme.* The film had no showing in Forest.

535 ***"I wish myself luck":*** Donald Triplett shared his yearbook and photographs with the authors.

536 **allow no harm:** Recollections about Donald Triplett's later years are from author interviews with Donald and Oliver Triplett, Celeste Slay, and Gene Walker.

537 **was befriended by:** Author interview with Reverend Brister Ware.

538 **"interest in the opposite sex":** Leo Kanner, "Follow-up Study of Eleven Autistic Children Originally Reported in 1943," *Journal of Autism and Childhood Schizophrenia* 1, no. 2 (1971): 119–45.

540 **"I wish I knew what his inner feelings":** Ibid., 122.

541 **"It was rather expected":** Donald Triplett interview.

Epilogue

550 **A 2013 study found:** Anne Roux, Kristy Anderson, Paul Shattuck, and Benjamin Cooper, "Postsecondary Employment Experiences Among Young Adults with an Autism Spectrum Disorder," *Journal of the American Academy of Child & Adolescent Psychiatry* 52, no 9 (2013): 931-39.

550 **more than half had never:** Shattuck et al., "Postsecondary Employment Experiences."

550 **Eight out of ten:** Kristy Anderson, Paul Shattuck, Benjamin Cooper, Anne Roux, and Mary Wagner, "Prevalence and Correlates of Postsecondary Residential Status Among Young Adults with an Autism Spectrum Disorder," *Autism* 8, no. 5 (2014).

550 **A Danish father named:** More information about Thorkil Sonne and his organization, the Specialists, can be found on his website at http://specialistpeople.com/.

550 **In late 2015, a New York:** More information about New York Collaborates for Autism launch of the Neighborhood Network of New York Community Living Program can be found on the organization's website at http://nyc4a.org/.

551 **In 2013, Connie and Harvey:** More information on California's Self Determination Program can be found on California's Department of Developmental Services website at http://www.dds.ca.gov/sdp/.

551 **in 2014, the College of William & Mary:** More information on John Elder Robison and the work he has begun at William and Mary College can be found on William and Mary's website at https://www.wm.edu/news/stories/2013/neurodiversity-advocate-robison-to-teach,-consult-at-wm123.php.

BIBLIOGRAPHY

Books

Allen, Arthur. *Vaccine: The Controversial Story of Medicine's Greatest Lifesaver.* New York: W. W. Norton, 2007.

Amaral, David, Daniel Geschwind, and Geraldine Dawson. *Autism Spectrum Disorders.* New York: Oxford University Press, 2011.

Attwood, Tony. *The Complete Guide to Asperger's Syndrome.* London: Jessica Kingsley, 2006.

Bailey, Jon S., and Mary R. Burch. *Ethics for Behavior Analysts, A Practical Guide to the Behavior Analyst Certification Board Guidelines for Responsible Conduct.* Mahwah, NJ: Lawrence Erlbaum Associates, 2005.

Barkins, Evelyn Werner. *Are These Our Doctors?* New York: Fell, 1952.

Baron-Cohen, Simon. *Mindblindness: An Essay on Autism and Theory of Mind.* Cambridge, MA: MIT Press, 1995.

———. *The Essential Difference: Male and Female Brains and the Truth About Autism.* New York: Basic Books, 2003.

Barr, Martin W. *Mental Defectives: Their History, Treatment, and Training.* New York: Arno Press, 1973.

Bashe, Patricia Romanowski, and Barbara L. Kirby. *The Oasis Guide to Asperger Syndrome: Advice, Support, Insight, and Inspiration.* New York: Crown, 2001.

Bentall, Richard P. *Doctoring the Mind: Is Our Current Treatment of Mental Illness Really Any Good?* New York: New York University Press, 2009.

Bettelheim, Bruno. *Love Is Not Enough: The Treatment of Emotionally Disturbed Children.* Glencoe, IL: Free Press, 1950.

———. *Truants from Life: The Rehabilitation of Emotionally Disturbed Children.* Glencoe, IL: Free Press, 1955.

———. *The Empty Fortress: Infantile Autism and the Birth of the Self.* New York: Free Press, 1967.

———. *Surviving, and Other Essays.* New York: Knopf, 1979.

Bettelheim, Bruno, and Alvin A. Rosenfeld. *The Art of the Obvious.* New York: Knopf, 1993.

Biklen, Douglas. *Let Our Children Go: An Organizing Manual for Advocates and Parents.* Syracuse, NY: Human Policy Press, 1974.

———. *Communication Unbound: How Facilitated Communication Is Challenging*

Traditional Views of Autism and Ability-Disability. New York: Teachers College Press, 1993.

———. *Contested Words, Contested Science: Unraveling the Facilitated Communication Controversy.* New York: Teachers College Press, 1997.

———. *Autism and the Myth of the Person Alone.* New York: New York University Press, 2005.

Blatt, Burton, and Fred Kaplan. *Christmas in Purgatory: A Photographic Essay on Mental Retardation.* Syracuse: Human Policy Press, 1966.

Brockett, L. P., and Edward Seguin. *Idiots and the Efforts for Their Improvement.* Hartford, CT: Case, Tiffany, 1856.

Bruckner, Leona S. *Triumph of Love: An Unforgettable Story of the Power of Goodness.* New York: Simon & Schuster, 1954.

Bruinius, Harry. *Better for All the World: The Secret History of Forced Sterilization and America's Quest for Racial Purity.* New York: Knopf, 2006.

Carey, Allison C. *On the Margins of Citizenship: Intellectual Disability and Civil Rights in Twentieth-Century America.* Philadelphia: Temple University Press, 2009.

Carley, Michael John. *Asperger's from the Inside Out: A Supportive and Practical Guide for Anyone with Asperger's Syndrome.* New York: Perigee, 2008.

Churchill, Don W. *Infantile Autism: Proceedings of the Indiana University Colloquium.* Springfield, IL: C. C. Thomas, 1971.

Clincal Practice Guidelines: Report of the Recommendations, Autism/Pervasive Developmental Disorders, Assessment and Intervention for Young Children (Age 0–3 Years). Publication 4216. Albany, NY: New York State Department of Health, 1999.

Clooney, Nick. *The Movies That Changed Us: Reflections on the Screen.* New York: Atria Books, 2002.

Cohen, Shirley. *Targeting Autism: What We Know, Don't Know, and Can Do to Help Young Children with Autism and Related Disorders.* Berkeley: University of California Press, 1998.

Coleman, Mary. *The Autistic Syndromes.* Amsterdam: North-Holland, 1976.

———. *The Neurology of Autism.* New York: Oxford University Press, 2005.

Copeland, James. Based on a diary by Jack Hodges. *For the Love of Ann.* London: Random House, 1973.

Crawley, Jacqueline N. *What's Wrong with My Mouse? Behavioral Phenotyping of Transgenic and Knockout Mice.* New York: Wiley-Liss, 2000.

Crossley, Rosemary. *Speechless: Facilitating Communication for People Without Voices.* New York: Dutton, 1997.

Crossley, Rosemary, and Anne McDonald. *Annie's Coming Out.* Reprint ed. Harmondsworth, UK: Penguin, 1984.

Cullen, Diane. *A Passion to Believe: Autism and the Facilitated Communication Phenomenon.* Boulder, CO: Westview Press, 1997.

Diagnostic and Statistical Manual of Mental Disorders. 3rd ed. Washington, DC: American Psychiatric Association, 1980.

Diagnostic and Statistical Manual of Mental Disorders: DSM-5. 5th ed. Washington, DC: American Psychiatric Association, 2013.

Diagnostic and Statistical Manual of Mental Disorders: DSM-IV-TR. 4th ed. Washington, DC: American Psychiatric Association, 2000.

Diagnostic and Statistical Manual of Mental Disorders: DSM-IV. 4th ed. Washington, DC: American Psychiatric Association, 1994.

Diagnostic and Statistical Manual of Mental Disorders: DSM-III-R. 3rd ed. Washington, DC: American Psychiatric Association, 1987.

Donnellan, Anne M. *Classic Readings in Autism.* New York: Teachers College Press, 1985.

Donohue, William T. *A History of the Behavioral Therapies: Founders' Personal Histories.* Reno, NV: Context Press, 2001.

Eliot, Stephen. *Not the Thing I Was: Thirteen Years at Bruno Bettelheim's Orthogenic School.* New York: St. Martin's Press, 2003.

Eyal, Gil. *The Autism Matrix: The Social Origins of the Autism Epidemic.* Cambridge, UK: Polity, 2010.

Feinstein, Adam. *A History of Autism: Conversations with the Pioneers.* Chichester, West Sussex, UK: Wiley-Blackwell, 2010.

Flack, Audrey. *Art & Other Miracles.* Unpublished ms.

Frances, Allen. *Saving Normal: An Insider's Revolt Against Out-of-Control Psychiatric Diagnosis, DSM-5, Big Pharma, and the Medicalization of Ordinary Life.* New York: HarperCollins, 2013.

Frank, John P. *My Son's Story.* New York: Knopf, 1952.

Frith, Uta. *Autism: Explaining the Enigma.* Oxford, UK: Basil Blackwell, 1989.

———. *Autism and Asperger Syndrome.* Cambridge, UK: Cambridge University Press, 1991.

Goldberg, Robert. *Tabloid Medicine: How the Internet Is Being Used to Hijack Medical Science for Fear and Profit.* New York: Kaplan, 2010.

Goldman, Lawrence. *Oxford Dictionary of National Biography: 2005–2008.* Oxford, UK: Oxford University Press, 2013.

Grandin, Temple. *Thinking in Pictures: And Other Reports from My Life with Autism.* New York: Doubleday, 1995. Expanded ed. 2006.

———. *Emergence: Labeled Autistic: A True Story.* New York: Grand Central, 1996.

Grant, Madison. *The Passing of the Great Race, Or, The Racial Basis of European History.* New York: Charles Scribner's Sons, 1916.

Greenberg, Gary. *The Book of Woe: The DSM and the Unmaking of Psychiatry.* New York: Blue Rider Press, 2013.

Greenfeld, Josh. *A Child Called Noah: A Family Journey.* New York: Holt, Rinehart and Winston, 1972.

Greenfeld, Karl Taro. *Boy Alone: A Brother's Memoir.* New York: Harper, 2009.

Grinker, Roy Richard. *Unstrange Minds: Remapping the World of Autism.* New York: Basic Books, 2007.

Guess, Doug. *Use of Aversive Procedures with Persons Who Are Disabled: An Historical Review and Critical Analysis.* Seattle: Association for Persons with Severe Handicaps, 1987.

Habakus, Louise Kuo. *Vaccine Epidemic: How Corporate Greed, Biased Science, and*

Coercive Government Threaten Our Human Rights, Our Health, and Our Children. New York: Skyhorse Publishing, 2011.

Haddon, Mark. *The Curious Incident of the Dog in the Night-Time.* New York: Vintage, 2004.

Hermelin, Beate. *Bright Splinters of the Mind: A Personal Story of Research with Autistic Savants.* London: Jessica Kingsley, 2001.

Hermelin, Beate, and Neil Connor. *Psychological Experiments with Autistic Children.* Oxford, UK: Pergamon Press, 1970.

Hill, John P. *Minnesota Symposia on Child Psychology.* Minneapolis: University of Minnesota Press, 1967.

Hollander, Eric. *Textbook of Autism Spectrum Disorders.* Washington, DC: American Psychiatric Publishing, 2011.

Houston, R. A., and Uta Frith. *Autism in History: The Case of Hugh Blair of Borgue.* Oxford, UK: Blackwell, 2000.

Howe, Samuel Gridley. *Report Made to the Legislature of Massachusetts, Upon Idiocy.* Boston: n.p., 1848.

Howe, Samuel Gridley, and Laura Elizabeth Howe Richards. *Letters and Journals of Samuel Gridley Howe: The Servant of Humanity.* Boston: Dana Estes, 1906.

Hunt, Morton M. *The Story of Psychology.* New York: Doubleday, 1993.

Imber, Jonathan B. *Trusting Doctors: The Decline of Moral Authority in American Medicine.* Princeton, NJ: Princeton University Press, 2008.

Itard, Jean-Marc-Gaspard. *The Wild Boy of Aveyron*, translated by George and Muriel Humphrey. Englewood Cliffs, NJ: Prentice-Hall, 1962.

Iversen, Portia. *Strange Son: Two Mothers, Two Sons, and the Quest to Unlock the Hidden World of Autism.* New York: Riverhead Books, 2006.

Jacobson, John W. *Handbook of Intellectual and Developmental Disabilities.* New York: Springer, 2007.

Jacobson, John W., Richard M. Foxx, and James A. Mulick. *Controversial Therapies for Developmental Disabilities: Fad, Fashion, and Science in Professional Practice.* Mahwah, NJ: Lawrence Erlbaum Associates, 2005.

Jimenez, Terese C. *Education for All: Critical Issues in the Education of Children and Youth with Disabilities.* San Francisco: Jossey-Bass, 2008.

Jones, Marshall R. *Miami Symposium on the Prediction of Behavior, 1967: Aversive Stimulation.* Coral Gables, FL: University of Miami Press, 1968.

Jones, Robert S. P. *Challenging Behaviour and Intellectual Disability: A Psychological Perspective* (Clevedon, UK: BILD Publications, 1993).

Joseph, Jay. *The Missing Gene: Psychiatry, Heredity, and the Fruitless Search for Genes.* New York: Algora Publishing, 2006.

Just, Marcel Adam, and Kevin A. Pelphrey, eds. *Development and Brain Systems in Autism.* Carnegie Mellon Symposia on Cognition Series. New York: Psychology Press, 2013.

Kanner, Leo. Unpublished autobiography. American Psychiatric Association Archives.

———. *Child Psychiatry, Etc.* 3rd ed. Oxford, UK: Blackwell Scientific Publications; Menasha Printed, 1957.

———. *Childhood Psychosis: Initial Studies and New Insights.* Washington, DC: V. H. Winston; distributed by Halsted Press Division, Wiley, New York, 1973.

Kaufman, Barry. *Son-Rise.* New York: Harper and Row, 1976.

Kirby, David. *Evidence of Harm: Mercury in Vaccines and the Autism Epidemic: A Medical Controversy.* New York: St. Martin's Press, 2005.

Klee, Ernst. *Persilscheine und falsche Passe. Wie die Kirchen den Nazis halfen* (Persil Certificates and False Passports: How the Church Aided the Nazis). Frankfurt, Germany: Fischer Taschenbuch-Verlag, 1991.

Klin, Ami, Fred R. Volkmar, and Sara S. Sparrow, eds. *Asperger Syndrome.* New York: Guilford Press, 2000.

Lane, Harlan L. *The Wild Boy of Aveyron.* Cambridge, MA: Harvard University Press, 1976.

Ledgin, Norm. *Diagnosing Jefferson: Evidence of a Condition That Guided His Beliefs, Behavior, and Personal Associations.* Arlington, TX: Future Horizons, 2000.

Levinson, Abraham. *The Mentally Retarded Child: A Guide for Parents.* New York: Day, 1952.

Lippman, Leopold D., and I. Ignacy Goldberg. *Right to Education; Anatomy of the Pennsylvania Case and Its Implications for Exceptional Children.* New York: Teachers College Press, 1973.

Lovaas, O. Ivar. *The Autistic Child: Language Development Through Behavior Modification.* New York: Irvington, 1977.

———. *Teaching Developmentally Disabled Children: The ME Book.* Baltimore: University Park Press, 1981.

Lyons, Tom Wallace. *The Pelican and After: A Novel About Emotional Disturbance.* Richmond, VA.: Prescott, Durrell, 1983.

Maurice, Catherine. *Let Me Hear Your Voice: A Family's Triumph over Autism.* New York: Knopf, 1993.

May, Elaine Tyler. *Homeward Bound: American Families in the Cold War Era.* New York: Basic Books, 1988.

McCarthy, Jenny. *Louder Than Words: A Mother's Journey in Healing Autism.* New York: Dutton, 2008.

McDonagh, Patrick. *Idiocy: A Cultural History.* Liverpool, UK: Liverpool University Press, 2008.

Meyer, Donald J., and Patricia F. Vadasy. *Sibshops: Workshops for Siblings of Children with Special Needs.* Baltimore: P. H. Brookes Publishing, 1994.

Mississippi State Sanatorium and Mississippi Tuberculosis Association. *Mississippi State Sanatorium: A Book of Information About Tuberculosis and Its Treatment in Mississippi.* 1939.

Mnookin, Seth. *The Panic Virus: A True Story of Medicine, Science, and Fear.* New York: Simon & Schuster, 2011.

Nadesan, Majia Holmer. *Constructing Autism: Unravelling the 'Truth' and Understanding the Social.* London: Routledge, 2005.

Noll, Steven. *Mental Retardation in America: A Historical Reader.* New York: New York University Press, 2004.

Offit, Paul A. *Autism's False Prophets: Bad Science, Risky Medicine, and the Search for a Cure.* New York: Columbia University Press, 2008.

Olmsted, Dan, and Mark Blaxill. *The Age of Autism: Mercury, Medicine, and a Man-Made Epidemic.* New York: Thomas Dunne Books/St. Martin's Press, 2010.

Park, Clara Claiborne. *The Siege.* New York: Harcourt, Brace & World, 1967.

Peek, Fran, and Stevens W. Anderson. *The Real Rain Man: Kim Peek.* 2nd ed. Salt Lake City, Utah: Harkness Publishing Consultants, 1996.

Pelka, Fred. *What We Have Done: An Oral History of the Disability Rights Movement.* Amherst: University of Massachusetts Press, 2012.

Pollak, Richard. *The Creation of Dr B: A Biography of Bruno Bettelheim.* New York: Simon & Schuster, 1997.

Porter, Roy. *The Confinement of the Insane International Perspectives, 1800–1965.* Cambridge, UK: Cambridge University Press, 2003.

Raines, Theron. *Rising to the Light: A Portrait of Bruno Bettelheim.* New York: Knopf, 2002.

Rimland, Bernard. *Infantile Autism: The Syndrome and Its Implications for a Neural Theory of Behavior.* New York: Appleton-Century-Crofts, Educational Division, Meredith Publishing, 1964.

Riordan, Hugh Desaix. *Medical Mavericks.* Volume 3. Wichita, KS: Bio-Communications Press, 2005.

Roberts, Andy. *Albion Dreaming: A Popular History of LSD in Britain.* Singapore: Marshall Cavendish, 2008.

Robison, John Elder. *Look Me in the Eye: My Life with Asperger's.* New York: Crown, 2007.

———. *Raising Cubby: A Father and Son's Adventures with Asperger's, Trains, Tractors, and High Explosives.* New York: Crown, 2013.

Rothman, David J. *The Discovery of the Asylum: Social Order and Disorder in the New Republic.* Boston: Little, Brown, 1971.

Rothman, David J., and Sheila M. Rothman. *The Willowbrook Wars.* New York: Harper & Row, 1984.

Sacks, Oliver W. *An Anthropologist on Mars: Seven Paradoxical Tales.* New York: Knopf, 1995.

Scheerenberger, R. C. *Deinstitutionalization and Institutional Reform.* Springfield, IL: Thomas, 1976.

Schopler, Eric, and Gary B. Mesibov. *The Effects of Autism on the Family.* New York: Plenum Press, 1984.

———. *Diagnosis and Assessment in Autism.* New York: Plenum Press, 1988.

———, eds. *Behavioral Issues in Autism.* New York: Plenum Press, 1994.

Schopler, Eric, Gary Mesibov, and Linda Kunce. *Asperger Syndrome or High-Functioning Autism?* New York: Plenum Press, 1998.

Schreibman, Laura Ellen. *The Science and Fiction of Autism.* Cambridge, MA: Harvard University Press, 2005.

Scott County History Book Committee. *History of Scott County, Missouri: History & Families.* Paducah, KY: Turner, 2003.

Sessums, Kevin. *Mississippi Sissy.* New York: St. Martin's Press, 2007.

Shapiro, Joseph P. *No Pity: People with Disabilities Forging a New Civil Rights Movement.* New York: Times Books, 1993.

Shattuck, Roger. *The Forbidden Experiment: The Story of the Wild Boy of Aveyron.* New York: Farrar, Straus and Giroux, 1980.

Shorter, Edward. *Doctors and Their Patients: A Social History.* New Brunswick, NJ: Transaction, 1991.

———. *A History of Psychiatry: From the Asylum to the Age of Prozac.* New York: John Wiley & Sons, 1997.

Silverman, Chloe. *Understanding Autism: Parents, Doctors, and the History of a Disorder.* Princeton, NJ: Princeton University Press, 2012.

Speers, Rex W., and Cornelius Lansing. *Group Therapy in Childhood Psychosis.* Chapel Hill: University of North Carolina Press, 1965.

Spiro, Jonathan Peter. *Defending the Master Race: Conservation, Eugenics, and the Legacy of Madison Grant.* Burlington: University of Vermont Press, 2009.

Spitz, Herman H. *Nonconscious Movements: From Mystical Messages to Facilitated Communication.* Mahwah, NJ: Lawrence Erlbaum Associates, 1997.

Spock, Benjamin. *The Common Sense Book of Baby and Child Care.* New York: Duell, Sloan and Pearce, 1946.

Stuesse, Angela Christine. *Globalization "Southern Style": Transnational Migration, the Poultry Industry, and Implications for Organizing Workers Across Difference.* PhD diss., University of Texas at Austin, 2008.

Sutton, Nina. *Bettelheim: A Life and a Legacy.* New York: Basic Books, 1996.

Tammet, Daniel. *Born on a Blue Day: Inside the Extraordinary Mind of an Autistic Savant.* New York: Free Press, 2007.

Taylor, Steven J. *Acts of Conscience: World War II, Mental Institutions, and Religious Objectors.* Syracuse, NY: Syracuse University Press, 2009.

Taylor, Steven J., and Douglas Biklen. *Understanding the Law: An Advocate's Guide to the Law and Developmental Disabilities.* Syracuse, NY: Human Policy Press, 1980.

Tinbergen, Niko, and Elisabeth A. Tinbergen. *Autistic Children: New Hope for a Cure.* London: Allen & Unwin, 1983.

Trapp, E. Philip, and Philip Himelstein. *Readings on the Exceptional Child: Research and Theory.* 2nd ed. New York: Appleton-Century-Crofts, 1972.

Trent, James W. *Inventing the Feeble Mind: A History of Mental Retardation in the United States.* Berkeley: University of California Press, 1994.

Ullmann, Leonard P., and Leonard Krasner. *Case Studies in Behavior Modification.* New York: Holt, Rinehart and Winston, 1965.

Unumb, Lorri Shealy, and Daniel R. Unumb. *Autism and the Law: Cases, Statutes, and Materials.* Durham, NC: Carolina Academic Press, 2011.

Volkmar, Fred R. *Encyclopedia of Autism Spectrum Disorders.* New York: Springer, 2013.

Volkmar, Fred R., Rhea Paul, Ami Klin, and Donald Cohen. *Handbook of Autism and Pervasive Developmental Disorders.* 3rd ed. Hoboken, NJ: John Wiley & Sons, 2005.

Wakefield, Andrew J. *Callous Disregard: Autism and Vaccines: The Truth Behind a Tragedy.* New York: Skyhorse Publishing, 2010.

Waltz, Mitzi. *Autism: A Social and Medical History.* Basingstoke, UK: Palgrave Macmillan, 2013.

Warren, Mary Lou "Bobo." *My Humpty-Dumpty: A Mother's View.* Unpublished ms.

Wilcox, Barbara. *Critical Issues in Educating Autistic Children and Youth.* Washington, DC: NSAC National Society for Children and Adults with Autism, 1981.

Williams, Donna. *Nobody Nowhere: The Extraordinary Autobiography of an Autistic.* New York: Times Books, 1992.

Wing, Lorna. *Autistic Children: A Guide for Parents.* New York: Brunner/Mazel, 1972.

———, ed. *Aspects of Autism: Biological Research.* London: Gaskell Psychiatry, 1988.

———. *The Autistic Spectrum: A Guide for Parents and Professionals.* London: Constable, 1996.

Wolman, Benjamin B. *Handbook of Treatment of Mental Disorders in Childhood and Adolescence.* Englewood Cliffs, NJ: Prentice-Hall, 1978.

Wright, Peter W. D., and Pamela Darr Wright. *Wrightslaw: Special Education Law.* 2nd ed. Hartfield, VA: Harbor House Law Press, 2007.

Young, Thomas. *Observations on Madness and Melancholy.* London: J. Callow, 1809.

Scholarly Articles

Abramson, Harold A. "The Use of LSD-25 in the Therapy of Children (A Brief Review)." *Journal of Asthma Research* 5 (1967): 139–43.

Allison, Helen Green. Paper presented at the University of Kent, September 18–20, 1987. Reprinted in *Aspects of Autism: Biological Research,* edited by Lorna Wing. London: Gaskell Psychiatry, 1988.

Anderberg D., A. Chevaliera, and J. Wadsworth "Anatomy of a Health Scare: Education, Income and the MMR Controversy in the UK." *Journal of Health Economics* 30, no. 3 (2011): 520.

Arkowitz, Hal, and Scott O. Lilienfeld. "Is There Really an Autism Epidemic?" *Scientific American* (online), December 6, 2007, http://www.scientificamerican.com/article/is-there-really-an-autism-epidemic/.

Asperger Felder, Maria. "Foreword." In *Asperger Syndrome,* edited by Ami Klin, Fred Volkmar, and Sara Sparrow. New York: Guilford Press, 2000.

Asperger, Hans. "Das Psychisch Abnormale Kind." *Wiener Klinische Wochenschrift* (1938): 1314–17.

———. "Pädagogische Therapie bei abnormen Kindern." *Medizinische Klinik* 35 (1939): 943–46.

———. "Die Autistischen Psychopathen im Kindesalter." *Archiv fur Psychiatrie und Nervenkrankheiten* 117 (1944): 76–136.

———. "Zur Differentialdiagnose des Kindlichen Autismus." *Acta Paedopsychiatrica* 35 (1968): 136–45.

———. "Problems of Infantile Autism (A Talk)." *Communication* (1979): 45–52.

———. "Autistic Psychopathy in Childhood." A translation of his 1944 paper by Uta Frith. In *Autism and Asperger Syndrome,* edited by Uta Frith. Cambridge, UK: Cambridge University Press, 1991, 37.

Asperger, Maria Felder. "Hans Asperger (1906–1980) Leben und Werk." In *Hundert Janfre Kind-in Jugendpsychiatries,* edited by R. Castell. Germany: V&R Unipress, 2008.

Atwell, Jessica, et al. "Nonmedical Vaccine Exemptions and Pertussis in California, 2010." *Pediatrics* 132, no. 4 (2013): 624–30.

Baker, Sidney M. "Learning About Autism." *Global Advances in Health and Medicine* 2, no. 6 (2013): 38–46.

Bakir, F., S. F. Damluji, L. Amin-Zaki et al. "Methylmercury Poisoning in Iraq." *Science* 181, no. 4096 (July 1973): 230–41.

Baron-Cohen, Simon, Alan Leslie, and Uta Frith. "Does the Autistic Child Have a Theory of Mind?" *Cognition* 21 (1985): 37–46.

Bauman, Margaret L. "Brief Report: Neuroanatomic Observations of the Brain in Pervasive Developmental Disorders." *Journal of Autism and Developmental Disorders* 26, no. 2 (1996): 199–203.

Bender, Lauretta. "Children's Reactions to Psychotomimetic Drugs." In *Psychotomimetic Drugs,* edited by D. H. Efron, 265–71. New York: Raven Press, 1970.

Bender, Lauretta, G. Faretra, and L. Cobrinik. "LSD and UML Treatment of Hospitalized Disturbed Children." *Recent Advances in Biological Psychology* 5 (1963): 85–92.

Bender, Lauretta, Lothar Goldschmidt, D. V. Siva Sankar, and Alfred M. Freedman. "Treatment of Autistic Schizophrenic Children with LSD-25 and UML-491." *Recent Advances in Biological Psychiatry* (1962): 170–79.

Berthier, M. L. "Corticocallosal Anomalies in Asperger's Syndrome." *American Journal of Roentgenology* 162, no. 1 (1994): 236–37.

Bettelheim, Bruno. "Individual and Mass Behavior in Extreme Situations." *Journal of Abnormal and Social Psychology* 38, no. 4 (1943): 417–52.

Bijou, Sidney. "Reflections on Some Early Events Related to Behavior Analysis of Child Development." *Behavior Analyst* 1, no. 19 (1996): 49–60.

Biklen, Douglas. "Communication Unbound: Autism and Praxis." *Harvard Educational Review* 60, no. 3 (1990): 291–315.

Bishop, Dorothy. "Forty Years On: Uta Frith's Contribution to Research on Autism and Dyslexia, 1966–2006." *Quarterly Journal of Experimental Psychology* 61, no. 1 (2008): 16–26.

Boynton, Janyce. "Facilitated Communication—What Harm It Can Do: Confessions of a Former Facilitator." *Evidence-Based Communication Assessment and Intervention* 6, no. 1 (2012): 3–13.

Brugha, T. S., L. Wing, J. Cooper, and N. Sartorius. "Contribution and Legacy of John Wing, 1923–2010." *British Journal of Psychiatry* 198, no. 3 (2011): 176–78.

Carter, M. P. "Twins with Early Childhood Autism." *Journal of Pediatrics* 71, no. 2 (1967): 303.

Challis, Natalia, and Horace W. Dewey. "The Blessed Fools of Old Russia." *Jahrbücher Für Geschichte Osteuropas, Neue Folge* D. 22, H. 1 (1974): 1–11.

———. "Basil the Blessed. Holy Fool of Moscow." *Russian History* 14, no. 1 (1987), 47–59.

Chance, Paul. "A Conversation with Ivar Lovaas About Self-Mutilating Children and How Their Parents Make It Worse." *Psychology Today* 7, no. 8 (1974): 76–84.

Chen, R., and F. Destefano. "Vaccine Adverse Events: Causal or Coincidental?" *Lancet* 351, no. 9103 (1998): 611–12.

Cooper, S. A., W. N. Mohamed, and R. A. Collacott. "Possible Asperger's Syndrome in a Mentally Handicapped Transvestite Offender." *Journal of Intellectual Disability Research* 37, no. 2 (1993): 189–94.

Creak, Mildred. "Schizophrenic Syndrome in Childhood: Progress Report (April, 1961) of a Working Party." *British Medical Journal* (1961): 889–90.

———. "Schizophrenic Syndrome in Childhood: Further Progress Report of a Working Party (April, 1964)." *Developmental Medicine & Child Neurology* 6, no. 5 (1964): 530–35.

Cummins, Robert, and Margot Prior. "Further Comment: Autism and Assisted Communication: A Response to Biklen." *Harvard Educational Review* 62, no. 2 (1992): 228–42.

Czech, Herwig. "'The Child Must Be an Unbearable Burden to Her Mother': Hans Asperger, National Socialism, and 'Race Hygiene' in World War II Vienna." Submitted in 2015 to *Molecular Autism.*

Czech, Herwig, and Lawrence A. Zeidman. "Walther Birkmayer, LDopa, and His Nazi Connections: Victim or Perpetrator?" *Journal of the History of the Neurosciences: Basic and Clinical Perspectives* (April 3, 2014): 19.

Dales, L., et al. "Time Trends in Autism and in MMR Immunization Coverage in California." *Journal of the American Medical Association* 285, no. 9 (2001): 1183–85.

Deer, Brian. "Comment: Reflections on Investigating Wakefield." *British Medical Journal* (online), February 2, 2010.

———. "Wakefield's 'Autistic Enterocolitis' Under the Microscope." *British Medical Journal,* April 15, 2010.

Denckla, Martha Bridge. "New Diagnostic Criteria for Autism and Related Behavioral Disorders—Guidelines for Research Protocols." *Journal of the American Academy of Child Psychiatry* 25, no. 2 (1986): 221–24.

Dickerson Mayes, Susan, Susan L. Calhoun, and Dana L. Crites. "Does DSM-IV Asperger's Disorder Exist?" *Journal of Abnormal Child Psychology* 29, no. 3 (2001): 263–71.

Donnellan, A. M., and G. W. LaVigna. "Myths About Punishment." In *Perspectives on the Use of Nonaversive and Aversive Interventions for Persons with Developmental Disabilities,* edited by A. C. Repp & N. N. Singh. Belmont, CA: Wadsworth Publishing, 1993.

Editors of *The Lancet*. "Retraction Statement" (regarding article: "Ileal-Lymphoid-Nodular Hyperplasia, Non-specific Colitis, and Pervasive Developmental Disorder in Children"). *Lancet* 375, no. 9713 (2010): 445.

Eisenberg, Leon. "Why Has the Relationship Between Psychiatry and Genetics Been So Contentious?" *Genetics in Medicine* 3 (2001): 377–81.

Eisenberg, Leon, and Leo Kanner. "Childhood Schizophrenia Symposium, 1955–56. Early Infantile Autism, 1943–55." *American Journal of Orthopsychiatry* 26 (1956): 556–66.

Fellowes, Sam. "Did Kanner Actually Describe the First Account of Autism? The Mystery of 1938." *Journal of Autism and Developmental Disorders* 45, no. 7 (2015): 2274–76.

Fisch, Gene S. "Autism and Epistemology IV: Does Autism Need a Theory of Mind?" *American Journal of Medical Genetics Part A* 161A, no. 10 (2013): 2464–80.

Folstein, Susan, and Michael Rutter. "Genetic Influences and Infantile Autism." *Nature* 265, no. 5596 (1977): 726–28.

Fombonne, Eric. "Epidemiology of Pervasive Developmental Disorders." *Pediatric Research* 65, no. 6 (2009): 591–98.

Foxx, R. M. "Commentaries on McEachin, Smith and Lovaas: Rapid Effects Awaiting Independent Replication." *American Journal of Mental Retardation* 97, no. 3 (1993): 375–76.

Freed, G. L. "Vaccine Policies Across the Pond: Looking at the U.K. and U.S. Systems." *Health Affairs* 24, no. 3 (2005): 755–57.

Freedman, A. M., E. V. Ebin, and E. Wilson. "Autistic Schizophrenic Children. An Experiment in the Use of D-lysergic Acid Diethylamide (LSD-25)." *Archives of General Psychiatry* 6 (1962): 203–13.

Frith, Uta. "Looking Back: The Avengers of Psychology." *Psychologist* (2009): 726–27.

Ganz, Jennifer B., Richard L. Simpson, and Emily M. Lund, "The Picture Exchange Communication System (PECS): A Promising Method for Improving Communication Skills of Learners with Autism Spectrum Disorders." *Education and Training in Autism and Developmental Disabilities* 47, no. 2 (2012): 176–86.

Giles, D. C. "'*DSM-5* Is Taking Away Our Identity': The Reaction of the Online Community to the Proposed Changes in the Diagnosis of Asperger's Disorder." *Health* (2014): 179–95.

Gilhool, Thomas. "The Uses of Litigation: The Right of Retarded Citizens to a Free Public Education." *Current Issues in Mental Retardation and Human Development* DHEVV Publication No. (OS) 73-86 (Dec. 1972): 27–38.

Gillette, Martha U., Thomas Roth, and James P. Kiley. "NIH Funding of Sleep Research: A Prospective and Retrospective View." *Sleep* 22, no. 7 (1999): 956–58.

Godlee, Fiona, Jane Smith, and Harvey Marcovitch. "Wakefield's Article Linking MMR Vaccine and Autism Was Fraudulent." *British Medical Journal* 342, no. 7452 (2011): 64–66.

Happé, Francesca. "The Weak Central Coherence Account of Autism." *Journal of Autism and Developmental Disorder* 36, no. 1 (2006): 5–25.

———. "Why Fold Asperger Syndrome into Autism Spectrum Disorder in the DSM-5?" Simons Foundation Autism Research Initiative, 2011, https://sfari.org/news-and-opinion/viewpoint/2011/why-fold-asperger-syndrome-into-autism-spectrum-disorder-in-the-dsm-5.

Harris, James. "Leo Kanner and Hans Asperger: Setting the Historical Record Straight." *Journal of the American Academy of Child and Adolescent Psychiatry* (August 2016): 729–35.

Harris, James, and Joseph Piven. "Correcting the Record: Leo Kanner and the Broad Autism Phenotype." *Spectrum News* (April 26, 2016).

Hepatitis Control Report. "Uproar over a Little-Known Preservative, Thimerosal, Jostles U.S. Hepatitis B Vaccination Policy." Summer 1999, http://www.hepatitiscontrolreport.com/articles.html.

Hermelin, Beate, and N. O'Connor. "Remembering of Words by Psychotic and Subnormal Children." *British Journal of Psychology* 58 (1967): 213–18.

Hobson-West, P. " 'Trusting Blindly Can Be the Biggest Risk of All': Organised Resistance to Childhood Vaccination in the UK." *Sociology of Health and Illness* 29, no. 2 (2007): 198–215.

Holden, C. "What's Holding Up 'Aversives' Report?" *Science* 249, no. 4972 (1990): 980.

Howard J. S., C. R. Sparkman, H. G. Cohen, G. Green, and H. Stanislaw. "A Comparison of Intensive Behavior Analytic and Eclectic Treatments for Young Children with Autism." *Research in Developmental Disabilities* 26, no. 4 (2005): 359–83.

Hurley, A. M., M. Tadrous, and E. S. Miller. "Thimerosal-Containing Vaccines and Autism: A Review of Recent Epidemiologic Studies." *Journal of Pediatric Pharmacology and Therapeutics* 15, no. 3 (July–September 2010): 173.

Iwata, Brian. "The Development and Adoption of Controversial Default Technologies." *Behavior Analyst* 11, no. 2 (1988): 149–57.

Kanner, Leo. "Exoneration of the Feebleminded." *American Journal of Psychiatry* 99 (1942): 17–22.

———. "Autistic Disturbances of Affective Contact." *Nervous Child* 2 (1943): 217–50.

———. "Problems of Nosology and Psychodynamics of Early Infantile Autism." *American Journal of Orthopsychiatry* (1949): 416–26.

———. "Infantile Autism and the Schizophrenias." *Behavioral Science* 10, no. 4 (1965): 412–20.

———. "The Specificity of Early Infantile Autism." *Acta Paedopsychiatrica* 25 (1958): 108–13.

———. "Follow-up Study of Eleven Autistic Children Originally Reported in 1943." *Journal of Autism and Childhood Schizophrenia* 1, no. 2 (1971): 119–45.

———. "Historical Perspective on Developmental Deviations." In *Psychopathology and Child Development*, edited by Eric Schopler, 7–17. New York: Springer, 1976.

Kapp, Steven, and Ari Ne'eman. "ASD in *DSM-5*: What the Research Shows and Recommendations for Change." *Policy Brief* (online), 2012.

Kasmini, K., and S. Zasmani. "Asperger's Syndrome: A Report of Two Cases from Malaysia." *Singapore Medical Journal* 6, no. 36 (1995): 641–43.

Kennedy, Foster. "The Problem of Social Control of the Congenital Defective: Education, Sterilization, Euthanasia." *American Journal of Psychiatry* 99 (1942): 13–16.

Kim, Y. S., B. L. Leventhal, Y.-J. Koh, E. Fombonne et al. "Prevalence of Autism Spectrum Disorders in a Total Population Sample." *American Journal of Psychiatry* 168, no. 9 (2011): 904–12.

Klin, Ami. "Young Autistic Children's Listening Preferences in Regard to Speech: A Possible Characterization of the Symptom of Social Withdrawal." *Journal of Autism and Developmental Disorders* 21, no. 1 (1991): 29–42.

Konziella, D. "Thirty Neurological Eponyms Associated with the Nazi Era." *European Neurology* 62 (2009): 56–64.

Korschun, Holly. "New Study Identifies Signs of Autism in the First Months of Life." Emory News Center (online), November 6, 2013.

Lee, Brian K., Cecilia Magnusson, Renee M. Gardner, Åsa Blomström et al.

"Maternal Hospitalization with Infection During Pregnancy and Risk of Autism Spectrum Disorders." *Brain, Behavior, and Immunity* 44 (2015): 100–105.

Lehr, Susan, and Robert Lehr. "Why Is My Child Hurting? Positive Approaches to Dealing with Difficult Behaviors. A Monograph for Parents of Children with Disabilities." Available online at http://eric.ed.gov/?id=ED334728.

Lord, Catherine. "A Multisite Study of the Clinical Diagnosis of Different Autism Spectrum Disorders." *Archives of General Psychiatry* 69, no. 3 (2012): 306–13.

Lotter, Victor. "Epidemiology of Autistic Conditions in Young Children." *Social Psychiatry* 1, no. 3 (1966): 163–73.

Lovaas, O. Ivar. "Behavioral Treatment and Normal Educational and Intellectual Functioning in Young Autistic Children." *Journal of Consulting and Clinical Psychology* 55, no. 1 (1987): 3–9.

Lovaas, O. Ivar, Robert Koegel, James Q. Simmons, and Judith Stevens Long. "Some Generalization and Follow-up Measures on Autistic Children in Behavior Therapy." *Journal of Applied Behavior Analysis* 6, no. 1 (1973): 131–65.

Lovaas, O. Ivar, Benson Schaeffer, and James Q Simmons. "Building Social Behavior in Autistic Children by Use of Electric Shock." *Journal of Experimental Research in Personality* 1 (1965): 99–105.

Lovaas, O. Ivar, and James Q. Simmons. "Manipulation of Self-Destruction in Three Retarded Children." *Journal of Applied Behavior Analysis* 2, no. 3 (1969): 143–57.

Lyons, Viktoria, and Michael Fitzgerald. "Did Hans Asperger (1906–1980) Have Asperger Syndrome?" *Journal of Autism and Developmental Disorders* 37 (2007): 2020–21.

Manfredi, C. P., and A. Maioni. "Reversal of Fortune: Litigating Health Care Reform in *Auton v. British Columbia.*" *Supreme Court Law Review* 29, no. 2 (2005): 129.

McClelland, R. J., D. G. Eyre, D. Watson, G. J. Calvert, and E. Sherrard. "Central Conduction Time in Childhood Autism." *British Journal of Psychiatry* 160, no. 5 (1992): 659–63.

McEachin, J. J., T. Smith, and O. I. Lovaas. "Long-Term Outcome for Children with Autism Who Received Early Intensive Behavioral Treatment." *American Journal of Mental Retardation* (1993): 359–72.

Mehler, Mark F., and Dominick P. Purpura. "Autism, Fever, Epigenetics and the Locus Coeruleus." *Brain Research Reviews* 59, no. 2 (2009): 388–92.

Mendres, Amber, and Michelle A. Frank-Crawford. "A Tribute to Sidney W. Bijou, Pioneer in Behavior Analysis and Child Development." *Behavior Analysis in Practice* 2, no. 2 (2009): 4–10.

Mesibov, Gary B. "Commentaries on McEachin, Smith and Lovaas: Treatment Outcome Is Encouraging." *American Journal of Mental Retardation* 97, no. 3 (1993): 379–80.

Miller, Judith, et al. "Autism Spectrum Disorder Reclassified: A Second Look at the 1980s Utah/UCLA Autism Epidemiologic Study." *Journal of Autism and Developmental Disorders* 43, no. 1 (2012): 200–10.

Miller, J., and S. Ozonoff. "Did Asperger's Cases Have Asperger Disorder? A Research Note." *Journal of Child Psychology and Psychiatry* 38, no. 2 (1997): 247–51.

Murch, Simon, et al. "Retraction of an Interpretation: Signed by Simon H Murch, Andrew Anthony, David H. Casson, Mohsin Malik, Mark Berelowitz, Amar

P. Dhillon, Michael A. Thomson, Alan Valentine, Susan E. Davies, John A. Walker-Smith." *Lancet* 363, no. 9411 (2004): 750.

Ne'eman, Ari. "The Future (and the Past) of Autism Advocacy, Or Why the ASA's Magazine, *The Advocate,* Wouldn't Publish This Piece." *Disability Studies Quarterly* 30, no. 1 (2010), http://dsq-sds.org/article/view/1059/1244.

O'Connor, N., and B. Hermelin. "Auditory and Visual Memory in Autistic and Normal Children." *Journal of Mental Deficiency Research* 11, no. 2 (1967): 126–31.

Ornitz, Edward M. "Childhood Autism—A Review of the Clinical and Experimental Literature." *California Medicine* 118, no. 4 (1973): 21–47.

Pickett, J., E. Xiu, R. Tuchman, G. Dawson, and C. Lajonchere. "Mortality in Individuals with Autism, with and Without Epilepsy." *Journal of Child Neurology* 8 (2011): 932–39.

Poland, G. A., and R. M. Jacobson. "Understanding Those Who Do Not Understand: A Brief Review of the Anti-Vaccine Movement." *Vaccine* 19, no. 17–19 (2001): 2440–45.

Premack, David, and Guy Woodruff. "Does the Chimpanzee Have a Theory of Mind?" *Behavioral and Brain Sciences* 1, no. 4 (1978): 515–26.

Primeau, Michelle, and Ruth O'Hara. "Exploring Sleep in Children with Autism." Simons Foundation Autism Research Initiative, July 30, 2013, http://sfari.org/news-and-opinion/viewpoint/2013/exploring-sleep-in-children-with-autism.

Prior, Margot, and Robert Cummins. "Questions About Facilitated Communication and Autism." *Journal of Autism and Developmental Disorders* 22, no. 3 (1992): 331–37.

Ramsay, Sarah. "Controversial MMR-Autism Investigator Resigns from Research Post." *Lancet* 358, no. 9297 (December 8, 2001): 1972.

Rimland, Bernard. "Megavitamin B_6 and Magnesium in the Treatment of Autistic Children and Adults." In *Current Issues in Autism: Neurobiological Issues in Autism,* edited by E. Schopler and G. Mesibov, 389-405. New York: Springer Science Business Media, 1987.

———. "Aversives for People with Autism." *Autism Research Review International* 2, no. 3 (1988): 3.

———. "*Rain Man* and the Savant Secrets." *Editors Notebook, Autism Research International Newsletter* 3, no. 1 (1989): 3.

———. "Autistic Crypto-Savants." *Autism Research International Newsletter* 4, no. 1 (1990): 7.

———. "In Defense of Ivar Lovaas (Editorial)." *Autism Research Review International* (1994): 3.

Risch, N., and K. Merikangas. "The Future of Genetic Studies of Complex Human Diseases." *Science* 273, no. 5281 (1996): 1516–17.

Ritvo, Edward R.–et al. "The UCLA–University of Utah Epidemiologic Survey of Autism: Prevalence." *American Journal of Psychiatry* (1989): 194–99.

Ritvo, Edward R., and B. J. Freeman. "National Society for Autistic Children Definition of the Syndrome of Autism." *Journal of Pediatric Psychology* 2, no. 4 (1977): 146–48.

Rogers, Sally, and Laurie Vismara. "Evidence-Based Comprehensive Treatments for Early Autism." *Journal of Clinical Child and Adolescent Psychology* 37, no. 1 (2008): 8–38.

Rutter, Michael. "Concepts of Autism: A Review of Research." *Journal of Child Psychology and Psychiatry* 9 (1968): 1–25.

———. "Childhood Schizophrenia Reconsidered." *Journal of Autism and Childhood Schizophrenia* 2, no. 3 (1972): 315–37.

———. "Diagnosis and Definition." In *Autism: A Reappraisal of Concepts and Treatment*, edited by Michael Rutter and Eric Schopler, 1–25. New York: Plenum Press, 1978.

———. "The Emanuel Miller Memorial Lecture 1998, Autism: Two-Way Interplay Between Research and Clinical Work." *Journal of Child Psychology and Psychiatry* 40, no. 2 (1999): 169–88.

Rutter, Michael, and Linda Lockyer. "A Five to Fifteen Year Follow-up Study of Infantile Psychosis." *British Journal of Psychiatry* 113 (1967): 1169–82.

Sallows, Glen, and Tamlynn Graupner. "Intensive Behavioral Treatment for Children with Autism: Four-Year Outcome and Predictors." *American Journal on Mental Retardation* 110, no. 6 (2005): 417–38.

Sanderson, Barbara A., and Daniel W. Kratchvil. "The Edison Responsive Environment Learning System or the Talking Typewriter Developed by Thomas A. Edison Laboratory." American Institutes for Research in the Behavioral Sciences, Palo Alto, California, January 1972.

Schechter, R., and J. K. Grether. "Continuing Increases in Autism Reported to California's Developmental Services System: Mercury in Retrograde." *Archives of General Psychiatry* 65, no. 1 (2008): 19–24.

Schirmer, Brita. "Autismus und NS-Rassengesetze in Österreich 1938: Hans Aspergers Verteidigung der 'Autistischen Psychopathen' gegen die NS-Eugenik." *Die neue Sonderschule* 47 (2002) 6: 460–64.

Schopler, Eric. "The Development of Body Image and Symbol Formation Through Bodily Contact with an Autistic Child." *Journal of Child Psychology and Psychiatry* 3, no. 3–4 (1962): 191–202.

———. "Parents of Psychotic Children as Scapegoats." *Journal of Contemporary Psychotherapy* 4, no. 1 (1971): 17–22.

———. "On Confusion in the Diagnosis of Autism." *Journal of Autism and Childhood Schizophrenia* 8, no. 2 (1978): 137–38.

———. "Editor's Note" preceding Margot Prior and Robert Cummins, "Questions About Facilitated Communication and Autism." *Journal of Autism and Developmental Disorders* 22, no. 3 (1992): 331.

———. "The Anatomy of a Negative Role Model." In *The Undaunted Psychologist: Adventures in Research,* edited by Garry G. Brannigan and Matthew R. Merrens. Philadelphia: Temple University Press, 1993.

———. "Ask the Editor: Are Autism and Asperger Syndrome (AS) Different Labels or Different Disabilities?" *Journal of Autism and Developmental Disorders* (1996): 109–10.

———. "Premature Popularization of Asperger Syndrome." In *Asperger Syndrome or High-Functioning Autism?*, edited by Eric Schopler, Gary B. Mesibov, and Linda J. Kunce, 385–400. New York: Plenum Press, 1998.

Schopler, Eric, Stella Chess, and Leon Eisenberg. "Our Memorial to Leo Kanner." *Journal of Autism and Developmental Disorders* 11, no. 3 (1981): 257–69.

Schopler, Eric, and Robert Reichler. "Parents as Co-therapists in the Treatment of Psychotic Children." *Journal of Autism and Childhood Schizophrenia* 1, no. 1 (1971): 87–102.

Schreibman, Laura. "Memories of Ole Ivar Lovaas, 'Never, Ever Dull.'" *Observer* (November 2010): 23.

Shah, Amitta, Nan Holmes, and Lorna Wing. "Prevalence of Autism and Related Conditions in Adults in a Mental Handicap Hospital." *Applied Research in Mental Retardation* 3, no. 3 (1982): 303–17.

Shah, Amitta, and Uta Frith. "Why Do Autistic Individuals Show Superior Performance on the Block Design Task?" *Journal of Child Psychology and Psychiatry* 34, no. 8 (1993): 1351–64.

Shattuck, P. T. "Prevalence of Autism in US Special Education: The Contribution of Diagnostic Substitution to the Growing Administrative Prevalence of Autism in US Special Education." *Pediatrics* 117, no. 4 (2006): 1028–37.

Simmons, J. Q., D. Benor, and D. Daniel. "The Variable Effects of LSD-25 on the Behavior of a Heterogeneous Group of Childhood Schizophrenics." *Behavioral Neuropsychiatry* 4, no. 1–2 (1972): 10–16.

Simmons, J. Q., S. J. Leiken, O. I. Lovaas, B. Schaeffer, and B. Perloff. "Modification of Autistic Behavior with LSD-25." *American Journal of Psychiatry* 122, no. 11 (1966): 1201–11.

Singer, Emily. "Folic Acid's Appeal." Simons Foundation Autism Research Initiative, March 26, 2013, http://sfari.org/news-and-opinion/blog/2013/folic-acids-appeal.

Singer, Judy. "Odd People In: The Birth of Community Amongst People on the 'Autistic Spectrum.'" BA diss., University of Technology, Sydney, 1998.

Smith, Tristram. "Outcome of Early Intervention for Children with Autism." *Clinical Psychology: Science and Practice* 6 (1999): 33–49.

"Special Education Teacher Vacancies, Cayuga-Onondaga BOCES." *Syracuse-Herald Journal*, July 20, 1991, Classifieds section.

Spinney, Laura. "Therapy for Autistic Children Causes Outcry in France." *Lancet* 370, no. 9588 (2007): 645–46.

Sullivan, Ruth. "Parents as Trainers of Legislators, Other Parents, and Researchers." In *The Effects of Autism on the Family*, edited by Eric Schopler and Gary Mesibov, 233–46. New York: Plenum Press, 1984.

———. "Foreword." In Temple Grandin, *The Way I See It: A Personal Look at Autism and Aspergers*. Arlington, TX: Future Horizons, 2008.

Szatmari, Peter, and Marshall B. Jones. "IQ and the Genetics of Autism." *Journal of Child Psychology and Psychiatry* 32, no. 6 (1991): 897–908.

Taylor, Brent, Elizabeth Miller, and Paddy Farrington. "Autism and Measles,

Mumps, and Rubella Vaccine: No Epidemiological Evidence for a Causal Association." *Lancet* 353, no. 916 (1999): 2026–29.

Van Krevelen, D. A. "Early Infantile Autism and Autistic Psychopathy." *Journal of Autism and Childhood Schizophrenia* (1971): 82–86.

Volkmar, Fred R., and Donald J. Cohen. "Classification and Diagnosis of Childhood Autism." In *Diagnosis and Assessment in Autism,* edited by Eric Schopler and Gary Mesibov, 71–89. New York: Plenum Press, 1988.

Volkmar, Fred R., and Ami Klin. "Asperger Syndrome and Nonverbal Learning Disabilities." In *Diagnosis and Assessment in Autism,* edited by Eric Schopler and Gary Mesibov, 107–22. New York: Plenum Press, 1988.

Volkmar, Fred R., and Brian Reichow. "Autism in *DSM-5*: Progress and Challenges." *Molecular Autism* 4 (2013): 13.

Wadman, Meredith. "Autism's Fight for Facts: A Voice for Science." *Nature* 479 (2001): 28–31.

Wakefield, A. J., et al. "RETRACTED: Ileal-Lymphoid-Nodular Hyperplasia, Non-Specific Colitis, and Pervasive Developmental Disorder in Children." *Lancet* 351, no. 9103 (1998): 637–41.

Wakefield, A. J., et al., "Enterocolitis in Children with Developmental Disorders." *American Journal of Gastroenterology* 95, no. 9 (2000): 2285–95.

Warren, Frank. "The Role of the National Society in Working with Families." In *The Effects of Autism on the Family,* edited by Eric Schopler and Gary Mesibov, 99–116. New York: Plenum Press, 1984.

Watson, John B. "Psychology as the Behaviorist Views It." *Psychological Review* 20 (1913): 158–77.

Wimmer, H., and J. Perner. "Beliefs About Beliefs: Representation and Constraining Function of Wrong Beliefs in Young Children's Understanding of Deception." *Cognition* 13, no. 1 (1983): 103–28.

Wing, Lorna. "Asperger's Syndrome: A Clinical Account." *Psychological Medicine* 11, no. 1 (1981): 115–29.

———. "The Relationship Between Asperger's Syndrome and Kanner's Syndrome." In *Autism and Asperger Syndrome,* edited by Uta Frith, 93–121. Cambridge, UK: Cambridge University Press, 1991.

———. "Past and Future of Research on Asperger Syndrome." In *Asperger Syndrome,* edited by Ami Klin, Fred R. Volkmar, and Sara S. Sparrow, 418–32. New York: Guilford Press, 2000.

———. "Reflections on Opening Pandora's Box." *Journal of Autism and Developmental Disorders* 35, no. 2 (2005): 197–203.

Wing, Lorna, Christine Bramley, Anthea Hailey, and J. K. Wing. "Camberwell Cumulative Psychiatric Case Register Part I: Aims and Methods." *Social Psychiatry* 3, no. 3 (1968): 116–23.

Wing, Lorna, and Judith Gould. "Severe Impairments of Social Interaction and Associated Abnormalities in Children: Epidemiology and Classification." *Journal of Autism and Developmental Disorders* 9, no. 1 (1979): 11–29.

Wolf, Montrose, Todd Risley, and Hayden Mees. "Application of Operant

Conditioning Procedures to the Behaviour Problems of an Autistic Child." *Behaviour Research and Therapy* 1, no. 2-4 (1963): 305–12.

Woodward, Katharine F., Norma Jaffe, and Dorothy Brown. "Psychiatric Program for Very Young Retarded Children." *Archives of Pediatrics & Adolescent Medicine* 108 (1964): 221–29.

Woodward, Katharine F., Miriam Siegel, and Marjorie Eustis. "Psychiatric Study of Mentally Retarded Children of Preschool Age: Report on First and Second Years of a Three-Year Project." *American Journal of Orthopsychiatry* 28, no. 2 (April 1958): 376–93.

Workman, Lance. "Interview: From Art to Autism." *Psychologist* 26, no. 12 (2013): 880–82.

Yell, M. L., and E. Drasgow. "Litigating a Free Appropriate Public Education: The Lovaas Hearings and Cases." *Journal of Special Education* 33 (2000): 205–14.

Zeliadt, Nicholette. "Diverse Dopamine Defects Found in People with Autism." Simons Foundation Autism Research Initiative, November 19, 2014, http://sfari.org/news-and-opinion/conference-news/2014/society-for-neuroscience-2014/diverse-dopamine-defects-found-in-people-with-autism.

Zirkel, P. A. "The Autism Case Law: Administrative and Judicial Rulings." *Focus on Autism and Other Developmental Disabilities* 17 (Spring 2002): 84–93.

Zirkel, Perry. "Case Law Under the IDEA: 1998 to the Present." In *IDEA: A Handy Desk Reference to the Law, Regulations, and Indicators,* 669–752. Albany, NY: LexisNexis, 2012.

Newspapers and Magazines

Allen, Arthur. "The Not-So-Crackpot Autism Theory." *New York Times Magazine,* November 10, 2002.

Ansen, David, Michael Reese, and Sarah Crichton. "Who's on First?" *Newsweek,* January 16, 1989.

Armentrout, Charles. "Mentally Ill Tots Crying for Love and Attention." *Charleston Gazette,* January 31, 1949.

———. "Huntington Hospital Fire Kills 14 Patients." *Charleston Gazette,* November 27, 1952.

"Autistic Child Brings Years of Toil as Loving Parents Strive to Help." *Daily Herald,* June 19, 1973.

Ballin, M. "Autistic Chidren: The Strangers in Our Midst." *McCall's,* November 1973.

Baum, Gary. "Hollywood's Vaccine Wars: L.A.'s 'Entitled' Westsiders Behind City's Epidemic." *Hollywood Reporter,* September 12, 2014.

Berton, Pierre. "The Dionne Years." *New York Times Magazine,* April 23, 1978.

Bettelheim, Bruno. "Joey, a Mechanical Boy." *Scientific American,* March 1959.

Blatt, B., and C. Mangel. "The Tragedy and Hope of Retarded Children." *Look,* October 31, 1967.

Blume, Harvey. "Neurodiversity: On the Neurological Underpinnings of Geekdom." *Atlantic,* September 1, 1998.

Boseley, Sarah. "Jab Warning 'Wrong'; WHO Chief Attacks Doctors over Claim of Vaccine Link with Autism." *Guardian,* March 12, 1998.

———. "*Lancet* Retracts 'Utterly False' MMR Paper." *Guardian,* February 2, 2010.

Buckley, Cara. "Man Obsessed with Trains Again Runs Afoul of Law." *New York Times,* November 11, 2006.

Buis, Micah. "Educating About Autism." *Vassar, The Alumnae/i Quarterly,* Fall 2006.

Casto, Harriet. "Archie, Autism and Another Time." *Advocate: Autism Society of America Magazine* 23, no. 3, 1991.

"Charge of Freeing Insane Is Repeated, Hopkins Doctor Says Girls Were Let Go to Provide Fees and Cheap Labor." *Baltimore Sun,* May 14, 1937.

Clark, Matt. "The Troubled Child." *Newsweek,* April 8, 1974.

Coles, Robert. "A Hero of Our Time." *New Republic,* March 4, 1967.

Cowley, Geoffrey. "Understanding Autism." *Newsweek,* July 30, 2000.

Cronin Fisk, Margaret. "Mercury's Legal Morass: A Surge of Lawsuits Allege That Vaccinations Triggered Autism." *National Law Journal,* March 20, 2002.

"Cruelty to Lunatics: Serious Charges Against a Pennsylvania Asylum." *New York Times,* March 31, 1890.

Dalphonse, Sherri. "Dustin and Me." *Washingtonian,* July 1, 1992.

Deer, Brian. "Focus: MMR: The Truth Behind the Crisis." *Sunday Times,* February 22, 2004.

———. "Revealed: MMR Research Scandal." *Sunday Times,* February 22, 2004.

———. "MMR Scare Doctor Planned Rival Vaccine." *Sunday Times,* November 14, 2004.

———. "Hidden Records Show MMR Truth." *Sunday Times,* February 8, 2009.

Editorial Board. "The Carefully Orchestrated Campaign Must Not Be Allowed to Stifle Real Debate." *Independent,* February 24, 2004.

Editorial Board. "Doctor's Secret." *Sun,* February 23, 2004.

Ervin, Mike. "Autism Group Founder: It's Time to Listen to What We Have to Say." *Independence Today,* June 13, 2013.

Estridge, Bonnie. "I Demand the Right to Clear My Name." *Express,* July 17, 2006.

Fraiser, Lorraine. "Anti-MMR Doctor Is Forced Out." *Telegraph,* December 2, 2001.

Fremont-Smith, Eliot. "Children Without an I." *New York Times Book Review,* March 10, 1967.

Frith, Maxine. "Measles Alert in MMR Crisis." *Evening Standard,* July 3, 2002.

Goleman, Daniel. "Researcher Reports Progress Against Autism." *New York Times,* March 10, 1987.

———. "Bruno Bettelheim Dies at 86—Psychoanalyst of Vast Impact." *New York Times,* March 14, 1990.

Gonzales, Daniel. "Critics Call It a Hoax but 100 Teachers Soon Will Gather to Learn More." *Syracuse Herald-Journal,* February 22, 1994.

Gramza, Janet. "Families Struggle with Schools, Governments." *Post-Standard* (Syracuse, New York), April 14, 1997.

Gross, Jane, and Stephanie Strom. "Autism Debate Strains a Family and Its Charity." *New York Times,* June 18, 2007.

Gunther, Marc, and Henry Goldblatt. "How GE Made NBC No. 1 When He Became NBC'S CEO." *Fortune,* February 3, 1997.

Hughes, David, and Jenny Hope. "MMR: The Betrayal of These Tragic Parents." *Daily Mail,* February 24, 2004.

Ito, Robert. "The Phantom Chaser: For Ivar Lovaas, UCLA's Controversial Autism Pioneer, a Life's Work Is Now Facing a Crucial Test." *Los Angeles Magazine,* April 2004.

Johannes, Laura. "New Hampshire Mother Overrode Doubts on New Use of Old Drug." *Wall Street Journal,* March 10, 1999.

Johnston, Lucy. "US Research on Controversial Vaccine May Vindicate Consultant Who Was Forced to Resign; New Tests Back Expert Who Sounded Alarm over Triple Jab for Children." *Sunday Express,* December 9, 2001.

Katz, D. R. "The Kids with the Faraway Eyes." *Rolling Stone,* March 8, 1979.

Kaufman, Joanne. "Campaign on Childhood Mental Illness Succeeds at Being Provocative." *New York Times,* December 14, 2007.

"Kelleys Win in 'Fitter Families' Contest." *Savannah Press,* November 6, 1924.

Kennedy Jr., Robert. "Deadly Immunity." *Rolling Stone* and *Salon,* July 14, 2005 (retracted by *Salon,* January 16, 2011).

Kingon, Jacqueline J., and Alfred H. Kingon. "The Words They Can't Say." Letter to the editor, *New York Times Magazine,* November 3, 1991.

Laurance, Jeremy. "Emotive and Controversial Issue That Splits Medical Profession." *Independent,* February 27, 1998.

———. "Health: Not Immune to How Research Can Hurt; Jeremy Laurance Talks to the Man at the Centre of the Controversy over the MMR Vaccine." *Independent,* March 3, 1998.

———. "A Doctor, the Distinguished Journal, and a Scare That Needs Never Have Happened; The MMR Controversy." *Independent,* February 22, 2004.

———. "I Was There When Wakefield Dropped His Bombshell." *Independent,* January 29, 2010.

Long, Colleen. "Darius McCollum, Serial Transit Impostor, Arrested 29 Times for Stealing Trains and Buses." Associated Press, August 12, 2013.

"Lorna Wing—Obituary," *Daily Telegraph,* June 9, 2014.

Lutz, Amy S. F. "You Do Not Have Asperger's." *Slate,* May 22, 2013.

Machacek, John. "No School for Bright Boy Suffering from Autism." *Binghamton Press,* February 22, 1966.

Macrae, Fiona, and David Wilkes. "Damning Verdict on MMR Doctor: Anger as GMC Attacks 'Callous Disregard' for Sick Children." *Daily Mail,* January 29, 2010.

Maisel, Albert. "Bedlam." *LIFE,* May 6, 1946.

Mason, Jan. "Child of Silence: Retrieved from the Shadow World of Autism: Katy Finds Her Voice." *LIFE,* September 15, 1987.

Maugh, Thomas. "State Study Finds Sharp Rise in Autism Rate." *Los Angeles Times,* April 16, 1999.

Mayor, Tracy. "A Disorder That's Defining an Era." *Child,* December 1, 2005.

McDougall, Liam. "MMR: Wakefield Welcomes Probe." *Sunday Herald,* February 20, 2004.

"Medicine: Frosted Children." *Time,* April 26, 1948.

Merose, Tamar. "The Children of the Fairies." *Ha'aretz,* August 24, 1973.
Morgan, John. "*ER*'s Anthony Edwards Curing Autism Now." *USA Today,* October 12, 2000.
Moser, Dan, and Alan Grant (photographer). "Screams, Slaps & Love: A Surprising, Shocking Treatment Helps Far-Gone Mental Cripples." *LIFE,* May 7, 1965.
Nash, J. Madeleine, and Amy Bonesteel. "The Secrets of Autism." *Time,* May 6, 2002.
Nava, Mary Ellen. "Readers' Comments, for Autistic Child Help." *Santa Barbara Press,* January 9, 1971.
Nelson, Harry. "New Help Seen in the Child Care Practitioner." *Geneva Times,* May 10, 1971.
"Nurses Tell of Cruelty." *San Bernardino Daily Sun,* August 11, 1903.
"Obituary: Albert Hoffmann." *Telegraph,* April 29, 2008.
Oppenheim, Rosalind C. "They Said Our Child Was Hopeless." *Saturday Evening Post,* June 17, 1961.
Park, Alice. "South Korean Study Suggests Rates of Autism May Be Underestimated." *Time,* May 9, 2011.
Patrick, William G. "Bizarre Withdrawal Symptoms Mark Infantile Autism Cases." *Salt Lake City Tribune,* March 17, 1967.
Putnam, Pat. "Sports Scrapbook." *Sarasota Journal,* September 13, 1957.
"Retarded Son Is Dead: Father Calls Police to Say He Shot Boy." *Santa Barbara Press,* January 6, 1971.
Roan, Shari. "A Quiet Advocate for the Child: Psychology: The Late Bruno Bettelheim Rewrote the Code of Treatment for Emotionally Disturbed Children." *Los Angeles Times,* March 16, 1990.
Sacks, Oliver. "A Neurologist's Notebook: An Anthropologist on Mars." *New Yorker,* December 27, 1993.
Shulins, Nancy. "Debate over Autism Communication Rages On." *Chicago Daily Herald,* May 16, 1994.
Silberman, Steve. "The Geek Syndrome." *Wired,* December 1, 2001.
Smith, Doug. "Autism Rates by State." *Los Angeles Times,* December 9, 2011.
Smith, Rebecca. "Andrew Wakefield—The Man Behind the MMR Controversy." *Telegraph,* January 29, 2010.
Sordyl, Samantha. "Creating an Asperger's Community." *Washington Post,* December 20, 2005.
Steel, Linda. "Parents: 'It Is Not About the Science. It's About Belief': Andrew Wakefield—the Doctor Who First Linked MMR and Autism—Has Resigned. But Does That Mean He Was Wrong About the Vaccine?" *Guardian,* December 5, 2001.
"The Trance Children" (Under "Mental Illness"). *Time,* August 1, 1969.
"The Words They Can't Say." *New York Times Magazine,* November 3, 1991.
Torres Al-anbi, Agnes. "*Rain Man* Puts Autism on the Map." *Orlando Sentinel,* December 22, 1988.
Trotter, Bill. "Deaths Motive Unknown; Recently Wed Woman Stabbed, Man Shot on Swans Island." *Bangor Daily News,* July 24, 2001.
Tsouderos, Trine, and Patricia Callahan. "Risky Alternative Therapies for Autism

Have Little Basis in Science: Alternative Therapies Amount to Uncontrolled Experimentation on Children, Investigation Finds." *Chicago Tribune,* November 22, 2009.

Vil, Ursula. "Mother of Slain Autistic Child Describes an Odyssey of Grief." *Los Angeles Times,* March 26, 1972.

———. "Lloyd Nolan Recalls Tragedy of Autism," *Los Angeles Times,* March 11, 1973.

Wallace, Amy. "An Epidemic of Fear: How Panicked Parents Skipping Shots Endanger Us All." *Wired,* October 19, 2009.

Wallace, Benjamin. "Is Everyone on the Autism Spectrum?" *New York Magazine,* October 28, 2012.

Warren, James. "Another Opinion: Chicago Adds to Doubts Raised About Bettelheim's Methods, Personality." *Chicago Tribune,* July 25, 1991.

Womack, Sarah. "Blair Silent over Leo's MMR Jab." *Telegraph,* December 21, 2001.

Wright, Lawrence. "Child-Care Demons." *New Yorker,* October 3, 1994.

Letter Collections

American Psychiatric Association Library and Archives. Drs. Dorothy and Irving Bernstein Reference Center, Arlington, Virginia

Personal Health Records of Donald Triplett, and the Leo Kanner Collection, Johns Hopkins Hospital. Medical Archives of the Johns Hopkins Medical Institutions, Baltimore, Maryland

Richard Pollak Collection of Bruno Bettelheim Research Materials 1863–2006. Box 12, Folder 10. Special Collections Research Center, University of Chicago Library, Chicago, Illinois

Film, Television, and Video

Behavioral Treatment of Autistic Children. Directed by Robert Aller. Focus International, 1988.

Change of Habit. Directed by William A. Graham. Universal Pictures, 1969.

Conjoint Parent-Therapist Teaching of a Pre-School Psychotic Child. Produced by the Child Research Project, University of North Carolina, 1967.

Crean, Robert. "Conall." *Directions 65.* ABC. Original airdate February 7, 1965.

Deer, Brian. "MMR—What They Didn't Tell You." *Dispatches.* Channel Four. Original airdate November 18, 2004.

Harry: Behavioral Treatment of Self-abuse. Produced by Richard Foxx. Research Press, 1980.

Histoire, Histoires D'autisme. Directed by Anne Georget. Gloria Films, 2000.

House of Cards. Directed by Michael Lessac. Miramax Films, 1993.

Infantile Autism: The Invisible Wall. Produced by the University of Oklahoma Medical Center. Featuring Bernard Rimland, Ruth Sullivan, and Joe Sullivan. Behavioral Sciences Audiovisual Laboratory, University of Oklahoma Medical Center, 1968.

A Minority of One. Directed by Mike Gavin. KNBC, Los Angeles. Original airdate May 1975.

Palfreman, Jon. "Prisoners of Silence." *Frontline*. Original airdate October 19, 1993.

Rain Man. Directed by Barry Levinson. United Artists Pictures, 1988.

Refrigerator Mothers. Directed by David Simpson, J. J. Hanley, and Gordon Quinn. Kartemquin Films, Fanlight Productions (distributor), n.d.

Temple Grandin. Produced by Emily Gerson Saines. Warner Bros., 2010.

Tuohy, Denis. *Panorama*. Episode 34. "Denis Tuohy Looks at the Care of Autistic Children in Britain." BBC 1. Original airdate October 21, 1974.

Victor, David. "The Foal." *Marcus Welby, M.D.* Original airdate September 30, 1969.

Willowbrook: The Last Great Disgrace. Directed by Al Primo. 1972. http://sproutflix.org/all-films/willowbrook-the-last-great-disgrace/.

"Wright Family Interviewed About Autism Speaks." *Today*. NBC. Original airdate February 25, 2005.

Press Releases, Online Posts, Organizational and Government Reports, Legal Filings, Lectures, Interviews, Newsletters, Legislation, Correspondence

Adventures in Aspergers (blog), adventuresinaspergers.com.

Allen, Arthur. "The Autism Numbers, Why There's No Epidemic." *Slate*, January 15, 2007, http://www.slate.com/articles/health_and_science/medical_examiner/2007/01/the_autism_numbers.html.

Autism Research Review International: Newsletter of the Autism Research Institute (Archives 1987–2006), www.autism.com/httpsdocs/ari/newsletter/arriindex.htm.

Autistic Self Advocacy Network. "An Urgent Call to Action: Tell NYU Child Study Center to Abandon Stereotypes Against People with Disabilities." Online statement. December 8, 2007, http://autisticadvocacy.org/2007/12/tell-nyu-child-study-center-to-abandon-stereotypes/.

———. "ASAN Condemns Presidential Appointment of Anti-Vaccine Activist Peter Bell." Press release. January 12, 2012, http://autisticadvocacy.org/?s=peter+bell.

Autism Science Foundation. "NAAR Founder Eric London Resigns from Autism Speaks." Press release. June 30, 2009, https://autismsciencefoundation.wordpress.com/2009/06/30/naar-founder-eric-london-resigns-from-autism-speaks-citing-disagreement-over-autismvaccine-research/.

Autism Speaks. "Autism Speaks Withdraws Support for Strategic Plan for Autism Research, Decries Unexpected Change in Final Approval Process." Press release. January 15, 2009, https://www.autismspeaks.org/about-us/press-releases/autism-speaks-withdraws-support-strategic-plan-autism-research-decries-unexp.

———. "Autism Speaks Demands an Urgent, New Response to the Autism Epidemic as CDC Updates Prevalence Estimates." Press release. March 29, 2012, https://www.autismspeaks.org/about-us/press-releases/cdc-autism-prevalence-1-88-autism-speaks-demands-response.

Burton, Dan. "Press Statement." Address, from *Congressional Record,* V. 148, Pt. 17, November 15, 2002, to December 16, 2002.

California Criminal Court. *The People of the State of California, Plaintiff, v. Alexander Gibson, Defendant.* Original Reporter's Transcript of Grand Jury Proceedings, Original Clerk's Transcript, January 12, 1971.

California Department of Developmental Services. "Changes in the Population of Persons with Autism and Pervasive Developmental Disorders in California's Developmental Services System: 1987 through 1998, Report to the Legislature." March 1, 1999, available at http://www.dds.ca.gov/Autism/docs/autism_report_1999.pdf.

Cantor, Nancy. "Imagining America; Imagining Universities: Who and What?" Chancellor's welcome address for the Imagining America Annual Conference at Syracuse University, September 7, 2007.

Centers for Disease Control and Prevention. "Prevalence of the Autism Spectrum Disorders (ASDs) in Multiple Areas of the United States, 2000 and 2002," http://stacks.cdc.gov/view/cdc/6864.

———. *Morbidity and Mortality Weekly Report,* March 28, 2014, http://www.cdc.gov/mmwr/pdf/ss/ss6302.pdf.

Combating Autism Act of 2006.

Court of Appeals of California, Second Appellate District, Division Two. Ruling, *People v. Gibson,* 23 Cal.App.3d 918, March 1, 1972.

Cure Autism Now. "Cure Autism Now Calls for Removal of Mercury-Based Preservative in Children's Vaccinations." PR Newswire, July 17, 2001.

Deer, Brian. "Amended Declaration of Brian Deer in Support of Defendants' Anti-SLAPP Motion to Dismiss." July 9, 2012, http://briandeer.com/solved/slapp-amended-declaration.pdf.

Despert, Louise. Letter to Leo Kanner, July 12, 1942. American Psychiatric Association collection, American Psychiatric Association.

General Medical Council. "GMC Fitness to Practice Hearing for Andrew Wakefield," http://wakefieldgmctranscripts.blogspot.com/2012/02/day-17.html.

Grant, Moosa V. P. "The President Reports," *National Society for Autistic Children, Inc., Newsletter,* Summer 1968.

Handley, J. B. "Paul Offit and the 'Original Sin' of Autism." Age of Autism (website). January 31, 2011, http://www.ageofautism.com/2011/01/paul-offit-and-the-original-sin-of-autism.html.

Immunization Safety Review Committee. *Immunization Safety Review: Vaccines and Autism*. Washington, DC: National Academies Press, 2004.

Kanner, Leo. Address given as recipient of Stanley R. Dean Research Award by the American Psychiatric Association, May 4, 1965, available at http://neurodiversity.com/library_kanner_1965.pdf.

———. Speech to National Society, Washington, DC, July 17, 1969. Transcription available at American Psychiatric Association Collection, American Psychiatric Association.

Kansas Bureau of Child Research. *Fitter Families for Future Firesides: A Report of the Eugenics Department of the Kansas Free Fair, 1920–1924*. Eugenics Committee of the United States of America, 1924.

Lovaas, O. I. "Special Report: Dr. Lovaas Comments on the Mistaking of His Work." *FEAT Newsletter,* 2000. "Clarifying Comments on the UCLA Young Autism Project."

McCravey, William. Letter to his grandson, Donald Triplett. June 22, 1943, provided to the authors by Oliver Triplett.

McIlwain, Lori. "Autism & Wandering: A Guide for Educators." National Autism Association, April 20, 2015, http://nationalautismassociation.org/autism-wandering-a-guide-for-educators/.

National Institutes of Health. *Mental Health: A Report of the Surgeon General.* Rockville, MD: US Department of Health and Human Services, 1999, available at http://profiles.nlm.nih.gov/ps/access/NNBBHS.pdf.

National Society for Autistic Children, Inc., Newsletter, June 1974. Archives of the Autism Society of America, Bethesda, Maryland.

New York State Department of Health. "Quick Reference Guide for Parents and Professionals: Autism/Pervasive Developmental Disorders," 1999, available at http://www.health.ny.gov/publications/4216.pdf.

Pace, Giacinta. "Philanthropist Wages Fight to Cure Autism, Suzanne Wright's Foundation Raises Money to Fund Research on Disorder." NBC News, November 12, 2009, www.nbcnews.com/id/33868343/ns/us_news-giving/t/philanthropist-wages-fight-cure-autism/#.VZ1HY_kgkqM.

Patches, Matt. "Remembering *Rain Man*: The $350 Million Movie That Hollywood Wouldn't Touch Today." Grantland, January 9, 2014, http://grantland.com/hollywood-prospectus/remembering-rain-man-the-350-million-movie-that-hollywood-wouldnt-touch-today/.

Pavlov, Ivan. Nobel Lecture: "Physiology of Digestion." December 12, 1904.

The People of the State of California, Plaintiff, v. Alexander Gibson, Defendant, Original Reporter's Transcript of Grand Jury Proceedings, January 12, 1971, Superior Court of the State of California for the County of Santa Barbara.

"Ransom Notes and Love Letters." Mom—Not Otherwise Specified (blog). December 10, 2007, http://momnos.blogspot.com/2007/12/ransom-notes-and-love-letters.html.

Reichler, Robert. Talk on "Early History of TEACCH." Winter InService, Division TEACCH, Chapel Hill, February 8, 2007.

SafeMinds. "SAFEMINDS Outraged That IOM Report Fails American Public." Press release. SafeMinds, May 18, 2004, http://www.safeminds.org/wp-content/uploads/2004/05/040518-PR10-BadIOMReport.pdf.

Schopler, Eric. Audio Interview with Gary Mesibov: Reminscences, June 18, 1988.

———. "Recollections of My Professional Development." Lecture, from "What Future for the Helping Professional?" Emma P. Bradley Symposium, October 22, 1971.

Seidel, Kathleen. "Autism and Lupron: Playing with Fire." Neurodiversity.com, February 19, 2006, http://web.archive.org/web/20120204153600/http://neurodiversity.com/weblog/article/83/autism-testosterone-lupron-playing-with-fire.

Sharp, Beverly. "Autism and Discrimination in British Columbia." Address to BC-NDP Women's Rights Committee. December 8, 1997.

Sinclair, Jim. "Don't Mourn for Us." Web post. November 3, 1993, http://www.autreat.com/dont_mourn.html..

"Statement from NAA Board Member Katie Wright Reported June 15, 2007."

Adventures in Autism (blog). June 15, 2007, http://adventuresinautism.blogspot.com/2007/06/statement-on-autism-speaks-from-katie.html.

The Pennsylvania Association for Retarded Children Et Al., Plaintiffs, v. Commonwealth of Pennsylvania Et Al., Defendants, US District Court, E.D. of Pennsylvania. May 5, 1972.

Treffert, Darald. "Rain Man, the Movie / Rain Man, Real Life." Wisconsin Medical Society, n.d., https://www.wisconsinmedicalsociety.org/.

United States Federal Census 1920. Census Place: Huntington Ward 7, Cabell, West Virginia; Roll: T625_1951; Page: 1B; Enumeration District: 193; Image: 504.

US Court of Federal Claims. "Claims for Vaccine Injuries Resulting in Autism Spectrum Disorder or Similar Neurodevelopmental Disorder, Autism-Update (Circular)." May 24, 2007, http://www.uscfc.uscourts.gov/sites/default/files/opinions/SWEENEY.Snyder081109a_0.pdf.

———. "Transcript of Proceedings. June 11, 2007: *Theresa Cedillo and Michael Cedillo v. Secretary of Health and Human Services,*" http://www.autism-watch.org/omnibus/cedillo2.pdf.

———. "Vaccine Program Background." Office of the Special Masters, the Autism Proceedings, 2010, www.uscfc.uscourts.gov/sites/default/files/vaccine_files/vaccine.background.2010.pdf.

US Department of Health and Human Services. "HHS Secretary Leavitt Announces Members of the New Interagency Autism Coordinating Committee." News release. November 27, 2007, https://iacc.hhs.gov/news/.

US House of Representatives. "Autism: Present Challenges, Future Needs—Why the Increased Rates?" Hearing Before the Committee on Government Reform, 106th Congress, Second Session, April 6, 2000.

———. "Mercury in Medicine—Are We Taking Unnecessary Risks?" Hearing Before the Committee on Government Reform, 106th Congress, Second Session, July 18, 2000.

US Public Health Service. Statement by PHS in "Notice to Readers: Thimerosal in Vaccines: A Joint Statement of the American Academy of Pediatrics and the Public Health Service." Centers for Disease Control, *Morbidity and Mortality Weekly Report* 48, no. 26 (July 9, 1999): 563–65.

US Senate. "Thimerosal and Autism Spectrum Disorders: Alleged Misconduct by Government Agencies and Private Entities." Executive summary for the Committee on Health, Education, Labor and Pensions, September 2007.

Wright, Bob, and Suzanne Wright. "Statement . . . from Co-Founders." Autism Speaks. 2007, web.archive.org/web/20071021232618/http://www.autismspeaks.org/wrights_statement.php.

A NOTE FROM THE AUTHORS

WITH EXTREMELY FEW EXCEPTIONS, THE FACTS AND EVENTS described in these pages originate in eyewitness accounts, confirming documents, and reliable third-party recollections. Such accounts were provided by individuals whom we interviewed directly or came to know through their writings or other evidence of their deeds, words, and thoughts. This documentary evidence includes books, journal articles, private correspondence, audio and video recordings, newspaper and magazine accounts, blog posts, text messages, medical records, oral and written tributes, transcripts of legal proceedings, and maps. As a rule, our sources are specified either in the text itself or in an endnote.

The exceptions concern some of the earliest interactions between Donald Triplett and his mother, Mary. Donald has little to share in the way of specific memories of those interactions, and only Mary knew what she was thinking and feeling during Donald's childhood, and she died in 1985. In her absence, we have imagined only a handful of details, all firmly rooted in what we do know about their circumstances. As one example: on the day she saw Donald do well in school—documented in a letter—we take it for granted that Mary was moved and excited, and we have stated as much. For another: we visited the Triplett family home and noticed a relatively busy street in proximity to the house; based on that, we have assumed that Mary was concerned about Donald's running into traffic. For a third: we used our experience of autism in general, and our knowledge of Donald's documented behaviors, to depict Mary as worried about Donald figuring out how to open the locks on windows. Elsewhere in the book, we have added minor narrative details only if we judged them to be highly plausible based on the totality of our research and interviews. For example, when we describe Donald's first driving lesson, we say that he has both hands high on the wheel at the start of it. This seems to us extremely likely, especially since, to this day, Donald has a distinctive way of gripping the wheel with both hands.

In three cases, we have avoided fully naming individuals in order to protect their privacy. In one case, we use no name at all; in a second, we use a first name only. The third case is that of a young woman who appears, at her own request, as "Junie Gibson." Junie derives from a childhood nickname.

Regarding names in general, we have chosen to use first names when referring to children and their parents, and last names for professionals such as scientists and educators. However, we found it difficult to apply our own rule consistently, since during the course of the narrative some parents become "professionalized," and some professionals become personally engaged with families. Therefore, some individuals appear by their first names sometimes and their last names at other times, according to the context.

Finally, we have occasionally used words that today are considered deeply offensive, such as "mentally retarded," "idiot," "feebleminded," and so forth. We want to make clear that we mean no offense and have used them only in a historical context, as used by professionals in another era. In their day, many of these words were clinical terms, used by professionals who sought only to be precise and intended no malice. That said, we have made efforts to minimize such usages, and to employ the terms commonly accepted today wherever context allows. Likewise, we almost always use the "people first" formulation when describing an individual with a disability. Thus, we usually write of "a boy with autism" rather than "an autistic boy." We have reversed this, however, when writing about individuals or groups that prefer the latter, such as many of those in the neurodiversity movement.

ACKNOWLEDGMENTS

Our list of those owed our deepest thanks for getting this book written starts where most authors conclude theirs: with our families, whose connection to autism is neither casual nor abstract. In the case of Caren's family, that connection comes through her oldest child, Michael "Mickey" McGuinness, who was diagnosed with autism in 1996. On John's end, it is his wife's brother, Dror Mishori, born in Israel in 1967, who is profoundly affected.

Mickey and Dror. Right there, those are two fine teachers of what the "autism experience" is about. But autism makes experts of family members too, and so, among other true authorities we want to acknowledge, first we thank these: John McGuinness, Mickey's dad and Caren's husband; and Jonah and Molly McGuinness, Mickey's brother and sister. His uncle, Michael Zucker, Caren's brother, belongs here too along with his aunt, Alison Porter.

Also Dror's family in the United States: his sister, Ranit Mishori, John's wife; their children, Ben and Noa Donvan, who are Dror's nephew and niece; his parents at home in Israel, Edna and Yaacov Mishori; and his younger sister, Osnat Weinstein.

We are indebted to these several near relatives, for permitting our subject to crowd their already crowded lives, for putting up with absences during travel undertaken for research, and for not always asking to change the subject, when we perhaps brought home more "autism talk" than everyone else in the house, already well versed in the topic, necessarily needed to hear. Their forbearance, and humor, made the long journey a lot more pleasant.

Caren also thanks the wider unofficial family of soulmates whose support over her first twenty years as an "autism mom" showed her the power of love and laughter in getting through almost anything. Most of these happen to be fellow mothers: Cheryl Brocco, Katy Barrett, Janet Boyle, Barbara Friedman, Julie Hartenstein, Ilene Lainer, Debbie Lankowsky, Kate O'Brian, Beth Sovern, and Betsy Stark. Liz Daibes and her family taught Caren a lesson in zen before she knew what the word meant, and showed the Zucker-McGuinness household a little sampling of Forest, Mississippi, in Bergen County, New Jersey.

In the same vein, John thanks Ken Weinstein, Amy Kauffman, Jeffrey Goldberg, Mark D'Anastatio, Elisa Tinsley, Jeanie Milbauer, Gerry Ohrstrom, Laurie Strongin, Allen Goldberg, David Dunning, and Jacqueline and John Bredar, for their own soulmate qualities—and for sustenance both moral and culinary. It also helped to have a short list of fellow writers/authors/producers, who are also friends, checking in from time to time, rooting for us, reading a chapter here or there, and providing fact-checking, advice on tone, lessons on book-writing, and encouragement overall. Thanks for the always well-timed assists from Rick Beyer, Ethan Bronner, Lisa Dallos, Sue Goodwin, Deborah Lewis, Richard Mark, Barbara Moses, Elissa Rubin, Chris Schroeder, Ken Stern, and Jay Winik. John also found enormous support from the driving forces behind his "other" big project of the last few years, moderating the Intelligence Squared US Debates, whose founders, Robert Rosenkranz and Alexandra Munroe, and superb executive producer, Dana Wolfe, understood early that the "distraction" would always be temporary. Their goodwill counted for a lot.

We got our running start at reporting on autism thanks to our bosses at ABC News, who heard us near the end of the last millennium when we suggested that autism was a topic worth covering regularly, but from the perspective of lives and science, and not as a compendium account of fads, miracles, and guys doing calendar calculations. As a result, in 2000, ABC became the first network to start treating autism as something of a real and serious beat—eventually branded *Echoes of Autism*—which, for nearly a decade, was ours. As television is so collaborative, credit for our work on *Nightline* and *World News* must be shared with the managers who found room for it and the colleagues who helped make it better and often beautiful, especially Akram Abi Hanna, Jon Banner, Tom Bettag, Tom Budai, Jeanmarie Condon,

Dennis Dunleavy, Tommy Fasano, Roy Garlisi, Charlie Gibson, James Goldston, Dan Green, Mimi Gurbst, Katie Hinman, Gerry Holmes, Peter Jennings, Tom Johnson, Sara Just, Ted Koppel, Cynthia McFadden, Tom Nagorski, Diane Sawyer, Stu Schutzman, Ben Sherwood, Roxanna Sherwood, Leroy Sievers, Madhulika Sikka, George Stephanopoulos, David Zapatka, and many others. Later, Caren continued the streak by producing the series *Autism Now* for the *PBS NewsHour,* where she shared credit with, and deeply admired, Robert MacNeil, Linda Winslow, and Ray Conley, who were committed to portraying autism in all of its subtle complexity.

Getting to know so many members of the autism community through our television work— people on the spectrum, as well as those trying to help and understand—served as a years-long seminar in the depth and the idiosyncrasy of autism. As subjects and participants in our early stories, these people are all present in this book, even if unnamed in the text. Standing out among them, from different points on the spectrum, are Jacob Artsen, Billy Bernard, Daniel Corcoran, Josh Devries, Paul DiSavino, Jamie Hoppe, Clayton Jones, Noah Orent, Andrew Parles, Isaiah Paskowitz, Madison Prince, Ian Rager, Victoria Roma, Kaede Sakai, and Mackenzie Smith. And among their family, teachers, and therapists: Jed Baker, Marlene DiSavino, Julie Fisher, Doug Gilstrap, Jan Hoppe, Susan Hamarich, Kenneth Hosto, Jimmy Jones, Judy Karasik, Jim Laidler, Don Meyer, Brenda Myers, Karrie Olick, "Izzy" Paskowitz, Craig, Jeffrey, and Lisa Parles, Christi Sakai, Karen Siff-Exkorn, Franklin Exkorn, and Jake Exkorn.

We also thank the editor in chief of *The Atlantic,* James Bennet, for publishing our original profile of Donald Triplett. Chris Orr's brilliant editing brought forth the best from that story (the title, "Autism's First Child," was his idea) and helped make us finalists for a 2011 National Magazine Award. The article's appearance also revived our interest in writing a book, an effort we had initiated in 2007 but let flag by 2010 (because TV takes so much time). It was John's wife who suggested that, if there was to be no book, we at least publish our account of Donald Triplett's life, which we had already researched, in a magazine.

Obviously, as the book in your hands attests, that proved a turning point. A further five years spent exploring autism's backstory leaves us with a great deal more people to thank, for giving of their time and expertise, in their homes, offices, clinics, labs, and libraries. These include the following—all of whom we met, in person (in most cases), by phone, or by Skype—between the spring of 2010 and the summer of 2015.

In Mississippi: Allen Breland, Bob Brown, Janelle Brown, Ralph Brown, Tom Burns, Millie Clark, Lisa Davis, Albert Earle Elmore, Buddy Lovett, John Madden, Jan Nester, James Rushing, John Rushing, Ralph Ryan, Sid Salter, Constance Slaughter-Harvey, Celeste Sly, David Tedford, Yvonne Theriot, Donald Triplett, Ingrid Triplett, Oliver B. Triplett III, Gene Walker, Thomas E. Walker Jr., Brister Ware, Suzanne Wilder, and Jamie Woods.

Elsewhere in North America: Dan Amaral, Susie Arons, Sid Baker, Alice Barton, Sharmila Basu, Peter Bearman, Liz Bell, Sallie Bernard, Ed Berry, Douglas Biklen, Janyce Boynton, Timothy Buie, Marc Bush, Joseph Buxbaum, Betty Camp, Norman Camp, Norman "Normie" Camp IV, Dick Cavett, Maynard Clark, Edwin Clayton, Shirley Cohen, Brenda Considine, Daniel Corcoran, Jacqueline Crawley, Moira Cray, Chris Crean, Katherine Crean, Lorenzo Dall'Armi, Gerry Dawson, Brenda Denzler, Brenda Deskin, Anne Donnellan, Leon Eisenberg, Lauren Elliot, Celine Ennis, Gal Evra, Liz Feld, Linda Fiddle, Julie Fisher, Audrey Flack, Hannah Flack, Arthur Fleischmann, Carly Fleischmann, Tammy Fleischmann, Meg Flynan, Michael Flynan, Michael Flynan Jr., Nell Floyd, Susan Folstein, Eric Fombonne, Richard Foxx, SueAnn Galante, Emily Gerson Saines, Daniel Geschwind, Junie Gibson, Bob Gilhool, Tom Gilhool, Deb Gordon, Judith Gould, Temple Grandin, Gina Green, Julius Griffin, Richard Roy Grinker, Lee Grossman, Kimberly Gund, Debbie Hagen, Martha Herbert, Irva Hertz-Picciotto, Saima Hossain, Tom Insel, Robert Ito, Portia Iversen, Brian Iwata, Rose Jochum, Suzanne Kaplan, Ami Klin, Lynn Koegel, Robert Koegel, Connie Lapin, Harvey Lapin, Shawn Lapin, Barry Levinson, Eric London, Karen London, Cathy Lord, Ann Lotter, John Maltby, Robert Marcus, Catherine Maurice, Gary Mayerson, Cece McCarton, Darius McCollum, Tony Meyers, David Minier, Linda Morrissey, Soma Mukhopadhyay, Tito Rajarshi Mukhopadhyay, Kevin Murray, Gail Mutrux, Mary Ellen Nava, Ari

Ne'eman, Craig Newschaffer, Paul Offit, Jon Pangborn, Joseph Piven, Alex Plank, Douglas Plank, Mary Plank, Arnold Pollak, Richard Pollak, Jalynn Prince, Barry Prizant, Ellen Rampell, Lyn Redwood, Denise Resnick, Gloria Rimland, Mark Rimland, Rick Rollens, Michael Rosen, Alvin Rosenfeld, Chris Saddler, Sid Salter, Bonnie Sanabia, Barb Savino, Greg Savino, Ross Savino, Craig Schaeffer, Lenny Schafer, Kathleen Seidel, Howard Shane, Paul Shattuck, Lori Shery, Jon Shestack, Chantelle Sicile-Kir, Bryna Siegal, Lorraine Slaff, Ilana Slaff-Galatan, Michelle Smigel, Robert Smigel, Mike Smith (Halifax), Tristram Smith, Cecile Snider, Stuart Spielman, Joe Sullivan, Ruth Sullivan, Rita Tepper, James Todd, Janet Twyman, Daniel Unumb, Lori Unumb, Judith Ursitti, Fred Volkmar, Mary Lou "Bobo" Warren, Aislinn Wendrow, Ian Wendrow, Julian Wendrow, Jim Wheaton, Suzette Wheaton, Philip Worden, Bob Wright, Suzanne Wright.

In France: Katrina Alt, Laurent Alt, Françoise Ayzac, Laurent Damon, Laurent Dillion, Pierre Delion, Diane Fraser, Eric Laurent, Sophie Roberts.

In Vienna: Herwig Czech and Arnold Pollak.

In Tel Aviv and Nazareth: Edna Mishori and Eti Dromi, and Juman Tannous.

In Copenhagen: Steen Thygesen, Thorkil Sonne.

In the UK: Miles Allison, Michael Baron, Simon Baron-Cohen, Adam, Heather, and Sandra Barrett, Brian Deer, Judith Gould, Hephzibah Kaplan, Jeremy Laurance, Janis McKinnon, Michael Rutter, Marion Stanton.

In South Africa: Claudia Ceresa, Kenneth Moeketsi, Mary Moeketsi, Phindle Nikosi, Sanele Nikosi, Jill Stacey, Louise Trichadt, Ronel Van Bijon, and the few dozen mothers and educators we met at schools and in tiny villages along the way.

There is also a small circle of sources whose names we pulled out of the above paragraphs to single out for special thanks, owing to their willingness to take calls from us repeatedly over the years, acting, as we thought of them, as our overall autism history brain trust. Each was especially good at pointing us to other writing and opening doors, often making introductions on our behalf. Therefore, we especially thank: Peter Bell, Michael John Carley, Stephen Edelson, Judy Favell,

Adam Feinstein (a most generous colleague, whose own book, *A History of Autism,* we highly recommend), Gerald Fischbach, Uta Frith, Pete Gerhardt, Ilene Lainer, Lee Marcus, Gary Mesibov, John Elder Robison, Andy Shih, Alison Singer, Bridget Taylor, and, for his unrelenting graciousness the several dozen times we phoned over eight or nine years, Oliver B. Triplett Jr.

We discovered repeatedly that professional librarians love the hunt, and have a magic touch for finding gold. We acknowledge the spirit and intrepidness of our fellow searchers at the National Library of Medicine in Bethesda, Maryland, especially Cynthia Burke, Ryan Cohen, Liliya Gusakova, Lalitha Kutty, Ellen Layman, Wanda Whitney, and Marcia Zorn. Thanks also to librarians Gary McMillan at the American Psychiatric Association, Arlene Shaner at the New York Academy of Medicine, and Virginia Gillham at the University of Guelph. The same goes for library staff at the Autism Society of America, Bowie State University, Brooklyn College Archives and Special Collections, Columbia University, Georgetown University, Howard University, Pennsylvania State University, the Martin Luther King Public Library of Washington, DC, the Medical Archives of the Johns Hopkins Medical Institutions, the New York Public Library, the Rockefeller Archive Center, the Teaneck and Tenafly, New Jersey, public libraries, the University of Chicago, and the University of the District of Columbia.

Finally, there were our allies at Penguin Random House, beginning with Molly Stern, Crown's publisher, who believed enough in our idea not only to buy it, but to take us at our word when we came back not once, but twice, to explain that another deadline extension would produce a better book. Throughout, Molly remained committed to providing us with all necessary support to continue and complete the research and writing. Early on, Vanessa Mobley's passion for the project played a vital role in helping us to choose which paths to go down. We thank Rachel Klayman, our editor, who inherited this book and embraced the mission with full enthusiasm and instant insight about its purposes and possibilities. She was our champion at 1745 Broadway. Her grit, flexibility, and well-sharpened talent for language carried us over the finish line. Publicist Sarah Breivogel brought talent, drive, and energy to the project of getting our book into the hands of as many readers as possible. Her already formidable multitasking skills were tested by dealing with not one but two authors who also work in the media and are used to being in charge, and she responded with grace. Danielle Crabtree brought her creative ideas and easy demeanor to the complex task of marketing our book, not only to mainstream readers but also to the autism community. We also thank the Crown team devoted to designing the book and telling the world what we had written: Chris Brand, Jon Darga, Lauren Dong, David Drake, Rachel Rokicki, Annsley Rosner, and Christine Tanigawa.

Outside the Crown kingdom, Jane Fransson has a special place in our hearts for her timely, devoted, and critical assist down the home stretch. We suspect she has lived past lives as an ER doctor, or perhaps as a magician, or maybe as a saint. We saw hints of all of those in her and in her performance as a pinch hitter. Thanks, Jane.

But most credit for this book's existing at all belongs to our personal guide to the publishing industry: our agent, Alia Hanna Habib. As mentioned above, our initial spurt of interest in writing a history had started to wane, when we published *The Atlantic* article in late 2010. Alia read the article, tracked us down, and, in one forty-minute phone conversation, showed us how and why a history of autism taking off from the life of Donald Triplett could turn into a book she would want to read herself. She had her own ideas for shape and tone, which sounded, frankly, eminently doable, and honest to the historical reality. In short, Alia sold *us* on starting over again. Then she taught us how to write a book proposal. Then she went out and sold the proposal. For the next five years, she kept up our nerve, told us the truth, and was always, always on our side. Truly, she is this book's godmother. We count that as a blessing.

INDEX

ABOUT THE AUTHORS

John Donvan is a correspondent for ABC News, and host and moderator of the Intelligence Squared U.S. Debates, which are heard on public radio and by podcast. During his journalism career, in addition to anchoring such broadcasts as ABC's *Nightline,* John served as chief White House correspondent, and held multiyear postings in London, Moscow, Jerusalem, and Amman, Jordan. He is the winner of three Emmys and the Overseas Press Club Award. He became interested in autism's impact on families upon meeting his wife, the physician and medical school professor Ranit Mishori, who grew up in Israel with a brother profoundly affected by autism. John also performs as a live storyteller with the group Story District. He has two children and lives in Washington, DC. (Twitter: @johndonvan)

Caren Zucker is a journalist and television producer who has reported on a broad range of subjects both domestically and internationally. As a producer for ABC's *World News* and *Nightline,* working alongside Peter Jennings, Charlie Gibson, and Diane Sawyer, she covered economic summits, presidential campaigns, social trends, and the Olympic Games. Emmy-nominated, she was honored for her part in ABC's coverage of 9/11 with two of television's most prestigious prizes, the Peabody and the Alfred L. DuPont awards. Her oldest son Mickey's autism diagnosis inspired a new direction in her reporting: to bring a better understanding of autism's realities. Zucker and her husband, NBC Sports senior producer John McGuinness, have three children and reside in New Jersey. (Twitter: @caren_zucker)

As a team, Donvan and Zucker have been collaborating on stories about autism since 2000. At ABC, they created the pioneering series *Echoes of Autism*, the first regular feature segment in network news devoted to understanding the lives of individuals and families living with autism. Their 2010 article in *The Atlantic*, "Autism's First Child," was shortlisted for the National Magazine Award and appeared in the paperback anthology *Best Magazine Writing of 2011.* Zucker also produced the series *Autism Now* for the *PBS NewsHour*. As two journalists with a personal connection to autism, they aim to inspire acceptance of and support for people on the spectrum by telling their stories with honesty and compassion.